THE INDEPENDENT GUIDE TO THE CONSTITUTION

THE INDEPENDENT GUIDE TO THE CONSTITUTION

Original Intentions, Modern Inventions

WILLIAM J. WATKINS JR.

INDEPENDENT INSTITUTE

Copyright © 2026 by Independent Institute

ISBN: 978-1-59813-422-3
eISBN: 978-1-59813-424-7
LCCN: 2025042775

Cataloging-in-Publication data on file with the Library of Congress

Independent Institute
100 Swan Way, Oakland, CA 94621-1428
Telephone: 510-632-1366
Fax: 510-568-6040
Email: info@independent.org
Website: www.independent.org

Cover Design: John Caruso
Cover Image: Wikimedia Commons / "Washington Presiding in the Convention 1787"
Interior Design: Jason Sunde

10 9 8 7 6 5 4 3 2 1

This book is dedicated to the memory of David Theroux.

TABLE OF CONTENTS

Topics subject to vigorous debates are in boldface.

PREFACE

PREFACE TO, AND USE OF, *The Independent Guide to the Constitution*

THIS WORK IS a plea for a revival of strict construction of the Constitution as articulated by America's first originalists. Men such as Thomas Jefferson, St. George Tucker, and John Taylor of Caroline elucidated principles that were both elegant and potent in their simplicity. Tucker, who wrote the first full-length exposition of the Constitution in 1803, set forth the North Star of constitutional interpretation: "that the powers delegated to the federal government, are, in all cases, to receive the most strict construction that the instrument will bear, where the rights of a state or of the people, either collectively, or individually, may be drawn in question."[1] Absent such a rule, Tucker predicted that "gradual and sometimes imperceptible usurpations of power, will end in the total disregard of all [the Constitution's] intended limitations."[2]

Advocacy of strict construction originalism* was a hallmark of the early republic.[3] For example, in 1791 when debating Congress's power to incorporate a bank, James Madison explained to the House of Representatives that they should be guided by "the meaning of the parties to the instrument" as found in "[c]ontemporary and concurrent expositions."[4] In a letter written in 1823 to Associate Justice William Johnson, whom he had nominated to the Supreme Court nineteen years earlier, Thomas Jefferson opined that "[o]n every question of construction [we should] carry ourselves back to the time when the Constitution was adopted, recollect the spirit manifested in the debates . . . instead of trying what meaning may be squeezed out of the text, or invented against it."[5] John Randolph of Roanoke, leader of the "Old Republicans"[6] in the House of Representatives, characterized strict construction as "the plain, common-sense construction of the Constitution."[7] Under such an approach, a "power will not lie, unless . . . the power is specifically given."[8] North Carolina's Nathaniel Macon, who served as Speaker of the House from 1801 to 1807, appealed to Federalist representations in the state ratifying conventions as he inveighed against the Sedition Act of 1798. Macon observed that almost all the Constitution's advocates in 1787–88 "declared explicitly that no power was granted

---

* Throughout this book, I use the terms "strict construction originalism" and "strict construction" to describe this originalism of the early republic. At its essence, strict construction means simply holding the Federalists and other friends of the proposed constitution to the promises they made about the strict confines of federal power.

to Congress whereby they could pass any law abridging the liberty of the press."[9] Based on these representations, Macon challenged constitutional interpretation that permitted the general government to criminalize political speech. John C. Calhoun, while serving as vice president, described "the Constitution itself" as "[t]he only safe rule interpretation."[10] If the constitutional text was susceptible to more than one interpretation, Calhoun urged recourse to "the history of the times" and consultation of authorities such as "the journals of the [Philadelphia] Convention" to aid in discovering original intent.[11] Abel Upshur, who served in the Virginia judiciary and as secretary of state for President John Tyler, summed up the Jeffersonian view as follows: "The strict construction for which I contend applies to the intention of the framers of the Constitution" and "will give to the Federal Government all power which it can beneficially exert."[12]

This Jeffersonian strict construction should not be confused with the originalism fashioned in the early 1980s by scholars associated with the Federalist Society.[13] Thoughtful observers should not give short shrift to the work of the modern originalists, but neither should they confuse late twentieth-century originalism with eighteenth-century and early nineteenth-century strict construction.[14]

Modern originalist scholars too often practice their craft in a manner that augments federal power rather than seeking to cabin it. The first originalists, on the other hand, sought to promote self-government and policy experimentation in the states. Yale Law School's Akhil Amar, who is an accomplished scholar and is at the top of the marquee when the conservative Federalist Society holds a

conference, is illustrative of modern originalism. Rather than promote Tucker's canon of construction, Amar has used his intellect and originalist credentials to encourage federal power. A prime example is Congress's power to regulate interstate commerce, which since the New Deal has been construed to confer a general power of legislation upon the federal government. In the face of modest efforts by the Rehnquist and Roberts Courts to curtail this power by limiting it to economic activity (which is still far beyond what the Framers and ratifiers envisioned), Amar has argued that commerce should encompass "all forms of intercourse in the affairs of life, whether or not narrowly economic or mediated by explicit markets."[15] Such an interpretation renders the other enumerated powers superfluous and transforms the federal union into a European-style unitary state. Jesse Merriam of Patrick Henry College makes a compelling case when he asserts that modern originalist theory "has been sufficiently flexible to accommodate a variety of decisions seemingly inconsistent with the relevant constitutional text and history."[16] Stanford University's Jonathan Gienapp has observed that modern "originalism can now seemingly permit . . . the broadest of broad construction" of the Constitution.[17] The fact that Justice Elena Kagan, an Obama appointee and a jurist with strong progressive leanings, announced at her confirmation hearing that "we are all originalists now" attests to the suppleness of modern originalist theory.[18]

Twentieth- and twenty-first-century critics of Jeffersonian strict construction and modern originalism are loosely described as living constitutionalists.[19] Under such a philosophy, interpreters do not apply rules found within the document in ways consistent with the original intention or original understanding in the early republic. Instead, they see the words of the Constitution as malleable reference points designed to bend and morph with evolving values and human aspirations. Certainty and restraint are exchanged for pliancy and dynamism. Some scholars, such as Georgetown University's Louis Michael Seidman, would go even further and read the Constitution "as a work of art, designed to evoke a mood or emotion, rather than as a legal document."[20] The ultimate result of living constitutionalism is the transfer of public policy decisions from elected state legislators to unelected federal judges—from politically accountable servants who may be voted out to appointed officials who serve for life.

Living constitutionalism is ascendant in the legal academy, and its adherents belong to both the right and left of the political spectrum. They believe in updating the Constitution by interpretation rather than through the amendment process set forth in Article V. For example, on the right is Harvard Law School's Adrian Vermeule, who champions "common good constitutionalism" based on his study of the classical tradition.[21] Vermeule contends that provisions of the federal Constitution such as the General Welfare Clause should be interpreted broadly to confer comprehensive authority to promote Americans' health, safety, and right relationship with the natural environment. He urges conservatives to stop complaining about the growth of the federal government and to accept that it "has acquired by prescription, over time, a *de facto* police power."[22]

On the left is Cass Sunstein, who also teaches at Harvard's law school. According to Sunstein, constitutional law must be rooted in "identifiable moral aspirations and commitments."[23] Only a theory of interpretation that produces his favored policy outcomes—what Sunstein calls "better results"—should be adopted.[24] Sunstein's aspirations and commitments undergird much of the Warren Court's jurisprudence and counsel against reforms limiting court power. Indeed, Justice William J. Brennan, a Warren Court stalwart who served on the Supreme Court from 1956 to 1990, described the "genius of the Constitution" as setting forth "great principles" susceptible to "adaptability . . . to cope with current problems and current needs."[25]

Sunstein, like many other many other living constitutionalists, rejects any form of originalism because the Framers represented "a small subset of the population . . . that included no women and not many Black people."[26] The only thing a just society can do, originalism's opponents contend, is ignore the Constitution of 1787 and focus on later amendments that protected individual freedoms and human rights.

These critics of the men of 1787 take for granted the modern world of written constitutions and governments chosen by the people. They forget (or ignore) that in 1787 most people in the world had no agency in choosing a form of government and could not imagine limiting their governments by adopting a written charter. In the words of Thomas Jefferson, the American experiment challenged the assumption "that man cannot be governed but by a rod of iron."[27] Rather than an unruly beast to be muscled about, the Framers recognized the people of each of the thirteen states as sovereign. Before the Constitution of 1787 could bind a people, they had to accept the document in specially called conventions where the constituent power—the ultimate authority—was exercised.[28] In advocating for that method of ratification, James Madison lectured that "it [was] indispensable that the new Constitution should be ratified in the most unexceptionable form, and by the supreme authority of the people themselves."[29] Such a method of creating a government was a major departure from all that preceded the American experiment.

Centralization was the governmental pattern in the eighteenth century, and the Framers rejected that model. The Framers championed real self-government, suited to smaller representative bodies closer to the people. The Constitution did not reduce the states to mere administrative subdivisions of the general government, but instead recognized their full authority over internal affairs. With respect to such matters as criminal justice, domestic relations, and public safety, the individual states stood as independent nations.[30] This division of power and functions, according to Thomas Ritchie, the editor of *The Richmond Enquirer* from 1804 to 1845, "present[ed] to us one of the grandest experiments that was ever made in political science."[31]

Jeffersonian strict construction is the preferred method of construction because it recognizes the exalted place of the people of the several states. Only the people—not judges, legislators, or executives—can grant powers to their servants in government. The second article of Virginia's declaration of rights avowed: "That all power is vested in, and consequently derived from, the people; that magistrates are their trustees and servants, and at all times amenable to them."[32] As explained by historian Gordon Wood, in the United States "all governmental officials, including the executive and judicial parts of the government, were agents of the people, not fundamentally different from the people's nominal representatives in the lower house of the legislatures."[33] Agency is a fiduciary relationship in which the principal appoints an agent to conduct designated business. The agent is subject to the principal's ultimate control and must account for his actions. The principal, then, is superior to the agent.[34] A country built on the premise that government functionaries are accountable to the people and subject to their control was a radical idea in 1780s. Today it is taken for granted by critics of the Framers.

When speaking of the "the people," however, to whom are we referring? In the context of the Constitution the answer is clear: the people of the several states and not the amalgamated American people.[35] The success of the Revolutionary War secured thirteen separate states in which thirteen peoples established governments to act as their agents. The Framers required that the Constitution of 1787 be ratified in separate state conventions. They recognized conventions as specially elected bodies in which the people exercised ultimate sovereignty. George Mason, who had been the drafter of Virginia's declaration of rights, made clear to his fellow delegates in Philadelphia that acceptance of the Constitution by that state legislatures would be insufficient: "The Legislatures have no power to ratify it. They are mere creatures of the State Constitutions, and cannot be greater than their creators."[36] Thus, the people of each state in adopting the Constitution took certain powers from their state governments and transferred them to the federal government. "[T]hey constituted a general government for special purposes," Jefferson wrote in his draft of the Kentucky

Resolution, "delegated to that government certain definite powers, reserving, each state to itself, the residuary mass of right to their own self-government."[37]

In further respect for the sovereignty of the people, the Constitution did not create a general government to oversee all affairs of a vast continent. Instead, the Framers created a general government with few and defined powers to handle only those matters that required continental cohesion.[38] In the words of James Madison in *Federalist* No. 45, the general government's powers would be exercised "principally on external objects, as war, peace, negotiation, and foreign commerce."[39] Because of federalism—whether it was rooted in Great Britain's salutary neglect, the independence of the Confederation period, or the design of the Constitution—American historian Forrest McDonald could aver that more eighteenth-century Americans had "probably . . . participated directly in government than had any other people on earth."[40]

The Anti-Federalists—opponents of ratification—expressed fears that a latitudinarian interpretation would transform the new general government into a Leviathan. (And, as I have argued elsewhere,[41] they have often turned out to be correct.) They demanded a second constitutional convention to address areas of concern. The Constitution's proponents defeated the demand for additional amendments prior to ratification but promised the Anti-Federalists that the first Congress would consider amendments requested by the various ratifying conventions.

Madison, elected a representative from Virginia, made good on that promise, and twelve amendments ultimately were submitted to the states for consideration. Ten were

ratified in short order. The preface to the proposed amendments recognized that, because "[t]he Conventions of a number of the States, having at the time of their adopting the Constitution expressed a desire in order to prevent misconstruction or abuse of its powers," it was necessary for "further declaratory and restrictive clauses" to be added to the Constitution.[42] Modern Americans call the ratified amendments the Bill of Rights. As evidenced by the prefatory language, these amendments applied only to the general government and not to the states. While this fact might seem curious to twenty-first-century Americans, we must remember that the people of the states were comfortable with their state governments and the states' bills of rights. It was the new general government that gave them pause. The American Revolution had been fought to secure self-government in the individual states. Many patriots worried about creating a new general government that could threaten the revolutionary achievement and rule with a heavy hand similar to the British Parliament.

The Framers were aware of the novelty of their experiment and that its success could provide hope for millions. In the Philadelphia Convention, Madison asserted that "it was more than probable we are now digesting a plan which in its operation would decide for ever the fate of Republican Government."[43] Benjamin Franklin observed that if republican government failed in the United States, "mankind may hereafter from this unfortunate instance, despair of establishing Governments by Human wisdom and leave it to chance, war and conquest."[44] In his first inaugural address, George Washington declared his belief that "preservation of the sacred fire of liberty, and the destiny of the Republican model of

Government, are justly considered as deeply, perhaps as finally staked, on the experiment entrusted to the hands of the American people."[45]

Strict construction originalism embraces popular sovereignty within the several states and the limited purposes of the federal government, whereas much of modern originalism and the totality of living constitutionalism reject the states as preexisting political communities ruled by sovereign peoples and a limited federal government that operates in just a few discrete areas. Some modern originalists might concede that strict construction originalism was a viable theory until the passage of the Fourteenth Amendment. They believe that the Fourteenth Amendment changed everything. For example, libertarian scholars Randy Barnett and Evan Bernick, in their book *The Original Meaning of the Fourteenth Amendment*, contend that "[n]othing in the Constitution of the United States is more important to contemporary American law and politics than the Fourteenth Amendment."[46] The Constitution of 1787's federalist structure, they argue, was vanquished with the Fourteenth Amendment's ratification in 1868. Similarly, exacting limitations on Congress's power were removed to allow for sweeping federal protection of individual rights.

Undoubtedly, the Fourteenth Amendment did result in changes to American constitutional government. Barnett and Bernick, however, overstate the intended results. The key to a proper understanding—consistent with strict construction originalism—is how Northern members of Congress explained the purpose of the Fourteenth Amendment to their constituents back home. They forecast no great revolution in the internal affairs of Northern states or those states' relationship

with the general government. So long as the Northern states treated black citizens and white citizens as equals under the law, the states that had remained loyal to the Union would continue as before. Senator Lyman Trumbull of Illinois, for example, announced that the amendment would have "no operation in Massachusetts, New York, Illinois, or most of the States in the Union" because such states levied no lawfare against freedmen.[47] The Fourteenth Amendment's purpose was to stop the Southern states from imposing second-class citizenship on former slaves. Other than commanding a color blindness in the law, the Fourteenth Amendment worked no great structural revolution.

Scholars, both left and right, have criticized aspects of the Supreme Court's opinion in the *Slaughterhouse Cases* (1872), but the Court's summary of the Reconstruction Amendments rings true:

> But, however pervading this sentiment [belief in a stronger general government], and however it may have contributed to the adoption of the amendments we have been considering, we do not see in those amendments any purpose to destroy the main features of the general system. Under the pressure of all the excited feeling growing out of the war, our statesmen have still believed that the existence of the State with powers for domestic and local government, including the regulation of civil rights[,] the rights of person and of property[,] was essential to the perfect working of our complex form of government, though they have thought proper to impose additional limitations on the States, and to confer additional power on that of the Nation.[48]

The Fourteenth Amendment does not undermine strict construction originalism. It wisely prohibits state and local government from discriminating against persons based on race, but also leaves the federal system's structural bones in place.

The Constitution of 1787 is the oldest written constitution still in use in the world. Its longevity compels our admiration and examination. It was not perfect, but it was the best government the people would approve. Considering its impact, we should be thankful that it was approved no matter how "unrepresentative" the Grand Convention and state ratifying conventions were in the eyes of moderns. Despite the wishes of Professor Seidman and others, it is not mere background music in the course of American law. It is to the American experiment what the Bible is to orthodox Christianity. In the book at hand—written for ordinary citizens seeking to make sense of competing constitutional claims—we see the beauty of American constitutionalism and grasp why we must preserve the inheritance that has been bequeathed to us. Strict construction originalism is perhaps the best available vehicle of constitutional preservation. Tucker's canon of interpretation should remain our North Star as the Constitution takes us further into the twenty-first century.

This book seeks to provide the average citizen with a resource. When trying to make sense of the modern dialogue surrounding the Constitution, citizens can turn to this clause-by-clause examination of the document. No provision is ignored or passed over. Each section gives a brief introduction to the constitutional provision, its history, distortions (if any) to the original intent that have arisen over time, and concrete solutions to return us to a constitutionalism congruent with original intent. The index is user-friendly and is designed to direct the reader to the relevant constitutional passage, even if all the citizen has for a guide is a buzzword such as "emolument" or "privacy." The table of contents is detailed. Topics subject to vigorous debates are noted in boldface type in the table of contents.

The citizen may desire to read the book cover to cover, garner additional resources from the notes, and continue constitutional studies with more specialized books. Or the reader may simply want a guide at hand when hot-button constitutional issues make headlines. This volume is designed to support either approach.

The book does not claim to have all the answers or to be an exhaustive discussion of the Constitution. It is a mere starting point for average Americans who care about their country and who are not content to leave interpretation of the Constitution to the federal judiciary.

It was the people of the several states gathered in conventions who debated and accepted the Constitution. They breathed life into the document. And it is the people of today who should continue to study, debate, and interpret their Constitution. May this book put the Constitution back in their hands.

Acknowledgments

This book would not have been possible without the support and encouragement of Mary Theroux, chief executive officer of the Independent Institute, Graham Walker, president of the Independent Institute, and Christoher B. Briggs, public affairs counsel of the Independent Institute. Their attention to detail and faith in the manuscript were instrumental in completing the work. Thanks are also due to Williamson M. Evers and William F. Shugart II for their helpful suggestions. A special debt of gratitude goes to Alice McLean, whose editorial "kicks in the pants" were both necessary and proper to turn a raw manuscript into a completed work. Cathy Cambron, copy editor extraordinaire, evinced much patience with her close reading of the book in its entirety.

ABBREVIATIONS

The following abbreviations are used throughout the notes.

Creating
Creating the Bill of Rights, ed. Helen E. Veit et al. (Johns Hopkins University Press, 1991)

Elliot's Debates
The Debates in the Several State Conventions on the Adoption of the Federal Constitution, ed. Jonathan Elliot, 7 vols. (J. B. Lippincott & Co., 1888)

Farrand's Records
The Records of the Federal Convention of 1787, ed. Max Farrand, 4 vols. (Yale University Press, 1966)

JCC
Journals of the Continental Congress, 1774–1789, 34 vols. (Library of Congress, 1904–37)

JM Notes
James Madison, *Notes of the Debates in the Federal Convention of 1787* (W. W. Norton and Company, 1987)

JS Exposition
Joseph Story, *A Familiar Exposition of the Constitution of the United States* (Regnery Gateway, 1986)

JW Works
Collected Works of James Wilson, ed. Kermit L. Hall & Mark David Hall, 2 vols. (Liberty Fund, 2007)

LDC
Letters of Delegates to Congress, 1774–1789, ed. Paul H. Smith, 24 vols. (Library of Congress, 1976–93)

PHD
The Pacificus-Helvidius Debates of 1793–74, ed. Morton J. Frisch (Liberty Fund, 2007)

SGT View
St. George Tucker, *View of the Constitution with Selected Writings*, ed. Clyde N. Wilson (Liberty Fund, 1999) [1803]

TAF
The Anti-Federalists: Selected Writings and Speeches, ed. Bruce Frohnen (Regnery, 1999)

TFC
The Founders' Constitution, ed. Phillip B. Kurland & Ralph Lerner, 5 vols. (Liberty Fund, 1987)

TRL
The Republic of Letters: The Correspondence Between Jefferson and Madison, ed. James Morton Smith, 3 vols. (W. W. Norton, 1995)

VCCG
We the States: An Anthology of Historic Documents and Commentaries Thereon, Expounding the State and Federal Relationship (Virginia Commission on Constitutional Government, 1964).

Purpose

The preamble is akin to a trial lawyer's opening statement to the jury. Painting with broad strokes, it sets forth the aims of the new charter of government. The Constitution's preamble is, in other words, an introductory statement that sets forth the purposes of the union.

Background and Development

The Framers were familiar with the use of preambles in the great legal documents of Anglo-American liberty. For example, prefatory statements appear in the Petition of Right of 1628, the Bill of Rights of 1689, and the Declaration of Independence of 1776. Hence, we should not be surprised that the Committee of Detail—the body charged with writing a draft constitution based on the Philadelphia Convention's agreements and compromises—would begin with a preamble.

The preamble provides historical insight into the purpose of the Constitution and is similar to the stated purposes of the Articles of Confederation, which announce the states' rights to "common defence, the security of their Liberties, and their mutual and general welfare."[1] The Constitution sought to improve on the existing structure, or design, of the union. Although the Articles of Confederation enabled the states to defeat the superpower that was Great Britain, and to preserve the rights of the people of the several states to govern themselves, the document contained serious flaws. Congress had no power to levy taxes to pay for the Revolutionary War, to formulate a unified policy over foreign trade, or to offer Massachusetts assistance in putting down an internal rebellion led by Daniel Shays. The Constitution of 1787 purported to empower the new federal government to fulfill the purposes of the original Confederation and served the purpose of making the union "more perfect" in effecting its broad goals. The Committee of Detail believed that the preamble would declare that a new constitution was "the only effectual mode . . . for curing th[e] insufficiency" of the Articles.[2]

Opponents of the Constitution sensed a sinister purpose behind the preamble. The Anti-Federalist who wrote under the pseudonym Brutus complained that if the preamble declared the ends of the new government, "it is obvious it has in view every object which is embraced by any government."[3] In other words, Brutus feared that the preamble would convey a broad national

1

police power whereby the new government could legislate on anything relating to the health, welfare, and morals of the entire citizenry. Similarly, Patrick Henry, in the Virginia ratifying convention, complained that the preamble signaled a "consolidated government," in which all power is collected in the center.[4] Henry predicated that the states would be little more than administrative subdivisions of the central government.

To counter Anti-Federalist rhetoric, the friends of the Constitution pointed to the enumeration of powers in Article I to show that no such consolidation was intended. The Constitution's specific provisions controlled and delegated to the general government only certain definite powers and thus left the states with abundant and broad authority over internal matters.[5] In the Virginia ratifying convention, James Madison assured Anti-Federalists that the states would have full power of legislation over "those great objects which immediately concern the prosperity of the people."[6] Alexander Hamilton in *Federalist* No. 17 scoffed at the idea that the general government had the power or desire to "divest the States of the authorities" relating to purely intrastate affairs.[7] Hamilton declared that the states, not the general government, would remain "the immediate and visible guardian of life and property."[8]

Distortions

It is black-letter law that a preamble is explanatory "and neither enlarges nor confers powers."[9] Consequently, the proponents of legislation cannot rely on the preamble when asserting that a bill is authorized by the Constitution. In his famed Report of 1800, Madison described resort to the preamble to support the constitutionality of a measure as "contrary to every acknowledged rule of construction."[10] The Supreme Court recognized the same understanding in *Jacobson v. Massachusetts* (1905), when it averred that the preamble "has never been regarded as the source of any substantive power conferred on the government of the United States, or on any of its departments."[11]

Nevertheless, proponents of omnipotence in the general government continually demand that the preamble be used to invigorate powers. In the late 1790s, when the Federalists sought to invest the government with the statutory power to punish speech and remove aliens deemed dangerous to the United States without due process of law, they cited the preamble along with other constitutional provisions.[12] They argued that the preamble established the general government as sovereign. Inherent in the attributes of sovereignty, they averred, was the power to deal with the citizens of foreign governments and to enact measures to protect the American people. Jeffersonian Republicans opposed the legislation and the use of the preamble but did not have the numbers to prevent the Federalists from passing the widely contentious and unpopular Alien and Sedition Acts. The harshness of these acts led to the Revolution of 1800 and the demise of the Federalists as a durable political party.

More than two hundred years later, cunning scholars make the same arguments as the Federalists. For example, law professors John W. Welch and James A. Heilpern contend that the preamble must assist "constitutional law [to] stay responsive to major social change" and be "construed dynamically."[13] Over the past two centuries, the limited government created by the Framers has already been stretched beyond recognition through dynamic interpretations. Like the Federalists of old, Welch and Heilpern suggest putting yet another arrow in the progressive quiver to assist Congress and judges in expanding the power fixed in Washington, DC.

On January 5, 2011, the House of Representatives adopted an amendment to House rules requiring that, to be accepted for introduction, all bills and joint resolutions must contain a constitutional authority statement specifically pointing to the provisions allowing the House to act on the bill or joint resolution. Despite the weight of authority indicating that prefatory statements do not confer power, legislators have proposed countless bills that cite the preamble as one of the constitutional grounds for legislation. Often, proposed bills will cite an enumerated power but also include a statement such as "additionally, the preamble to the Constitution provides support of the authority to enact legislation to promote the General Welfare."[14]

The preamble is also distorted by assumptions that "the People" in the preamble refers to the American people as one consolidated body rather than the political communities of the different states. As early as 1793, Chief Justice John Jay, in *Chisholm v. Georgia* (1793), described the preamble as evidencing a national body: "Here we see the people acting as sovereigns of the whole country; and in the language of sovereignty, establishing a Constitution by which it was their will."[15] Such a claim runs counter to the mode of ratification (separate conventions in each state) and Madison's clear teaching in *Federalist* No. 39: "[T]his assent and ratification is to be given by the people, not as individuals composing one entire nation; but as composing the distinct and independent States

to which they respectively belong."[16] Had there been one national act of ratification, the states of North Carolina and Rhode Island would not have been outside the union for a time until their separate state conventions decided to adopt the Constitution. But they were outside the union when the first Congress convened in New York City in March 1789. As a result, the United States at that time was a union of eleven states, with North Carolina and Rhode Island charting their own courses.

Confusion remains rampant about whether ratification was a national or a confederal act. The average civics student typically assumes that the amalgamated people of the United States ratified the Constitution. Students are surprised to learn that two states were outside the union when the general government began operation and that there were separate state conventions because popular sovereignty was located in the people of thirteen separate preexisting communities.

Students are not the only ones confused. So too are Supreme Court justices. In *Cohens v. Virginia* (1821), Chief Justice John Marshall declared that sovereignty, described as the "supreme and irresistible power to make or to unmake, resides only in the whole body of the people; not in any sub-division of them."[17] Marshall, who participated in the Virginia ratification debates, certainly knew better, but he was determined to elevate the power of the general government and to reduce that of the states. Hence, he attempted to erase from history the fact that ratification was an act of the subdivisions—the people of the several states.

Scholars such as Yale's Akhil Amar concede that the Constitution was ratified by citizens of distinct political communities. Amar contends, however, that the act of ratification was "the world's largest corporate merger," which created a single and indissoluble united people.[18] Although Amar is a distinguished scholar, his merger theory would not have been accepted by citizens living at the time of ratification. Had the friends of the Constitution advertised it as creating a single and indissoluble united people, the people of the several states would have rejected the document. Indeed, multiple state ratifying conventions declared that the powers delegated to the general government could be resumed. Such declarations would have been futile if such resumption required the consent of the amalgamated people as a whole. As John Taylor of Caroline noted in *Construction Construed and Constitutions Vindicated*, "[n]ot a single one of the United States would have consented to have dissolved its people, to have reunited them into one great people . . . so ignorant of local circumstances, and so different in local habits."[19]

Perhaps the best evidence of the Framers' view of the people of the several states was the August 6, 1787 report of the Committee of Detail, which read:

> We the people of the States of New Hampshire, Massachusetts, Rhode-Island and Providence Plantations, Connecticut, New-York, New-Jersey, Pennsylvania, Delaware, Maryland, Virginia, North-Carolina, South-Carolina, and Georgia, do ordain, declare, and establish the following Constitution for the Government of Ourselves and our Posterity.[20]

The Framers understood that the ultimate sovereigns—those charged with making, altering, or abolishing fundamental law—were the people in their thirteen separate preexisting communities.[21] But they also realized that some of the political communities might decide to remain outside the new union. Hence, they removed the list of states from the preamble. The removal of the list of sovereign states was a wise decision because, as noted above, Rhode Island and North Carolina did not ratify until long after the other eleven and thus remained outside the union for a time. There is nothing in the records of the Philadelphia Convention to indicate that the removal of the list of states evidenced a change in theory about the locus of ultimate sovereignty.[22]

In sum, the Framers never contemplated one great national act of ratification. The one motion made in Philadelphia to convene a national ratification convention never was seconded and thus was not discussed.[23] Hence, the people organized in their separate states are the parties to the constitutional compact.

This ratification procedure is an acknowledgment of popular sovereignty; in other words, the people of a republic (and in the American situation, there were thirteen separate republics) possess ultimate authority and are the creators and modifiers of fundamental law. Acceptance of popular sovereignty was a significant departure from the British system, in which Parliament retained ultimate authority. In the words of William Blackstone, Parliament could "change and create and create afresh even the Constitution of the kingdom," and "no authority upon earth" could alter a command of Parliament.[24] Not in America. The people of the several states retained ultimate power.

Discussion and Solutions

Just as jurors, when deciding a case, are prohibited from treating the lawyers' opening statements as evidence, so too are government officials prohibited from using the preamble as constitutional support for statutory law or other official measures. Citizens must always remember that the preamble is a prefatory statement and neither supports nor enlarges the powers delegated to the federal government. Resort to the preamble—when politicians invoke, for instance, "the People"—should immediately raise red flags with the citizenry.

Those who support limited government must fight to maintain the principle articulated in *Jacobson*, which states that the preamble is not the source of any substantive power. Activist scholars such as Welch and Heilpern argue that *Jacobson* was "flawed" and "meaningless."[25] They urge the Supreme Court to overrule or simply decline to apply *Jacobson* when presented with arguments about the scope of the preamble. As shown above, the *Jacobson* Court got it right on the preamble. The structure of the Constitution—specific enumerated powers instead of a broad general power of legislation—and responses by the friends of the Constitution to Anti-Federalist arguments demonstrate that the preamble is not a source of substantive power.

The House of Representatives would be wise to further amend House rules to prohibit use of the preamble in statements of constitutional authority. The preamble can add nothing to an enumerated power, and its repeated citation will aid progressive arguments that a developing consensus favors energizing the preamble. As a body politic, we would be better off forbidding constitutional authority statements than continuing to allow the preamble to be trotted out in support of congressional legislation.

Two years before the *Cohens* decision, in an unguarded moment of candor in *McCulloch v. Maryland* (1819), Chief Justice Marshall observed that "[n]o political dreamer was ever wild enough to think of breaking down the lines which separate the states, and of compounding the American people into one common mass. Of consequence, when they act, they act in their states."[26] The "American people" can undertake no act of constitutional significance. The amalgamated population, for example, cannot amend the Constitution, elect a president, or elect a member of Congress.

Appeals to "the People" often signal the use of rhetoric, such as when a politician seeks to use the lives of other people's children in some militaristic endeavor or tries to explain why a slaughter of soldiers was appropriate. One must immediately think of Abraham Lincoln's speech at Gettysburg when dedicating a new national cemetery.[27] Lincoln needed his audience to believe that the death of 51,000 men at Gettysburg was necessary so that "government of the people, by the people, for the people, shall not perish from the earth."[28] His speech fails to explain why allowing the Confederate states to secede in peace would have threatened the type of government Lincoln presumably believed to be embodied in the original union.

No mechanism exists that can prohibit politicians from rhetorical bombast in the name of "the People." Accordingly, citizens should remain on guard when lofty language is used. Appeals to a people incapable of any act of constitutional significance is but a smoke screen to undertake some unconstitutional act or to sacrifice lives at the altar of power.

ARTICLE I
SECTION 1

ALL LEGISLATIVE POWERS herein granted shall be vested in a Congress of the United States, which shall consist of a Senate and House of Representatives.

Purpose

In republican governments, the legislative power predominates. Consequently, a constitution must specify where this power resides. In the United States, laws for the union are to be made in the two houses of Congress and no other place. Should the executive, judiciary, or another entity appear to exercise lawmaking power, Article I, Section 1 is a beacon to point the way back home.

Background and Development

The Confederation had a unicameral Congress that served as the heart of the union. Tasks we associate with the presidency or the judiciary belonged to Congress under the Articles. It created laws, executed laws, and served as an appellate court for disputes between states "concerning boundary, jurisdiction, or in any cause whatever."[29] The Confederation had no other branches of government to check Congress. It is not an overstatement to say that Congress was the Confederation.

The Congress created by the Constitution of 1787 is the legislative branch of the general government. Legislative power refers to the "[m]aking or giving of laws" and "pertain[s] to the function of law-making or to the process of enactment of laws."[30] The full power of legislation for the general government—but only as "herein granted" by specific constitutional provisions—resides in the two houses

of Congress and nowhere else.[31] This accords with separation-of-powers principles, which dictate that the legislative, executive, and judicial powers should be kept separate and distinct.

According to political scientist M. J. C. Vile, "[t]he doctrine of separation of powers is clearly committed to a view of political liberty an essential part of which is the restraint of governmental power, and that this can best be achieved by setting up divisions within the government to prevent the concentration of such power in the hands of a single group of men."[32] In *Federalist* No. 47, James Madison averred that the accretion of powers "in the same hands, whether of one, a few, or many, and whether hereditary, self-appointed, or elective, may justly be pronounced the very definition of tyranny."[33] Hence, we see strong statements of separation of powers in state constitutions predating the Constitution of 1787. The Massachusetts Constitution of 1780 stated the predominant view as follows:

> In the government of this Commonwealth, the legislative department shall never exercise the executive and judicial powers, or either of them: The executive shall never exercise the legislative and judicial powers, or either of them: The judicial shall never exercise the legislative and executive powers, or either of them: to the end it may be a government of laws and not of men.[34]

Congress comprises two houses and thus is a bicameral body. Bicameralism was standard among the state governments, with eleven states out of thirteen opting for bicameral legislatures after declaring independence from Great Britain.[35] During the Philadelphia Convention, Virginia's George Mason described popular support for bicameralism as follows: "The people of America, like all other people, are unsettled in their minds, and their principles fixed to no object, except that a republican government is best, and the legislature ought to consist of two branches."[36] Madison expected the legislative power to "predominate" in the general government and thus saw bicameralism as a necessary check on Congress.[37] In remarks at the Philadelphia Convention, Madison explained that with important business passing through two separate chambers, the people would be protected from (1) a betrayal of their liberties by Congress and (2) illiberal but perhaps popular legislation prompted by "temporary errors" or passions.[38] James Wilson of Pennsylvania argued that two legislative branches secured the first purposes of government, because if one house endeavored to "depart from the principles of the constitution," the other house would draw it back to the firm foundations of fundamental law.[39]

Under the Great Compromise (or the Connecticut Compromise, as it is often called), representation in the House of Representatives is based on population, while that in the Senate is based on the equality of the states. The division between the large states (favoring proportional representation) and the small states (favoring equal representation) did not first arise at the Philadelphia Convention. The issue came up in the drafting of the Articles of Confederation. The larger states demanded a vote based on their larger populations, and the smaller states viewed an equal vote as the only way to protect their liberties. Samuel Chase of Maryland urged a compromise voting scheme for the confederation: Each colony would have one vote on matters of "life and liberty," but on money issues "the voice of each colony should be proportioned to the number of it's [*sic*] inhabitants."[40] Roger Sherman of Connecticut also pleaded that middle ground be sought. He proposed that two votes be taken on issues concerning the confederacy: one by states and the other by population. Ultimately, the large states, fearing that no union would be formed absent a concession, agreed to continue the practice of equal state voting that had been implemented by the First Continental Congress.

Fundamentally, the Great Compromise in Philadelphia was a retooling of Sherman's proposed middle ground. Oliver Ellsworth of Connecticut observed that the new Constitution would be "partly national" and "partly federal."[41] Proportional representation in the House "was conformable to national principles & would secure the large states against the small."[42] "An equality of voices [in the Senate] was conformable to the federal principles and was necessary to secure the small states against the large."[43] Rather than two votes in a unicameral body, the Philadelphia Convention followed the advice of Connecticut and created two legislative chambers chosen by very different means and constituencies. Absent some security for the small states that feared being swallowed by the large, the Constitution of 1787 would have been an impossibility.

In defending the compromise of the New York ratifying convention, Alexander Hamilton declared that insistence on a Congress based on population or wealth would have been ludicrous. "Would it have been wise and prudent in [the Philadelphia Convention], in this critical situation," Hamilton asked, "to have deserted" the union by being inflexible?[44] Hamilton told opponents that if they called another convention, "they will have the same difficulties to encounter, the same clashing interests to reconcile."[45]

Distortions

The Constitution's grant of legislative power has been distorted by the rise of the administrative state. Broad powers are in the hands of unelected officials instead of Congress. In the early 1940s, political theorist James Burnham observed that power had been "slipping away from parliaments" to "an interconnected group of administrative boards, commissions, [and] bureaus."[46] He traced this trend to World War I and believed that "[n]o development of this period is more obvious and indisputable."[47] Burnham, of course, described what he termed as the rise of the managerial society. Citizens in this society who want to know what the law is should not "look up the records . . . of parliament" or another representative body.[48] Instead, they must turn to "the rules, regulations, laws, decrees" that are "issued from an interconnected group of administrative boards, commissions, bureaus—or whatever other name may be used for comparable agencies."[49]

Burnham observed that Congress's most important laws were not direct legislation, but rather delegations of congressional power "to one or another agency largely outside of its control."[50] As a result, "[t]he bureaus are the sovereign bodies of the unlimited state of

managerial society."[51] The superintendence of the administrative state, Burnham believed, "is carried on by new men, a new type of men. It is, specifically, the managerial type."[52] In other words, the administrative state was ruled by experts.

The administrative state arose not by accident but intentionally. As Hillsdale College's Ronald J. Pestritto has observed, President Woodrow Wilson in the early years of the twentieth century "urged Congress to abandon the business of legislating on the details of policy, leaving that responsibility to the experts in the bureaucracy who were best suited for it."[53] Wilson's Hegelian preference for expert rule is evident in his scholarly articles as well as in his political efforts. He believed in inevitable historical progress in three stages: (1) absolute rulers with the unchecked power of administration; (2) constitutional government, in which administration is more difficult because of limited government; and (3) administrative rule "where the people abandon their fear of unchecked administrative power."[54] During stage three, rule is by "educated experts in the bureaucracy, insulated from the pressures of narrow self-interest," who "were to see more clearly than the people themselves the objective public will, and were to know best the administrative means necessary to achieve it."[55] Shielding the experts from political control, under Wilson's theory, "was a means of purifying government—of keeping policy decisions above the fray of traditional political machinations."[56]

This purification has resulted in entities such as the Federal Trade Commission, the Securities and Exchange Commission, and the Commodity Futures Trading Commission exercising quasi-legislative, quasi-executive, and quasi-judicial powers. These agencies, based on a broad command from Congress, make the rules that govern us, enforce the rules they have made, and adjudicate challenges to their directives. Whereas in the federal and state governments—pursuant to written constitutions—these functions are assigned to different departments of government, in the administrative state the functions are performed under one roof.

The benefits of separation of powers and bicameralism are lost in the administrative state. When the power to regulate securities, for example, is concentrated in a federal agency, this one entity exercises all legislative, executive, and judicial power concerning securities regulation. Such a concentration, the Framers recognized, was the very definition of tyranny. Restraint of government is rejected for empowerment of government. Moreover, the benefits of bicameralism are lost. An agency rule does not have to pass through two different bodies (the House and Senate), where compromise or a flat-out refusal to enact the rule are possibilities. The agencies are echo chambers bereft of the limitations and the purposeful push toward deliberation found in the tripartite design.

An administrative state is also contrary to popular sovereignty (discussed in the previous section on the preamble). Because the people have never transferred power to a fourth branch of government, the administrative state is ultra vires. The principals (the people) have never authorized the administrative state (the agent) to act on their behalf. Under acknowledged concepts of agency law, arrangements made by an agent are binding on the principal only if they are within the authority actually granted or reasonably apparent to the

agent. In the American case, neither the Constitution of 1787 nor its amendments grant power or imply that power might be granted. Thus, claims that experts in the bureaucracy can bind the people are false. In fact, the first principles of the American Revolution counsel against such usurpation.

The administrative state also offends the nondelegation doctrine. Under the nondelegation doctrine, Congress is not permitted to delegate its legislative power to any other branch or entity. The nondelegation doctrine is a derivative of the separation of powers and popular sovereignty. The English philosopher John Locke is clear that "[t]he legislative cannot transfer the power of making laws to any other hands: for it being a delegated power from the people, they who have it cannot pass it over to others."[57] Similarly, Thomas Jefferson instructs that it is forbidden for legislators to undertake "a transfer of their powers into other hands and other forms, without consulting the people."[58]

The Tariff Act of 1922 dealt a blow to the nondelegation doctrine when Congress, the president, and the Supreme Court all agreed that Congress could delegate to the president the authority to increase custom duties. The Supreme Court averred that "the Congress has found it frequently necessary to use officers of the executive branch within defined limits, to secure the exact effect intended by its acts of legislation, by vesting discretion in such officers to make public regulations interpreting a statute and directing the details of its execution, even to the extent of providing for penalizing a breach of such regulation."[59] Thus, so long as Congress provides the president or an agency with an "intelligible principle" on how to achieve Congress's desired result, "such legislative action is not a forbidden delegation of legislative power."[60]

The Supreme Court during the New Deal did use the nondelegation doctrine on two occasions to strike down delegations of legislative authority. Under the National Industrial Recovery Act (NIRA), Congress permitted the president via executive order to prohibit the transportation in commerce of petroleum produced in excess of the amounts permitted by states. In *Panama Refining Co. v. Ryan* (1935), the Supreme Court held that an executive order issued under the NIRA was an unconstitutional delegation of congressional power.[61] Similarly, in *A.L.A. Schechter Poultry Corporation v. United States* (1935), the Court considered whether Congress in the NIRA could permit the executive to regulate industries by instructing them to develop their own business codes—that is, to create government-sponsored cartels.[62] The Court found this an unconstitutional delegation of legislative power because of an absence of a clear statutory standard to guide the president. Since 1935, the Supreme Court has not struck down any act of Congress based on the nondelegation doctrine.

There have been recent rumblings about a revival of the nondelegation doctrine. In *Gundy v. United States* (2019), a majority of the Supreme Court rejected a nondelegation argument against the Sex Offender Registration and Notification Act (SORNA), in which Congress delegated to the U.S. attorney general authority to impose the statute's registration provisions on sex offenders who sustained convictions before the enactment of SORNA.[63] Interestingly, three justices dissented (Neil Gorsuch, John Roberts, and Clarence Thomas), arguing that the "intelligible

principle" test has no basis in the Constitution and thus that a serious use of the nondelegation doctrine should be reconsidered. Since the decision in *Gundy*, Justices Brett Kavanaugh and Amy Coney Barrett have joined the Court. In *FCC v. Consumers' Research* (2025), the Court had an opportunity to utilize the nondelegation doctrine when considering congressional authorization permitting the FCC to determine the amounts that telecommunications carriers must contribute to subsidize telephone service to low-income households.[64] The Court held that Congress had provided the agency with intelligible principles and avoided a resurrection of the nondelegation doctrine. While the decision was a disappointment to critics of the administrative state, it does not prevent future nondelegation challenges to other statutory schemes.

Discussion and Solutions

While a judicial revival of the nondelegation doctrine would be welcome, Americans fool themselves if they believe that unelected judges offer the solution. Americans are right to praise recent decisions such as *Loper Bright Enterprises v. Raimondo* (2024), in which the Court held that administrative agencies are not more competent than the judiciary to interpret statutes they administer.[65] This decision ended the era of *Chevron* deference, in which agency interpretations were upheld if they met the low bar of reasonableness.[66] Citizens must not forget that the modern judiciary—with its preference for policymaking over declaration of preexisting law—is a problem itself. While more rigorous judicial review might be an ingredient in the recipe for reform, further investigation is warranted.

Elsewhere I have argued that perhaps only the constituent power—the people of the several states gathered in conventions—can serve as the needed check.[67] Because this nullification option is drastic, we should consider, to borrow a phrase from Peter B. McCutchen, "second best" options as well.[68] Whatever remedy or combination of remedies is chosen, Americans must recognize that the administrative state as structured undermines the constitutional order and must be dealt with sooner or later.

To counter the administrative state, Congress might be armed with a legislative veto. With a legislative veto, a simple majority in Congress could nullify any controversial administrative actions. Not only could Congress render agency decisions void, but the existence of such a veto would likely improve the quality of administrative decision-making.

One must recognize that Congress created the administrative state and thus has the power to abolish it. At this advanced stage in the development of managerialism, however, Congress is unlikely to take such a bold action. With the legislative veto, however, it could slowly chip away at some of the administrative state's worst excesses. Admitting that Congress created the administrative apparatus does not necessarily mean that a future Congress will decline to use the legislative veto. Today, Congress often passes difficult decisions to the agencies in order to avoid potential backlash during the next election cycle. But will Congress always be an entity desirous of passing the buck? Maybe not. Thus, we should provide it with the necessary tools to limit the administrative state, even if they are unlikely to be used in this decade. As things currently stand, Congress does not have a legislative

veto and cannot have it because of the Court's Presentment Clause jurisprudence.

In *I.N.S. v. Chadha* (1983), the Supreme Court considered a portion of the Immigration and Nationality Act authorizing either the House or the Senate to invalidate and suspend deportation rulings of executive branch officials.[69] This was not the first time Congress had used a "legislative veto." Indeed, prior to *Chada*, the national legislature included such provisions in "200 separate laws over a period of 50 years."[70] The Court discussed the Presentment Clause and concluded that congressional invalidation of executive branch directives was an exercise of legislative power and thus subject to the lawmaking process outlined in Article I, Section 7 (that is, both houses should have passed the measure and presented it to the president for his consideration). The Court sympathized with the need to oversee and control administrative agencies but gleaned from the text and debates in Philadelphia an "unmistakable expression of a determination that legislation by the national Congress be a step-by-step, deliberate and deliberative process."[71]

In dissent, Justice Byron White recognized the problem with the majority's decision:

> The prominence of the legislative veto mechanism in our contemporary political system and its importance to Congress can hardly be overstated. It has become a central means by which Congress secures the accountability of executive and independent agencies. Without the legislative veto, Congress is faced with a Hobson's choice: either to refrain from delegating the necessary authority, leaving itself with a hopeless task of writing laws with the

requisite specificity to cover endless special circumstances across the entire policy landscape, or in the alternative, to abdicate its law-making function to the executive branch and independent agencies. To choose the former leaves major national problems unresolved; to opt for the latter risks unaccountable policymaking by those not elected to fill that role.[72]

Whether by a constitutional amendment or by the Court overturning precedent, we should dispense with *Chada*, and the legislative branch should be armed with a tool to restrict the rule of the managers. As pointed out earlier, this is a "second best" option that accepts that the modern administrative state

will not be dismantled overnight. Boston University's Gary Lawson traced the explosion of the administrative state to the New Deal and averred that "[f]aced with a choice between the administrative state and the Constitution, the architects of our modern government chose the administrative state, and their choice has stuck."[73] We must never forget that the administrative state is unconstitutional. As a result, any measures—even modest ones—to roll it back should be welcomed. We must combat the administrative state with modest tools such as revival of the nondelegation doctrine and legislative veto. If these prove insufficient, more potent measures must be examined.

SECTION 2, CLAUSE 1

THE HOUSE OF Representatives shall be composed of Members chosen every second Year by the People of the several States, and the Electors in each State shall have the Qualifications requisite for Electors of the most numerous Branch of the State Legislature.

Purpose

Frequent elections are necessary to promote the accountability of representatives to the people. Such accountability is critical to republican government. In addition, the Constitution sets forth who chooses members of the lower house and determines the qualifications for electors—namely, the people of the several states. Because of divergent voting laws throughout the union, the Framers tied qualifications to state practice.

Background and Development

Unlike the Articles of Confederation, the Constitution allows the general government to operate directly on the people. Consequently, the Framers determined that the people of the several states should elect the members of the lower house. At the Philadelphia Convention, Virginia's George Mason described the House of Representatives as "the grand repository of the democratic principles of the Government"[74] and a "security for the rights of the people."[75] James Wilson of Pennsylvania believed that popular election of the House would serve as "the corner Stone" and "foundation of the fabric" of the general government.[76]

The two-year term for representatives was a compromise between three years, as proposed in the Virginia Plan, and one year, as advocated by many delegates. Most of the delegates agreed that frequent elections were necessary for the popular branch of the legislature. Edmund Randolph of Virginia observed that "[t]he people were attached to frequency of elections."[77] Because of the difficulty posed by travel for the representatives in returning home and the electors in the states' backcountry trekking to the polls, a two-year term seemed more reasonable. In *Federalist* No. 52, Madison argued that elections every two years were frequent enough so that House members would depend on the people and sympathize with their local circumstances.[78]

Many Anti-Federalists criticized the two-year term and contended that "where annual elections end, tyranny begins." The Anti-Federalist writing as Cato charged "that biannual elections for representatives are a departure from the safe democratical principles of annual ones."[79] In the Massachusetts ratifying convention, Dr. John Taylor expressed disapproval of biannual elections: "Annual elections have been the practice of this state ever since its settlement, and no objection to such a mode of electing has ever been made. It has, indeed, sir, been considered as the safeguard of the liberties of the people; and the annihilation of it, the avenue through which tyranny will enter."[80]

In defending biannual elections, friends of the Constitution focused on the limited powers delegated to Congress. In the Massachusetts ratifying convention, Fisher Ames

conceded "that annual elections may be highly fit for the state legislature" possessed with a general power of legislation.[81] But the general government, according to Ames, had no such broad power, because "[t]he objects of their power are few and national."[82] Christopher Gore supported Ames on the propriety of biannual elections and observed that "the powers of the whole government are limited to certain national objects, and are accurately defined."[83]

Under the Constitution, the persons permitted to vote for representatives are the same ones who are allowed to vote for the most numerous branch of the state legislature. No amalgamated mass of "American people" chooses representatives. Instead, the people acting within their individual states do. At the Philadelphia Convention, some delegates suggested setting a uniform national voting-eligibility standard, such as an individual's status as a freeholder. Others opposed such endeavors vehemently. For example, Oliver Ellsworth of Connecticut supported allowing the states to determine voter qualifications because "[t]he right of suffrage was a tender point, and strongly guarded by most of the State Constitutions." Moreover, he believed that if the proposed Constitution set requirements that disenfranchised some citizens who were used to voting in state legislative elections, then they would "not readily subscribe to the National Constitution."[84]

Friends of the Constitution also touted the voter-qualification tie with the state houses of representatives as a strong bulwark against the destruction of the state governments. For example, Eleazer Brooks, at the Massachusetts ratifying convention, exclaimed that it would be "impossible that the state governments should be annihilated by the general government" because of Article I, Section 2, Clause 1.[85] Similarly, James Wilson of Pennsylvania reasoned that this section shows that "the existence of state legislatures is . . . essential to the existence of the general government."[86]

Since ratification, amendments to the Constitution have restricted the states from excluding voters on grounds of race, sex, failure to pay taxes, and age (persons eighteen years or older may vote).[87]

Distortions

Nothing in Section 2 mandates that states be divided into congressional districts. After ratification, many states chose to have representatives elected at large. Federal law, under guise of regulating the times, places, and manner of elections pursuant to Article I, Section 4, now requires election of House members by district. In *Wesberry v. Sanders* (1964), the Supreme Court held that the principle of "one man, one vote" applies to House elections: "We hold that, construed in its historical context, the command of Art. I, s 2, that Representatives be chosen 'by the People of the several States' means that as nearly as is practicable one man's vote in a congressional election is to be worth as much as another's."[88] Though that might be a laudable idea, in the years after ratification, states adopting congressional districts attempted to create them with roughly equal populations but did not get close to the Court's "one man, one vote" standard. The Court has not shied away from demanding mathematical precision in drawing district lines. In *Karcher v. Daggett* (1983), the Court struck down a New Jersey redistricting plan wherein "the largest district

is less than one percent greater than the population of the smallest district."[89]

Discussion and Solutions

"One man, one vote" is an additional, extraconstitutional requirement that should be jettisoned. As Justice John Marshall Harlan noted in a dissenting opinion in 1962, there is "nothing . . . in the Federal Constitution which expressly or impliedly supports the view that state legislatures must be so structured as to reflect with approximate equality the voice of every voter. Not only is that proposition refuted by history . . . but it strikes deep into the heart of our federal system."[90] Justice Harlan further observed that acceptance of "one man, one vote" "would require us to turn our backs on" principles of deference "for the judgment of state legislatures on matters of basically local concern."[91]

Similarly, Justice Clarence Thomas has noted, "in embracing one person, one vote, the Court has arrogated to the Judiciary important value judgments that the Constitution reserves to the people."[92] There are multiple possible answers to the question of how much voting strength an individual citizen should have. It is reasonable to conclude that "individual voting strength must sometimes yield to countermajoritarian checks"—for example, in an effort to control the effect of factions.[93] Neither the Constitution nor political theory dictates that "one man, one vote" is the only orthodox way to design a republican government. The U.S. Senate and the Electoral College are but two examples in the federal Constitution in which the Framers rejected "one man, one vote."

In a federal system, the states serve as laboratories of democracy. Our fifty states should be permitted to design their institutions based on local circumstances, traditions, and new innovations. Just as scholars demonstrated the shaky ground of *Roe v. Wade* (1973) and thus contributed to its ultimate demise, so should we expose "one person, one vote" for the fallacy it is.

SECTION 2, CLAUSE 2

NO PERSON SHALL be a Representative who shall not have attained to the Age of twenty five Years, and been seven Years a Citizen of the United States, and who shall not, when elected, be an Inhabitant of that State in which he shall be chosen.

Purpose

This provision sets certain minimum constitutional qualifications to serve in the House of Representatives. The Framers believed that a representative should have significant life experience, be attached to the United States, and have substantial ties to the people of the state elevating him to federal office.

Background and Development

The Philadelphia Convention debated various qualifications for membership in the House, including requiring property holdings and prohibiting public debtors from serving. Some delegates opposed specifying any qualifications for representatives and preferred to leave the matter with the people. Ultimately, the Convention chose the three qualifications listed in this provision.

George Mason of Virginia was one of the leading proponents for qualifications. Noting that when he was a young man, his opinions "were too crude & erroneous to merit influence on public measures," Mason proposed that a House member be at least twenty-five years old.[94] Other delegates observed that young men had often been assets to their countries. James Wilson declared

that there were "[m]any instances" where "signal services" were "rendered in high stations to the public before the age of 25."[95] A majority sided with Mason and agreed that a person should have some meaningful life experiences before serving in the national legislature.

Mason also suggested the seven-year citizenship requirement. He "did not chuse to let foreigners and adventurers make laws for us & govern us" and argued that recent arrivals needed to live in America a significant period to garner local knowledge.[96] Oliver Ellsworth of Connecticut "thought seven years of residence was by far too long a term" and that some shorter period "would be proper."[97] The majority preferred the lengthier term and accepted seven years.

A House member must be an "inhabitant" of the state rather than a "resident." The Framers chose the former designation for fear that the latter could exclude people who traveled frequently for employment purposes. Madison stated that the term "resident" might "exclude persons absent occasionally for a considerable time on public or private business."[98] The delegates agreed with him and voted unanimously to strike "resident" and insert "inhabitant."

Distortions

In the 1990s, a substantial movement developed to limit the terms of representatives and senators. Multiple states affirmed the importance of a rotation in office and imposed term limits on their congressional delegations. Arkansas amended its state constitution to prohibit an otherwise-eligible candidate for Congress from appearing on the ballot if that candidate already had served three terms in the House or two terms in the Senate. The Supreme Court reviewed the matter in *U.S. Term Limits, Inc. v. Thornton* (1995) and held "that neither Congress nor the States . . . possess the power to supplement the exclusive qualifications set forth in the text of the Constitution."[99] The majority's holding met with a powerful dissent from Justice Clarence Thomas: "Nothing in the Constitution deprives the people of each State of the power to prescribe eligibility requirements for the candidates who seek to represent them in Congress. The Constitution is simply silent on this question. And where the Constitution is silent, it raises no bar to action by the States or the people."[100]

Thomas's position is the same as Thomas Jefferson's. In an 1814 letter to Joseph C. Cabell, Jefferson observed that the Constitution "does not declare, itself, that the member shall not be a lunatic, a pauper, a convict of treason, of murder, of felony, or other infamous crime, or a non-resident of his district."[101] The Constitution does not prohibit, Jefferson continued, "the State power of declaring these, or any other disqualifications which its particular circumstances may call for."[102]

Discussion and Solutions

The decision in *U.S. Term Limits* should be corrected either by constitutional amendment or by the Court overturning its precedent. Rotation in office—what we would call term limits—dates back to ancient Athenian democracy. In the fourth and fifth centuries BC, Athenians prohibited anyone from serving on the five-hundred-person ruling council for longer than two years. Aristotle held that in a constitutional state "citizens rule and are ruled by turns," since "the natures of the citizens are equal."[103] Hence, this vaunted philosopher was an early champion of term limits.

Rotation in office was a critical part of the Articles of Confederation's efforts to limit congressional power. Under Article V, "no person shall be capable of being a delegate for more than three years in any term of six years."[104] According to historian Gordon Wood, motivating factors for this provision were fears of establishment of an American ruling aristocracy and the belief that public service should be open to men as talented as (or perhaps more talented than) the old guard.

The Constitution of 1787 is silent on term limits; that silence raised the ire of Anti-Federalists. "ROTATION, that noble prerogative of liberty, is entirely excluded from the new system of government, and great men may and probably will be continued in office during their lives," predicted An Officer of the Late Continental Army.[105] Similarly, Mercy Otis Warren, writing as a Columbian Patriot, abjured that "[t]here is no provision for a rotation, nor any thing to prevent the perpetuity of office in the same hands for life; which by a little well timed bribery, will probably be done, to the exclusion of men of the best abilities from their share in the offices of the government."[106]

Term limits might not be a panacea for the political ailments of the country, but the states should be allowed to impose them on members of their congressional delegations. If the experiment does not produce the desired results, the states can return to the present system of possible perpetual reelection. We should at least give federal rotation in office a chance.

SECTION 2, CLAUSE 3

REPRESENTATIVES AND DIRECT Taxes shall be apportioned among the several States which may be included within this Union, according to their respective Numbers, which shall be determined by adding to the whole Number of free Persons, including those bound to Service for a Term of Years, and excluding Indians not taxed, three fifths of all other Persons. The actual Enumeration shall be made within three Years after the first Meeting of the Congress of the United States, and within every subsequent Term of ten Years, in such Manner as they shall by Law direct. The Number of Representatives shall not exceed one for every thirty Thousand, but each State shall have at Least one Representative; and until such enumeration shall be made, the State of New Hampshire shall be entitled to chuse three, Massachusetts eight, Rhode-Island and Providence Plantations one, Connecticut five, New-York six, New Jersey four, Pennsylvania eight, Delaware one, Maryland six, Virginia ten, North Carolina five, South Carolina five, and Georgia three.

Purpose

To foster fairness in direct taxation and representation, the original Constitution required apportionment of representatives and direct taxes based on population. Slaves were counted as three-fifths of a person. Southerners wanted slaves counted as whole persons, to increase the Southern states' voting strength, and Northerners did not want them counted at all, to increase the Northern states' voting strength. The three-fifths figure represented a compromise. The taxation component ensured that the South would not import slaves just to increase political power. To ensure an accurate count, the Constitution provides for a decennial census.

Background and Development

The issue of counting slaves for some purposes was not unique to the Philadelphia Convention. The matter came up during the debates on the Articles of Confederation regarding the payment of common expenses for the union. John Dickinson's original draft of the Articles provided that all expenses for war, the common defense, or the general welfare would be paid out of a common treasury, "which shall be supplied by the several

Colonies in Proportion to the Number of Inhabitants of every Age, Sex and Quality, except Indians not paying Taxes."[107] Samuel Chase of Maryland questioned the fairness of allocating expenses based on the numbers of all inhabitants. Chase suggested that the number of white inhabitants should be the standard, because slaves were property. The Dickinson provision, Chase claimed, had the effect of taxing the Southerner's investment and thus gave the Northern farmer an economic advantage.

John Adams challenged Chase's reasoning. He maintained that the number of laborers in a state, regardless of their status, was a true measure of wealth and the ability to contribute to the Confederation. "[T]hat the condition of the laboring poor in most countries, that of the fishermen particularly in the Northern states," Adams contended, "is as abject as that of slaves. It is the number of laborers which produce the surplus for taxation, and numbers therefore indiscriminately are a fair index of wealth."[108]

After much debate, the Congress rejected the amendment offered by Chase. The vote, to no one's surprise, was along sectional lines. The states voting against the amendment were New Hampshire, Massachusetts, Rhode Island, Connecticut, New York, New Jersey, and Pennsylvania. It was in their collective interest that slaves be counted as freemen for congressional revenue purposes. The states with large slaveholdings understood that they would have to pay less if expenses were allocated based on the number of white inhabitants. While some general denunciations of slavery were voiced, historian Merrill Jensen has observed that the debate on that provision of the Articles "had little of the humanitarian

about it. It was a matter of simple addition and subtraction."[109] Congress eventually abandoned Dickinson's proposal to count heads and instead divided the states' contributions to the national government's expenses on the basis of land values.

This same issue arose in Philadelphia concerning representation and taxation. In making the calculus of power, Southerners wanted slaves counted as whole persons to increase the Southern states' voting power in Congress; Northerners did not want slaves to be counted at all for the same parochial reason. William Paterson of New Jersey observed that slaves were not counted in allocating representation within Southern state legislatures and questioned why slaves, as a species of property, should augment Southern numbers in Congress. Rufus King of Massachusetts explained the matter succinctly: As the richest members in the Confederation, the Southern states "would not league themselves with the Northern unless some respect were paid to their superior wealth."[110] King reasoned that wealthy states with relatively small white populations (for example, South Carolina) likely would contribute more to the federal treasury than many states with larger numbers of freemen. Thus, counting slaves as three-fifths of a free person was a compromise between the two sections.

Gouverneur Morris of Pennsylvania, who expressed strong moral objections to slavery, urged that the formula for apportioning representation should be the same for apportioning taxes. Several delegates admitted the equity in Morris's motion, including George Mason, who also feared "embarrassments might be occasioned to the Legislature by it."[111] Morris acknowledged Mason's concern and agreed to limit his motion to direct taxes, thus omitting indirect taxes on imports, exports, and consumption. James Wilson of Pennsylvania supported Morris's modified motion and believed that the Northern public would find the three-fifths clause more palatable if it applied to both direct taxation and representation. He and other Northerners also viewed Morris's proposal as discouraging the slave states from importing large numbers of Africans to increase their political power in Congress, because such importations would also increase their tax burdens.

With representation and taxation tied to the number of free inhabitants and bondsmen, some method of periodically counting the population was needed. Edmund Randolph of Virginia suggested that a regular census be taken; Mason agreed that such a counting "was essential" to a "fair representation."[112] Randolph also acknowledged that the census should be under the direction of the general government, because the states "will be too much interested to take an impartial one for themselves."[113]

The final portion of this clause provides the number of representatives allotted per state prior to the first decennial census in 1790. George Mason properly described this as a "conjectur[e] as to the actual populations of the states."[114]

Distortions

Although the words "actual Enumeration" seem to require a detailed count of the population, in *Utah v. Evans* (2002), the Supreme Court held that the Census Clause allows Congress to estimate population numbers when conducting the decennial census.[115] The Court averred that because the Constitution allows Congress to direct the manner of the enumeration, estimates are allowed. The majority's conclusion met with a strong dissent from Justice Clarence Thomas: "The text, history, and a review of the original understanding of the Census Clause confirm that an actual enumeration means an actual count, without estimation. While more sophisticated statistical techniques may be available today than at the time of the founding, the Framers had a great deal of familiarity with alternative methods of calculating population. They decided to constitutionalize the arduous task of an actual enumeration.[116]

Another relevant question is whether the federal government, pursuant to the decennial census, may do more than simply conduct a count. The operation plan of the modern census often seeks information that will be used to calculate everything from employment and crime rates to health and educational background. The text, however, does not support asking such questions.

The Constitution provides that the "number of Representatives shall not exceed one for every thirty thousand" inhabitants but is silent on how large a district can be. Initially, drafts provided for one representative for every forty thousand inhabitants, but George Washington and others successfully obtained an adjustment based on concerns about inadequate representation.

During the ratification debates, opponents of the Constitution remained concerned that one representative for every thirty thousand people was insufficient to foster a true representative body. In the Virginia convention, George Mason observed that "to make representation real and actual," the number of representatives needed to be adequate to allow the representatives "to mix with the people, think as they think, feel as they feel," and be "thoroughly acquainted with their interest and condition."[117]

In the main, the pro-Constitution Federalists did not disagree with the Anti-Federalists on the representation issue. "It is a sound and important principle that the representative ought to be acquainted with the interests and circumstances of his constituents," wrote James Madison in *Federalist* No. 56.[118] James Wilson of Pennsylvania did not challenge Madison's view of representation, but contended that because the federal government's powers were few and defined, representatives did not need to be as numerous as in the state assemblies.

Madison assured Anti-Federalist critics that "the number of representatives will be augmented from time to time in the manner provided by the Constitution."[119] Madison estimated that within fifty years, the House would have four hundred members. It did not turn out that way. Only 242 congressional seats were filled in 1839. After the 1910 census, with the population of more than 92 million, the number was increased to 435 from 394. But there the growth stopped. In 1929, Congress fixed the number of representatives at 435, where it remains today, even though our population now exceeds 300 million. The initial first amendment to the Bill of Rights would have required at least one representative for every fifty thousand persons. This was an effort to ensure that representation remained somewhat meaningful. It failed ratification by just one state.

Discussion and Solutions

We are poorer as a republic because of Congress's refusal to augment the number of representatives in the House. Based on the 2010 census, each member of Congress represents approximately 710,767 people. We kid ourselves if we believe this is true representation. The Founders—both Federalists and Anti-Federalists—would have concerns about such numbers. America's large districts make it impossible for representatives to be acquainted with the interests and circumstances of their constituents. This is especially so today because the federal government legislates on matters that in prior generations were considered the province of state and local governments.

Undoubtedly, many would protest that a significant enlargement would make the House too unwieldy. Such an objection assumes that meaningful debate takes place on the floor of Congress. In reality, however, most of the work is done in committees and by committee staff. Expansion of the House would have little effect on the process.

Moreover, technology makes casting ballots easier and could speed Congress's work, even with increased membership. With a computer, internet access, and a phone, members of Congress could do as other Americans do: telecommute. Large representative bodies are common in other countries, and the ratios make them more representative than our lower house: 62 million people in the United Kingdom elect 650 members of Parliament, one for every 95,000 residents; Japan's 127 million people elect 480 representatives, one for every 264,000 residents; France's National Assembly has 577 members, each representing 118,000 people.

Expansion of Congress would help in other ways. It would be easier for third-party candidates to compete in elections, because in smaller districts the price of reaching voters would drop. To effectively campaign in districts of 710,767 people, politicians need a sizable war chest, but retail politics matters more in small ones. Lower costs mean less influence for those big donors.

Whether by means of a constitutional amendment or by pressure on Congress to proceed with statutory changes, the number of representatives should be increased. The number 435 is not magical, and it makes a mockery of representative democracy. So what is the proper number? Reasonable people can disagree on whether the number of representatives should double or triple. Reasonable people can also question whether the size of the United States is inimical to a meaningful representation in Congress. Perhaps Montesquieu was correct in his assessment that "[i]t is natural for a republic to have only a small territory; otherwise it cannot long subsist."[120] What is important is not the fixation on the right number, but a push to move beyond 435. Once a majority of Americans agree on the obsolescence of 435, next steps can be addressed.

SECTION 2, CLAUSE 4

WHEN VACANCIES HAPPEN in the Representation from any State, the Executive Authority thereof shall issue Writs of Election to fill such Vacancies.

Purpose

The people are entitled to representation. If a representative, for example, resigns or dies while in office, the Constitution commands the governor of the state to call for an election to fill the vacant seat.

Background and Development

The Framers did not disagree on the need for a mechanism to fill vacant House seats. The governor of the state experiencing the vacancy is required to hold an election to fill the empty seat. This provision ensures that the people of a state do not go unrepresented. It also ensures that the popular branch, in the event of some catastrophe, will have enough members to conduct national business.

Distortions

In *American Civil Liberties Union of Ohio, Inc. v. Taft* (2004),[121] the Sixth Circuit Court of Appeals considered the refusal of the governor of Ohio to issue writs of election when the House expelled an Ohio representative a little more than two months before the scheduled end of the 107th Congress. The governor announced that he would not call a special election because of "the cost of an election, the difficulty presented by redistricting that was to take effect for the regularly scheduled election in 2002, the small length of time an elected replacement could be expected to serve, and the uninterrupted continuation of constituent services by the Clerk of the House."[122] The court held that "Article I, section 2, clause 4 is mandatory, requiring the state's executive to issue a writ to fill a vacancy in the House."[123] The court recognized that "there may be instances where the time remaining in the congressional term is truly de minimis, thereby excusing the executive from issuing the writ," but that the five months between the vacancy in Ohio and the meeting of the next Congress was not de minimis.[124]

Discussion and Solutions

The states have an interest in having their people represented in the House and the Senate. Decisions on when to issue writs of election to fill a vacancy belong to the governors of the states. Consequently, courts should avoid intruding into state political affairs absent a circumstance in which the people will be without a representative for a substantial length of time—twelve to twenty-four months. It is mandatory that a governor issue writs of election, but nothing is amiss if a governor waits upon a general election absent an extraordinary passage of time. Despite the assertions of the Sixth Circuit, five months between the vacancy and the meeting of the next Congress is a modest passage of time. Judges should refrain from interfering in such matters absent an extremity.

SECTION 2, CLAUSE 5

THE HOUSE OF Representatives shall chuse their Speaker and other Officers; and shall have the sole Power of Impeachment.

Purpose

As an independent representative body, the House is not beholden to the executive and thus chooses its own presiding officer. Consistent with British practice, the House is the only body that can begin the process of impeachment by drafting articles of impeachment.

Background and Development

The role of the House in choosing its own Speaker and bringing charges through impeachment follows British practice. In the mother country, the House of Commons elects its Speaker subject to approval by the Crown. The Speaker, as the chief officer and highest authority of the House of Commons, chairs debates, maintains order, and calls on members to speak. The Speaker also represents the Commons to the monarch and the House of Lords.

The unicameral Confederation Congress did not elect a "Speaker" but did choose a "president" to officiate. In November 1781, Maryland's John Hanson became the first "President of the United States in Congress Assembled." Many of the state and colonial assemblies, in the British tradition, chose Speakers presiding over their lower houses.

With the Constitution of 1787, the Framers likely crafted the fifth clause based on the Massachusetts Constitution of 1780, which states: "The House of Representatives . . . shall choose their own Speaker; appoint their own officers, and settle the rules and orders of proceeding in their own house."[125] The words "their own" highlight the desire to prohibit executive interference with legislative business, such as the colonies experienced at the hands of royal governors. No Speaker has been selected who was not also a member of the House, but some scholars argue that the House could choose a Speaker from outside its own ranks.[126] The choice of a Speaker is the first order of business at the beginning of the House's two-year term. To be elected Speaker, a candidate must receive a majority of all votes cast. The Speaker's function in the House is largely a matter of political traditions that have taken shape over time.

The "Power of Impeachment" means the right to accuse a public official of a crime or some form of malfeasance. In essence, the House acts as a grand jury and can return an "indictment" (articles of impeachment in practice) against the alleged offender, who is then tried by the Senate. In so empowering the House, the Framers followed the British model, in which the House of Commons decides whether an impeachment should be instituted. As noted by George Washington University Law School's Jonathan Turley, "[t]here is no constitutional guidance as to how impeachment inquiries are to be raised, conducted, or concluded in the House, nor is there any requirement to conduct House proceedings under oath."[127] Controversies over matters such as late impeachments, individuals subject to impeachment, and what acts are impeachable are covered in subsequent sections.

Section 3, Clause 1

The Senate of the United States shall be composed of two Senators from each State, chosen by the Legislature thereof, for six Years; and each Senator shall have one Vote.

Purpose

The Framers intended the Senate to represent the states in the national legislature; therefore, the state legislatures chose members of the upper house. The equality of votes in the Senate signifies the equal dignity and sovereignty of the states. The six-year terms are intended to provide strength and stability in the national legislature. The Senate's small size (as compared with the House) is intended to promote coolheaded deliberation.

Background and Development

The Virginia Plan, which framed the Convention's debate from the beginning, contemplated an upper house.[128] Members of the upper house were to be nominated by the state legislatures and to be chosen by the lower house. Edmund Randolph of Virginia explained that he envisioned the Senate as a much smaller chamber than the House to avoid "the passionate proceedings to which numerous assemblies are liable."[129] He believed that much of the independent states' problems stemmed from the "follies of democracy" and that "a good Senate" would likely provide a necessary check on democratic excesses.[130]

John Dickinson of Delaware suggested that senators should be chosen by the state legislatures. He contended that the legislatures could reflect "the Sense of the States" better than popular election.[131] He further wanted "the Senate to consist of the most distinguished characters, distinguished for their rank in life and their weight of property, and bearing a strong likeliness to the British House of Lords."[132] Election by the state legislatures, more so than popular election, he said, likely would produce senators of stature. Not only would the agency of the state legislatures lead to a Senate populated with men of substance, but it would also cause the Senate to have different interests from the House and "produce a collision between the different authorities which should be wished for in order to check each other."[133]

Roger Sherman of Connecticut agreed with Dickinson that the states should choose senators. Attempting to appeal to the nationalists, he pointed out that under Dickinson's proposal, "the particular states would thus become interested in supporting the National Government."[134] George Mason of Virginia, who supported election of senators by the state legislatures, focused on state self-defense rather than support of the new government. Efforts to craft the other departments of government, Mason noted, had focused on self-defense. Why should the states not have such a mechanism? Similarly, William Samuel Johnson of Connecticut feared that the states "would be at the mercy of the Genl. Govt." without some instrument for self-defense.[135]

Of course, self-defense to the small states meant an equal vote in the Senate. Large-state delegates saw equality of representation in the upper chamber as bringing the evils of the Confederation into the new government. Certain delegates on both sides professed a desire for the union to dissolve rather than compromise their positions on equality. Fortunately,

as discussed above, delegates accepted the Connecticut Compromise and moved on to other business. In *Federalist* No. 62, Madison candidly admitted that the Senate was the result of compromise and that the equal vote for each state "is at once a constitutional recognition of the portion of sovereignty remaining in the individual states, and the instrument for preserving that residuary sovereignty."[136] Senators were thought of at the founding as ambassadors of the states to the general government.

Gouverneur Morris of Pennsylvania suggested that each state have three senators to create a "numerous body."[137] Mason objected that three senators per state would make the upper house too numerous. Most of the delegates agreed with Mason; Morris's motion garnered only Pennsylvania's approval. Immediately after rejecting Morris's proposal, the delegates agreed unanimously on two senators per state.

Regarding the terms of senators, the delegates considered a variety of proposals, including service during good behavior or terms as short as four and as long as nine years. The Convention ultimately settled on six years. In the New York ratifying convention, Alexander Hamilton defended the Senate and its six-year terms as providing needed "*strength and stability* in the organization of our government."[138] To be in a position to "correct the prejudices, check the intemperate passions, and regulate the fluctuations, of a popular assembly," Hamilton argued that the Senate "should hold its authority during a considerable period."[139]

Anti-Federalists were suspicious of the Senate. For example, Centinel described the Senate as "a baneful aristocracy" because of the "unequal representation of the several

States," its "members being appointed for the long term of six years," and there being no term limits; this meant "they might be continued for life, which would follow of course from their extensive means of influence, and that possessing a considerable share in the executive as well as legislative, it would become a permanent aristocracy, and swallow up the other orders in the government."[140]

Like Centinel, Cato objected "that no attention has been paid to either the numbers or property in each state in forming the senate; that the mode in which they are appointed and their duration, will lead to the establishment of an aristocracy."[141] Anti-Federalist John DeWitt was no fan of the Great Compromise and complained that "[f]ive pounds in the Senate has an equal voice with fifty, and about five hundred thousand of the inhabitants the same number of votes with the remaining three million."[142]

Luther Martin of Maryland, in his *Genuine Information*, doubted that the senators would truly be representatives of the states. Martin argued that "for six years the senators are rendered totally and absolutely independent of their States, of whom they ought to be the representatives, without any bond or tie between them."[143] He feared that during such a long term "they may join in measures ruinous and destructive to their States, even such as should totally annihilate their State governments, and their States cannot recall them, nor exercise any controul over them."[144]

Distortions

With the ratification of the Seventeenth Amendment in 1913, senators are now elected by the people of the several states rather than the state legislatures. For years the Senate embodied the federative aspect of the Constitution. This was undone in 1913. Today, the states have no representation in the federal government and thus no means of self-defense. (The full effects of this change will be discussed in the section on the Seventeenth Amendment.)

Discussion and Solutions

As a structural matter, the Senate continues to serve many purposes intended by the Framers. The longer terms for senators, despite the change to popular elections, continues to promote stability in the portion of the legislature most concerned with foreign affairs. The Senate continues to serve the interests of bicameralism, since a bill must be approved by both houses of Congress before presentation to the president.

SECTION 3, CLAUSE 2

IMMEDIATELY AFTER THEY shall be assembled in Consequence of the first Election, they shall be divided as equally as may be into three Classes. The Seats of the Senators of the first Class shall be vacated at the Expiration of the second Year, of the second Class at the Expiration of the fourth Year, and of the third Class at the Expiration of the sixth Year, so that one third may be chosen every second Year; and if Vacancies happen by Resignation, or otherwise, during the Recess of the Legislature of any State, the Executive thereof may make temporary Appointments until the next Meeting of the Legislature, which shall then fill such Vacancies.

Purpose

Although senators serve longer terms than representatives or the president, one-third of senators are subject to election every two years. This one-third figure preserves institutional knowledge because the Senate's most important tasks are related to foreign affairs—an area where continuity is critical. However, the frequency of elections reminds all senators that accountability to those who chose them must not be forgotten.

Background and Development

One-third of the senators are subject to election every two years. The current class system was suggested by Nathaniel Gorham of Massachusetts when he made a motion for six-year terms, "one third of the members to go out every second year."[145] In the Massachusetts ratifying convention, Fisher Ames argued that this served as an "effectual *check* upon the power of the Senate."[146] He believed that senators, seeing colleagues stand for election every two years, would keep cognizant of their duties to the state legislatures and their status

as representatives of a sovereign state. Such security, Ames averred, "affords just ground to believe that it will be, in practical theory, a *federal* republic."[147]

In complying with this constitutional provision, the first Senate divided its membership into thirds, but also ensured that each state's senatorial allotment fell into different classes. Hence, senators from the same state are not subject to reelection in a given year. The three-class system was no innovation but followed state practice. For example, "Delaware's senate and Pennsylvania's unicameral council were divided into three classes on a one-year election rotation, while upper houses in Virginia and New York had four classes and yearly elections."[148]

Should a vacancy arise when the state legislature is not in session, the governor may make a temporary appointment. At the Philadelphia Convention, Virginia's Edmund Randolph urged that the provision was necessary because "[i]n some States the Legislatures meet but once a year" and a position of such consequence as senator should not go unfilled for an extensive period.[149]

SECTION 3, CLAUSE 3

NO PERSON SHALL be a Senator who shall not have attained to the Age of thirty Years, and been nine Years a Citizen of the United States, and who shall not, when elected, be an Inhabitant of that State for which he shall be chosen.

Purpose

The constitutional qualifications to serve as a senator reflect the particular purposes of the upper chamber. The Framers believed that older and more experienced men would likely be immune to democratic impulses pushing for ill-conceived legislative action. As for the lengthy citizenship requirement, the Framers hoped that such a time lapse would diminish, if not erase, a person's attachment to his land of origin.

Background and Development

In *Federalist* No. 62, Madison explained that "the nature of the senatorial trust" required "greater extent of information and stability of character" associated with mature age.[150] Regarding the Senate's role in ratifying treaties with foreign nations, Madison explained that a senator ought to be "thoroughly weaned from prepossessions and habits incident to foreign birth and education."[151]

At the Philadelphia Convention, Gouverneur Morris of Pennsylvania argued for a fourteen-year citizenship requirement to avoid "admitting strangers into our public Councils."[152] Pierce Butler of South Carolina agreed that foreigners "bring with them, not only attachments to other Countries; but ideas of Govt. so distinct from ours that in every point of view they are dangerous."[153] Madison warned against such a lengthy citizenship requirement because he believed that adoption of the Constitution

would give "stability" to the American government and thus cause "great numbers of respectable Europeans . . . to transfer their fortunes hither."[154] He believed that a fourteen-year requirement would unnecessarily discourage them from coming to America. The nine-year requirement was a compromise between Morris's proposal and acknowledgment that the Senate residency requirement should be lengthier than the House's seven-year requirement.

Perhaps the most famous case of an individual denied a Senate seat because of inability to meet the citizenship requirement was that of Albert Gallatin, who was elected by Pennsylvania in 1793. Gallatin was born in Switzerland and came to the United States in 1780. In arguing for his status as a citizen for the requisite time, Gallatin pointed out that he "had contributed money and services to the Revolution, that he had bought land in what is now Maine, and that he had taken oaths of loyalty to both Massachusetts and Virginia."[155] However, because of the transfer of sovereignty from Great Britain to the thirteen newly independent states, proof of citizenship for those who had not formerly been British subjects was tricky. Gallatin also was a staunch Jeffersonian and was a critic of Secretary of the Treasury Alexander Hamilton's financial plan. The Federalist-controlled Senate, which had no sympathy for Gallatin's political principles, ruled that he could not meet his burden of establishing citizenship for nine years and thus determined that he was ineligible to serve. Gallatin would later be elected to the House of Representatives and serve as secretary of the treasury for Presidents Thomas Jefferson and James Madison.

A senator must be an inhabitant of the state from which the individual is chosen at the time of election. Regarding the age and citizenship requirements, the Senate will receive into membership a person who did not meet these two requirements when elected but who met them prior to assuming office.

Distortions

The constitutional requirements to serve as a senator remain in place. In 1790, when the life expectancy of for white males was thirty-eight years, a person meeting the senatorial age requirements was far along into adulthood. The honor of a selection to the Senate was often a crowning achievement for a distinguished public servant. In modern America, however, where perpetual adolescence is endemic, thirty years of age is often not the season of maturity.

Discussion and Solutions

Although an upward revision to the minimum age might be desirable (say, to forty or fifty years of age), such a correction is not a priority. With Congress no longer bound by enumerated powers, the president usurping congressional powers over foreign affairs, and the administrative state serving as the real lawgiver in modern America, a constitutional amendment requiring senators to have greater life experience is far down the list of initiatives deserving significant time and capital to achieve.

SECTION 3, CLAUSE 4

THE VICE PRESIDENT of the United States shall be President of the Senate, but shall have no Vote, unless they be equally divided.

Purpose

With an even number of senators, tie votes are a possibility. The vice president presides over the Senate and casts deciding votes when necessary.

Background and Development

At the Philadelphia Convention, several delegates expressed concern about the vice president's role in the Senate. George Mason of Virginia thought the vice president's duties in the Senate "mixed too much the Legislative & Executive" and would interfere in the Senate's work.[156] Considering the expected propinquity between the president and vice president, Elbridge Gerry of Massachusetts quipped that "[w]e might as well put the President himself at the head of the Legislature."[157] Roger Sherman of Connecticut feared that without the position as presiding officer in the Senate, the vice president "would be without employment."[158] (Sherman's sentiments were echoed years later when the colorful John Nance Garner of Texas—the thirty-second vice president—described the office as not being "worth a bucket of warm spit.")

The Convention ultimately approved the vice president presiding over the Senate and casting tiebreaking votes. Absent this approval, a sitting senator would have presided and cast tiebreaking votes, or, as the presiding officer, the senator would have been denied a vote in the ordinary course of Senate business. In either case, the equality of the Senate would have been undermined. In the former case, a state would have had more power than its sister states; in the latter case, less power.

Anti-Federalists, similar to Mason in Philadelphia, did not approve of the vice president's role in the Senate. In the North Carolina ratifying convention, opponents of the Constitution "apprehend[ed] that all the legislative power granted by this Constitution are not vested in a Congress consisting of the Senate and the House of Representatives, because the Vice-President has a right to put a check on it."[159] Scholars have noted that "anti-Federalists remained so committed to keeping executive and legislative powers actually and symbolically detached from one another that their member Senators did not acknowledge the vice presidential role of the nation's first vice president, John Adams, instead recognizing him only as Senate president when he presided over the chamber."[160]

In the early republic, vice presidents spent a great deal of time presiding over the Senate. Adams, serving as Washington's vice president, "operated in a manner not unlike a modern Senate majority leader, helping to shape the Senate's agenda and organizing and intervening in debate."[161] In modern times, the vice president spends more time on executive branch business and rarely presides over the Senate. Such a role is incongruent with how Thomas Jefferson, serving as vice president during John Adams's presidential term, viewed the office: "I consider my office as constitutionally confined to legislative functions, and that I could not take any part whatever in executive consultations, even were it proposed."[162]

Distortions

The vice presidential role has evolved from the days when Jefferson viewed his duties as more legislative than executive. The rise of political parties and designation of official presidential running mates (see the discussion of the Twelfth Amendment) has changed the way we view the office. Moreover, as noted by constitutional scholar Joel K. Goldstein, "The New Deal, World War II, and the Cold War changed American government in ways that drew the Vice Presidency closer to the executive branch."[163] Few modern Americans would characterize the vice president's job duties as more legislative than executive. Most forget the role of presiding in the Senate because this duty has become ceremonial. Nonetheless, the vice president still has an important role under Article I: breaking tie votes in the Senate.

Discussion and Solutions

The vice presidency has developed through the years. Ratification of the Twelfth Amendment, which recognized the rise of political parties and allowed designation of a vice presidential candidate on the ticket, was bound to push the vice president toward the executive branch. Also, the growth of government during the twentieth century made it inevitable that the president would call upon the vice president for assistance in managing the executive branch. The Senate still requires someone to break tie votes, and the modern vice president remains the logical candidate despite being firmly ensconced in the executive branch. Although the office is somewhat different from that originally envisioned, the need and desire for correction is minuscule.

SECTION 3, CLAUSE 5

THE SENATE SHALL chuse their other Officers, and also a President pro tempore, in the Absence of the Vice President, or when he shall exercise the Office of President of the United States.

Purpose

Although the Constitution dictates that the vice president presides over the Senate, the upper house enjoys independence since it has the liberty to choose its own officers and can elect a president pro tempore to preside in the absence of the vice president.

Background and Development

Similar to the House, the Senate has the power to choose its officers, except for the vice president, who serves as the presiding officer. Should the vice president be absent from the Senate or assume the presidency of the union, the upper house must elect a president pro tempore to preside.

In the early republic, the Senate did not believe it had the authority to choose a president pro tempore while the vice president was present in the chamber. Consequently, it became a custom for the vice president to withdraw from the Senate just before the end of a session so that senators could fill the position. These efforts were necessary because under statute, the president pro tempore followed the vice president in the order of succession to the presidency. If both the president and vice president, say, were killed in an attack while the Senate was not in session, it might require many weeks for the senators to assemble and elect a president pro tempore. In cases when no president pro tempore had been named, early statutory law provided that the Speaker of the House would become president.

In 1890, the Senate decided that the president pro tempore could be elected and hold office whether the vice president was present or absent. Dating from this change in constitutional interpretation, the post has typically been held by the most senior senator of the majority party. "The President Pro Tempore is treated as a continuing officer in the sense that a Senator selected in one Congress remains in that office in the following Congress."[164] Serving as president pro tempore is one of the highest posts of honor that can be conferred on a member of the Senate.

Distortions

The 1890 rule change remains a reasonable interpretation of the Constitution and thus not a distortion. The change was an advance because it dispensed with the inefficient practice of holding an election every time the vice president was not present. When there are two reasonable interpretations of the Constitution—especially with respect to ministerial matters—Congress has the freedom to adopt the interpretation most conducive to carrying out its business.

Discussion and Solutions

Under the current presidential succession statute, the House's Speaker and the Senate's president pro tempore are first and second in line, respectively, if there is neither a president nor a vice president. In our age of mass terrorism, there is a real possibility that the president and vice president might both be killed in a single event. One must question whether it is wise for the most senior senator of the majority party to be, in theory, so close to assuming presidential power when such a senator might be in his dotage and toward the end of his career. This is not an infirmity with the constitutional provision at hand but is worth considering as a matter of wise policy.

In 2022, Senate Democrats apparently realized the dangers mentioned above when they elected Senator Patty Murray of Washington, their second-longest-serving member, as president pro tempore of the Senate rather than Senator Dianne Feinstein of California, their longest-serving member. Murray's nomination was a break from precedent dating back to the 1940s and was undoubtedly occasioned by widespread concerns about the eighty-nine-year-old Feinstein's cognitive abilities. Feinstein died in 2023 and never gave up her Senate seat despite hospitalizations and an obvious decline in her mental faculties.

SECTION 3, CLAUSE 6

THE SENATE SHALL have the sole Power to try all Impeachments. When sitting for that Purpose, they shall be on Oath or Affirmation. When the President of the United States is tried, the Chief Justice shall preside: And no Person shall be convicted without the Concurrence of two thirds of the Members present.

Purpose

Impeachment was a serious matter to the Framers, and they provided a constitutional sketch for bringing charges and adjudicating cases. Based on articles of impeachment brought by the House, the Senate hears evidence and determines whether to convict. Because of the gravity of such a proceeding against the president, the chief justice of the Supreme Court presides over the trial. A supermajority is required for a verdict of guilt.

Background and Development

The House serves as the grand jury for impeachments, and the Senate serves as the trial court. Much of the debate in the Philadelphia Convention concerning impeachment focused on impeachment of the president. Most of the delegates agreed that the Constitution should contain a mechanism to remove a corrupt or unfit chief executive. John Dickinson of Delaware suggested that the president be removable upon the request of a majority of state legislatures. Others preferred that Congress should possess such a power.

George Mason of Virginia opined that "[s]ome mode of displacing an unfit magistrate is rendered indispensable by the fallibility of those who choose, as well as by the corruptibility of the man chosen."[165] Mason, however, feared making the executive "the mere creature" of Congress.[166]

Gouverneur Morris of Pennsylvania agreed with Mason regarding the chief magistrate's office depending on Congress and questioned how the president could be a check on Congress if he was subject to impeachment. Charles Pinckney of South Carolina also feared that Congress would "effectually destroy" the president's independence if granted the sword of impeachment.[167] He envisioned the House and Senate combining to toss the president out of office if he opposed a measure favored by both chambers. (The impeachment of Andrew Johnson for violation of the Tenure of Office Act shows Pinckney's concerns were real. Johnson's firing of Secretary of War Edwin Stanton without Congress's permission was the ostensible impetus for impeachment, although the real reason was Reconstruction policy. Johnson and his predecessor, Abraham Lincoln, favored a lenient treatment of the former Confederate states, whereas Congress favored more severe measures. Efforts to impeach Johnson meant to remove him as an obstacle to radical Reconstruction.)[168]

James Madison objected to the Senate serving as a trial court and preferred that the Supreme Court or some other tribunal should judge the matter. Despite Madison's objections, the Convention followed the British model regarding the role of the upper house. In *Federalist* No. 65, Alexander Hamilton questioned whether a body other than the Senate would be august enough to sit as a court of impeachment. Hamilton doubted whether the Supreme Court possessed "the degree of credit and authority" needed to sit impartially and to persuade the people of the justness of the verdict.[169] He also argued that the "awful discretion" exercised by a court of impeachment "to doom to honor or to infamy" eminent members of the community "forbids the commitment of the trust to a small number of persons" such as the Supreme Court.[170]

During ordinary impeachment proceedings, the vice president sits as the presiding officer of the Senate. However, when the president is on trial, the chief justice of the Supreme Court presides. In North Carolina's ratifying convention, Archibald Maclaine explained that the provision took into account that "the Vice-President might be connected" in committing the crime with the president, and, if not, the vice president might have a conflict of interest in desiring to rise to the presidency "and endeavor to influence the Senate against" the defendant.[171]

To be convicted, two-thirds of the members present (under a juror's oath to render a just verdict) must vote "aye." The supermajority provision departs from British practice, in which conviction in the House of Lords required only a simple majority vote.

Some Anti-Federalists criticized the power vested in the Senate to try impeachments. In the Virginia ratifying convention, John Tyler complained that "the power of trying impeachments, added to that of making treaties, was something enormous, and rendered the Senate too dangerous."[172] George Mason believed that because the Senate provided the president with advice and consent on certain issues, senators became his counselors, and this made them suspect as a trial court. In Pennsylvania, opponents of the Constitution also mentioned the advice and consent power and asserted that the Senate would not convict those they had agreed to appoint.

Hamilton's assertion that no institution other than the Senate would be august enough to sit as a court of impeachment has proved correct. Despite the turmoil of the Trump years, high-level impeachments are uncommon, and the Senate remains the natural body to hear and decide these cases.

SECTION 3, CLAUSE 7

JUDGMENT IN CASES of impeachment shall not extend further than to removal from Office, and disqualification to hold and enjoy any Office of honor, Trust or Profit under the United States: but the Party convicted shall nevertheless be liable and subject to Indictment, Trial, Judgment and Punishment, according to Law.

Purpose

The Constitution sets forth the punishment for an official convicted in cases of impeachment. The guilty party is removed from his office and is barred from holding high office in the federal government. The disgraced official is still subject to prosecution in the criminal courts and cannot claim that impeachment proceedings act as a bar to further punishment.

Background and Development

In Great Britain, a person impeached and convicted in the House of Lords could face various penalties ranging from a fine to death. Moreover, British impeachment was not limited to officeholders but also extended to private citizens. The Framers of the Constitution restricted the possible punishment to removal from office and disqualification from holding "any Office of honor, Trust or Profit under the United States." In so doing, they also rejected the British practice of subjecting private citizens to impeachment proceedings. In the North Carolina ratifying convention, some worried that private citizens, state officeholders, or both would be subject to federal impeachment proceedings. Proponents of the Constitution in North Carolina such as Archibald Maclaine pointed to the plain text of the provision and assured colleagues that "none but officers of the United States are impeachable."[173]

An individual convicted in the Senate may not plead res judicata (a prohibition on further litigation of a matter already decided) if subsequently indicted in criminal court. The Constitution is clear that "the Party convicted shall nevertheless be liable and subject to Indictment, Trial, Judgment and Punishment, according to Law." For example, if the House of Representatives issued articles of impeachment against a sitting president for violations of campaign finance laws and the Senate did not convict, the president could still face criminal charges for his actions. The U.S. Justice Department, however, has a long-standing policy that a sitting president cannot be indicted. The policy is based on separation of powers concerns and fear that a criminal prosecution of a sitting president would prevent the president from performing constitutionally assigned duties. After leaving office, the president can face criminal charges for conduct that occurred while in office.

In *Trump v. United States* (2024), the Supreme Court addressed the issue of a former president's immunity from prosecution.[174] Under a separation-of-powers analysis, the Court held that a former president has absolute immunity from criminal prosecution for actions within his conclusive and preclusive constitutional authority. Absent such broad immunity, the Court feared that the president's ability to perform his job would be inhibited by the threat of prosecution for, say, signing congressional legislation or granting a pardon. For other official acts, a former president has a presumptive immunity that can be rebutted by the prosecution. The Court declared that there is no immunity for unofficial acts. Critics of the decision raised concerns that immunity for former presidents would render them above the law and have transformative effects on the office of the presidency.

Distortions

During the second impeachment proceeding brought against Donald Trump, the issue arose whether "late impeachments" are authorized by the Constitution—that is, whether the Senate can convict a charged official after the official leaves office. The House voted to impeach Trump on January 13, 2021, while he was still president, but it did not deliver the single article of impeachment to the Senate until January 25, 2021, after Trump had returned to private life. Trump argued that at the time of the Senate trial he was not president, vice president, or an officer of the United States; therefore, he should not face a trial in the Senate.

Proponents of late impeachment argued that removal from office and disqualification

from holding a future office are separate penalties; therefore, late impeachment is allowable because a person in Trump's situation nonetheless could be disqualified from future offices of honor. Linguistically, that argument is a canard. The provision's mention of "disqualification to hold and enjoy any Office of honor, Trust, or Profit under the United States" is the dependent clause in the sentence. Hence, the disqualification language is not an independent provision separable from the penalty of removal.

Proponents of late impeachment also pointed to the British proceeding against Warren Hastings, the first governor-general of India. The House of Commons impeached Hastings for mismanagement and corruption after he had left office. Hastings was tried in the House of Lords and acquitted. The Framers certainly were familiar with the Hastings proceedings; George Mason during the Philadelphia Convention even mentioned him by name while discussing what sort of malfeasance should be impeachable. But just because the Framers were aware that late impeachment was possible under the British constitution does not support the proposition that they adopted it for the American system. Late impeachment was not discussed at the Philadelphia Convention.

In a case far removed from the founding, late impeachment was allowed in the 1876 matter of former Secretary of War William Belknap. After the House discovered Belknap's receipt of kickbacks for Western trading-post rights, it launched an investigation. Seeking to avoid impeachment, Belknap resigned just hours before the House voted on the matter. By a simple majority vote, the Senate decided that it had jurisdiction and went forward with a trial. House impeachment managers were unable to garner the requisite two-thirds vote needed to convict because a substantial minority of senators had concerns about jurisdiction.

Similar to the Belknap case, in a simple majority vote of 55–45, the Senate rejected Trump's motion to dismiss and accepted the doctrine of late impeachment. Again, much like Belknap, Trump avoided conviction because a substantial minority in the Senate retained doubts about jurisdiction. Because impeachment is inherently political, one must question the precedential value of this vote for future impeachment proceedings. Moreover, we should take notice that even the foremost expert and advocate of late impeachments, Michigan State's Brian C. Kalt, admits that "the question of late impeachability is close and unsettled."[175]

Discussion and Solutions

The issue of late impeachments is far from settled. Because impeachment is as much a political process as it is a judicial one, varying interpretations should be expected in the partisan world of Washington, DC. High-profile impeachment proceedings remain a rarity in American constitutional history; therefore, the issues surrounding late impeachments will arise infrequently.

The text, in this author's opinion, does not support late impeachment. But if we desire to settle the matter in favor of late impeachments, we could adopt provisions similar to the Delaware and Virginia constitutions of 1776, which specifically indicate that the executive may be impeached "when he is out of office."[176] Such a change would require a constitutional amendment. As infrequently as the issue arises, the benefit of an amendment is not worth the effort required. But absent such an amendment, impeachment should be reserved for an offender who holds office. We should not twist the words of the Constitution in favor of late impeachment just so that a political figure will be barred from holding and enjoying an office of honor. Such a decision ultimately rests with the people at the ballot box.

SECTION 4, CLAUSE 1
THE TIMES, PLACES and Manner of holding Elections for Senators and Representatives, shall be prescribed in each State by the Legislature thereof; but the Congress may at any time by Law make or alter such Regulations, except as to the Places of chusing Senators.

Purpose

The state legislatures are charged with passing laws setting the times, places, and manner of electing members of Congress. The Framers, however, feared that in times of political turmoil the states might refuse to hold elections for senators and representatives and thus cripple the federal government by depriving it of a legislative branch. Consequently, this provision allows Congress to step in and legislate concerning the time, places, and manner of elections for senators and representatives.

Background and Development

At the Philadelphia Convention, Madison argued that congressional oversight for federal elections was necessary for two reasons. First, he worried that if a state legislature had a favorite policy or candidate, "they would take care so as to mold their regulations as to favor the candidates they wished to succeed."[177] Such gamesmanship would be unscrupulous and should be banned from federal elections. Second, Madison feared that the states might "fail or refuse altogether" to hold elections for the House.[178] If the states did so, they could destroy the national government.

Charles Pinckney and John Rutledge, both of South Carolina, questioned giving Congress any power to interfere with state election laws for senators and representatives. They believed that the states "could & must be relied on in such cases."[179] Madison challenged Pinckney and Rutledge because "[i]t was impossible to foresee all the abuses that might be made of the discretionary power."[180]

The Anti-Federalists distrusted the power granted to Congress in the Time, Place, and Manner Clause. They were concerned that Congress could use this power to make it onerous for ordinary people to vote. Congress might make the place of voting difficult to attend by establishing it far away from the bulk of the populace. Or Congress might set the time for voting during harvest, when it would be almost impossible for citizens to leave the fields and to travel to polling places. "Congress may establish a place, or places," wrote Cato, "at either the extremes, center, or outer parts of the states; at a time and season too, when it may be very inconvenient to attend; and by these means destroy the rights of election."[181]

Brutus shared Cato's concern. "The proposed Congress may make the whole state one district, and direct, that the capital . . . shall be the place for holding the election."[182]

Centinel saw the Time, Place, and Manner Clause in a more sinister light. He believed that the clause was necessary to give the national government legitimacy after it had destroyed the several states. "[W]hen the state legislatures drop out of sight," he averred, "from the necessary operation of this government, then Congress are to provide for the election and appointment of representatives and senators."[183]

Some of the Constitution's opponents expressed concern that Congress would use the Time, Place, and Manner Clause to alter state voting requirements in an effort to perpetuate themselves in office. Federalists such as John Steele of North Carolina quickly assured Anti-Federalists that "[t]he power over the manner of elections does not include that of saying who shall vote."[184] Rufus King in Massachusetts and Edmund Randolph in Virginia made similar representations to their respective conventions.[185]

The Anti-Federalists were not persuaded by the Federalists' promises about the limited scope of the Time, Place, and Manner Clause. Multiple state conventions demanded amendments to this clause. Virginia, for example, proposed the following: "That Congress shall not alter, modify, or interfere in the times, places, or manner of holding elections for senators and representatives, or either of them, except when the legislature of any state shall neglect, refuse, or be disabled, by invasion or rebellion, to prescribe the same."[186]

In *Federalist* No. 59, Alexander Hamilton averred that only in "extraordinary circumstances" would Congress alter state election laws.[187] Despite Hamilton's promise, Congress has not been shy in legislating pursuant to this clause. For example, in 1842 Congress required that all House members be elected by district and later decreed that each district be compact and contiguous.

The clause specifically prohibits Congress from regulating the place of choosing senators. Because senators originally were elected by the state legislatures, this provision ensured that Congress would not have the power to decide where state legislatures meet.

Distortions

The clause drew much attention in the 2020 election when the Pennsylvania Supreme Court altered state statutory law by extending the deadline for receipt of mail-in ballots. The state legislature "permitted all voters to cast their ballots by mail but unambiguously required that all mailed ballots be received by 8 p.m. on election day."[188] The legislature also "made it clear that, in its judgment, the COVID-19 pandemic did not call for any change in the election-day deadline."[189] Despite the clear law written by the legislature, the Pennsylvania supreme court "decreed that mailed ballots need not be received by election day" and crafted its own rule: Ballots could be counted if "postmarked on or before election day and . . . received within three days thereafter."[190]

When considering a motion to expedite the petition for review of the Pennsylvania supreme court's decision, three U.S. Supreme Court justices expressed "a strong likelihood that the State Supreme Court decision violates the Federal Constitution" because the Constitution confers "on state legislatures, not state courts, the authority to make rules governing federal elections."[191] Ultimately, the Court declined to hear the Pennsylvania case.

The Pennsylvania case aside, Congress and the federal courts use Section 4, Clause 1 to regulate voter qualifications—a subject alien to this provision. For example, in *Arizona v. Intertribal Council* (2013),[192] the Supreme Court held that Arizona could not demand that persons registering to vote provide documentary proof of citizenship. Because Congress via Section 4, Clause 1 had directed state officials to use a federal form during voter registration, this law preempted Arizona from imposing proof of citizenship requirements to combat voter fraud. Thus this constitutional provision, which was intended to allow the federal government to protect itself from efforts meant to destroy the national legislature, has been used as a weapon to prevent the operation of reasonable state laws.

Discussion and Solutions

The Federalists made solid arguments that the general government, for purposes of self-defense, needed the power to act if the states refused to hold elections for senators and representatives. In theory, the states could deprive the general government of a functioning legislative branch. But the remedy for this possibility found in Section 4, Clause 1 placed unnecessary power in the national legislature.

During the ratification debate, multiple states suggested that the Constitution be amended to prohibit Congress from interfering with the times, places, or manner of holding elections *except* when a state legislature refused—or was unable to—hold elections for federal officeholders. Virginia's proffered amendment is quoted above. Such an amendment would have given Congress the power of self-defense without allowing it to interfere with matters best governed by the states. It is disquieting that Section 4, Clause 1 could be used to prevent a state from requiring a voter to show proof of citizenship at a polling place.

Americans should resurrect Virginia's suggested amendment and thus curb abuse of the Time, Place, and Manner Clause. Congress should be equipped with the power to defend itself, but neither it nor the courts should be allowed to manage state election procedures.

Section 4, Clause 2

The Congress shall assemble at least once in every Year, and such Meeting shall be on the first Monday in December, unless they shall by Law appoint a different Day.

Purpose

The Framers established basic guidance on when Congress should meet. They believed there would be enough business to require an annual gathering of senators and representatives. This provision also makes clear that Congress has full authority to set the date of the constitutionally required annual meeting. Such authority furthers the goal of congressional independence from the executive.

Background and Development

Under the British constitution, the Crown had the power to convene, prorogue, or dissolve Parliament. English history is littered with examples of arrogant monarchs refusing to call parliaments and instead trying to rule by extraconstitutional measures. The Stuarts in the 1600s were perhaps the worst offenders. Charles I, for example, did not summon a parliament from March 1629 to April 1640. He lived off forced loan repayments from his subjects and revived medieval revenue sources that his predecessors had long ago abandoned.

The Framers ensured that the chief executive would have no such power in the American system by providing in the constitutional text for at least one annual meeting of Congress. At the Philadelphia Convention, Nathaniel Gorham of Massachusetts "thought it necessary that there should be one meeting at least every year as a check on the Executive department."[193] Gouverneur Morris of Pennsylvania was against this requirement. He doubted that "[t]he public business" would require it.[194] Rufus King of Massachusetts also opposed an annual meeting because "legislating too much" was a "vice" that should not be encouraged.[195] King further observed that the powers of the general government "were but few" and focused predominantly on "commerce and revenue."[196] "When these should be once settled," King argued, "alterations would be rarely necessary & easily made."[197]

George Mason of Virginia thought the annual meeting requirement would be "essential to the preservation of the Constitution."[198] He believed that "[t]he extent of the Country will supply business."[199] Connecticut's Roger Sherman agreed that Congress would have enough work to require an annual meeting. He pointed to the Western territories and the "varying state of our affairs in general."[200]

A majority of delegates agreed with the wisdom of an annual meeting; however, they contemplated changing the meeting date from December to May. Madison championed a May date because December "would require the travelling to & from the seat of Govt in the most inconvenient seasons of the year."[201] James Wilson of Pennsylvania did not challenge Madison's statement about the difficulty of travel, but instead reminded him that "[t]he Winter is the most convenient time to conduct business."[202] Oliver Ellsworth of Connecticut elaborated on Wilson's statement: "The summer will interfere too much with private business, that of almost all the probable members of the Legislature being more or less connected with agriculture."[203] The effort to substitute May for December failed miserably and garnered the votes of only two state delegations.

Prior to adoption of the Twentieth Amendment, a new Congress convened for its first session in December—a full thirteen months after its election. The Congress's second session began the following December, just shortly after the election of a new Congress. These lame-duck sessions lasted for no more than a few months. Now, the terms of senators and representatives end at noon on the third day of January of the year following elections. This is the same day a new Congress assumes office.

SECTION 5, CLAUSE 1

EACH HOUSE SHALL be the Judge of the Elections, Returns and Qualifications of its own Members, and a Majority of each shall constitute a Quorum to do Business; but a smaller Number may adjourn from day to day, and may be authorized to compel the Attendance of absent Members, in such Manner, and under such Penalties as each House may provide.

Purpose

An independent legislature should choose the time of its meetings and judge the elections and qualifications of its members. It may also impose discipline upon its members as needed. In England by the 1620s, Parliament's power to examine election returns was well established and served as a model for Americans. The quorum requirement ensures that no small faction can hijack proceedings and conduct business when the bulk of their colleagues are out of town.

Background and Development

To preserve the independence of the legislative branch and to promote separation of powers, the Senate and House of Representatives have the power to judge the elections, returns, and qualifications of their own members. Justice Joseph Story in his exposition of the Constitution described that power as "common to all the legislative bodies of the States" and consistent with the practices of "other free governments."[204] This constitutional provision was consistent with British precedent allowing the

House of Commons to judge the constitutional qualifications of members-elect.

Of course, the power to judge election returns and qualifications (like all powers) is subject to abuse. Prior to the American Revolution, the Commons refused to seat the outspoken radical John Wilkes because of certain writings and other conduct. The Commons even went so far as to declare Wilkes's opponent as the winner of the election despite Wilkes having received a sizable majority of votes. In 1782, the Commons officially recognized its improper conduct in the Wilkes matter and voted to expunge from its journals various resolutions against Wilkes. The rights of parliamentary electors thus were vindicated, and the Commons rejected the broad authority it had previously claimed to judge the qualifications of members-elect. Americans, like their British Whig[205] counterparts, were familiar with Wilkes's battles with Parliament. The cry of "Wilkes and Liberty!" resonated on both sides of the Atlantic and influenced the framing of Section 5, Clause 1.

In *Powell v. McCormack* (1969), the Supreme Court held that in judging the qualifications of a member-elect, the House is limited to considering the constitutional qualifications spelled out in Article I, Section 2 (namely, age, citizenship, and residency requirements).[206] The House had refused to seat Adam Clayton Powell Jr. because of corrupt actions that occurred in a previous Congress and prior to his reelection. Because Powell met the standing qualifications prescribed in the Constitution, the Court held that the House should have seated Powell before considering possible sanctions or expulsion.

A majority of each house constitutes a quorum to do business. That requirement sparked debate at the Philadelphia Convention. Nathaniel Gorham of Massachusetts believed that less than a majority should constitute a quorum; "otherwise great delay might happen in business, and great inconvenience from the future increase in members."[207] George Mason of Virginia favored the majority requirement because "it would be dangerous to the distant parts to allow a small number of members of the two Houses to make laws."[208] Oliver Ellsworth of Connecticut believed that people would oppose the Constitution if laws could be passed "by a few men."[209] Gouverneur Morris of Pennsylvania proposed to fix the quorum at thirty-three members in the House and fourteen in the Senate, but the Convention declined to set a certain number. Ultimately, the majority requirement prevailed, to provide the people with confidence that gamesmanship by a small minority could not result in legislation.

Anti-Federalist objections to the quorum requirement were tied to belief that the House was too small to properly represent the people. This sentiment was expressed by Melancton Smith in the New York ratifying convention: "I confess, to me they hardly wear the complexion of a democratic branch; they appear the mere shadow of representation. The whole number, in both houses, amounts to ninety-one; of these forty-six make a quorum; and twenty-four of those, being secured, may carry any point. Can the liberties of three millions of people be securely trusted in the hands of twenty-four men?"[210]

Until the late 1800s, the House believed the quorum requirement made it necessary for a majority of the members to vote on any matter submitted to the House. It was not uncommon for the opposition to break the quorum by refusing to vote. In 1890, Speaker Thomas Brackett Reed of Maine changed the House rules so that the names of members present but not voting could be entered and counted for purposes of determining a quorum. That change in rules was challenged in the Supreme Court in *United States v. Ballin* (1892). The Court held that "[a]ll . . . the constitution requires is the presence of a majority."[211] It declined to hold that the quorum requirement could be satisfied only by counting voting members.

The mention of a smaller number adjourning from day to day allows for the legislature's business to carry over while avoiding the need to call daily for a quorum.

By authorizing the House and Senate to compel the attendance of absent members, the Framers sought to thwart efforts by a recalcitrant minority to defeat the quorum requirements. Perhaps the most famous use of this power involved the passage of the controversial Alien and Sedition Acts in 1798. Many senators had left Washington for their homes, and the Senate thus could not muster a quorum. Pursuant to Senate rules, the minority present charged the sergeant at arms with bringing absent members back to the chamber. The rule also required detained senators to pay the expenses incurred by the sergeant at arms in chasing them down. A quorum was achieved that summer, and Congress passed legislation denying due process to foreigners and prohibiting criticism of the national government.

Under modern practice, the Senate presumes a quorum exists unless and until a senator suggests there is no quorum or demonstrates there is no quorum. When the issue of a quorum is raised, the clerk calls the roll, and the Senate cannot resume business until a majority of senators respond or by unanimous consent abandon the quorum call. Quorum calls are typically not made to secure an actual quorum but rather to allow a break in business so that senators can engage in informal discussions and negotiate to achieve agreement on an issue.

Similarly, the House presumes a quorum is present unless a lack of a quorum is shown conclusively. House rules allow a member to question the presence of a quorum only when a vote is taking place. If a majority of members do not respond to the quorum call, business must cease until a quorum is present.

Distortions

In *U.S. Term Limits v. Thornton* (1995), the Supreme Court placed great reliance on the *Powell v. McCormack* decision in holding that the states cannot mandate rotation in office for their federal representatives and senators. (This issue is discussed under Article I, Section 2, Clause 2.) *Powell* need not have been read so broadly. *Powell* should have been interpreted solely to limit Congress from imposing additional qualifications upon its own members. The case did not confront the issue of whether the people of a state may impose qualifications in addition to age, citizenship, and residency requirements.

Discussion and Solutions

Absent the stretching of *Powell* by the *U.S. Term Limits* decision, Section 5, Clause 1 is unexceptional and, to paraphrase Justice Story, an incident of free governments. The clause has roots in the British constitution and in the American Constitution promotes the dignity and independence of the national legislature. No remedies need be discussed other than rotation in office, which is addressed in conjunction with Section 2, Clause 2.

SECTION 5, CLAUSE 2

EACH HOUSE MAY determine the Rules of its Proceedings, punish its Members for disorderly Behaviour, and, with the Concurrence of two thirds, expel a Member.

Purpose

With the power to determine their own rules, the Framers sought to protect the House and Senate from interference instigated by the executive and judicial branches. The separate bodies may also punish members to keep good order and, in extraordinary circumstances, expel a member by supermajority vote.

Background and Development

Justice Joseph Story described the clause as representing the types of powers "usually granted to legislative bodies."[212] Without such a grant, Story continued, "it would be utterly impracticable to transact the business of the nation at all, or at least, to transact it with decency, deliberation, and order."[213]

The power of the House and Senate to set their own rules is significant and has led to the House Rules Committee becoming the command-and-control center of the popular branch. It oversees legislation reported out by other committees and decrees how much debate time is allowed, the number and types of amendments permitted once a bill reaches the House floor, and many other consequential matters. The rules put in place often determine whether the bill passes or is obstructed.

Initially, the expulsion provision as crafted by the Philadelphia Convention required only a majority. James Madison of Virginia thought that rule dangerous because a majority faction could abuse its power to expel members of the minority. Gouverneur Morris of Pennsylvania preferred to retain the majority requirement because he feared that an unjust minority could "keep in a member who ought to be expelled."[214] The majority of delegates agreed with Madison: Ten states voted in favor of the supermajority requirement, and one state was divided on the issue. (At the Convention each state enjoyed one vote. A vote one way or another required the consent of a majority of the state's delegation. If the delegation's votes ended in a tie, the state could not vote on a proposed constitutional provision.)

Historically, the penalty of expulsion has been limited to disloyal conduct (for example, support of the Confederate States of America) or violation of a criminal law that relates to an abuse of the violator's official position (such as bribery). Since the formation of the government under the Constitution of 1787, only six House members have been expelled.[215] The Senate has expelled fifteen members in its history.[216] Fourteen of the Senate expulsions were for support of the Confederacy. The Supreme Court has noted that "[t]he right to expel extends to all cases where the offense," in the judgment of the Senate or House, "is inconsistent with the trust and duty of a member."[217]

In practice, the House has adopted procedures for censure and reprimand. Both require only a majority vote; neither term is mentioned or defined specifically in the Constitution. With censure, the violator must stand in the well of the House while the Speaker reads the censure resolution. With a reprimand, the violator does not have to stand in the well and instead receives a copy of the written rebuke. The Senate may censure or reprimand a senator, but it has eschewed adopting formal terminology as the House has done. Party caucuses also serve as means of discipline. The caucuses can strip a member of committee leadership positions, revoke seniority, impose a fine, or deprive a member of other privileges.

Section 5, Clause 2 remains relevant. The 118th Congress, from its inception, faced calls to expel George Santos (R-NY) because of the multiple lies he crafted during his House campaign about his background and accomplishments. The demand for expulsion grew after Santos was federally indicted for fraud related to campaign finances. Prosecutors charged Santos with identity theft, making unauthorized charges on his donors' credit cards, and making false statements to help him qualify for additional financial and logistical support from the Republican Party's national committee. The criminal charges proved his undoing, and Santos became the sixth member to be expelled in the history of the House. The vote was 311–114, exceeding the two-thirds requirement by 21 votes. Republicans who voted against expulsion argued that the vote was premature because the criminal charges against Santos had not been adjudicated. (Santos pleaded guilty in April 2024 and one year later was sentenced to 87 months in federal prison.) They also likely had in mind that the Republican House majority was minuscule and that Santos's exit would narrow it even further.

Had he not been criminally indicted, Santos probably would have been censured or reprimanded by House leadership and permitted to serve out his term. The frequency of House elections provides the people ample opportunity to make their own judgments about a representative. As a result, expulsion is a tool that is used sparingly. Santos's conduct was so egregious, however, that Congress decided to act.

SECTION 5, CLAUSE 3

EACH HOUSE SHALL keep a Journal of its Proceedings, and from time to time publish the same, excepting such Parts as may in their Judgment require Secrecy; and the Yeas and Nays of the Members of either House on any question shall, at the Desire of one fifth of those Present, be entered on the Journal.

Purpose

Members of Congress are responsible to their constituents. To assist constituents in judging the public conduct of Congress, this provision requires the keeping and publication of a journal of proceedings.

Background and Development

This provision is very similar to one appearing in the Articles of Confederation. Under the Articles, Congress was required to "publish the journal of their proceedings monthly, except such parts thereof relating to treaties, alliances or military operations, as in their judgement require secrecy; and the yeas and nays of the delegates of each State on any question shall be entered on the journal, when it is desired by any delegates of a State."[218]

In the Philadelphia Convention, James Madison of Virginia and John Rutledge of South Carolina, both having served as delegates to the Confederation Congress, moved that the Constitution contain a similar journal requirement. Oliver Ellsworth of Connecticut opposed the provision. He believed that the new Congress would "not fail to publish their proceedings from time to time."[219] James Wilson of Pennsylvania disagreed with Ellsworth and averred that citizens "have a right to know what their Agents are doing or have done, and it should not be an option of the Legislature to conceal their proceedings."[220] He also observed that the Articles contained a similar provision and "not retaining it would furnish the adversaries of the reform a pretext by which weak & suspicious minds may be easily misled."[221]

As for the journal's contents, the Supreme Court has noted that "in respect to the particular mode in which, or with what fullness, shall be kept the proceedings of either house relating to matters not expressly required to be entered on the journals; whether bills, orders, resolutions, reports, and amendments shall be entered at large on the journal, or only referred to and designated by their titles or by numbers,—these and like matters were left to the discretion of the respective houses of congress."[222]

Both houses have rules allowing for secret sessions. In recent years, the secrecy has been invoked for certain matters related to national defense, international relations, and impeachment. Because of its role in approving treaties and deliberating as a court of impeachment,

the Senate is more likely to declare a closed session than is the House.

The one-fifth requirement for recording yeas and nays was seen as an improvement upon the practice of the Confederation Congress, which permitted one delegate from one state to require floor votes to be tabulated. Some members of the Confederation Congress complained that much time was wasted recording votes on trifling and unimportant matters. (Today, in both the House and Senate, votes are usually conducted as voice votes. However, members of those bodies may request roll call votes.)

In the Virginia ratifying convention, Patrick Henry questioned the value of a journal requirement in light of other provisions. "We are told that the yeas and nays shall be taken, and entered on the journals. This, sir, will avail nothing: it may be locked up in their chests, and concealed forever from the people; for they are not to publish what parts they think require secrecy: they *may think*, and *will think*, the whole requires it."[223] He also believed that the expression "*from time to time*" was "very indefinite and indeterminate," possibly "extending to a century."[224] George Mason thought that the Confederation's journal requirement was superior. He pointed out that, under the Articles, the proceedings were "to be published monthly" and secrecy was limited "to treaties, alliances, or military operations."[225]

Madison disagreed with Anti-Federalist contentions in the ratifying convention: "If one fifth of the members present think the measure erroneous, the votes of the states are to be taken upon it, and entered on the journals. Every gentleman here ought to recollect that this is some security, as the people will thereby know those who advocate iniquitous measures."[226]

Although Virginia ratified the Constitution, it also requested that Section 5, Clause 3 be amended. Virginia proposed the following: "That the journals of the proceedings of the Senate and House of Representatives shall be published at least once in every year, except such parts thereof, relating to treaties, alliances, or military operations, as, in their judgment, require secrecy."[227]

Distortions

Henry was wrong that Congress would attempt to hide its actions from the American people. Congress is open about its actions, and the people are at best ambivalent about its many transgressions of the Constitution. Scottish historian Alexander Tytler observed that "[a] democracy cannot exist as a permanent form of government. It can only exist until a majority of voters discover that they can vote themselves largesse out of the public treasury."[228] Americans long ago discovered this fact, and they are content to let Congress abuse its powers so long as entitlement funds continue to flow. Although

Henry's arguments about the journal and secrecy were sound, Congress's penchant for spending has superseded the dangers he feared.

Discussion and Solutions

Life in Congress is akin to life in a fishbowl. CSPAN, the internet, and the twenty-four-hour news cycle provide the public with substantial information about the events in Congress. While the mainstream media is often biased in its reporting of congressional business, alternative websites abound where the people can find the truth.

The journal requirement might seem antiquated in modern America, but in its day it served the purposes of governmental transparency and accountability. As stated above, our problem is not that Congress conceals its actions, but that the people do not seem to care as long as the largesse from the public treasury continues to flow. The only concrete solution this book can offer is for the people to reclaim their position as independent citizens making their own livings.

SECTION 5, CLAUSE 4

NEITHER HOUSE, DURING the Session of Congress, shall, without the Consent of the other, adjourn for more than three days, nor to any other Place than that in which the two Houses shall be sitting.

Purpose

Either house of Congress must get the other's consent before adjourning for more than three days. This provision fosters cooperation between the two chambers and affirms the independence of the legislative branch from the other two departments of government.

Background and Development

At the time of the Constitution's drafting, the king in Great Britain could prorogue or dissolve Parliament at any time. Monarchs, especially the Stuarts, used this power to avoid dealing with issues that had the potential to curb the royal prerogative. No such comprehensive power is given to the president under the U.S. Constitution.

The upper and lower houses of Congress are expected to coordinate schedules in carrying out their business. That provision forbids either house from adjourning for more than three days or conducting business at a location different from the other during the congressional session without the express consent of the other chamber. In other words, nether house has the power to keep Congress from meeting and executing its constitutional duties. If the houses cannot agree on a time for adjournment, Article II, Section 3, Clause 1, authorizes the president to "adjourn them to such Time as he shall think proper." The president never has been called upon to exercise that power, since the Senate and House have worked together in setting schedules.

In the Virginia ratifying convention, James Monroe feared that the provision would render the lower house dependent upon the Senate. Monroe believed that representatives would be "prevented . . . from returning home, or adjourning, without [the Senate's] consent; and, as this might increase their influence unduly, he thought it improper."[229] George Mason was also concerned that the Senate could prevent "the other house from adjourning" and might "worry them into any thing."[230]

Madison was surprised that anyone objected to this provision. He argued that it would "be very exceptionable to allow the senators, or even the representatives, to adjourn, without the consent of the other house, at any season whatsoever, without any regard to the situation of public exigencies."[231] He recognized "[t]hat it was possible, in the nature of things, that some inconvenience might result from it; but that it was as well secured as possible."[232] If the Senate attempted to prevent an adjournment, Madison averred that "it would but serve to irritate the representatives without having the intended effect, as the President could adjourn them."[233]

SECTION 6, CLAUSE 1

THE SENATORS AND Representatives shall receive a Compensation for their Services, to be ascertained by Law, and paid out of the Treasury of the United States. They shall in all Cases, except Treason, Felony and Breach of the Peace, be privileged from Arrest during their Attendance at the Session of their respective Houses, and in going to and returning from the same; and for any Speech or Debate in either House, they shall not be questioned in any other Place.

Purpose

The compensation provision is an anti-corruption measure. Public servants receiving no salary or an inadequate one face the temptation to use their offices for personal financial gain. Hence, members of Congress are paid out of the U.S. Treasury. The protections for speech and privilege against civil arrests secure members' independence in the performance of their duties.

Background and Development

The Framers rejected the British model, in which members of Parliament were not entitled to compensation. Unpaid legislators, most of the Framers believed, are more susceptible to the temptations of bribery and other corrupt practices to support themselves. The delegates at the Philadelphia Convention discussed congressional compensation vigorously. Should the states or the new federal government be responsible for congressional pay? James Madison of Virginia argued that payment from state governments "would create an improper dependence."[234] Alexander Hamilton of New York agreed with Madison. He opined that "[t]hose who pay are the masters of those who are paid."[235] Hamilton wanted Congress beholden to the national Treasury rather than the various state treasuries.

Virginian George Mason supported compensation coming from the national government and conjectured further that different states would appropriate different amounts of money for the legislators. Differences in pay, Mason believed, would undermine the principle of equality among representatives.

Oliver Ellsworth of Connecticut thought that the state legislatures should be Congress's paymasters. He noted that divergent local circumstances would make it difficult to set one standard of pay. "What would be deemed therefore a reasonable compensation in some States," Ellsworth argued, "in others would be very unpopular, and might impede the system."[236] Nathaniel Gorham of Massachusetts distrusted the states to determine compensation for their congressional delegations and complained that they "were always paring down salaries in such a manner as to keep out

of offices men most capable of executing the functions of them."[237]

Charles Cotesworth Pinckney of South Carolina believed that a distinction should be made between senators and representatives. Because the upper house "was meant to represent the wealth of the Country, it ought to be composed of persons of wealth; and if no allowance was to be made for representatives the wealthy alone would undertake the service."[238] Benjamin Franklin of Pennsylvania agreed that senators should be uncompensated and observed that many delegates to the Philadelphia Convention likely would be chosen as senators and thus would be open to the charge that they created lucrative appointments for themselves.

Ellsworth made the point that if the Senate was to represent the states, then senators should be paid by the states. Madison opposed the states having any role in senatorial compensation. He feared that such a role would make the senators mere agents of the state legislatures rather than "impartial umpires & Guardians of justice."[239] Jonathan Dayton of New Jersey supported Madison. He "considered the payment of the Senate by the States as fatal to their independence."[240]

Ultimately, the delegates agreed that all members of Congress should receive compensation and that pay would come from the federal Treasury. The amount of compensation is set by law and is subject to the president's veto, just like any other bill.

In the Virginia ratifying convention, Patrick Henry objected that "[t]he pay of the members is, by the Constitution, to be fixed by themselves, without limitation or restraint. They may therefore indulge themselves in the fullest extent. They may make their compensation as high as they please."[241] He believed that congressional pay should be set by the state legislatures. Madison acknowledged a "theoretic inconvenience of leaving to Congress the fixing their compensations" but thought that it was "more than counterbalanced by" preventing the state legislatures from destroying the general government by starving representatives and senators.[242]

For most of American history, Congress received pay adjustments by passing a bill and presenting it to the president for his signature. While Congress can still do this, most adjustments occur under the Ethics Reform Act of 1989.[243] Under the statute, a formula is utilized incorporating changes in private sector wages and salaries as measured by the Employment Cost Index (ECI). Congress automatically receives the cost-of-living adjustment (COLA) unless it is prohibited by statute, it revises the adjustment, or "the annual base pay adjustment of GS [General Service] employees is established at a rate less than the scheduled adjustment for Members, in which case Members would be paid the lower rate."[244] Under the Twenty-Seventh Amendment, a pay increase cannot go into effect during the term of a sitting Congress. Lower federal courts have held that "the COLA provision of the Ethics Reform Act of 1989 is constitutional because it did not cause any adjustment to congressional compensation until after the election of 1990 and the seating of the new Congress."[245] In other words, because no COLA had gone into effect until after an intervening election (namely, the election of 1990), subsequent COLAs are constitutional.

The clause also concerns the privilege from arrest for members of Congress while attending a congressional session or traveling to and from the sessions. This privilege does not apply to criminal cases, as evidenced by the words "except Treason, Felony and Breach of the Peace." At the time of the framing, arrest for civil (noncriminal) law violations were common. The Framers feared that the process could be abused and the people could be deprived of representation for a significant time. In *Williamson v. United States* (1908), the Supreme Court examined this clause and affirmed that it does not contain any privilege relating to criminal offenses.[246] In so holding, the Court noted that the constitutional language "is the form in which the privilege is stated by Sir Edward Coke, and in which it is usually expressed by the English writers on parliamentary law."[247] Hence, the Framers followed British practice by limiting the privilege to civil arrests. Members of Congress, however, are subject to civil process and civil actions.[248]

The final part of the constitutional provision at hand secures freedom of speech and debate in Congress. The Articles of Confederation contained a similar provision: "Freedom of speech and debate in Congress shall not be impeached or questioned in any court or place out of Congress."[249] This language of the Articles can be traced to the English Bill of Rights, which declared that "[t]he freedom of speech and debates or proceedings in parliament ought not to be impeached or questioned in any court or place out of parliament."[250] Throughout English history, the Stuarts often threatened members of Parliament with civil and criminal actions for statements made during debates. James Wilson, in his law lectures, described this provision as necessary to "enable and encourage a representative of the publick to discharge his publick trust with firmness and success."[251]

As for the extent of the privilege, Thomas Jefferson in his manual on parliamentary procedure observed that "it is restrained to things done in the House in a Parliamentary course."[252] The Supreme Court has recognized that "[t]he heart of the Clause is speech or debate in either House."[253] The Court has extended the privilege to cover more than comments made on the floor of the national legislature but has held that the other matters "must be an integral part of the deliberative and communicative processes by which Members participate in committee and House proceedings with respect to the consideration and passage or rejection of proposed legislation or with respect to other matters which the Constitution places within the jurisdiction of either House."[254]

In *Hutchinson v. Proxmire* (1979), a research professor sued a U.S. senator for defamation because the senator had bestowed the "Golden Fleece" award on a federal agency owing to its funding of the professor's research measuring aggression in animals.[255] The senator spoke in the upper chamber about the research and later sent out a newsletter to constituents that contained passages from his speech. The Court held that the Speech and Debate Clause did not protect the senator's statements made in the newsletter. The newsletter, the Court reasoned, was not "essential to the deliberations of the Senate" or "part of the deliberative process."[256]

Distortions

Some scholars, such as Yale's Akhil Reed Amar, have argued that the Arrest Clause extends to the president of the United States.[257] Such a view has no basis in the text or history of the Constitution. The Arrest Clause

is found in Article I, which pertains to Congress. Moreover, the clause does not mention the president. While perhaps there is a policy argument that the president should have the same immunity as members of Congress, the text of the Constitution does not support such an argument. To reach the result Amar proposes would take a constitutional amendment.

Discussion and Solutions

The Framers were wise to insist on compensation for members of Congress. Even though the current $174,000 per year sounds princely to most Americans, many members resort to sleeping in their offices because they cannot afford to establish a residence in Washington, DC. Absent congressional compensation, only the wealthiest of Americans could contemplate serving in the national legislature.

Court interpretations of Section 6, Clause 1 have been reasonable. The Framers never contemplated immunity from arrest in criminal cases. A contrary interpretation would prevent members of Congress from being brought to justice for serious crimes. Moreover, limiting the speech protections to matters "essential to the deliberations" of Congress or "part of the deliberative process" is equitable. Once a member decides to address issues outside of the safety of a congressional chamber, that member enjoys no special protections beyond those of an ordinary citizen.

Finally, despite policy arguments that a sitting president should enjoy immunity under the Arrest Clause, courts and commentators should reject any attempt to interpret the Constitution to reach such a result. Article V sets forth the proper amendment process and mentions nothing about creative construction.

SECTION 6, CLAUSE 2

NO SENATOR OR Representative shall, during the Time for which he was elected, be appointed to any civil Office under the Authority of the United States, which shall have been created, or the Emoluments whereof shall have been encreased during such time; and no Person holding any Office under the United States, shall be a Member of either House during his Continuance in Office.

Purpose

Members of Congress should not be tempted to create positions or increase the salary for positions if they might personally benefit from an appointment to the office. Moreover, to the extent a member is offered a preexisting office for which the compensation has not been increased, the member must resign from Congress and is barred from holding two offices at the same time.

Background and Development

The Framers were concerned about corruption infesting the government, but they also wanted to encourage talented individuals to seek high office. As proposed originally, Section 6, Clause 2 would have prevented members of Congress from seeking or holding federal office during their terms of service and for one year afterward. James Wilson of Pennsylvania opposed such a stringent measure. Wilson believed that "we ought to hold forth every honorable inducement for men of abilities to enter service of the public."[258] To prove his point, he used the example of war. If a military conflict erupted and men with the best tactical minds were in Congress, the government would "lose the benefit of their services."[259]

George Mason of Virginia inveighed against dishonesty. He urged the Convention to "shut the door against corruption."[260] He expressed admiration for many facets of the British system but lamented that "by the sole power of appointing the increased officers of government, corruption pervades every town and village in the kingdom."[261] John Rutledge of South Carolina agreed with Mason. He urged that the proposed constitution make members of the national legislature ineligible for other offices.

Alexander Hamilton of New York opposed any provision that would deter the talented men of the republic from seeking federal offices. He described man's "prevailing passions" as "ambition and interest."[262] Government needed to harness those passions "to make them subservient to the public good."[263] Hence, Hamilton announced his opposition to all measures that would ignore human motivations and deprive the government of the services of the natural aristocracy.

Charles Pinckney of South Carolina agreed with Hamilton. He believed that making members of Congress ineligible for other offices "was degrading to them."[264] He asserted further that election to the national legislature demonstrated the confidence of the people, and thus members of Congress were prime candidates for other public offices.

John F. Mercer of Maryland defended the British system unabashedly. He feared that if the president could not appoint members of the national legislature to other offices, this lack of influence would render him "a mere phantom of authority."[265]

James Madison advocated for a compromise position that would become part of the Constitution. "[N]o office ought to be open to a member," Madison averred, "which may be created or augmented while he is in the legislature."[266] The term "emolument" fits with the idea of "augmented," inasmuch as dictionaries at the time defined an emolument as "[p]rofit" or "advantage."[267]

The delegates also appreciated the arguments about military preparedness and limited the restriction to civil offices. The original proposal barred members from state offices, but it was struck because the delegates believed that the states might desperately need the services of their best and brightest.

In 1937, President Franklin D. Roosevelt nominated Senator Hugo Black from Alabama to the Supreme Court. Black ultimately was confirmed, but during his first appearance on the Court, members of the bar objected because, inter alia, during his time in the Senate, Congress had voted to increase the justices' retirement benefits. Although the plain words of the Constitution appeared to disqualify Black, the Supreme Court sidestepped the issue in *Ex parte Levitt* (1937) by holding that the lawyer challenging Black's appointment lacked standing.[268]

In recent years, Congress and the president have utilized the "Saxbe fix" to handle similar issues related to the Emoluments Clause. In 1973, President Richard M. Nixon sought to appoint Senator William Saxbe as attorney general. Saxbe, however, had been a senator when Congress raised the attorney general's annual pay from $35,000 to $60,000. The problem was "fixed" by lowering the attorney general's salary back to $35,000 so that Saxbe would receive no pecuniary benefit from the salary increase adopted while he was in office. Saxbe fixes have been utilized by multiple administrations since 1973.

Under the final clause of Section 6, the Framers prohibited members of Congress from holding other offices under the United States simultaneously. The clause prohibits any movement toward parliamentary government and seeks to strike at corruption. Members of Congress are not to be bought by the chief executive with offers of high-paying offices or appointments. If a member of Congress does accept a position in the executive or judicial branch (and the position was not created nor its benefits raised while the member was in Congress), the member must resign from the national legislature.

Because the final clause is not limited to civil offices, some commentators have questioned whether members of Congress may hold commissions in the Armed Forces Reserve.[269] Much as it did with Hugo Black's appointment to the Supreme Court, in *Schlesinger v. Reservists Committee to Stop the War* (1974), the Supreme Court ducked the issue of members of Congress holding commissions in the reserves by finding that the plaintiffs had no standing to bring a legal action.[270]

Distortions

One must question whether a "Saxbe fix" is legitimate, since constitutional disability arises when the pay or benefits related to an office are increased by Congress. If the member of Congress holds congressional office at the time, then the member should not be eligible for a judicial or executive office for which the pay was raised. This is a bright-line rule, and there is no constitutional mechanism to annul the effects of the increase.[271] Moreover, only a neophyte would believe that Senator Saxbe or Senator Black were the best available candidates for attorney general or justice of the Supreme Court. While prohibitions of Saxbe fixes would marginally decrease the pool of candidates for an appointment, in a nation of 331 million, there is a surfeit of qualified individuals to fill important offices.

Discussion and Solutions

The legislative, judicial, and executive branches have all demonstrated cowardice in facing cases implicating the Emoluments Clause. The clause sets forth a bright-line rule. President Roosevelt should have simply picked someone else to serve on the Court, and the Senate should never have confirmed Black because of the constitutional violation. The Supreme Court did no better when it hid behind the standing doctrine and refused to adjudicate the case.

Similarly, a "Saxbe fix" is really no constitutional fix at all in the face of the plain language. President Nixon could have selected from a number of qualified lawyers who did not suffer from the constitutional infirmity that Senator William Saxbe did. The president, courts, and Congress should eschew questionable "fixes" and adhere to the plain meaning of the Emoluments Clause. The people, media, and pundits should pressure Congress when it ignores Section 6, Clause 2. No amendments or legislative proposals are needed. In this matter, the three branches of government should just adhere to the Constitution as it exists.

Section 7, Clause 1
All Bills for raising Revenue shall originate in the House of Representatives; but the Senate may propose or concur with Amendments as on other Bills.

Purpose

Increases in revenue are typically derived from taxation, and the people shoulder the burdens of increased taxation; therefore, the Constitution requires that all bills raising revenue must originate in the House—the body chosen by the people.

Background and Development

Part of the Great Compromise between the large and small states resulted in the House having the sole authority to originate revenue bills. Benjamin Franklin of Pennsylvania remarked that this provision and "the equality of votes in the Senate" were "essentially connected by the compromise which had been agreed to."[272] Moreover, the Origination Clause follows the British practice that all bills raising taxes must originate in the House of Commons. However, under the British constitution, the House of Lords had no power to amend revenue bills. At the time of the Philadelphia Convention, "[s]even state constitutions required the lower legislative house to originate money bills, with only three permitting the upper body to amend such bills."[273]

George Mason of Virginia put great emphasis on the House having the authority to originate revenue bills, because "the purse strings should be in the hands of the Representatives of the people."[274] Similarly, Elbridge Gerry of Massachusetts observed that "[t]axation & representation are strongly associated in the minds of the people, and they will not agree that any but their immediate representatives shall meddle with their purses."[275] James Wilson of Pennsylvania disagreed with Mason and Gerry. He believed that the Senate should be able to originate revenue bills because most important matters delegated to the new government were connected with money. Charles Pinckney of South Carolina observed that his state experienced strife because of its origination clause, which was honored in the breach and was a source of friction between the upper and lower houses.

Edmund Randolph of Virginia proposed amending the Origination Clause to apply only to bills whose purpose was to raise revenue. The thrust of his proposal "was to prevent all potential bills that might incidentally raise revenue from being excluded from Senate origination."[276] Although Randolph's proposal was rejected, the courts have interpreted the clause in the spirit of Randolph's proposed amendment.

In the Virginia ratifying convention, William Grayson disapproved of permitting "the Senate to propose or concur with amendments to money bills."[277] Grayson "looked upon the power of proposing amendments to be equal, in principle, to that of originating."[278]

He pointed out that "[t]he lords in England had never been allowed to intermeddle with money bills. He knew not why the Senate should."[279] In response, Madison acknowledged that "[t]he gentlemen who composed the Convention divided in opinion concerning the utility of confining this to any particular branch. Whatever it be in Great Britain, there is a sufficient difference between us and them to render it inapplicable to this country."[280]

Distortions

In *United States v. Munoz-Flores* (1990), a defendant challenged, inter alia, the constitutionality of a special assessment fee imposed under statute on all persons convicted of federal misdemeanors on grounds that the bill originated in the Senate rather than the House.[281] Referring to prior precedents, the Court observed that "revenue bills are those that levy taxes in the strict sense of the word, and are not bills for other purposes which may incidentally create revenue."[282] The Court described this "general rule to mean that a statute that creates a particular governmental program and raises revenue to support the program, as opposed to a statute that raises revenue to support Government generally," is not a revenue bill within the meaning of the clause.[283] The special assessment fee, according to the Court, was simply a measure to support a government program (the Crime Victims Fund) and thus not a revenue bill.

The Origination Clause has been diminished further by congressional practice coupled with judicial interpretations. For example, in *Sissel v. United States Department of Health and Human Services* (2014), a plaintiff challenged the Patient Protection and

Affordable Care Act (ACA) on grounds that it violated the Origination Clause.[284] Of note is the history of the bill, which originated in the House with the modest purpose of amending the first-time homebuyers' credit for members of the military and certain federal employees. The Senate, however, gutted the bill and replaced its contents with health insurance reforms. Because the Supreme Court had earlier upheld the ACA under Congress's taxing power and the full text of the ACA came from the Senate, Sissel asked that the statute be declared unconstitutional under the Origination Clause.

The D.C. Circuit Court of Appeals held that despite the ACA being affirmed based on the taxing power, the purpose of the bill was to increase the number of Americans with health insurance. As such, it was not a revenue bill under the Origination Clause's meaning, and it did not matter that the Senate simply deleted the full text of the House bill and created a new statutory scheme.

Discussion and Solutions

As the history of the ACA shows, our government plays games with the Origination Clause. Americans should take issue with the fact that the Senate gutted a bill received

from the House and replaced its contents with health insurance reforms supposedly enacted under Congress's taxing power. Of course, the House acquiesced to the Senate's tactic, and President Obama happily signed the ACA into law. When given the opportunity to rectify this situation, federal judges claimed with a straight face that ACA had little to do with revenue but instead sought to increase the number of Americans with health insurance.

Randolph's suggestion was that the Origination Clause apply only to bills whose primary purpose was to raise revenue. He wanted to prevent all potential bills that might incidentally raise revenue from being excluded from Senate origination. Randolph's proposal was rejected by the Philadelphia Convention. Unfortunately, we act as if his proposal won acceptance. The Constitution of 1787 should be interpreted to construe the term "money bills" in a broad fashion and thus prohibit Senate shenanigans as seen with the ACA. Members of the House should jealously guard the origination power and refuse to act on proposed legislation from the Senate that raises revenue—whether they agree with the underlying policy or not—to protect the balance established by Section 7, Clause 1.

SECTION 7, CLAUSE 2

EVERY BILL WHICH shall have passed the House of Representatives and the Senate, shall, before it become a Law, be presented to the President of the United States; If he approve he shall sign it, but if not he shall return it, with his Objections to that House in which it shall have originated, who shall enter the Objections at large on their Journal, and proceed to reconsider it. If after such Reconsideration two thirds of that House shall agree to pass the Bill, it shall be sent, together with the Objections, to the other House, by which it shall likewise be reconsidered, and if approved by two thirds of that House, it shall become a Law. But in all such Cases the Votes of both Houses shall be determined by yeas and Nays, and the Names of the Persons voting for and against the Bill shall be entered on the Journal of each House respectively. If any Bill shall not be returned by the President within ten Days (Sundays excepted) after it shall have been presented to him, the Same shall be a Law, in like Manner as if he had signed it, unless the Congress by their Adjournment prevent its Return, in which Case it shall not be a Law.

Purpose

With the Presentment Clause, the Framers set forth a fairly detailed procedure for how a bill becomes law. A bill must be approved by both the lower and upper house and must be presented to the president for consideration. If the bill is rejected or vetoed, Congress can override the negative by a two-thirds vote. The president cannot prohibit a bill from becoming law by inaction. If after ten days the president has taken no action, the bill becomes law as if the president had signed it, unless an adjournment cuts short the ten-day period.

Background and Development

At the Philadelphia Convention, the debate about presentment and veto centered on the eighth resolution of the Virginia Plan, which called for a council of revision composed of the executive and "a convenient number of the National Judiciary."[285] The council would

be charged to "examine every act of the National Legislature" and the state legislatures before they would be allowed to operate.[286] A number of delegates raised concerns about having the judiciary involved in vetoing statutes. Elbridge Gerry of Massachusetts believed that the proposal in the Virginia Plan established "an improper coalition between the Executive & Judiciary departments."[287] Caleb Strong of Massachusetts agreed with Gerry that "the power of making ought to be kept distinct from that of expounding, the laws."[288] Luther Martin of Maryland thought it improper to include the judges on the council. "Join them with the Executive in the Revision," Martin said, "and they will have a double negative" because the judges will be asked to review laws in legal cases.[289] Such concerns about separation of powers prevailed, and the Framers disentangled the judiciary from presidential veto.

The judiciary aside, the presidential veto was itself controversial. Pierce Butler of South

Carolina reminded his colleagues that throughout the world "Executive power is in a constant course of increase."[290] He chastised the Convention for acting as if "we had nothing to apprehend from an abuse of the Executive power."[291] Benjamin Franklin of Pennsylvania stressed how colonial governors exercised veto powers to extort money from the legislature. Good laws could not be passed, Franklin remarked, "without a private bargain" with the governor.[292] Roger Sherman of Connecticut protested against enabling "any one man to stop the will of the whole."[293] If the measure met with the approval of the national legislature, Sherman thought it should become law.

James Madison of Virginia and James Wilson of Pennsylvania championed veto power for the executive. They doubted that the power would be used often and believed its mere existence could dissuade the national legislature from passing ill-conceived laws. Madison, contending that the executive would be weak, predicted that a veto never would be contemplated absent the backing of a substantial portion of Congress.

The Convention ultimately accepted presidential veto power. In *Federalist* No. 73, Alexander Hamilton summed up the reasons for lodging such a power with the president: "The primary inducement to conferring the power in question upon the Executive is, to enable him to defend himself; the secondary one is to increase the chances in favor of the community against the passing of bad laws, through haste, inadvertence, or design."[294] Hamilton acknowledged that the veto "does not turn upon the supposition of superior wisdom or virtue in the Executive."[295] Instead, it rests "upon the supposition that the legislature will not be infallible" and that the possibility

of a presidential negative might lead to mature reflection.[296]

Proponents of the Constitution also emphasized the limited nature of the veto as opposed to the absolute power of the British monarch. In the North Carolina ratifying convention, James Iredell observed that "[i]n a republican government, it would be extremely dangerous to place [the veto] in the power of one man to put an absolute negative on a bill proposed" by Congress.[297] Iredell described the veto designed by the Philadelphia Convention as "a happy medium between the possession of an absolute negative, and the executive having no control whatever on acts of legislation."[298]

While some Anti-Federalists concurred that presidential veto authority was needed, others asserted, in the words of the Pennsylvania minority, that "[t]he president is to have control over the enacting of laws, so far as to make the concurrence to two thirds of the representatives and senators present necessary, if he should object to the laws."[299] This was, in their view, a violation of separation-of-powers principles. Similarly, Impartial Examiner argued that a veto was suited to a monarch in a government of mixed interests such as the British constitution, but that such an analysis did not apply to a republic in which all officers were servants of the people.[300] The Federal Farmer in his letters believed the executive should have some part in a negative of legislative bills, but he preferred that such a power be exercised jointly by the president and judiciary in a council of revision following the New York model.[301]

Presentment Clause issues typically have arisen in the context of the modern administrative state. For example, in *I.N.S. v. Chadha* (1983), the Supreme Court considered a portion of the Immigration and Nationality Act authorizing either the House or the Senate to invalidate and suspend deportation rulings of executive branch officials.[302] It was not the first time Congress had used a "legislative veto." Indeed, prior to *Chada* the national legislature included such provisions in "200 separate laws over a period of 50 years."[303] Nevertheless, the Court concluded that a constitutional violation existed because congressional nullification of executive branch directives was an exercise of legislative power and thus required presentment to the president. The Court recognized the need to check administrative agencies, but interpreted the Philadelphia Convention's debates as requiring "that legislation by the national Congress be a step-by-step, deliberate and deliberative process."[304] (For a full discussion of the problems presented by *Chada*, refer to the first section of Article I discussed above.)

In *Clinton v. City of New York* (1998), the Court considered the constitutionality of the Line Item Veto Act, which allowed the president to cancel certain provisions in appropriations legislation before signing it into law: "(1) any dollar amount of discretionary budget authority; (2) any item of new direct spending; or (3) any limited tax benefit."[305] The Court held that "[i]n both legal and practical effect, the President [by using the cancellation authority] has amended" acts of the national legislature "by repealing a portion of each."[306] Hence, the Court believed that if it allowed the Line Item Veto Act to stand, "it would authorize the President to create a different law—one whose text was not voted on by either House of Congress or presented to the President for signature."[307] Justice Scalia entered a vigorous dissent, arguing that presidents throughout American history had made decisions declining to spend appropriations and that the Act's

cancellation provision was "no different from what Congress has permitted the President to do since the formation of the Union."[308] Although many state governors have been granted line-item veto authority, at the federal level, presidential vetoes are all-or-nothing.

The very last portion of Section 7 deals with the so-called pocket veto, whereby the president holds on to a bill without approving or rejecting it at the end of a legislative session and, in effect, vetoes the bill by dormancy. Unlike the return veto, the Constitution does not require the president to return the bill to the national legislature with his objections. If Congress still desires the bill to become law, then when it reconvenes, the bill has to be reintroduced, approved by both houses, and presented to the president for his consideration.

Distortions

The pocket veto universally is recognized as valid when a Congress adjourns sine die—that is, the legislative session comes to an end while a newly elected Congress waits to convene. The real question is whether the pocket veto may be exercised during an intersession adjournment or an intrasession adjournment. The former occurs when Congress takes a respite between its two scheduled sessions; the latter, when Congress breaks within one of the two scheduled sessions.

The text of the Constitution simply refers to an adjournment and makes no distinction between sine die, intersession, or intrasession adjournments. In the *Pocket Veto Case* (1929), the Supreme Court held that "the determinative question in reference to an 'adjournment' is not whether it is a final adjournment of Congress or an interim adjournment, such as an adjournment of the first session, but whether it is one that 'prevents' the President from returning the bill to the House in which it originated within the time allowed."[309] That precedent, however, has been eroded over time. Through a series of decisions from the Supreme Court and the lower federal courts, current jurisprudence indicates "that the pocket veto is not available during brief intra- and intersession adjournments where the House of origin appoints an agent to receive the veto message from the President."[310]

Discussion and Solutions

The *Pocket Veto Case* (1929) got it right on the adjournment issue as it relates to the presidential veto. The determinative matter is whether there is an adjournment—not a final adjournment, but an adjournment. The commonsense understanding of this case should be revived. Public interest litigators should seek an opportunity to bring the issue of pocket vetoes back to the Supreme Court docket.

The Line Item Veto Act discussed above highlights another area of possible reform. Under the Constitution, every bill passed by both houses of Congress must be presented to the president, who must sign the bill into law or return it to Congress. Understanding that the president's options are limited, Congress often attaches special-interest riders to gigantic funding bills. Members of Congress engage in logrolling: They vote for wasteful projects furthering local interests offered on a quid pro quo basis. The president cannot reject the riders and amendments without vetoing the entire bill. Logrolling was not a concern in the early republic because no one envisioned the massive bills passed today dealing with

diverse subject matter and loaded with pork. The only appropriations bill passed by the first Congress in 1789 contained fewer than two hundred words. Not so anymore.

The Constitution of the Confederate States of America contained a line-item veto provision.[311] The Confederate Framers believed that the U.S. Congress had abandoned the splendid simplicity of the first Congress and embarked on a course of abusive spending practices. They lamented that the president's hands had been tied by the all-or-nothing veto found in the U.S. Constitution. The Confederate Framers allowed their president to veto individual line items that he deemed improvident spending. They hoped this would impose a check on congressional fiscal misbehavior.

It is interesting that the Confederate Framers explicitly incorporated a line-item veto in their constitution rather than relying, as did Justice Scalia, on historical practice, which entailed Congress authorizing money to be spent on a particular item at the president's discretion. While it is worth considering the Confederate example of specifically granting the president a line-item veto, we should be careful. The modern presidency (discussed under Article II) exercises significantly more power than envisioned by the Philadelphia Convention and the state ratifying conventions. We definitely have a spending problem in American government. But the "cure" of further empowering the president might be worse than the disease of profligate spending by Congress. Institutional responsibility would not be advanced by the line-item veto; the lack of responsibility via delegation of legislative functions is one of our greatest challenges.

Section 7, Clause 3

Every Order, Resolution, or Vote to which the Concurrence of the Senate and House of Representatives may be necessary (except on a question of Adjournment) shall be presented to the President of the United States; and before the Same shall take Effect, shall be approved by him, or being disapproved by him, shall be repassed by two thirds of the Senate and House of Representatives, according to the Rules and Limitations prescribed in the Case of a Bill.

Purpose

The Philadelphia Convention sought to prevent Congress from avoiding presidential vetoes by designating legislation as something other than a "bill." Hence, this provision exists to prevent gamesmanship to determine whether or not legislation must be presented to the president.

Background and Development

At the Philadelphia Convention, James Madison of Virginia noted "that if the negative of the President was confined to bills; it would be evaded by acts under the form and name of Resolutions, votes &c."[312] Section 7, Clause 3 was proposed by Edmund Randolph of Virginia and approved by the Convention with only New Jersey voting in the negative.

In *Hollingsworth v. Virginia* (1798), a litigant challenged the validity of the Eleventh Amendment, inter alia, on grounds that Congress never presented it to the president under Section 7, Clause 3.[313] However, under the constitutional amendment procedure, the text provides that "Congress, whenever two thirds of both Houses shall deem it necessary, shall propose Amendments to this Constitution."[314] The text makes no mention of the president having any role in the amendment process, and no part of the Bill

of Rights proposed by the first Congress was presented to the president. A unanimous Supreme Court rejected the challenge and held that the Eleventh Amendment was enacted properly. In a footnote, Justice Chase observed specifically that "[t]he negative of the President applies only to the ordinary cases of legislation: He has nothing to do with the proposition, or adoption, of amendments to the Constitution."[315] Similarly, the Constitution authorizes Congress to declare war and mentions nothing about presentment of declarations to the president. Since a declaration of war is not "ordinary legislation," one would expect the rule in *Hollingsworth* to govern that matter as well.

Distortions

Some scholars argue that *Hollingsworth* was wrongly decided. Sopan Joshi, who currently serves as assistant to the solicitor general, relies on Article I, Section 7 to argue that Congress must submit proposed constitutional amendments to the president.[316] This is a suspect interpretation because the Constitution requires a two-thirds majority in each house to pass constitutional amendments. That is the same number required to override a presidential veto, and thus it would be illogical for the Constitution to require presentment and the possibility of a veto when Congress has started the process with a supermajority sufficient to override a veto.

Discussion and Solutions

Madison's comments in Philadelphia and the *Hollingsworth* decision indicate that the key to this clause is "ordinary legislation." If a matter partakes of the character of legislation, then Congress must present it to the president for consideration. Declarations of war and proposed constitutional amendments, however, are not ordinary legislation and do not have to be presented to the president. Hence, we should resist efforts by Joshi and others to impose a presentment requirement for amendments and similar extraordinary matters. The Constitution imposes no such condition.

SECTION 8, CLAUSE 1

THE CONGRESS SHALL have Power To lay and collect Taxes, Duties, Imposts and Excises, to pay the Debts and provide for the common Defence and general Welfare of the United States; but all Duties, Imposts and Excises shall be uniform throughout the United States;

Purpose

Dominant opinion in 1787 held that the national legislature should have an independent source of revenue so it could pay debts and perform the functions expressly delegated to it. Section 8, Clause 1 is an expression of this judgment.

Background and Development

Taxation

The Confederation Congress had no power to tax; it subsisted on "requisitions" from the states. Scholars estimate that by the end of 1780, the "costs of the war had outstripped receipts from the states by nearly forty to one."[317] In March 1780, James Madison complained to Thomas Jefferson that funding concerns were endangering the revolution and provided a list of problems: "Our army threatened with an immediate alternative of disbanding to living on free quarter; the public Treasury empty; public credit exhausted."[318] During his last years, Madison contemplated the challenges of the Confederation period and described Congress's lack of an independent revenue source as "the radical infirmity" of America's first constitution.[319]

In light of those concerns, on February 3, 1781, Congress requested that the states give it the power to levy a 5 percent duty on imports.[320] The money received would be allocated to retiring past debts and financing the war. Under the Articles, all alterations of the charter had to be approved unanimously by all thirteen states. Initially, it appeared that the states would adopt the impost proposal and give Congress an independent source of revenue. By the middle of 1782, all states except Rhode Island had approved the amendment. Rhode Island did not agree to the amendment because it wanted the money from duties for its own use and raised sundry objections. Congress sent a delegation to Rhode Island to persuade it to join the other states on this matter, but while the delegation was en route, Virginia withdrew its acceptance of the impost. Hearing the news, the delegation turned back and admitted that the impost was dead.

In 1783, Congress again tried to persuade the states to grant it the power to levy an impost. Congress urged that such a power was "indispensably necessary to the restoration of public credit."[321] Congress proposed that the moneys received would be used only to retire the national debt and that the power to levy an impost would lapse twenty-five years hence. To address concerns about armies of congressional tax collectors swarming the states, Congress provided that the collectors of the duties would be appointed by the states but would be removable from office by Congress. This time, it was not Rhode Island that scuttled the impost, but New York. The state collected a substantial amount of revenue from duties placed on imports. New York did not want to compete with the confederacy for these funds and thus refused to augment Congress's powers.

With Section 8, Clause 1, the Philadelphia Convention secured an independent source of funding for the union. For the most part, Anti-Federalist critics did not oppose the idea of Congress having some power to tax. As mentioned above, in both 1782 and 1783 supermajorities of the states favored allowing the Confederation Congress to impose a tax on imports.

Some suggested, however, that the requisition system be kept with modifications. For example, William Symmes in the New York ratifying convention averred that "if each state had its proportion of some certain gross sum assigned, according to its numbers, and a power was given to Congress to collect the same, in case of default in the state, this would not have been a safer Constitution."[322] Otherwise, he feared that Americans would be burdened "with a standing army of ravenous collectors,—harpies, perhaps, from another state, but who, however, were never known to have bowels for any purpose, but to fatten on the life-blood of the people."[323]

Similarly, Virginia's Patrick Henry exclaimed that he was willing to give Congress only the conditional power of direct taxation, "that is, after non-compliance with requisitions."[324] George Mason aligned with Henry on this matter: "An indispensable amendment in this case, is, that Congress shall not exercise the power of raising direct taxes till the States shall have refused to comply with the requisitions of Congress."[325]

Another common complaint raised by opponents of the Constitution was the Convention's failure to distinguish between internal and external taxes. According to an Anti-Federalist writing as the Federal Farmer, external taxes "are import duties, which are laid on imported goods," and these duties typically are "collected in a few seaport towns, and of a few individuals."[326] Only small numbers of officials are needed to collect these taxes, he continued, "and they can be carried no higher than trade will bear, or smuggling [will] permit."[327] Internal taxes, on the other hand, encompass such things as "poll and land taxes, excises, duties on all written instruments," and "may fix themselves on every person and species of property in the community."[328] Such broad taxes also require more federal involvement in their enforcement, and that troubled the Anti-Federalists.

The distinction between internal and external taxation was integral to the events leading to the American Revolution. The hated Stamp Act of 1765 was the first direct internal tax levied on the North American colonies by the British Parliament. By raising the distinction between internal and external taxes, the Anti-Federalist writers hoped to remind Americans of the Revolution's assumption that internal taxes were the province of state assemblies and not the central government. "When I recollect how lately congress, conventions, legislatures, and people contended in the cause of liberty, and carefully weighed the importance of taxation," the Farmer observed, "I can scarcely believe we are serious in proposing to vest the powers of laying and collecting internal taxes in a government so imperfectly organized for such purposes."[329]

General Welfare

Opponents of the Constitution also saw its "general welfare" language as conferring a plenary power on the national government. In a letter to Edmund Randolph, Virginia's Richard Henry Lee feared that those two words permitted Congress "[t]o judge of what may be for the general welfare" and to pass laws "with every possible object of human legislation."[330] George Mason, during the Virginia ratifying convention, similarly believed that "the power of providing for the general welfare may be perverted to" the destruction of the union.[331] William Grayson, in that same convention, complained that Congress "had an indefinite power to provide for the general welfare, he thought there were great reasons to apprehend great dangers."[332] In the New York ratifying convention, John Williams reasoned that "if the Congress should judge it a proper provision,

for the common defence and general welfare, that the state governments should be essentially destroyed, what, in the name of common sense, will prevent them? Are they not constitutionally authorized to pass such laws?"[333]

Friends of the Constitution pushed back against the Anti-Federalists' arguments. Edmund Randolph, during the Virginia ratifying convention, asserted that the "rhetoric of the gentleman has highly colored the dangers of giving the general government an indefinite power of providing for the general welfare. I contend that no such power is given."[334]

James Madison, writing in *Federalist* No. 41, rejected the notion that the General Welfare Clause "amounts to an unlimited commission to exercise every power which may be alleged to be necessary for the common defense or general welfare."[335] Such an objection might have weight, Madison noted, but for the careful enumeration of powers that followed this introductory language. Madison continued:

> For what purpose could the enumeration of particular powers be inserted, if these and all others were meant to be included in the preceding general power? Nothing is more natural nor common than first to use a general phrase, and then to explain and qualify it by a recital of particulars. But the idea of an enumeration of particulars which neither explain nor qualify the general meaning, and can have no other effect than to confound and mislead, is an absurdity, which, as we are reduced to the dilemma of charging either on the authors of the objection or on the authors of the Constitution, we must take the liberty of supposing, had not its origin with the latter.[336]

In other words, if "general welfare" was the goal, then why bother to give Congress the power to regulate commerce, establish post offices, and to raise an army and navy? Surely those matters are for the general welfare and no specific enumeration would be required.

Although Hamilton collaborated with Madison on the *Federalist*, it did not take him long to reject the explanation of general welfare articulated in *Federalist* No. 41. During George Washington's first administration, Secretary of the Treasury Hamilton presented to Congress a Report on Manufactures. In this report, Hamilton urged that measures should be taken to render the United States independent of foreign nations for military and other essential purposes. Hamilton suggested protective tariffs, government monetary support for certain industries, government grants to inventors, internal improvements, and the payment of the travel expenses of skilled foreigners who emigrated to the United States.

Hamilton anticipated constitutional objections to his program and argued in his report that the General Welfare Clause provided the authority to raise and spend money for purposes not specifically enumerated in the Constitution. "The phrase ['general welfare'] is as comprehensive as any that could have been used," Hamilton lectured, "because it was not fit that the constitutional authority of the Union to appropriate its revenues should have been restricted within the narrower limits than the 'general welfare,' and because this necessity embraces a vast variety of particulars, which are susceptible neither of specification nor of definition."[337] So long as its goals are in the interest of the nation, Congress may spend money as it sees fit.

In his Report of 1800, Madison addressed Hamilton's interpretation of the General Welfare Clause directly. Madison pointed out that the Articles of Confederation also contained a general welfare provision and that the "similarity in the use of these phrases in the two great federal charters, might well be considered, as rendering their meaning less liable to be misconstrued."[338] The general welfare language of the Articles of Confederation had never been understood to grant powers outside of their enumeration in the Articles, and thus neither should that same language be construed broadly in the Constitution of 1787. Madison characterized the assertions of Hamilton's Report on Manufacturers as "extraordinary" and chided Congress for failing to rebuke Hamilton for such an untenable interpretation of the General Welfare Clause.[339] A government bound only by ideas of the general welfare, Madison continued, would be granted unlimited jurisdiction. Before Congress spends money, it must first point to an enumerated power. If no such enumerated power is found, then no expenditure is authorized.

Uniformity Clause

The Uniformity Clause is the final provision of Section 8, Clause 1; it seeks to ensure that no one jurisdictional subdivision or parochial interest oppresses another by discriminatory duties, imposts, and excises. For example, a tariff that imposes a 5 percent rate on goods imported into Northern states and a 10 percent rate on goods imported into Southern states would be unconstitutional. In the *Head Money Cases* (1884), the Supreme Court dealt with an "excise duty on the business of bringing passengers from foreign countries into this by ocean navigation."[340] The Court averred that such a tax "is uniform and operates precisely alike in every port of the United States where such passengers can be landed."[341] The Court set forth the basic rule of the Uniformity Clause by noting that a tax is uniform if it "operates with the same force and effect in every place where the subject of it is found."[342] A tax, of course, may have disparate effects and not violate the Uniformity Clause. For example, a tax on the purchase of snow shovels would disproportionally affect Northern states, but it operates with the same force in Florida as it does in Maine.

Distortions

An Uncontrollable Spending Power

The Supreme Court considered the General Welfare Clause in *United States v. Butler* (1936),[343] when it reviewed provisions of the Agricultural Adjustment Act of 1933. In that statute, Congress sought to maintain a balance between agricultural production and consumption to stabilize prices for farmers. In defending the statute, the government claimed that the General Welfare Clause authorized Congress to spend money for "anything conducive to national welfare."[344] Because Congress believed that the raising of farm prices would be conducive to the good of the whole, Congress should be allowed to appropriate money and to spend it to achieve that ultimate goal. The Court accepted this argument and held that the spending of money "is not limited by the direct grants of legislative power found in the Constitution."[345]

In 1987, the Court opined further on the power of Congress to spend for the general welfare. In *South Dakota v. Dole* (1987),[346] the Court considered a challenge to the constitutionality of conditioning a state's receipt

of federal highway funds on the adoption of a minimum drinking age of twenty-one. If a state declined to raise the drinking age, it would lose 5 percent of funds it otherwise would receive from Congress. The Court affirmed the Hamiltonian position announced in *Butler* and set forth the "limits" of the General Welfare Clause. First, the Court noted that the spending must be for general public purposes and that Congress is the best judge of whether spending meets that requirement. Second, a statute tying some state action to the receipt of funds must be unambiguous so that states may "exercise their choice knowingly, cognizant of the consequences of participation."[347] Third, the conditions imposed must be related to a federal interest in a particular national project. Finally, Congress may not impose a condition if it violates some other constitutional provision.

With the drinking age, the Court held that the spending at issue was designed to promote the general welfare because Congress found that lower drinking ages gave young people an incentive to mix alcohol with automobiles. Young people traveled across state lines in search of jurisdictions with lower drinking ages. A dangerous situation thus arose on the nation's roads, which permitted Congress to act. The statute imposing the conditions clearly set forth the "rules," so South Dakota could make a knowing and intelligent decision. Such encouragement of state action, the Court ruled, was well within the spending power.

In *National Federation of Independent Business v. Sebelius* (2012), the Court confronted the expansion of Medicaid through the Patient Protection and Affordable Care Act of 2010 (ACA).[348] Created in 1965, the Medicaid program offered federal funds to assist the states in providing medical care to pregnant women, children, the blind, and other discreet classes. To receive the federal moneys, states are required to "comply with federal criteria governing matters such as who receives care and what services are provided at what cost."[349] The ACA required the states to cover all adults "with incomes up to 133 percent of the federal poverty level"—a dramatic expansion.[350] States that refused to expand Medicaid were threatened with the loss of all federal Medicaid funding. As the Court noted, "Medicaid spending accounts for over 20 percent of the average State's total budget, with federal funds covering 50 to 83 percent of those costs."[351] The Court found that such a consequence amounted to impermissible coercion and that the states could not have foreseen that Congress would have expanded Medicaid as part of the bid for universal coverage. The Court distinguished *Dole* because states faced a loss of only 5 percent of highway funds and thus had a meaningful choice to adopt or not adopt twenty-one as the drinking age.

While the Court's result with Medicaid expansion is a welcome restriction on the spending power, Americans must not lose sight that the spending power as approved in *Butler* and *Dole* remains and is incongruent with the Constitution. Congress can tax state citizens and slide this money back to the state governments if they spend the money as directed by Congress. The spending is not required to be in furtherance of any enumerated power.

Not Really Uniform

The Supreme Court has held that the Uniformity Clause does not prohibit all geographically defined classifications. In *United States v. Ptasynski* (1983), the Court dealt with the Crude Oil Windfall Profit Tax Act of 1980 and the tax exemption for oil produced north of the Arctic Circle or in other rugged areas of Alaska.[352] In light of the history of the Uniformity Clause, the Court observed that when Congress chooses to frame a tax in geographic terms, "we will examine the classification closely to see if there is actual geographic discrimination."[353] The Court upheld the exemption because the national legislature was not attempting to favor Alaska over other states and the statute reflected "Congress' considered judgment that unique climactic and geographic conditions require that oil produced from this exempt area be treated as a separate class of oil."[354] In other words, because it was so expensive to drill and operate Alaskan oil wells, profits were smaller than for wells in the lower forty-eight, and thus windfall profits from rising oil prices were not likely. With its ruling in *Ptasynski*, the Supreme Court endorsed "benign" discrimination under the Uniformity Clause. Discrimination with the best of intentions, of course, is still discrimination and should have no sanction in the Court's Uniformity Clause jurisprudence.

Discussion and Solutions

One of the pillars of the modern puissant national government is the Spending Clause. Had the friends of the Constitution asserted that Congress could spend money unrelated to the enumerated powers, the new plan of government would never have been ratified. The Constitution was sold to the people as creating a government of few and defined powers. The modern Hamiltonian interpretation of general welfare is inconsistent with the key promise that the national government would have limited jurisdiction. Moreover, when used as a tool to persuade states to enact policies they otherwise would not, the spending power amounts to bribery or coercion and further denigrates the states' place in the union.

It is late in the game, but we need to return to the original understanding of Congress's power to spend money. Congress should be limited to spending on matters within its delegated powers. Matters outside the enumerated powers should be left to the states and the people. Whether by a constitutional amendment ("Congress shall spend no federal funds unsupported by an enumerated power appearing in Article I, Section 8 or an Amendment to this Constitution"), congressional restraint, or the Supreme Court rethinking *Butler*, a revision is necessary to revive a limited government.

Of course, the problem might take care of itself if we adopted a balanced budget amendment. An amendment prohibiting an increase of the outstanding debt of the United States absent a three-fifths vote of both the House and Senate would have salutary effects.[355] In 2022, the annual deficit was $1.4 trillion. Had a balanced budget amendment been in place, Congress would have been required to make substantial cuts in spending or to muster three-fourths of both houses to avoid the amendment's requirements. Gaining the agreement of three-fourths of the members of both houses is a substantial hurdle, and absent a war or similar calamity Congress is unlikely to achieve such unanimity. If Congress is required to make real and extensive budget cuts, this would naturally limit its ability to freely spend federal funds to coerce the states.

Another possibility would be a single-subject amendment. Too often members of Congress use appropriations riders to offer or gain support for a bill. As noted by author John Menton, this practice "can . . . result in billions of dollars of excessive spending" as the riders bring "government money unnecessarily to the home districts of members."[356] The Confederate Constitution addressed spending riders and omnibus legislation with the following: "Every law, or resolution having the force of law, shall relate to but one subject, and that shall be expressed in the title." Such an addition to the U.S. Constitution would be a marked improvement. Congress would be prevented from, say, attaching spending riders to a bill whose chief purpose is to criminalize the counterfeiting of our currency. Limiting bills to a single subject would prevent omnibus legislation and perhaps give members a chance to read and understand the key focus of legislation without worrying about what unrelated matter might be hidden in pages of nongermane material.

SECTION 8, CLAUSE 2
TO BORROW MONEY on the credit of the United States;

Purpose

To meet emergencies brought on by war or other calamities, the government of the union must be able to borrow money. Taxes can be raised at a later time, but in the midst of a crisis the borrowing power is essential.

Background and Development

Under the Articles of Confederation, Congress had the power "to borrow money or emit bills on the credit of the United States."[357] During the American Revolution, Congress issued paper money eleven times and, by the end of hostilities, had printed approximately $214,550,000 in "Continentals." Owing to increases in its supply, the currency did not retain its value—hence the still-used phrase "not worth a Continental."

At the Philadelphia Convention, the provision's language originally followed that of the Articles: "[t]o borrow money, and emit bills on the credit of the United States."[358] Gouverneur Morris of Pennsylvania moved to strike the words "bills on the credit." In 1787, "bills of credit" were paper instruments "intended to circulate as money but . . . not redeemable in gold and silver."[359] Today, they would be described as "fiat money." Morris stated that if the United States were creditworthy then "such bills would be unnecessary; if they had not, unjust and senseless."[360] Oliver Ellsworth of Connecticut agreed with Morris. He proclaimed that "this is a favorable moment to shut the door against paper money."[361] Paper money, Ellsworth observed, "may do harm, never good."[362] George Read of Delaware spoke in even stronger terms. He thought that "the words, if not struck out, would be as alarming as the mark of the beast in Revelation."[363] Edmund Randolph of Virginia and several other delegates agreed that paper money was a scourge, but they did not want to tie the hands of the new government because one "could not foresee all the occasions that might arise."[364] The Convention voted nine states to two to strike the words. In commenting on the vote, Madison penned the following: "Striking out

the words cut off the pretext for a paper currency, and particularly for making the bills a tender either for public or private debts."[365]

Anti-Federalists expressed concern about Congress's power to borrow. Brutus observed that "Congress may mortgage any or all revenues of the union, as a fund to loan money upon, and it is probable in this way, they may borrow of foreign nations, a principal sum, the interest of which will be equal to the annual revenues of the country."[366] Brutus envisioned a substantial national debt, unlikely ever to be retired. Hence, he believed it was "unwise and improvident to vest in the general government, a power to borrow at discretion, without any limitation or restriction."[367] He suggested that the Constitution require a two-thirds congressional majority to permit borrowing.

In discoursing on the power, St. George Tucker in his *View of the Constitution* associated the borrowing of money with war and the repayment of debts incurred because of military conflict. In war, Tucker wrote, "debt is almost unavoidable" and borrowing "[t]he least burdensome mode of contracting debt."[368] Tucker also was aware of the danger posed by this power outside of the common defense: "[W]here loans are voluntarily incurred, upon the principle that public debt is a blessing, or to serve the purposes of aggrandizing a few at the expense of the nation, in general, or of strengthening the hand of government, . . . nothing can be more dangerous to the liberty of the citizen, nor more injurious to remotest posterity, as well as to present generations."[369]

Distortions

It was war that undermined the clear intent of the Framers to forbid fiat money. In

1862, Congress passed a statute authorizing the secretary of the treasury to issue notes "receivable in payment of all taxes, internal duties, excises, debts, and demands of every kind due to the United States."[370] Those "greenbacks" (so named because their backs were printed in green ink) were not redeemable in gold or silver. In the *Legal Tender Cases* (1870), the Supreme Court upheld their constitutionality for pragmatic reasons, noting that "[i]f it be held by this court that Congress has no constitutional power, under any circumstances, or in any emergency, to make treasury notes a legal tender for the payment of all debts (a power confessedly possessed by every independent sovereignty other than the United States), the government is without those means of self-preservation."[371] By 1884, the Supreme Court had abandoned any reliance on the exigencies of war and held that "the power to makes notes of the government a legal tender in payment of private debts" was inherent in the federal government's sovereignty "and not expressly withheld from congress by the constitution."[372]

Discussions and Solutions

Despite the efforts of the Framers, we have a fiat currency tied to nothing of extrinsic value. (The constitutional requirement of hard money is discussed in Section 8, Clause 5.) It is easily manipulated by government and makes inflation as simple as cranking a printing press. The Framers tried to shut the door against paper money, but the waging of an offensive war against the Confederate states ushered in the world of greenbacks. The change was brought about by appeals to vague concepts such as inherent sovereignty and self-preservation rather than the words of the Constitution and the history of its framing and ratification.

The United States should return to a gold standard. The dollar must be repegged to gold at somewhere near prevailing rates. Such a stable currency would fend off inflation and necessitate retrenchment. The general government would have no choice but to stop inflating, balance the budget, and reduce the scope of the current welfare state. Are the American people, taught from an early age to expect cradle-to-grave benefits from the general government, ready for such a change? Probably not. Americans have yet to realize that they have no entitlement to the earnings of others and that the government's borrowing places financial burdens on their children and grandchildren. Only if the American mindset changes to embrace personal responsibility can a return to gold money be possible.[373]

Moreover, in 2022 the general government spent $1.4 trillion more than it took in. By 2033, the Congressional Budget Office estimates that the interest on the debt will be in the neighborhood of $1.4 trillion. This sort of recklessness counsels reconsidering Brutus's proposal that the Constitution be amended to require a two-thirds congressional majority to permit any borrowing. Without some significant reform, the United States will eventually drown in a sea of debt and spend much of its revenues on paying interest without retiring any principal. A simple majority makes it too easy to borrow money. The two-thirds requirement would force Congress to wrestle with difficult financial decisions rather than postponing a fiscal reckoning for a future generation.

Section 8, Clause 3

To regulate Commerce with foreign Nations, and among the several States, and with the Indian Tribes;

Purpose

Congress needed a commerce power to establish the United States as a great free trade zone where goods could travel from Georgia to Massachusetts without being encumbered by multiple internal customs duties. Congress also needed the power to put the full weight of the union behind negotiations with foreign powers to obtain favorable trade arrangements and to counter mercantilist policies enacted by European states.

Background and Development

Foreign Commerce

After the signing of the Treaty of Paris, Great Britain refused to negotiate a commercial treaty with the United States. The mother country's decision, according to St. George Tucker, "was unquestionably dictated at first by a knowledge of the inability of congress to extort terms of reciprocity" and by a "want of unanimity among the states, which, under the existing confederation, was a perpetual bar to any restriction upon her commerce with the whole of the states."[374]

Britain and France, the natural trading partners of the newly free and independent but confederated states, imposed discriminatory restrictions on American trade in short order. As part of the empire, the colonies had enjoyed a lucrative trade with the British West Indies. With the colonies outside of the British fold, Parliament excluded American vessels from the West Indies. Parliament also only allowed American vessels to transport American goods to Britain. Subjects in Canada, for example, could not contract with American shipowners for the transportation of their raw materials to the mother country. Such dictates and restrictions hit Americans hard in their pocketbooks.

At the Philadelphia Convention, the delegates accepted Congress's need for a commerce power. The main focus of debate was whether to trust a congressional majority with the power to pass "navigation acts" (statutes regulating shipping and foreign trade) or whether a two-thirds requirement should be necessary. As exporters of staple crops, the Southern states favored an open trading system with few restrictions. The Northern states, on the other hand, wanted to build up their shipping fleets, which likely would mean higher rates for Southerners transporting their crops to foreign markets. Southerners also realized that if Northern manufacturers were successful in placing tariffs on foreign goods, the actions could result in retaliation and thus a loss of some market shares. Because the Southern states would be a minority in both houses, George Mason of Virginia argued that the Northern states could, by a mere majority vote, wreck the Southern economy with commercial restrictions. He believed that a two-thirds voting requirement was necessary for the defense of Southern economic interests.

Nathaniel Gorham of Massachusetts protested that "[i]f the Government is to be so fettered as to be unable to relieve the Eastern States what motive can they have to join in" the union.[375] The delegates appeared to be at an impasse.

Luther Martin of Maryland, in his *Genuine Information*, reported that the dispute over commercial regulations was decided by a committee. In exchange for allowing the slave trade to continue until 1808, the Southern states agreed to abandon "the restrictive clause relative to navigation acts."[376]

Clearly, all sides agreed that Congress should have the power to regulate commerce for the benefit of deepwater shipping and foreign trade. The mercantilist impulse to obtain a favorable balance of trade was the primary impetus for the commerce power. In the Virginia ratifying convention, Edmund Randolph observed that "England has arisen to the greatest height, in modern times, by her navigation act, and other excellent regulations."[377] By implication, Randolph believed the United States could do the same if Congress had the power to pass an American navigation act. On the Anti-Federalist side, Agrippa approved of giving the union the power "to regulate trade with foreigners."[378] But he preferred that this power be added to the Articles of Confederation instead of granting it in a new charter.

Interstate Commerce

The clause also gives Congress the power to regulate commerce "among the several States." James Madison described the purpose of Congress's power to regulate interstate commerce in *Federalist* No. 42:

A very material object of this power was the relief of the States which import and export through other States, from the improper contributions levied on them by the latter. Were these at liberty to regulate trade between State and State, it must be foreseen that ways would be found out, to load articles of import and export, during the passage through their jurisdiction, with duties which would fall on the makers of the latter, and on the consumers of the former.[379]

Madison observed further that even in loose confederations such as Switzerland, "each Canton is obliged to allow merchandizes, a passage through its jurisdiction into other Cantons, without an augmentation of the tolls."[380] Tensions between states are reduced and the individual states prosper if goods can pass freely without internal trade barriers.

In *Federalist* No. 11, Hamilton also explained that the interstate commerce power would promote a great free trade zone within the union: "An unrestrained intercourse between the States themselves will advance the trade of each, by an interchange of their respective productions, not only for the supply of reciprocal wants at home, but for exportation to foreign markets."[381] With state jealousies quieted and goods flowing freely across America, Hamilton predicted that "[t]he veins of commerce in every part will be replenished, and will acquire additional motion and vigour from a free circulation of the commodities of every part."[382]

Other proponents of the Constitution echoed Madison and Hamilton. For example, State Soldier (possibly Virginia's George Nicholas) predicted that "[c]ommerce, then, freed from the oppressive hand of state jealously and local interest, traversing the whole continent and seeking your commodities, would stamp a higher value on all your property."[383]

As the term "interstate commerce" implies, the Framers had in mind trade between persons of one state and another. As Justice Thomas has noted, "[a]t the time the original Constitution was ratified, 'commerce' consisted of selling, buying, and bartering, as well as transporting for these purposes."[384] Purely internal selling or exchange—intrastate trade—was excluded. The great Virginia legal scholar St. George Tucker observed matter-of-factly that by delegating to Congress the power to regulate commerce "among" the states, the Constitution left "the regulation of internal commerce of each state, to the states, respectively."[385] Federalist Tench Coxe discerned that items were not injected into interstate commerce until they were involved in a sale or exchange with a citizen of another state. Consequently, Coxe believed Congress lacked the authority to pass inspection laws pursuant to the commerce power, even though the growing or production of quality items was "a matter of the utmost importance to commerce of the several states, and the honor of *the whole*."[386] Indeed, Chief Justice Marshall, in *Gibbons v. Ogden* (1824), followed Coxe's reasoning and held that state laws governing the quality of goods destined for the stream of commerce were proper because "[t]hey act upon the subject, before it becomes an article of foreign commerce, or of commerce among the states."[387] Seventy-one years later, the Supreme Court continued to make distinctions between matters internal to a state and the ultimate placing of an article in the flow of commerce. In *United States v. E.C. Knight Co.* (1895), the Supreme Court recognized that "[c]ommerce succeeds to manufacture, and is not part of it."[388] Consequently, it held that Congress could not use the Commerce Clause to prohibit businesses from acquiring substantial manufacturing facilities that the Sherman Anti-Trust Act decreed to be a monopoly in restraint of trade. Unfortunately, the Court abandoned the manufacturing/commerce distinction during the New Deal.

Indian Commerce Clause

The final component of the commerce power focuses on the Indians. The Indians are referred to specifically because of a provision in the Articles whereby Congress was charged with "regulating the trade, and managing all affairs with Indians, not members of any of the states, providing that the legislative right of any state within its own limits be not infringed or violated."[389] Determining the status of Indian tribes living in the United States proved to be confusing. Were the tribes "foreign nations," loose associations of individuals, or domestic dependent nations operating under the guardianship of the national or state governments? To determine whether an Indian residing within the borders of a state was a "member" of a state only complicated the matter. Add to the mix the prohibition against infringing state legislative prerogatives, and the Confederation Congress's power to regulate trade with the Indians under the Articles was useless. Hence, Indians were named specifically in the Commerce Clause of the Constitution.

Distortions

In modern times, the Commerce Clause has become the source of vast power. Under the guise of regulating interstate commerce, Congress has enacted federal criminal statutes, civil rights laws, and health care programs. Prior to 1937, for the most part, the Commerce Clause was exercised to regulate the exchange or trading of goods between people in different states. Franklin Delano Roosevelt's New Deal legislative program changed that interpretation radically. A key part of the New Deal program was the National Labor Relations Act of 1935. Enacted pursuant to the Commerce Clause, the Act promoted collective bargaining and forbade employers from discouraging union activity. In *NLRB v. Jones & Laughlin Steel Corp.* (1937),[390] a steel manufacturer challenged the Act as infringing the states' reserved power to regulate labor relations. The company argued that the manufacturing process preceded and was separate from the interstate selling and shipment of steel; therefore, federal regulation of employment relations could not be a valid exercise of the commerce power.

The Supreme Court rejected the company's reasoning and held that employee unionization, though an intrastate activity, bore such a close relationship to interstate commerce that congressional regulation was proper. "Although activities may be intrastate in character when separately considered," wrote the Court's majority, "if they have such a close and substantial relation to interstate commerce that their control is essential or appropriate to protect that commerce from burdens and obstructions, Congress cannot be denied the power to exercise that control."[391] Because labor unrest contains the possibility of obstructing the flow of steel products across state lines, the Court held the regulated activity to fall within Congress's reach.

The commerce power expanded further when the Court upheld provisions of the Agricultural Adjustment Act of 1938. In an effort to raise wheat prices, that statute allowed the federal government to set quotas on the amount of wheat grown. Farmers could plant a certain amount of acreage for the growing of wheat. If they planted more than their allotment, they faced monetary penalties. Roscoe C. Filburn brought suit to challenge the Act. For the 1941 crop, the government allotted Filburn 11.1 acres of wheat. Filburn instead planted twenty-three acres, and the regulators demanded that he pay a $117.11 fine.

In his lawsuit, Filburn argued that the wheat beyond his allotted 11.1 acres was destined for home consumption. He objected to marketing quotas that embraced not just what he sold to others, but what he used to feed livestock and to provide for his family. Filburn urged the Supreme Court to find that such activity was purely local and thus beyond the reach of the interstate commerce power. In *Wickard v. Filburn* (1942), the Court rejected Filburn's arguments and noted that a local activity may be regulated "if it exerts a substantial economic effect on interstate commerce."[392] While the Court conceded that Filburn's few acres might not seem to have a substantial effect on the national market, the Court stated that the matter must be looked at in the aggregate. "That [Filburn's] own contribution to the demand for wheat may be trivial by itself is not enough to remove him from the scope of federal regulation where, as here, his contribution, taken together with that of many others similarly situated, is far from trivial."[393] Because wheat produced for home consumption by Filburn and other farmers could affect the market, since demand would drop, the government could dictate the quantity of wheat grown by Filburn.

In recent years, the Supreme Court has sought to impose some limits on the commerce power. For example, in *United States v. Lopez* (1995), the Court struck down a federal statute prohibiting possession of firearms near school premises.[394] The government argued that the statute was a regulation of "commerce" because guns could disrupt schools, undermine classroom education, and therefore result in a less productive national workforce. The Court rejected the government's argument, holding that such a broad interpretation of "commerce" would permit Congress to regulate almost every activity in the United States and would infringe on many areas traditionally of state concern.

Similarly, in *National Federation of Independent Businesses v. Sebelius* (2012), the Supreme Court refused to uphold the Obamacare individual mandate to purchase health insurance as a valid exercise of the commerce power.[395] (The Court ultimately upheld the mandate under the taxing power.) In so holding, the Court observed that "[t]he individual mandate, however, does not regulate existing commercial activity. It instead compels individuals to become active in commerce by purchasing a product, on the ground that their failure to do so affects interstate commerce."[396] If Congress could "regulate individuals precisely because they are doing nothing [this] would open a new and potentially vast domain to congressional authority."[397] "[C]ountless decisions an individual could potentially make [would be brought] within the scope of federal regulation, and—under the Government's theory—empower Congress to make those decisions for him."[398] This was a bridge too far for the Court.

Although the Supreme Court, in *Dobbs v. Jackson Women's Health Organization* (2022),[399] held that the Constitution does not protect a "right" to abortion, certain activists are working to codify abortion rights in statutory law. In doing so, they rely on the Commerce Clause and the assertion that abortion procedures are an economic activity subject to congressional regulation. This is a tenable interpretation of post–New Deal Commerce Clause jurisprudence—even though it is alien to the Framers' Commerce Clause.

Discussion and Solutions

The Commerce Clause, along with the spending power, is a primary pillar of the modern state. Moderns have interpreted commerce to mean "economic activity," rather than the traffic in goods. *Wickard v. Filburn* is a prime example of how the original intent of the Commerce Clause has been twisted to promote omnipotence in Congress. If Congress can tell a farmer how much wheat he is allowed to grow for personal consumption, what activity is beyond federal control? While cases such as *Lopez* are welcome, such modest rulings still leave the modern commerce power intact.

The ruling in *Wickard v. Filburn*, the substantial effects test, and the concept of commerce as "economic activity" must be rejected and abandoned as incongruent with the Framers' Constitution. The failure to do so invests Congress with a general police power alien to our charter of government. *The Independent Guide* suggests a constitutional amendment clarifying the scope of the Commerce Clause: "Congress shall make no law pursuant to its commerce power acting upon an object before it becomes an article of interstate or foreign commerce, nor shall Congress have the power to regulate an item or activity solely because it alone, or in the aggregate, could substantially affect commerce or economic activity." The amendment would leave Congress with substantial authority to regulate the traffic in goods among the states and with foreign countries but would curtail efforts to use the commerce power as a general police power.

SECTION 8, CLAUSE 4

TO ESTABLISH AN uniform Rule of Naturalization, and uniform Laws on the subject of Bankruptcies throughout the United States;

Purpose

In a union whose member states entrust their federal government to handle foreign relations, it follows that naturalization rules should be uniform throughout the federation. Similarly, in a union with uninhibited travel among the states, it inures to everyone's benefit to have a uniform statutory scheme for handling a person's or entity's inability to pay debts justly acquired.

Background and Development

With the Revolutionary War at an end, the individual states were free to establish their own naturalization requirements. Under the Articles of Confederation, "the free inhabitants of each of these states, paupers, vagabonds and fugitives from Justice excepted, shall be entitled to all privileges and immunities of free citizens in the several states."[400] Scholars have noted that that provision of the Articles "effectively permitted an alien to seek naturalization in a state with permissive naturalization practices and then move to a state with tighter restrictions, and still be entitled to all the incumbent rights of naturalized citizens in the second state."[401]

In *Federalist* No. 42, James Madison observed that "[t]he dissimilarity in the rules of naturalization, has long been remarked as a fault in our system."[402] For this reason, there was little debate or controversy in Philadelphia about vesting the federal government with the power to establish uniform rules of naturalization.

In the early republic, some dispute arose concerning whether the federal government's power over naturalization preempted the states from legislating in the same field. In 1817, the Supreme Court, in *Chirac v. Chirac's Lessee*, noted that "the power of naturalization is exclusively in congress" and definitively settled the matter.[403] Moreover, as early as 1802, Congress made clear that following enactment of the first naturalization law in 1790, naturalizations under state statutes were valid only if citizenship had already been granted.

Congress's bankruptcy power is located in the same clause as its naturalization power, apparently because the delegates sought "uniformity" for both. In the Philadelphia Convention, the only discussion of the bankruptcy power took place when Roger Sherman of Connecticut expressed concern because some bankrupts were sentenced to death in the mother country. Gouverneur Morris of Pennsylvania brushed that apprehension aside and averred that he saw no danger of Congress abusing its delegated power.

In *Federalist* No. 42, Madison commented briefly on the bankruptcy power: "The power of establishing uniform laws of bankruptcy, is so intimately connected with the regulation of commerce, and will prevent so many frauds where the parties or their property may lie or be removed into different States, that the expediency of it seems not likely to be drawn into question."[404]

According to scholars, "[a]t the time of our founding, it was common to use the term 'bankruptcy' with respect to proceedings for the liquidation of a trader and to refer to 'insolvency' laws when discussing how individuals could obtain a discharge from debtor's prison."[405] No federal bankruptcy law applied to persons other than merchants until 1841. The historical record thus supports Madison's connection of bankruptcy power "with the regulation of commerce." However, the Supreme Court has held that the congressional bankruptcy power is not limited to merchants and that individuals other than traders may be covered by federal statutes.[406] More generally, it has been determined that "[f]ederal bankruptcy law suspends state bankruptcy and insolvency laws so far as they are in conflict with it. An act which is not in conflict with but assists the National Act is not suspended."[407]

Distortions

The naturalization power is often cited as one of the enumerated powers, giving Congress plenary power over immigration.[408] But because the Constitution does not specifically mention immigration, it is often claimed that the federal government alone controls immigration because such a power is an incident of sovereignty. Estimates vary, but there are at least 11 million illegal aliens currently residing in the United States. The federal government has proved itself unable or unwilling to curb the flow of people entering the country from the southern border. Unless it deals with what amounts to an invasion, states may realize that naturalization and immigration are two separate matters. The former is delegated to the federal government, whereas the latter is not.

While such an assertion of state power might seem odd to modern ears, both James Madison and Thomas Jefferson in the late 1790s argued that certain congressional statutes touching on immigration were unconstitutional infringements on state power. For example, the Alien Friends Act of 1798 empowered the president to expel all aliens that he deemed dangerous to the peace and safety of the United States.[409] An alien who was expelled and later returned to the United States could be imprisoned by the president for so long as he deemed the public safety to require the alien's incarceration.

In his Kentucky Resolution of 1798, Jefferson declared the Alien Friends Act void on the grounds "that alien friends are under the jurisdiction and protection of the laws of the State wherein they are; and that no power over them has been delegated to the United States."[410] James Madison concurred with Jefferson's arguments about the statute. He believed alien friends to be under state law and subject to punishment only in the state where they resided. Alien enemies—subjects or citizens of countries with which the United States was at war—were a different matter. Madison believed that Congress's war powers granted it jurisdiction over alien enemies.

Discussion and Solutions

Perhaps Americans should revisit the constitutional theory of these two giants as we contemplate our current immigration fiasco. We have assumed Congress has the constitutional authority to regulate immigration, and that assumption is working to our detriment. Recent polling shows that the American people are concerned about the level of legal and illegal immigration.[411] An open borders policy, such as existed during the Biden administration, generates a massive demographic and cultural shift. In the age of terrorism, it is also a convenient way for our enemies to easily cross into the United States and plan attacks. Moreover, the economic prospects of the American working class are dimmed in the flood of cheap (and illegal) labor. If the federal government will not undertake reasonable measures in the realm of immigration, perhaps the states should. Jefferson and Madison would endorse such an approach.

Texas Governor Greg Abbott, for example, has challenged the conventional wisdom on national supremacy in immigration law. He launched Operation Lone Star, an initiative to secure the state's southern border, stop the smuggling of drugs and contraband, and interdict transnational criminal activity. Texas officials have erected multiple barriers to keep illegal immigrants and others out. Multiple governors have offered National Guard units to assist Texas with these measures of self-defense. A significant confrontation with national authorities seemed likely, but the election of Donald Trump in 2024 eased tensions between the states and the general government. Conflict could reemerge if the federal judiciary rejects Trump's executive actions or if a Democrat is elected president in 2028. Perhaps a confrontation is inevitable and will help revive the distinction between immigration and naturalization. At the very least, the confrontation might persuade the federal government to enforce the immigration statutes in the U.S. Code, which is all Texas and the other states really desire.

SECTION 8, CLAUSE 5

To COIN MONEY, regulate the Value thereof, and of foreign Coin, and fix the Standard of Weights and Measures;

Purpose

The provision permits Congress to provide for facilities to mint coins that circulate as money. Similarly, the setting of uniform weights and measures is granted as a commercial aid. Standard weights and measures make it easier for merchants to buy and sell goods in interstate and foreign commerce.

Background and Development

Under the Articles, Congress had "the sole and exclusive right and power of regulating the alloy and value of coin struck by their own authority, or by that of the respective states—fixing the standard of weights and measures throughout the united states."[412] The Confederation did not have the power to regulate the value of foreign coin. That omission, in the words of Joseph Story, threatened to "destroy any uniformity in the value of current coin,[413] since the respective states might, by different regulations, create a different value in each."[414]

As mentioned in the discussion of Section 8, Clause 2, the Framers sought to ban fiat money. As economist Richard H. Timberlake has explained, the power to coin money "meant that Congress should provide the practical facility for minting coins."[415] Indeed, Justice Stephen J. Field reached the same conclusion when dissenting in *Juilliard v. Greenman* (1884): "It is to mould metallic substances into forms convenient for circulation and to stamp them with the impress of government authority."[416] The power to regulate the value of money, according to Timberlake's study, "meant that Congress would specify a weight of fine gold or fine silver as a precise quantity of dollars."[417] Justice Field likewise noted that the Framers intended American coinage "to be composed principally, if not entirely, of the metals of gold and silver."[418] The end result, in the words of Justice Field, is that Congress has "the power to make coins of precious metals a legal tender, for that alone which is money can be a legal tender."[419]

Regarding the power to fix weights and measures, scholars associate it with the regulation of commerce. A uniform set of weights and measures, for example, makes it easier for a merchant to buy and sell goods in interstate and foreign commerce. The power to set weights and measures largely has been ignored by Congress. In 1866, Congress permitted use of the metric system but has never mandated its general use. The prevalent English ("imperial") system of weights and measures never has been approved by statute; congressional

acquiescence and custom allow it to survive throughout the United States.

Distortions

Although Justice Field's analysis was true to the text and intention of the Framers, it was a dissenting opinion. A majority of the Supreme Court viewed the federal government as a unitary state created as a mirror image of the European governments. Because the European states possessed the power to create fiat money as an incident of sovereignty, the *Juilliard* majority concluded that "congress has the power to issue the obligations of the United States in such form, and to impress upon them such qualities as currency for the purchase of merchandise and the payment of debts, as accord with the usage of sovereign governments."[420]

Discussion and Solutions

In the words of libertarian scholar Bettina Bien Graves, "[t]here is no reason, technically or economically, why the world today, even with its countless wide-ranging and complex commercial transactions, could not return to the gold standard and operate with gold money. The major obstacle is ideological."[421] Honest money would necessitate the federal government abandoning inflation as monetary policy, limiting spending to revenues, and curtailing, if not forsaking, the nanny state. With many Americans dependent on government for health care (Medicare), old-age pensions (Social Security), and food (the Supplemental Nutrition Assistance Program, or SNAP, formerly known as the Food Stamp Program), such a curtailment of government spending would not be popular. But benefits would be enormous: prevention of inflation from consuming workers' wages, encouragement to save and provide for oneself, stable prices, and avoidance of boom-and-bust cycles. Honest money could be the rule once again if we simply adhered to the Constitution.

Representative Alex X. Mooney (R-WV) is an advocate of the gold standard and has introduced the Gold Standard Restoration Act in Congress.[422] The Act requires the U.S. Treasury and the Federal Reserve to publicly disclose all gold holdings and to peg the Federal Reserve note (U.S. dollar) to a fixed weight of gold at its market price. Dollar bills would be redeemable for and exchangeable with gold. The relevant portions of the Act are as follows:

> Not later than the date that is 24 months after the date of the enactment of this Act—
> (1) the Secretary of the Treasury (in this Act hereafter referred to as the "Secretary") shall define the Federal reserve note dollar in terms of a fixed weight of gold, based on that day's closing market price of gold;
> (2) Federal reserve banks shall make Federal reserve notes redeemable for and exchangeable with gold at the fixed price determined under paragraph (1) and create processes that facilitate such redemptions and exchanges between member banks and the public; and
> (3) if a Federal reserve bank does not fulfill its duties under paragraph (2), the Secretary shall make the redemption or exchange as guarantor and place a corresponding first and paramount lien on all assets of such bank.[423]

The introductory portion of the legislation observes that the dollar "has lost more than 40 percent of its purchasing power since 2000, and 97 percent of its purchasing power since the passage of the Federal Reserve Act in 1913."[424] Obviously, continuation of this trend will rob Americans of their savings and prosperity. The Gold Standard Restoration Act is legislation worth supporting.

SECTION 8, CLAUSE 6

TO PROVIDE FOR the Punishment of counterfeiting the Securities and current Coin of the United States;

Purpose

Because the Framers rejected counterfeiting as coming within the definition of treason as in the British system, they chose to add a separate provision indicating that counterfeiting was nonetheless a crime punishable by Congress.

Background and Development

Under British law, counterfeiting was a form of treason and was punished frequently by parliamentary bills of attainder (special acts of the legislature inflicting capital punishment on a person). The Framers rejected British practice and in Article III defined treason specifically to exclude counterfeiting. In

Article I, Section 9, the Framers also forbade bills of attainder. Although the power to punish counterfeiting arguably is a necessary and proper incident to the Coinage Clause, the Convention likely adopted Clause 6 out of an abundance of caution to show that counterfeiting was unlawful even though it no longer was treasonous.

Evidence from the Philadelphia Convention on counterfeiting is sparse. Gouverneur Morris of Pennsylvania suggested that the Constitution "provide for the punishment of counterfeiting in general."[425] In support of that power, Morris pointed out that "[b]ills of exchange for example might be forged in one State and carried into another."[426] Another delegate suggested that it "might be politic to provide by national authority for the punishment" of counterfeit foreign securities.[427] When Oliver Ellsworth of Connecticut moved to add the Counterfeiting Clause to the Constitution, his motion received unanimous approval with no debate.

The Supreme Court has interpreted the Counterfeiting Clause to vest the federal government with the exclusive power to punish the creation of counterfeit currency.[428] However, the Court recognized that the states have concurrent jurisdiction to punish the passing of counterfeited money.[429] The passing of bogus coins or currency, the Court reasoned, is a fraud against the people of the states and thus falls under the states' police power.

Legal scholars such as Lewis D. Solomon have pointed out that "[t]he anti-counterfeiting provision reinforces the Framers' intent to limit 'Money' to coin. By distinguishing between 'the Securities and current Coin of the United States,' the Constitution authorizes the United States Congress to punish counterfeiting 'Money' of the United States, composed of 'regulate[d]' domestic and foreign 'Coin,' and 'Securities' which are promises to pay 'borrow[ed] Money.'"[430]

Distortions

The Counterfeiting Clause has not been a great source of congressional power. It is one of the few legitimate sources of criminal statutory law used by Congress. Broad construction of other constitutional provisions, however, has rendered the Counterfeiting Clause superfluous. Modern interpretations allow Congress to create fiat money and assert that protection of the paper money is an inherent power. Hence, if for any reason the people chose to repeal the Counterfeiting Clause, congressional anti-counterfeiting statutes would live on as if nothing had happened.

Discussion and Solutions

Today, the federal government retains the exclusive power to punish the creation of counterfeit instruments and shares with the states the authority to punish the uttering of counterfeit instruments. But for the Framers' desire to separate counterfeiting from treason, this provision likely would not be in the Constitution. It is, and remains, a proper matter of federal authority.

SECTION 8, CLAUSE 7
TO ESTABLISH POST Offices and post Roads;

Purpose

The postal power exists to promote communication between the citizens of the union, to aid commerce, and to enable the exchange of ideas.

Background and Development

Under the Articles, Congress was charged with "establishing and regulating post-offices from one state to another, throughout all the united states, and exacting such postage on the papers passing through the same, as may be requisite to defray the expenses of the said office."[431] The Articles specified that this power was "exclusive." The language in the Constitution of 1787 is far less verbose and simply grants Congress the power to establish post offices and post roads. By its terms, it is not an exclusive power.

At the Philadelphia Convention, Benjamin Franklin of Pennsylvania wanted to include the power to create canals. James Wilson supported Franklin's motion, but Oliver Ellsworth of Connecticut objected that the expense would fall on all the states while the benefits would "accrue to the places where the canals may be cut."[432] James Madison attempted to go further than Franklin by suggesting a power to grant corporate charters. Madison averred that his "primary object was to secure an easy communication between the States."[433] Ultimately, the attempt to enlarge the postal power failed, with eight states opposing a modification.

St. George Tucker described a national postal system as "one of the most beneficial establishments which can be introduced by any government" because it "provid[es] the means of intercourse between the citizens of remote parts of the confederation," contributes to commerce, and encourages the flow of ideas.[434]

The extent of Congress's power under the clause is disputed. Constitutional law scholar Robert Natelson has argued that the founding generation, based on their experience with the British postal system, would have understood the power as "comprehend[ing] all actions necessary to make the system work."[435] Natelson believes that the power includes the "purchasing, maintaining, and operating packet boats; laying out, constructing, and maintaining posts, toll gates, and post roads; hiring and directing postal employees and contractors."[436]

Thomas Jefferson, however, questioned such a broad reading of the postal power. After hearing of James Madison's 1796 proposal to survey the national post road running from Maine to Georgia and to prepare for extensive work on the road, Jefferson urged Madison to reconsider. Jefferson questioned whether the power to establish post roads allowed the federal government to construct the roads or merely to designate preexisting roads as post roads. "If the term be equivocal," Jefferson wrote, "(and I really do not think it so) which is the safer construction?"[437] Jefferson feared such an interpretation as allowing "the majority of Congress to go to cutting down mountains and bridging of rivers."[438] If Madison thought his interpretation was too restrictive, Jefferson suggested that the matter be referred to the states for consideration of an amendment.

As president, James Monroe articulated a Jeffersonian understanding of the postal power. "President Monroe believed that Congress merely was given the power to select pre-existing roads and that the States, under their police power, could decide whether or not they would permit Congress to appropriate state land in order to construct postal roads."[439] As late as 1845, at least one member of the Supreme Court disputed Congress's claimed power to construct new roads rather than designating existing roads to facilitate the moving of the mails.[440]

In the main, the Supreme Court has interpreted the postal power broadly. For example, in *Ex Parte Jackson* (1877), the Court asserted: "The framers of the Constitution meant to create an establishment as an entirety; not merely to designate the places at which mails should be taken up and delivered, and the routes by which they should be transported from point to point. Full, sovereign control over the whole subject was given, to be exercised by any appropriate means."[441]

Distortions

In line with the exclusive power granted, the Confederation Congress established a postal monopoly via statute. Only the government's postal service could carry "letters, packets, or other despatches" for hire.[442] The Congress created by the Constitution of 1787 continued with the Confederation's postal laws and did not enact a new law until 1792.

Despite no specific mention of a monopoly power, Congress granted the exclusive right to the postal service of carrying "any letter or letters, packet or packets, other than newspapers, for hire or reward."[443] Members of Congress worked hard to increase postal routes for constituents in an effort to curry favor and win reelection. According to Yale Law School's George L. Priest, "[o]btaining a new postal route for one's district became an expected perquisite, a simple means for any Congressman to endear himself to his constituents."[444]

The Supreme Court likewise has upheld Congress's granting of a monopoly for the carrying of "first class" letters to the United States Postal Service (formerly the U.S. Post Office).[445] Individualist Lysander Spooner and others have argued that Congress cannot create a postal monopoly. They point to the rejection of the "sole and exclusive" language in the Articles as an indication that the Framers did not intend to give Congress monopoly power over mails. Spooner contended that the power to establish post roads was separate and distinct from any power to prohibit competition. "The simple grant of an authority," argued Spooner, "whether to an individual or a government, to do a particular act, gives the grantee no authority to forbid others to do acts of the same kind."[446]

Discussion and Solutions

To the extent a postal monopoly was once necessary and proper to establishment of the postal service, it is no longer the case. Email and other virtual services have made snail mail unnecessary. The postal service is losing billions of dollars as Americans turn to the internet and postal unions fight automation technologies. Chris Edwards of the Cato Institute notes that in the name of universal service, "Congress imposes a rigid monopoly on the nation so that we can continue to receive mainly 'junk mail' in our mailboxes six days a week."[447] Put simply, a universal service requirement for paper mail does not square with the modern economy. Congress should have listened to Spooner long ago.

SECTION 8, CLAUSE 8

TO PROMOTE THE Progress of Science and useful Arts, by securing for limited Times to Authors and Inventors the exclusive Right to their respective Writings and Discoveries;

Purpose

Protection of intellectual property rights is intended to encourage innovation and the revelation of the particulars of new inventions. The innovator receives the right to exclude others from marketing, manufacturing, or using the innovator's creation.

Background and Development

Grants of exclusive rights to inventors can be traced back to the late 1400s and the city-state of Venice.[448] In Venice and other medieval cities, guilds developed a respect for what we today call intellectual property. The knowledge of how to do something, the guilds believed, was just as valuable as the finished product, if not more so.

In Anglo-American history, letters patent were associated with the monarch's prerogative powers and often had little to do with innovation. Elizabeth I was notorious for using her authority to grant monopolies by issuing letters of patent (exclusive rights) for such mundane matters as the sale of foodstuffs and playing cards. These patents had nothing to do with creating novel concepts or tools and instead were mechanisms to confer economic privileges on the monarch's favorites.

The abuse of letters of patent led Parliament to pass the Statute of Monopolies of 1623. The statute forbade monopolies, but it provided an important exception. Under the statute, the "true and first inventor" of a new manufacture was granted the sole right to make and commercialize the invention for up to fourteen years.[449] Parliament decided on fourteen years because at least two apprentices could be trained in the new industry during that time. (Customarily, an apprentice served a seven-year term.) Hence, the statute became the first codified patent law in Anglo-American history.

The United States' first constitution, the Articles of Confederation, contained no national protection for intellectual property. Instead, such matters were left to the thirteen states. That changed with the Constitution of 1787. Little debate arose in Philadelphia on the granting of exclusive rights to authors and inventors. In his expository writings on the Constitution, Joseph Story observed that for authors and inventors to have any property interest in their works, "it is manifest that the power of protection must be given to, and administered by, the General Government."[450] Otherwise, a "patent, granted by a single State, might be violated with impunity."[451] Story lamented that authors and inventors often had died in poverty and neglect even though the world "derived immense wealth from their labors."[452] A patent for a limited time was a "poor reward" for the spirit of innovation, but Story concluded that this solution best balanced the interests of the intellectual property holder and society.

Thomas Jefferson, on the other hand, questioned the very idea that inventions could be the property of one person. "Inventions then cannot, in nature, be a subject of property," Jefferson wrote.[453] "Society may give an exclusive right to the profits arising from them, as an encouragement to men to pursue ideas which may produce utility, but this may or may not be done, according to the will and convenience of the society, without claim or complaint from anybody."[454] By law of nature, Jefferson believed, the moment an idea is divulged, "it forces itself into the possession of every one."[455] Ideas were meant to spread rapidly across the globe, Jefferson averred, and exist for the betterment of all mankind. Jefferson saw intellectual property as a prime example of a "pure public good."

The U.S. Patent Act of 1790, the first American statute on the topic, provided that a person who had "invented or discovered any useful art, manufacture, engine, machine, or device, or any improvement therein not before known" could apply for a patent.[456] A critical requirement set forth in the statute was that the application specify or describe the invention in such a way as to enable people of ordinary skill in the art pertinent to the patent to make and use the invention. The disclosure had to contain a written description of the invention showing that the inventor was in possession of the invention at the time the application was filed. The application had to offer the "best mode" of practicing the invention contemplated by the inventor. If granted a patent, the inventor would enjoy for fourteen years "the sole and exclusive right and liberty of making, constructing, using, and vending to others to be used, the said invention or discovery."[457]

We currently are governed by the Patent Act of 1952. The law provides that "whoever invents or discovers any new and useful process, machine, manufacture, or composition of matter, or any new and useful improvement thereof, may obtain a patent."[458] Like its predecessors, the law recognizes that patent rights are not awarded automatically. The inventor must apply to the U.S. Patent and Trademark Office (USPTO). Inventors must disclose their ideas thoroughly and claim rights to their inventions. If the patent examiners approve an application, a patent is issued and is good for twenty years.

Distortions

Despite an exponential increase in technology, Congress has clung to the one-size-fits-all patent policy—a policy that made sense in the early republic but has little relation to modern circumstances. Patent holders typically enjoy an exclusive right that runs for twenty years from the date on which the patent is issued, but this system ignores that technological progress proceeds at different paces in different industries. Whereas a longer patent term might be proper for a manufacturing process, technologies such as software have much shorter lifespans because of the rapid changes in computer technology.

Discussion and Solutions

A five-year term for software would be more appropriate and would prevent non-practicing entities (patent trolls) from using grossly outdated patents to target new inventions. Trolls obtain patents not for the purpose of producing an invention or a technology, but for the sake of lucrative lawsuits. They garner all the benefits of patent protection but offer society no benefit. They are parasites. Hence, Congress should consider reforms that account for the pace of certain technologies.

Furthermore, patent law could borrow from trademark law and require that a plaintiff prove the intention of "use." A person or entity may file a trademark application based on the intent to use the mark in commerce.

This means that the applicant must have a bona fide, demonstrable intention to actually use the mark—that is, to sell products to the public with the mark attached. The right to a trademark can be lost if the holder abandons or stops using the mark. Likewise, patent holders who never show any intention of using the technologies covered would lose their right to sue. Trolls would undoubtedly try to devise nominal uses of the technology to meet the use requirement, but the courts could evaluate the alleged use and determine whether it represents a good faith attempt to practice the invention or is merely a minimal effort meant to secure an open courthouse door.

SECTION 8, CLAUSE 9
TO CONSTITUTE TRIBUNALS inferior to the supreme Court;

Purpose

The Constitution does not mandate the creation of lower federal courts. Instead, it gives Congress the discretion to use the state courts as the trial courts for the union or to create a system of federal courts. The first Congress chose the latter option.

Background and Development

The Articles of Confederation contained a modest judicial power. Under Article IX, Congress had the power to appoint judges to try "piracies and felonies committed on the high seas" and to hear "appeals in all cases of captures."[459] When petitioned by a state in a boundary dispute, Congress could appoint judges to hear the case if the states could not agree on arbitrators. Congress itself was "the last resort on appeal" for boundary issues.[460] The Articles provided for a similar mechanism for the settling of competing private claims based on conflicting state land grants. But that was the extent of the Confederation's judicial branch.

At the Philadelphia Convention, the Virginia Plan called for the creation of "one or more supreme tribunals, and of inferior tribunals to be chosen by the National Legislature."[461] The delegates eventually decided on one supreme tribunal, but differed on whether inferior tribunals were necessary.

John Rutledge of South Carolina urged that "the State Tribunals might and ought to be left in all cases to decide in the first instance [with] the right of appeal to the supreme national tribunal being sufficient to secure the national rights & uniformity of Judgmts."[462] Rutledge feared "encroachment on the jurisdiction of the States" and believed that the people would be less likely to adopt a constitution providing for multiple courts.[463] Roger Sherman of Connecticut agreed with Rutledge and spoke about the unnecessary expense of inferior federal courts "when the existing State Courts would answer the same purpose."[464] Edmund Randolph of Virginia countered that state courts could "not be trusted with the administration of the National laws."[465] Madison likewise protested that the new government needed inferior federal courts "dispersed throughout the Republic" and empowered to decide "*many* cases."[466] Ultimately Madison and James Wilson of Pennsylvania proposed a compromise that would not mandate the creation of lower federal courts, but leave the matter to the judgment of Congress.

Anti-Federalists were concerned about this compromise. Luther Martin of Maryland in his *Genuine Information* predicted that a system of inferior federal courts "would eventually absorb and swallow up the State judiciaries, by drawing all business from them to the courts of the general government."[467] Virginia's George Mason objected that "inferior federal courts are to be as numerous as Congress may think proper" with the end result being the degrading of state courts.[468] Samuel Spencer, in the North Carolina ratifying convention, averred that "[t]here does not appear to me any kind of necessity that the federal court should have jurisdiction in the body of the country."[469] He believed that "in the body of a state, the jurisdiction of the courts in that state might extend to the carrying into execution the laws of Congress."[470]

The first Congress ultimately chose to create a system of inferior federal courts in the Judiciary Act of 1789. Under the law, Congress established a Supreme Court with six justices, three circuit courts, and thirteen district courts. Jurisdiction over civil cases arising under the Constitution, laws, or treaties was left to the state courts. "By contrast," as noted by constitutional law scholar Donald H. Ziegler, "Congress gave the lower federal courts virtually all of the original criminal arising under jurisdiction possible under Article III."[471] Although most Americans cannot imagine a federal judicial system without myriad federal appellate courts and trial courts, the Constitution does not mandate the existence of any federal court other than the Supreme Court. The Constitution gave Congress wide discretion about establishing inferior federal courts and how many to establish. The first Congress chose to create a system of inferior federal courts, and such a decision was undoubtedly within its powers.

SECTION 8, CLAUSE 10

To DEFINE AND punish Piracies and Felonies committed on the high Seas, and Offences against the Law of Nations;

Purpose

Piracy, crimes on the high seas, and offenses against the law of nations all implicate foreign commerce, relations between sovereign nations, or both. Therefore, the Constitution properly grants Congress—the exclusive agent of the states in foreign affairs—the power to pass criminal statutes in these areas.

Background and Development

Under the Articles of Confederation, Congress had the power of "appointing courts for the trial of piracies and felonies committed on the high seas."[472] But it lacked the power to define and punish offenses against the law of nations (that is, obligations established by treaty and customary international law).[473] In 1781, a congressional committee recommended that the states "enact punishments against violators of the law of nations," but only a few states took action.[474]

At the Philadelphia Convention, the draft constitution initially included a version of the clause within a federal criminal jurisdiction power that encompassed counterfeiting, piracy and felonies committed on the high seas, and offenses against the laws of nations.[475] That consolidation was undone, and the ultimate version "merely authorizes Congress to enact federal criminal statutes defining and prescribing punishment for Piracy and Offences against the law of nations, and divests the States of criminal jurisdiction over these matters."[476]

In *Federalist* No. 42, James Madison described the clause as properly belonging to the general government, thus much improving the Articles of Confederation. Madison believed that the Articles raised a danger that "any indiscreet member [could] embroil the confederacy with foreign nations."[477]

St. George Tucker, in his *View of the Constitution*, averred that "[t]he true ground of granting these powers to congress seems to be, the immediate and near connection and relation which they have to the regulation of commerce with foreign nations."[478] Such commerce, Tucker noted, was conducted almost exclusively on the high seas. Tucker also believed that when Congress had to decide on questions of war and peace, the law of nations often would be the primary guide, buttressing the relevant powers' assignment to the general government.

The Supreme Court has interpreted this clause broadly. In *United States v. Arjona* (1887), the Court held that the Offenses Clause allowed Congress to punish conduct that could give rise to state responsibility, observing that "if the thing made punishable is one which the United States are required by their international obligations to use due diligence to prevent, it is an offense against the law of nations."[479] In other words, Congress may address conduct that international law authorizes, but does not mandate, a nation to punish.

In *Ex parte Quirin* (1942), which dealt with proceedings against Nazi saboteurs, the Supreme Court recognized that Congress may establish military commissions "to try persons for offenses which, according to the rules and precepts of the law of nations, and more particularly the law of war, are cognizable by" the commissions.[480] In *Hamdan v. Rumsfeld* (2006), the Supreme Court struck down the military tribunals established by former President George W. Bush to try Guantánamo Bay detainees because they had not been authorized by Congress.[481]

Distortions

The primary danger of this clause is that Congress might choose to define broad matters as crimes without support of the developed law of nations. Congress, the president, and the courts should make a searching inquiry of obligations established by treaty and customary international law before claiming to legislate under Section 8, Clause 10.[482] Otherwise, there is a danger that Section 8, Clause 10 could be abused to support legislation outside the scope of the delegated powers. Indeed, a few activist legal scholars have urged Congress to look for an international consensus on, for example, the inhumanity of the death penalty, and then use the Offenses Clause to ban the death penalty in all American states.[483] Rutgers's Beth Stephens argues that the Offenses Clause "provides heretofore unrecognized support for a broad interpretation" to permit the federal government "to regulate areas traditionally governed by the states."[484]

Discussion and Solutions

Stephens occupies a minority position in her claims about the Offenses Clause. *The Independent Guide* recommends that judges, legislators, and citizens should continue to resist the arguments of Stephens and her fellow travelers. Whereas Stephens suggests abandoning principles of federalism in exchange for an Offenses Clause that frees Congress from its enumerated powers, *The Independent Guide* argues that Congress has already strayed too far from what the Framers intended. Taking the tack proposed by Stephens would enable Congress to regulate any conduct that is recognized by a handful of countries as being an offense against the law of nations. This, however, is decidedly not the law of nations as understood by the Framers, who aimed to limit Congress to enumerating the elements of offenses that have been clearly established in international law.

SECTION 8, CLAUSE 11

To DECLARE WAR, grant Letters of Marque and Reprisal, and make Rules concerning Captures on Land and Water;

Purpose

The Framers, based on the British experience, believed that the executive was likely to lead the country into unnecessary wars that were outside of the national interest. Rather than allow the executive to determine war and peace, the Framers lodged this power in Congress.

Background and Development

The American experience with the war power is unique. As Louis Fisher has noted, in the 1780s, "existing models of government in Europe placed the war power securely in the hands of the monarch."[485] The Confederation and Constitution of 1787 marked a significant departure from this norm.

Under the Articles, Congress had "the sole and exclusive right and power of determining on peace and war," except when an individual state had been invaded or faced imminent danger.[486] The Philadelphia Convention initially considered granting the new Congress the power to "make war."[487] James Madison of Virginia and Elbridge Gerry of Massachusetts moved to replace "make" with "declare."[488] They suggested that such a change would allow "the Executive the power to repel sudden attacks" but not commence hostilities.[489] Pierce Butler of South Carolina favored giving the executive the control over war and peace; his suggestion brought a harsh rebuke from Gerry, who "never expected to hear in a republic a motion to empower the Executive alone to declare war."[490] George Mason of Virginia agreed with Gerry and "was for clogging rather than facilitating war."[491] The Convention ultimately agreed with Madison and Gerry's motion, with seven states voting in the affirmative.

In Pennsylvania's ratifying convention, James Wilson assured his colleagues that the Constitution would not "hurry us into war" because "the important power of declaring war is vested in the legislature at large" and not the president.[492] Whereas the ambitions of kings are prone to carry countries into conflict, Wilson believed that "nothing but our national interest can draw us into a war" with the power lodged in Congress.[493] The concern about the executive branch's war powers was expressed succinctly in a letter from Madison to Jefferson a decade after ratification. "The constitution supposes, what the History of all Govts demonstrates," explained Madison, "that the Ex. is the branch of power most interested in war, and prone to it."[494] For that reason, the Philadelphia Convention "vested the question of war in the Legisl."[495]

Madison elaborated on that decision when expressing concern about President Washington's issuance of the Neutrality Proclamation in 1793. France and Great Britain were at war, and the 1778 Treaty of Alliance with France bound the United States to defend the French West Indies and prohibited aid to the enemies of France. Neutrality was the prudent course for the young nation, but many commentators at the time worried that Washington's action usurped Congress's power to declare war. Executive action, as a practical matter, could negate or weaken Congress's options in dealing with hostilities.

Writing as Helvidius, Madison addressed the Philadelphia Convention's delegation of the war power to Congress. "In no part of the constitution is more wisdom to be found," Madison declared, "than in the clause which confides the question of war or peace to the legislature, and not to the executive department."[496] Placing the war powers in the hands of a unitary chief executive, Madison observed, "would be too great for any one man; not such as nature may offer as the prodigy of many centuries, but such as may be expected in the ordinary successions of magistracy."[497] Madison described war as "the true nurse of executive aggrandizement" because the president directs the armed forces and thus has the opportunity to promote and benefit his associates.[498] Moreover, "[i]t is in war, finally, that laurels are to be gathered; and it is the executive brow they are to encircle. The strongest passions and most dangerous weaknesses of the human breast; ambition, avarice, vanity, the honourable or venial love of fame, are all in conspiracy against the desire and duty of peace."[499] Madison foresaw that presidents who are described as "great" often are wartime presidents, and the natural drive for greatness thus will cause executives to commit the nation to conflict.

In conjunction with the power to declare war, Congress also has the power to "grant Letters of Marque and Reprisal." "Letters of marque and reprisal are commissions from a recognized government to private parties to use their vessels to plunder and destroy the ships of an enemy; the vessels are 'privateers.'"[500] Privateering played a critical role in the American Revolution. Approximately seven hundred ships were commissioned as privateers, and they neutralized almost as many British vessels. Although privateers were authorized to sell captured vessels through court proceedings, they had to do so lawfully. If they could not prove the enemy status of a vessel or if they used unreasonable methods, they could be liable for damages. Congress last issued letters of marque and reprisal during the War of 1812.

The power to "make Rules concerning Captures on Land and Water" allows Congress to establish procedures governing privateers' captures of vessels and their cargoes, which typically are enforced in prize courts. If a capture is determined to have been lawful, privateers are granted good title to seized property.

Distortions

Although the executive branch certainly exercised broad authority in foreign affairs throughout American history, the year 1950 was the first time that a president formally adopted the position that he could send troops abroad to fight without congressional authorization. President Harry S. Truman relied on a resolution of the United Nations Security Council when he sent troops to aid South Korea after it was invaded by its neighbor to the north. Secretary of State Dean Acheson pointedly advised Truman against going to Congress and seeking its approval to enter the fight on the Korean peninsula. The move enlarged presidential power at the expense of Congress, and the effects are still felt today.

Congress has not declared war since World War II, but the United States has been involved in various military actions, including in Korea, Vietnam, Kuwait, Iraq, Afghanistan, and the former Yugoslavia. In some situations, the executive has consulted with Congress and received Authorization for Use of Military Force (AUMF). The first AUMF was issued in 1955 when President Dwight D. Eisenhower requested authority to protect Formosa (now known as Taiwan) from the People's Republic of China. The AUMF permitted Eisenhower to "employ the Armed Forces of the United States as he deems necessary for the specific purpose of securing and protecting Formosa and the Pescadores against armed attack."

While it certainly is laudable that Eisenhower consulted Congress and sought some blessing for deploying U.S military forces in and around Formosa, the AUMF of 1955 established a broad and unconstitutional precedent whereby Congress abdicated its constitutional authority and gave the president carte blanche over the use of force. Congress passed the most recent AUMF in 2001 after the 9/11 suicide attacks. Congress authorized the president "to use all necessary and appropriate force against those nations, organizations, or persons *he determines* planned, authorized, committed, or aided the terrorist attacks that occurred on September 11, 2001 or harbored [terrorists], in order to prevent any future acts of international terrorism."⁵⁰¹

Prolonged wars and efforts at nation-building are the natural result of congressional grants of power to the president that the executive does not possess under the Constitution. Voters are also deprived of the ability to applaud or rebuke Congress for its use of the war power during biennial elections. In other words, representatives are no longer responsible to the people for decisions to involve American forces in military actions around the globe. The president, with congressional blessing, assumes a power reminiscent of Britain's eighteenth-century monarchs.

Of course, at times Congress has tried to act to limit the president's claims of ultimate power over the armed forces. Truman's actions in Korea and the undeclared Vietnam War led Congress to adopt the War Powers Resolution in 1973. The resolution commands the president to consult with Congress before "introducing United States Armed Forces into hostilities or into situations where imminent involvement in hostilities is clearly indicated by the circumstances."⁵⁰² If the president does put troops in harm's way absent a declaration of war, he has forty-eight hours in which to report to Congress about the circumstances of the action and about the estimated duration of the involvement. After sixty days of the use of troops, the president must terminate American involvement in the conflict unless Congress has declared war, extended the sixty-day period, or is unable to meet because of an attack on the United States. Notwithstanding the sixty-day period, the president must withdraw troops from hostilities "if the Congress so directs by joint resolution."⁵⁰³

As noted by constitutional law scholars Bruce Ackerman and Oona Hathaway, "[s]ince the adoption of the War Powers Resolution in 1973, modern presidents have repeatedly asserted the constitutional authority to commit troops without seeking congressional approval, but have nonetheless sought and received the congressional authorization that the War Powers Resolution requires (putting aside cases authorized by UN Security Council resolution)."⁵⁰⁴ Even when presidents do seek congressional approval, they are still in a position to coerce Congress and increase executive authority.

The executive's disregard for Congress's war powers was evidenced in a March 2012 exchange between Secretary of Defense Leon Panetta and the Senate on possible American intervention in the Syrian civil war. Panetta told the Senate that if the Obama administration decided that war with the Syrian government was in our best interests, he could not promise that Congress would be consulted. Panetta did indicate that the administration would seek an international mandate, but he made clear that Congress would not exercise veto power over the use of force in Syria.

Discussion and Solutions

Congress has largely abandoned its constitutional role as the body that determines war and peace. The president leads on these matters, and Congress follows. This formula has led to perpetual wars and aggressive military actions (including bombings, cruise missile strikes, and drone attacks) based on the president's judgment and discretion. Congress must reassert its constitutional role. The people's representatives should decide whether American forces are deployed into a hot zone—not the president.

The War Powers Resolution, however, recognizes executive power far outside the constitutional scope. One could argue that, rather than limiting presidential power, the resolution codifies presidential excesses. Congress should resort to the power of the purse and exercise oversight of spending decisions. This was the norm in early American history. The

lack of oversight gives presidents the liberty to enter conflicts with discretionary funds.

Congress should also censure a president for unilateral use of military force. In January 2024, when President Biden ordered American fighter jets to strike Yemen's Houthi rebels who were menacing commercial shipping in connection with the Israel-Hamas war, thirty House members signed a letter urging the Biden administration to request congressional authorization before ordering more attacks.[505] The letter set forth the constitutional bounds of the war powers and discussed the War Powers Resolution. This communication should have been signed by the entire House—even by members agreeing that action against the rebels was warranted.

Section 8, Clause 12

To RAISE AND support Armies, but no Appropriation of Money to that Use shall be for a longer Term than two Years;

Purpose

Because the Constitution delegates to Congress the power to declare war, the Framers believed that Congress was the proper organ to raise military forces. Delegating such a matter to the executive would be incongruent with the plan to limit presidential authority. In light of concerns about standing armies being inimical to the rights of the people, there is a two-year limit on the use of monetary appropriations.

Background and Development

Under the Confederation, Congress could engage in war and raise forces, but only with

the assent of nine states. Soldiers, sailors, and armaments were financed by requisitions on the states. The Articles provided that Congress would inform each state of its manpower quota, and the states would be responsible for raising and equipping the troops, with the promise of congressional reimbursement.

At the Philadelphia Convention, the delegates considered the power of Congress "[t]o raise armies" and, on a motion of Nathaniel Gorham of Massachusetts, added the words "and support."[506] Elbridge Gerry of Massachusetts expressed concern that unlike under the Articles, the new Congress would not be constrained in maintaining a standing army in times of peace, which he and many other delegates considered a threat to liberty. Gerry suggested that such a broad power would lead to serious opposition in the states' ratifying conventions. Gerry and Luther Martin of Maryland argued that in peacetime, the armies should be limited to small numbers of men. Jonathan Dayton of New Jersey opposed such a restriction on Congress because "a standing force of some sort may, for ought we know, become unavoidable."[507] John Langdon of New Hampshire rebuked Gerry for his "distrust of the Representatives of the people."[508] Ultimately, the Convention rejected the proposal to limit the size of a peacetime army; however, it did prohibit any military appropriations longer than two years.

Gerry was correct in believing that the enhanced powers granted to the national legislature over military matters would lead to opposition in the states. The English Whig tradition and its distrust of standing armies was gospel for many Americans. English Whigs—those favoring parliamentary power rather than royal power—pointed to sundry instances wherein armies were deployed not to defend a realm but to control it. In his *Wealth of Nations*, Adam Smith took up the subject of armies and reminded readers of the dangers of military establishments. Smith pointed to the harm done to the Roman Republic by Julius Caesar. After he was ordered by the Senate to stand trial in Rome, Caesar marched on Rome with a legion and seized power. He centralized the governing apparatus and became a dictator in perpetuity.

In addition to experience, Whigs reasoned that a standing army is inimical to a free state. Soldiers typically are housed together in forts and strongholds and thus are separated from daily interaction with the common people.

Soldiers also are governed by different laws than civilians are and must submit to the orders of a commanding officer. Prolonged separation from the rest of society and submission to the rigors of military life, the Whigs believed, fostered a foreignness that could be abused by those in authority.

Whiggish principles and lessons from history taught the American colonists that constitutions should be drafted to forbid the maintenance of a standing army in peace time. The Virginia Declaration of Rights framed the prohibition as follows: "that standing armies, in time of peace, should be avoided, as dangerous to liberty; and that, in all cases, the military should be under strict subordination to, and governed by, the civil power."[509]

In Massachusetts's ratifying convention, Samuel Nason described standing armies as a "bane of republican government" and reminded his colleagues that George III mobilized soldiers from a standing British force to perpetrate the Boston Massacre and to fight against American independence.[510] Indeed, the king's maintenance of standing armies in the colonies, without the consent of their legislatures, was a grievance listed in the Declaration of Independence. Virginia patriot George Mason predicted in his state's convention that once Congress created a standing force, "the people [would] lose their liberty."[511]

Alexander Hamilton, in *Federalist* No. 8, brushed aside concerns about standing armies. He argued that the real danger of standing armies would be present if the states rejected the Constitution of 1787. Hamilton contended that the smaller states would need to keep professional armies trained and staffed to protect them against their larger neighbors. "Thus we should in a little time see established in every part of this country," Hamilton wrote, "the same engines of despotism, which have been the scourge of the old world."⁵¹²

Anti-Federalists remained skeptical about the two-year period. At the Massachusetts ratifying convention, Samuel Thompson questioned whether the British people "ever allow[ed] Parliament to vote an army but for one year? But here we are giving Congress power to vote an army for two years—to tax us without limitation; no one to gainsay them, and no inquiry yearly."⁵¹³ Thomas Dawes, in the same convention, responded that the "army must expire of itself in two years after it shall be raised, unless renewed by representatives, who, at that time, will have just come fresh from the body of the people. It will share the same fate as that of a temporary law, which dies at the time mentioned in the act itself, unless revived by some future legislature." Hence, he saw no danger in the two-year period.⁵¹⁴

Distortions

Until the Civil War, the United States did not have a national military draft. The armed forces of the North and South initially depended on volunteers, often induced by systems of paying bounties to enlistees. In the *Selective Draft Law Cases* (1918), the Supreme Court held that "[i]t may not be doubted that the very conception of a just government and its duty to the citizen includes the reciprocal obligation of the citizen to render military service in case of need, and the right to compel it."⁵¹⁵ The Court noted that, prior to independence, conscription was common in the British Empire and, in the Revolutionary War, the states resorted to enforced military service to fulfill their quotas of soldiers.

Many prominent American statesmen, however, have denied that the general government has the power to conscript citizens. When a draft was considered during the War of 1812, Daniel Webster of Massachusetts was a vigorous opponent. "Where is it written in the Constitution," thundered Webster, "in what article or section is it contained that you may take children from their parents and parents from their children and compel them to fight the battles of any war which the folly or the wickedness of government may engage in?"⁵¹⁶ Because of such opposition, the proposed conscription bill failed.

Today, the U.S. armed forces consist of approximately 1.3 million service members. The United States maintains eight hundred military bases in more than seventy countries and territories overseas. The armed forces are all volunteers; a draft has not been in place since the early 1970s, when the Vietnam War was still underway and widespread protests prompted President Nixon to end it. Young men of prime military age are nevertheless required to register for possible conscription.

Our significant standing military force is primarily deployed for nondefensive aims. America has a highly interventionist foreign policy in which our military serves to spread democracy, to nation-build, and to retaliate against perceived threats to the international liberal order. The disaster in Afghanistan is the most recent example of the failure of this policy.

Discussion and Solutions

In place of this militaristic foreign policy and improper use of the armed forces, American liberty at home should be a shining example that other countries choose to emulate. If we must export our principles by force, they have likely become warped because of misuse at home and thus are not attractive to nations abroad. A foreign policy based on liberty at home would negate any arguments for the Selective Service System (a precursor to a draft) and the likelihood that America's youth would be needed to fight on foreign shores. As Doug Bandow, a former adviser to President Ronald Reagan, observed, "[t]he most effective way to prevent foreign adventure—like Vietnam—is to rely on a volunteer military that people can shut down by simply refusing to join."[517]

Senator Rand Paul (R-KY) has introduced bipartisan legislation to abolish the Selective Service System. "It has been nearly 50 years since the draft was last used," Senator Paul observed. He went on to note, "I've long stated that if a war is worth fighting, Congress will vote to declare it and people will volunteer. This outdated government program no longer serves a purpose and should be eliminated permanently."[518] Congress should adopt this bipartisan legislation and be done with the draft. If a cause lacks volunteers, it is not a cause worth forcing upon the unwilling.

Section 8, Clause 13
To provide and maintain a Navy;

Purpose

Based upon the successes of the Royal Navy, the Framers understood the utility of naval power. The Framers viewed a standing navy as less dangerous than its land-based counterpart. Nonetheless, they ensured that Congress and not the executive would make decisions about the scope and use of naval warships.

Background and Development

The Articles empowered Congress "to build and equip a navy."[519] At the Philadelphia Convention, the initial draft constitution granted Congress the authority "[t]o build and equip fleets" but was changed to its present wording with no recorded debate.[520] Unlike the power to raise armies, Clause 13 elicited little discussion.

In *Federalist* No. 4, John Jay commented that "[w]e have heard much of the fleets of Britain, and the time may come, if we are wise, when the fleets of America may engage attention."[521] Jay argued further that Britain became a sea power because the resources of England, Wales, Scotland, and Ireland had been marshaled by one national government. Had those four parts of the empire continued as independent states, Jay wrote, "it is easy to perceive how soon they would each dwindle into comparative insignificance."[522] Accordingly, Jay urged ratification of the Constitution so that the resources of the thirteen states could be administered to further the goal of making the United States a great maritime power.

Some Anti-Federalists expressed concern about aspirations for the United States to be a naval power. For example, William Grayson, in the Virginia ratifying convention, feared that efforts to fulfill Jay's vision would "irritate the nations of Europe against us" because "[c]ommerce and navigation are the principal sources of their wealth."[523] Grayson also observed that equipping a navy would entail great expense and questioned whether the United States should devote the enormous sums necessary to become a maritime power. Moreover, Grayson believed that a large navy primarily would benefit the commercial states of the North. Anticipating a future sectional conflict, he predicted that "the Southern States will be in the power of the Northern States."[524]

Today, the U.S. Navy has more than 336,000 personnel on active duty and 290 deployable combat vessels. Six future presidents served in the Navy during World War II: John F. Kennedy, Lyndon Johnson, Richard M. Nixon, Gerald Ford, Jimmy Carter, and George H. W. Bush.

SECTION 8, CLAUSE 14
TO MAKE RULES for the Government and Regulation of the land and naval Forces;

Purpose

The Framers sought to establish a system of military law tailored to the regimens of military discipline, which differentiates military from civilian life.

Background and Development

The Philadelphia Convention added Clause 14 to a draft of the Constitution, as recorded in Madison's *Notes*, "from the existing Articles of Confederation."[525] No debate arose. As observed by Cleveland State University's David F. Forte and the Foreign Policy Research Institute's Mackubin Owens, "[t]he central purpose of the clause is the establishment of a system of military law and justice outside the ordinary jurisdiction of the civil court. Tradition and experience taught the Framers that the necessities of military discipline require a system of jurisprudence separate from civilian society."[526]

Today, the basis for our military justice system is the Uniform Code of Military Justice (UCMJ). That statutory scheme was signed into law in 1950 by President Harry S. Truman. After World War II, a more modern and equitable justice system for service members was suggested. More than 16 million Americans served in the armed forces during the war and saw the deficiencies of the system, such as the harsh punishments and significant discretion of commanders in meting out justice. Prior to the UCMJ, "military justice in the United States had remained virtually unchanged since the time of the Revolutionary War when the Articles of War governed the Army disciplinary system while the Navy followed the Articles of Government for the Navy."[527] Following enactment of the UCMJ, criminal procedure closely follows the civilian model. Practically all constitutional protections associated with the civilian system are available to accused military personnel, and trained legal professionals (judge advocates) work at all levels of the system.

Distortions

In *Solorio v. United States* (1987), the Supreme Court held that the language of the Military Regulations Clause is "plenary" and that the jurisdiction of a military court depends solely on the accused's status as a member of the armed forces, and not on the "service connection" of the offense charged.[528] Hence, a military court can exercise jurisdiction over a service member when the alleged crime was committed off base, the accused person was off duty, and the victim had no connection with the military.

Discussion and Solutions

Military trials of soldiers who committed offenses with no connection to the armed forces have raised suspicion in American history. The concern has been that a military court might insulate the offender from a harsher civilian punishment. In *O'Callahan v. Parker* (1969), the Supreme Court held that there must be a service-related connection between the crime and a soldier's military duties for a military court to handle the matter rather than a civilian court.[529] Of course, in *O'Callahan*, the Court's primary concern was loss of broad constitutional protections for an accused if the matter was handled in a military versus a civilian setting. This decision was overruled in 1987 in *Solorio v. United States* in favor of the plenary power, as discussed above. Though the result reached in *O'Callahan* might have been based on the wrong reasons, the service-related requirement does have appeal. Civilian victims have an interest in having an offender brought to justice in courts controlled by civilian authorities. *Solorio*, on the other hand, provided a bright-line rule that is easy to implement and does not entangle the federal courts in military justice.

SECTION 8, CLAUSE 15
To PROVIDE FOR calling forth the Militia to execute the Laws of the Union, suppress Insurrections and repel Invasions;

Purpose

Because of the suspicion surrounding standing armies, the Framers expected that state militias would be integral in meeting emergencies such as invasions, insurrections, and defiant refusals to abide by the laws of the union. The militia's closeness to the people would foster greater trust in these troops than in a professional force.

Background and Development

The Virginia Plan proposed that the national legislature should have the power to "call forth the force of the Union against any member of the Union failing to fulfill its duties under the articles thereof."[530] It did not take Madison long to rethink the efficacy of that proposal. Just two days after the introduction of the Virginia Plan, Madison declared that "[a] union of States containing such an ingredient seemed to provide for its own destruction."[531]

Madison observed that use of force against a state "would probably be considered by the party attacked as a dissolution of all previous compacts by which it might be bound."[532] He averred to the Convention that he hoped a government would be formed that rendered such a clause unnecessary. The Convention agreed unanimously to postpone any consideration of the force clause found in the Virginia Plan.

The New Jersey Plan contained a similar provision regarding enforcement of federation dictates. According to the New Jersey Plan, "if any State, or any body of men in any State shall oppose or prevent the carrying into execution" federal statutory or treaty law, "the federal Executive shall be authorized to call forth the power of the Confederated States . . . to enforce and compel an obedience to such Acts, or an observance of such Treaties."[533]

After the report of the Committee of Eleven, which was formed to reach a compromise between the large and small states, Gouverneur Morris of Pennsylvania moved to strike the mention of treaties in the Militia Clause "as being superfluous, since treaties were to be 'laws.'" The Convention accepted Morris's change unanimously. He then suggested further edits that molded the Militia Clause into its present form.

Luther Martin of Maryland, in his *Genuine Information*, reported no objection at the Convention to giving the federal government some power to execute confederal law, suppress insurrections, and repel invasions. "But," Martin observed, "it was thought by some, that this power ought to be given with certain restrictions."[534] For example, Martin suggested that only a fraction of a state's militia should be required to leave the state at the command of the national government.

In *Federalist* No. 29, Alexander Hamilton described the power of calling forth the militia "in time of insurrection and invasion" as "natural incidents to the duties of superintending the common defence, and of watching over the internal peace of the confederacy."[535] As for calling forth the militia to enforce federal laws, James Madison averred in the Virginia ratifying convention that "[i]f resistance should be made to the executions of the laws, it ought to be overcome" by the people rather than a standing army.[536] Madison also argued that "[t]he most effectual way to guard against a standing army is to render it unnecessary."[537] And "[t]he most effectual way to render it unnecessary, is to give the general government full power to call forth the militia, and exert the whole natural strength of the Union, when necessary."[538]

Virginia's George Mason feared that Congress would abuse this power by, for example, requiring the Georgia militia to march to New Hampshire when other militia units were much closer. Mason believed "[t]his would harass the people so much that they would agree to abolish use of the militia, and establish a standing army."[539] He argued for an amendment to prevent a militia unit from being marched beyond the limits of an adjoining state and for one that required the permission of the militia unit's home state legislature before a deployment far away.

In the early republic, Congress delegated the power to call forth the militia to the president. For example, a statute enacted in 1795 provided that "whenever the United States shall be invaded or be in imminent danger of invasion from any foreign nation or Indian tribe, it shall be lawful for the President of the United States to call forth" the militia.[540]

During the War of 1812, governors of several New England states asserted that they, rather than the president, had the power to determine whether an exigency existed that would allow the militia to be summoned. In *Martin v. Mott* (1827), the Supreme Court interpreted the 1795 law and held "that the authority to decide whether the exigency has arisen, belongs exclusively to the President, and that his decision is conclusive upon all other persons."[541]

SECTION 8, CLAUSE 16

TO PROVIDE FOR organizing, arming, and disciplining, the Militia, and for governing such Part of them as may be employed in the Service of the United States, reserving to the States respectively, the Appointment of the Officers, and the Authority of training the Militia according to the discipline prescribed by Congress;

Purpose

To ensure its effectiveness, the Framers delegated to Congress the important tasks of arming, organizing, and disciplining the militia. Leaving such matters fully in the hands of the states, many believed, would invite neglect of this important force.

Background and Development

The militia "is an Anglo-Saxon institution ... composed of all subjects and citizens capable of bearing arms."[542] Blackstone traced the militia system to Alfred the Great (848/849 – 899) who "by his prudent discipline made all the subjects of his dominion soldiers."[543] Scholars have noted that the English "concept of a general militia differed radically from the continental feudal system, which limited the right of bearing arms and the duty of fighting in defense to a relatively small and wealthy class."[544]

The militia in the American colonial period was partly a social institution, partly a police force, and partly an army. The colonial militias typically comprised all free male citizens able to bear arms in times of danger. When the militia mustered to drill, the assembly turned into a community event at which the people discussed political affairs and enjoyed fellowship. The muster often ended with celebration and the enjoyment of whiskey, rum, or beer. Such revelry should not induce us to believe that militia duty was not a serious matter. As observed by historian Saul Cornell, "[f]or Americans living on the edge of the British Empire, in an age without police forces, the militia was essential for the preservation of public order and also protected Americans against external threats."[545] Militia service was as much a part of citizenship as jury duty or exercise of the franchise. Members of the colonial militias were required to muster with muskets, gunpowder, and shot, as well as other specified gear; they were subject to fines if not so equipped.

The delegates to the Philadelphia Convention were divided over granting the national government authority over the states' militias. Elbridge Gerry of Massachusetts protested that the Convention might as well disarm the people "as to take command from the States, and subject them to the Genl. Legislature."[546] He regarded national control over the militia as "Despotism."[547] Luther Martin of Maryland agreed with Gerry and predicted later that national control over the militia would deprive the states of a means to defend themselves "against arbitrary encroachments of the general government."[548] Other delegates, such as Charles Cotesworth Pinckney of South Carolina, stressed the need for uniformity and believed that the states would see the wisdom in surrendering authority over their militias. Madison feared that leaving the states with the power to discipline the militia would invite neglect of those important forces. "The Discipline of the militia is evidently a *National* concern," Madison argued, "and ought to be provided for in the *National* Constitution."[549]

The Constitution's provisions dealing with the militia and armies represented a compromise between the classic Whig position and the nationalists' desire for a permanent professional military force. Congress could raise a standing force, but the militia remained an important component of defense. Congress could call the militia into service to repel invasions, suppress rebellions, and execute the laws of the union. The Constitution empowered Congress to organize, arm, and discipline the militia. The states retained the power to appoint officers and to train the units in ways consistent with congressional guidelines.

The Militia Act of 1792 was the first congressional measure passed governing the armed forces. All able-bodied white men between the ages of eighteen and forty-five were to be enrolled for militia duty. Congress required each man to provide his own musket and other necessary equipment. Congress provided that the states should organize and train the militias by the standards each state set.[550] The law remained on the books until it was repealed by the Dick Act in 1903. The militia was officially renamed and became the National Guard. No longer would the militia comprise all able-bodied males of certain ages; instead, it would be a selected group of volunteers organized along the lines of a regular army. In 1908, Congress provided further that when it called the National Guard into service, units so mobilized could be compelled to serve abroad. The requirement of overseas service contradicted the constitutional command that the militia could be called forth only to suppress insurrection, repel invasions, or execute the laws of the union. In 1912, the judge advocate general of the U.S. Army held that the overseas service requirement exceeded Congress's authority under the Constitution.

Distortions

Experience in the Spanish-American War, America's first major war of interventionism, persuaded the national government that it needed to be able to count on the militias to serve abroad and not limit themselves to the purposes prescribed by the Constitution. To circumvent the constitutional issue of foreign service identified by the judge advocate general, in World War I the federal government simply drafted members of the National Guard into regular army units. In 1933, Congress established a "dual enlistment" system, whereby every person joining a State Guard simultaneously joins the National Guard of the United States, a wholly federal reserve force. Thus, rather than having to draft guardsmen to serve abroad, Congress simply deploys the National Guard of the United States overseas.

Discussion and Solutions

An imperialistic foreign policy required conversion of the militia to the National Guard and a "dual enlistment." The National Guard is rarely used for domestic concerns such as repelling invasions or executing the laws of the union. Instead, the primary purpose is to supplement or relieve regular army units stationed in myriad foreign lands and engaged in fighting unending wars. This is contrary to the Framers' view of the militia and marks the ascendency of the modern warfare state.

Americans need to reacquaint themselves with Washington's Farewell Address and his advice to "steer clear of permanent alliances with any portion of the foreign world" and to configure our armed forces in a "defensive posture."[551] "Harmony, liberal intercourse with all nations," Washington said, "are recommended by policy, humanity, and interest."[552]

Such advice should be heeded as we rethink the American militarism that drives our foreign policy and use of the National Guard.

Another solution would be to follow the lead of Governor Ron DeSantis (R-FL), who in 2022 reestablished the Florida State Guard, an entity distinct from the National Guard and responsive to the governor.[553] Florida is not alone in this endeavor; twenty-three states and Puerto Rico have established and maintained these units. Under Florida law, the State Guard "shall be used exclusively within the state, or to provide support to other states . . . and may not be called, ordered, or drafted into the armed forces of the United States."[554] The State Guard is made up of volunteers and is a tool for the governor to use to deal with emergencies and disasters. The creation of state guards is not counter to federal law and is authorized by Title 32 of the United States Code. State Guards have roots in the historical militia and offer men and women the opportunity to serve their state outside of the federal uniformed services.

SECTION 8, CLAUSE 17

To exercise exclusive Legislation in all Cases whatsoever, over such District (not exceeding ten Miles square) as may, by Cession of particular States, and the Acceptance of Congress, become the Seat of the Government of the United States, and to exercise like Authority over all Places purchased by the Consent of the Legislature of the State in which the Same shall be, for the Erection of Forts, Magazines, Arsenals, dock-Yards, and other needful Buildings;

Purpose

The Framers believed that the federal government, like the state governments, should possess complete authority over the seat of

government to prevent insults and interruptions. They feared that if the capital was located in a state, the federal government would be too dependent on that state for protection.

Background and Development

Commotion over the location of the national capital arose under the Articles of Confederation. In June 1783, disgruntled continental soldiers marched on Philadelphia to complain about their lack of pay. Congress requested that the Pennsylvania state government mobilize its militia to defend the Confederation's delegates, but the state refused. Although the soldiers disbanded quickly and no persons or property were injured, Congress adjourned to Princeton, New Jersey, because the delegates were insulted by Pennsylvania's lack of assistance. The move suited many delegates who disliked the social and commercial center that was Philadelphia. The big-city milieu made it difficult to keep discussion confidential and also seemed to breed a push for centralization.

In October 1783, with multiple states offering property for the creation of a federal enclave, Congress created two seats of government: one near Trenton, New Jersey, and the other near Georgetown, Maryland. Pending construction in those two locations, "Congress was to alternate between Annapolis and Trenton."[555] In late 1784, Congress abandoned the idea of dual seats of government. The delegates instead planned to locate the capital somewhere on the Delaware River and began conducting governmental business in New York City.

At the Philadelphia Convention, George Mason of Virginia introduced questions about siting the seat of government. Mason suggested that the Constitution prohibit placing the seat of government in the same location as a state capital. Mason feared that positioning in a state capital would cause improper

mixture of the two governments and also would "produce disputes concerning jurisdiction."[556] Gouverneur Morris of Pennsylvania expressed sympathy for Mason's motion but believed that the proposal would alienate the people of Philadelphia and New York City; both cities hoped to be chosen as the new capital. Elbridge Gerry of Massachusetts supported the motion and went on to observe further that most Americans did not want the seat of government to be near an existing state capital or a large commercial city. Pierce Butler of South Carolina "was for fixing by the Constitution the place, & a central one" for the new seat of government.[557]

James Madison of Virginia thought that "[t]he necessity of a central residence of the Govt wd be much greater under the new than the old Govt" both because officers of the new government would be more numerous and because many of them would be chosen "more from the interior parts of the States."[558] He also expected more private citizens to visit the capital to petition the government or bring business to it. Accordingly, he argued, the general government should be in a position to "contemplate with the most equal eye, and sympathize most equally with every part of the nation."[559]

In defending the Enclave Clause in the Massachusetts ratifying convention, Caleb Strong referenced the Confederation Congress's flight from Philadelphia. According to Strong, the lesson of that move was "that the erection of a federal town was necessary, wherein Congress might remain protected from insult."[560] Similarly, Edmund Pendleton, in the Virginia ratifying convention, averred that the Enclave Clause necessarily "gives [Congress] power over the place, so as to be secured from any interruption in their proceedings."[561] In *Federalist* No. 43, Madison observed that all the state legislatures enjoyed complete authority over their seats of government for purposes of preventing insults and interruptions. He inveighed further against how dangerous it would be for the general government to depend on any one state for protection. Because forts and other federal buildings would be erected with public money and would house the property of the general government, Madison contended that "they should be exempt from the authority" of any particular state.[562]

Anti-Federalists feared the Enclave Clause would be used to skirt the enumeration of powers. Citizens meeting at Harrisburg, Pennsylvania, demanded that the power "be qualified by a proviso that such right of legislation extend only to such regulations as respect the police and good order thereof."[563] In the Virginia ratifying convention, George Mason "thought there were few clauses in the Constitution so dangerous as that which gave Congress exclusive power of legislation within ten miles square."[564] Mason believed that by implication this power "was capable of any extension, and would probably be extended to augment the congressional powers."[565]

The capital came to the Potomac River because of a compromise brokered by Secretary of State Thomas Jefferson. A key part of Secretary of the Treasury Alexander Hamilton's financial plan involved assuming state Revolutionary War debts. Hamilton argued that because the debts were incurred for the benefit of all colonies' independence, the debts should be paid jointly rather than severally. He understood that if one or two states defaulted or were slow in repaying justly incurred debts, the credit of the whole union would

be impaired. He also hoped to enhance the stature of the national government by having the nation's wealthiest creditors look to it for payment rather than to the individual states. He struggled to get his proposal through Congress, because states that had dutifully paid down their debts already objected to bailouts of states that had made little or no effort to satisfy their creditors.

Madison opposed Hamilton's debt-assumption plan. Virginia had repaid a large percentage of its debts, and his constituents did not fancy being taxed for the benefit of other states. Jefferson arranged a dinner at which he, Madison, and Hamilton agreed to a compromise. Hamilton would persuade his allies to locate the nation's capital along the Potomac River, and Jefferson and Madison would urge Virginia congressmen to support assumption. The compromise worked. Hamilton got a key part of his financial plan through Congress, and the Virginians secured a southern location for the national government's capital.

In 1788 and 1789, Virginia and Maryland ceded the territory comprising the seat of government. Under the legislation creating a district not exceeding ten miles square and accepting the ceded territory, Congress directed President George Washington to obtain a proper survey and to approve the construction of suitable buildings for the government's public offices. The legislation provided that Philadelphia would serve as the national capital until December 1800, when the government would move to the new federal city.[566] Congress met for the first time in the District of Columbia on November 21, 1800.

SECTION 8, CLAUSE 18

TO MAKE ALL Laws which shall be necessary and proper for carrying into Execution the foregoing Powers, and all other Powers vested by this Constitution in the Government of the United States, or in any Department or Officer thereof.

Purpose

The Necessary and Proper Clause makes explicit that when a power is delegated, then all incidents essential to the exercise of the power are also given.

Background and Development

The Necessary and Proper Clause is a creature of the Committee of Detail, which was established by the Philadelphia Convention to draft a document reflecting the compromises and agreements reached by the delegates. No discussion of the clause took place at the Convention prior to its drafting. According to Georgetown University Law Center's Randy Barnett, "the likely explanation for the lack of debate surrounding the Clause" is that "if the power to make law was already thought implicit in the enumerated powers scheme, then it is not surprising that the Clause would provoke no discussion at the Convention."[567] In other words, because the delegates anticipated that Congress would pass legislation to carry into effect its enumerated powers, a statement to that effect aroused little concern.

But outside the Philadelphia Convention, great concern about the scope of the so-called Sweeping Clause emerged. Opponents of the Constitution contended that the clause nullified the enumerated powers. "Under such a clause as this," asked the Anti-Federalist writer known as An Old Whig, "can any thing be said

to be reserved and kept back from Congress? Can it be said that the Congress have no power but what is *expressed*?"[568] The clause reminded An Old Whig of the Declaratory Act of 1766, in which Parliament claimed the power to pass legislation governing the colonies in all cases whatsoever. That hated act of Parliament, An Old Whig opined, "was not more extensive" than the Necessary and Proper Clause.[569] The Federal Farmer concurred with An Old Whig's analysis. The anonymous author believed that with the Sweeping Clause tacked onto the enumerated powers, "it is almost impossible to have a just conception of [Congress's] powers, or of the extent and number of the laws which may be deemed necessary and proper to carry them into effect."[570]

Centinel believed that Congress could claim powers not granted and that these powers could, in turn, threaten the state governments. "Whatever law congress may deem necessary and proper for carrying into execution any of the powers vested in them, may be enacted," wrote Centinel, "and by virtue of this clause they may control and abrogate any and every of the laws of the state governments, on the allegation that they interfere with the execution of their powers."[571] Brutus similarly feared that such a comprehensive power might "be exercised in such a manner as entirely to abolish the state legislatures."[572]

In Pennsylvania's ratifying convention, James Wilson dismissed the objections raised by the Anti-Federalists. According to Wilson, the Sweeping Clause "is saying no more than that the powers we have already particularly given shall be effectually carried into execution."[573] Alexander Hamilton, in *Federalist* No. 33, described the effect of the clause similarly. "And it is *expressly* to execute these powers that the sweeping clause, as it has been affectedly called, authorizes the national legislature to pass all *necessary* and *proper* laws," explained Hamilton. "If there is any thing exceptionable, it must be sought for in the specific powers upon which this general declaration is predicated."[574] Seen in that light, Hamilton continued, the Necessary and Proper Clause, which "may be chargeable with tautology or redundancy, is at least perfectly harmless."[575]

Distortions

The breadth of the Sweeping Clause was tested early during Washington's first term as president. In 1791, Secretary of the Treasury Hamilton recommended that Congress establish a national bank. Hamilton described the bank as "an institution of primary importance to the prosperous administration of [national] finances, and . . . of the greatest utility in the operations connected with the support of public credit."[576] Hamilton informed Congress that the "most enlightened commercial nations" had established national banks and that the United States should follow suit.[577]

Hamilton recommended a bank with $10 million in capital and twenty-five thousand shares of stock. Private investors would own twenty thousand shares, with the national government holding the remainder. The bank would issue its own notes in excess of its assets and thus engage in fractional reserve banking.

Hamilton believed that gold and silver should not be means of paying private debts and hoped that the country's specie would be collected in the vaults of the national bank. Paper money would circulate while the gold and silver collected interest and buttressed the bank's power.

Hamilton touted the ability of a national bank to assist the government in great emergencies. In case of war or threatened invasion, large amounts of capital would already have been collected in one place to support government war financing. Hamilton also claimed that "[t]he facilitating of the payment of taxes" would be another benefit of a national bank.[578] A person short of money could obtain loans from the bank to answer the call of the tax collector. In addition, a taxpayer would not be burdened with the "trouble, delay, expense, and risk" of transferring gold and silver to the national Treasury.[579] Bank notes would make the process easier and quicker for all parties involved.

Hamilton's bank ignited an impassioned debate in the House of Representatives. Southerners charged that the bank would benefit the mercantile interest centered in the North while doing nothing for the yeoman farmers. They also questioned its constitutionality. Even if a national bank would be conducive to the financial health of the union, whence, they asked, did the power to charter this corporation come?

To answer that question, the bank's proponents advanced remarkably broad theories of constitutional interpretation on the floor of Congress. Fisher Ames of Massachusetts opined that "Congress may do what is necessary to the end for which the constitution was adopted."[580] And just what were the ends? According to Theodore Sedgwick, who also represented Massachusetts, "the public good and general welfare" were the ultimate ends.[581] Elbridge Gerry concurred with his neighbors from Massachusetts and pointed Congress to the preamble of the Constitution. Providing for the common defense and general welfare, he observed, were the great objects of the Constitution and should guide interpretation of the enumerated powers. John Lawrence of New York argued that there was nothing in the Constitution that expressly forbade a bank and declared that "we ought not to deduce a prohibition by construction."[582] He continued, "A full uncontrollable power to regulate the fiscal concerns of this Union, is a primary consideration in this Government; and, from hence, it clearly follows, that it must possess the power to make every possible arrangement conducive to that great power."[583]

Congressman James Madison was shocked as he listened to the arguments of his colleagues. The construction put forward, Madison alleged, would destroy the system of enumerated powers crafted in Philadelphia. Madison reminded his fellow representatives that the Philadelphia Convention had in fact considered enumerating the power of incorporation but decided against delegating such a power to Congress. He reminded them that if no powers pertaining to creation of a national bank had been enumerated, then the bank had to be necessary and proper for carrying out one of the listed powers. To the extent that an enumerated power could be cited, Madison said that the Sweeping Clause must be interpreted "according to the natural and obvious force of terms and the context" and thus "be limited to the means *necessary* to the *end*, and incident to the *nature*, of the specified powers."[584] As constitutional law scholars Gary Lawson and Patricia B. Granger have pointed out, to Madison

"necessary" referred to a "fit[] between the executory law and valid government ends," whereas "proper" contemplated "executory laws to be the laws that are particularly within the jurisdiction and competence of Congress—that is, laws that do not tread on the retained rights of individuals or states."[585] Remote implications of constitutional language should not be relied upon, Madison warned the Congress, or else the national government may "reach every object of legislation."[586]

Despite Madison's criticism, Congress passed the bank bill and sent it to President Washington for his signature. Washington, however, was uncomfortable with the legislation and asked Attorney General Edmund Randolph and Secretary of State Thomas Jefferson to offer opinions on the bill. Both Randolph and Jefferson believed that the bill was unconstitutional. Randolph's thoughts were summed up in the penultimate paragraph of his opinion: "[L]et it be propounded as an eternal question to those who build new powers on this clause, whether the latitude of construction, which they arrogate will not terminate in an unlimited power in Congress."[587]

In his response, Jefferson began with the Tenth Amendment: "The powers not delegated to the United States by the Constitution, nor prohibited by it to the States, are reserved to the States respectively, or to the people."[588] Jefferson described the amendment as the foundation of constitutional interpretation. "To take a single step around the powers of Congress," he warned, "is to take possession of a boundless field of power, no longer susceptible of any definition."[589] Jefferson examined the enumerated powers and concluded that all of them could be executed without the creation of a bank. Jefferson acknowledged that the bank might make the collection of taxes more convenient, but he denied that convenience and necessity were synonyms. The word "necessary," in Jefferson's view, restrained the national government "to those means, without which the grant of power would be nugatory."[590]

The opinions of Randolph and Jefferson certainly worried Washington. As he mulled the matter, he asked Hamilton to offer his opinion on the constitutionality of the bank. After studying Randolph's and Jefferson's opinions, Hamilton complied and asserted that the analysis of his cabinet colleagues "would be fatal to the just and indispensable authority of the United States."[591] A means was necessary, according to Hamilton, so long as it was useful or helpful to the exercise of a delegated power. Pointing to recent federal legislation erecting lighthouses and buoys for facilitating commerce, Hamilton observed that while navigational aids were helpful to ships participating in the carrying trade, they were not strictly necessary. But few people complained that the lighthouses and buoys were authorized in contravention to the Constitution. "If the end be clearly comprehended within any of the specified powers, and if the measure have an obvious relation to that end, and is not forbidden by any particular provision of the constitution," Hamilton reasoned, "it may safely be deemed to come within the compass of the national authority."[592]

Impressed with Hamilton's arguments, Washington signed the bank bill into law.

The Supreme Court joined the debate on the Bank of the United States almost thirty years later when it heard the case of *McCulloch v. Maryland* (1819).[593] The charter of the original bank expired in 1811. A charter for the Second Bank of the United States was issued in 1816—with the approval of President James Madison. Madison believed that the public had accepted a national bank as constitutional, and thus he abandoned his earlier opposition.

Chief Justice Marshall rightly began the analysis by asking whether "Congress [has] power to incorporate a bank."[594] He admitted readily that no enumerated power existed allowing the chartering of a national corporation and then turned to consider whether creation of a bank was incidental to some other enumerated power. Like Hamilton before him, Marshall took note of the powers to raise taxes, borrow money, regulate commerce, and raise military forces. The government must "be allowed to select the means" of carrying out its delegated powers, so long as the means are "convenient, or useful, or essential."[595] Marshall implied further that the means had to bear a reasonable fit or relationship to the ultimate end proposed. "Let the end be legitimate, let it be within the scope of the constitution, and all means which are appropriate, which are plainly adapted to that end, which are not prohibited, but consist with the letter and spirit of the constitution, are constitutional."[596] Based on those principles, the Court upheld the chartering of the Second Bank of the United States.

Debate about the scope of the Sweeping Clause continues in the twenty-first century. Modern constructions and arguments stretch the clause beyond even what Hamilton and Marshall envisioned. In *United States v. Comstock* (2010),[597] the Supreme Court considered the constitutionality of a statute permitting the civil incarceration of sexually dangerous persons beyond the periods of their criminal sentences.

The Supreme Court framed the issue as follows: "The question presented is whether the Necessary and Proper Clause . . . grants

Congress authority to enact the statute before us."[598] Surprisingly, the Court did not frame the issue as whether the civil commitment statute carried into effect an enumerated power granted in the Constitution. In upholding the statute, the court reasoned that because Congress can enact criminal laws pursuant to its enumerated powers and the operation of prisons is incidental to that power, it follows that Congress can detain a sexually dangerous federal prisoner for as long as that person is deemed a danger to society.

That reasoning is questionable. While Congress may have the power to enact criminal laws and to detain individuals convicted of violating those laws, it does not follow that Congress may enact statutes to keep individuals in custody after their prison terms end. The power to construct and operate prisons is not an independent grant of power under the Constitution.

Discussion and Solutions

The Anti-Federalists were correct to be suspicious of the Necessary and Proper Clause.

While it is true that, under the common law, a grant is accompanied by those incidents that are necessary for the grant to have effect, the interpretations of Hamilton and Marshall transformed the idea of necessity into simple convenience. In the words of the great Virginia Judge Spencer Roane, "[t]hat man must be a deplorable idiot who does not see that there is no earthly difference between an unlimited grant of power and a grant limited in its terms, but accompanied with unlimited means of carrying it into execution."[599] Nationalists eager to augment the enumerated powers of Congress have given the Sweeping Clause an extensive interpretation that denigrates from the promise of a limited government. The modern Supreme Court is happy to continue in the Hamiltonian tradition, as evidenced by its ruling in *Comstock*. One step in returning to a federal government with few and defined powers will require resurrecting Jefferson's insistence that "necessary" extends only to those means that must accompany the delegated power so that it is not rendered nugatory.

SECTION 9, CLAUSE 1

THE MIGRATION OR Importation of such Persons as any of the States now existing shall think proper to admit, shall not be prohibited by the Congress prior to the Year one thousand eight hundred and eight, but a Tax or duty may be imposed on such Importation, not exceeding ten dollars for each Person.

Purpose

This provision is a compromise between delegates who realized that the transatlantic slave trade was inhumane and should be stopped immediately and delegates from the slaveholding states who believed further importation of slaves advanced important economic interests. Under the compromise, Congress could tax slave imports and abolish the slave trade in 1808.

Background and Development

Under the Articles of Confederation, Congress had no power to regulate or prohibit the slave trade. As James Wilson observed in the Pennsylvania ratifying convention, the states in the Confederation "may admit the importation of slaves as long as they please."[600] Wilson characterized Section 9, Clause 1 "as laying the foundation for banishing slavery out of this country" because Congress could ban the international slave trade under its power to regulate foreign commerce.[601]

At the Philadelphia Convention, and in response to a motion from a Committee of Detail charged with creating a draft constitution conformable to the resolutions agreed upon by the Convention, Charles Cotesworth Pinckney of South Carolina made clear that absent some security for the institution of slavery, he would be bound to oppose any new plan of government. The Committee of Detail heard his words and in their draft documents prohibited the federal government from interfering with the slave trade. But that recommendation ignited more debate on the subject.

In response to arguments by Luther Martin of Maryland that further importation of slaves "was inconsistent with the principles of the revolution and dishonorable to the American character," John Rutledge of South Carolina suggested focusing on interests. He said the issue of slave importation was one of economic interest, and interest would determine whether the Southern states joined the new union.[602] Oliver Ellsworth of Connecticut urged the Convention to leave slave importation to the individual states. "The old confederation," Ellsworth said, "had not meddled with this point, and he did not see any greater

necessity for bringing it within the policy of the new one."[603]

George Mason of Virginia (who was a slave owner) described the slave trade as an "infernal traffic."[604] He also criticized the peculiar institution as "produc[ing] the most pernicious effects on manners" and making "[e]very master of slaves . . . a petty tyrant."[605] Mason believed that the federal government "should have the power to prevent the increase of slavery."[606]

Charles Pinckney of South Carolina defended the institution against Mason's attacks. He observed that slavery had existed throughout the world and that great civilizations such as Greece and Rome sanctioned slavery. He expected that if the Southern states "were let alone," they probably would cease importing slaves.[607] But the "attempt to take away the right" to import slaves would "produce serious objections to the Constitution which he wished to see adopted."[608]

With tempers flaring over slavery, the Convention created the Committee of Eleven to try to find a middle ground. The committee recommended acknowledging congressional power over the slave trade, but suggested that the power be suspended for twelve years. It also recommended allowing a tax on slave importation and striking out the supermajority requirement for Congress to pass a navigation act.

Charles Cotesworth Pinckney moved to extend the suspension period until 1808. Madison objected that such a lengthy term would be "more dishonorable" than ignoring the issue altogether.[609] Pinckney's motion succeeded by a vote of seven states to four. The majority proved to be an interesting coalition, as New Hampshire, Massachusetts,

Connecticut, and Maryland voted with three Deep South states.

Vexed by the majority's vote, Gouverneur Morris of Pennsylvania urged that the clause allowing importation specify North Carolina, South Carolina, and Georgia, so the world would know exactly which states favored continuation of the slave trade. He also wanted the word "slave" inserted to avoid any ambiguity. Other delegates reminded him that such a list would offend the people of those three states and likely would work against ratification. Regaining his composure, Morris withdrew his motion.

The Convention agreed to a tax on the importation of slaves. To act otherwise, Mason argued, would "be equivalent to a bounty on the importation of slaves."[610] The Convention approved a "tax or duty" not to exceed ten dollars per slave.

In December 1806, in his sixth annual message to Congress, President Thomas Jefferson reminded the legislators of "the approach of the period at which you may interpose your authority constitutionally, to withdraw the citizens of the United States from all further participation in those violations of human rights" bound up in the international slave trade.[611] Although no law banning the trade could take effect until 1808, Jefferson averred that early action by Congress might prevent further expeditions that could not be completed prior to the new statute's effective date. Congress acted on Jefferson's suggestion, and on New Year's Day

1808 the importation of African slaves into the United States was banned. Prior to 1808 all states in the union except South Carolina "had outlawed the foreign slave trade on their own authority."[612]

Jefferson's sixth annual message marked the second time that he had successfully endeavored to end the international slave trade. In 1777, Jefferson was part of a committee that revised Virginia's laws. Jefferson and his colleagues drafted a bill banning the importation of slaves from Africa. This legislation was introduced in the Virginia legislature by James Madison and was adopted in 1778.[613]

Modern activists, employing extreme presentism, engage in heated rhetoric about the existence of slavery in the antebellum period in the United States. They would do well to remember, as Oxford University's Nigel Biggar has pointed out, that "[b]efore about 1770, few [anywhere in the world] condemned the institution of slavery as such."[614] Moreover, the impetus for abolition of the slave trade came from western Christianity—specifically English dissenters and nonconformists.[615] Because the United States had roots in the dissenting Protestant tradition, it was one of the first Western countries to abolish the slave trade. Only Denmark (1792) and Great Britain (1807) took action before the United States. Although we regret that slavery ever existed in the United States, we can take pride that our government was in the vanguard of efforts to end the horrors of the middle passage.

SECTION 9, CLAUSE 2

THE PRIVILEGE OF the Writ of Habeas Corpus shall not be suspended, unless when in Cases of Rebellion or Invasion the public Safety may require it.

Purpose

Consistent with their ancient rights as Englishmen, the Framers ensured that any person imprisoned could apply to a judge to test the validity of the confinement. The Constitution allows congressional suspension of habeas protection only in cases of invasion or rebellion.

Background and Development

In his *Commentaries*, William Blackstone described habeas corpus as "the most celebrated writ in English law."[616] The writ of habeas corpus ad subjiciendum is a legal mechanism requiring that the custodian of a prisoner bring the prisoner before a court for a determination of the lawfulness of incarceration. While bills of rights serve as guideposts for the people to monitor government infringements on their liberties, the "Great Writ" provides a mechanism by which a person can challenge a loss of personal freedom. Historian Anthony Gregory has described the development of habeas corpus in England as "rocky," since it "evolved from a privilege of officials and a method for judges to amass money and power into a clarion call for justice and . . . an instrument to secure the rights of the falsely detained."[617]

Initially, the provision read: "The privileges and benefit of the Writ of Habeas corpus shall be enjoyed in this Government in the most expeditious and ample manner: and shall not be suspended by the Legislature except upon the most urgent and pressing occasions, and for a limited time not exceeding __ months."[618]

The Framers likely modeled the provision on the Massachusetts Constitution of 1780: "The privilege and benefit of the writ of habeas corpus shall be enjoyed in this commonwealth, in the most free, easy, cheap, expeditious, and ample manner, and shall not be suspended by the legislature, except upon the most urgent and pressing occasions, and for a limited time, not exceeding twelve months."[619]

Charles Pinckney and John Rutledge, both of South Carolina, urged strong protections for writs of habeas corpus. Gouverneur Morris of Pennsylvania then suggested wording almost identical to that ultimately adopted: The writ could not be suspended absent a rebellion or invasion. Even with those limitations, many opponents of the Constitution saw danger and believed the exceptions would swallow the whole. For example, Luther Martin of Maryland ventured that when a state disagreed with an action of the general government, the latter would declare the state to be in rebellion and arrest critics of national policy. In the Massachusetts ratifying convention, Samuel Nason complained that the provision was "exceeding[ly] loose" and desired that the Constitution specify the maximum time period for permissible suspension.[620]

Distortions

Although this clause appears in Article I (concerning the powers of Congress) and in England the writ could be suspended only by Parliament, the first federal suspension of habeas corpus was instituted by President Abraham Lincoln. Approximately two weeks after the surrender of Fort Sumter to Confederate forces, Lincoln suspended the Great Writ in the area between Washington, DC, and Philadelphia so the army could deal with dissenters and Southern sympathizers. Historian Clinton Rossiter has recognized that Lincoln's actions were done "in the face of almost unanimous opinion that the constitutional clause regulating the suspension of the writ of habeas corpus was directed to Congress alone."[621]

On May 26, 1861, Union soldiers arrested John Merryman, a pro-Confederate Maryland state legislator. He was charged with treason for seeking to hinder U.S. troop movements from Baltimore to Washington. His lawyer sought a writ of habeas corpus, but General George Cadwalader, the commander of Fort McHenry where Merryman was imprisoned, refused to produce him for a hearing.

In *Ex parte Merryman* (1861), Chief Justice Roger B. Taney, who was sitting as a circuit judge, rebuked Lincoln: "He certainly does not faithfully execute the laws if he takes upon himself legislative power by suspending the writ of habeas corpus, and the judicial power also, by arresting and imprisoning a person without due process of law."[622] Despite Taney's ruling that only Congress could suspend habeas corpus and his direction that the clerk of court transmit the case record to the White House, General Cadwalader and President

Lincoln simply ignored the chief justice's order and continued to hold Merryman at Fort McHenry.

Taney was not alone in his rebuke of Lincoln. Senator James A. Bayard Jr. of Delaware described suspension as "the highest act of legislative discretion" and counseled that only Congress could "determine the question of whether the public safety" required temporary suspension of the Great Writ.[623] He scoffed at the idea that the president could suspend the writ or that Congress could delegate the power of suspension to the president. Having such a power vested in the legislative branch, Bayard argued, was a "great guard for the liberty of the citizen against the aggression of power."[624] Accepting that the power of suspension existed in the executive, Bayard averred, would be tantamount to abandoning republican government in favor of a tyrannical government.

Prior to the late 1850s, state court judges could exercise habeas review over federal prisoners. Decentralized enforcement of habeas power terminated in *Ableman v. Booth* (1859), when a unanimous Supreme Court held that state habeas authority did not extend to prisoners held by the federal government.[625] A federal district court, the Court lectured, "has exclusive and final jurisdiction by the laws of the United States; and neither the regularity of its proceedings nor the validity of its sentence could be called in question in any other court, either of a State or the United States, by habeas corpus or any other process."[626]

During the war on terror, the Supreme Court for the first time in American history extended the constitutional right to habeas corpus to alien enemies detained abroad by American military units.[627] The Court took this step despite congressional legislation (the

Detainee Treatment Act) providing the critical protections that habeas corpus typically guarantees. The Court also ignored precedent dating from World War II in which it had held that German prisoners confined abroad had no right to request the writ of habeas corpus.[628]

Discussion and Solutions

The Great Writ ensures that any person suffering imprisonment can apply to the courts to test the validity of the confinement. As demonstrated by the actions of President Lincoln, habeas corpus is rendered an ineffectual parchment barrier when government uses the force of arms to shove it aside. Merryman did not receive relief, but his treatment teaches us about the importance of the writ and why we should demand that our officials scrupulously honor it.

Todd E. Pettys of the University of Iowa College of Law reminds us that "[t]hroughout the first half of the nineteenth century, it was widely believed—among state courts, federal officials, and legal commentators alike—that state courts had the power to provide relief to individuals being extra-judicially detained, regardless of whether the federal government was the sovereign responsible for the confinement."[629] Perhaps the time has come to reconsider the *Ableman* decision and thus allow state habeas authority to extend to prisoners held by the federal government. This would mean more protections for individuals suffering confinement.

SECTION 9, CLAUSE 3
NO BILL OF Attainder or ex post facto Law shall be passed.

Purpose

The Framers prohibited legislation declaring a person guilty of a crime. Under the Constitution, conviction and punishment require proceedings in a court of justice in accordance with the law of the land. Similarly, a deed that was neutral or innocent under the law when it was done may not be made subject to punishment later because of legislation purporting to be retroactive.

Background Development

A bill of attainder is a legislative act inflicting capital punishment on persons believed guilty of serious offenses without a conviction in the ordinary course of justice. St. George Tucker described bills of attainder as "state-engines of oppression in the last resort."[630] One of the most notable bills of attainder in English history targeted the Earl of Stafford, a friend and adviser of Charles I. In 1640, the Commons impeached Stafford for alleged treasonous conduct. The case managers struggled in the House of Lords, and it appeared that an acquittal would ensue. To avoid Stafford's exoneration, the Commons and the Lords passed a bill of attainder. The king, feeling the great public pressure, gave his royal assent. On May 12, 1641, Stafford was executed on Tower Hill. The proceedings against Stafford were purely political.

Nothing resembling due process was followed in the matter.

During the American Revolution, multiple colonies enacted legislation resembling bills of attainder. The statutes typically targeted Crown loyalists, declared them guilty, and appropriated their property. According to legal historian Duane L. Ostler, "New York alone raised $3,600,000 this way, by passing 11 separate bills of attainder between 1777 and 1784."[631] Because the legislation did not impose the death penalty, it is more properly described as "bills of pains and penalties." Nonetheless, such statutes closely resemble the English bill of attainder because of the lack of process accorded their targets.

According to St. George Tucker, an ex post facto law makes an action that was neutral or innocent at the time committed "to have been a crime" and subject to punishment.[632] In *Federalist* No. 84, Alexander Hamilton noted that "[t]he creation of crimes after the commission of the act" was a "most formidable instrument[]of tyranny" and had no place in the national government.[633]

In the Philadelphia Convention, Elbridge Gerry of Massachusetts and James McHenry of Maryland moved to include in the Constitution the prohibition of bills of attainder and ex post facto laws. Gouverneur Morris of Pennsylvania and Oliver Ellsworth of Connecticut agreed readily with prohibiting bills of attainder but thought the mention of ex post facto laws was unnecessary. Ellsworth declared "that there was no lawyer, no civilian who would not say that ex post facto laws were void of themselves."[634] James Wilson of Pennsylvania believed that the Convention would appear "ignorant of the first principles of Legislation" if it included the ex post facto

provision in the Constitution.[635] Hugh Williamson of North Carolina countered that such a prohibition in his state's constitution had done much good, and at a minimum "the Judges can take hold of it" and strike ex post facto laws. Ultimately, the Convention agreed unanimously to a prohibition of bills of attainder. Regarding ex post facto laws, seven states voted for the provision, three voted no, and one was divided.

Although the traditional understanding of bills of attainder involved capital punishment, the Supreme Court has expanded the prohibition's scope. For example, in *United States v. Brown* (1965), the Court held that "the Bill of Attainder Clause was not to be given a narrow historical reading . . . but was instead to be read in light of the evil the Framers had sought to bar: legislative punishment, of any form or severity, of specifically designated persons or groups."[636] In *Brown*, the Court struck down a statute making it crime for members of the Communist Party to serve as officers or employees of labor unions.

Under prevailing Supreme Court precedent, the Ex Post Facto Clause applies only to criminal laws. In *Calder v. Bull* (1798), the Court held that "[t]he restraint against making any ex post facto laws was not considered, by the framers of the constitution, as extending to prohibit the depriving a citizen even of a vested right to property; or the provision, 'that private property should not be taken for public use, without just compensation,' was unnecessary."[637] In other words, the Court contended that had the Ex Post Facto Clause applied to civil laws, the Takings Clause of the Fifth Amendment and the constitutional prohibitions against interfering with contracts would have been unnecessary.[638]

Of course, legislatures are prohibited from circumventing the Ex Post Facto Clause by camouflaging criminal penalties in civil form. The Supreme Court has noted that "it is the effect, not the form, of the law that determines whether it is ex post facto."[639]

Distortions

Progressive lawyers and judges have devised novel arguments concerning the Bill of Attainder Clause. For example, in *Center for Equal Protection, Inc. v. Bruning* (2012), a federal district court in Nebraska held that the state's constitutional provision declaring that marriage can exist only between one man and one woman was a violation of the Bill of Attainder Clause.[640] (The decision was overturned a year later by the Eighth Circuit Court of Appeals.) The district court ruled that the state constitutional provision targeted homosexuals and deprived them of a trial "before preventing the legal recognition of same-sex relationships."[641] The district court found that by constitutionalizing the traditional definition of marriage, the provision punished homosexuals by preventing them from petitioning elected officials to effect political change through the democratic process.

Such an argument could be used to attack any constitutional provision that creates classifications. For example, a state choosing to prohibit, say, marijuana in the text of its constitution would face arguments from cannabis users that they are punished without a trial because they cannot use the ordinary political process to legalize the drug. The *Bruning* court went far beyond the Framers' understanding of a bill of attainder. Although the bill of attainder issue is moot as to same-sex marriage because of *Obergefell v. Hodges* (2015),[642] *Bruning* shows just how far theorists will distort clear constitutional provisions.

Discussion and Solutions

In a republican government, no law should be passed declaring a person guilty of a crime or imposing punishment for an act that was innocent when performed. Section 9, Clause 3 prohibits such laws. As a matter of policy, the provision serves "to assure that legislative acts give fair warning of their effect and permit individuals to rely on their meaning until explicitly changed."[643] It "also restricts governmental power by restraining arbitrary and potentially vindictive legislation."[644] Section 9, Clause 3 remains intact and thus requires no proposed amendments or legislative initiatives.

SECTION 9, CLAUSE 4
NO CAPITATION, OR other direct, Tax shall be laid, unless in Proportion to the Census or Enumeration herein before directed to be taken.

Purpose

If Congress resorts to direct taxation (that is, taxes on people's lives, homes, or productive occupations), it must be levied in proportion to population and thus avoid partiality in the imposition of burdens.

Background and Development

The Constitution does not define the term "direct tax." In identifying the articles subject to direct taxes in the Virginia ratifying convention, John Marshall included "[l]ands, slaves, stock of all kinds, and a few other articles of domestic property."[645] Oliver Ellsworth of Connecticut observed in his state's ratifying convention that direct taxes often fall upon "the tools of a man's business, or the necessary utensils of his family."[646] Similar to Marshall and Ellsworth, the Anti-Federalist writing as the Federal Farmer averred that direct taxes would target "polls, lands, houses, labour, &c."[647] Legal historian Robert G. Natelson concludes that "[a] tax was direct if it was imposed on people's lives, homes, or on the productive occupations by which they supported and expressed themselves. Direct taxes, in other words, were levies on living and producing."[648]

A capitation, of course, is simply "a tax or imposition upon the person."[649] Often it is referred to as a "head tax."

St. George Tucker explained the apportionment requirement aptly as "check[ing] any possible disposition in congress towards partiality in the imposition of burdens."[650] Indeed, apportionment of direct taxes was the custom in England and was followed, for the most part, in the several states prior to the ratification of the Constitution. Natelson emphasizes the Framers' belief that the business of government should be based on fiduciary principles and stresses that the apportionment rule, though part of a compromise dealing with representation and taxation, was "one of several constitutional provisions designed to assure the impartial treatment of both individuals and states."[651] Hugh Williamson of North Carolina articulated the impartiality principle succinctly in 1792 during a debate in the House when he described the "clear and obvious intention" of the provision as ensuring that "Congress might not have the power of imposing unequal burdens; that it might not be in their power to gratify one part of the Union by oppressing another."[652]

Although the Constitution empowered Congress to raise revenue by direct taxation, most of the Framers believed that direct taxes would be imposed only rarely. In the Massachusetts ratifying convention, Thomas Davies proclaimed that most federal revenue would come from customs duties but that in "extraordinary cases," such as war, Congress should be permitted to levy direct taxes.[653] Francis Dana made a similar point in the same convention when he averred that "it was not to be supposed that [Congress] would levy [direct taxes] unless the impost and excise should be found insufficient in case of a war."[654]

Distortions

In 1794, Congress followed the recommendation of Alexander Hamilton, the secretary of the treasury, to enact a tax on carriages. James Madison opposed the tax because he believed it was direct and thus should be apportioned. Supporters of the tax described it as an "excise"—that is, a tax on the consumption of selected commodities—and thus not subject to apportionment. Madison countered that a proper excise tax involved the sale of a commodity, but not a tax on the postsale fact of ownership of the property.

The matter ultimately was decided by the Supreme Court in *Hylton v. United States*

(1796).[655] Hamilton argued the government's case and convinced the justices that the "direct taxes" referred to in the Constitution involved only poll taxes and land taxes. Taxes on personal goods, Hamilton averred, were outside the meaning of direct taxation. Accordingly, the carriage tax was upheld, and the Court adopted a functional rule in considering taxes: "If it is proposed to tax any specific article by the rule of apportionment, and it would evidently create great inequality and injustice, it is unreasonable to say, that the Constitution intended such tax should be laid by that rule."[656] The principle of such a rule was illustrated by Justice Chase in *Hylton*. "Suppose two States, equal in census, to pay 80,000 dollars each, by a tax on carriages, of 8 dollars on every carriage; and in one State there are 100 carriages, and in the other 1000. The owners of carriages in one State, would pay ten times the tax of owners in the other. A. in one State, would pay for his carriage 8 dollars, but B. in the other state, would pay for his carriage, 80 dollars."[657] Of course, what Chase ignored was that "inequality and injustice" could have been avoided had Congress crafted the tax as a true selective excise or consumption tax, which would have been a constitutional indirect tax, and thus spared the Court the intellectual gymnastics necessary to save an extraconstitutional statute.

In *Springer v. United States* (1880), the Supreme Court upheld a tax on incomes imposed during the Civil War as an excise or duty.[658] Based on this precedent, Congress added an income tax to the Wilson-Gorman Tariff of 1894, which provided for a 2 percent tax on all individual and corporate incomes but also included a $4,000 exemption for individuals. The tax on incomes was part of the progressive program to bridle big business. "The income tax," writes economic historian Robert Higgs, "was seen by proponents and opponents alike as primarily an instrument of redistribution; in the parlance of the time it was 'class legislation.'"[659] In *Pollock v. Farmers' Loan & Trust Co.* (1895), the Court reevaluated *Hylton* and *Springer* to hold that the Constitution required apportionment because the taxes imposed on personal income from real estate investments and property such as stocks and bonds were direct.[660] The initial *Pollock* opinion, which was divided evenly and vacated on reargument, shed better light on the direct-versus-indirect distinction than the final *Pollock* decision. According to Chief Justice Fuller's initial opinion, "[o]rdinarily, all taxes paid primarily by persons who can shift the burden upon some one else, or who are under no legal compulsion to pay them, are considered indirect taxes; but a tax upon property holders in respect of their estates, whether real or personal, or of the income yielded by such estates, and the payment of which cannot be avoided, are direct taxes."[661]

The *Pollock* decision was overturned in 1913 by the Sixteenth Amendment: "The Congress shall have power to lay and collect taxes on incomes, from whatever source derived, without apportionment among the several States, and without regard to any census or enumeration."

Discussion and Solutions

The Sixteenth Amendment applies only to income taxes. Thus, other direct taxes must still be apportioned. *Pollock* reexamined the *Hylton* view of direct taxation and provided a definition more congruent with original intent. This is quite relevant as progressive scholars are urging adoption of a wealth tax to reduce inequality.[662] In making constitutional arguments for the tax, they take a Hamiltonian approach and thus try to limit direct taxation to poll and land taxes. We should adhere to the *Pollock* distinction that taxes on property holders in respect of their estates, whether real or personal, or of the income yielded by such estates, are direct taxes.

SECTION 9, CLAUSE 5
NO TAX OR Duty shall be laid on Articles exported from any State.

Purpose

The wealth of the Southern states depended on their ability to export crops and sell them on the world market. To protect their trade, the delegates from those states demanded this constitutional provision.

Background and Development

Representing a state that depended on the ability to sell its staples freely on the world market, Charles Cotesworth Pinckney of South Carolina informed the Philadelphia Convention that absent a prohibition on export taxation, he would oppose any new Constitution. Similarly, his fellow South Carolinian Pierce Butler "was strenuously opposed to a power over exports[] as unjust and alarming to the staple States."[663] George Mason of Virginia observed that the commercial states of the North "have an interest different from the five" Southern states and could use their superior numbers to stifle free trade.[664]

Elbridge Gerry of Massachusetts agreed with the Southerners on the export taxation issue. He did not trust Congress with such a power because "[i]t might be exercised partially, raising one [part of the country] and depressing another."[665] Gerry also feared that a power to tax exports could be used to force the staple states to grant additional powers to the general government and thus "enable the Genl Govt to oppress the States, as much as Ireland is oppressed by Great Britain."[666]

Gouverneur Morris of Pennsylvania opposed making any distinction between import and export taxes. He believed it would "be inequitable to tax imports without taxing exports."[667] James Madison did not want to prohibit Congress from taxing exports and instead suggested a supermajority requirement to enact such levies. Such a modification was rejected, six states to five.

In *United States v. IBM Corp.* (1996), the Supreme Court considered whether a tax on premiums paid to foreign insurers protecting export shipments against loss violated the Export Taxation Clause.[668] In striking the tax down, the Court observed that "our cases have broadly exempted from federal taxation not only export goods, but also services and activities closely related to the export process."[669] The Court recognized that "[a] tax on policies insuring exports is not, precisely speaking, the same as a tax on exports," but acknowledged the two were functionally similar and thus came within the scope of the Export Taxation Clause.[670]

The delegates in Philadelphia sought to relieve concerns that the commercial states would tax exports and thus disadvantage the Southern states. Hence, there is a total ban on export taxation. The federal government has asked that the Supreme Court loosen the interpretation of the clause, but so far the Court has refused.[671] The Court should continue its efforts to give the text its plain and ordinary meaning. Although the original concerns prompting the clause might have dissipated, gamesmanship with any one part of the Constitution invites similar misconduct with other parts.

SECTION 9, CLAUSE 6

NO PREFERENCE SHALL be given by any Regulation of Commerce or Revenue to the Ports of one State over those of another: nor shall Vessels bound to, or from, one State, be obliged to enter, clear, or pay Duties in another.

Purpose

Congress is prohibited from enacting regulations that give preference to one state port over another. This provision commands that state ports be treated equally and thus serves to promote harmony in the union.

Background and Development

This provision arose from concerns expressed by delegates from Maryland. Daniel Carroll and Luther Martin believed "that under the power of regulating trade the General Legislature, might favor the ports of particular States, by requiring vessels destined to or from other States to enter and clear thereat."[672] The Marylanders feared that Congress would bow to the influence of the Old Dominion and require vessels to stop in Virginia and clear customs before entering the port of Baltimore. Several suggestions to prohibit preferential treatment of states and ports were referred to a committee composed of one member from each state. The committee recommend language very similar to what was ultimately adopted.

Justice Joseph Story, in his exposition of the Constitution, observed that the provision "cuts off the power to require that circuity of voyage, which under the British colonial system, was employed to interrupt American commerce before the revolution."[673] He also noted that it prohibited Congress from regulating commerce in ways that injured the particular interests of one state. In reviewing the Port Preference Clause, the Supreme Court has interpreted it in a narrow fashion.

In *Pennsylvania v. Wheeling and Belmont Bridge Co.* (1855), the Court considered a federal statute authorizing the construction of a bridge across the Ohio River at Wheeling, Virginia [now West Virginia], which allegedly obstructed and caused losses to steamboat operators bound for Pittsburgh.[674] Pennsylvania argued that the proposed bridge amounted to giving a preference to the port of Wheeling. The Court held that even if the statute incidentally benefited Wheeling over Pittsburgh, the Port Preference Clause prevented only the granting of a direct preference to the ports of one state over those of another. The Court observed that the Constitution "seems to import a prohibition against some positive legislation by congress to this effect, and not against any incidental advantages that might possibly result from the legislation of congress upon other subjects connected with commerce, and confessedly within its power."[675]

SECTION 9, CLAUSE 7

NO MONEY SHALL be drawn from the Treasury, but in Consequence of Appropriations made by Law; and a regular Statement and Account of the Receipts and Expenditures of all public Money shall be published from time to time.

Purpose

Congress has the power of the purse; therefore, no money may be drawn from the Treasury absent appropriate legislation. Neither the president, the courts, nor the technocrats running various administrative agencies have any claim on public funds absent congressional action. To promote transparency, an accounting must be published from time to time so the people can examine the use of funds.

Background and Development

The theory behind the Appropriations Clause is traced to British constitutional history. During the 1600s, the Stuart kings went to great lengths to govern from funding sources unrelated to parliamentary appropriation. Charles I, for example, governed for approximately eleven years without summoning a parliament. He demanded forced loans from his subjects, resurrected medieval practices such as destraint of knighthood (in essence a tax on small landholders), and levied fines on subjects living on lands that at one time had been part of the royal forest. A key component of the Glorious Revolution was the establishment of full parliamentary control over fiscal matters. Nonappropriated funding sources were eliminated, and constraints were imposed on how the monarchy could use appropriated funds.

Edward S. Corwin, the great Princeton political scientist, characterized the Constitution's Appropriations Clause as "the most important single curb in the Constitution on Presidential power."[676] Fundamentally, the executive may not spend money unless it has been appropriated by direct legislative action. Because the power of the purse is connected intimately with representation, the Framers provided that revenue bills could originate only in the House (the Origination Clause previously discussed) and provided further that Congress as a whole—not the executive or judiciary—would make decisions on the spending of public funds. In *Federalist* No. 58, James Madison described Congress's power of the purse as "the most compleat and effectual weapon with which any constitution can arm the immediate representatives of the people, for obtaining redress of every grievance, and for carrying into effect every just and salutary measure."[677] At the Virginia ratifying convention, John Marshall touted Congress's power of the purse, since the power cannot be held by the people at large but required "interposition of their representatives." Who better to control the purse strings, Marshall asked, than legislative "representatives, who are accountable for their conduct?"[678]

In light of Congress's duty to the public, the Framers also required publication of an accounting of the sources and uses of public moneys from time to time. In the Virginia ratifying convention, George Mason complained that the "time to time" language was too "loose" and "might afford opportunities of misapplying the public money, and sheltering those who did it."[679] Patrick Henry similarly objected that "time to time" would allow indefinite extensions and thus the national legislature "may carry on the most wicked and pernicious of schemes under the dark veil of secrecy. The liberties of a people never were, nor ever will be, secure, when the transactions of their rulers may be concealed from them."[680] In the New York ratifying convention, Melancton Smith remonstrated "that 'from time to time' might mean from century to century, or any period of twenty or thirty years."[681]

Madison defended the provision in the Virginia ratifying convention. He believed that publication at "short, stated periods" would cause unnecessary problems because of the extensive amounts of time needed to reconcile accounts and detect errors.[682]

Distortions

After the 2008 financial crisis, Congress created the Consumer Financial Protection Bureau (CFPB) and tasked it with enforcing consumer protection laws and ensuring that all consumers have access to markets for consumer financial products. Under the Dodd-Frank Act, the CFPB is not funded through the congressional appropriations process. The CFPB receives funding directly from the Federal Reserve, and its receipt of money is not subject to review by congressional appropriations committees. Under statutory law, the Federal Reserve is directed to "transfer to the Bureau from the combined earnings of the Federal Reserve System, the amount determined by the [CFPB's] Director to be reasonably necessary to carry out the authorities of the Bureau under Federal consumer financial law, taking into account such other sums made available to the Bureau from the preceding year."[683]

As the statute indicates, Congress intentionally designed the CFPB to insulate it from Congress's budgetary oversight. This is akin to Parliament granting the monarchy a free hand in determining its financial needs—a constitutional heresy in the British system. The CFPB's unique funding system, in the view of *The Independent Guide*, is contrary to the Appropriations Clause and amounts to congressional abdication of its power of the purse.

The Supreme Court, however, does not agree with this book's analysis of the issue. In *CFPB v. Community Financial Services Association of America, Ltd.* (2024), the Court held that Congress has broad discretion in how it appropriates public money.[684] So long as Congress specifies the source and purpose of the funding, the Appropriations Clause is satisfied. Thus, by specifying the Federal Reserve as the source of funds to operate the agency, Congress satisfied its constitutional duty. In dissent, Justice Samuel Alito alleged that the majority had allowed Congress to "sign away" its duty to "monitor and control the expenditure of public funds."[685]

Discussion and Solutions

The decision in *Community Financial Services* is concerning. As noted by the Supreme Court in an earlier decision, "[t]he established rule is that the expenditure of public funds is proper only when authorized by Congress, not that public funds may be expended unless prohibited by Congress."[686] This is a sound rule and especially serves to limit the executive. The CFPB's self-funding mechanism is of questionable constitutional parentage. The Supreme Court has spoken on the matter, but its decision does not prevent Congress from reevaluating the constitutionality of the CFPB's funding. It is fiscally dangerous to insulate from appropriations oversight an agency exercising significant powers over consumer financial markets. Congress needs to rethink the blank check written to the CFPB and bring its funding back within constitutional requirements.

SECTION 9, CLAUSE 8

NO TITLE OF Nobility shall be granted by the United States: And no Person holding any Office of Profit or Trust under them, shall, without the Consent of the Congress, accept of any present, Emolument, Office, or Title, of any kind whatever, from any King, Prince, or foreign State.

Purpose

An established order of nobility is antithetical to republican government; therefore, the Framers forbade the granting of titles and the formation of artificial ranks. Always concerned about corruption, they also forbade any officer of the United States—absent the consent of Congress—from accepting any gift or title conferred by a foreign state.

Background and Purpose

In his *Commentaries*, William Blackstone opined that "[t]he distinction of rank and honours is necessary to every well-governed state."[687] Blackstone believed that individuals should be rewarded for exemplary public service and that such distinctions would spur others to emulate the holders of noble titles. In addition, Blackstone believed that in a mixed system of government such as Great Britain, the nobility was necessary for supporting the rights of the monarch and the people "by forming a barrier to withstand the encroachments of both."[688] Nobles, Blackstone wrote, "are reared from among the people" to support the monarchy and "preserve[] that gradual scale of dignity, which proceeds from peasant to the prince."[689]

Not surprisingly, the Articles of Confederation, written as the American states embraced popular sovereignty, rejected noble titles. Article VI forbade either Congress or the individual states from granting "any title of nobility."[690] An established order of nobility, most Americans agreed, was antithetical to republican government. In a letter to George Wythe penned in 1786 while serving in France, Thomas Jefferson expressed this sentiment when he suggested that "[i]f anybody thinks that kings, nobles, or priests are good conservators of the public happiness, send him here. It is the best school in the universe to cure him of that folly."[691] Such an opinion of established orders caused Jefferson and others to view organizations such as the Society of the Cincinnati with suspicion. The Society was a fraternal association of Continental Army officers founded in May 1783. Membership was hereditary, and members were permitted to wear a gold medal as a badge of distinction. The Society's skeptics worried that the creation of a preeminence by birth would eventually produce an order antithetical to republican liberty. South Carolina's Aedanus Burke predicted that the Cincinnati would create two classes of citizens: "the patricians or nobles and the rabble."[692] Ascendency of the Society's nobles, Burke feared, "would give a fatal wound to civil liberty through the world."[693]

Unsurprisingly, the Philadelphia Convention followed the Articles and prohibited the new government from granting noble titles. In discoursing on the Convention's decision to follow the Articles, St. George Tucker described this prohibition as "indispensably necessary to preserve the several states in their democratic form, tone and vigor."[694]

The Articles also forbade "any person holding any office of profit or trust under the United States, or any of them" from acquiring "any present, emolument, office or title of any kind whatever from any King, Prince or foreign State."[695] The provision was meant to prevent corruption—namely, a foreign state buying the favor of an individual serving in or working on behalf of the confederal or state governments. "Nothing can be more dangerous to any state," wrote Tucker, "than influence from without, because it must be invariably bottomed upon corruption from within."[696]

During the Confederation period, it became customary for diplomats receiving gifts to disclose them to Congress and seek permission to keep the item. For example, when Louis XVI "gifted Benjamin Franklin a snuff box bearing a royal portrait surrounded by 408 diamonds," Franklin gave the box to Congress and asked permission to retain it.[697] Congress granted the request.

The Philadelphia Convention followed the Articles and the Confederation's practice by specifically allowing the acceptance of gifts, emoluments, and so on with the consent of Congress. The consent requirement mandated disclosure, and disclosure typically defeats the purpose of bribes or other extravagant gifts.

In *Federalist* No. 22, Alexander Hamilton noted that "[o]ne of the weak sides of republics . . . is that they afford too easy an inlet to foreign corruption."[698] Hamilton believed that a commoner elevated by the votes of his fellow citizens to high office would face great temptation when presented with requests for favors from foreign governments. The Foreign Emoluments Clause is designed to promote transparency and thus to remove much of the temptation.

Distortions

The Foreign Emoluments Clause recently garnered attention when Donald J. Trump assumed the presidency in 2017. Prior to taking office, President Trump disposed of his publicly traded and liquid investments. He put his illiquid assets (for example, hotels, golf courses, and commercial properties) into a blind trust. He also resigned from all official positions with the Trump organization and turned over management of the businesses to his adult sons.

Lawsuits brought by law professors, state attorney generals, and members of Congress asserted that Trump's actions were inadequate for compliance with the Foreign Emoluments Clause. The plaintiffs argued that the Constitution was violated every time, for instance, a foreign diplomat booked a room in a Trump hotel or paid for a meal in a Trump restaurant while Trump was in the Oval Office. These lawsuits sought to force the president to sell all his holdings and to disclose his tax returns so foreign payments could be tracked.

Trump countered that the Foreign Emoluments Clause did not prohibit his companies from engaging in market transactions on the same terms as any other citizen or private business.

His lawyers pointed to early presidential practice wherein Presidents Washington, Jefferson, Madison, and Monroe all owned massive plantations and sold agricultural commodities in Europe. Undoubtedly, some of their customers were foreign governments, but no political opponent ever raised the specter that they were violating the Constitution.

This litigation was undoubtedly brought to harass a populist president and had little to do with vindicating constitutional rights. A decision on the matter was not reached during Trump's first term in office. Accordingly, the Supreme Court declared the emoluments litigation moot.

The Foreign Emoluments Clause was also raised in Trump's second administration when he expressed excitement over a Boeing 747-8 jet estimated to be worth $400 million that Qatar offered as a replacement for Air Force One. Defense Secretary Pete Hegseth accepted the gifted plane on behalf of the government. Because the plane is not a personal gift to Trump, it likely is not a violation of the Foreign Emoluments Clause. Had the plane been given to a Trump business entity or to the president as a personal gift, then a constitutional problem would exist.

Discussion and Solutions

Section 9, Clause 8 was designed to protect the republican character of our government. To the extent our citizenry no longer retains the plucky independence of their forefathers, it is not because of the creation of noble ranks by the government. The Framers could not have foreseen the rise of what James Burnham called "new men"—that is, members of the managerial class who organize and direct society through their positions in the bureaucracy, the media, and the corporate world. The managers are what Jefferson feared the Society of Cincinnati would become.

SECTION 10, CLAUSE 1

NO STATE SHALL enter into any Treaty, Alliance, or Confederation; grant Letters of Marque and Reprisal; coin Money; emit Bills of Credit; make any Thing but gold and silver Coin a Tender in Payment of Debts; pass any Bill of Attainder, ex post facto Law, or Law impairing the Obligation of Contracts, or grant any Title of Nobility.

Purpose

This clause restricts the states from infringing on Congress's war and foreign affairs powers. It is designed to prevent the actions of one state from dragging the entire union into a war or a sensitive diplomatic situation. It also restricts the states from issuing fiat currency and passing debt-relief measures that would cause injustice to creditors. Finally, the clause prohibits anti-republican actions such as granting noble titles and passing bills of attainder.

Background and Development

Under the Confederation, the states had to receive the consent of Congress before entering into a treaty and could grant letters of marque and reprisal only after Congress had declared war. The Philadelphia Convention restricted the power of the states in foreign affairs further by expressing the intent that the general government make all decisions about war and peace for the federation. Consequently, the Constitution prohibits the states from entering into long-term relationships with other powers, because those relationships could push the United States into war or some other delicate foreign policy situation. Similarly, the power to issue letters of marque and reprisal is vested in Congress alone. In discussing those matters in *Federalist* No. 44, James Madison observed that the changes were "justified by the advantage of

uniformity in all points which relate to foreign powers; and of immediate responsibility to the nation in those, for whose conduct the nation itself is to be responsible."[699]

As discussed previously, the Continental Congress's inflationary emissions of fiat money led the Philadelphia Convention to reject a federal power to issue bills of credit (that is, paper circulating as money but not redeemable in gold and silver). During the Confederation period, multiple states likewise emitted substantial sums of paper money. The results were akin to the experience of the Continental Congress with the steadily depreciating "continentals." The states of Rhode Island and North Carolina were hit especially hard by severe inflation.

Rhode Island not only issued copious quantities of paper money but also enacted criminal penalties for those who refused to accept it. Alleged violators could be tried without a jury in a special court and had no right of appeal. Rhode Island declined to send delegates to the Philadelphia Convention because it knew that efforts would be made to restrict or prohibit the issuance of fiat money.

In discussing the defects of the Confederation, Edmund Randolph of Virginia observed to the Philadelphia Convention that "the havoc of paper money had not been foreseen" by the drafters of the Articles.[700] Similarly, James Madison, in the preface to his notes on the federal convention, complained about the "internal administration of the States" where "a violation of Contracts had become familiar in the form of depreciated paper made a legal tender."[701]

The absolute prohibition on the states creating money came from James Wilson of Pennsylvania and Robert Sherman of Connecticut. They believed it would be folly to give the states any wiggle room regarding monetary policy. Nathaniel Gorham of Massachusetts objected to the absolute prohibition and suggested that requiring the consent of Congress would be sufficient to stifle the most dangerous state fiat-money projects. Sherman countered that "this is a favorable crisis for crushing paper money."[702] If the Congress permitted paper money to circulate, he feared that the currency's friends would marshal their full resources and cunning to influence national councils. Eight states agreed with Wilson and Sherman. Just one state voted in the negative, and one was divided. In light of the chaos caused by paper money, James Madison in *Federalist* No. 44 declared that "the prohibition to bills of credit must give pleasure to every citizen in proportion to his love of justice, and his knowledge of the true springs of public prosperity."[703]

The Contracts Clause is related to the prohibitions on paper money. Because of the economic downturn following the Revolutionary War, many states sought to aid debtors by enacting legislation "suspending the collection of debts, remitting or suspending the collection of taxes, providing for the emission of paper money, delaying legal proceedings, etc."[704] At the Philadelphia Convention and in the context of state debt-relief laws, Rufus King of Massachusetts urged the delegates to add language from the newly adopted Northwest Ordinance to prohibit states from interfering with private contracts. The Ordinance, of course,

acknowledged that "in the just preservation of rights and property, it is understood and declared, that no law ought ever to be made, or have force in the said territory, that shall, in any manner whatever, interfere with or affect private contracts or engagements, bona fide, and without fraud, previously formed."[705]

Gouverneur Morris of Pennsylvania complained that inserting such a provision into the Constitution "would be going too far."[706] Morris feared that King's suggestion would affect the many laws related to filing legal claims. George Mason of Virginia worried that unforeseen events might require some kind of "proper & essential" interference.[707] In his *Genuine Information*, Luther Martin of Maryland engaged the issue more directly. Martin argued that at times of public distress, it was proper for the state legislatures to pass laws interfering with contracts, closing courthouses, and authorizing debtor installment payments. Absent such measures, nothing would "prevent the wealthy creditor and moneyed man from totally destroying the poor though even industrious debtor."[708] The Convention sided with King's proposal, but the reference to "private contracts" was dropped in favor of the broader language found in the Constitution.

In the early years of the republic, the Supreme Court applied a broad interpretation to the Contracts Clause. For example, in *Fletcher v. Peck* (1810)[709] and *Dartmouth College v. Woodward* (1819),[710] the Court held that the clause was not limited to private agreements but also encompassed state charters. Although the clause was adopted with debtor-creditor relationships in mind, the Court, true to the text, has interpreted it as applying to all contracts.[711] In *Ogden v.*

Saunders (1827),[712] the Court held that the clause applied only to a state law prejudicing performance of an extant contract retroactively, but not to future contracts affected by state police power regulations (laws providing for the health, safety, and welfare of the people). In the words of Justice Bushrod Washington, state "municipal law" is "a part of the contract, and travels with it wherever the parties may be found."[713]

The prohibitions on states passing bills of attainder, ex post facto laws, and grants of noble titles rest in republican principles. Measures lacking in due process or intentionally creating an aristocracy are counter to the sense of justice that should pervade a commonwealth. In *Federalist* No. 44, Madison described such unjust measures as "contrary to the first principles of the social compact, and to every principle of sound legislation";[714] in other words, such measures have no redeeming value in a republican government. Thus, the prohibitions against them should apply equally to the states and the federal government.

An exception to this principle, however, is in the bar to state laws impairing the obligation of contracts. Elbridge Gerry of Massachusetts suggested that Congress, as well as the states, should be prevented from interfering with contracts. No delegate seconded his motion, and thus there was no discussion of Gerry's proposal.

Distortions

The demise of the Contracts Clause came in *Home Building & Loan Ass'n v. Blaisdell* (1934), in which the Court considered the Minnesota Mortgage Moratorium Law, which allowed a mortgagor in default to apply in state court for an extension of the redemption period.[715] Although such debtor relief legislation was the prime reason for the Contracts Clause, the Court held that "[t]he economic interests of the state may justify the exercise of its continuing and dominant protective power notwithstanding interference with contracts."[716] The Court crafted a reasonableness standard of review whereby the legislation must address a legitimate government end and the statutory framework must be rational "and appropriate to that end."[717] In essence, *Blaisdell* meant that banks had to carry bad debt. That undermined the economy, the banks' ability to remain open, and the ability of private parties to agree on contractual terms that would remain binding. In a vigorous dissent, Justice George Sutherland accused the majority of transforming clear provisions of the Constitution into "a mere collection of political maxims to be adhered to or disregarded according to the prevailing sentiment of the legislative or judicial opinion in respect to the necessities of the hour."[718]

Discussion and Solutions

Blaisdell should be overruled. The Framers intended the Contracts Clause to prevent debt-relief measures that deprived a creditor of the benefit of the bargain. While one can sympathize with legislators desiring to offer aid to debtors, such aid must not come at the expense of the creditor as per the clear terms of the Constitution. To embrace *Blaisdell*, in the words of Justice Sutherland, is to turn the Constitution into a collection of maxims that we can follow or disregard as the situation dictates.

SECTION 10, CLAUSE 2

NO STATE SHALL, without the Consent of the Congress, lay any Imposts or Duties on Imports or Exports, except what may be absolutely necessary for executing it's inspection Laws: and the net Produce of all Duties and Imposts, laid by any State on Imports or Exports, shall be for the Use of the Treasury of the United States; and all such Laws shall be subject to the Revision and Controul of the Congress.

Purpose

This provision is designed to promote peace and harmony among the states by placing restrictions on import and export taxes. Absent congressional approval, such taxes are prohibited, and the "net Produce" of allowable taxes is designated for federal use. Consequently, the motivations for such taxes—state revenue and commercial advantage—have been removed.

Background and Development

The Framers of the Constitution desired that the United States be a great free trade zone. Internal trade barriers caused strife among the states and threatened the stability of the union. "As early as 1779, the problems posed by interstate trade barriers had become acute enough to warrant a request by the Continental Congress urging the States 'to repeal all laws or other restrictions laid on the inland trade between the said states.'"[719] Unfortunately, the states ignored the suggestion.

James Madison was concerned about states that lacked their own deepwater ports being "taxed by their neighbors, thro whose ports, their commerce was carried on."[720] As an example, Madison described New Jersey as "a cask tapped at both ends" because of the policies of New York's harbors and the port of Philadelphia.[721] North Carolina, situated between Virginia and South Carolina, was "a patient bleeding at both arms."[722] At the Massachusetts ratifying convention, Thomas Dawes observed that "it is well known that different states now pursue different systems of duties in regard to each other" and that under the Articles "we have not secured even our domestic traffic that passes from state to state."[723] The constitutional cure for this exploitation among the states was the Import-Export Clause.

Anti-Federalists feared that the Import-Export Clause imposed improper restrictions on the states. Brutus concluded that because no state could "lay any duties, or imposts, on imports, or exports, but by consent of the Congress; and then the net produce shall be for the benefit of the United States," then the only mechanism left for a state to raise revenue was "direct taxation."[724] And because the Congress enjoyed the "power to lay and collect taxes, in any way they please," the state governments would struggle to raise money.[725] Without proper funding, Brutus believed the state governments would "dwindle away" and one consolidated government rise in their place.[726]

In the Virginia ratifying convention, George Mason observed that "[f]or forty years we have laid duties on tobacco, to defray the expenses of inspection, and to raise incidental revenue for the state."[727] He believed it "unjust and unreasonable" for Congress to have control over this practice when many members would have no background in the tobacco market and would be unfamiliar with the needs and situation in Virginia.[728]

Distortions

The Framers designed the clause to apply to domestic as well as foreign imports. Early Supreme Court decisions recognized equal treatment.[729] However, in *Woodruff v. Parham* (1868), the Supreme Court held that clause referred only to foreign trade, not domestic trade among the states.[730] Nonetheless, the Court has still struck down discriminatory state taxation of interstate commerce through its negative Commerce Clause jurisprudence (that is, because Congress is empowered to regulate interstate commerce, it follows that the states cannot discriminate against interstate commerce even if the federal government has declined to regulate a particular activity). Much of the Court's negative Commerce Clause jurisprudence is congruent with the original intent behind the Import-Export Clause, which undoubtedly applied to foreign and domestic shipments of goods. But this congruence does not cure the

fact that the Constitution contains no negative Commerce Clause. As Justice Clarence Thomas has observed, "the real Commerce Clause adopted by the People merely empowers Congress" to regulate commerce and "says nothing about prohibiting state laws that burden commerce. Much less does it say anything about authorizing judges to set aside state laws they believe burden commerce" based on some dormant power.[731] Fidelity to the written Constitution requires jettisoning such a judge-made doctrine.

Discussion and Solutions

The solution to the negative Commerce Clause issue is simple. Justice Thomas has urged his colleagues "to shed ourselves of our nontextual negative Commerce Clause and all the accompanying multifactor balancing tests we have employed, and instead merely apply what appears to me to be the relevant provision of the Constitution": the Import-Export Clause.[732] *Woodruff* should be overruled, and the Court should interpret the Import-Export Clause in the same way the Framers of the Constitution did.

SECTION 10, CLAUSE 3

NO STATE SHALL, without the Consent of Congress, lay any Duty of Tonnage, keep Troops, or Ships of War in time of Peace, enter into any Agreement or Compact with another State, or with a foreign Power, or engage in War, unless actually invaded, or in such imminent Danger as will not admit of delay.

Purpose

Matters touching upon foreign affairs such as war, formal compacts or agreements, and the use of military force belong to the general

government under the Constitution. This division of authority prevents one state from dragging the entire union into a war or dispute without the thoughtful consent of its sister states.

Background and Development

The Articles of Confederation restricted states from maintaining warships or armies, engaging in armed conflict, and entering into treaties or agreements. The intent was to prevent one state from taking action that might draw the entire union into a conflict or diplomatic imbroglio. Similar restrictions were adopted in the federal Constitution. An exception is made for a pressing danger that does not allow for close consultation with Congress.

At first blush, the prohibitions on agreements or compacts seem redundant with the provisions of Section 10, Clause 1, banning the states from entering into treaties, alliances, and confederations. A significant distinction exists, however. As St. George Tucker has noted, treaties, alliances, and confederations "relate ordinarily to subjects of great national magnitude and importance, and are often perpetual, or made for a considerable period of time."[733] Agreements and compacts, according to Tucker, touch upon "transitory or local affairs" and "cannot possibly affect any other interest but that of the parties."[734] Hence, the states may enter into these arrangements with the consent of Congress.

The Tonnage Clause prevents a state "from taxing vessels solely for the privilege of entering, trading in, or lying in a port" without congressional approval.[735] Scholars have recognized that "[i]f such duties could be levied, friction among the states might increase, and national unity might be strained."[736] The Tonnage Clause was pushed by New Hampshire's John Langdon at the Philadelphia Convention. Langdon was insistent "that the regulation of tonnage was an essential part of the regulation of trade, and that the States ought to have nothing to do with it."[737]

Distortions

Supreme Court case law has interpreted the Compact Clause to encompass two types of agreements, only one of which requires congressional approval. In *U. S. Steel Corp. v. Multistate Tax Commission* (1978), the Court held that a compact requires congressional approval if it (1) permits "the member States to exercise any powers they could not exercise in its absence," (2) transfers "sovereign power" to any agency or commission, and (3) does not permit each state to "adopt or reject the rules and regulations of the Commission."[738] In shorthand: If the compact increases a state's power vis-à-vis the federal government, then the parties should seek congressional approval. When Congress does approve an interstate agreement, it becomes binding federal law. An example of an interstate agreement not requiring congressional approval is a compact settling a boundary dispute: It is a purely local affair between states and does not augment state power relative to the federal government.

Discussion and Solutions

The Supreme Court's interpretation of the Compact Clause is one of the few instances in which the Court has improperly curtailed congressional power and given the states greater leeway. The plain words of the clause apply to all compacts and not just compacts that invade federal supremacy. The solution is obvious: a return to an interpretation that encompasses all state compacts—not just the ones the courts believe pose a risk to federal authority.

SUMMATION

Article I is the engine of the Constitution. The power of legislation—but only that delegated by the people of the several states—rests in Congress. Article I, Section 8 specifies the enumerated powers Congress may use. If a power is not delegated, then Congress may not act. This is the heart of strict construction originalism. The national government's authority, in the words of Madison, "is a grant of particular powers only, leaving the general mass in other hands."[739] Rather than engaging in constitutional gymnastics to "discover" additional authority in one of the specified powers, Congress should instead seek a constitutional amendment to honestly augment its functions. Advocates of centralization and expansive federal power have employed the Commerce Clause, the Spending Clause, and other delegated powers as catch-all grants. Consequently, Congress claims the power to dictate to farmers how many acres of wheat they may plant on private property, to command the states to spend money for purposes unrelated to the delegated powers, and to create federal agencies to micromanage our lives.

The administrative state is a creature alien to our Constitution. Congress has improperly delegated its powers to a fourth branch of government foreign to our written charter. This fourth branch generates a stream of regulations for businesses and individuals to navigate. The administrative state exercises quasi-legislative, quasi-executive, and quasi-judicial powers. But no bureaucrat appears on a ballot for the people to reject or applaud. By design, the managers who direct the administrative state are unaccountable to the ultimate sovereigns. This is anathema to republican government.

Congress and its Frankenstein monster operate outside the bounds of the Constitution. The task is to rein both in without the former suffering the fate of Dr. Frankenstein.

ARTICLE II
SECTION 1, CLAUSE 1

THE EXECUTIVE POWER shall be vested in a President of the United States of America. He shall hold his Office during the Term of four Years, and, together with the Vice President, chosen for the same Term, be elected, as follows.

Purpose

The Constitution, unlike the Articles of Confederation, established a distinct executive department. The president is vested with the authority to execute duly enacted laws of the United States. This power is separate and distinct from the legislature's lawmaking power and the judiciary's work of interpreting laws in cases and controversies.

Background and Development

Executive power, as defined by Thomas Jefferson in his draft of a constitution for Virginia, comprised "those powers only, which are necessary to execute laws (and administer the government), and which are not in their nature either legislative or judiciary."[1] Jefferson made clear that Virginia's governor would have no prerogative powers such as the British monarch exercised. Jefferson specifically noted that the governor could never declare war, erect courts, or establish offices. Jefferson's view of executive power was born in the American Revolution and meant, in the words of historian Gordon Wood, "the effectual elimination of magistracy's major responsibility for ruling the society."[2] State governors, presidents, or executive councils enforced laws promulgated by the legislatures. Their power ended there.

Political scientist M. J. C. Vile notes that the early state constitutions frequently are portrayed as providing for "weak" executives but correctly challenges that description based on separation of powers, because "a 'strong executive' is a contradiction in terms."[3] Certainly, Americans realized that the Articles of Confederation were defective because, among other reasons, no independent executive branch had been created. There was a president, but his job was to preside over the Congress. It was a ceremonial position and lacked independent authority. As the states prepared to send delegates to Philadelphia to rethink the powers of the general government, few contemplated rekindling the magistracy's responsibility for ruling the society.

At the Grand Convention, James Wilson of Pennsylvania, one of the more conservative delegates, stated that "[t]he only powers he considered strictly Executive were those of executing laws, and appointing officers, not appertaining to and appointed by the

Legislature."[4] He opined further that the Crown's prerogative powers were not "a proper guide in defining the Executive power."[5] Jefferson and Wilson, the former very Whiggish and the latter more conservative, agreed in large part on the scope and function of executive power.

From the outset, delegates in Philadelphia contemplated a separate executive department. The seventh point of the Virginia Plan resolved that "a National Executive be instituted" who would "execute the National laws" and "enjoy the Executive rights vested in Congress by the Confederation."[6] The major debate at the Philadelphia Convention was not over the existence or definition of executive power, but whether the executive should be unitary or plural. Wilson suggested a unitary executive, and John Rutledge of South Carolina was of the same mind. Rutledge "was for vesting the Executive power in a single person" because one man "would feel the greatest responsibility and administer the public affairs best."[7] Rutledge, however, made clear that the power to declare war or peace—which was vested in the Confederation Congress—should not be conferred on the executive.

Edmund Randolph of Virginia opposed a unitary executive. He believed that by considering a single person for the office, the delegates were relying improperly on the British government as a prototype and were sowing the seeds of an American monarchy. He held that the necessary characteristics of an executive department—"vigor, dispatch & responsibility"—could exist "in three men, as well as in one man."[8] Moreover, to balance the union's different interests, Randolph suggested that the "three members of the Executive . . . be drawn from different portions of the Country."[9]

Wilson believed that a plural executive would be disastrous and "foresaw nothing but uncontrouled, continued, & violent animosities" disturbing the public's business.[10] He feared that the three (or even a majority of two) executive officeholders would be unable to agree, and thus the execution of laws would be frustrated. Elbridge Gerry of Massachusetts presumed similarly that three persons would "be extremely inconvenient in many instances, particularly in military matters."[11]

Roger Sherman of Connecticut did not believe that the Constitution should mandate a one-person executive or plural executive. He thought the national legislature should have discretion to make the decision "as experience might dictate."[12] Sherman's views were shaped by his understanding that the executive is "nothing more than an institution for carrying the will of the Legislature into effect."[13]

Ultimately, by a vote of seven states to three, the delegates consented to a unitary executive.

As for the term length of the executive, proposals at the Philadelphia Convention ranged from three years to indefinitely contingent on good behavior (that is, proper and peaceable conduct like that of a typical law-abiding citizen). Intermixed with the length of the president's term was the question of reeligibility for the office. Gouverneur Morris of Pennsylvania believed that the possibility of reelection provided a "great motive" to the honest execution of duties.[14] Alexander Hamilton made a similar point in *Federalist* No. 72, when he argued that "the desire of reward is one of the strongest incentives to human conduct."[15] The possibility of reward by reelection, Hamilton believed, would encourage noble conduct. Hamilton also frowned on excluding a man from office who had invaluable experience and might be needed by the country to steer it through a crisis. No constitutional bar should be raised, Hamilton said, to the electors continuing a good man in office when a crisis was imminent.

Virginia's James McClurg was a staunch proponent of "good behavior." He believed that executive independence was akin to judicial independence and should be handled in like manner. McClurg's observations were cheered by Gouverneur Morris and Delaware's Jacob Broom.

George Mason frowned on McClurg's remarks. Mason argued that it would be "impossible to define the misbehavior in such a manner as to subject it to a proper trial."[16] He also doubted whether the executive would submit to such a trial. Mason described an executive with such a tenure as "a softer name only for an Executive for life."[17] And to install an executive for life, to Mason, left but a small step to a hereditary monarchy. If such a step toward monarchy were taken, Mason predicted that he or his children would surely live to see a war of revolution.

The Framers settled on a term of four years with reeligibility for holding office. Joseph Story described the duration of office as "adequate and satisfactory."[18] He noted that a term of four years is "a period intermediate between the term of office of the Representatives, and that of the Senators."[19]

Anti-Federalists were suspicious that the Philadelphia Convention had attempted to make the president a king. "[T]here is to be a great and mighty President," thundered Patrick Henry in the Virginia ratifying convention, "with very extensive powers—the powers of a king."[20] Rawlins Lowndes, in the South Carolina ratifying convention, lamented the impending transition to monarchy in America. He believed the transition would be easy and that "the President was the man proper for this appointment" based on the vast powers granted to him in the Constitution.[21] An Old Whig asked that someone show him "what important prerogative the King of Great-Britain is entitled to, which does not also belong to the President?"[22] Similarly, Philadelphiensis predicted that the president would "be a king to all intents and purposes, and one of the most dangerous kind too."[23]

In response to these arguments, Federalists compared the British monarch's power to the president's and concluded that Anti-Federalist fears were misplaced. Tench Coxe, writing as An American Citizen, pointed out that the president had no authority over religion, could not appoint members to the upper house, lacked the ability to prorogue Congress, and would be forced to use much of his power in cooperation with the legislature (in appointing officers and making treaties). John Stevens Jr., writing as Americanus, offered a similar list of differences and added a lack of "dangerous prerogatives . . . such as the sole power of making war and peace—making treaties, leagues, and alliances, the collection, management, and expenditure of an immense revenue."[24] He indicated that he could list additional prerogatives that were inapplicable to the American situation but declined to say more because "none of [them] . . . are invested in the President" according to the Constitution.[25]

Distortions

The Vesting Clause

From the early republic until today, citizens have disputed whether the first nine words of

Article II conveyed broad, undefinable powers to the president or whether those words simply named the executive to whom certain definite powers were delegated by other provisions of Article II. Alexander Hamilton, in his Pacificus newspaper essays, took the former approach when arguing for George Washington's presidential authority to issue the Neutrality Proclamation of 1793. Faced with yet another conflict between Great Britain and France, Washington declared that the United States would "adopt and pursue a conduct friendly and impartial towards the belligerent powers"—a wise course for the young country.[26] Although the Constitution grants Congress the power to declare war and requires the Senate's approval of any treaty, Hamilton contended that those two policy matters were specific exceptions to the universal understanding of executive power and that outside such constitutionally enshrined exceptions, the opening words of Article II vested full executive power in the president. Accordingly, the president under the rubric of executive power could conduct foreign affairs as he saw fit.

A key point for Hamilton was the different wording used in the opening words of Articles I and II. In Article I, the Constitution specifies that Congress is vested with "[a]ll legislative power *herein* granted."[27] Article II omits the words "herein granted" and simply states that the executive power is vested in the president. Hamilton argued that this difference in language meant that Congress was limited by its enumerated powers, whereas the president enjoyed full executive power "subject only to the *exceptions* and *qu[a]lifications* which are expressed in the instrument."[28] As examples of exceptions, Hamilton pointed to the Senate's role in the appointment of officers and

making treaties. He also noted that only the Senate and House together could declare war. But for these exceptions spelled out in the Constitution, Hamilton contended that such matters would belong to the president based on the common understanding of executive power. The exceptions, Hamilton urged, "are to be strictly construed—and ought to be extended no further than is essential to their execution."[29] Constitutional law scholar Robert Natelson has observed that "[n]either [Hamilton], nor any other Federalist, seems to have suggested before ratification that the first sentence of Article II was a grant, as well as a designation."[30] This theory would arise only after ratification, as Hamilton sought to shape the American presidency.

Madison, serving in the House of Representatives and writing in the newspapers as Helvidius, challenged Hamilton's expansive definition of general executive power. Madison recognized that celebrated authors such as Locke and Montesquieu had similar views of executive power as Hamilton, but pointed out that their examinations were tainted by the monarchical context. They wrote "before these subjects were illuminated by the events and discussions which distinguish a very recent period" (namely, the rise and adoption of republican government in the United States).[31] Madison denied that the making of treaties or declaring war should ever be considered as an executive power in a republic. "The natural province of the executive magistrate is to execute laws," Madison wrote, "as that of the legislature is to make laws. All his acts therefore, properly executive, must presuppose the existence of the laws to be executed."[32] In other words, for a president to "execute" a law or a treaty, it must already exist because of action in the legislative branch. Similarly, a republican declaration of war is entirely a legislative act and produces a new code for the executive to implement. Madison also pointed out that Hamilton's association of treaties and executive power was in direct contradiction to Hamilton's discourse on executive power in *Federalist* No. 75. In discussing presidential powers further, Madison focused on Article II's specific grants and accused Hamilton of attempting to import royal prerogatives into American constitutionalism.

Madison did not address Hamilton's textual argument based on the "herein granted" language in Article I. While one could argue that his silence is a concession to the strength of Hamilton's argument, we should note that the Philadelphia Convention's debates evinced no intent to have divergent vesting clauses in Articles I and II. The difference is solely a product of the Committee of Style. Both vesting clauses originally mirrored each other, but the Committee of Style added the "herein granted" language to Article I.[33]

Had Madison addressed this matter, he could have done no better than Justice James Clark McReynolds, who challenged the Hamiltonian argument in *Myers v. United States* (1926), a case that dealt with the president's powers to remove executive branch officials:

> I hardly suppose, if the words "herein granted" had not been inserted, Congress would possess all legislative power of Parliament, or of some theoretical government, except when specifically limited by other provisions. Such an omission would not have overthrown the whole theory of a government of definite powers, and destroyed the meaning and effect of the particular

enumeration which necessarily explains and limits the general phrase. When this article went to the committee on style it provided, "The legislative power shall be vested in a Congress," etc. The words "herein granted" were inserted by that committee September 12, and there is nothing whatever to indicate that anybody supposed this radically changed what already had been agreed upon. The same general form of words was used as to the legislative, executive, and judicial powers in the draft referred to the committee on style. The difference between the reported and final draft was treated as unimportant.[34]

The language of Article II's Vesting Clause and the Hamiltonian interpretation have had significant consequences in modern times. When John Yoo, who is currently a law professor at the University of California, Berkeley, served as deputy assistant attorney general, he sanctioned the torture of enemy combatants held outside the United States based, in part, on the Vesting Clause. In the infamous torture memos, Yoo wrote:

> The structure of the Constitution demonstrates that any power traditionally understood as pertaining to the executive—which includes the conduct of warfare and the defense of the nation—unless expressly assigned to Congress, is vested in the President. Article II, Section I makes this clear by stating that the "executive Power shall be vested in a President of the United States of America." That sweeping grant vests in the President the "executive power" and contrasts with the specific enumeration of the powers—those "herein"—granted to Congress in Article I.[35]

Yoo also argued that the Vesting Clause confers upon the president all the powers possessed by George III during the American Revolution. During the war on terror, Yoo's views sanctioned "enhanced interrogation techniques" such as waterboarding, which simulates an execution by drowning.

Executive Orders and Actions

According to the Department of Justice, "Executive Orders (EOs) are official documents . . . through which the President of the United States manages the operations of the Federal Government."[36] The orders are based on "the President's authority under the Constitution and statute (sometimes specified)."[37] The orders are "published in the Federal Register, and they may be revoked by the President at any time. Although Executive Orders have historically related to routine administrative matters and the internal operations of federal agencies, recent Presidents have used Executive Orders more broadly to carry out policies and programs."[38]

Executive orders have been around since the Washington administration. Indeed, one of Washington's first acts was to direct officers of the Confederation government to prepare reports on the state of American affairs. Scholars have noted that "[i]n the first years of our republic, executive orders were used primarily to regulate government employees, to transfer property among governmental departments or to establish national holidays or days of mourning."[39] Over time, they have become vehicles whereby the president usurps Congress's power to make the laws.

President Washington issued eight executive orders during his two terms in office, and his successors were similarly modest in

their use of the device.[40] This changed with the Lincoln administration and the Reconstruction presidencies. Ulysses S. Grant, for example, issued 217 executive orders during his two terms in office.[41] The numbers declined after Reconstruction but shot up to 1,081 executive orders under Theodore Roosevelt. The wartime presidencies of Woodrow Wilson and Franklin Roosevelt followed the TR pattern of substantial use of executive orders. Modern presidents typically issue several hundred executive orders during their tenure—a far cry from TR, but still a substantial number.

An example of executive usurpation is President Barack Obama's Deferred Action for Childhood Arrivals (DACA), an executive action that provided temporary protection from deportation for illegal aliens who entered the United States as children. DACA beneficiaries, approximately eight hundred thousand aliens, were also permitted to apply for driver's licenses, Social Security numbers, and work permits. DACA originated because President Obama was frustrated that Congress had not passed immigration reform to protect the so-called Dreamers from deportation. In a Rose Garden ceremony, Obama declared that it would be wrong "to expel these young people who want to staff our labs, or start new businesses, or defend our country simply because of the actions of their parents—or because of *the inaction of politicians*."[42] The decision to ignore immigration law was characterized by President Obama and his supporters as merely an act of prosecutorial discretion. Such a characterization was false.

Two years prior to DACA, when Hispanic voters pressed Obama on immigration reform, he answered them as follows: "I am president, I am not king. I can't do these things just by myself. We have a system of government that requires the Congress to work with the executive branch to make it happen. I'm committed to making it happen, but I've gotta have some partners to do it."[43] President Obama, a former constitutional law professor, earned an A for his 2010 answer but an F for the 2012 DACA program. His earlier remarks show that he knew the truth: Reform of immigration law requires congressional action. Frustrated with congressional inaction, Obama simply assumed the mantle of a king and handled the Dreamer problem himself. DACA might or might not be wise public policy—reasonable people can disagree. But honest critics must admit DACA was unconstitutional. Obama could point to no constitutional provision or statute granting him such power.

A more recent example of presidential policymaking is Donald Trump's second administration. Trump signed numerous executive orders that sought to bypass Congress's role in the federal system. One order instructed the secretary of education to "take all necessary steps to facilitate the closure of the Department of Education and return authority over education to the States and local communities."[44] The Department of Education was created by Congress in 1979. As a creature of congressional legislation, its dismantling will require a repeal of the earlier law. Although the goal of Trump's executive order is popular with many libertarians and conservatives, the means is improper and should be rejected by them.

Discussion and Solutions

Thomas Jefferson described the executive as a mere "machine erected by the constitution for the performance of certain acts according to laws of action laid down for" him.[45] This minimalist view of the presidency has been traded for something resembling kingship. Americans must reject the assertions that the Vesting Clause grants the president unenumerated executive power akin to that possessed by George III. If we do not, the result will be further untrammeled power and aggrandizement of the presidency. The practical result is a claimed power to torture enemy combatants—a decision that evinces hubris and inhumanity. Moreover, the use of executive orders to legislate rather than regulate government employees violates basic separation-of-powers principles. Unfortunately, too many members of Congress who share the president's party affiliation and policy preferences are content to grant the executive extensive powers. They should show loyalty to the Constitution rather than a results-oriented approach to presidential power.

ARTICLE II

SECTION 1, CLAUSE 2

EACH STATE SHALL appoint, in such Manner as the Legislature thereof may direct, a Number of Electors, equal to the whole Number of Senators and Representatives to which the State may be entitled in the Congress: but no Senator or Representative, or Person holding an Office of Trust or Profit under the United States, shall be appointed an Elector.

Purpose

The Electoral College grants each state the same number of votes for president as its total congressional delegation. It serves as a special congress to choose the president but does not have the deficiencies that the U.S. Congress would have if tasked to elect a president (for example, fostering an unhealthy dependency of the executive on the national legislature).

Background and Development

The Philadelphia Convention spent considerable time debating the proper method by which to choose a president. Delegates proposed election by the national legislature, the people, state chief executives, state legislatures, and the Senate. The seventh resolve of the Virginia Plan, which formed the primary basis of debate, proposed election by the national legislature. Roger Sherman of Connecticut approved that mode and favored "making him dependent on that body, as it was the will of that which was to be executed."[46] Sherman feared that an executive not beholden to the legislature would produce tyranny. Gouverneur Morris of Pennsylvania disagreed with Sherman and others supporting congressional election of the president. Morris warned that if the executive were dependent on the legislature, "they can perpetuate & support their usurpations by the influence of the tax gathers & other officers, by fleets armies &c."[47]

Dependency on the legislature, Morris concluded, was a recipe for "[c]abal & corruption."[48]

James Wilson of Pennsylvania urged election of the president by the people. He noted that several states had success with popularly elected magistrates and believed that "[t]he objects of choice in such cases must be persons whose merits have general notoriety."[49] George Mason of Virginia opposed Wilson's suggestion. Mason "conceived [that] it would be as unnatural to refer the choice of a proper character for chief Magistrate to the people, as it would, to refer a trial of colours to a blind man."[50] Mason believed that the country was too large for the people "to judge of the respective pretensions of the Candidates."[51]

Deeply opposed to the national legislature's involvement in choosing the president and sensing strong opposition to popular election, Wilson offered an alternative in which the states would be divided into districts and the voters qualified to cast ballots in House races would choose "electors of the Executive magistracy."[52] Gerry "liked the principle of" Wilson's idea but feared it would cause much angst to "the State partisans."[53] He also doubted the people had the wisdom to choose electors because they were "too little informed of personal characteristics in large districts."[54] Initially, only two states (Pennsylvania and Maryland) voted in favor of Wilson's Electoral College.

The delegates continued to struggle with the method of electing the president. Luther

Martin of Maryland sought to revive the Electoral College idea by proposing that the electors be appointed by the state legislatures rather than being chosen by the people. On its face, Martin's suggestion addressed the concerns raised by Gerry regarding the bypassing of the state legislatures and the people's lack of knowledge. Martin's plan, however, was voted down and received the support of only two states.

Division among the delegates continued, and the matter was referred to the Committee of Eleven chaired by David Brearley of New Jersey. The committee accepted an Electoral College system and suggested that "[e]ach State shall appoint in such manner as its Legislature may direct, a number of electors equal to the whole number of Senators and members of the House of Representatives."[55] While it was expected that the state legislatures would choose the electors, the clause gave the legislatures wide latitude in adopting other methods, such as popular election.

Morris explained the committee's reasoning to the Convention using six main points. First, Morris averred that "the danger of intrigue & faction" was obviated.[56] Key to that statement was the fact that the electors did not meet in one central location to enable mass lobbying. Also, the college was not a preexisting body like the Congress. Thus, political manipulators would have difficulty targeting the electors in the months before the election. Second, Morris indicated that the Electoral College removed the necessity of a single-term presidency. In a system where the president was chosen by Congress, he would be tempted to bend to the legislature's will to secure reelection. With the Electoral College, the issue of dependence on Congress was solved. Third, the system of impeachment would be more secure. If Congress chose the

president and the Senate served as the jury to hear the case, the senators would be hesitant to convict a man of their own choosing. Fourth, Morris observed that "[n]o body had appeared to be satisfied with appointment by the Legislature."[57] Although both the Virginia and New Jersey Plans contemplated that the legislature would choose the executive, multiple objections had been raised about dependency on Congress, eligibility for a second term, and the length of the single term necessitated by congressional election. The Electoral College solved all these difficulties. Fifth, many delegates were concerned about direct election by the people when many citizens would not have knowledge of continental figures. The Electoral College relieved apprehensions about popular election. In his sixth and final point, Morris cited "the indispensable necessity of making the Executive independent of the Legislature."[58] Separation-of-powers principles dictated that the president could not be a mere creature of the legislature, subject to its whims. The Electoral College ensured that the president would not be beholden to Congress, at least regarding his election.

In *Federalist* No. 68, Alexander Hamilton praised members of the Electoral College as "most capable of analyzing the qualities" of potential presidential candidates.[59] "A small number of persons," Hamilton averred, "selected by their fellow citizens from the general mass, will be most likely to possess the information and discernment requisite to so complicated an investigation."[60] The Electoral College, Hamilton explained further, avoided cabal and intrigue because it was not a "preexisting bod[y] of men who might be tampered with before hand to prostitute their votes."[61]

Members of the national legislature and persons holding office in the general government are prohibited from serving as electors. This provision was the handiwork of Rufus King and Elbridge Gerry, both of Massachusetts. Madison's *Notes* reveal no discussion of this matter—only that it passed unanimously. Joseph Story, in his exposition of the Constitution, explains that this prohibition exists for "the purpose of excluding all undue influence in the Electoral College."[62]

Anti-Federalists thought the Electoral College unnecessarily complicated and dangerous. Republicus questioned why "a free people should first resign their right of suffrage into other hands besides their own."[63] He believed that the people were the proper body to choose the president and questioned the legitimacy of the office without a popular vote. "Therefore if any people are subjected to an authority which they have not thus actually chosen—even though they may have tamely submitted to it—yet it is not their legitimate government."[64] Mercy Otis Warren, writing as a Columbian Patriot, objected that the Electoral College was "tantamount to the exclusion of the voice of the people in the choice of their first magistrate."[65] The choice of the president would be vested, not in the country's sovereigns, but "in an aristocratic junto, who may easily combine in each state to place at the head of the union the most convenient instrument for despotic sway."[66]

Distortions

The Electoral College continues to be controversial—especially after the 2016 election when Hillary Clinton won the popular vote but lost the election to Donald Trump. "I believe we should abolish the Electoral College and select our president by the winner of the popular vote, same as every other office," Clinton has said.[67] Representative Alexandria Ocasio-Cortez

(D-NY) is even more dismissive of the Electoral College: "It is well past time we eliminate the Electoral College, a shadow of slavery's power on America today that undermines our nation as a democratic republic."[68] In contrast, *The Independent Guide* argues that it would be foolhardy to eliminate the Electoral College based on sour grapes from the 2016 election.

There are many benefits of the Electoral College. For example, it encourages presidential candidates to campaign across the country and to listen to a variety of interests. They encounter Americans from different walks of life and backgrounds with very different concerns. The candidates are forced out of their comfort zones as they interact with the diverse citizenry. With a popular vote, candidates would likely focus on large urban centers such as New York City, Los Angeles, and Atlanta. They would ignore "flyover country" for the millions of votes concentrated in cities. Thus, the Electoral College encourages coalition-building and forces candidates to engage the center rather than catering only to the whims of progressive urbanites.

The Electoral College discourages fraud. There is little benefit to stuffing ballot boxes in Los Angeles, because California is solidly Democratic and extra votes could not deliver more electors to the candidate of choice. California has fifty-four electoral votes, and fraud activity cannot make that number any bigger. If there were a national popular vote, however, large urban areas would be fertile grounds for bad actors hoping to influence the total vote count. Hence, temptation to engage in fraud is lessened with the Electoral College.

Finally, the Electoral College promotes federalism. There is no such constitutional entity as "the American people." Voters act within their states when they choose representatives, senators, and presidential electors. The United States is a federation that allows for great diversity in the community of states. The Electoral College recognizes this federative aspect and furthers the Framers' goal of establishing a representative republic rather than a democracy. This federative feature is worth keeping.

Discussions and Solutions

Americans must resist the siren songs of a national popular vote. The Electoral College is an inventive way for choosing a president that emphasizes the federative nature of the union. It allows the larger states such as California and Florida to have a significant role in presidential elections without rendering the smaller states irrelevant. While the AOCs of the country would prefer that presidential candidates listen only to the progressives of large urban centers, the Electoral College requires that candidates consider a multitude of viewpoints. The Electoral College should be embraced and protected.

SECTION 1, CLAUSE 3

THE ELECTORS SHALL meet in their respective States, and vote by Ballot for two Persons, of whom one at least shall not be an Inhabitant of the same State with themselves. And they shall make a List of all the Persons voted for, and of the Number of Votes for each; which List they shall sign and certify, and transmit sealed to the Seat of the Government of the United States, directed to the President of the Senate. The President of the Senate shall, in the Presence of the Senate and House of Representatives, open all the Certificates, and the Votes shall then be counted. The Person having the greatest Number of Votes shall be the President, if such Number be a Majority of the whole Number of Electors appointed; and if there be more than one who have such Majority, and have an equal Number of Votes, then the House of Representatives shall immediately chuse by Ballot one of them for President; and if no Person have a Majority, then from the five highest on the List the said House shall in like Manner chuse the President. But in chusing the President, the Votes shall be taken by States, the Representation from each State having one Vote; A quorum for this Purpose shall consist of a Member or Members from two thirds of the States, and a Majority of all the States shall be necessary to a Choice. In every Case, after the Choice of the President, the Person having the greatest Number of Votes of the Electors shall be the Vice President. But if there should remain two or more who have equal Votes, the Senate shall chuse from them by Ballot the Vice President.

Purpose

The Framers set forth detailed instructions on the mechanics of choosing a president through the Electoral College. This provision instructs the electors on meeting, voting, and transmitting the ballots. It further instructs on the counting of ballots and what to do if a candidate does not garner a majority of ballots.

Background and Development

The Constitution directs that the electors meet in their respective states to cast ballots. Each elector must vote for two persons, one of whom is not an inhabitant of the elector's state. The Framers believed that a dispersion of electors rather than one central meeting place in the union would prevent malevolent forces from influencing the choice of a president. By requiring at least one vote for a person from another state, the Framers sought to prevent the electors from simply favoring friends and colleagues from their own jurisdictions.

Under this clause, each state's electors are to draw up lists of all persons receiving votes for the presidency and the number of votes every candidate received. The certified list is then transmitted to the president of the Senate at the seat of the general government. The person with the largest number of votes, provided that the vote total represents a majority of electors appointed, becomes president. The person in second place becomes vice president. If two individuals garnering Electoral College majorities end up in a tie, then the House of Representatives, voting by states (with each state having one vote), chooses one of the two candidates as president. If no person receives a majority of electoral votes, the House voting by states chooses a president from among the top five vote recipients.

The initial report from the Brearley Committee provided that the Senate, rather than the House, would choose the president if no one candidate received a majority of electoral votes. Virginia's George Mason predicted that "nineteen times in twenty the President would be chosen by the Senate."[69] He opined further that the Senate was "an improper body for the purpose."[70] Charles Pinckney of South Carolina agreed that the Senate on most occasions would choose the president. In a system without political parties, Pinckney and others believed that the electors would cast votes for local or regional figures rather than a continental figure. He also complained that "the same body of men which will in fact elect the President [are] his Judges in case of an impeachment."[71] Many other delegates expressed reservations about the Senate's role and feared that the upper house would become a ruling aristocracy. Roger Sherman of Connecticut suggested that the House would be a more appropriate body for choosing a president, and his motion passed by a substantial majority—ten states to one. Before the House can act in a tied presidential election, two-thirds of the state delegations in the House must be present.

The person who was the runner-up in the electoral vote becomes vice president. If two or more runners-up tie, the Senate is tasked with choosing the vice president.

Distortions

Section 1, Clause 3 was repealed in 1804 by ratification of the Twelfth Amendment. The Framers of the Constitution did not foresee the rise of national political parties. Indeed, they associated parties with "factions." During the debate on the Constitution, Madison described a faction as "a number of citizens, whether amounting to a majority or minority of the whole, who are united and actuated by some common impulse of passion, or of interest, adverse to the rights of other citizens, or to the permanent and aggregate interests of the community."[72]

Alexander Hamilton's financial plan, the French Revolution, and disputes over foreign policy led to the rise of political parties in the United States. The Federalist Party of Hamilton championed commercial interests, a pro-British foreign policy, and a liberal interpretation of the Constitution to energize the new government. The Republican Party of Jefferson and Madison championed agriculture, a pro-French foreign policy, and an interpretation of the Constitution meant to limit national power. To use the terms of British political discourse, the Federalists were a "Court" party, determined to expand the ambit of the new government, while Republicans were a "Country" party, ever on guard against the slightest hint of corruption or usurpation of power.

Once George Washington retired from public service and the Federalist and Republican parties wrestled for control of the national government, serious flaws were exposed in the constitutional mechanism for choosing a president and vice president. In the 1796 election, Federalist John Adams won seventy-one electoral votes to Republican Thomas Jefferson's sixty-eight. Jefferson became Adams's vice president, and tensions mounted because the two men held irreconcilable views of constitutional construction, foreign policy, and the development of the United States.

In the next presidential election, matters became more complicated. Despite a bitter campaign and Federalist assertions that a vote for Jefferson was a "sin against God," Jefferson and Aaron Burr (who was viewed by Republicans as their vice presidential candidate) tied, with seventy-three electoral votes each. Adams received sixty-five electoral votes, and Charles Pinckney (viewed by the Federalists as Adams's vice presidential candidate) received sixty-four. The tie between Jefferson and Burr could have been avoided had one

elector cast his vote for someone other than Burr. But electors feared that the election would be close, and Republican electors thus were understandably skittish about throwing away votes. The tie resulted in the presidential election being thrown to the House of Representatives. Federalists in the House were determined to prevent a Jefferson presidency and therefore cast their votes for Burr to prevent Jefferson from receiving the votes of a majority of the states. Deadlock ensued for multiple votes. The tide turned when Republican Samuel Smith informed Federalist leaders that Jefferson was not inclined to dismiss Federalist members of the civil service for political reasons. Upon hearing that news, James Bayard, Delaware's sole representative, urged his fellow Federalists to relent. On the thirty-sixth ballot, Federalist congressmen from Maryland and Vermont declined to vote, an act that shifted these two states toward Jefferson's column. South Carolina and Delaware abstained, and Jefferson was elected to the presidency.

Discussion and Solutions

The elections of 1796 and 1800 exposed serious flaws in the Framers' method for electing a president. The Framers did not envision the rise of political parties and the difficulties that Section 1, Clause 3 would present with elections and governance. Fortunately, the troubles were solved by the Twelfth Amendment, which was ratified in 1804 and required electors to designate a president and vice president. (Contentions in the 2020 election about the extent of the vice president's power to resolved disputed electoral votes will be addressed under the section on the Twelfth Amendment.)

ARTICLE II

SECTION 1, CLAUSE 4

THE CONGRESS MAY determine the Time of chusing the Electors, and the Day on which they shall give their Votes; which Day shall be the same throughout the United States.

Purpose

The Framers reasoned that if all electors in the separate states voted on the same day, the risk of intrigues and conspiracies in electing a president would be reduced. Hence, the Constitution delegates to Congress the time of choosing electors and when they meet to cast ballots.

Background and Development

Under the Constitution, all electors must vote at separate locations (state capitals) on the same day, but Congress may set a time for the choosing of electors. Discoursing on the benefits of this provision at the Philadelphia Convention, Gouverneur Morris of Pennsylvania observed: "As the Electors would vote at the same time throughout the U.S. and at so great a distance from each other, the great evil of cabal was avoided. It would be impossible to corrupt them."[73]

In commenting on the provision in the North Carolina ratifying convention, James Iredell averred that voting on the same day would "prevent the danger of influence" and political intrigues.[74] "Had the time of election been different in different states," Iredell continued, "the electors chosen in one state might have gone from state to state, and conferred with the other electors, and the election might have been carried under undue influence."[75]

In 1845, Congress declared that the first Tuesday after the first Monday in November to be the uniform date on which the states appoint their electors. The November Tuesday was selected "because it came after the fall harvest but before the weather got bad enough in much of the country to restrict travel."[76] Tuesday was chosen over Monday so Christians could observe the Sabbath on Sunday and avoid traveling to the polls.

Under federal law, electors meet in their respective states to cast ballots on the Monday following the second Wednesday of December.

SECTION 1, CLAUSE 5

NO PERSON EXCEPT a natural born Citizen, or a Citizen of the United States, at the time of the Adoption of this Constitution, shall be eligible to the Office of President; neither shall any Person be eligible to that Office who shall not have attained to the Age of thirty five Years, and been fourteen Years a Resident within the United States.

Purpose

The eligibility requirements for the presidency ensure that the president is mature in years, familiar with the American situation because of residency, and tied to the destiny of the country through citizenship.

Background and Development

The Constitution establishes three eligibility criteria for the office of the presidency: age (thirty-five years or older), residency (fourteen years a resident within the United States), and citizenship (natural-born or naturalized at the time the Constitution was adopted).

Joseph Story praised the age requirement because "solid wisdom and experience" were needed to carry out the duties of the executive department.[77] A person in the "middle age of life," Story asserted, would have developed "character and talents" and lost the "passions of youth."[78] Modern Americans often do not appreciate that attaining the age of thirty-five was a significant achievement in 1787. Life expectancy for white males in the United States was thirty-eight years at the time the Constitution was drafted. Thus, a person meeting the age requirement in the early years of the republic had lived a long life.

As for the residency requirement, the Framers wanted the president to have a firm attachment to the United States and an appreciation for American political principles. A thirty-five-year-old candidate would have resided in the United States for a substantial fraction of his life. The Framers expected that such a period would "purge" attachments or habits foreign to the American character. The fourteen-year period likely can be calculated cumulatively rather than consecutively. An early draft of the residency provision prohibited someone serving as president "who has not been in the whole, at least 14 years a resident."[79] The deletion of "in the whole," scholars argue, "was not intended to alter the provision's meaning."[80] Practice supports such an interpretation. For example, Herbert Hoover ran for the presidency in 1928, when he had not been a resident for fourteen consecutive years because he had been working in Europe organizing food relief programs in connection with World War I and its aftermath. But when his residency was measured cumulatively, Hoover met the requirement.

To be eligible for the presidency, a candidate must be a natural-born citizen or have held U.S. citizenship at the time the Constitution was adopted. Undue foreign influence concerned the Framers. For example, during the Philadelphia Convention, John Jay wrote George Washington and urged that "a strong check to the admission of Foreigners into the administration of our national Government" be incorporated in the Constitution.[81] Jay also urged that no one but a "natural born citizen" should ever have command of the American army.[82] Jay and others feared that wealthy European nobles could settle in the United States and use their riches to buy supporters and offices. The most desirable office would be that of chief executive officer for the general government.

Who is a natural-born citizen? According to constitutional law scholar Lawrence B. Solum, "[t]here is general agreement on the core of its meaning. Anyone born on American soil whose parents are citizens of the United States is a natural born citizen."[83] Moreover, "[a]nyone whose citizenship is acquired after birth as a result of naturalization is not a natural born citizen."[84] To understand the term "natural-born citizen" thoroughly, we must resort to English common law, because "[t]he language of the Constitution cannot be interpreted safely except by reference to the common law and to British institutions as they were when the instrument was framed and adopted."[85]

In his *Commentaries*, Blackstone observes that "[t]he first and most obvious division of the people is into aliens and natural-born subjects. Natural-born subjects are such as are born within the dominions of the crown of England, that is, within the ligeance, or as it is generally called, the allegiance of the king; and aliens, such as are born out of it."[86] The idea of allegiance was critical to Blackstone; he stressed that "[n]atural allegiance is such as is due from all men born within the king's dominion immediately upon their birth."[87] The bonds of natural allegiance, Blackstone taught, were strong and based on "a debt of gratitude" for the king's protection to subjects born within his dominions.[88] Blackstone did recognize an exception for the children of ambassadors and other ministers who were serving the Crown abroad. In sum, "under common law, 'natural born' meant born within the protection of the monarch (and thus, as a natural matter, owing allegiance to the person who provided protection)."[89] Madison affirmed this common-law understanding in a speech to the House representatives in 1789: "It is an established maxim that birth is a criterion of allegiance. Birth . . . derives its force sometimes from place, and sometimes from parentage; but . . . place is the most certain criterion; it is what applies in the United States."[90]

Distortions

Activists complain that under the Constitution, "over 20 million American citizens are excluded from this part of the American Dream if they would like to become President, because one must be a natural-born citizen of the United States to do so."[91] They grumble that "[o]ut of the G7 countries (Canada, France, Germany, Italy, Japan, the United Kingdom, and the United States), the United States is the only of these wealthy democracies with the natural-born citizen requirement to run as a candidate in an election to be the Head of Government or Head of State."[92] Activists call for Supreme Court intervention or a constitutional amendment.

The Framers did not share the modern fixation on equality of outcomes. They had real concerns about foreign influence and took the modest step to require that the president be a natural-born citizen. Issues of dual loyalty pose real concerns; the Founders took a practical step to ensure that dual loyalty did not despoil the executive branch.

While today it seems unlikely that a European noble would move to the United States and embark upon a program of purchasing friends and offices, dangers still exist. Europeans are less the concern than those from anti-republican countries such as China, Russia, and the oil-rich nations of the Middle East. We should not make it easier for foreign governments to infiltrate the highest office in the land.

Discussion and Solutions

In our history, forty-five men have held the office of president. The fact that 20 million Americans are prevented from the remote possibility of holding the presidency should cause no loss of sleep. Foreign-born Americans can serve in the House, Senate, Supreme Court, and other powerful offices within the general government. The three eligibility requirements for the presidency set forth in the Constitution are reasonable and should be perpetuated. Americans should oppose calls for a constitutional amendment or the Supreme Court to "redefine" what it means to be a natural-born citizen.

Section 1, Clause 6

In Case of the Removal of the President from Office, or of his Death, Resignation, or Inability to discharge the Powers and Duties of the said Office, the Same shall devolve on the Vice President, and the Congress may by Law provide for the Case of Removal, Death, Resignation or Inability, both of the President and Vice President, declaring what Officer shall then act as President, and such Officer shall act accordingly, until the Disability be removed, or a President shall be elected.

Purpose

The Framers ensured that the executive branch would continue to function and have an identifiable leader if the sitting president died, resigned, or was otherwise unable to carry out the duties of office. After one of those events, the powers and duties of the presidency devolve on the vice president.

Background and Development

Most Americans cannot imagine a presidential system without a vice president to assume the reins of power if something happened to the president. Interestingly, neither the Virginia Plan nor the New Jersey Plan contemplated a vice president. The office was not created until the waning days of the Convention and is something of a fluke related to the original structure of the Electoral College. The Committee of Eleven feared that electors would favor candidates from their own states when voting for president. Accordingly, the committee proposed that each elector would cast equal, undesignated votes for two persons. Only one of the two candidates could be from the elector's home state. The committee reasoned that electors would be forced to vote for at least one person from another state, and this person would likely be a continental figure.

Creation of the office of vice president provided, in the words of Pepperdine's Edward J. Larson, a more "principled explanation . . . for giving each elector two votes for President."[93] Delegates could explain to the people that the two-vote mechanism existed because electors were choosing two officeholders: a president and vice president. Such an explanation sounded much better than telling folks it was a trick to counteract local biases. "Therefore, the Committee decided that the candidate receiving the second-highest number of votes (even if they came from a minority of the electors) would hold a new office of Vice President."[94]

Vice presidential succession is logical—especially when considering the Electoral College as designed by the Philadelphia Convention. The vice president would be the "runner-up" in presidential voting and thus be a man of continental reputation and honor. Indeed, giants such as John Adams and Thomas Jefferson served as vice presidents under the original system.

Does Section 1, Clause 6 confer the office of president on the vice president or just presidential duties? The vagueness of this provision was exposed when President William Henry Harrison died on April 2, 1841, and John Tyler, Harrison's vice president, declared himself the new president.[95] Some questioned Tyler's actions and argued that he had only become the acting president. The powers and duties of the presidency, they argued, devolved on him but not the office itself. Congress accepted Tyler's presidential claim and thus established the precedent that the office, rather than just its functions, transfers to the vice president when the presidency is vacant.

The provision also allows Congress to establish an order of succession beyond the vice president as head of the executive branch. The Constitution is silent on what would happen if, say, a terrorist bombing killed both the president and vice president. Hence, Congress must have the power to provide for someone else to run the executive branch. The second Congress enacted the first Succession Act in 1792. Under that statute, the Senate's president pro tempore, followed by the Speaker of the House, would succeed if the vice president were incapacitated or otherwise unable to serve. The Act required a special election to fill the vacancy unless it occurred late in the last full year of a presidential term. Congress also required the Senate's president pro tempore and the House's Speaker to meet the constitutional requirements of age, residency, and citizenship.

The succession law was changed after President James A. Garfield died from an assassin's bullet in 1881. At the time of his death, the offices of president pro tempore and Speaker were vacant because the newly elected House had not yet convened and partisan bickering prevented the Senate from electing a president pro tempore. The Succession Act of 1886 removed the Speaker and president pro tempore from the order of succession and replaced them with cabinet officers "in the chronological order in which their departments were created, provided they had been duly confirmed by the Senate and were not under impeachment by the House."[96]

We currently are governed by the Presidential Succession Act of 1947, which provides that "if both the presidency and vice presidency are vacant, the Speaker succeeds, acting as president (after resigning the speakership and House seat). If there is no Speaker, or if the Speaker does not qualify, the president pro tempore succeeds, acting as president under the same requirements."[97] President Harry Truman suggested that Congress enact those changes because he believed that it would be more appropriate for elected officials to serve as president than unelected cabinet officials.

The Constitution also provides that the duties of the presidency will devolve to the vice president when the president suffers a disability. At the Philadelphia Convention, Delaware's John Dickinson asked, "What is the extent of the term 'disability' & who is to be the judge of it?" No one could answer his question. The problem Dickinson detected was highlighted with the assassination of President Garfield, who lingered seventy-nine days before expiring. Garfield "was unconscious or suffering hallucinations" for much of the time, but because of disagreements among cabinet officials, "Vice President Chester Arthur refused to become Acting President, and the Secretary of State ran the government."[98]

The uncertainties presented by Clause 6 largely have been addressed by the Twenty-Fifth Amendment, which was ratified on February 10, 1967. The amendment addresses the transition of power if a president is unfit or unable to serve. It also specifies the process for selecting a new vice president in the case of a vacancy.

Section 1, Clause 7

The President shall, at stated Times, receive for his Services, a Compensation, which shall neither be encreased nor diminished during the Period for which he shall have been elected, and he shall not receive within that Period any other Emolument from the United States, or any of them.

Purpose

So that candidates who are not wealthy may seek the presidency, the Constitution provides that the president shall be paid for his services. Congress may not increase or reduce a president's salary while he is serving a term of office. This prevents Congress from exerting improper influence over the executive.

Background and Development

The Virginia Plan provided a salary for the nation's chief executive, but such compensation was opposed by Pennsylvania's Benjamin Franklin. The wizened statesman argued that the two passions that drive men are ambition and avarice. When the two are separated, passions can drive men to positive pursuits; however, when joined, they produce "the most violent effects" and attract selfish individuals who lack a noble concern for the people.[99] Combining stature and monetary gain in the presidency, Franklin feared, would cause dishonorable men to seek the office. Alexander Hamilton of New York seconded the motion, but only as a gesture of esteem for Franklin. Madison's *Notes* indicate that the motion "was treated with great respect, but rather for the author of it, than from any apparent conviction of its expediency or practicability."[100] The Framers believed that reasonable compensation was necessary to prevent limiting the office to the very rich.

In addition to offering compensation, Clause 7 prohibits Congress from increasing or reducing it during the president's term of office. In *Federalist* No. 73, Hamilton explained that giving Congress a power over the salary of a sitting president "could render him as obsequious to their will."[101] Congress could "reduce him by famine, or tempt him by largesse, to surrender at discretion his judgment to their inclinations."[102]

On a motion of Franklin and John Rutledge of South Carolina, the Framers also prohibited the president, while in office, from receiving "any other Emolument" from the states. That provision prevents the states from corrupting a president by offering money or other things of value to support or oppose a particular legislative agenda.

The issue of the Domestic Emoluments Clause arose when Ronald Reagan assumed the presidency in 1981. As the retired governor of California, Reagan received vested retirement benefits from the Golden State. Some commentators questioned whether the pension constituted a prohibited emolument. In a written opinion, the Office of Legal Counsel (OLC) at the Department of Justice concluded that Reagan's receipt of state retirement checks did not violate the Constitution. OLC focused on the facts that the benefits resulted from public service that had terminated six years before he became president and were vested under state law, and that California could not deprive Reagan of his pension legally. Those findings indicated that the state had no leverage over President Reagan, and thus his receipt of benefits did not fall within the intended purposes of the Domestic Emoluments Clause.

SECTION I, CLAUSE 8

BEFORE HE ENTER on the Execution of his Office, he shall take the following Oath or Affirmation:—"I do solemnly swear (or affirm) that I will faithfully execute the Office of President of the United States, and will to the best of my Ability, preserve, protect and defend the Constitution of the United States."

Purpose

An oath of office solemnizes the occasion and impresses upon the executive that he will answer for any misdeeds, if not to the people, then ultimately to God. The Constitution does not specify who administers the oath, but typically the chief justice of the Supreme Court does so on Inauguration Day when the president is sworn into office.

Background and Development

The Committee of Detail originated the presidential oath. Initially, the oath was short: " I ____ solemnly swear,—or affirm,—that I will faithfully execute the office of President of the United States."[103] Virginians George Mason and James Madison moved to add "and will to the best of my judgment and power preserve protect and defend the Constitution of the U.S."[104] The only recorded discussion is a remark by James Wilson of Pennsylvania that "the general provision for oaths of office, in a subsequent place, rendered the amendment unnecessary."[105] The amendment passed with seven states voting in the affirmative.

An oath was a serious matter at the time of the Constitution's framing. For example, the Westminster Confession of Faith, well-known to the colonists as a systematic exposition of Reformed theology, explains that "[a] lawful oath is a part of religious worship, wherein, upon just occasion, the person swearing solemnly calleth God to witness what he asserteth, or promiseth, and to judge him according to the truth or falsehood of what he sweareth."[106] The Confession further instructs that "[t]he name of God only is that by which men ought to swear, and therein it is to be used with all holy fear and reverence. Therefore, to swear vainly, or rashly, by that glorious and dreadful Name; or, to swear at all by any other thing, is sinful, and to be abhorred."[107] "Whosoever taketh an oath ought duly to consider the weightiness of so solemn an act," the Confession continues, "and therein to avouch nothing but what he is fully persuaded is the truth."[108]

One might interject that the presidential oath mentions nothing about God. Such an assertion is correct but ignores the precedent set by George Washington. When Washington took the oath of office, he ensured that a Bible was present and added the words "so help me God." Northwestern's James E. Pfander notes that "So Help Me God has been a regular feature of the event ever since, an outcome that would not have surprised the precedent-conscious first president."[109] He further observes that "[i]n a real sense, then, we have a religious oath of office as a result of a constitutional amendment adopted through the precedent-setting action of the nation's first chief executive."[110]

Distortions

Some presidents have cited the oath's language as a source of additional powers. Lincoln, for example, contended that his duty to "preserve, protect and defend the Constitution of the United States" sanctioned his suspension of habeas corpus—a power clearly belonging to Congress and not the president.

(Lincoln's unconstitutional suspension of the Great Writ is discussed in conjunction with Article I, Section 9, Clause 2.) "The fact that the President takes an oath 'to preserve and protect' the Constitution," Edward S. Corwin writes, "does not authorize him to exceed his own powers under the Constitution on the pretext of preserving and protecting it."[111] The presidential oath is not a well of implied powers that can be drawn from as necessary.

Discussion and Solutions

Americans must reject claims by the executive that the oath of office is a source of power. A president who does claim additional powers is violating his oath and obviously does not care about the Almighty or the people who formed a limited government under the Constitution. Such a president should be rejected at the ballot box.

Section 2, Clause 1

The President shall be Commander in Chief of the Army and Navy of the United States, and of the Militia of the several States, when called into the actual Service of the United States; he may require the Opinion, in writing, of the principal Officer in each of the executive Departments, upon any Subject relating to the Duties of their respective Offices, and he shall have Power to grant Reprieves and Pardons for Offences against the United States, except in Cases of Impeachment.

Purpose

The Framers did not entrust the president with broad, undefined executive power. They learned from British history and their experience with George III that executive power must be circumscribed. Therefore, the powers of the president are set forth in the Constitution, with

the lion's share of them in Article II, Section 2. The Convention's work, in the words of Temple Law School's Robert J. Reinstein, "do[es] not suggest a residue of unspecified powers that can be characterized as 'executive' in nature."[112]

Background and Development

Early during the Philadelphia Convention, James Madison suggested that before the delegates chose between a unitary or plural executive, they ought to first make a decision on the extent of executive power. He suggested an enumeration to include the "power to carry into effect the national laws, to appoint to offices in cases not otherwise provided for, and to execute such other powers not Legislative nor Judiciary in their nature as may be from time to time delegated by the national Legislature."[113] No delegate objected to the idea of an enumeration, although delegates certainly had different ideas about the extent of executive power. The Committee of Detail listed the president's powers to include executing national laws, commanding the armed forces, pardoning offenders (except for impeachment), and directing military operations.[114] This idea of stated powers remained throughout the deliberations and was refined by the Committee of Style.

The chief executive serves as commander in chief of the armed forces (the army, navy, and militia when called into national service). In *Federalist* No. 69, Alexander Hamilton described this power as "amount[ing] to nothing more than the supreme command and direction of the military and naval forces, as first General and Admiral of the confederacy."[115] The Constitution's opponents objected that the president could assume personal command of military forces—even if he had no prior military experience—and that his powers resembled those of the British monarch. Supporters of the Constitution countered, in the words of North Carolina's James Iredell, that "secrecy, dispatch, and decision" were

critical to military operations and that military command "ought to be delegated to one person only."[116] The president was the natural repository of such power. Iredell pointed out further that the king has the power to declare war and to raise fleets and armies. Under the Constitution, however, those powers are delegated to Congress, thus making the office of commander in chief less likely to be abused.

The president is authorized to require written opinions from the executive department heads. That authority originated from discussions at the Philadelphia Convention about creating a council of state to advise the president. The original proposal provided that the president could "submit any matter to the discussion of the Council of State, and he may require the written opinions of any one or more of the members."[117] The Convention ultimately rejected the creation of such a body because some delegates feared that it could serve as a shield for the chief executive to hide behind rather than accept full responsibility for decisions. The Opinions Clause is a remnant of the initial proposal to create a council of state.

The power of granting pardons was first suggested by South Carolina's Charles Pinckney, who proposed that the executive "have the power to grant pardons and reprieves, except in impeachments."[118] Edmund Randolph of Virginia urged that treason cases should be excluded from the pardoning power. He especially feared that the executive "may himself be guilty" and that traitors might be his accomplices in the crime.[119] James Wilson of Pennsylvania answered by pointing out that if the president was guilty of treason, he could be impeached and removed from office. Wilson believed that the pardon power should include treason, and a substantial majority of delegates agreed; they rejected Randolph's motion.

The final wording of the pardon power limits it to offenses against the United States and thus excludes crimes under state law. A pardon and a reprieve are separate concepts. The former remits the penalties of a law violation, whereas the latter merely suspends them.

Distortions

The principal controversy concerning Section 2, Clause 1 deals with designation of the president as commander in chief. Advocates of broad presidential power, such as UC Berkeley's John Yoo, argue that the "provision confers substantive constitutional power upon the executive branch to engage military forces in hostilities."[120] The advocates of a strong commander of the nation's military forces deny that the president must secure congressional approval in the form of a declaration of war or otherwise. The only meaningful constitutional limit on presidential war-making, they argue, is Congress's power over the purse. Thus, Yoo and his colleagues argue that the president can use the military as he sees fit until Congress withdraws funding so that the military operation cannot continue.

Such an interpretation, however, renders Congress's power to declare war and issue letters of marque and reprisal as mere nullities. It also ignores the arguments advanced by influential friends of the Constitution during the debate on ratification in which they assured the people that, unlike the British monarch, the president could not push the country into war unilaterally. Congress, they told the people, controlled such decisions based on its delegated powers. (Those matters are discussed more fully under Article I, Section 8, Clause 11.) Louis Fisher, scholar in residence at the Constitution Project, contends that "[b]road definitions of the President's role as commander in chief in contemporary times would have astonished the framers, particularly when this title is meant to justify and empower the president to take offensive actions against other nations without coming first to Congress for approval."[121]

Indeed, when President George Washington was confronted with unrest between settlers and the Creek Nation, he refused to authorize military action that was not purely defensive. Washington had been advised by General Andrew Pickens to raise an army of five thousand men and to attack the Creeks residing near the Georgia border. Washington rebuffed suggestions by Pickens and others by pointing to the Constitution. Washington observed that "[t]he Constitution vests the power of declaring war with Congress; therefore no offensive expedition of importance can be undertaken until after they have deliberated upon the subject, and authorized such a measure."[122] Congress did not authorize offensive maneuvers, and consequently Washington did not make war upon the Creeks.

In 1805, the United States and Spain quarreled over the boundaries of the Louisiana Purchase. Spain asserted that Spanish Texas extended into what is modern-day Louisiana, and the United States claimed that the new American territory extended to the Rio Grande or at least the Sabine River (the border existing today between the states of Louisiana and Texas). Spain severed diplomatic relations with the United States, and the Sabine River was the location of much saber-rattling by both sides.

In December 1805, President Thomas Jefferson sent a special message to Congress in which he informed the legislature of the disputes and Spain's apparent intent to encroach on American possessions. Jefferson explained that he was informing Congress of the disturbances because "Congress alone is constitutionally invested with the power of changing our condition from peace to war."[123] Based on this constitutional design, he wrote, "I have thought it my duty to await their authority for using force in any degree which could be avoided."[124] Jefferson did take the step of instructing "the officers stationed in the neighborhood of the aggressions to protect our citizens from violence," but he looked to Congress to authorize a more aggressive posture.[125]

Abraham Lincoln and the Civil War transformed the understanding of the division of power between Congress and the chief executive in time of war. As Martin S. Sheffer, a professor emeritus of political science at Tuskegee University, has commented, "Lincoln's imaginative combining of the commander-in-chief" clause and other constitutional provisions shaped a "notion of presidential war power independent of legislative authority" that was "virtually unlimited" and "created the notion of constitutional dictatorship in the United States."[126] Lincoln's aggressive constitutional interpretation led to a suspension of habeas corpus, a blockade of southern ports, and the Emancipation Proclamation. Those actions served as precedent for Franklin Roosevelt in the months before World War II, when he "engaged in negotiations over military and foreign affairs with Great Britain, sent troops to the North Atlantic, ordered Nazi U-boats shot on sight, and declared a state of 'unlimited national emergency.'"[127]

In April 1952, President Harry Truman ordered the secretary of commerce to seize and operate the nation's steel mills. Workers were threatening to strike, and Truman worried about an interruption of steel production while American troops fought in Korea. The steel companies challenged Truman's action, and the case eventually made its way to the Supreme Court. In *Youngstown Sheet & Tube Co. v. Sawyer* (1952), the government argued that the "President was acting within the aggregate of his constitutional powers as the Nation's Chief Executive and the Commander in Chief of the Armed Forces of the United States."[128] The Court rejected that argument, averring that "we cannot with faithfulness to our constitutional system hold that the Commander in Chief of the Armed Forces has the ultimate power as such to take possession of private property in order to keep labor disputes from stopping production."[129] Congress, the Court continued, wielded such powers under the Commerce Clause, but that constitutional provision did not translate into expanded executive powers.

Discussion and Solutions

As previously discussed (under Article I, Section 8, Clause 11), Congress attempted to limit the president's claims of ultimate power over the armed forces with the War Powers Resolution in 1973. The resolution directs presidential consultation with Congress and sets forth a timetable for reporting to Congress and withdrawing troops unless Congress takes certain actions. Modern presidents deny that they must consult Congress before committing troops. While cheering the spirit of the War Powers Resolution (limiting presidential power), one must nonetheless recognize that the resolution accepts extraconstitutional executive authority over the armed forces. Congress must demand a complete return to the allocation of powers set forth in the Constitution of 1787. Our commander in chief does not possess the power to deploy the military as he sees fit. Offensive operations without congressional action are prohibited.

To counter executive overreach with the armed forces, Congress should resort to the power of the purse and exercise oversight of spending decisions. This was the norm in early American history. As noted by Boston University School of Law's Alan L. Feld, in previous decades, "[a]n appropriation bill for a department might have one line for salaries, another for office supplies, and another for rent."[130] While perhaps such minute detail is not possible in modern government, a modest shift back toward detail and oversight is needed. The modern lack of oversight gives presidents the liberty to enter conflicts with discretionary funds and leaves Congress as a mere spectator.

Section 2, Clause 2

He shall have Power, by and with the Advice and Consent of the Senate, to make Treaties, provided two thirds of the Senators present concur; and he shall nominate, and by and with the Advice and Consent of the Senate, shall appoint Ambassadors, other public Ministers and Consuls, Judges of the supreme Court, and all other Officers of the United States, whose Appointments are not herein otherwise provided for, and which shall be established by Law: but the Congress may by Law vest the Appointment of such inferior Officers, as they think proper, in the President alone, in the Courts of Law, or in the Heads of Departments.

Purpose

The direction of public policy is in the hands of elected and appointed officials. Just as the Constitution sets forth the mode of election for critical offices, it also directs who controls the appointment power: the president, with the advice and consent of the Senate. For appointment of inferior officials, Congress has discretion in deciding who (for example, the president, courts, or cabinet officers) shall make these hiring decisions. Section 2, Clause 2 also provides that in the making of treaties, the president acts with the advice and consent of the Senate.

Background and Development

The Appointment Power

At the Philadelphia Convention, Pennsylvania's James Wilson argued that appointments should be delegated to a single executive officer to promote responsibility in government. John Rutledge of South Carolina feared that such power in one man's hands would indicate the Convention's preference for monarchial government rather than the republican form. Madison objected to the executive having the sole power of appointing judges and other officers. He preferred that the Senate be delegated the authority to make important appointments.

Massachusetts's Nathaniel Gorham suggested combining the appointment power in the president and the Senate. He observed that the Bay State employed such a system in its constitution and that the arrangement had worked well. This proposal did not immediately win over a majority of delegates. They disputed over whether the executive or Senate would have a better knowledge of individuals worthy of a high appointive office. Gouverneur Morris of Pennsylvania averred that the Senate "was too numerous for the purpose; as subject to cabal: and as devoid of responsibility."[131] Some delegates doubted whether either the president or Senate would be suitable.

The delegates ultimately referred the matter of the appointment power to the Brearley Committee, which recommended, as Gorham suggested earlier, that it be shared between the president and Senate. Despite the vigor of prior debates on the appointment power, the Convention unanimously accepted the Brearley Committee's resolution.

Section 2, Clause 2 addresses directly the appointment procedure but does not mention removal. Can the president, for example, dismiss a department head, or must the president act only with the advice and consent of the Senate? In the words of James Madison writing to Thomas Jefferson, this question "gave birth to a very interesting constitutional" examination in the first Congress, with competing ideas being offered.[132] Madison reported that ultimately the view of removal triumphed, holding that "the Executive power, being generally vested in the President, and the Executive function of removal not expressly taken away, it remained with the President."[133] He further described this

"as most consonant to the text of the Constitution, to the policy of mixing the Legislative and Executive Departments as little as possible, and to the requisite responsibility and harmony of the Executive Department."[134]

Following the decision of the first Congress, the Supreme Court has held that "as a general matter" the president may "remove those who assist him in carrying out his duties"; without this removal power, the president "could not be held fully accountable for discharging his own responsibilities."[135] The Court has recognized two exceptions to the general rule for (1) multimember bipartisan commissions, whose expert members check and balance one another, and (2) inferior government officers with no policymaking duties.[136] In these limited circumstances, Congress can impose good-cause tenure provisions (that is, limiting removal to causes such as neglect of duty or malfeasance in office).

In *Seila Law LLC v. Consumer Financial Protection Bureau* (2020),[137] the Supreme Court struck down legislation providing for the Consumer Financial Protection Bureau (CFPB) to be led by a single director removable only for inefficiency, neglect of duty, or malfeasance in office. Such a director, the Court held, did not fit within the judicially recognized exceptions to the president's removal power; thus, the removal limitations violated separation-of-powers principles. "These lesser officers," the Court explained, "must remain accountable to the President, whose authority they wield."[138] Because "[t]he CFPB's single-Director structure contravenes this carefully calibrated system by vesting significant governmental power in the hands of a single individual accountable to no one," the Court detected a significant constitutional problem.[139]

The appointment of inferior officers is left to Congress. They may vest such power in the president, courts, or heads of executive branch departments. The Constitution does not define "inferior officers," but the courts have recognized "that 'inferior officers' are officers whose work is directed and supervised at some level by others who were appointed by Presidential nomination with the advice and consent of the Senate."[140] As *Seila Law* demonstrates, this congressional power over the appointment of inferior officers is not plenary.

The Treaty Power

An early draft of the Constitution placed the treaty power in the Senate. Maryland's John Francis Mercer objected because he believed that "[t]his power belonged to the Executive department."[141] Mercer supposed that Congress would have a role regardless, because "[t]reaties would not be final so as to alter the laws of the land, till ratified by the legislative authority."[142] Similar to the appointment power, the treaty power proved contentious and was settled by the Committee of Eleven's recommendation that the power to make treaties be vested in the president with the advice and consent of two-thirds of the Senate.

As observed by constitutional scholar Louis Fisher, "[t]he phrase 'advice and consent' implies that the Senate will have an opportunity to shape the content of a treaty. If it had been the intent of the framers to limit the Senate to voting yes or no to a treaty prepared exclusively by the President, the word 'advice' is superfluous and the phrase should have been reduced to a simple 'consent.'"[143] In *Federalist* No. 64, John Jay understood that the president would not simply present a treaty to the Senate for an up-or-down vote. In the

"forming" and negotiation of a treaty, Jay wrote that the president "must . . . act by the advice and consent of the senate."[144]

In preparation for negotiating a treaty with Southern Indian tribes in 1789, Washington personally visited the Senate Chamber for advice on instructions to be given to the commissioners who would meet with Indian representatives. Unfortunately, the meeting did not go well. The Senate did not want to rely on information provided by Secretary of War Henry Knox, and noise from the street made it difficult for anyone to hear the exchange. Washington believed that the trip was a waste of his time and avoided any further personal visits to discuss treaty negotiations. He resolved to deal with the Senate in writing when seeking its advice.

The two-thirds requirement for Senate approval can be traced to concerns about differing sectional interests. Those concerns were no mere specter, but evinced themselves just prior to the Philadelphia Convention during negotiations with Spain. In early 1784, Spain had closed the lower Mississippi River to American commerce, a blow to Americans migrating to the West who demanded relief. The Confederation Congress authorized John Jay to negotiate with Spanish envoy Don Diego de Gardoqui about various commercial and political matters. Jay's instructions forbade him from ceding navigation rights to the Mississippi; Gardoqui's instructions precluded him from acquiescing to American navigation of the river. Realizing that he could obtain substantial concessions for American merchants and traders (most of whom resided in the Northern states), Jay asked Congress for permission to abandon American claims to use of the Mississippi River for a period of thirty years. In a sectional vote, the Northern states voted as a block to agree to Jay's request, while all states from Maryland southward voted against altering his instructions. Although the North won the vote on instructions, no treaty would be concluded, because the Articles of Confederation required a supermajority of nine states before any treaty was adopted. The vote on instructions showed that the supermajority would be impossible to obtain.

On the mechanics of the treaty power, Anti-Federalists objected to the exclusion of the House of Representatives. The exclusion of the House smelled of aristocratic machinations. "And from this power of making treaties, the house of representatives, which has the best chance of possessing virtue, and public confidence, is entirely excluded," complained Hampden.[145] "Indeed, I see nothing to hinder the president and senate, at a convenient crisis, to declare themselves hereditary and supreme, and the lower house altogether useless, and to abolish what shadow of the state constitutions remain by this power alone."[146]

The Anti-Federalists also opposed the treaty power because they believed that the president and Senate could use treaties to override constitutional protections. This argument and modern issues related to the treaty power are addressed in connection with the Supremacy Clause and Article VI.

Distortions

Today, partly because of Washington's unsatisfactory visit to the Senate Chamber, preparations for treaty negotiations and the negotiations themselves are often handled by the executive branch alone. We must remember, however, that Washington did not exclude the Senate from the negotiation process. As Fisher has noted, "Washington continued to seek the advice of Senators, but he did that through written communications rather than personal appearances."[147] Of course, other presidents, such as Woodrow Wilson, believed that the Senate's role was to simply accept a treaty negotiated by executive branch officials. Such an attitude led to the Senate rejecting the Versailles Treaty, which President Wilson had personally negotiated to end World War I and to create the League of Nations.

Discussion and Solutions

The Constitution and common sense indicate that the president should consult with senators early on in developing instructions for officials negotiating treaties and that Senate advice should be requested throughout the treaty-making process. The idea that the executive is the sole organ in foreign negotiations is anathema to the Framers' Constitution. As Alexander Hamilton observed in *Federalist* No. 75 about the treaty power, "[t]he history of human conduct does not warrant that exalted opinion of human virtue which would make it wise in a nation to commit interests of so delicate and momentous a kind as those which concern its intercourse with the rest of the world to the sole disposal of a magistrate, created and circumstanced, as would be a president of the United States."[148]

> ## SECTION 2, CLAUSE 3
> THE PRESIDENT SHALL have Power to fill up all Vacancies that may happen during the Recess of the Senate, by granting Commissions which shall expire at the End of their next Session.

Purpose

The Framers of the Constitution did not expect the Senate to be in session most of the time. In the early republic, Senate recesses of six to nine months were common. The Recess Appointments Clause allows the executive branch to function despite the death, resignation, or removal of key appointees while the Senate is in recess.

Background and Development

The Recess Appointments Clause was suggested late in the Philadelphia Convention and was agreed to without debate.[149] Anti-Federalists objected that the clause would give the president too much power. Archibald Maclaine, in the North Carolina ratifying convention, countered that the clause was necessary for good government. "Congress are not to be sitting at all times," Maclaine explained, "they will only sit from time to time, as the public business may render it necessary. Therefore the executive ought to make temporary appointments."[150] Maclaine doubted whether any other organ of government could possess the power. "[T]he President must do this business, the North Carolinian stated, "or else it will be neglected; and such neglect may occasion public inconveniences."[151] In *Federalist* No. 67, Alexander Hamilton described the clause as a "supplement" to the regular method of appointing officials and necessary because "it would have been improper to oblige [the Senate] to be continually in session for the appointment of officers."[152]

By its clear language, the clause applies only to "Vacancies that may happen during the Recess of the Senate." In other words, a vacancy that occurs while the Senate is in session should not be filled via the Recess Appointments Clause when the Senate leaves the Capitol for a recess. Even Hamilton, never one to shy away from broad constitutional interpretations meant to energize the executive, continued to interpret the clause in a limited manner. In a discussion with the secretary of war about the possibility that President Adams could fill vacancies that happened prior to a Senate recess, Hamilton responded, "It is clear, that independent of the authority of a special law, the President cannot fill a vacancy which happens during a session of the Senate."[153]

Distortions

The Recess Appointments Clause has been abused in modern times. Presidents claim that they can make recess appointments if the Senate takes a short break. The fact that the vacancy existed long before the Senate's pause proves no deterrent. A good example of the abuse comes from January 2012 and President Barak Obama's "recess appointments" of three members of the National Labor Relations Board. In January 2012, the Senate took a break from ordinary business but continued to hold pro forma sessions every three days. Obama used the break to spring into action. The matter eventually made it to the Supreme Court.

In *N.L.R.B. v. Noel Canning* (2014), the Court disregarded the clear text of the Constitution and held that the Recess Appointments Clause applies to vacancies that occur prior to a recess.[154] The Court also interpreted "the recess of the Senate" to include breaks between the two formal sessions of the Senate ("inter-session recesses") and brief intra-session breaks that last more than ten days. The ten-day rule crafted by the Court is alien to the constitutional text and merely represents what the majority of justices believed to be reasonable. The Court invalidated three recess appointments of President Obama during a three-day adjournment of the Senate, holding that a three-day interval was too brief to allow the president to take advantage of the Recess Appointments Clause.

In a separate opinion, Justice Scalia pointed out that "in the founding era, the terms 'recess' and 'session' had well-understood meanings in the marking-out of legislative time. The life of each elected Congress typically consisted (as it still does) of two or more formal sessions separated by adjournments '*sine die*,' that is, without a specified return date."[155] He would

have limited the Recess Appointments Clause to breaks between the formal sessions of the Senate and required the vacancy to have arisen during the recess. Aside from the plain language of the clause on the arising issue, Justice Scalia pointed to historical practice and understanding in the early presidential administrations that the vacancy had to occur during a Senate recess. To hold otherwise, he feared, would allow the president to nullify the Senate's role in the appointment process.

Discussion and Solutions

The Supreme Court should reconsider the *Noel Canning* decision and interpret the Recess Appointments Clause in accordance with the plain text and intentions of the Framers. A vacancy that happens during a session of the Senate is not subject to a recess appointment. Only a vacancy that occurs during a recess is permitted to be filled by the president. As for what counts as a recess, the Court should limit recess appointments to breaks between the formal sessions of the Senate. The ten-day rule crafted by the Court has no basis in the Constitution and must be rejected. Because of the length of modern Senate sessions, recess appointments should be rare events.

SECTION 3

HE SHALL FROM time to time give to the Congress Information of the State of the Union, and recommend to their Consideration such Measures as he shall judge necessary and expedient; he may, on extraordinary Occasions, convene both Houses, or either of them, and in Case of Disagreement between them, with Respect to the Time of Adjournment, he may adjourn them to such Time as he shall think proper; he shall receive Ambassadors and other public Ministers; he shall take Care that the Laws be faithfully executed, and shall Commission all the Officers of the United States.

Purpose

This provision deals primarily with the executive's relationship to Congress. Because the president is on duty throughout his term—there are no sessional breaks—the Framers expected him to have detailed information about the state and operation of the government. Therefore, the Constitution requires him to report to Congress and to recommend legislation that he believes is necessary. In case of an emergency, he can call Congress to convene. If the two houses cannot agree on the time of adjournment, he becomes the arbiter and makes the decision. Because Congress is not in continuous session, the Constitution directs that he will receive foreign ambassadors. Finally, he must faithfully execute duly enacted laws and commission officers of the United States.

Background and Development

What modern Americans know as the State of the Union address was simply known as the annual address until the twentieth century. The constitutional command to communicate information to Congress specifies no particular form or timing. Undoubtedly, the Framers believed that the president, with

an intimate involvement in administering the general government, would have access to detailed knowledge about its operation that would be helpful to Congress. In the words of St. George Tucker, "as it is indispensably necessary to wise deliberations and mature decisions, that they should be founded upon the correct knowledge of facts, and not upon presumptions, which are often false, and always unsatisfactory; the constitution has made it the duty of the supreme executive functionary, to lay before the federal legislature, a state of such facts as may be necessary to assist their deliberations on the several subjects confided to them by the constitution."[156]

Although Presidents Washington and Adams delivered annual addresses to Congress personally, Thomas Jefferson ended this practice as too much resembling a monarchical tradition. Jefferson chose to have his message sent to Congress in writing. Until the presidency of Woodrow Wilson, a written message was the standard practice of Jefferson's successors. According to political scientist Keith E. Whittington, "Woodrow Wilson began the process of converting the annual message into its modern form," taking advantage of "an opportunity to present himself as a political leader and ultimately speak over the heads of the assembled Congress to the people broadly."[157] The advent of modern mass media has ensured that every president since Franklin Roosevelt has delivered the State of the Union address in person.

In addition to communicating information to Congress, the president is charged with making policy recommendations "as he shall judge necessary and expedient." In his *View of the Constitution*, Tucker observed that because of the president's work in administering the government, he often will be one of the first to recognize deficiencies in existing laws or the need for new laws. Thus, it is appropriate for him to periodically make recommendations to Congress. His recommendations, however, carry no affirmative duty for Congress to follow them. The introduction of legislation is purely a matter for members of the legislative branch.

"[O]n extraordinary Occasions," the president can convene Congress or either house. The Framers realized that in case of an invasion or a similar emergency, the president would need to summon Congress, because the legislative branch possesses critical powers such as raising armies, maintaining a navy, and calling forth the militia. Moreover, finalizing a treaty might require expeditious Senate action and counsel the calling of a special session rather than waiting for the next formal session. Because in modern times Congress remains in session virtually year-round, the last president to convene a special session was Harry Truman in the summer of 1948. With his approval rating at 36 percent, Truman executed an effective political maneuver by calling both houses of Congress back into session and demanding that the Republican majority take action on Democratic policy initiatives.

The "do-nothing" Congress did not pass Truman-approved legislation, and Truman blamed the Republicans for the rising cost of living and uncertainty facing the nation. In November 1948—and to the surprise of many pundits—Truman won reelection by defeating Governor Thomas Dewey of New York.

The president can adjourn Congress only when an impasse between the two houses prevents agreement on the timing of adjournment. No president ever has exercised adjournment power.

The Constitution assigns the executive the duty of receiving ambassadors and other ministers. Because the Framers expected Congress to take lengthy breaks between sessions, the president was the logical choice for that task. In *Federalist* No. 69, Alexander Hamilton described the president's receiving of ambassadors as "more a matter of dignity than authority."[158] Hamilton also stated that a presidential role in diplomatic matters is "more convenient" than "convening the Legislature, or one of its branches, upon every arrival of every foreign minister."[159]

In defending President Washington's Neutrality Proclamation of 1793, however, Hamilton, writing as Pacificus, urged that the power to receive ambassadors and other foreign ministers invested the president with the power to recognize new regimes arising from revolution or other events. Hence, the chief executive may "decide the obligations of the Nation with regard to foreign Nations" because they touch the operation of treaties and other issues of international intercourse.[160] Writing as Helvidius, Madison responded that the clause in question does no more than identify "the department of government, most proper for the ceremony of admitting public Ministers, of examining their credentials, and of authenticating their title to the privileges annexed to their character by the law of nations."[161]

The Constitution directs that the president "shall take Care that the Laws be faithfully executed." According to William Rawle, who was appointed by George Washington as U.S. district attorney for Pennsylvania and later wrote a commentary on the Constitution, "[e]very individual is bound to obey the law, however objectionable it may appear to him, the executive power is not only to obey, but to execute it."[162] James Wilson interpreted this provision as giving the president "authority, not to make, or alter, or dispense with the laws, but to execute and act the laws, which were established."[163] Undoubtedly, the Take Care Clause harkened back to the principles of England's Glorious Revolution and the assertion in the English Bill of Rights that "the pretended power of suspending laws or the execution of laws by regal authority without consent of parliament is illegal."[164] The impetus behind that provision of the Bill of Rights was James II's suspension of a statutory scheme setting requirements for holding office in England. The Framers sought to ensure that the president, outside of his enumerated constitutional powers, did not attempt to set aside laws of the United States.

In the context of the modern administrative state, a debate has arisen about whether the president can ensure faithful execution of the laws when the heads of independent agencies often are removable only for cause or whether the current "doctrine surrounding removal power strikes a fragile balance between the complexities of an administrative state" and executive accountability.[165] (Article II, Section 2, Clause 2 discusses issues surrounding

the removal power.) "One main reason why the administrative agencies are said to be left 'independent'—a term that needs some real explication—of the President," writes Richard Epstein of the New York University School of Law, "is that Congress wishes to create a system whereby its own powers can be delegated in ways that do not lead to a corresponding increase in the scope of Presidential power."[166] Thus, Congress expands the scope of government—typically by using its commerce and spending powers—by creating agencies and at the same time deprives a rival branch from fully sharing in (or interfering with) the growth of government.

The Commissions Clause demands that the president commission "all" officers of the United States. A commission is an official document "empowering a person or persons to do certain acts, or to exercise the authority of an office."[167] The commission requirement, according to Joseph Story, "introduces uniformity and regularity into all the departments of the government, and furnishes an indisputable evidence of rightful appointment."[168]

Distortions

As mentioned above, the Constitution's Take Care Clause was meant to prevent the executive from mimicking the Stuart kings and their penchant for suspending statutory schemes enacted by Parliament.[169] Thus, it should be read as a restriction on executive machinations of aggrandizement. Unfortunately, it has too often been used by presidents to expand their powers. For example, Abraham Lincoln appealed to the Take Care Clause when he unilaterally suspended the writ of habeas corpus—a power the

Constitution confers on Congress in Article I. (Lincoln's suspension is discussed in conjunction with Article I, Section 9, Clause 2.) Harry Truman cited the Take Care Clause when he seized the nation's steel mills because he did not want a labor dispute to disrupt American steel production during the conflict in Korea. (Truman's action is discussed in conjunction with Article II, Section 2, Clause 2.)

Of course, the Take Care Clause can be violated when a president refuses to enforce the law. For example, when President Obama gave temporary legal status to Dreamers—illegal immigrants brought to the United States as children—he ignored the Take Care Clause, since statutory law conferred no special status and required deportation. (The DACA initiative is discussed in conjunction with Article II, Section 1, Clause 1.)

During Richard Nixon's administration, the Take Care Clause received attention because of impoundment—presidential delay or refusal to spend congressionally appropriated funds. In the last years of his administration, Nixon impounded approximately $12 billion in congressional appropriations. Nixon asserted that the president has a duty "to impound funds, and that is not to spend money, when the spending of money would mean either increasing prices or increasing taxes for all the people."[170] Congress objected that the Constitution does not contain a line-item veto and that the Take Care Clause required Nixon to follow congressional direction in spending the money. Nixon also cited the Take Care Clause as forbidding him to mechanically spend money without considering all laws and how the spending might impact other legislative goals such as reducing inflation. The Supreme Court has never ruled on

the constitutionality of impoundments,[171] but as constitutional scholar Louis Fisher has noted, "[a]lmost every court in which this issue was litigated rejected the administration's theory of inherent power not to spend appropriated funds, and in 1974 Congress passed legislation to limit the President's power over impoundment."[172]

Impoundment has been used by presidents of various political parties. Thomas Jefferson, for example, declined to spend $50,000 appropriated for gunboats to protect the Mississippi River because the Louisiana Purchase removed the specter of military conflict. Congress supported Jefferson's handling of the matter. Although the Jefferson impoundment seems commonsensical, there is a great danger in the impoundment power. Impoundment is tantamount to a suspending power, which the Take Care Clause was intended to prevent. Considering that the modern Congress is in session most of the year, a president faced with a situation like that encountered by Jefferson can easily request that Congress reconsider an appropriation. If Congress agrees there has been a change in circumstances, it can rescind the appropriation. Absent congressional action directing that the money not be spent, however, a president should with due diligence execute the law as passed by Congress.

Discussion and Solutions

When a president cites the Take Care Clause for some action that does not involve enforcing a preexisting statute, citizens should be on high alert. A power grab is underway that will have a deleterious effect on the people's rights. Similarly, when a president chooses to ignore a statute that requires execution—and there are no concerns about the statute's constitutionality—citizens should remind him that there is no suspending power in the Constitution and that the Stuart kings are not models for American government. A president who abuses the Take Care Clause should not be reelected to the executive magistracy. If the malfeasance is done in a president's final term and with the approval of his political party, voters should remove that party from power for years to come.

Section 4

The President, Vice President and all civil Officers of the United States, shall be removed from Office on Impeachment for, and Conviction of, Treason, Bribery, or other high Crimes and Misdemeanors.

Purpose

A government officer found guilty in the Senate during an impeachment proceeding must be removed from office. Such an individual is shown to be untrustworthy and dangerous to the country's welfare.

Background and Development

As discussed previously, the House of Representative may impeach (bring charges) against the president, vice president, and all civil officers of the United States for treason, bribery, and other high crimes and misdemeanors. The Senate sits as a trial court and determines whether the charges are proven. If the Senate returns a verdict against the accused, that person shall be removed from office.

A critical question concerns the limits on impeachment. Treason against the United States is defined in the Constitution as "levying War against them, or in adhering to their Enemies, giving them Aid and Comfort."[173] Bribery is not defined in the Constitution but is understood widely as "[t]he offering, giving,

receiving, or soliciting of something of value for the purpose of influencing the action of an official in the discharge of his or her public duties."[174] An interpretation issue arises with the phrase "high crimes and misdemeanors." Should the meaning be construed, as Gerald Ford once argued on the floor of the House, as "whatever a majority of the House of Representatives considers them to be at a moment in history," or should the words carry with them some other structural restriction?[175]

When considering a version of this clause that limited impeachment to treason and bribery, Virginia's George Mason objected that many "great and dangerous offenses," such as attempts to subvert the Constitution, would not be impeachable.[176] Mason urged that "maladministration" be added to the list of impeachable offenses; his motion was seconded by Elbridge Gerry of Massachusetts. Madison objected that "maladministration" was so vague that the president would serve at the pleasure of the Senate. Gouverneur Morris of Pennsylvania doubted whether a maladministration provision would ever be effective. Frequent presidential elections, he believed, would be the cure for maladministration. After Madison's and Morris's comments, Mason substituted "high crimes and misdemeanors against the State" for "maladministration.[177] The revised provision passed by a vote of 8–3. The delegates later agreed unanimously to strike the word "State" and to substitute "United States" to "remove ambiguity."[178] Eventually, the Committee on Style deleted "against the United States," and the clause assumed its present form.

The debates in Philadelphia and in the state conventions do not address the meaning of "high crimes and misdemeanors," a term of art taken from English impeachment proceedings. According to legal historian Stephen B. Presser, "'high Crimes and Misdemeanors' . . . are acts that are inconsistent with the obligations and duties of office, that involve putting personal or partisan concerns ahead of the interests of the people, and that demonstrate the unfitness of the man to the office."[179] That definition aligns with Alexander Hamilton's discussion of impeachable acts in *Federalist* No. 65: "those offenses which proceed from the misconduct of public men, or, in other words, from the abuse or violation of some public trust. They are of a nature which may with peculiar propriety be denominated POLITICAL, as they relate chiefly to injuries done immediately to the society itself."[180] Hence, high crimes and misdemeanors are not limited to acts punishable by the criminal law but extend to political acts in violation of the public trust.

Are members of Congress "civil officers of the United States" and thus subject to impeachment proceedings? In 1798, the first articles of impeachment ever returned by the House of Representatives targeted William Blount, who had served as a senator from Tennessee and was expelled by the Senate approximately six months before the House voted to impeach him. Blount's troubles related to a conspiracy to have Indians and frontiersmen attack Spanish Florida and Louisiana to facilitate the transfers of those possessions to Great Britain. The Senate ultimately ruled that it did not have jurisdiction to try Blount, but the record is unclear about why the Senate reached that conclusion. Blount's lawyers moved to dismiss the proceeding on multiple jurisdictional grounds, including that Blount no longer was a member of the Senate, senators were not civil officers of the United States, and his misdeeds were not connected to his public duties. Because the Senate never specified the grounds supporting the lack of jurisdiction, we do not know whether the upper house concluded that members of Congress are exempt from impeachment.[181] The lower house obviously did not think so when it approved the articles of impeachment.

Many intellectual heavyweights of the Founding period took for granted that members of Congress were impeachable. For example, Virginia's Edmund Randolph withheld his signature from the Constitution in part because the Senate would be forced to judge its own members in cases of impeachment. In a letter to the Virginia legislature, Randolph specifically suggested an amendment to "provid[e] a tribunal instead of the Senate for the impeachment of Senators."[182] Patrick Henry raised a similar concern at Virginia's ratifying convention: "Are members of the Senate responsible? They may try themselves, and, if found guilty on impeachment, are only to be removed from office."[183]

Distortions

Some scholars have applauded the arguments of Blount's lawyers that "the primary purpose of impeachment and disqualification under the Framers' Constitution was to check the executive and judicial branches, and thus impeachment and disqualification should not apply to legislative seats."[184] Although executive and judicial officials were foremost in the Framers' minds when considering impeachment, and Blount is the only member of Congress ever to have faced impeachment, it does not follow that members of Congress cannot be impeached. While expulsion or some other forms of discipline are more likely to be imposed on members engaging in egregious conduct, impeachment is not a constitutionally prohibited option.

Discussion and Solutions

Members of Congress do not have special standing to avoid impeachment. The Blount matter does not answer the question, because the reasons for the Senate's finding of no jurisdiction were not specified. The debates in the ratifying conventions indicate that the people believed that representatives and senators were subject to impeachment. Constitutional interpretation requires that the intent of the ratifiers controls.

SUMMATION

Article II creates and governs the presidency. The Framers designed the presidency with the intention of avoiding the expansive powers of the British monarch. The president was to be no king. Especially in the realm of foreign affairs, the president has loosed himself from the chains of the Constitution. Although Congress has the power to declare war, raise armies, and fund the military, the president treats the armed forces as his personal security force. He claims the power to commit American troops to hot spots across the globe without consulting Congress. Such claims cannot be supported under a strict construction originalism.

Just as Congress has abused its delegated powers, the president has crafted very broad interpretations of his role as commander in chief and his duty to take care that the laws be faithfully executed. President Truman's contention that he could seize and operate American steels mills is a prime example. Today, George III would feel comfortable in the Oval Office, surrounded by advisers explaining that the powers of an American president are inherently the same as those of eighteenth-century British monarchs.

We must revive true constitutional principles and the understanding that presidential power is limited to the objects enumerated in Article II. The president is not a king with a vast reservoir of power existing outside the Constitution. In designing Article II, the Framers specifically rejected the idea that the executive magistracy exists to direct and govern society. The rejected European model must not be revived.

ARTICLE III
SECTION 1

THE JUDICIAL POWER of the United States, shall be vested in one supreme Court, and in such inferior Courts as the Congress may from time to time ordain and establish. The Judges, both of the supreme and inferior Courts, shall hold their Offices during good Behaviour, and shall, at stated Times, receive for their Services, a Compensation, which shall not be diminished during their Continuance in Office.

Purpose

The Framers believed that the federal judicial power should be wielded by an independent department of government. Consequently, the Constitution establishes a judicial branch consisting of the Supreme Court and lower courts created at Congress's discretion. To ensure judicial independence, judges hold their office during good behavior and cannot have their compensation decreased while in office.

Background and Development

Most Americans take for granted that the federal courts are a separate and independent branch of government. We forget that for many years in England, the judicial power was considered a branch of the executive department. The king was the font of all justice, and judges were his agents. In the words of James I, "[a]s kings borrow their power from God, so judges from kings; and as kings are to account to God, so judges unto God and kings."[1] If the judges were presented with a question concerning the king's prerogative,

James instructed them to "deal not with it till you consult with the king or his Council."[2]

The 1701 Act of Settlement granted tenure to English judges during "good behavior," which means the proper and peaceable conduct expected of law-abiding citizens. They no longer were removable at the whim of the king. The Act of Settlement, however, did not extend to the colonies. Thus, the colonists complained in the Declaration of Independence that the king "has made judges dependent on his will alone, for the tenure of their offices, and the amount and payment of their salaries."[3]

The grievances against the king did not translate immediately into establishment of the U.S. state judiciaries as independent, coequal branches of government. For instance, in revolutionary South Carolina and New Jersey, the judiciary was not considered to be a separate and autonomous branch of government. Such arrangements surprise modern readers as violating basic separation-of-powers principles. Modern Americans, unlike the generation that lived as British subjects, do not associate judicial power with the executive branch. Moreover, since the executive branch often was synonymous with oppressive royal governors, much power gravitated toward the colonial/state legislatures. Ultimate acceptance in America of popular sovereignty (that is, the principle that all government actors are but agents of the sovereign people) assured the judiciary's place as a coequal branch of government.

Under the Articles of Confederation, judicial power was circumscribed. Congress had the power to appoint judges to "try piracies and felonies committed on the high seas" and to hear "appeals in all cases of capture."[4] When petitioned by a state in a boundary dispute, Congress could appoint judges to hear the case if the states could not agree on arbitrators. Congress itself was "the last resort on appeal" of the matter.[5] The Articles provided a similar mechanism for the settling of competing private claims based on conflicting state land grants. That was the extent of the judicial structure, however.

At the Philadelphia Convention, the Virginia Plan contemplated the creation of a national judiciary consisting "of one or more supreme tribunals, and of inferior tribunals to be chosen by the National Legislature."[6] Judges would hold office "during good behavior" and receive salaries that could not be increased or diminished while in office.[7] Once discussion began, the delegates altered the language of the proposal to provide for just one supreme court.

Selection by the national legislature proved contentious. Pennsylvania's James Wilson argued that "[i]ntrigue, partiality, and concealment were the necessary consequences" when "numerous bodies" made appointments.[8]

Madison agreed with Wilson on the unfitness of the legislature for appointing judges. He did not want to leave judicial appointments solely in the hands of the president, however, and he suggested that the involvement of the Senate would be appropriate.

Nathaniel Gorham of Massachusetts feared that the Senate, though smaller than the House, would be too numerous to make judicial appointments. He suggested that judges be appointed by the president with the advice and consent of the Senate. He observed that Massachusetts had adopted that mode of appointment and it had worked well. Wilson continued to advocate for executive power but stated that if the delegates disagreed with him, the Massachusetts model would be acceptable.

Luther Martin of Maryland and Roger Sherman of Connecticut both preferred that the power to make judicial appointments be lodged in the Senate. As representatives of the states, senators would be knowledgeable about the character and fitness of prospective federal judges. Moreover, judges should be called from myriad sections and states—something Martin and Sherman believed the Senate could accomplish better than the president.

After much more debate about the proper body, along with a decisive vote rejecting presidential control of judicial selection, it appeared that the Senate would be responsible for judicial appointments. Several compromise proposals requiring executive involvement failed. Later in the proceedings, however, the Convention asked the Committee of Eleven to resolve multiple matters, including appointments. The Committee of Eleven suggested a compromise providing that the "President . . . shall nominate and by and with the advice and consent of the Senate shall appoint . . .

Judges of the Supreme Court."[9] On September 7, 1787, the delegates accepted this language unanimously, ultimately tailoring it to apply to all federal judges.

The matter of inferior courts stirred much debate. John Rutledge of South Carolina opposed the Virginia Plan's design of creating lower federal courts. Rutledge suggested one supreme court, with state courts charged with deciding "all cases in the first instance."[10] The right to appeal to the supreme court, Rutledge argued, would be sufficient to secure uniformity and national rights. Roger Sherman of Connecticut agreed, adding that a system of federal courts would be expensive.

Madison feared that the number of appeals would become oppressive, making a system of inferior federal courts essential. Madison believed that local prejudices would make just outcomes improbable in state courts; federal trial courts insulated from such prejudices were the logical answer. John Dickinson of Delaware supported Madison and observed that creation of a national legislature counseled the creation of a national judiciary.

Ultimately, the delegates reached a compromise: Congress would be authorized to create lower federal courts but was not required to do so. Hence, Congress could choose to utilize state courts or to create a new system of courts.

The Virginia Plan prohibited increases or decreases in judicial pay. The concern was legislative dependence. The Framers did not want Congress to be able to punish judges by pay cuts for certain decisions nor to influence a decision by the prospect of a pay raise. Realizing that economic conditions were bound to change, with the possibility of inflation, recession, and other events, the delegates prohibited pay cuts but allowed for pay raises. Economic practicalities dictated that the dangers of improper salary increases could not be avoided.

The concept of service during good behavior was endorsed by both the Virginia Plan and the New Jersey Plan. As mentioned above, judicial dependence on the king's will was listed as one of the grievances against George III in the Declaration of Independence. The Framers did not want federal judges to be a servile class dependent on the will of the executive or Congress. In *Federalist* No. 78, Alexander Hamilton described good behavior as "the best expedient which can be devised in any government, to secure a steady, upright and impartial administration of the laws."[11] He also observed that such tenure "is conformable to the most approved of the state constitutions."[12]

In his *View of the Constitution*, St. George Tucker opined that the judiciary's obligation to support the Constitution "would be nugatory" without the safeguards of judicial independence built into the salary provisions and tenure for good behavior.[13] Judicial independence, Tucker observed, "is not less necessary to the liberty and security of the citizen, and his property, in a republican government than in a monarchy."[14] The danger of party spirit in the elected branches, Tucker believed, required preservation of "a calm, temperate, upright, and independent judiciary" to check the scorched-earth tactics of political parties.[15]

Anti-Federalists saw the federal judicial power as a danger. At the Philadelphia Convention, George Mason complained that the federal judiciary was "so constructed and extended, as to absorb and destroy the judiciaries of the several states."[16] Brutus believed the federal judiciary would be "independent of the people, of the legislature, and every power under heaven. Men placed in this situation will generally soon feel themselves independent of heaven itself."[17]

Federalists countered, in the words of Alexander Hamilton, that the judiciary had no say in matters of the purse or sword and thus was "the least dangerous" branch.[18] Lacking the ability to enforce its decisions, Hamilton observed that the judiciary would be forced to rely on the executive "for the efficacy of its judgments," and that would be an additional check.[19]

Distortions

Justice Story and other nationalists have argued that Article III's Vesting Clause requires the creation of lower federal courts. In *Martin v. Hunter's Lessee* (1816), Story asserted "that congress are bound to create some inferior courts, in which to vest all that jurisdiction which, under the constitution, is exclusively vested in the United States, and of which the supreme court cannot take original cognizance."[20] Story did not believe that state courts could adjudicate, for example, crimes against the United States and argued that lower federal courts were necessary to hear such cases.

Story's reasoning overlooks the compromise in the Philadelphia Convention whereby Congress was given the discretion—not the mandate—to establish lower federal courts. In light of this history, commentators observe that "it is virtually inconceivable that the phrase 'shall be vested' was intended to require the creation of lower federal courts."[21] Moreover, contrary to Story's assumption, state courts have jurisdiction to hear federal

claims and are competent to receive such jurisdiction. A strong argument exists that the Supremacy Clause requires state courts to hear cases falling under the judicial power as set forth in Article III.[22]

Modern nationalist scholars, such as Northwestern University's Steven G. Calabresi, follow in Story's footsteps and argue that the Vesting Clause of Article III confers broad judicial power rather than simply establishing a third branch of government.[23] The motive for such a contention related to Article III is the desire to unmoor executive power from the enumerations in Article II. To expand Article II's Vesting Clause consistency requires a similar interpretation for Article III's Vesting Clause. Of course, the real prize is presidential power falling under Article II. In other words, modern advocates of augmented presidential powers look for authority disconnected from the specifics set forth in the Constitution. Such advocacy promises to create uncontrollable entities. Without the particular enumeration of powers in Article II and specifications of jurisdiction in Article III, there is no yardstick by which to measure the authority of these two branches. The president and judiciary would be independent entities unfettered by the chains of the Constitution.

Discussion and Solutions

Our system of federal courts is not likely to be reduced or abandoned. We should remember, however, that these courts are not mandatory. Justice Story was wrong in his assessment of the Vesting Clause. If ever we desire systematic reform and rethink the first Congress's decision to create lower federal courts, the opening words of Article III pose no barrier. Moreover, Article III's Vesting Clause does not confer sweeping and nebulous power on the federal courts. Their powers are limited to the specifications of the Constitution. Americans should not be fooled by the clever arguments of nationalist scholars.

SECTION 2, CLAUSE 1

THE JUDICIAL POWER shall extend to all Cases, in Law and Equity, arising under this Constitution, the Laws of the United States, and Treaties made, or which shall be made, under their Authority;—to all Cases affecting Ambassadors, other public Ministers and Consuls;—to all Cases of admiralty and maritime Jurisdiction;—to Controversies to which the United States shall be a Party;—to Controversies between two or more States;—between a State and Citizens of another State,—between Citizens of different States,—between Citizens of the same State claiming Lands under Grants of different States, and between a State, or the Citizens thereof, and foreign States, Citizens or Subjects.

Purpose

The Constitution does not grant an imprecise judicial power. It specifies the types of cases that federal courts may decide. These jurisdictional grants are affirmative grants of authority. Although some of the categories are broad, the extent of the judicial power is nonetheless enumerated.

Background and Development

The judicial power extends to all cases in law and in equity arising under the Constitution, treaties, or statutory law. Historically, law and equity formed two separate court systems in England. The former was very rules-based and construed claims for relief strictly, while the latter provided more flexibility and considered matters that could not be raised at law. For example, in a contracts case at law, a litigant could not raise fraud in the inducement of the agreement but could do so in a court of equity.[24] In the words of legal scholar

Thomas O. Main, "[e]quity moderates the rigid and uniform application of law by incorporating standards of fairness and morality into the judicial process."[25]

The Report of the Committee of Detail presented to the Convention on August 6, 1787, omitted any mention of equitable jurisdiction. Samuel Johnson of Connecticut suggested that federal jurisdiction should extend to equity as well as law and thus moved to modify the text. George Read of Delaware "objected to vesting these powers in the same Court," but Johnson's motion passed.[26] Hence, the federal judiciary does not have a separate system of courts for legal and equitable remedies. We should not read too much into that institutional choice because, as legal scholar John R. Kroger has noted, "no delegates mentioned, much less discussed, the character, function, or purpose of the proposed federal equity powers."[27]

The "arising under" language occurs early in the Convention's proceedings: "That the jurisdiction of the national Judiciary shall extend to cases arising under laws passed by the general Legislature, and to such other questions as involve National peace and harmony."[28] William Samuel Johnson of Connecticut moved to insert the words "this Constitution" as part of the "arising under" clause.[29] Madison "doubted whether it was not going too far to extend the jurisdiction of the Court generally to cases arising Under the Constitution, & whether it ought not to be limited to cases of a Judiciary Nature."[30] But because the delegates agreed that Johnson's motion would extend only to cases "of a Judiciary nature," it was approved unanimously.[31] In other words, the courts could consider the Constitution in cases involving opposing parties but could not act as a roving constitutional commission.

South Carolina's John Rutledge suggested inclusion of "treaties made or which shall be made."[32] The delegates agreed unanimously. In *Owings v. Norwood's Lessee* (1809), Chief Justice Marshall observed that "[t]he reason for inserting that clause in the constitution was, that all persons who have real claims under a treaty should have their causes decided by the national tribunals. It was to avoid the apprehension as well as the danger of state prejudices."[33]

In sum, the judicial power extends to cases arising under the Constitution, statutory law, and treaties. Lawyers often refer to jurisdiction granted in those three domains as "federal question" jurisdiction.[34] The Supreme Court interpreted the phrase "arising under" in Section 2, Clause 1 so broadly that it encompasses every case wherein federal law potentially forms an ingredient of a claim.[35]

The Supreme Court has made exceptions for "political questions"—cases that raise constitutional issues but are better left to the elected branches of government. For example, in *Oetjen v. Central Leather Co.* (1918), an issue arose about the recognition of a revolutionary government in Mexico in relation to a dispute about the ownership of certain goods that had been seized during the Mexican Revolution.[36] The Court held that "[t]he conduct of the foreign relations of our government is committed by the Constitution to the executive and legislative—'the political'—departments of the government, and the propriety of what may be done in the exercise of political power is not subject to judicial inquiry or decision."[37]

In a more recent case, *Nixon v. United States* (1993), a district judge was impeached and the Senate named a committee to take testimony and receive evidence.[38] The judge asked the Supreme Court to hold that the Constitution required the full Senate to exercise these duties. The Court declined to wade into impeachment procedures and held that the matter was a political question that was better decided by the good judgment of the Senate without judicial interference.

The judicial power extends "to all Cases affecting Ambassadors, other public Ministers and Consuls." Little disagreement arose at the Philadelphia Convention that federal jurisdiction should extend to ambassadors and other foreign ministers. Even the more conservative New Jersey Plan proposed to empower the judiciary to hear "all cases touching the rights of Ambassadors."[39] In *Federalist* No. 80, Alexander Hamilton noted that federal jurisdiction over foreign emissaries has "an evident connection with the preservation of national peace."[40]

Under the Constitution, jurisdiction also extends to admiralty and maritime matters. The Confederation Congress had the authority to establish "courts for the trial of piracies and felonies committed on the high seas" and "for receiving and determining finally appeals in all cases of captures."[41] Thus, admiralty and maritime jurisdiction already resided with the federation, and little controversy surfaced about continuing that treatment in the new government. In *Chisholm v. Georgia* (1793), Chief Justice John Jay noted that admiralty and maritime jurisdiction properly was vested in the federal courts "because, as the seas are the joint property of nations, whose right and privileges relative thereto, are regulated by the law of nations and treaties, such cases necessarily belong to national jurisdiction."[42]

Federal courts have jurisdiction over any case to which the United States is a party. Chief Justice Jay noted the wisdom in that provision: When the whole union has an interest in a controversy, "it would not be equal or wise to let any one State decide and measure out the justice due to others."[43]

If "Controversies between two or more States" arise, the federal courts have jurisdiction. The Confederation Congress served as "the last resort on appeal, in all disputes and differences now subsisting, or that hereafter may arise between two or more states concerning boundary, jurisdiction, or any other cause whatever."[44] Considering that such a provision could be found in the Articles, it followed logically that jurisdiction over disputes between states would be taken up by the federal judiciary. In *Chisholm*, Chief Justice Jay opined that such jurisdiction promoted "domestic tranquility" because "the contentions of States should be peaceably terminated by a common judicatory."[45]

Federal jurisdiction applies in disputes "between a State and Citizens of another State" and "between a State . . . and foreign States,

Citizens or Subjects." The relevant clauses are referred to collectively as the Citizen-State Diversity Clauses of Article III. Those clauses provide a neutral forum for resolving disputes involving disparate parties. The Framers believed that a state government would have an unfair advantage when litigating in its own court system against outsiders.

These clauses raised the issue of sovereign immunity, "[a] judicial doctrine which precludes bringing suit against a government without its consent."[46] Do the Citizen-State Diversity Clauses operate as a waiver of sovereign immunity? In *Federalist* No. 81, Alexander Hamilton considered the question and observed that "it is inherent in the nature of sovereignty not to be amenable to the suit of an individual *without its consent*. . . . Unless, therefore, there is a surrender of this immunity in the plan of the convention, it will remain with the States and the danger intimated must be merely ideal."[47] Hamilton would never claim that sovereign immunity was surrendered in the plan of the Convention and reassured the states that they could not be sued in federal court without their consent. At the Virginia ratifying convention, Madison averred that the clauses did not grant individuals the power "to call any state into court."[48] The intended end, he continued, was that a state that sought to sue an individual had to file its lawsuit in federal court. John Marshall agreed with Madison and argued that "[i]t is not rational to suppose that a sovereign power should be dragged before a court."[49]

In sharp contrast, the Supreme Court in the 1793 *Chisholm* ruling believed it was rational to drag a sovereign power before a court. Chisholm, a citizen of South Carolina and an executor of an estate, brought suit in federal court against Georgia to recover a Revolutionary War debt. Georgia refused to answer or appear in court on the ground of sovereign immunity. The Court rejected Georgia's immunity defense and held that the Citizen-State Diversity Clauses operated as a waiver of such immunity.

The *Chisholm* decision, as noted by the Supreme Court in *Hans v. Louisiana* (1890), "created such a shock of surprise throughout the country that, at the first meeting of congress thereafter, the eleventh amendment to the constitution was almost unanimously proposed, and was in due course adopted by the legislatures of the states. This amendment, expressing the will of the ultimate sovereignty of the whole country, superior to all legislatures and all courts, actually reversed the decision of the supreme court."[50] The Eleventh Amendment provides: "The Judicial power of the United States shall not be construed to extend to any suit in law or equity, commenced or prosecuted against one of the United States by Citizens of another State, or by Citizens or Subjects of any Foreign State."

Jurisdiction extends to disputes "between Citizens of different States." That provision was adopted because the Framers thought that local courts were unlikely to be fair to an outsider when litigating against a native son. By statute, Congress routinely has limited judicial diversity jurisdiction to a certain amount in controversy. Currently, the amount in controversy must exceed $75,000.[51]

The judicial power also extends to controversies "between Citizens of the same State claiming Lands under Grants of different States." The Framers were aware of the importance of land boundaries and the disputes that could arise about them. As mentioned above,

the states delegated to the Confederation Congress the authority to decide boundary disputes. This power in the Constitution is a logical extension of that found in the Articles. In *Town of Pawlet v. Clark* (1815), Justice Story observed that "[t]he constitution intended to secure an impartial tribunal for the decision of causes arising from the grants of different states; and it supposed that a state tribunal might not stand indifferent in a controversy where the claims of its own sovereign were in conflict with those of another sovereign."[52]

Distortions

Judicial review, a subject debated hotly today, barely was mentioned at the Convention. The few references to judicial review we do have are in connection with a proposed council of revision. The eighth resolution of the Virginia Plan suggested that the executive and "a convenient number of the National Judiciary, ought to compose a Council of revision with authority to examine every act of the National Legislature before it shall operate."[53] If the council found a particular legislative act objectionable, it could veto the measure. The national legislature could override the veto if two-thirds of both houses again passed the act.

After the delegates agreed to a single executive, they turned to the proposed council of revision. Elbridge Gerry of Massachusetts objected to including the judiciary in the council because "they will have a sufficient check against encroachments on their own department by their exposition of the laws, which involved a power of deciding on their Constitutionality." Gerry continued by observing that "[i]n some States the Judges had actually set aside laws as being against the Constitution. This was done too with general approbation."[54]

Maryland's Luther Martin echoed Gerry's broad sentiments that judges—separate and distinct from the council—had the power to rule on the constitutionality of laws. "In this character" (as judicial officials), Martin noted, "they will have a negative on the laws."[55]

Rufus King of Massachusetts shared Gerry's misgivings about the composition of such a council and cited separation-of-powers concerns. "Judges ought to be able to expound the law as it should come to them," King averred, "free from the bias of having participated in its formation."[56] George Mason of Virginia, in addressing the council of revision, observed that when ruling from the bench, judges "could impede in one case only, the operation of law."[57] Sitting on the council, judges could have a say on every unjust law and affect more than just a single case.

James Wilson articulated a sweeping understanding of judicial review when he noted that "[t]he judiciary ought to have an opportunity of remonstrating against projected encroachments on the people as well as themselves."[58] He recognized, that in interpreting laws, the judges "would have an opportunity of defending their constitutional rights." In his opinion, however, that was not enough. "Laws may be unjust, may be unwise, may be dangerous, may be destructive," Wilson observed, "and yet may not be so unconstitutional as to justify the Judges in refusing to give them effect."[59] Oliver Ellsworth of Connecticut also spoke in favor of including federal judges in the council, noting that it would give more "firmness to the Executive"

and it would give an additional opportunity for the judiciary to defend itself.[60]

Despite forceful arguments for creating a council of revision composed of judges and the executive, the eighth resolution of the Virginia Plan was defeated. Without question, the delegates offering opinions on the matter seemed to have contemplated some form of judicial review of enacted legislation. When deciding an actual case or controversy, they expected the judges to strike down unconstitutional laws. The purpose of that power was twofold: for the judges to defend (1) their own constitutional authority and (2) the rights of the people.

In setting boundaries of judicial review, James Wilson articulated what we know as the doubtful-case rule.[61] A court should not negative an act of the legislature unless the act is a blatant violation of the Constitution. If any doubt about the legitimacy of a statute arises, it should be resolved in favor of the people's representatives by permitting the law to stand. Close calls are not the business of the judiciary. Wilson's remarks indicate that the Framers had some understanding of the threat of "judicial activism" and expected the judiciary to exercise its power modestly.

After the Philadelphia Convention, Alexander Hamilton in *Federalist* No. 78 offered a defense of the power of judicial review under the proposed Constitution. Hamilton began with the proposition that an act contrary to Congress's enumerated powers is void.[62] Hamilton viewed the people as the ultimate sovereigns who would be expressing their will by adopting the Constitution. The people's Constitution thus would be superior to statutory law. If Congress could pass a law outside of its delegated powers, Hamilton reasoned, it would "affirm that the deputy is greater than his principal."[63]

Hamilton focused on the fact that the proposed Constitution placed written limits on government power, something unknown under the British constitution. Those limitations, he argued, could be preserved only in "the courts of justice; whose duty it must be to declare all acts contrary to the manifest tenor of the constitution void."[64] To Hamilton, courts served as an "intermediate body between the people and the legislature . . . to keep the latter within the limits assigned to their authority."[65] This judicial power did not place the judiciary above the legislature, Hamilton averred, but rather put the people above both.

Hamilton reiterated James Wilson's stress on the doubtful-case rule. Judges should strike a law down only when an "irreconcilable variance" arose between a statute and the Constitution.[66] That interpretation suggests that the courts should act only if a duly passed law is implacably opposed to the clear meaning of the Constitution. If reasonable persons, acting in good faith, can harmonize the statute with the Constitution, no "irreconcilable variance" exists. If it is possible to square the statute and Constitution, but the judges nonetheless overturn the law, they have "substitute[d] their own pleasure to the constitutional intentions of the legislature" and thus have "exercised WILL instead of JUDGEMENT."[67]

In sum, the endorsement of judicial review as expressed by many delegates to the Philadelphia Convention and the state ratifying conventions is consistent with the evolution of sovereignty in American thinking. Under the British constitution, Parliament could make or unmake any law as it saw fit. Although courts interpreted parliamentary statutes, a court could not declare an act of Parliament void. In America, by 1787 most commentators agreed that the people possessed ultimate sovereignty. Hence, the delegates to Philadelphia and to the various state conventions understood that the courts would play a role unknown to the British system. No longer did a particular branch of government wield ultimate sovereign power. The legislative branch certainly predominated, but with a written constitution all three branches were charged with interpreting the document's contours. Hence, a form of judicial review was a natural outcome of the Revolution and was expected by the Constitution's drafters and ratifiers.

Although Chief Justice John Marshall's opinion in *Marbury v. Madison* (1803) is taught in law schools as the classic exposition and acceptance of the doctrine of judicial review, the Virginia decision in *Kamper v. Hawkins* (1793) is worth study. It is not tainted with the political gamesmanship resting at the heart of *Marbury* whereby Marshall sought to score points against the Jefferson administration. *Kamper* also provides a more cogent explanation of why judicial review is appropriate for a republic based on popular sovereignty.

In 1792, Virginia passed a statute giving state general court judges the power "of granting injunctions to stay proceedings on any judgment" obtained in the general courts and to "proceed to the dissolution or final hearing of all suits commencing by injunction."[68] An injunction is a court order prohibiting a person from taking a certain act or ordering a person to undo a wrong.[69] *Kamper* involved the constitutionality of the legislature's granting of equitable jurisdiction to the state's general court judges. At this time in American law, there was sharp distinction between legal and equitable remedies, with injunctions allotted to the equitable camp. Thus, only judges sitting in chancery courts—courts of equity—could grant injunctions and hear suits seeking injunctive remedies. Virginia followed this distinction, and until the 1792 statute, jurisdiction over suits seeking injunctive relief was reserved for the state chancery court.

Initially, Judge Spencer Roane was presented with a motion in the law courts for an injunction to stay proceedings on a judgment. Since one of the parties challenged the statute on the ground that it circumvented constitutional provisions requiring judges to be appointed by the joint ballot of both houses of legislature followed by an executive commission for good behavior, Roane adjourned proceedings so that the en banc general court could decide the case.

The matter was heard on November 17, 1793. The judges present included some of Virginia's finest legal minds: St. George Tucker, John Tyler, James Henry, Spencer Roane, and William Nelson. All five judges issued separate opinions on the propriety of judicial review and the validity of the statute. Interestingly, all five judges discoursed on the American Revolution and how Virginia and the other colonies rejected the doctrine of parliamentary sovereignty and embraced popular sovereignty. Judge Tyler (father of a future president) described parliamentary sovereignty as "an abominable insult upon the honor and good sense of our country." The only things sovereign in the commonwealth, Tyler declared, were "the God of Heaven and our constitution."[70]

Had Virginia retained parliamentary sovereignty, the judges realized that it would be unthinkable for a court to review the legislature's work. Indeed, Judge Roane observed that because of the historical limits placed on judges by parliamentary omnipotence, he initially "doubted how far the judiciary were authorized to refuse to execute a law" enacted by the legislature.[71] But because the people of Virginia were sovereign and had delegated powers to the governor, legislature, and judiciary through a written constitution, Roane realized that the people's constitution must control statutory law. "[T]he legislature," Roane wrote, "have not power to change the fundamental laws," and thus "the judiciary may and ought to adjudge a law unconstitutional and void, if it be plainly repugnant to the letter of the Constitution, or the fundamental principles thereof."[72]

Roane and his colleagues, with certain nuances in the separate opinions, held that the statute was "repugnant to the fundamental principles of the Constitution, in as much as the judges of the general court have not been balloted for and commissioned as judges in the chancery, pursuant to . . . the Constitution."[73]

In appreciating the influence of *Kamper*, we must recognize that it was not an opinion lost in dusty law reports. The case report was published in Philadelphia in 1794. The editor described the case's import as involving "the dearest rights and interests of the community, by its creating a ground of nice and critical enquiry between the legislative and judicial departments" of Virginia.[74] Believing that *Kamper* had implications outside of Virginia, the editor included a copy of the federal Constitution with the case report, because the opinions of the five judges applied "not only to the respective States, but to the co-relative departments of the federal government."[75]

Judicial review must be understood through the lens of departmentalism, which is best explained by Thomas Jefferson in his September 11, 1804, letter to Abigail Adams. In responding to Mrs. Adams's criticism of Jefferson's decision to pardon the men convicted under the Sedition Act, Jefferson averred that "nothing in the Constitution has given [the judges] a right to decide for the Executive, more than the Executive to decide for them" on the constitutionality of the Sedition Act.[76] Alluding to separation-of-powers principles, Jefferson observed that both branches "are equally independent in the sphere of action assigned to them."[77] Although he believed that the Sedition Act was unconstitutional, he conceded that "[t]he judges, believing the law constitutional, had a right to pass a sentence of fine and imprisonment."[78] Likewise, "the Executive, believing the law to be unconstitutional, was bound to remit the execution of it."[79] Jefferson summed up his understanding of the Constitution as follows: "That instrument meant that its co-ordinate branches should be checks on each other. But the opinion which gives to judges the right to decide what laws are constitutional, and what are not, not only for themselves in their own sphere of action, but for the Legislature & Executive also, in their spheres, would make the judiciary a despotic branch."[80]

Jefferson realized that the coordinate branches would occasionally disagree on matters of constitutional interpretation. Rather than any one branch having the power to decide for the others, he envisioned the people acting through the ballot box or in a convention making the final decision. As early as 1783, Jefferson believed that a convention of the people was the proper body to settle irreconcilable disputes of interpretation. In his 1783 draft of a constitution for Virginia, Jefferson provided

that any two branches of the government by a two-thirds vote in each branch could summon a constitutional convention for altering or correcting breaches of the constitution.[81] Throughout his career, Jefferson continued to believe that the people acting in convention were the final arbiters of fundamental law.[82]

Similarly, Virginia jurist Abel Upshur recognized the independence of the Supreme Court and averred that "[i]n most cases . . . no higher authority in the interpretation of the Constitution is known in our systems, and none better could be desired."[83] However, "in questions of political power, involving the rights of the States in reference to the Federal Government," Upshur denied that any branch of the federal government could be the final umpire. Like Jefferson, he believed that a state convention possessed the authority "to construe its own contracts and agreements, and to decide upon its own rights and powers."[84]

Although judicial review naturally flows from principles of popular sovereignty, judicial supremacy does not. Judicial review is the "[p]ower of courts to review decisions of another department or level of government."[85] Judicial supremacy holds that courts are the final arbiters of the meaning of the Constitution. The modern concept of judicial supremacy would shock the founding generation, including John Marshall himself. As noted by constitutional law expert Alexander Bickel, "[a]nalytically, supreme judicial autonomy is not easily reconciled with any theory of political democracy, Madisonian or majoritarian."[86]

Viewed against the backdrop of the American Revolution and the reasoning of *Kamper*, an aggrandizing interpretation of early federal cases recognizing judicial review cannot stand. *Marbury*, which will be discussed in the next section, was but a federal version of *Kamper*. It simply affirmed that the judiciary is a coequal branch of government that must consider the Constitution when presented with an actual case or controversy. To read more into *Marbury* undermines popular sovereignty and puts the Supreme Court in a position once occupied by the Stuarts and later the British Parliament. Such a view of the judicial power is antithetical to republican government.

Discussion and Solutions

Concerned citizens, when they inveigh against the usurpations of the Supreme Court, should be careful to distinguish between judicial review and judicial supremacy. The former is rooted in the American Revolution and our Constitution. The latter is hocus-pocus created by anti-republican forces who prefer the rule of elite lawyers to the elected branches of government. In understanding the role of the courts, we should turn to *Kamper* and the doubtful-case rule expressed by multiple Founding Fathers. Judicial supremacy makes the Supreme Court not a coequal branch but the dominant branch of government. This is not what our Founders intended. Had Americans desired for an artificial body to exercise ultimate power, they could have stayed in the British Empire and submitted to Parliament. At least some portion of the citizenry elected members of Parliament and could check them at the ballot box. In the case of the Supreme Court, no body of electors provides the least check.

Scholars, judges, and lawyers should renew focus on departmentalism. In this doctrine we have the promise of true separation of powers and equality among the branches of government. The Supreme Court would remain a significant institution; however, departmentalist theory would return the Court to its proper place in the constitutional system.

To make such matters clear, an explicit departmentalist amendment to the Constitution should be considered: "The three branches of the federal government—legislative, executive, and judicial—are coequal in their authority to interpret the Constitution of the United States. The final word on constitutional interpretation rests with the people of the several states as the creators of the federal Constitution."

SECTION 2, CLAUSE 2

IN ALL CASES affecting Ambassadors, other public Ministers and Consuls, and those in which a State shall be Party, the supreme Court shall have original Jurisdiction. In all the other Cases before mentioned, the supreme Court shall have appellate Jurisdiction, both as to Law and Fact, with such Exceptions, and under such Regulations as the Congress shall make.

Purpose

The Constitution sets forth the Supreme Court's power to hear cases in the first instance and in its appellate role. Congress may regulate the Court's appellate jurisdiction, but not the Court's original jurisdiction. The protection of original jurisdiction furthers the separation of powers and the Court's independence.

ARTICLE III

Background and Development

Original jurisdiction is a court's power "to consider a case in the first instance."[87] The Supreme Court has original jurisdiction in two matters: (1) cases involving ambassadors and other public ministers, and (2) disputes to which a state is a party. A court of first instance sits as a trial court, receives physical evidence, hears witness testimony, and issues a decision. The modern Supreme Court typically appoints a special master to conduct a trial and to submit a report to the justices. In earlier days, however, the members of the Court did such work themselves.

In the famed case of *Marbury v. Madison* (1803),[88] for example, the Court sat as a trial court and received evidence. The issue at bar was whether Secretary of State James Madison could withhold a commission appointing William Marbury as a justice of peace in the District of Columbia. Madison withheld the commission because Marbury was a midnight appointment made by former President John Adams as he was leaving the city after losing the presidential election to Thomas Jefferson. The Supreme Court castigated Madison for failing to deliver the commission but claimed that it could not apply the statutory remedy of issuing a writ of mandamus, which commands an official to take a particular act. The Court's power to issue the writ was granted in section 13 of the Judiciary Act of 1789. The Court held that Congress exceeded its power in "expanding" original jurisdiction to include issuance of writs of mandamus (in reality, Congress did not expand the Court's original jurisdiction but provided a tool for it to use in cases wherein jurisdiction already had been established). Chief Justice John Marshall likely adopted the

strained reading of section 13 to prevent the Jefferson administration from ignoring an order from the Supreme Court and thus diminishing the Court's prestige. Nevertheless, *Marbury* established federal judicial review and stands for the proposition that the Court's original jurisdiction is fixed by the Constitution, and Congress may not alter it by statute.

Aside from the two categories of cases mentioned, the Court has appellate jurisdiction in other matters. "The term 'appellate jurisdiction,' Chief Justice Marshall explained in *Marbury*, "is to be taken in its largest sense, and implies in its nature the right of superintending the inferior tribunals."[89] According to the Constitution, Congress has broad authority over the Court's appellate jurisdiction.

Under a plain reading of the Exceptions Clause, so long as a matter does not fall within the Court's limited grant of original jurisdiction, Congress can alter or abolish the Supreme Court's power to hear a case. The debates at the Philadelphia Convention are not extremely helpful when interpreting the Exceptions Clause. The Committee on Detail drafted the Exceptions Clause, and we do not have a record of the Committee's deliberations. Statements made during the state ratification debates support a broad reading of the clause, however.

For example, when responding to Patrick Henry's attack on the creation of the federal judiciary, friends of the Constitution in Virginia's ratifying convention pointed to the Exceptions Clause as a powerful weapon in the hands of the people's representatives. John Marshall highlighted Congress's authority over the Court's appellate jurisdiction: "Congress is empowered to make exceptions to the appellate jurisdiction, as to law and fact, of the Supreme Court. These exceptions certainly go as far as the legislature may think proper for the interest and liberty of the people."[90] Similarly, in *Federalist* No. 81, Alexander Hamilton avowed "that the supreme court will possess an appellate jurisdiction, both as to law and fact, in all cases referred to them, but subject to any exceptions and regulation which may be thought advisable."[91]

The Supreme Court read the Exceptions Clause broadly in *Ex parte McCardle* (1868),[92] which dealt with a newspaper editor who was imprisoned by federal military authorities for his criticism of Reconstruction policy. Confined under the Military Reconstruction Act of 1867, McCardle sought a writ of habeas corpus challenging his imprisonment. The lower court denied relief, and McCardle appealed to the Supreme Court. Before the Court rendered its decision, Congress repealed the statute granting the Court appellate jurisdiction to hear the case.

McCardle's lawyer argued that Congress's motive for stripping jurisdiction was improper. He pointed out that Congress simply wanted to stop the Court from deciding the case so that the policies of "radical" Reconstruction would not be hindered. He doubted further that, as a constitutional matter, Congress could tamper with the Supreme Court's jurisdiction. The Court brushed aside those concerns and denied that the justices had a power "to inquire into the motives of the legislature."[93] The Court recognized congressional power to make exceptions to appellate jurisdiction and dismissed the appeal: "It is quite clear, therefore, that this court cannot proceed to pronounce judgment in this case, for it has no longer jurisdiction of the appeal."[94]

Opponents of the Constitution were concerned about appellate jurisdiction as both to law and fact. They feared it would result in the end of jury trials in civil cases and permit a second trial of criminal cases at the appellate level. In *Federalist* No. 81, Hamilton explained that the reference to "law and fact" was meant to encompass a variety of cases, including those of a civil law nature, such as prize cases, in which reexamination of facts "might be essential to the preservation of the public peace."[95] Ultimately, concerns about jury trials and findings of fact in common-law cases were answered by the Seventh Amendment: "In Suits at common law, where the value in controversy shall exceed twenty dollars, the right of trial by jury shall be preserved, and no fact tried by a jury, shall be otherwise re-examined in any Court of the United States, than according to the rules of the common law."[96]

Distortions

Despite the Constitution's text, explanations of the text, and *McCardle*, some scholars argue that Congress cannot divest the Court of jurisdiction over broad classes of cases such as abortion or capital punishment.[97] They suggest that the Supreme Court must sign off on any "stripper act" and, when reviewing Congress's efforts, subject the legislation to strict scrutiny. Yale's Akhil Amar argues that if Congress does strip the Supreme Court's appellate jurisdiction in a class of cases, some other federal court must retain jurisdiction over those cases. He bases this argument on Article III's Vesting Clause, which he contends conferred broad judicial power rather than simply establishing a third branch of government. (The Vesting Clause is considered under Article III, Section 1.)

Discussion and Solutions

Despite the gasps of nationalists, Congress's removal of federal court jurisdiction is not uncommon. Scholars report that since the 1940s, hundreds of stripper bills have been enacted.[98] Just to give one prominent example, in 1932, Congress with the Norris-LaGuardia Act "stripped the federal courts of the power to issue injunctions in labor disputes."[99] The first section of the statute reads as follows: "No court of the United States . . . shall have jurisdiction to issue any restraining order or temporary or permanent injunction in a case involving or growing out of a labor dispute."[100]

As noted by the University of South Carolina's William J. Quirk, "[h]igh-profile" stripping proposals garner attention because such an exercise of Congress's power "contradict[s] the Court's public image that it has the last word" on all constitutional matters.[101] Claimed restrictions on exercise of congressional authority by Amar and others nullify the Exceptions Clause and seek to elevate the Court to a position of ultimate sovereignty in the American system. We should resist their rhetoric and hold to the precedent of *McCardle*. The federal judiciary is unelected and unaccountable to the American people. The Exceptions Clause allows an accountable branch to check a federal judiciary that enjoys making public policy rather than interpreting the law.

SECTION 2, CLAUSE 3

THE TRIAL OF all Crimes, except in Cases of Impeachment, shall be by Jury; and such Trial shall be held in the State where the said Crimes shall have been committed; but when not committed within any State, the Trial shall be at such Place or Places as the Congress may by Law have directed.

Purpose

The Framers valued the right to a jury trial—especially in criminal cases. Section 2, Clause 3 recognizes the importance of this right and requires that federal criminal jury trials be held in the state where the crime was committed. Hence, a defendant alleged to have committed a federal offense in South Carolina cannot be forced to travel to Washington, DC, to have the matter adjudicated.

Background and Development

A major complaint in the Declaration of Independence was George III's deprivation "in many cases[] of the benefits of Trial by Jury."[102] Juries in prerevolutionary America possessed virtually unlimited power to determine both law and fact.[103] Judges often were relegated to deciding pretrial motions and other ministerial matters.[104] If judges took actions tending to undermine customary rights or republican government, citizens expected that the jurors would check them by ignoring or overturning the judges' opinions and determinations.[105] In modern practice, jurors decide questions of fact, whereas judges determine questions of law.

Clause 3 of Section 2 applies to criminal cases. At the Philadelphia Convention, several delegates raised concerns about the omission of civil cases. In response to those concerns, Nathaniel Gorham of Massachusetts stated that "[i]t is not possible to discriminate equity cases from those in which juries are proper."[106] No doubt he had in mind that in courts of "chancery and admiralty . . . civil cases regularly proceeded without a jury."[107] Hence, including civil cases in clause 3 would sweep too broadly.

The singling out of criminal cases for jury trials concerned many Anti-Federalists. For example, the Federal Farmer opined that the federal criminal cases would be uncommon and would be limited to counterfeiting, crimes at sea, and crimes against the law of nations. Civil trials, on the other hand, would be more numerous. Consequently, he found it suspicious that jury trial would be secured for the handful of criminal cases but ignored for civil disputes.[108] Other commentators argued that by specifying trials by jury for criminal cases, juries would be barred in civil cases under the maxim *expressio unius est exclusio alterius*—the explicit mention of one thing is the exclusion of another. As stated previously, those and other objections led to the Seventh Amendment's provision of jury trials in civil cases.

In *Schick v. United States* (1904), the Supreme Court held that the guarantee of a jury trial for "crimes" does not extend to petty offenses.[109] The Court asserted that "crimes" under the common law did not include minor offences; therefore, it would be improper to give "crimes" a broader meaning in the

Constitution. The modern Court has determined that "[a]n offense carrying a maximum prison term of six months or less is presumed petty, unless the legislature has authorized additional statutory penalties so severe as to indicate that the legislature considered the offense serious."[110]

Federal criminal trials must be held in the state where the crime was committed. If the crime did not occur in a state, Congress may direct the place of trial. The venue provision caused much angst among Anti-Federalists because it would allow for a criminal trial at any location in the state where an offense was alleged to have occurred. A defendant residing in New York along the Canadian border could be compelled to stand trial in New York City—a location hundreds of miles away, where the defendant would be unknown to the inhabitants.

In the Massachusetts ratifying convention, Abraham Holmes concluded that in criminal proceedings under the Constitution, "a person shall not have a right to insist on a trial in the vicinity where the act was committed, where a jury of the peers would, from their local situation, have an opportunity to form a judgment of the *character* of the person charged with the crime, and also to judge the *credibility* of witnesses."[111] Samuel Spencer of North Carolina, in his state's convention, reminded his colleagues that "[o]ne reason of the resistance to the British government was, because they required that we should be carried to the country of Great Britain, to be tried by juries of that country."[112] The colonists, however, "insisted on being tried by juries of the vicinage, in our own country. I think it therefore proper that something explicit should be said with respect to the vicinage."[113] Jurors who knew the accused, the parties to a lawsuit, or both, many Americans believed, were in a better position to adjudicate disputes than judges alone or juries of strangers.

James Madison attempted to address concerns about the juries of the vicinage in the Sixth Amendment to the Constitution. In the House of Representatives, the draft of the Sixth Amendment sent to the Senate provided for an "impartial jury of the vicinage" in criminal cases.[114] As a result of compromises between the House and Senate, the final language read an "impartial jury of the State and district wherein the crime shall have been committed."[115] "District" refers to federal judicial districts to be created by Congress. The geographical sizes of federal judicial districts would be determined by statutory law and thus are creatures of the ordinary political process.

Distortions

Federal jury trials in criminal cases are becoming a rarity. According to the Pew Research Center's analysis of data from 2018, eighty thousand people were defendants in federal criminal cases that year, and only 2 percent of these defendants went to trial.[116] Most defendants enter guilty pleas rather than risk a jury trial. The system of federal sentencing guidelines, although advisory and not mandatory, rewards defendants who accept responsibility and do not put the government to the burdens of trial. Moreover, the professionalization of federal law enforcement officers has resulted in high-quality investigations and indictments. The need for criminal jury trials has diminished.

Discussion and Solutions

Federal jury trials likely would increase if the sentencing guidelines were abandoned and Congress abolished (especially in drug cases) mandatory minimum sentences. The mandatory minimums encourage defendants to plea-bargain with the government rather than risk a significant prison sentence that the judge is powerless to reduce no matter what mitigating factors exist. Plea-bargaining is often considered by law-and-order advocates as a method for defendants to avoid the full consequences of their actions, whereas progressive reformers complain that defendants are punished too severely because of prosecutorial discretion in charging decisions. The truth is that a plea agreement is a contract between the government and defendant in which each party accepts a certain outcome because they believe it is in their best interests. Such contracts promote efficiency in the system and provide agreed-upon outcomes. "Plea-bargaining" is not a dirty word.

If increased frequency of criminal jury trials is (or should be) a public policy goal, Congress is the body that must act. The judiciary is not the cause of the decline in jury trials and cannot act to increase them. Jury selection, trial preparation, and trials are time-consuming. A significant increase in federal jury trials would cause delays in the administration of justice that would displease the courts, the defense bar, prosecutors, and the public.

SECTION 3, CLAUSE 1

TREASON AGAINST THE United States, shall consist only in levying War against them, or in adhering to their Enemies, giving them Aid and Comfort. No Person shall be convicted of Treason unless on the Testimony of two Witnesses to the same overt Act, or on Confession in open Court.

Purpose

Treason is the only crime defined in the Constitution. The Framers chose a narrow definition of treason to prohibit a repressive government from abusing political opponents.

Background and Development

"Treason is the breach of the allegiance which a person owes to the state under whose protection he lives, and the most serious crime known to the law."[117] In the Pennsylvania ratifying convention, James Wilson observed that historically, much evil had been done in the prosecution of treasonous conduct. Broad definitions and draconian penalties, Wilson averred, were "great sources of danger and persecution[] on the part of government."[118] Indeed, William Blackstone recognized in his *Commentaries* that under "the ancient common law, there was a great latitude left in the breast of the judges, to determine what was treason, or not so: whereby the creatures of tyrannical princes had opportunity to create abundance of constructive treasons; that is, to raise, by forced and arbitrary constructions, offenses into the crime and punishment of treason which never were suspected to be such."[119] In England, even "spoken or written words criticizing the king," riotous behavior, or counterfeiting could be considered treasonous.[120] Thus, the holders of Britain's reins of

power often succumbed to the temptation of prosecuting subjects expressing certain political opinions.

At the Philadelphia Convention, the Committee of Detail was responsible for the narrow scope of the treason clause. The language adopted was "largely derived from the Statute of 25 Edward III—an English treason statute that was enacted in 1350."[121] It also shares much in common with Virginia's treason statute of 1776, which declared treasonous the levying of war against the commonwealth, adhering to the commonwealth's enemies, and giving them aid and comfort.[122]

James Madison initially criticized the narrow definition and urged the Convention to allow more discretion to Congress in defining treason. He was unable to persuade his colleagues and in the *Federalist Papers* praised the Convention for "inserting a constitutional definition of the crime, fixing the proof necessary for conviction of it, and restraining the Congress."[123]

Maryland's Luther Martin, in his *Genuine Information*, recounted how he urged the Convention to exclude from the definition of treason one or more states making war on the United States. Martin believed that the general government would be likely to use arbitrary power and thus trigger a natural right of the people and their state governments to resist. Absent the urged exception, Martin feared that patriots defending their rights would be branded as traitors and punished as such. He believed that the laws of war and of nations should control a conflict between the general government and one or more states. Martin lamented that he could not garner a majority in Philadelphia for his proposal and thus the states were at the mercy of the general government.

After limiting treason to levying war against the United States, adhering to the country's enemies, or giving them aid and comfort, the Constitution sets forth proof requirements. A conviction is impermissible absent the testimony of two witnesses to the same overt act or a confession in open court. Virginia's 1776 statute similarly required "the evidence of two sufficient and lawful witnesses, or [an accused's] voluntary confession."[124] Akhil Amar of Yale Law School notes that "[i]n specifying certain rights of treason defendants above and beyond those of all other accused persons," the Framers provided substantial protections.[125]

The Supreme Court had an early opportunity to consider the Treason Clause in *Ex parte Bollman* (1807), which dealt with men assisting Aaron Burr in his plan to overthrow the American government in New Orleans.[126] Erick Bollman and Samuel Swarthout conspired with Burr to subvert the government; however, the plot was foiled before any attack could be made. Chief Justice Marshall did not approve of the conspiracy against the government but held that a mere conspiracy is not treason. "To conspire to levy war, and actually to levy war," Marshall observed, "are distinct offences. The first must be brought into open action by the assemblage of men for a purpose treasonable in itself, or the fact of levying war

cannot have been committed. So far has this principle been carried, that . . . it has been determined that the actual enlistment of men to serve against the government does not amount to levying of war."[127] Because there was no actual assemblage of men to carry out Burr's plan, the efforts of Bollman and Swarthout fell short of the Constitution's definition of treason. Had there been an assembly, Marshall clarified that any person who had aided the plot could have been charged with treason.

To many Americans, the most obvious case of treason in our history is that of Jefferson Davis and other high-profile leaders of the Confederacy. So why was Davis not tried for treason? The intent was to try him. Union calvary captured Davis on May 10, 1865, near Irwinville, Georgia. Troops transported him to Fort Monroe, Virginia, where he was held pending trial.

Davis certainly had levied war against the United States. Had his case gone to trial, the question would have been whether Davis owed allegiance to the United States. If he did not, he could not be convicted of treason. Davis would have argued that when Mississippi left the union, his duties to the union ceased because his allegiance to the United States was based on his status as a citizen of Mississippi. When his state withdrew from the federation, he had no remaining relationship to the federation.

Davis's treason trial was scheduled to begin on February 15, 1869, in Richmond, the city that formerly served as the capital of the Confederacy and where Davis directed Confederate armies and resources. The Constitution sets venue for criminal cases as the state where the crime was committed. Hence, Virginia was the spot (although many radical

Republicans argued that Davis was constructively present in any state—North or South—where the Confederate army conducted raids or engaged in hostilities).

As the government prepared its case, certain matters crystalized. There would be no factual disputes with Davis about his leadership of the Confederacy, the prosecution of the war, or the actions of Confederate forces. The only real issue would be the legality of secession. Davis would argue that the United States came into being by secession from Great Britain, that ultimate sovereignty resides in the people of the several states, and that just as state conventions determined whether to join the union, they could determine when to leave the union. Because a duly called convention voted to withdraw Mississippi from the union, Davis would assert that he owed no allegiance to the United States when he assumed the presidency of the Confederacy. Realizing that such important matters would be decided by Southerners sitting on the jury, the government prosecutors got a case of the jitters.

A hung jury or an acquittal would undermine the North's justification for the war: preservation of the union against illegal secessionist acts of various states. Even a conviction would do little to advance the idea of an indestructible union. The trial of arms had settled the matter, and a verdict form marked "guilty" would not bring back to life or heal the 642,427 casualties suffered by Union forces. Davis's lawyers filed a motion to dismiss the indictment, arguing that Section 3 of the Fourteenth Amendment, which disallowed former Confederates from holding public office if they had previously taken an oath to support the Constitution, already punished Davis for treason and thus prevented any further penalty. The judges presiding over Davis's case split on the issue, which triggered an appeal to the Supreme Court. While the case was on appeal, Davis's indictment was nol-prossed; the Government declared that it was unwilling to prosecute after President Johnson issued a general pardon to all participants in the rebellion. In reality, the government had long realized the pitfalls in a Davis treason prosecution and was happy to dispose of the case.

SECTION 3, CLAUSE 2

THE CONGRESS SHALL have Power to declare the Punishment of Treason, but no Attainder of Treason shall work Corruption of Blood, or Forfeiture except during the Life of the Person attainted.

Purpose

The Constitution limits Congress in punishing treason to protect innocent family members who were not involved in their relative's crimes. The traitor's heirs are allowed to inherit as if there had been no treason. The government may obtain property through forfeiture proceedings, but only during the traitor's lifetime.

Background and Development

Under English common law, a person convicted of treason suffered death, the forfeiture of all real and personal property, and the "corruption of blood." Corruption of blood prevented the traitor's children from inheriting through or from the convicted parent. The hardships imposed on a traitor's dependents and other blood kin were meant to provide an extraordinary level of deterrence.

The Framers recoiled at punishing individuals other than the person actually convicted of treason and thus prohibited the corruption of blood. Eleven years before the drafting of the Constitution, Virginia in its treason statute of 1776 prohibited any punishment in treason cases that "work[ed] any corruption of blood."[128] The Philadelphia Convention followed the wisdom of Virginia and, in the words of James Madison, prohibited "extending the consequences of guilt beyond the person of its author."[129] The Supreme Court has concurred in this understanding of the purpose of the provision: "No one ever doubted that it was a provision introduced for the benefit of the children and heirs alone; a declaration that the children should not bear the iniquity of the fathers. Its purpose has never been thought to be a benefit to the traitor, by leaving in him a vested interest in the subject of forfeiture."[130]

SUMMATION

Article III creates a separate and independent judicial branch. Unlike the British system so familiar to the Framers, the American judiciary—by virtue of popular sovereignty—can review decisions of other departments of government. If, for example, Congress passes a law in blatant violation of the Constitution, the federal courts must declare it void. Judicial review, however, is much different from the modern doctrine of judicial supremacy whereby the Supreme Court is the final arbiter of the Constitution. The Framers would have been aghast that a branch of government—on the model of the British Parliament—claims such authority over fundamental law. Through judicial supremacy, the Supreme Court often makes public policy, such as when it created a fundamental right to abortion in *Roe v. Wade*.

The Court has difficulty resisting the temptation to operate as a roving constitutional convention. It believes it can improve upon the written Constitution, but in reality, in attempting to do so the Court undermines the rule of law. Reacquaintance with the principles of strict construction originalism would do much to promote judicial modesty rather than judicial overreach.

ARTICLE IV
SECTION 1

FULL FAITH AND Credit shall be given in each State to the public Acts, Records, and judicial Proceedings of every other State. And the Congress may by general Laws prescribe the Manner in which such Acts, Records and Proceedings shall be proved, and the Effect thereof.

Purpose

The Full Faith and Credit Clause exists so that the records, acts, and judicial proceedings of one state will be accepted in another state as conclusive of the matter decided. This practice promotes efficiency and prevents a bad actor from thwarting a judgment by simply relocating to another state. Nonetheless, Congress is vested with broad power under the Effects Clause to enact legislation limiting the extra-territorial application of certain state policy decisions.

Background and Development

The Articles of Confederation provided that "[f]ull faith and credit shall be given in each of these states to the records, acts and judicial proceedings of the courts and magistrates of every other state."[1] The Articles sought to preclude, for example, a judgment debtor from fleeing to another state and requiring the creditor to bring a new action and prove the debt all over again. The intent was that the creditor could just bring a simple action to enforce the judgment procured in another state. Obviously, the language from the Articles was incorporated into the first sentence of Article IV, with only minor alterations.

At the Philadelphia Convention, North Carolina's Hugh Williamson questioned the addition of legislative acts in a draft provision of the Full Faith and Credit Clause and preferred to stick with the original language of the Articles. In response, James Wilson of Pennsylvania and Samuel Johnson of Connecticut explained that the language meant "that Judgments in one State should be the ground of actions in other States, & that acts of the Legislatures should be included, for the sake of Acts of insolvency."[2] In other words, the clause would operate in the same manner as under the Articles but would also allow a debtor discharged under the laws of a particular state to plead the operation of an applicable sister-state statute.

The mention of state insolvency laws caused Charles Pinckney of South Carolina to urge a uniform federal bankruptcy regime. James Madison supported Wilson and Johnson, and also agreed with Pinckney about the necessity of federal bankruptcy laws. Madison "wished [that] the Legislature might be authorized to provide for the *execution* of Judgments in other States, under such regulations as might be expedient."[3] Perhaps prompted by Madison's comments, Gouverneur Morris of Pennsylvania suggested a role for Congress in establishing "the interstate rules for the acknowledgment of all legal acts of a state and the effect these acts would have."[4] Morris's proposal ultimately was transformed into the second sentence of the Full Faith and Credit Clause: "And the Congress may by general Laws prescribe the Manner in which such Acts, Records and Proceedings shall be proved, and the Effect thereof."

The current implementing statute provides that authenticated acts, records, and judicial proceedings "shall have the same full faith and credit in every court within the United States and its Territories and Possessions as they have by law or usage in the courts of such State, Territory or Possession from which they are taken."[5]

Scholars debate whether the Framers intended the Full Faith and Credit Clause to go beyond governing the evidentiary effect given to out-of-state judgments and thus touch choice-of-law questions, or whether the clause is limited to guaranteeing that the acts, judgments, and records of other states would be received as evidence and deemed conclusive.

Distortions

In more recent years, the Full Faith and Credit Clause garnered much attention when Congress passed and then-President Bill Clinton signed the Defense of Marriage Act (DOMA), which declared that states were not required to recognize same-sex marriages performed in other states. The statute, passed pursuant to the second sentence of the Full Faith and Credit Clause, was prompted by rumblings from the state of Hawaii that it would legalize same-sex marriage. Opponents of DOMA pointed to the first sentence of the clause and the words "shall be given." They contended that this command removed from Congress discretion in exempting certain records or judgments from the clause's operation. Proponents relied on the Effects

Clause—the second sentence—and contended that Congress is empowered to specify by statute how states are to treat the laws of other states. Absent the power to limit the amount of full faith and credit given, proponents of DOMA contended, the Effects Clause would have been superfluous.

When litigation involving DOMA reached the Supreme Court in *United States v. Windsor* (2013), the justices did not consider the Effects Clause because a majority held that the statute violated the Fifth Amendment's guarantee of equal protection by "interfer[ing] with the equal dignity of same-sex marriages."[6] DOMA, however, was a constitutional exercise of Congress's broad power under the Effects Clause to regulate the extraterritorial application of controversial state policy decisions. Scholars have described such an exercise of congressional authority as "an eminently federal function that . . . does not improperly trench on state sovereignty," because it leaves individual states with the power to express their own view of marriage.[7]

Discussion and Solutions

DOMA's opponents would have erased the Effects Clause from the Constitution with their desire to promote progressive policy positions. As the legislature for the union, Congress is empowered to regulate the extraterritorial application of certain state policy decisions. Such power is congruent with federalism and should be respected because it leaves states free to set their own internal policies on controversial issues. DOMA, we must remember, did not prohibit any state from adopting same-sex marriage. It only permitted states to choose whether they would adhere to the traditional definition of marriage or adopt another definition.

SECTION 2, CLAUSE 1

THE CITIZENS OF each State shall be entitled to all Privileges and Immunities of Citizens in the several States.

Purpose

When state or local government confers certain privileges to state citizens, a visitor from another state must share equally in the benefits bestowed. "Privileges and Immunities," however, were not understood to encompass political rights such as suffrage.

Background and Development

The Articles of Confederation contained the following language about the privileges and immunities of citizens: "The better to secure and perpetuate mutual friendship and intercourse among the people of the different states in this union, the free inhabitants of each of these states, paupers, vagabonds and fugitives from Justice excepted, shall be entitled to all privileges and immunities of free citizens in the several states."[8] The term "privileges and immunities" is properly defined "as legal benefits granted to citizens or groups by official grace."[9] Privileges and immunities were creatures of local law that could be altered or abolished by the lawmaking process. They must be distinguished from what the Founders would have characterized as inalienable or natural rights.[10]

An early interpretation of the Constitution's Privileges and Immunities Clause in New York held that "[i]t means only that citizens of other states shall have equal rights with our own citizens, and not that they shall have different or greater rights."[11] In Maryland, a court ruled that "it means that the citizens of all the states shall have the peculiar advantage of acquiring and holding real as well as personal property, and that such property shall be protected and secured by the laws of the state, in the same manner as the property of the citizens of the state is protected."[12] As constitutional scholar Kurt Lash has noted, the tendency in the early republic was to read the clause as securing "to sojourning state citizens equal access to a limited set of local state-conferred rights. These rights did not include political rights such as suffrage, and they excluded any liberty not granted by the state to its own citizens."[13]

Distortions

Many scholars contended that privileges and immunities encompass "fundamental rights." That language is derived from dicta in Justice Bushrod Washington's *Corfield v. Coryell* (1823) opinion, in which he ruled that the Privileges and Immunities Clause did not prohibit New Jersey from excluding citizens of other states from taking oysters located in New Jersey's waters.[14] Washington concluded that wild game ("fugitive property") and other natural resources were held by the citizens of New Jersey in common and, hence, it was reasonable to restrict noncitizens from harvesting those resources in an effort to manage and protect the oyster beds. Although it was unnecessary to the opinion, Washington went on to describe privileges and immunities as fundamental rights belonging to the citizens of all free governments; he then enumerated certain rights falling within the definition, such as life, liberty, and the acquisition of property. Robert Bork has correctly described *Corfield* as a "singularly confused opinion" and observed that most commentators "have always thought that the article IV clause simply prevented a state from discriminating against out-of-staters in favor of their own citizens."[15] (The importance of *Corfield* for Republicans and abolitionists will be discussed in the section on the Fourteenth Amendment.)

The modern Court has adopted the "fundamental rights" language of *Corfield*. For example, in *Baldwin v. Fish & Game Commission of Montana* (1978), the Court considered a challenge to Montana's system of charging out-of-staters more for an elk hunting license than residents.[16] The Court found no fault with Montana's treatment of out-of-staters because "[w]hatever rights or activities may be 'fundamental' under the Privileges and Immunities Clause, we are persuaded, and hold, that elk hunting by nonresidents in Montana is not one of them."[17] Hunting, according to the Court was "recreation and a sport" and thus "deprived [no one] of a means of a livelihood."[18]

In *Supreme Court of New Hampshire v. Piper* (1985), the U.S. Supreme Court struck down a New Hampshire rule that required a lawyer seeking admission to the state bar to be a New Hampshire resident.[19] The Court declared that "the opportunity to practice law should be considered a 'fundamental right'" and thus within the ambit of the Privileges and Immunities Clause.[20] In the realm of business, the Court reinforced its belief that the clause protects the fundamental "privilege" of a citizen of state A to do business in state B on terms substantially equal with those available to state B's citizens.

Discussion and Solutions

The *Corfield* dicta is a weak foundation upon which to build an understanding of privileges and immunities. The clause does nothing more than secure visitors from other states limited legal benefits granted by official grace. Political rights are excluded from the clause's scope. Courts and commentators should resist the temptation to expand judicial power by an aggressive interpretation of the Privileges and Immunities Clause. Distinctions between residents and nonresidents should be allowed so long as the state has a rational basis for the distinction.

SECTION 2, CLAUSE 2

A PERSON CHARGED in any State with Treason, Felony, or other Crime, who shall flee from Justice, and be found in another State, shall on Demand of the executive Authority of the State from which he fled, be delivered up, to be removed to the State having Jurisdiction of the Crime.

Purpose

As a matter of comity, the Constitution requires that fugitives from justice be extradited to the requesting state. No state should become a sanctuary for fugitives and thus disrupt the peaceful relations of the union.

Background and Development

The Articles of Confederation commanded that "[i]f any Person guilty of, or charged with, treason, felony, or other high misdemeanor in any state, shall flee from Justice, and be found in any of the united states, he shall upon demand of the Governor or executive power of the state from which he fled, be delivered up, and removed to the state having jurisdiction of his offence."[21] Obviously, Section 2, Clause 2 is substantially the same as the provision found in the Articles. The clause is based on principles of comity. At base, comity is the deference one jurisdiction extends to the otherwise nonbinding laws, acts, or resolutions of another jurisdiction. It is a reciprocal courtesy that exists between friendly states.

Under the Constitution, states have a duty to return fugitives from justice to the requesting state. According to the Supreme Court, "[t]he purpose of the Clause was to preclude any state from becoming a sanctuary for fugitives from justice of another state and thus 'balkanize' the administration of criminal justice among the several states."[22] Once an extradition request is made, the state receiving it has a limited number of issues to determine: "(a) whether the extradition documents on their face are in order; (b) whether the petitioner has been charged with a crime in the demanding state; (c) whether the petitioner is the person named in the request for extradition; and (d) whether the petitioner is a fugitive."[23] If all four factors are met, the fugitive must be returned. If the executive still refuses to return the fugitive, the requesting state can seek a writ of mandamus in federal court.

Distortions

In *Kentucky v. Dennison* (1861), the governor of Kentucky sought the extradition from Ohio of a fugitive who had been charged with enticing and assisting the escape of slaves. Kentucky complied with all provisions of the federal extradition statute, but Ohio refused to turn over the fugitive on grounds that no such crime existed under Ohio law.[24] Kentucky sought a writ of mandamus from the U.S. Supreme Court to force Ohio to deliver the fugitive. The Court declined to issue the writ. In examining the Extradition Clause, the Court observed that "when the Constitution was framed, and when this law was passed, it was confidently believed that a sense of justice and of mutual interest would insure a faithful execution of this constitutional provision by the Executive of every State, for every State had an equal interest in the execution of a compact absolutely essential to their peace and well being in their internal concerns, as well as members of the Union."[25] Because the Extradition Clause did not proclaim "it shall be his duty" to turn over the fugitive, the Court held "there is no power delegated to the General Government, either through the Judicial Department or any other department, to use any coercive means to compel him."[26]

In *Puerto Rico v. Branstad* (1987), the Court overruled *Kentucky v. Dennison* as "the product

of another time."[27] The Court held that a writ of mandamus can issue to require a state governor to turn over a fugitive from justice.

Discussion and Solutions

The Supreme Court correctly overruled *Dennison*, which was decided on the eve of Civil War. The Extradition Clause is not a suggestion to state governors; it is a constitutional command. Therefore, it is proper that the Supreme Court has the power to issue a writ of mandamus in appropriate cases.

SECTION 2, CLAUSE 3

NO PERSON HELD to Service or Labour in one State, under the Laws thereof, escaping into another, shall, in Consequence of any Law or Regulation therein, be discharged from such Service or Labour, but shall be delivered up on Claim of the Party to whom such Service or Labour may be due.

Purpose

This provision allowed slaveowners to recover a slave who had escaped to another state.

Background and Development

The Fugitive Slave Clause was modeled on the Northwest Ordinance. Although the Ordinance prohibited slavery in the Northwest Territory, it also provided "[t]hat any person escaping into the same, from whom labor or service is lawfully claimed in any one of the original States, such fugitive may be lawfully reclaimed and conveyed to the person claiming his or her labor or service as aforesaid."[28]

The Fugitive Slave Clause initially was suggested by Pierce Butler and Charles Pinckney,

both of South Carolina. Pennsylvania's James Wilson observed that the proposal would impose great public expense in the state where the slave was found. Roger Sherman of Connecticut complained that he "saw no more propriety in the public seizing and surrendering a slave or a servant, than a horse."[29] Butler withdrew his motion until the next day, when it was adopted without objection. Unanimity emerged from a compromise wherein the Southerners withdrew demands for requiring a supermajority for commercial legislation in exchange for Northerners agreeing to protections for slavery. During South Carolina's ratifying convention, Charles Cotesworth Pinckney boasted that "[w]e have obtained a right to recover our slaves in whatever part of

America they may take refuge, which is a right we had not before."[30]

Believing that the clause granted it a power to legislate, Congress passed the Fugitive Slave Act of 1793, which allowed a claimant "to seize or arrest" a fugitive and bring the person before a judicial officer.[31] After establishing for the court that the person was indeed a fugitive slave, the owner would receive a certificate allowing him to seize and repatriate the runaway.

The first Supreme Court case delving into the matter of fugitive slaves was *Prigg v. Pennsylvania* (1842), in which the Court held that the Fugitive Slave Act of 1793 trumped a Pennsylvania law that prohibited removal of runaways.[32] The Court also noted that state officials were not required to assist in the enforcement of the Fugitive Slave Act. That led to numerous states passing laws prohibiting their officers from enforcing the federal statute.

As part of the Compromise of 1850, a new fugitive slave law was passed that required federal officers to assist in the location and apprehension of runaways. Judicial sabers were drawn over the new statute, with the Wisconsin Supreme Court, in *In re Booth* (1854), declaring it to be unconstitutional.[33] On the eve of the Civil War, the U.S. Supreme Court overturned the decision, but the Wisconsin Supreme Court refused to file the mandate—typically a certified copy of the judgment and a copy of the court's opinion—upholding the Fugitive Slave Act of 1850.[34] The ratification of the Thirteenth Amendment, abolishing slavery in the United States, rendered the Fugitive Slave Clause a nullity.

SECTION 3, CLAUSE 1

NEW STATES MAY be admitted by the Congress into this Union; but no new State shall be formed or erected within the Jurisdiction of any other State; nor any State be formed by the Junction of two or more States, or Parts of States, without the Consent of the Legislatures of the States concerned as well as of the Congress.

Purpose

The Constitution specifically provides for the admission of new states to the union; however, it also seeks to protect existing states from dismemberment.

Background and Development

The third section of Article IV delineates the power of Congress to admit new states to the union. The original provision considered at the Philadelphia Convention explicitly provided that new states would be admitted on the same terms as the original states. Gouverneur Morris of Pennsylvania objected, because he foresaw substantial expansion in the Western territories and "did not wish however to throw the power into their hands."[35] Hugh Williamson of North Carolina agreed with Morris. He added that the only reason the small states enjoyed power equal to that of large states in the Senate was because of the status accorded them under the Confederation. New states would be a different matter, and thus Congress should have discretion on the terms of admission. Virginia's George Mason warned that the people of the West should be treated as friends and equals. Otherwise, they would see themselves as enemies of the East. Madison believed that Morris's motion "degraded" the West and spoke against it.[36] Nine states supported Morris, and thus the language about equality between old and new states was eliminated from the draft. The Supreme Court, however, has adopted the "equal-footing doctrine" concerning new states and has held they "have the same rights, sovereignty and jurisdiction . . . as the original States possess within their respective borders."[37]

Morris also moved to ensure that existing states with claims to Western lands had to consent before their western counties could be admitted as states. This motion passed as well. In working on the Committee of Style, Morris edited the language agreed upon so that the text of the Constitution technically forbids the creation of new states out of existing states—"but no new State shall be formed or erected within the Jurisdiction of any other State;"—a feat accomplished by the use of a semicolon to separate that provision from the provision concerning the junction of states and the consent requirement. According to constitutional scholar William Michael Treanor, "Morris changed the provision so that new states could never be created from the boundaries of existing states, making the language about permission from the state legislature and Congress inapplicable to the creation of new states from land within existing states."[38]

If read literally, with Morris's semicolon, the Constitution prohibited the creation of Kentucky and Tennessee because they were derived from the territories of Virginia and North

Carolina, respectively. Both states were admitted in the early days of the republic, and no one challenged the propriety of their creation. Despite Morris's best efforts, the prevailing view is that "new states may be formed out of an existing state provided all parties consent: the new state, the existing state, and the Congress."[39]

Distortions

The most constitutionally questionable creation of a state concerns West Virginia. When President Abraham Lincoln made clear that he would use military power to force the states of the Deep South back into the union, Virginia's hand was forced. The Old Dominion held a referendum on secession, and the measure was adopted by a vote of 132,201–37,451. Unhappy with the majority's decision to leave the federation, leaders from thirty-nine northwestern Virginia counties decided to start the process of forming their own government, known as the Restored or Reorganized Government of Virginia. The northwestern area never identified with the eastern plantation owners who controlled political authority. The northwestern folks were subsistence farmers leasing land or owning small parcels. After Union troops occupied northwestern Virginia, the leaders of the breakaway counties pushed for statehood.

President Lincoln recognized the government of West Virginia, and in 1864 Congress passed an enabling act to formally admit the new state to the union. The government of Virginia never consented to the carving off of its western counties and thus the provisions of Article IV were ignored by Lincoln and the Republican Congress. "By adopting the position that West Virginia was free to join the union under its own will without the express sanction of Virginia," independent scholar Dave Benner writes, "Lincoln had unwittingly embraced the principle he was willing to plunge the country into war over—secession."[40]

Discussion and Solutions

It is too late to reunify Virginia and West Virginia. Nonetheless, we should remember the constitutional irregularities that led to the creation of a new state. Such remembrance should cause us to resolve to respect the boundaries of sovereign states and to insist upon the consent required in the Constitution. Ignoring the historical violence done to Section 3, Clause 1 only numbs us to violations of other constitutional provisions occurring in our own time.

SECTION 3, CLAUSE 2

THE CONGRESS SHALL have Power to dispose of and make all needful Rules and Regulations respecting the Territory or other Property belonging to the United States; and nothing in this Constitution shall be so construed as to Prejudice any Claims of the United States, or of any particular State.

Purpose

This provision ensures that Congress has the power to govern the territories and dispose of federal property.

Background and Development

The Philadelphia Convention said nothing about the Property Clause to guide constitutional interpretation. In *Federalist* No. 38, James Madison lamented that the Confederation Congress had formed new states and established territorial governments "without the least color of constitutional authority."[41] Madison was referring to the Northwest Ordinance of 1787, which he regarded as good policy that simply lacked a foundation in fundamental law. The Northwest Ordinance, of course, dealt with myriad issues such as intestate succession, territorial government, and slavery. In 1789, the first Congress to operate under the new Constitution reenacted the ordinance. While the Northwest Ordinance prohibited slavery, the Southwest Ordinance enacted in 1790 for the territories south of the Ohio River prohibited federal interference with the peculiar institution. The early case law interpreted Congress's power under the Property Clause as existing "without limitation."[42]

The last passage of Clause 2 provides that "nothing in this Constitution shall be so construed as to Prejudice any Claims of the United States, or of any particular State" to the territories. The language was inserted because disputes persisted about the boundaries of certain states in lands ceded by the Crown. Madison realized that some states would distrust Supreme Court adjudication of boundary issues, because the Court was part of the general government. To be "neutral and fair," Madison suggested specific language recognizing the legitimate claims of particular states.

In 1819, the issue of Congress's authority to govern the territories became heated when New York Congressman James Tallmadge Jr. proposed that his colleagues allow Missouri's admission as a state if slavery was phased out. All slaves born after Missouri's admission to the union would be emancipated upon reaching the age of twenty-five. Tallmadge's proposal struck Thomas Jefferson and many others as a fire bell in the night. The compromises reached at the Philadelphia Convention had allowed the North and South to live together in peace. Jefferson saw that the arrangement was in danger if the issue was injected into national politics. He also doubted whether Congress could, in the words of historian Kevin R. C. Gutzman, "impose conditions on a territory that would remain binding once it became a state."[43] Such restrictions would be the death of the doctrine that all states entered the union on equal footing.

The Missouri Compromise resolved the issue of slavery in the territories for a time by admitting Missouri as a slave state and prohibiting slavery from territories lying north of thirty-six degrees and thirty minutes latitude— roughly dividing the area of the Louisiana Purchase between North and South. The issue of Congress's power in the territories inflamed sectionalism; the slaveholding states viewed efforts to exclude slavery from the territories as intentional discrimination meant "to deprive the Southern states of equality in the Union."[44] Southerners took umbrage that Northerners could access and settle all commonly held land in the West, but that slave-owning citizens were limited to certain areas of the continent.

Realizing that the union was about to break apart over territorial expansion, the Supreme Court, in *Dred Scott v. Sandford* (1857), attempted definitively to resolve the matter.[45] Chief Justice Roger Taney, inter alia, held the Missouri Compromise to be unconstitutional on the ground that Congress had no power to forbid or abolish slavery in the territories. "[A]n act of Congress which deprives a citizen of the United States of his liberty or property," Taney wrote, "merely because he came himself or brought his property into a particular Territory of the United States, and who had committed no offence against the laws, could hardly be dignified with the name of due process of law."[46] This was a substantive reading of the Fifth Amendment's Due Process Clause. As political scientist Carl Brent Swisher has noted, "[t]he due process phrase had been used prior to this time chiefly as a restriction upon judicial process rather than on the content of legislation."[47] Such an interpretation of due process was ultra vires. In addition, Taney held that blacks could not be citizens of the United States because they were not part of the people forming the political community of an independent America. This latter contention was challenged by Justice Benjamin R. Curtis in a vigorous dissent. He suggested that at least five states at the time of the Constitution's ratification enfranchised blacks, many blacks likely voted for members of state ratifying conventions, and thus blacks actively participated in establishing fundamental law. Rather than set national policy and prevent calamity, *Dred Scott* angered Northerners and demonstrated that the animosity between the sections had gone too far to be quelled by judicial pronouncement. The flawed *Dred Scott* decision was the last judicial effort to limit Congress's power in the territories.

Distortions

According to the modern Supreme Court, Congress enjoys plenary power over the territories subject to (1) structural constitutional limitations, (2) fundamental constitutional rights, and (3) the necessity of a rational basis for congressional action.[48] In *Kleppe v. New Mexico* (1976), the Court observed that "while the furthest reaches of the power granted by the Property Clause have not yet been definitively resolved, we have repeatedly observed that the power over the public land thus entrusted to Congress is without limitations."[49] *Kleppe* concerned the Wild Free-Roaming Horses and Burros Act, which prohibited capturing or killing unbranded and unclaimed horses and burros on public lands of the United States. Because wild burros were interfering with ranchers by eating their feed and bullying cattle, the state entered federal land, captured the burros, and sold them at auction. The state contended that the statute was unconstitutional because "the Clause grants Congress essentially two kinds of power: (1) the power to dispose of and make incidental rules regarding the use of federal property; and (2) the power to protect federal property."[50] The state further reasoned

that "the first power is not broad enough to support legislation protecting wild animals that live on federal property; and the second power is not implicated since the Act is designed to protect the animals, which are not themselves federal property, and not the public lands."[51] The Court rejected the state's argument and found that Congress's power over public land was vast and boundless.

Discussion and Solutions

Modern readers should not think that Congress's power over territories or property belonging to the United States is inconsequential. The federal government owns approximately 640 million acres, representing 28 percent of all land within the United States. Most of it is in the West. A general police power over such vast land holdings represents an immense reservoir of authority and is incongruent with a constitution conferring limited authority on the general government and reserving substantial powers in the several states.[52] The limitations proposed by New Mexico in *Kleppe* were reasonable and should be revisited when the Court is presented with an opportunity.

SECTION 4

THE UNITED STATES shall guarantee to every State in this Union a Republican Form of Government, and shall protect each of them against Invasion; and on Application of the Legislature, or of the Executive (when the Legislature cannot be convened) against domestic Violence.

Purpose

The Framers believed that the union could survive only if its members adhered to

the republican model. The rise of monarchy was a great fear in the American Whig tradition. Consequently, the Constitution limits membership in the union to guard against monarchical innovations. Moreover, the union was designed so the states would present a united front to foreign powers. From this premise, it follows that the union should protect the states from invasion.

Background and Development

The impetus for the Guarantee Clause originated in John Dickinson's draft of the Articles of Confederation. Under the Dickinson draft, once the boundary of a colony was agreed upon, "all the other Colonies shall guarantee to such Colony the full and peaceable Possession of, and the free and entire Jurisdiction in and over the Territory included within such Boundaries."[53] The draft also empowered Congress to limit the boundaries of colonies that claimed vast holdings under royal charters. Western land claims were major points of contention. The states with no vast claims (Maryland, Pennsylvania, Delaware, New Jersey, and Rhode Island) wanted congressional control of Western lands because they objected that states with claims running to the Pacific Ocean could sell acreage to defray substantial costs incurred in fighting the British. The landless states believed that possible sale of Western lands should benefit the whole. Because Virginia's delegates made clear that they would not countenance the stripping away of the Old Dominion's chartered boundaries, the final version of the Articles dropped the boundary guarantee and Congress's power to determine boundaries.

At the Philadelphia Convention, the eleventh resolve of the Virginia Plan provided that "a Republican Government & the territory of each State, except in the instance of a voluntary junction of Government & territory, ought to be guarantied by the United States to each State."[54] Objections were made about territorial guarantees, and the resolve was amended to cover republican constitutions and existing laws—thus omitting any mention of state boundaries.[55]

Virginia's Edmund Randolph defended the revised language on the ground that "a republican government must be the basis of our national union; and no state ought to have it in their power to change its government into a monarchy."[56]

Gouverneur Morris of Pennsylvania worried about securing state laws and mentioned that Rhode Island had many objectionable ones. Delegates then discussed the central purpose of the clause and identified its key objectives as fostering republican government and protecting the states against commotions and violence. Undoubtedly, many delegates had in mind Shays' Rebellion in Massachusetts, when debt-ridden farmers took up arms to close courthouses and thus prevent foreclosure proceedings from moving forward. After a brief engagement in 1787, state militia units caused the rebels to disperse, but the armed resistance to state laws concerned many people throughout the Confederation.

Other delegates expressed concern about guaranteeing state constitutions. They realized that as time revealed flaws in them, revisions would be needed. These delegates did not want to lock the states into constitutions that could not be improved by the people. Rather than securing state constitutions, James Wilson of Pennsylvania suggested a guarantee encompassing protection of "a Republican form of Government" and use of federal forces in case of "foreign & domestic violence."[57]

Massachusetts's Elbridge Gerry and Maryland's Luther Martin thought that the general government should not be given license to interfere in internal state conflicts. Gerry opposed "letting loose the myrmidons of the U. States on a State without its own consent." He stressed that had the Confederation intervened in Shays' Rebellion, "[m]ore blood would have been spilt."[58] Concerned about overreaching by the general government, the Convention inserted a requirement that the state legislature, or the executive when the legislature could not be convened, must request assistance in cases of domestic disturbances before federal forces are mobilized to quell them.

In explaining the Guarantee Clause in *Federalist* No. 43, Madison averred that "[i]n a confederacy founded on republican principles, and composed of republican members, the superintending government ought clearly to possess authority to defend the system against monarchical innovations."[59] Madison noted that the confederacy in ancient Greece was undone when Macedon joined its ranks and Macedon's king infused a monarchical form of government into the system. Madison opined further that the only restriction on states altering their governing institutions was "that they shall not exchange republican for anti-republican Constitutions."[60]

According to William Rawle's commentaries on the Constitution, if the people of a state determine to adopt, for example, a limited monarchy, the state would have "to retire from the Union."[61] To the extent that a state prefers membership in the union, it "must retain the character of representative republics."[62] Abraham Lincoln rejected Rawle's reasoning and in 1861 contended

that his invasion of the South was aimed at preserving republican forms of government in the seceded states. Lincoln claimed that if a state could leave the union, then it could discard the republican formula. To prevent the latter, Lincoln acted to coerce the Southern states back into the union.

So what makes a government republican? Most of the Founders agreed that popular sovereignty and rule of the majority were the two pillars of republican government.[63] Popular sovereignty means that ultimate power resides in the people. They have the power to erect a government, alter it, or abolish it. Officers of government exercise only delegated powers; they are the agents, and the people are the principals. The majority rules in a republic when the people choose representatives and these representatives vote the sense of their constituents. A majority is usually 50 percent plus one. Of course, constitutions can require supermajorities for certain decisions and immunize other matters from the political process.

The Supreme Court has held that the question whether a state has a republican form of government is a political question and thus should be decided by the elected branches of government rather by the federal courts.[64]

Distortions

The greatest distortion of the Guarantee Clause was Lincoln's appeal to the clause in launching the Civil War. Lincoln viewed the union as sacrosanct and, in his crusade to maintain it, he resorted to novel interpretations of multiple constitutional provisions, including the Guarantee Clause. While one might or might not agree with the idea of union as the ultimate American political principle, one must acknowledge abuse of the clause. The secession of states did not threaten the republican form of states choosing to remain in the union. Moreover, the potential of states outside of the union to abandon republican principles—not the actual abandonment of the principles—offers the general government myriad excuses to meddle in various state affairs based on the potential that some state action could ultimately infringe upon national powers. Under such an interpretation, it is difficult if not impossible to identify tangible limits on the Guarantee Clause.

Discussion and Solutions

Americans should exercise caution when political leaders appeal to the Guarantee Clause. Much damage can be done in the name of aspirational provisions of the Constitution. Popular sovereignty and majority rule are simple concepts that national leaders should be unable to exploit. Fundamental law is the work of the people acting in constituent bodies and ordinary law is passed by majorities in duly constituted legislatures. We would do well to preserve both concepts.

SUMMATION

Article IV governs interstate relations. States must give full faith and credit to the records, acts, and judicial proceedings of other states. When states grant certain nonpolitical privileges to their citizens, visitors from other states must share equally in the benefits bestowed. Fugitives from justice must be extradited in an expeditious manner to prevent any state from becoming a sanctuary for criminal actors. The Constitution contemplates the admission of new states but also protects existing states from a loss of territory absent their consent. No state may depart from the republican model of government and thus inject monarchial principles into the union. The Framers believed that anti-republican institutions posed a danger and could spread dangerous doctrines throughout the federation.

ARTICLE V

THE CONGRESS, WHENEVER two thirds of both Houses shall deem it necessary, shall propose Amendments to this Constitution, or, on the Application of the Legislatures of two thirds of the several States, shall call a Convention for proposing Amendments, which, in either Case, shall be valid to all Intents and Purposes, as Part of this Constitution, when ratified by the Legislatures of three fourths of the several States, or by Conventions in three fourths thereof, as the one or the other Mode of Ratification may be proposed by the Congress; Provided that no Amendment which may be made prior to the Year One thousand eight hundred and eight shall in any Manner affect the first and fourth Clauses in the Ninth Section of the first Article; and that no State, without its Consent, shall be deprived of its equal Suffrage in the Senate.

Purpose

The Framers knew that their Constitution was not perfect and that experience is a great teacher. An amendment procedure was necessary to allow for corrections and reformation. But a reasonable amendment procedure should also protect the people from ill-conceived constitutional change. Hence, the Framers sought to achieve a balance, so that the Constitution would be neither impossible to amend nor too easily changed.

Background and Development

The Articles of Confederation required that changes in the compact "be agreed to in a Congress of the United States, and be afterwards confirmed by the legislatures of every State."[65] The unanimity requirement proved to be the Articles' undoing. To pay the Revolutionary War debt, Congress needed an independent source of revenue. Twice, twelve states agreed to grant Congress the power to levy a tax on imports, and twice, one recalcitrant state torpedoed the effort (Rhode Island in the first instance and New York in the second).

Accordingly, the Framers of the Constitution rejected unanimous consent, opting instead to require three-fourths of the states to approve proposed amendments.

Madison's *Notes* record that a few delegates questioned the need for an amendment procedure. In response, Virginia's George Mason explained that a workable amendment procedure was essential. "The plan now to be formed will certainly be defective," Mason said, "as the Confederation has been found on trial to be."[66] Good judgment, he continued, counseled that "it will be better to provide for [revisions], in an easy, regular and Constitutional way than to trust to chance and violence."[67] Mason also stressed that amendments ought not depend solely on the national government because of concerns about abuse of power and possible refusal to consent to salutary alterations in the government. Elbridge Gerry of Massachusetts also argued that a reasonable amendment procedure would stabilize the new government since "[t]he novelty & difficulty of the experiment requires periodical revision."[68]

As the Convention completed its work, the draft of the amendment article provided that upon "the application of the Legislatures of two thirds of the States in the Union, for an amendment of this Constitution, the Legislature of the U.S. shall call a convention for that purpose."[69] Gerry feared that the states could exploit the amendment procedure to "bind the Union to innovations that may subvert the State-Constitutions."[70] Gerry asked that the amendment process be reconsidered, and his motion was seconded by New York's Alexander Hamilton. Hamilton, however, admitted candidly that his concerns were different from Gerry's. Hamilton feared that the state legislatures would only seek amendments to preserve state powers. To promote energy in the new government, Hamilton believed that the national legislature should have an important role in calling and structuring a convention to consider needed alterations in the form of government. Madison agreed that the amendment procedure should be reconsidered because of "the vagueness of the terms, 'call a Convention for the purpose.'"[71]

Upon further discussion, what is now Article V provided that Congress could send proposed amendments to the states for ratification if (1) two-thirds of Congress agreed to a proposed amendment or (2) two-thirds of the state legislatures requested an amendment. Amendments would be valid only after ratification by three-fourths of the state legislatures or conventions called to approve or reject them. Mason thought that the procedure was "exceptionable & dangerous" because "the proposing of amendments is in both the modes to depend, in the first immediately, in the second, ultimately, on Congress."[72] With Congress in charge of the amendment process, he predicted that "no amendments of the proper kind would ever be obtained by

the people, if the Government should become oppressive."[73] To address Mason's concerns, Gouverneur Morris of Pennsylvania and Gerry moved to amend the Article V to require a constitutional convention on the application of two-thirds of the states. This motion passed unanimously.

The clause of the amendment procedure prohibiting amendments dealing with the slave trade prior to 1808 was requested by John Rutledge of South Carolina. He wanted to ensure that the bargained-for protections of the slave trade could not be revoked via an amendment. Roger Sherman of Connecticut suggested adding language guaranteeing security for the small states to ensure they could not be dispossessed of equal voices in the Senate. The attainment of an equal vote in the Senate provided a structural protection for the smaller states, and Sherman preserved this compromise in perpetuity.

The Anti-Federalists believed the amendment process was too difficult and objected to congressional control over the procedure. An Old Whig observed that "[p]eople once possessed of power are always loth to part with it; and we shall never find two thirds of a Congress voting or proposing any thing which shall derogate from their own authority and importance, or agreeing to give back to the people any part of those privileges which they have once parted with."[74] The Federal Farmer also expected that Congress would "be exceedingly artful and adroit in preventing any measures" limiting national power.[75] If such alterations could be obtained, they would come from "great exertions and severe struggles on the part of the common people."[76]

In the Virginia ratifying convention, Patrick Henry took aim at the amendment procedure. He echoed the words of An Old Whig and the Farmer regarding the unlikelihood that Congress would ever agree to amendments that limited national power. Henry also objected that "four of the smallest States, that do not collectively contain one-tenth of the population of the United States, may obstruct the most salutary and necessary amendments."[77] The minority, he averred, should not be able to prevent the majority from amending the Constitution.

Virginian Wilson Carey Nicholas challenged the Anti-Federalist critique. He agreed that if the amendment power had rested solely in Congress, then the Anti-Federalists would have had grounds to object. He was keen to point out that "there is another mode provided, besides that which originates with Congress."[78] He touted the convention procedure of Article V as a guarantee that the states could procure needed constitutional alterations. In the North Carolina convention, James Iredell denied that Congress could block amendments. He averred that "it is provided that Congress shall call such convention, so that they will have no option."[79]

As the Anti-Federalists feared, all constitutional amendments have originated in Congress. In originating amendments, Congress is not required to present them to the president as it would do with ordinary legislation.[80] The task of recommending amendments to the states thus belongs to the legislative branch alone.

Because the number of states requesting a convention to amend the Constitution has never met the high bar set, one can only speculate about whether such a convention would be limited or unlimited in its scope. If the states requested a convention to consider proposing a balanced budget amendment, for instance, would the convention be prohibited from also considering amendments on matters such as abortion or capital punishment? The Constitution provides that "Congress . . . on the application of two-thirds of the Legislatures of the several States, shall call a convention for proposing amendments." The plain language at the end of the sentence seems to suggest that a convention would be unrestricted in scope and could propose amendments on a variety of subjects.

Distortions

Outside of the first ten amendments, which were ratified in 1791 and were necessary to somewhat assuage Anti-Federalist angst, constitutional amendments (for the most part) have augmented national power rather than curtailed it. In recent years, polls have shown that large majorities of the people have favored constitutional limits on congressional power such as a balanced budget amendment, term limits, and prohibitions on imposing unfunded mandates on the states.[81] Yet Congress, the body that largely controls the amendment process, has refused to act. The Anti-Federalists foresaw this result and would not be surprised by congressional efforts to increase and secure power. Common sense dictates that seldom will those imbibing the intoxicants of power seek to reduce their intake on their own initiative.

In a federal system, any state should be able to propose a constitutional amendment without the involvement of Congress. If the originating state can persuade three-fourths of the others to ratify, then it becomes a part of the Constitution. The result, in the words of the University of South Carolina School of

Law's William Quirk, is that "[t]he people, acting through their states, would be able, through an orderly and manageable process, to reclaim powers previously granted to, or assumed by, the federal government."[82]

Discussion and Solutions

In remembrance of Professor Quirk, *The Independent Guide* proposes the following: "An amendment proposed by one or more of the several states shall be valid to all intents and purposes, as part of this Constitution, when ratified by the legislatures of three-fourths of the several states, or by conventions in three-fourths thereof." Such an amendment procedure would give the states and the people a fighting chance to defend themselves against a consolidated national government that continually operates in an extraconstitutional manner. The adoption of a new amendment procedure would open the door for constitutional change. Excluding the Bill of Rights and the exceptional circumstances under which Congress drafted it, the Constitution has been amended only seventeen times since 1791. The trials, complexities, and inadequacies of the Constitution have demonstrated the need for revisions, but Congress has not acted.

Madison warned in *Federalist* No. 43, that an amendment procedure should not "render the Constitution too mutable."[83] But he did expect that amendments, as necessary, would be proposed to augment or reduce national power. "Had the power of making treaties, for example, been omitted, however necessary it might have been," Madison explained during the national bank controversy, "the defect could only have been lamented or supplied by an amendment of the constitution."[84] As flaws became visible, the Constitution would be altered via the deliberative process outlined in Article V. But enough effort and work had to go into the procedure to interdict the passions of faction.

Today our Constitution is "amended" by judicial interpretations and congressional fervor for expanded power. Article V's congressionally directed amendment process has rendered the Constitution too mutable, but not because amendments are offered willy-nilly. Instead, the powerlessness of the states to police constitutional boundaries through amendments permits the national government to contort our constitutional charter.

Scholars can make the case for various amendments to the Constitution, but none is as necessary as a new procedure whereby we strip Congress of its monopoly on constitutional change. As outlined in the Virginia Plan, the states should be able to propose amendments without the involvement of the national government. Were such a procedure in place, the national government's powers might still be few and defined rather than broad and indeterminate.

> ## ARTICLE VI
> ## SECTION 1
>
> ALL DEBTS CONTRACTED and Engagements entered into, before the Adoption of this Constitution, shall be as valid against the United States under this Constitution, as under the Confederation.

Purpose

With this provision, the Framers articulated to the Confederation's creditors that a change in the charter of government would not equal a cancellation of justly acquired debts. The new general government would recognize the same obligations as the Confederation Congress.

Background and Development

The Articles of Confederation provided that "[a]ll bills of credit emitted, monies borrowed, and debts contracted by, or under the authority of Congress, before the assembling of the United States, in pursuance of the present confederation, shall be deemed and considered as a charge against the United States, for payment and satisfaction whereof the said United States, and the public faith are hereby solemnly pledged."[85] The provision recognized that debts incurred by the Continental Congress before formal confederation would be honored as valid debts of the United States. And the debt accumulated throughout the American Revolution in the forms of foreign loans, bonds, and fiat currency (bills of credit) was astronomical. Some estimates place it at $75 million, which translates to $2.5 billion in today's dollars.[86]

Much as the drafters of the Articles recognized the need to make good on the obligations of the Continental Congress, the Philadelphia Convention accepted the necessity of assuaging creditors' angst. During the Convention, Pennsylvania's James Wilson stated that "some provision on the subject would be proper in order to prevent any suspicion that the obligations of the Confederacy might be dissolved along with the Government under which they were contracted."[87] Answering a claim that the specific wording of Wilson's provision missed the mark, Elbridge Gerry of Massachusetts declared "it essential that some explicit provision should be made on this subject, so that no pretext might remain for getting rid of the public engagements."[88] Virginia's Edmund Randolph agreed on the need for an unambiguous provision, because Congress would be unable to act on Revolutionary War debts or any other matter unless a specific power was conferred on it. Madison also thought a specific provision would be prudent lest someone attempt to argue that the Revolution "destroyed the political identity of the Society" and thus contracts and debts were canceled.[89] Madison elaborated on his conclusion in *Federalist No. 43*, when he characterized the clause as being inserted "for the satisfaction of foreign creditors of the United States, who cannot be strangers to the pretended doctrine that a change in the political form of civil society, has the magical effect of dissolving its moral obligations."[90]

In the early 1790s, Congress agreed to assume the Revolutionary War debt of the states. Alexander Hamilton was the chief proponent of debt assumption. He realized that in trying to establish national credit, the reputation of the country would suffer if an impoverished or recalcitrant state failed to service its debts accumulated during the war. Republicans feared this was simply a plan to enrich speculators, since many state bonds had been purchased for pennies on the dollar from their original holders. A compromise was reached when Thomas Jefferson and James Madison agreed to support debt assumption if Hamilton and his supporters would agree to locate the new national capital on the Potomac River. Debt assumption undoubtedly assisted in establishing national credit and also increased the prestige of the general government as numerous state creditors looked to it for payment rather than the state legislatures.

SECTION 2

THIS CONSTITUTION, AND the Laws of the United States which shall be made in Pursuance thereof; and all Treaties made, or which shall be made, under the Authority of the United States, shall be the supreme Law of the Land; and the Judges in every State shall be bound thereby, any Thing in the Constitution or Laws of any State to the Contrary notwithstanding.

Purpose

The Constitution attempted to avoid disputes between the general and state governments through the enumeration of powers. The general government would focus on foreign relations, war and peace, and commercial intercourse. The state governments would legislate on internal matters relating to the health, welfare, and morals of the people. Recognizing that conflict between the two levels of government was a possibility, the Framers adopted the Supremacy Clause as a rule of priority. The Constitution, along with statutes and treaties made pursuant to it, would trump state laws to the contrary.

Background and Development

The Articles of Confederation contained a precursor of the Supremacy Clause: "Every state shall abide by the determinations of which the united states in congress assembled, on all questions which by this confederation are submitted to them."[91] The Virginia Plan, however, proposed a much more radical method of promoting the supremacy of the general government. In the sixth resolve, the Virginia Plan recommended that Congress have a veto on "all laws passed by the several States contravening in the opinion of the National Legislature the articles of Union."[92] At the suggestion of Pennsylvania's Benjamin Franklin, the delegates inserted at the clause's end "or any treaties subsisting under the authority of the Union."[93] Charles Pinckney of South Carolina wanted to broaden the veto power to all state laws that Congress believed to "be improper."[94] The South Carolinian believed that "such a universality of the power was indispensably necessary to render it effectual" and "that the States must be kept in due subordination to the nation."[95] Madison seconded the motion, noting that such a veto was "absolutely necessary to a perfect system."[96] Madison feared that without a national legislative veto on state laws, "the only remedy will lie in an appeal to coercion."[97]

Massachusetts's Elbridge Gerry objected that such a power in the general government would "enslave the States."[98] Gouverneur Morris of Pennsylvania, a friend of energetic government, believed that Congress's proposed negative would hinder ratification because the states would view such a veto with disgust. Maryland's Luther Martin was shocked at the attempt to give Congress a negative and predicted "that the States, particularly the smaller, would never allow a negative to be exercised over their laws."[99] After a vigorous debate, the motion to arm Congress with veto power over states laws failed by a vote of seven to three.

Following rejection of the proposed negative, Martin suggested a supremacy clause:

> that the Legislative acts of the U.S. made by virtue & in pursuance of the articles of Union, and all Treaties made & ratified under the authority of the U.S. shall be the supreme law of the respective States, as far as those acts or treaties shall relate to the said States, or their Citizens and inhabitants—& that the Judiciaries of the several States shall be bound thereby in their decisions, any thing in the respective laws of the individual States to the contrary notwithstanding.[100]

The clause clearly was meant as an alternative to Congress's veto power, and it triggered very little debate. The Committee of

Detail changed Martin's phraseology from "the Judiciaries of the several States" to "the judges in the several States,"[101] excluding juries from the clause and making it clear that the provision applied to national as well as state judges. The committee supported other revisions, including changing "supreme law of the respective states" to "supreme law of the land."[102] Without question, the Supremacy Clause envisioned federal and state judges reviewing the constitutionality of legislation, because they too were bound by "the supreme law of the land." The Constitution required them to exercise judgment on just what constituted "supreme law" and thus contemplated judicial review.

Anti-Federalists sensed great danger with the Supremacy Clause. An Old Whig believed the provision granted Congress "supreme legislative power, without control."[103] Brutus agreed with this assessment and contended that the Supremacy Clause created "a complete [government], and not a confederation."[104] He lamented that "all ideas of confederation are given up and lost."[105] A Federal Republican saw the Supremacy Clause as cementing "the whole country . . . into one large system of lordly government."[106]

Alexander Hamilton scoffed at Anti-Federalist contentions that the Supremacy Clause created a "hideous monster."[107] Hamilton asserted that the general government's power would not change if the Supremacy Clause were deleted. The clause was "only declaratory of a truth, which would have resulted by necessary and unavoidable implication from the very act of constituting a Federal Government."[108]

In his commentary on the Constitution, St. George Tucker believed there would "be little room for collision" between the states and general government, because the former's powers were "enumerated, defined, and limited to particular objects" such as foreign relations and war and peace.[109] Insofar as the states likely would legislate only "within their own domestic concerns," conflict with national policies seemed doubtful.[110] Absent the Constitution's careful division between the general and state governments, Tucker thought it as "extraordinary" that "a people jealous of their liberty, and not insensible to the allurements of power, should have entrusted the federal government with such extensive authority as this article conveys."[111]

In adjudicating a case presenting a potential conflict between federal and state law, a court must first identify the enumerated power supporting federal authority. Second, the court must determine whether the federal action falls within the proper scope of the enumerated power. If the federal law is constitutionally legitimate, then the court must determine whether a conflict exists between the two laws. If it does, "[t]he Supremacy Clause supplies a rule of priority" and requires the court to hold that the state law is displaced by the federal law.[112]

Distortions

In modern jurisprudence, Supremacy Clause issues most often arise in connection with "preemption." This is a "[d]octrine adopted by the U.S. Supreme Court holding that certain matters are of such a national, as opposed to local, character that federal laws preempts or takes precedence over state laws."[113] Preemption of state laws can take three possible forms: express, field, and conflict. "Express preemption occurs when a federal statute explicitly states that it overrides state or local law."[114] Field preemption occurs "when federal law so thoroughly occupies a legislative field as to make it reasonable to infer that Congress left no room for the states to act."[115] Conflict preemption "exists if it would be impossible for a party to comply with both local and federal requirements or where local law stands as an obstacle to the accomplishment and execution of the full purposes and objectives of Congress."[116]

Modern preemption doctrine acts very much like the congressional veto that Congress rejected in favor of the Supremacy Clause. Supreme Court litigator Paul Wolfson recognizes that "an attempt to distinguish between the congressional veto rejected by the Framers and the preemption doctrine in force today along enumerated-powers lines fails because the limitations on congressional power set forth in Article I, Section 8 are practically no limitations at all."[117]

Preemption doctrine defers to congressional claims to override state laws or permits a complex regulatory regime to stand as evidence that there is no room left for state action. The Framers believed that the states and general government would enjoy concurrent powers over various matters, but preemption doctrine rejects this. Simply put, preemption doctrine frequently disrespects our federal constitutional structure.

Justice Clarence Thomas has objected that the Supreme Court "has pre-empted state law based on its interpretation of broad federal policy objectives, legislative history, or generalized notions of congressional purposes that are not contained within the text of federal law."[118] "Congressional and agency musings," Thomas observes, "do not satisfy the Article

I, § 7, requirements for enactment of federal law and, therefore, do not pre-empt state law under the Supremacy Clause."[119]

Discussion and Solutions

The Supreme Court should renounce the freewheeling, extratextual preemption doctrine that invites, in the words of Justice Thomas, "judicially manufactured policies," allowing the Court to strike state laws as improper obstacles to the full accomplishment of a federal regulatory regime.[120] Preemption doctrine must focus on a real conflict between a state law and the text of a federal statute or regulation. And, of course, the federal statute or regulation must be within the bounds of an enumerated power. A federal policy—whether declared by the Court or a regulatory body—is not "law" under the Supremacy Clause.[121] Hence, the Court must return to constitutional basics when considering preemption issues.

Section 3

The Senators and Representatives before mentioned, and the Members of the several State Legislatures, and all executive and judicial Officers, both of the United States and of the several States, shall be bound by Oath or Affirmation, to support this Constitution; but no religious Test shall ever be required as a Qualification to any Office or public Trust under the United States.

Purpose

The Framers viewed an oath as a serious matter. An oath solemnizes the event and impresses upon believers that they will answer for misdeeds in the age to come. In the spirit of religious toleration, one may by affirmation promise to support the Constitution. Section 3 specifically prohibits any religious test to hold office. The main thrust of the Oaths Clause was to impress upon state officials their role in executing federal law, not as competitors with the general government but as necessary partners in it.

Background and Development

The Virginia Plan proposed "that the Legislative Executive & Judiciary powers within the several States ought to be bound by oath to support the articles of Union."[122] Edmund Randolph of Virginia believed that the Oaths Clause would bind state officials to the national system and contribute to strengthening the new government's support. Roger Sherman of Connecticut opposed the clause on grounds that it improperly trespassed on state jurisdiction. North Carolina's Hugh Williamson believed that national officers should swear a reciprocal oath to support state constitutions. Reciprocal oaths were rejected because members of the federal government, in the words of Madison's *Federalist* No. 44, "have no agency in carrying the State Constitutions into effect."[123]

The delegates eventually agreed on a clause and, according to Hillsdale College's Matthew

Spalding, it "helps to fulfill the Framers' plan to integrate the states into the electoral, policy-making, and executory functions of the federal union."[124] In deference to the Quakers' religious view that oaths improperly create one standard of truthfulness for daily living and another for special occasions, the oath-taker may "affirm" rather than "swear."

The Philadelphia Convention agreed unanimously that religious tests should not be required for holding office in the general government. Although there is nothing in Madison's *Notes* to explain the decision, in the Massachusetts ratifying convention Rev. Daniel Shute provided a general rationale for the prohibition. Shute observed that religious tests would disqualify otherwise capable men from office and would do nothing to deter rapscallions, because "[u]nprincipled and dishonest men will not hesitate to subscribe to anything that may open the way for their advancement, and put them in a situation the better to execute their base and iniquitous designs."[125] Reverend Shute believed that "there are worthy characters among men of every denomination—among the Quakers, the Baptists, the Church of England, the Papists; and even among those who have no other guide, in the way to virtue and heaven, than the dictates of natural religion."[126] He contended that the best security was not a religious test but the people's choosing of men known for ability, probity, and character.

SUMMATION

To quiet the fears of the Confederation's creditors, the Framers expressly declared that a change in the charter of government would not equal a cancellation of justly acquired debts. The United States would make good on its obligations. Despite the careful enumeration of powers in the Constitution, the Framers realized that conflict between the general and state governments was a possibility. Therefore, the Framers adopted the Supremacy Clause, declaring that the Constitution, along with statutes and treaties made pursuant to it, would trump state laws to the contrary. In light of the role that state officials have in executing federal law, the Constitution requires them to take an oath to support it.

ARTICLE VII

THE RATIFICATION OF the Conventions of nine States, shall be sufficient for the Establishment of this Constitution between the States so ratifying the Same.

Purpose

The Framers recognized that only the people of the several states acting in separate conventions could exercise ultimate authority in modifying their state constitutions and adopting the federal Constitution. Hence, mere legislatures were not allowed to ratify the fundamental charter for the union. The

Framers also realized that the Constitution might not receive approval in all the states; therefore, they provided that it would go into effect once nine states ratified it. The Constitution was only in effect in those states that ratified it, however. States had the option of staying outside the new union.

Background and Development

The Virginia Plan's fifteenth resolve contemplated that the work of the Philadelphia Convention "after the approbation of Congress . . . be submitted to an assembly or assemblies of Representatives, recommended by the several Legislatures to be expressly chosen by the people, to consider & decide thereon."[127] In supporting that resolve, Madison argued "that the new Constitution should be ratified in the most unexceptionable form, and by the supreme authority of the people themselves."[128] Pennsylvania's James Wilson agreed with Madison and was firm in his position that the new Constitution should be submitted to the people "and not to the *Legislatures*, for ratification."[129] George Mason of Virginia elaborated on the matter: "The Legislatures have no power to ratify it. They are the mere creatures of the State Constitutions, and cannot be greater than their creators."[130] Connecticut's Oliver Ellsworth, in commenting on the desire for the people to ratify, observed that "a new sett of ideas seemed to have crept in since the articles of Confederation were established. Conventions of the people, or with power derived expressly from the people, were not then thought of."[131]

The idea of the people holding ultimate authority was not an entirely new idea. For example, in its Declaration of Rights, adopted about three weeks before the Declaration of Independence, Virginia averred that "all power is vested in, and consequently derived from, the People."[132] But the use of special conventions called into existence to wield sovereign power was innovative. As noted by historian Gordon Wood, "in the context of eighteenth-century thought the idea of a legal body existing outside of the representative legislature and making law which the legislature could not make was . . . a radical innovation in politics."[133] By the time Alexis de Tocqueville visited the United States in the early 1830s, he could aver that "[w]henever the political laws of the United States are to be discussed, it is with the doctrine of sovereignty of the people that we must begin."[134]

The first state to call a special convention to draft a constitution and then to submit this product to the people was Massachusetts. In so doing, Massachusetts became the model of popular sovereignty in the making of constitutions.[135] That innovation in the theory of government did not come from the state's leading politicians, but rather from town meetings of farmers and tradesmen.[136] The elites envisioned government continuing as it had before, only without interference from royal officials or Parliament. The people wanted a new frame of government that guaranteed certain rights and, most important, elicited the consent of the governed.

Between the Declaration of Independence and the Massachusetts Constitution of 1780, most of the former colonies adopted constitutions in their legislative branches. That should not be surprising insofar as a parliament, under British constitutional theory, could make or unmake fundamental law. Massachusetts taught Americans the difference between legislative power and constituent power. Only the people can exercise the latter, while their agents exercise the former *after* the people make a delegation of authority in a constitution. In his *Notes on the State of Virginia*, Thomas Jefferson praised Massachusetts for its chosen method of adopting a constitution and urged his state to follow its example: "[T]o render a form of government unalterable by ordinary acts of assembly, the people must delegate persons with special powers. They have accordingly chosen special conventions to form and fix their government."[137]

The Constitution was submitted not to one national convention, but to individual state conventions. Gouverneur Morris of Pennsylvania moved for a single national convention, but no delegate seconded the proposal to even allow its discussion. Separate state conventions, the Framers realized, were necessary for ratification because the people of each state, in adopting the Constitution of 1787, also were amending their state constitutions. For instance, to the extent that a state constitution granted the legislature the power of regulating trade with foreign nations, other states in the union, and Indian tribes, the people of the state had to reassume that power and then confer it on the general government. No one other than the people of a state themselves could do so. Accordingly, the states as political societies in their highest sovereign capacities are the parties to the constitutional compact.

Nine of the thirteen states were required to ratify the Constitution before it went into effect. And, when in effect, its jurisdiction would extend only to the ratifying states. Daniel Carroll of Maryland believed that all thirteen states should be required to ratify because the existing Confederation had been adopted unanimously and, moreover, unanimous consent was prescribed for amending the Articles. Pennsylvania's James Wilson believed seven was an appropriate number because it constituted a simple majority of the states. Considering the problems facing the several states and recognizing the weight of Carroll's reasoning, Wilson urged his colleagues not to be overscrupulous in adhering to the Articles' unanimity requirement. Other delegates suggested that eight, nine, and ten were the optimum numbers for ratification. Virginia's George Mason favored nine because certain momentous decisions in the Confederation Congress required the assent of nine states, and he believed that the number nine would be familiar to the people and meet with their approval. The Framers ultimately decided on ratification by nine states.

The Framers debated whether to submit the plan of government to Congress for approval. Wilson made clear that such a move would doom it to failure. If Congress did not endorse the Constitution, then the state legislatures would decline to call ratification conventions. He foresaw Rhode Island, a state that did not send delegates to Philadelphia, never voting for the Constitution in Congress and thus torpedoing a new government. The other delegates recognized the wisdom in Wilson's words and omitted any reference to congressional approval of the Constitution.

Post-ratification, the great legal minds of the United States taught their students about the people's power to adopt or abolish government. The American understanding of popular sovereignty was eventually enshrined in Blackstone's *Commentaries*—albeit in St. George Tucker's 1803 annotated version of the text. In his Appendix A to the first volume of the *Commentaries*, Tucker made clear that the British concept of sovereignty did not survive the American Revolution. Tucker described the people as possessing "indefinite and unlimited power."[138] If a mere legislature exceeded a grant of power found in a constitution, Tucker stated that the resulting statute offended "against a greater power from whom all authority, among us, is derived" and that the offending act should be opposed.[139] With such annotations, Tucker attempted to render Blackstone usable for American lawyers brought up in the republican tradition.

Similarly, James Wilson lectured on the people's authority while teaching at the College of Philadelphia, which is now the University of Pennsylvania. Wilson explained to his students that "[t]he supreme power of the people is a doctrine unknown and unacknowledged in the British system of government. The omnipotent authority of parliament is the dernier resort."[140] In the United States, on the other hand, "no prerogative or government can be set up as coequal with the authority of the people. The supreme power is in them; and in them, even when a constitution is formed, and government is in operation, the supreme power still remains."[141] Government operates based on a delegation of power from the people. The people choose how much authority to delegate, to whom, and for what period of time. The people are the ultimate sovereigns.

Distortions

Americans have lost appreciation for the importance of popular sovereignty and its locus. While Americans might have some general idea that "the people" are the source of power, they typically assume that the amalgamated people of the nation adopted the Constitution. Indeed, some leading men in the early republic asserted similar views. For example, James Wilson, in the Pennsylvania ratifying convention, argued that the Constitution was established by "the people of the United States" and thus there was not "the least trace of a compact in that system."[142] By "compact," Wilson meant a contract or agreement between two or more parties. Based on his assertion that the amalgamated people ratified, he argued that only one party existed, and thus the Constitution could not be a compact.

The majority of modern scholars agree with Wilson. For example, Yale's Akhil Amar asserts that "[o]nly the People of the United States as a whole are sovereign."[143] While one must respect the intellectual heft of a Wilson or Amar, their conclusions about sovereignty and the compact are counter to the plain language of Article VII and the method used to adopt the Constitution. Had "the American people" adopted the Constitution, North Carolina and Rhode Island could never have been outside the union; but they were, until their own conventions ratified and accepted the Constitution.

Edmund Pendleton, in the Virginia ratification convention, described the Constitution as "the only government founded in real compact."[144] If the compact among the states was ever violated, Pendleton assured Virginians that the people of Virginia could assemble in a convention and "wholly recall our delegated powers."[145] Of course, it was not just Virginians who described the work of the Philadelphia Convention as a compact. Pennsylvania's Gouverneur Morris, an advocate of an energetic national government, explained that he came to Philadelphia "to form a compact for the good of America" and was "ready to do so with all the States" as parties.[146]

In their Kentucky and Virginia Resolutions, Jefferson and Madison both described the Constitution as a compact among the states. By "compact," they meant an agreement or contract between independent parties giving rise to rights and obligations. Thinking in terms of compacts was second nature to the Revolutionary War generation. In protesting against the assumptions of power by Parliament, the colonists repeatedly appealed to the "principles of the English Constitution, and the several charters and compacts" to vindicate their rights.[147] Legendary Jefferson scholar Dumas Malone has observed that in the late eighteenth century, "this view of [the Constitution] was widely held."[148] Fundamental to understanding the Constitution as a compact was the process in which the people of the several states ratified the Constitution. According to Madison in his Report of 1800, "[t]he Constitution of the United States was formed by the sanction of the states, given by each in its sovereign capacity."[149] Thus, Madison reasoned that the states "are consequently parties to the pact from which the powers of the Federal Government result."[150]

Scholars such as Amar reject the compact theory because if it is correct, then South Carolina's nullification of the tariff in 1832 and the secession of the Southern states in 1860–61 must be reconsidered. The nationalist view of the Constitution has become part of modern America's civic religion. Those who do challenge this aspect of the civic religion cannot expect to hold positions at Yale or even a midlevel state college.

Amar and others ignore that the independent states forming the union would not exist absent a secession from the British Empire. Every American revolutionary was a believer and a participant in secession. The Constitution, drafted just four years after the Treaty of Paris ended the War of Independence, did not reject our revolutionary principles. Had pro-ratification forces claimed that after ratifying, a state could not leave the union, we would still be governed by the Articles of Confederation. The people were already leery about the proposed federal government, and three state ratification conventions explicitly claimed the power to reassume powers delegated to the federal government—in other words, to secede.

In the early 1790s, senators from New England were frustrated with Southern insistence that the United States retaliate against the British because of affronts to American commerce. Senators Rufus King and Oliver Ellsworth (from New York and Connecticut, respectively) approached Senator John Taylor of Virginia to discuss a peaceful dissolution of the union. Nothing came from the talks, but more significantly, no one doubted their propriety.

As Thomas Jefferson, author of the Declaration of Independence, noted in 1819, "if any state in the union will declare that it prefers separation . . . to a continuance in union . . . I have no hesitation in saying 'let us separate.'"[151] Alexis de Tocqueville, after his study of American government, came to the following conclusion: "If one of the states chose to withdraw its name from the contract, it would be difficult to disprove its right of doing so."[152] Belief in secession was practically universal in the early American republic. The celebrated American historian Robert Remini has noted that Andrew Jackson in the 1830s was "the first and only statesman of the early national period to deny publicly the right of secession."[153] After the Civil War, in *Texas v. White* (1868), the Supreme Court weighed in on secession when deciding the ownership of certain financial instruments.[154] The Court opined that the union was indissoluble, and thus secession was unthinkable.

Discussion and Solutions

Americans should embrace the decentralized federal structure found in the Constitution of 1787. This structure is at the heart of strict construction originalism. Federalism allows preexisting political communities—the states—to govern themselves based on differences in culture, climate, political philosophy, and various other factors. We do not require a national one-size-fits-all remedy for every ill that befalls us, nor should our diverse peoples be fitted for the bed of Procrustes.

Part of embracing a real federalism is acknowledging and embracing the role of the state conventions, which point to the locus of ultimate sovereignty: the people of the several states. Acceptance of the compact theory also raises mechanisms of self-defense, such as a state veto and secession. Certainly, such remedies should never be used for light and transient causes. But their mere existence might deter governmental overreach from Washington, DC.

Friends of centralization, of course, argue that the Civil War settled the issue, and the Supreme Court agreed in *Texas v. White* (1868). But the Reconstruction Congress also agreed that blacks and whites should attend segregated schools in Washington, DC, and separate-but-equal was established Supreme Court precedent for years. Fortunately, "settled" constitutional mistakes can always be rectified.

AMENDMENTS

A Note on the Bill of Rights

IN THE WANING days of the Philadelphia Convention, Virginia's George Mason asked the delegates to preface the Constitution with a bill of rights. Mason explained that a federal bill of rights "would give great quiet to the people," and he believed a suitable declaration of rights "might be prepared in a few hours."[1] Elbridge Gerry of Massachusetts made the formal motion to fashion an enumeration of rights, and Mason seconded the motion. Roger Sherman of Connecticut asserted that the various state declarations of rights were not repealed by the Constitution and thus would be sufficient to protect the people's liberties. Mason countered that the Constitution's Supremacy Clause would make national laws "paramount to State Bills of Rights," and thus an additional security was needed.[2] James Madison's *Notes* show that the debate ended here and that the Gerry-Mason motion was defeated by a vote of ten states to none (with Massachusetts abstaining).

In refusing to give Mason's suggestion proper attention, the Philadelphia Convention blundered. Unwittingly, the delegates provided Anti-Federalists with ammunition that they masterfully used in the ratification debates. "There are certain rights which we have always held sacred in the United States," wrote the Federal Farmer, "and recognized in all our constitutions, and which, by the adoption of the new constitution in its present form, will be left unsecured."[3] The Federal Farmer did not object to national laws taking precedence over state laws; but he did believe that "national laws ought to yield to unalienable or fundamental rights."[4] A Maryland Farmer shared the Federal Farmer's concern about fundamental rights. In times of passion and heated debate, the Maryland Farmer explained, the natural rights of individuals would likely be "lost" if "not clearly and expressly ascertained" in the governing document.[5]

Brutus emphasized that the principles of the national compact "ought to have been clearly and precisely stated, and the most express and full declaration of rights to have been made—But on this subject there is almost an entire silence."[6] Universal experience, Brutus reasoned, compelled the inclusion of a declaration of rights in the Constitution. Those in power "have been found in all ages ever active to enlarge their powers and abridge the public liberty."[7] This thirst for power "has induced the people in all countries, where any sense of freedom remained, to fix barriers against the encroachments of their rulers."[8] Using England as an example, Brutus pointed to the Magna Carta and the English Bill of Rights as "the boast, as well as the security, of that nation."[9] Considering the importance of such great charters in Anglo-American liberty, Brutus found it "astonishing, that this grand security, to the rights of the people, is not to be found in this constitution."[10]

Staunch Federalists rejected claims that a national bill of rights was necessary. James Wilson, for example, argued that bills of rights were proper in state constitutions, in which the people "invested their representatives with every right and authority which they did not in explicit terms reserve."[11] The federal Constitution, Wilson averred, was different. Absent an express delegation of power, the federal government could not act. "[I]t would have been superfluous and absurd to have stipulated with a federal body of our own creation," Wilson proclaimed, "that we should enjoy those privileges of which we are not divested, either by the intention or the act that has brought the body into existence."[12] Wilson then gave the example of freedom of the press. "[W]hat control can proceed from the Federal government to shackle or destroy that sacred palladium of national freedom?" Wilson asked.[13] Had the people delegated "a power similar to that which has been granted for the regulation of commerce . . . to regulate literary publications, it would have been as necessary to stipulate that the liberty of the press should be preserved inviolate."[14] Because the Constitution mentioned nothing about publications, Wilson reasoned that Congress could not limit the dissemination of information and opinion. An amendment declaring that Congress could not interfere with the press, Wilson claimed, would be dangerous. "[T]hat very declaration might have been construed to imply that some degree of power was given, since we undertook to define its extent."[15]

In several state ratifying conventions, the Anti-Federalists made strong arguments to conditionally ratify the Constitution or to call a second convention to consider a bill of rights and structural amendments. In preparing for the Virginia ratifying convention, Madison wrote to Jefferson, who was serving as the American minister in Paris, that "[t]he preliminary question will be whether previous alterations shall be insisted on or not? Should this be carried in the affirmative, either a conditional ratification, or a proposal for a new Convention will ensue. In either event, I think the Constitution and the Union will be both endangered."[16]

Ratification was certainly endangered, but respected statesmen (such as George Wythe in Virginia and John Hancock in Massachusetts) urged ratification without conditions. These men spoke of the blessings of union, the defects of the Articles, and the hard work of the Philadelphia Convention. They acknowledged shortcomings in the Constitution and suggested that a few well-designed amendments—obtained after ratification—might cure the infirmities. The arguments of such statesmen carried the day. Although ratifying, Massachusetts, New York, Virginia, and other states submitted proposed amendments and requested that the first Congress consider them promptly. Indeed, Federalist assurances that amendments would be considered in good faith was an unwritten pact of ratification.

To the chagrin of Federalists, demands for a bill of rights and substantive amendments did not die after ratification of the Constitution. Anti-Federalists continued to express serious concerns about the lack of safeguards for individual liberty and the broadly worded provisions granting power to the new government. For example, in September 1788, delegates from Philadelphia and thirteen Pennsylvania counties met in Harrisburg to consider steps in a post-ratification world. The delegates agreed that the citizenry should acquiesce in the formation of the general government, but they worried about the Constitution's effects on future generations. The national compact, they averred, "contains in it some principles which may be perverted to purposes injurious to the rights of free citizens."[17] The document also contained "some ambiguities which may probably lead to contentions incompatible with order and good government."[18] Hence, the delegates resolved that "early" and "considerable amendments are essentially necessary."[19] They recommended that the Pennsylvania legislature petition Congress for a second convention to convene and consider revision of the Constitution.

Madison's continental reputation and campaign-trail endorsement of amendments earned him a seat in the House of Representatives. Although the first Congress was overwhelmingly Federalist in composition, Madison knew he needed to make good on his promises of amendments to the Constitution. Two states (Rhode Island and North Carolina) remained outside the union because of perceived defects in the Constitution, and Virginians were keeping a close eye on his efforts.

Because the House was preoccupied with pressing business in the early months of its existence, Madison waited until June 8, 1789, to offer his proposals. Madison acknowledged that the House was busy, but he urged that the members "should commence the enquiry, and place the matter in such a train as to inspire a reasonable hope and expectation, that full justice would eventually be done to so important a subject."[20] He further assured Federalists that he "had no design to propose any alterations which . . . could affect [the Constitution's] main structure of principles, or do it any possible injury."[21] Madison did not want radical amendments, but just enough to quiet Anti-Federalists and to demonstrate that he and other Federalists were acting in good faith.

Madison's proposals for amendments were met with skepticism. Roger Sherman of Connecticut thought that "the necessity of amendments would be best pointed out by the defects, which experience may discover in the constitution."[22] Georgia's James Jackson compared the Constitution to a ship "that has never been put to sea." Until the voyage was undertaken and ocean conditions were experienced, "we can not determine with any precision, whether she sails upon an even keel or no."[23] Hence, he believed that any amendments offered would be "speculative and theoretical."[24]

Madison pressed on despite the consternation of many in the House. The resolutions he submitted, which will be examined below, were ultimately crafted by the House and Senate into twelve amendments that were sent to the states. Ten of those were ratified quickly and became what we know as the Bill of Rights.

Today, when we think of the Bill of Rights and landmark Supreme Court cases, we typically think of restrictions on actions of the states. It does not occur to modern Americans that the Bill of Rights applied only to the general government. As the preamble to the Bill of Rights declares, "further declaratory and restrictive clauses" were adopted because the state conventions wanted some security to "prevent misconstruction and abuse of" powers delegated to the general government.[25] The people of the states were satisfied with their own bills of rights and restrictions on state power appearing in the various state constitutions.

Even the Supreme Court in 1833 recognized the limited applicability of the federal Bill of Rights. Writing for the Court in *Barron v. Baltimore* (1833), Chief Justice Marshall observed that during the late 1780s, "fears were extensively entertained that" certain powers "might be exercised in a manner dangerous to liberty."[26] He continued:

> In almost every convention by which the Constitution was adopted, amendments to guard against the abuse of power were recommended. These amendments demanded security against the apprehended encroachments of the General Government—not against those of the local governments. In compliance with a sentiment thus generally expressed, to quiet fears thus extensively entertained, amendments were proposed by the required majority in Congress and adopted by the States. These amendments contain no expression indicating an intention to apply them to the State governments. This court cannot so apply them.[27]

From the 1920s to the present, the Supreme Court has "incorporated" most of the rights found in the first eight amendments and applied them against the states. To do so, the Court has held that the Fourteenth Amendment, enacted after the Civil War, was intended to nationalize fundamental rights. Hence, the Court holds that these rights have been "incorporated" via the Fourteenth Amendment's Due Process Clause. (The arguments for and against incorporation are addressed in the section on the Fourteenth Amendment.)

To generations of Americans who have lived on this side of incorporation, it is difficult to appreciate the natural limits of the Bill of Rights as applying to only federal action. It is even more difficult to reconcile the original intent behind many of the amendments with the result of incorporation. For example, the First Amendment left the states to decide whether they would have established churches, and one state (Massachusetts) kept its established church until 1833. Yet today the First Amendment is applied not just to prevent state-established churches but to ban nativity scenes from state government property. State policy decisions that were never intended to be within the purview of the Constitution form the heartland of the Supreme Court's blockbuster decisions. In what follows, *The Independent Guide* will examine the amendments to the Constitution, the intent behind the amendments, and developments in American law that cannot be squared with strict construction originalism.

AMENDMENT I (RATIFIED 1791)

CONGRESS SHALL MAKE no law respecting an establishment of religion, or prohibiting the free exercise thereof; or abridging the freedom of speech, or of the press; or the right of the people peaceably to assemble, and to petition the Government for a redress of grievances.

Purpose

The First Amendment is addressed specifically to the U.S. Congress and deals with broad topics of religion, speech, and the people's influence over the government. It prohibits Congress from establishing a national church or compelling Americans to worship God in a congressionally sanctioned manner. Because open discussion of political issues and the character of leaders and would-be leaders is critical to the functioning of a representative democracy, free speech and the press are secured by the amendment. The rights to assemble and petition government are also protected because of their relation to representative democracy. A democratic system should encourage the people to gather to discuss matters important to the body politic and to demand that their leaders address pressing issues.

Background and Development

Several states proposed amendments dealing with speech, the press, religious freedom, and petitioning the general government. The Virginia ratifying convention's proposals provide an excellent example of the broad concerns in these three areas:

15th. That the people have a right peaceably to assemble together to consult for the common good, or to instruct their representatives; and that every freeman has a right to petition or apply to the legislature for redress of grievances.

16th. That the people have a right to freedom of speech, and of writing and publishing their sentiments; that the freedom of the press is one of the greatest bulwarks of liberty, and ought not to be violated. . . .

20th. That religion, or the duty which we owe to our Creator, and the manner of discharging it, can be directed only by reason and conviction, not by force or violence; and therefore all men have an equal, natural, and unalienable right to the free exercise of religion, according to the dictates of conscience, and that no particular religious sect or society ought to be favored or established, by law, in preference to others.[28]

Since James Madison narrowly won a seat in the U.S. House of Representatives, campaigning on the promise of amending the Constitution to address the concerns of Anti-Federalists, it is likely that Madison referred to Virginia's proposed amendments when introducing the subject in the House.

Establishment and Free Exercise

Many scholars point out correctly that Madison was especially interested in religious freedom and was the author of the 1785 Memorial and Remonstrance Against Religious

Assessments. In that document, Madison successfully defeated an effort to revive Virginia state taxes for the support of ministers and teachers laboring in Christian churches. Prior to the Revolution, Virginia tax dollars supported Anglican clergy members, but the church was disestablished in 1779. However, some Virginians, such as Patrick Henry, wanted to revive the tax and distribute the proceeds to support Protestant Christianity.

In the words of historian Kevin R. C. Gutzman of Western Connecticut State University, the Memorial and Remonstrance diagrammed "the whole American Enlightenment case for religious freedom."[29] Madison argued that man's status "as a subject of the Governor of the Universe" takes precedence over his membership in civil society; therefore, religion (which is a matter between man and God) "is wholly exempt from [society's] cognizance."[30] Madison objected to the establishment of Christianity over other religions because he feared that a government with such power would likely begin to favor certain denominations over others. He further opined that Christ's kingdom does not need state support because the Bible promised that the very gates of hell would not prevail against the church universal.

One must be careful, however, in transposing Madison's personal views into any language contained in amendments to the Constitution. Madison, like most Federalists, did not believe that amendments or a Bill of Rights were required and was forced to acquiesce to them because of the traction gained by Anti-Federalist arguments. Moreover, the push for amendments was intended to protect the states and their citizens from encroachment of the national government. Although

Madison and other Founders might have held "American Enlightenment" views on religion and the state, the proper forums in which to advance those views were in the states themselves. The design of the Constitution of 1787 was to leave such matters as religion, speech, and the press in the hands of individual state governments. Hence, we should not assume that Madison and the other Founders believed that the federal Constitution or the national legislature was the proper venue for pursuing their policy preferences on religious establishment, religious exercise, freedom of the press, speech, and so on.

On June 8, 1789, Madison offered a list of proposed amendments to the House. Madison drafted the amendments to be incorporated into the body of the Constitution rather than placed at the end. (Americans can thank Roger Sherman of Connecticut for insisting that the original constitutional text be preserved and that amendments be appended to the document.) Madison's fourth resolution provided a foundation for what would become our First Amendment:

> That in article 1st, section 9, between clauses 3 and 4, be inserted these clauses, to wit, The civil rights of none shall be abridged on account of religious belief or worship, nor shall any national religion be established, nor shall the full and equal rights of conscience be in any manner, or on any pretext infringed.
>
> The people shall not be deprived or abridged of their right to speak, to write, or to publish their sentiments; and the freedom of the press, as one of the great bulwarks of liberty, shall be inviolable.
>
> The people shall not be restrained from peaceably assembling and consulting for

their common good, nor from applying to the legislature by petitions, or remonstrances for redress of their grievances.[31]

Concerning protections for religion, some in Congress opposed such an amendment because the Constitution gave Congress no power to establish churches or interfere with worship. They saw no reason to amend the Constitution when there was no power needing limitation or clarification. Daniel Carroll of Maryland spoke in favor of the amendment because "it would tend more toward conciliating the minds of the people to the government than almost any other amendment he had heard proposed."[32] Others in Congress expressed concern that the provision could harm the cause of organized religion. Madison countered this by explaining that the simple purpose of an amendment protecting religion was so "Congress should not establish a religion, and enforce the legal observation of it by law, nor compel men to worship God in any manner contrary to their conscience."[33]

In the annals of constitutional interpretation, Madison's cogent explanation for the amendment's purpose concerning religion has been ignored in favor of one line in a letter that President Thomas Jefferson wrote to the Danbury Baptists wherein he described the First Amendment as "building a wall of separation between church and State."[34] In 1878, the Supreme Court took this one line and described it as "accepted almost as an authoritative declaration of the scope and effect of the amendment thus secured."[35]

The idea of a "wall of separation" hardly fit the American situation in the states or the more limited federal government. We must remember that in 1775, on the eve of the American Revolution, nine of the thirteen colonies had established churches. Massachusetts continued with an established church until 1833. Three days after approving the First Amendment, the first Congress authorized the appointment of paid chaplains for the House and Senate. The first Congress also reenacted the Northwest Ordinance, which proclaimed that "[r]eligion, morality, and knowledge, being necessary to good government and the happiness of mankind, schools and the means of education shall forever be encouraged."[36] This same Congress also asked that President Washington "recommend to the people of the United States a day of public thanksgiving and prayer, to be observed by acknowledging with grateful hearts the many and signal favors of Almighty God, especially by affording them an opportunity peaceably to establish a form of government for their safety and happiness."[37] As observed by Justice Joseph Story in his exposition of the Constitution, "at the time of the adoption of the Constitution, and the amendments to it . . . the general, if not the universal, sentiment in America was, that Christianity ought to receive encouragement from the State, so far as such encouragement was not incompatible with the private rights of conscience, and the freedom of religious worship."[38] While Jefferson's "wall of separation" has proved to be a catchy phrase, it is far removed from the American situation or the work of the first Congress.

The final form of the House's effort that was sent to the Senate made clear that protections for religion applied to Congress alone—not the states. Protections for speech and for remonstrances for the redress of grievances were phrased in more general terms. Had Madison had his druthers, the states would also have been restricted in interfering with the rights of conscience and a free press. The Senate, as representatives of the state legislatures, rejected House proposals to limit state power. Indeed, the states had requested amendments to guard against the powers of the general government, not the state governments. Thus, the proposals of Madison's fourth resolution on religion, speech, and petitioning were condensed into one proposed amendment that applied to Congress.

Concerning the "free exercise" component of the First Amendment, Stanford's Michael W. McConnell notes that "[e]ach of the thirteen states, with only one exception (Connecticut) guaranteed religious liberty in its constitution, often using the terminology 'free exercise of religion.'"[39] McConnell identifies two common elements from state free exercise provisions: (1) independence on the part of the individual believer's conscience from the state's judgment about appropriate worship, and (2) a limitation of free exercise so it does not interfere with the peace and safety of the state. In a 1986 report to the U.S. attorney general on the historical meaning of free exercise guarantees, a survey of colonial and state practice concluded that "free exercise clauses secured the religious practices of religious institutions, and in particular, the minority sects, and that they alone could judge their own doctrines and affairs."[40] As for government interference, the report concluded that "until those activities threatened public peace and safety or infringed the rights of others," the state "had no right to interfere" with religious practices.[41]

Speech and the Press

To determine the Founders' understanding of freedom of speech and of the press, resort must be had to the common law. The standard common-law rule was that a person could not be stopped from publishing a matter; however, the publisher was not insulated from civil or criminal penalties once the publication was circulated. Moreover, a person who spoke or published matter defamatory of the government or intended to stir up commotions or treason was subject to prosecution for sedition. Although the common law is clear, we should not assume that the general government has the power to prosecute a person for a publication so long as there is no prior restraint or to drag critics into court for public criticisms of the government. Congress must always first point to an enumerated power before acting. During the ratification debates, the Federalists were clear that Congress had no power to interfere with speech or the press. For example, in *Federalist* No. 84, Alexander Hamilton, questioning the need for a bill of rights, asked, "For why declare that things shall not be done which there is no power to do? Why, for instance, should it be said, that the liberty of the press shall not be restrained, when no power is given by which restrictions may be imposed?"[42]

Despite the Federalist assurances about the lack of congressional power, in 1798 Congress passed and President John Adams signed the Sedition Act, which at its essence made criticism of the general government a crime. To enact this measure, members of the Federalist Party claimed to rely on inherent powers, federal common law, and the Necessary and Proper Clause. They could not point to a specific enumerated power to support the statute. The Republican opposition rallied to the First Amendment and propelled itself into the libertarian vanguard concerning speech and press. In his Report of 1800, Madison argued that because the United States is grounded in principles of popular sovereignty and republicanism, "the freedom of the press requires that it should be exempt, not only from previous restraints by the executive, as in Great Britain; but from legislative restraint also" and "the subsequent penalty of laws."[43] In a republic, Madison reasoned, the people require broad freedom to examine the conduct and character of public officials. This can only happen when printing and discourse are freed from the standards of the common law.

Similarly, in his 1803 edition of Blackstone, St. George Tucker argued for an "absolute freedom of the press" in place of the common-law rule of no prior restraints. Tucker averred that "[e]very individual, certainly, has a right to speak, or publish, his sentiments on the measures of the government: to do this without restraint, control, or fear of punishment for doing so, is that which constitutes the genuine freedom of the press."[44] Tucker and other Republicans recognized, however, that the several states possessed a broad police power and in the absence of a state constitutional provision could restrict freedom of speech in a manner forbidden to Congress.

Petition and Assembly

The right of the people to assemble and petition government is tied to republicanism, in which officials are agents and the people principals. An agent acts on behalf of a principal and is not greater than the principal. The rights of assembly and petition ensure that the people have the freedom to examine the conduct of their agents in the government and to make their views known.

Scholars describe the right of assembly as a "conduit through which those assembled could critically reflect on their perceptions of reality and reach an end goal."[45] The right to petition the government was a critical component of English history, with the Bill of Rights of 1689 asserting a "right of the subjects to petition the king" and forbidding "all commitments and prosecutions for such petitioning."[46]

Great debate resulted in the House on the subject of petitioning Congress. Thomas Tudor Tucker of South Carolina wanted the amendments to specifically allow constituents to instruct their representatives. Many members opposed Tucker's suggestion because they believed a right to instruct would strip the representatives of the duty to deliberate and use best judgment. George Clymer of Pennsylvania protested that Tucker's proposal "would destroy the very spirit of representation itself" and "render[] Congress a passive machine instead of a deliberative body."[47] Massachusetts's Elbridge Gerry disagreed with Clymer's analysis. Because the people were the ultimate sovereign, Gerry "could not conceive why they had not the right to instruct and direct their agents at their pleasure."[48] After much discussion, Tucker's suggestion was rejected.

Distortions

Modern Supreme Court jurisprudence is far afield from the original understanding of the First Amendment. Part of the problem is that via the doctrine of incorporation (discussed under the Fourteenth Amendment), the First Amendment is now applied to the states. Thus, provisions that were intended to preserve state freedom of action are now used to prohibit conduct. What follows is an overview of the distortions in areas of religion, freedom of speech, and freedom of association.

Establishment and Free Exercise

Rather than the First Amendment prohibiting the establishment of a state-sponsored church, for example, beginning in 1971 the Court employed the *Lemon* test to determine whether modest aid to religion amounts to an establishment. As set forth in *Lemon v. Kurtzman* (1971), government can aid religion only if (1) the primary purpose of the assistance is secular, (2) the assistance neither promotes nor inhibits religion, and (3) there is no excessive entanglement between church and state.[49] In *Lemon*, the Court held that state funding for private, nonsecular schools amounted to a prohibited establishment of religion. Jurists and scholars acknowledge that the *Lemon* test has proved vague and difficult to apply. *Lemon* has led to unpredictable results in the lower courts and often the exclusion of religion from the public square despite the history and practice from the founding era. Justice Antonin Scalia went so far as to describe the *Lemon* test as "some ghoul in a late-night horror movie that repeatedly sits up in its grave and shuffles abroad . . . frightening the little children and school attorneys."[50]

It does not take much for the Supreme Court to find a prohibited establishment of religion. For instance, in *Allegheny County v. ACLU* (1989), the Court held that a nativity scene on the main staircase of the county courthouse was an unconstitutional establishment of religion.[51] The Court indicated that had the nativity scene been accompanied by Santa Claus, reindeer, and other secular decorations, the nativity scene would have passed constitutional muster.

State displays of the Ten Commandments are subject to a similar quixotic jurisprudence. In *McCreary County v. ACLU* (2005), the Court held that a prominent display of the Ten Commandments in two county courthouses was constitutionally impermissible because of a "predominantly religious purpose" behind the display.[52] The same day, in *Van Orden v. Perry* (2005), the Court upheld a display of the Ten Commandments on the grounds of the Texas state capitol because it was part of a display celebrating "the State's political and legal history."[53] "The inclusion of the Ten Commandments monument in this group," the Court declared, "has a dual significance, partaking of both religion and government. We cannot say that Texas' display of this monument violates the Establishment Clause of the First Amendment."[54]

In *Kennedy v. Bremerton School District* (2022), the Supreme Court observed that the *Lemon* test had been distilled to whether a reasonable person would believe that the challenged government action was an endorsement of religion.[55] Rather than an endorsement test, the Court made clear that "the Establishment Clause must be interpreted by reference to historical practices and understandings"—that is, the original meaning and history of the prohibition against an establishment of religion.[56] The Court rejected a school district's claim that it was constitutionally required to prohibit a football coach from kneeling at midfield after a game to offer a short prayer of thanks. Rather than preventing an establishment, the Court found that the school district "single[d] out private religious speech for special disfavor."[57]

The Court's Establishment Clause jurisprudence had led governments to discriminate against religious schools. In *Carson v. Makin* (2022), the Court dealt with state benefit programs that allowed public funds to go to private schools, but specifically prohibited religious schools from receiving money.[58] Maine created a tuition assistance program for parents living in school districts without state-funded secondary schools. The program permitted parents to designate a public or private secondary school to which they desired to send their children, and state funds would follow the children to help defray costs. Most private schools were eligible to receive the payments, but only if they were "nonsectarian." Lower courts upheld the restriction, and the Supreme Court reversed. The Court emphasized that "a neutral benefit program in which public funds flow to religious organizations through the independent choices of private benefit recipients does not offend the Establishment Clause."[59] The program parameters amounted to "discrimination against religion."[60]

As for the Free Exercise Clause, the Supreme Court has averred in *Employment Division v. Smith* (1990), that a generally applicable rule that does not target a specific religious practice will not violate the Constitution.[61] *Smith* involved two drug rehabilitation counselors who were fired because they used peyote (a hallucinogen derived from a cactus plant) "for sacramental purposes at a ceremony of the Native American Church, of which both are members."[62] The state denied the men

unemployment benefits because their termination was for cause, since they had consumed a prohibited controlled substance. The therapists argued that the denial of unemployment benefits unconstitutionally burdened their free exercise rights and urged the Court to hold that governmental actions substantially burdening religious practice be justified by a compelling state interest. The Court declined to exercise such a rigorous standard of review for fear that "[a]ny society adopting such a system would be courting anarchy."[63]

Believing that the Court had undermined constitutional protection of free exercise, Congress passed in 1993 the Religious Freedom Restoration Act (RFRA). RFRA prohibits the federal government from substantially burdening the exercise of religion absent demonstration that the rule or law (1) furthers a compelling governmental interest and (2) is the least restrictive means of furthering that compelling governmental interest. Multiple states have enacted their own versions of RFRA.

In *Burwell v. Hobby Lobby Stores, Inc.* (2014), the Supreme Court applied RFRA in a case where Christian business owners objected to an Obamacare mandate requiring them to pay for health insurance coverage for four birth control methods that prevented a fertilized egg from developing by inhibiting its attachment to the uterus.[64] Because of their belief that life begins at conception, the Christian business owners felt that they would be aiding and abetting the murder of unborn children if they funded these methods. The Court held that the Christian business owners did not have to pay for the four methods that they believed induced abortion. The Court assumed that the government had a compelling interest in providing cost-free contraceptives but found that the mandates of Obamacare were not the least restrictive means of furthering that interest.

Speech and the Press

Since the Supreme Court declared that homosexual marriage is a fundamental right in *Obergefell v. Hodges* (2015), federal courts have struggled with balancing freedom of speech and this newly discovered right. For example, in *303 Creative LLC v. Elenis* (10th Cir. 2021), the Tenth Circuit Court of Appeals dealt with a Colorado public accommodations statute that the state averred required a website designer to create web pages and graphics for same-sex weddings despite the designer's personal religious beliefs that marriage is between one man and one woman.[65] The Tenth Circuit did not doubt the designer's sincere belief but held that Colorado had a compelling interest in ensuring equal access to publicly available goods and services and thus the state could coerce the designer to offer her services to homosexual couples planning weddings.

The Supreme Court dodged a similar situation involving a Colorado baker in 2018.[66] But when presented with an appeal from the Tenth Circuit decision in *303 Creative* in 2023, the Court surprisingly reaffirmed that "the First Amendment protects an individual's right to speak his mind regardless of whether the government considers his speech sensible and well intentioned or deeply misguided."[67] The Court found that the wedding websites created by the designer qualify as "pure speech" within the ambit of the First Amendment. To hold otherwise, "would allow the government to force all manner of artists, speechwriters, and others whose services involve speech to

speak what they do not believe on pain of penalty."[68] Such a result "would not respect the First Amendment; more nearly, it would spell its demise."[69]

Not only does the First Amendment protect an individual's right to speech with which government disagrees, but it also prevents government from discriminating against a speaker's viewpoint. In *Shurtleff v. City of Boston* (2022), the Court encountered the city of Boston's refusal to allow the group Camp Constitution to fly a Christian flag on a pole outside City Hall.[70] Boston had permitted hundreds of private groups to use of the flagpole to fly banners such as the gay pride flag, the Chinese flag, and the Juneteenth flag. The city had never denied a request until Camp Constitution asked to fly a Christian flag. The lower courts sided with Boston and held that flying private groups' flags from City Hall's third pole amounted to government speech, and thus Boston could not be compelled to endorse Camp Constitution's message.

The Supreme Court rejected Boston's government speech argument because the city had no policy setting forth that the flagpole was reserved for the city's speech and because it had never denied a request by a private group to fly a flag. The Court held that it was too late in the game for Boston to craft a government speech argument: "When the government encourages diverse expression— say, by creating a forum for debate—the First Amendment prevents it from discriminating against speakers based on their viewpoint."[71]

Under Supreme Court case law, most pornographic material is considered protected speech unless it falls into the category of obscenity. In *Miller v. California* (1973), the Court adopted a three-part test for obscenity:

(1) whether the average person, applying contemporary community standards, would find that the work, taken as a whole, appeals to the prurient interest; (2) whether the work depicts or describes, in a patently offensive way, sexual conduct specifically defined by applicable state law; and (3) whether the work, taken as a whole, lacks serious literary, artistic, political, or scientific value.[72] Most efforts to ban adult pornography fail under the *Miller* test unless the material is "patently offensive 'hard core' sexual conduct."[73] States may regulate non-obscene pornography as to the time, place, and manner of its distribution (through, for example, zoning ordinances and licensing for businesses).

Petition and Assembly

As for the rights to petition and assemble, the Supreme Court has collapsed these safeguards into its free speech jurisprudence. For example, in *De Jonge v. Oregon* (1937), the Court declared that "[t]he right of peaceable assembly is a right cognate to those of free speech and free press."[74] In examining laws that regulate assemblies of the people and their speech, the Court has averred that "[g]overnment may impose reasonable restrictions on the time, place, or manner of protected speech, provided the restrictions are justified without reference to the content of the regulated speech, that they are narrowly tailored to serve a significant governmental interest, and that they leave open ample alternative channels for communication of the information."[75]

Today, Congress treats petitions from the people as formalities by often entering them into the public records without debate or a response to the petitioners. In earlier days,

petitions were taken more seriously. Abolitionists in the 1830s presented sundry petitions to Congress calling for an end to slavery. In an effort to preserve peace between the sections, in the mid-1830s the House adopted a "Gag Rule" requiring that all such abolitionist petitions would be tabled without the taking of further action. In 1844, at the urging of Representative and former President John Quincy Adams, the Gag Rule was lifted. This was a symptom and sign of increasing animosity between the sections.

Discussion and Solutions

The Court's First Amendment jurisprudence needs to return to its historical roots. In adjudicating a case, the Court should examine the founding and inquire what Americans then understood to be an establishment of religion, or free exercise of religious beliefs, or the right to freely examine public actions and characters. Only such an analysis of original understanding can free us from the misguided musings of the Supreme Court.

The idea of a "wall of separation" between government and religion might or might not be wise policy. One thing is sure, however: It is not mandated by the First Amendment. The Establishment Clause prevents the general government from establishing a national church. It does not disallow, for example, tuition payments to sectarian schools while blessing the same payments to private non-sectarian schools. Nor does it require a town hall to sprinkle in reindeer, elves, and Charlie Brown's Christmas tree for a nativity scene to pass constitutional muster. Modern establishment jurisprudence would be comical if it were not enveloping such a weighty subject.

Free exercise principles are also far less complicated than the Court's jurisprudence. So long as government does not interfere with religious practices and doctrines, free exercise is respected.

As for speech and the press, we are in an age of compelled speech, when government seeks to force individuals to express viewpoints with which they disagree. Government is in the virtue-signaling business and expects us to follow its lead. In the early republic, government expected citizens to revile the French and support American war preparedness. Today, government expects us to perform obeisance to certain protected classes and praise their activities and lifestyles. Both then and now, the power of the state is employed. The First Amendment, however, forbids government from forcing citizens to voice "proper" opinions or to hide their views.

AMENDMENT II (RATIFIED 1791)

A WELL REGULATED Militia, being necessary to the security of a free State, the right of the people to keep and bear Arms, shall not be infringed.

Purpose

An armed populace is a deterrent to governmental oppression. The Second Amendment sought to prevent the general government from disarming Americans and thus depriving them of the ability to defend themselves and to check unjust rulers.

Background and Development

Anti-Federalists and various state conventions believed that the federal Constitution should explicitly disclaim any power of the general government to disarm the people. Indeed, the venerable English Bill of Rights provided "[t]hat the subjects which are Protestants may have arms for their defense suitable to their condition and as allowed by law."[76] This provision resulted from the actions of James II when certain "Protestants were disarmed while Catholics were permitted arms and positions in government and the army."[77] The English also realized the importance of arms when James raised large numbers of troops and marched them on London in an effort to intimidate the populace.

In the forefront of the Anti-Federalists' thoughts were attempts by the British army to disarm the colonists in the years leading up to the American Revolution. The royal governor of Massachusetts, General Thomas Gage, routinely ordered redcoats to execute warrantless seizures of firearms and ammunition. As noted by Second Amendment scholar Stephen J. Halbrook, "[t]he Crown's attempts to disarm the colonists" was "a contributing grievance in the chain of events leading to the American Revolution" and subsequent state and federal constitutional provisions protecting the people's right to possess firearms.[78]

The Virginia ratification convention urged that the following amendment be added to the Constitution of 1787: "Seventeenth, That the people have a right to keep and bear arms; that a well regulated Militia composed of the body of the people trained to arms is the proper, natural and safe defence of a free State."[79] The New Hampshire ratification convention suggested this language: "Congress shall never disarm any Citizen unless such are or have been in Actual Rebellion."[80] The minority in the Pennsylvania convention demanded a declaration stating:

> That the people have a right to bear arms for the defense of themselves and their own state, or the United States, or for the purpose of killing game; and no law shall be passed for disarming the people or any of them, unless for crimes committed, or real danger of public injury from individuals; and as standing armies in the time of peace are dangerous to liberty, they ought not to be kept up; and that the military shall be kept under strict subordination to and be governed by the civil powers.[81]

The Federal Farmer (likely New York Anti-Federalist Melancton Smith or a close associate), in his writings against the Constitution, observed that "to preserve liberty, it is essential that the whole body of the people always possess arms, and be taught alike, especially when young, how to use them."[82]

Acknowledging the concern about the possession of arms, Madison included the following in his resolution on amendments of June 8, 1789: "The right of the people to keep and bear arms shall not be infringed; a well armed, and well regulated militia being the best security of a free country: but no person religiously scrupulous of bearing arms, shall be compelled to render military service in person."[83] Madison's language closely followed Virginia's except that he substituted "state" for "country" and added language to protect

conscientious objectors from military service.

Just ten days after Madison introduced his resolution to the House, the Philadelphia *Federal Gazette* published Federalist Tench Coxe's "Remarks on the First Part of the Amendments to the Federal Constitution." Coxe, writing as "A Pennsylvanian," described Madison's proposal on arms as "confirm[ing]" the people's "right to keep and bear their private arms."[84] Coxe noted that the amendment would ensure the people could defend themselves if civil rulers raised military forces that "might pervert their power to the injury of their fellow-citizens."[85]

The House altered Madison's proposal so that the language about the importance of the militia preceded the statement about the people's right to bear arms. This order was preserved in the Senate, and the statement about contentious objectors was dropped.

Although the Second Amendment is the only amendment with such a prefatory clause, that kind of clause was not out of the ordinary. According to Eugene Volokh of the UCLA School of Law, frequently "[s]tate Bills of Rights contained justification clauses for many of the rights they secured."[86] However, these justification clauses "should not be read as a condition on the operative clause[s]."[87] "When you mean to check government authority," Volokh explains, "you do this by imposing specific commands on the government, even if they sometimes don't match your purposes perfectly, rather than by letting the government decide how it thinks the purposes can best be served."[88]

Recognizing the history behind the Second Amendment, the Supreme Court held in *District of Columbia v. Heller* (2008), that the amendment protects an individual right to possess a firearm unconnected with service in a militia.[89] In so holding, the Court rejected the progressive interpretation that the Second Amendment prohibits the federal government only from abolishing state militias or their modern equivalent, the National Guard. In *McDonald v. City of Chicago* (2010), the Court held that the Second Amendment's individual right to keep and bear arms applies against the states via the Fourteenth Amendment.[90]

In *New York State Rifle & Pistol Ass'n, Inc. v. Bruen* (2022), the Supreme Court held that ordinary, law-abiding citizens have a Second Amendment right to carry a handgun for self-defense outside the home.[91] It also struck down a New York licensing regime that conditioned "issuance of a license to carry on a citizen's showing of some additional special need" for self-defense.[92] The Court held that the special need requirement was alien to the Second Amendment's text and the historical understanding of the right to bear arms. The dissenting justices opposed the majority's reliance on historical understanding and urged a test that balances "the serious dangers and consequences of gun violence that led States to regulate firearms" against the interest in possessing a firearm.[93] The approach urged by the dissenting justices would give judges significant leeway to uphold sundry laws restricting gun use or possession.

The *Heller* interpretation of the Second Amendment as protecting an individual right to bear arms is supported by early commentators. St. George Tucker described the right to bear arms as "the true palladium of liberty" and inherent in the natural right of self-defense.[94] William Rawle opined that because of the Second Amendment, "[n]o clause in the Constitution could by any rule of construction be conceived to give Congress a power to disarm the people."[95] Echoing Tucker, Joseph Story described the Second Amendment "as the palladium of the liberties of a republic; since it offers a strong moral check against the usurpations and arbitrary power of rulers."[96]

Distortions

There is a strong movement in progressive circles to resurrect an understanding of the Second Amendment as restricted to militia service. Like the majority of Americans, they lament the gun violence in our major cities (most of which have had strict gun laws in place for decades) and hope that new gun control measures will make a difference despite the failure of the old ones. These activists pine[97] for the days of *United States v. Miller* (1939), in which the Supreme Court upheld provisions of the National Firearms Act prohibiting transportation of a sawed-off shotgun in interstate commerce.[98] The Court held that "[i]n the absence of any evidence tending to show that possession or use of a shotgun having a barrel of less than eighteen inches in length at this time has some reasonable relationship to the preservation or efficiency of a well regulated militia, we cannot say that the Second Amendment guarantees the right to keep and bear such an instrument."[99] *Miller* contained only a cursory examination of the Second Amendment's history, and the matter was not fully briefed because the defendants made no appearance in the case.

Other progressives call for the repeal of the Second Amendment. For example, the advocacy group MoveOn complains that "[t]his anachronistic, poorly worded amendment prevents us from passing real gun control measures that will be effective in stopping the ongoing gun slaughter. It should be no more a constitutional right to own a gun than to own a car."[100] For MoveOn and others on the left, the Second Amendment is an inconvenience that must be erased so law-abiding citizens will be disarmed in the face of rising crime and government overreach.

Discussion and Solutions

Heller resurrected the historical Second Amendment grounded in the natural right of self-defense. Americans should continue to insist on an interpretation of the right to bear arms as centered on individual rights rather than on militia service. Moreover, they should oppose any effort to repeal the Second Amendment. Left-wing activists seek to ban the most useful weapons for self-defense—handguns—so that only criminals and agents of the state will possess them. The Second Amendment stands in the way of such a servile outcome and thus is worthy of a vigorous intellectual defense. The United States does not have a gun problem but a criminality problem. Stricter penalties, more law enforcement officers, and swift prosecutorial action are preferable to impairing law-abiding citizens' use and possession of firearms.

In addition, we must be on watch for theories of interpretation that render the individual right a nullity. For example, after he perceived that the *Heller* majority would take an individual-rights approach, Justice Stephen Breyer proffered an interest-balancing inquiry whereby the courts would measure gun restrictions against government interests such as reducing the level of handgun violence and protecting dense urban populations. So long as a government can demonstrate that its regulation furthers the interests proffered and the limitation on the Second Amendment is not disproportionate to those interests, Justice Breyer concluded that the regulation should be upheld. As Justice Scalia pointed out in *Heller*, "[t]he very enumeration of the right takes out of the hands of government—even the Third Branch of Government—the power to decide on a case-by-case basis whether the right is *really worth* insisting upon."[101] We should take these words to heart and be vigilant against variants of the Breyer test when they percolate up through the lower federal courts.

AMENDMENT III (RATIFIED 1791)

NO SOLDIER SHALL, in time of peace be quartered in any house, without the consent of the Owner, nor in time of war, but in a manner to be prescribed by law.

Purpose

The Third Amendment protects the sanctity of our homes by prohibiting the government from quartering its troops in private homes during time of peace without the consent of the owner. In wartime, troops may be quartered in homes in accordance with the law as set forth by Congress.

238 THE INDEPENDENT GUIDE TO THE CONSTITUTION

Background and Development

In the prefatory section of the English Bill of Rights, the lords and commons levied various charges against James II, including the "raising and keeping a standing army within this kingdom in time of peace without consent of Parliament, and quartering soldiers contrary to law."[102] Although an act of Parliament prohibited lodging soldiers in private homes, James ignored the statute and quartered large numbers of troops with the populace. His raising and billeting of troops thus became a contributing cause of the Glorious Revolution.

Although the colonists and the mother country sparred over the quartering of troops prior to the 1770s, the Quartering Act of 1774 angered colonists because it allowed for the quartering of troops in private homes. Undoubtedly, remembrance of the Quartering Act of 1774 sparked Anti-Federalists and state conventions to demand a constitutional amendment. The Virginia ratifying convention urged the following language: "That no soldier in time of peace ought to be quartered in any house without the consent of the owner, and in time of war in such manner only as the law directs."[103]

In his resolution of June 8, 1789, Madison proposed language very similar to that requested by Virginia: "No soldier in time of peace be quartered in any house, without consent of the owner; nor at any time, but in a manner warranted by law."[104] This wording, with minor changes, ultimately became our Third Amendment.

Distortions

The Third Amendment has sparked little litigation. It has made appearances in the Warren Court's extraconstitutional privacy jurisprudence. In *Griswold v. Connecticut* (1965), the Supreme Court struck down a Connecticut law prohibiting the use of contraceptives as unconstitutionally intruding upon marital privacy.[105] In determining that the Constitution protected a general right to privacy, the Court cited the Third Amendment (among other provisions of the Bill of Rights) and held that the penumbras from these amendments give life and substance to a privacy right. Such misuse of the amendment finds no support in its history and drafting. The amendment deals with the billeting of soldiers in private homes and was not intended to be a source of judicial power to invalidate state police power measures.

Discussion and Solutions

The *Griswold* Court's abuse of the Third Amendment is a reminder of how clearly worded constitutional provisions can be manipulated by those seeking to aggrandize their own power. *Griswold*'s jurisprudence serves as Exhibit A in the argument for originalism's efforts to restrain judicial power while honoring the intent of the Framers and ratifiers. Proponents of originalism must oppose efforts by the courts to co-opt provisions of the Bill of Rights for use in their own extraconstitutional projects—even when we might agree with certain policy objectives such as individual choice about the use of contraceptives. Skillful judicial manipulation typically constitutionalizes a policy preference and further removes the people from the process of self-government. Scholars, lawyers, and citizens must demand that Supreme Court opinions not stray from the clear original intent behind provisions such as the Third Amendment. When they do stray, alarms should sound from elected representatives, the media, and diners sitting at the lunch counter in the corner café. The question is not whether adults should have access to contraceptives, to use the *Griswold* facts as an example, but whether the unelected and unaccountable or the elected and accountable should make such decisions.

AMENDMENT IV (RATIFIED 1791)

THE RIGHT OF the people to be secure in their persons, houses, papers, and effects, against unreasonable searches and seizures, shall not be violated, and no Warrants shall issue, but upon probable cause, supported by Oath or affirmation, and particularly describing the place to be searched, and the persons or things to be seized.

Purpose

The first clause of the Fourth Amendment announces the right to be free from "unreasonable searches and seizures." The second clause provides the basic measure of what constitutes a reasonable search. A government actor must obtain a warrant from a magistrate and establish probable cause for the belief that, say, contraband will be found in a location. The government actor must swear by oath or affirmation and describe with particularity the place to be searched and the things to be seized.

Background and Development

Writs of assistance used by royal customs agents in the colonies to search for goods that had been smuggled (that is, no duty on the goods had been paid to the Crown) were an impetus for our Fourth Amendment. These writs allowed British officials "to search anyone's property without warning or even probable cause."[106] In 1761, when asked to help in enforcing the writs of assistance, James Otis (serving as the chief government attorney in the colony of Massachusetts) resigned his post and represented the smugglers pro bono because of his belief that such writs were counter to the British constitution. Otis challenged the writs as forbidden general warrants because they described no location with particularity and the complainant had sworn no oath regarding facts showing probable cause. A general warrant, Otis complained, "places the liberty of every man in the hands of every petty officer."[107] Otis lost the case, but his arguments gained currency throughout the colonies.

Fuel was added to the colonial fire when the British government in London used general warrants to seize the papers of opposition politician John Wilkes, who had published comments critical of the British ministry in his newspaper, *The North Briton*. Armed with general warrants, government officials searched approximately five houses and arrested almost fifty people. Wilkes and his colleagues brought trespass actions against the government officials. In multiple cases decided between 1763 and 1765, courts held that the general warrants were contrary to the common law. Juries awarded Wilkes and his friends monetary damages. The colonists followed the Wilkes affair with much interest and believed the rulings vindicated Otis's constitutional arguments.

Critics of the Constitution of 1787 seized on the people's hatred of general warrants to question the work of the Philadelphia Convention. Patrick Henry, speaking in the Virginia ratifying convention, questioned why the Framers did not protect citizens from "general warrants, by which an officer may search suspected places, without evidence of the commission of a fact, or seize any person without evidence of his crime."[108] The Anti-Federalist writing as Brutus predicted that the general government would exercise broad authority in "granting search warrants, and seizing persons, papers, or property."[109] Hence, he believed that for "the security of liberty" the Constitution needed a specific provision to protect the people against unreasonable searches and seizures.[110]

The Virginia ratifying convention demanded a federal declaration of rights averring the following:

> Fourteenth, That every freeman has a right to be secure from all unreasonable searches and seizures of his person, his papers and his property; all warrants, therefore, to search suspected places, or seize any freeman, his papers or property, without information upon Oath (or affirmation of a person religiously scrupulous of taking an oath) of legal and sufficient cause, are grievous and oppressive; and all general Warrants to search suspected places, or to apprehend any suspected person, without specially naming or describing the place or person, are dangerous and ought not to be granted.

The New York ratifying convention proposed similar language in its ratification message.

Acknowledging the concern about general warrants and unreasonable searches, Madison included the following in his resolution on amendments of June 8, 1789: "The rights of the people to be secured in their persons, their houses, their papers, and their other property from all unreasonable searches and seizures, shall not be violated by warrants issued without probable cause, supported by oath or affirmation, or not particularly describing the places to be searched, or the persons or things to be seized."[111] With minor changes, this proposal became our Fourth Amendment.

Distortions

In *Wolf v. Colorado* (1949), the Supreme Court held that the core of the Fourth Amendment, described as "security . . . against arbitrary intrusion by the police," was "enforceable against the States through the Due Process Clause" of the Fourteenth Amendment.[112] In *Mapp v. Ohio* (1961), the Court went further and held that evidence obtained by searches and seizures in violation of the Fourth Amendment is inadmissible in a state court. This is known as the exclusionary rule. The exclusionary rule was first applied to federal law enforcement officers in *Weeks v. United States* (1914).[113] The purpose of the exclusionary rule is to deter police misconduct. A police officer faced with the knowledge that critical evidence could be excluded if proper procedures are not followed will likely err on the side of caution in preserving a putative defendant's constitutional rights.

While the exclusionary rule might be good policy, it is alien to the Framers' Fourth Amendment. As evidence by the Wilkes case discussed above, at common law the remedy for an unreasonable search and seizure was a trespass action against the offending government officials and an award of damages. The Framers assumed that the remedy for a Fourth Amendment violation, in the words of Princeton's Bradford P. Wilson, "was met by the remedial aspect of the common law regarding unreasonable searches and seizures."[114] The Supreme Court, believing that the common law's remedy was insufficient, constitutionalized the exclusionary rule. To the extent that the remedy for a Fourth Amendment violation needed updating, one must question whether judicial amendment of the Bill of Rights was the appropriate vehicle. Congress, for example, could simply have amended the Federal Rules of Evidence to exclude evidence recovered during an unreasonable search and seizure. Such rulemaking would allow a more flexible approach and permit adjustments as circumstances dictate.

The Supreme Court has recognized multiple exceptions to the exclusionary rule. Among the most important are the inevitable discovery doctrine and the good-faith exception. Under the inevitable discovery doctrine, if the evidence in question would have been inevitably discovered through lawful means, a trial court is not required to suppress the evidence. According to the good-faith exception, evidence obtained by police officers with a good-faith belief that they are acting pursuant to the law (that is, acting pursuant to a search warrant issued by a judge that is later found to have been legally defective) is not required to be suppressed.

Current Fourth Amendment jurisprudence is closely tied to *Katz v. United States*

(1967), in which the Court held that the Fourth Amendment was violated by agents attaching an eavesdropping device to the outside of a public phone booth to capture Katz's transmission of illegal gambling information.[115] In a departure from jurisprudence employing a property-based approach, the Court averred that "the Fourth Amendment protects people, not places."[116] Concurring in *Katz*, Justice John Marshall Harlan II suggested that a Fourth Amendment violation occurs when police officers violate a person's "reasonable expectation of privacy."[117] Justice Harlan's analysis quickly became the North Star of Fourth Amendment jurisprudence.

Since *Katz's* departure from the historic property-based approach, results in Fourth Amendment cases are factually specific and can veer toward the quixotic. The Court has found that overnight house guests have a reasonable expectation of privacy in the home they are visiting (*Minnesota v. Olson* [1990]),[118] but individuals present in a home for a short business transaction do not have such an expectation (*Minnesota v. Carter* [1998]).[119] A person in lawful possession of a rental car "has a reasonable expectation of privacy in it even if the rental agreement does not list him or her as an authorized driver" (*Byrd v. United States* [2018]).[120] Passengers in a car (rental or otherwise) do not have a reasonable expectation of privacy in the vehicle (*Rakas v. Illinois* [1978]).[121]

Discussion and Solutions

Modern Fourth Amendment jurisprudence—with its exclusionary rule and focus on people's reasonable expectation of privacy—might be good policy. Policy, however, is a matter for legislatures, not jurists. The federal and state legislatures should make the decision whether the common law's remedy for an unreasonable search and seizure (a trespass action) is an insufficient deterrent to police misconduct. A legislature might adopt an exclusionary rule or empower a court to enjoin police misconduct or to impose criminal sanctions against offending officers. A legislature might require a law enforcement officer to be suspended without pay for two weeks if they are found to have violated the Fourth Amendment. There are myriad options and, unlike the Supreme Court, *The Independent Guide* advocates state experimentation so that state governments can serve as true laboratories of democracy.[122] Unfortunately, the Court has short-circuited legislative policy decisions and designed its own regime. So long as we claim to live in a republic, we should insist that the courts exit the policy arena and allow elected officials to make such decisions.

AMENDMENT V (RATIFIED 1791)

NO PERSON SHALL be held to answer for a capital, or otherwise infamous crime, unless on a presentment or indictment of a Grand Jury, except in cases arising in the land or naval forces, or in the Militia, when in actual service in time of War or public danger; nor shall any person be subject for the same offence to be twice put in jeopardy of life or limb; nor shall be compelled in any criminal case to be a witness against himself, nor be deprived of life, liberty, or property, without due process of law; nor shall private property be taken for public use, without just compensation.

Purpose

The Fifth Amendment provides protections for important rights related to criminal trials, such as grand jury presentment, prohibitions against double jeopardy and compulsory incrimination, and due process. It also requires government to pay just compensation when it uses the power of eminent domain.

Background and Development

The Constitution's silence on safeguards for federal criminal trials concerned the Anti-Federalists. In the Massachusetts ratifying convention, Abraham Holmes protested that nothing in the Constitution protected the rights of an accused in a federal criminal case.

Examining the Constitution, Holmes could not discern whether an accused had a right to grand jury presentment or other common safeguards. "These are matters of by no means small consequence," Holmes explained, "yet we have not the smallest constitutional security that we shall be allowed the exercise of these privileges."[123] Holmes admitted that Congress might pass fair rules for criminal cases; but if they did so, it would be owing "to the goodness of men, and not in the *least degree* owing to the goodness of the Constitution."[124] The Massachusetts ratifying convention suggested that the Constitution be amended to state "[t]hat no person shall be tried for any crime, by which he may incur an infamous punishment, or loss of life, until he be first indicted by a grand jury, except in such cases as may arise in the government and regulation of the land and naval forces."[125] The Virginia ratification convention similarly demanded constitutional protection for grand jury presentment.

In his June 8 resolution, Madison suggested that "in all crimes punishable with loss of life or member, presentment or indictment by a grand jury, shall be an essential preliminary."[126]

Grand Jury Presentment

In English common law, according to William Blackstone, a presentment "is the notice taken by a grand jury of any offense from their own knowledge or observation, without any bill of indictment laid before them at the suit of the king."[127] We are more familiar with the government proceeding in front of the grand jury with an indictment, which is "a written accusation of one or more persons of a crime . . . presented" to a grand jury.[128] Hence, when modern lawyers speak of grand jury presentment, they envision the government prosecutor presenting an indictment and evidence to a grand jury. Blackstone described the grand jury as "usually gentlemen of the best figure in the county." A grand jury panel under the common law must be "twelve at least, and not more than twenty-three."[129] Today, federal rules require that a grand jury must have sixteen members present for a quorum.

For an indictment to be found valid at common law and today, at least twelve members of the grand jury must endorse it as a "true bill"—meaning that probable cause exists to show that the accused is likely guilty. Blackstone described the grand jury as one of a "strong and two-fold barrier, of a presentment

and a trial by jury, between the liberties of the people, and the prerogative of the crown."[130] In a republican government, the Founders believed that the grand jury remained essential to protect citizens from oppressive government prosecutions. The Supreme Court has described the grand jury's historic function as "provid[ing] a shield against arbitrary or oppressive action, by insuring that serious criminal accusations will be brought only upon the considered judgment of a representative body of citizens acting under oath and under judicial instruction and guidance."[131]

The text of the Fifth Amendment contains an exception to the grand jury requirement: "arising with the land or naval forces, or in the militia, when in actual service in time of War or public danger." The Supreme Court has interpreted the words "when in actual service in time of War or public danger" as applying only to the militia. The Fifth Amendment does not require grand jury presentment for crimes committed by service members in the land or naval forces.

Double Jeopardy

The Fifth Amendment's Double Jeopardy Clause traces its origins back to English common law. In addressing double jeopardy in the context of capital litigation, Blackstone observed that "no man is to be brought into jeopardy of his life, more than once for the same offence. And hence it is allowed as a consequence, that when a man is once fairly found not guilty upon any indictment, or other prosecution . . . he may plead such acquittal in bar of any subsequent accusation for the same crime."[132]

The New York ratifying convention demanded that the Constitution be amended to declare "[t]hat no Person ought to be put twice in Jeopardy of Life or Limb for one and the same Offence, nor unless in case of impeachment, be punished more than once for the same Offence."[133] Maryland similarly desired an amendment to ensure that there be no "second trial after acquittal."[134] According to the University of Notre Dame's G. Robert Blakely, "[a]ll state constitutions drafted prior to the Bill of Rights contained a double-jeopardy provision."[135] In light of state demands and state bills of rights, Madison's June 8 resolution proposed the following amendment: "No person shall be subject, except in cases of impeachment, to more than one punishment, or one trial for the same offence."[136] In debates in the House, Samuel Livermore of New Hampshire described a double jeopardy provision as "essential" and understood settled law in Great Britain and the United States as prohibiting second trials after an acquittal.[137]

The main controversy surrounding the Double Jeopardy Clause is the Supreme Court's dual-sovereignty doctrine. Under this theory, "a single act gives rise to distinct offenses—and thus may subject a person to successive prosecutions—if it violates the laws of separate sovereigns."[138] Because the states are separate sovereigns from the general government, a state prosecution does not bar a later federal prosecution of the same person for the same crime (or vice versa). In *Gamble v. United States* (2019), in which the defendant was prosecuted in both state and federal court for illegally possessing a firearm, the Supreme Court revisited the dual-sovereignty doctrine and affirmed its applicability.[139] "We have long held that a crime under one sovereign's laws is not 'the same offence' as a crime under the laws of another sovereign."[140] Key to the Court's

reasoning is that although the defendant's conduct under consideration in state and federal court is the same, the offenses are different (even if the elements of the crime are the same) because different sovereigns have criminalized the behavior. Justice Thomas concurred in the judgment and admitted that he was initially skeptical of the dual-sovereignty doctrine, but there was not enough in the historical records to change his mind. "The founding generation foresaw," Justice Thomas wrote, "very limited potential for overlapping criminal prosecutions by the States and the Federal Government" since they understood Congress to have a very limited criminal jurisdiction; "therefore[,] [they] had no reason to address the double jeopardy question that the Court resolves today."[141]

Self-Incrimination

Enshrined in the Fifth Amendment is the right against self-incrimination in criminal cases. The Virginia and New York ratifying conventions both believed a federal bill of rights should protect accused persons from giving evidence against themselves. Indeed, scholars note the privilege "was included in the constitutions of eight states prior to the adoption of the Fifth Amendment."[142] In light of the history and specific demands from the states, one should not be surprised that Madison included a right against self-incrimination in his June 8 resolution.

The most famous self-incrimination decision is *Miranda v. Arizona* (1966), in which the Warren Court held that the prosecution cannot use statements "stemming from custodial interrogation of the defendant unless it demonstrates the use of procedural safeguards effective to secure the privilege against self-incrimination."[143] *Miranda* requires law enforcement officers to inform individuals in custody of their right of silence, that any statement they do make may be used as evidence against them, and that they have a right to the presence of an attorney. The Court's conclusion that a failure to give *Miranda* warnings per se equates to a violation of the privilege against compelled self-incrimination stirred criticism.

Prior to *Miranda*, courts simply examined a confession to ensure that it was voluntary—that is, not coerced. In dissent, Justice Harlan observed that the *Miranda* decision was nothing "but the Court's own fine spun conception of fairness which I seriously doubt is shared by many thinking citizens in this country."[144] In other words, *Miranda* was nothing but the Warren Court making public policy.

In *Dickerson v. United States* (2000), the Court had the opportunity to hold that *Miranda* warnings were "prophylactic" and not constitutional.[145] The Court doubled down on *Miranda* and held that the rule announced was indeed constitutional and thus could not be superseded by federal or state statutes measuring the voluntariness of confessions.

Due Process

The Fifth Amendment's Due Process Clause prohibits deprivations of life, liberty, or property without due process of law. The idea of due process dates back to chapter 39 of the Magna Carta, which provides that "[n]o freeman shall be taken, imprisoned, or disseized, or outlawed, or exiled, or in any way harmed—nor we will go upon or send upon him—*save by the law of the land*."[146] By the end of the fourteenth century, Englishmen

viewed "due process of law" and "law of the land" as interchangeable phrases.[147] By the time the colonists arrived in North America, due process meant that before the government could punish a person for some act or omission, government had to resort to the courts and use "established and nondiscriminatory procedures" under "pre-existing laws."[148]

Early treatise writers supported this understanding. For example, St. George Tucker examined the Fifth Amendment's Due Process Clause and instructed that due process "is by indictment or presentment of good and lawful men, where such deeds be done in due manner, or by writ original of the common law." Tucker further stated that due process "must then be had before a judicial court, or a judicial magistrate."[149] William Rawle in his treatise saw the due process clause as intimately connected with the other procedural guarantees contained in the Bill of Rights, such as grand jury presentment, the right to counsel, and the right to confront witnesses at trial. According to Rawle: "It follows from all the antecedent precautions, that 'no one can be deprived of life, liberty, or property, without due process of law,' and the repetition of this declaration is only valuable as it exhibits the summary of the whole, and the anxiety that should never be forgotten."[150] Hence, Rawle saw the Due Process Clause as having no independent significance other than as an exclamation point on other procedural guarantees.

The modern Supreme Court has held that "the central meaning of procedural due process" is notice of proposed deprivation of liberty or property and an opportunity to be heard at a meaningful time and in a meaningful manner.[151] The Court has broadly defined the liberty and property interests at stake and has imposed procedural due process requirements on such matters as the termination of welfare benefits and public employment.[152] Interests in continued employment and benefits "are not created by the Constitution. Rather, they are created and their dimensions are defined by existing rules or understandings that stem from an independent source such as state law—rules or understandings that secure certain benefits and that support claims of entitlement to those benefits."[153]

The Court has also read a substantive requirement into due process. Substantive due process will be discussed in the section on the Fourteenth Amendment.

Takings Clause

The final words of the amendment are known as the Takings Clause: "nor shall private property be taken for public use, without just compensation." No state ratification convention suggested such a clause, since no eminent domain power was delegated to Congress. Madison, perhaps appreciating possible future uses of the Necessary and Proper Clause, included the forerunner of the clause in his June 8 resolution: No person shall "be obliged to relinquish his property, where it may be necessary for public use, without a just compensation."

The thrust of the Takings Clause is clear. If government, say, desires a particular piece of property to build a base for military training, the government must pay the owner of the property a fair market value. In 1922, the Supreme Court recognized that the clause also applied to regulatory takings—that is, when government regulation limits the use of property to the extent that the owner is effectively denied the reasonable use or value of the property.[154] This principle was affirmed in *Lucas v. South Carolina Coastal Council* (1992), when the Court found that a state law, aimed at controlling erosion on barrier islands, that banned construction on beachfront property amounted to seizing all economic value from the property owner and thus was a taking.[155]

As for what constitutes "public use," the Court has rejected the obvious "use by the public" as the proper definition. In *Kelo v. City of New London* (2005), the Court held that public use can consist of a government taking a home from one person and giving it to another in expectation that the second person will develop the property and increase the city's tax base.[156] *Kelo* arose out of an economic development plan in New London, Connecticut. The New London Development Corporation (NLDC), a private corporation chartered to assist the New London city council, created a plan to revitalize ninety acres of the city in connection with a proposed Pfizer pharmaceutical facility. Among other things, the plan called for the building of a waterfront conference hotel, restaurants, shopping centers, and parking facilities.

The city approved the plan in January 2000 and authorized the NLDC to acquire the property through purchases or the power of eminent domain exercised in the city's name. Some residents entered into voluntary transactions with the NLDC, but other residents refused. One such resident was Wilhelmina Dery. Ms. Dery had lived in the same house since her birth in 1918. Her home had been in the family for more than one hundred years, was in good repair, and provided a view of the waterfront. The subjective value of this home to Ms. Dery was far more than the NLDC's offer; therefore, she filed a lawsuit arguing that government could not take property for the private use of other owners simply because the new owners might make more productive use of the property. She contended that the text of the amendment permitted the taking of private property only if the public had a right to employ it (as in the case of public roads, public parks, and so on).

The Court rejected Ms. Dery's appeal to the words of the Takings Clause in favor of the NLDC's assurance that the exercise of eminent domain was part of a carefully considered development plan. In essence, the Court erased the words "public use" from the amendment and substituted the words "public purpose."

Distortions

The most troubling aspect of the Court's Fifth Amendment jurisprudence is its desire to make public policy rather than interpret preexisting law. The *Miranda* decision is the poster child for the Court acting as a legislature. The requirement that a police officer read certain warnings to a person in custody might be good policy, but it is not the Court's role to make policy. *Miranda*, to echo Justice Harlan, is nothing but the Court's own idea of what fairness should look like.

The Court has not only added requirements to an amendment but has also deleted safeguards that do not coincide with the Court's preferred outcomes. *Kelo* marked a troubling day for property holders, when the Court discarded the Takings Clause's public use requirement and crafted a public purpose provision that allows governments to take property and give it to developers if the government believes the transfer will increase its revenues.

Discussion and Solutions

Although every citizen who has watched a cop show such as *Hawaii Five-O* or *NYPD Blue* assumes *Miranda* is just a natural part of policing, we should not resign ourselves to the permanence of the Warren Court's policy pronouncements. Maybe the famous warnings should stay; maybe they should go. Whatever the case, the ultimate decision belongs to elected officials who are accountable to the people. Americans should insist that the accountable branches of government set the rules for how police treat individuals in custody. State legislatures can hold hearings, receive testimony from law enforcement and the criminal defense bar, examine arrest statistics, and make an informed choice about the place of warnings. A court, on the other hand, is limited to hearing from the parties in the distinct case and controversy before it.

Americans should also demand that the Court respect the plain text of the amendment, including "public use." The *Kelo* decision invites the powerful and politically connected to lobby government to transfer private property to them. The rightful owners are left with no remedy. Property ownership is placed in a precarious position because of the Court's departure from the constitutional text. *Kelo* should be overruled when public use issues are presented again.

AMENDMENT VI (RATIFIED 1791)

IN ALL CRIMINAL prosecutions, the accused shall enjoy the right to a speedy and public trial, by an impartial jury of the State and district wherein the crime shall have been committed, which district shall have been previously ascertained by law, and to be informed of the nature and cause of the accusation; to be confronted with the witnesses against him; to have compulsory process for obtaining witnesses in his favor, and to have the Assistance of Counsel for his defence.

Purpose

A criminal trial is a serious matter in which an accused faces possible loss of life, liberty, and property. The Sixth Amendment secures the rights of an accused to have a speedy and public trial, all charges explained, a jury to decide issues of fact, confrontation of adverse witnesses, the assistance of counsel, and the ability to procure and call defense witnesses.

Background and Development

To appreciate the Sixth Amendment, one must understand the importance the Founders attached to juries. As recounted previously in the discussion of Article III, the Founders believed that juries were barriers against tyranny. While today many Americans see judges as guardians of liberty, the jury occupied this position for the Founders because juries could reject unconstitutional statutes and refuse to convict in unjust proceedings.

During the Massachusetts ratifying convention, Abraham Holmes said it was a universal maxim "that the safety of the subject consists in having a right to a trial as free and impartial as the lot of humanity will admit of."[157] Holmes believed that a person should be tried by "a jury of the peers [who] would, from their local situation, have an opportunity to form a judgment of the *character* of the person charged with a crime, and also judge of the *credibility* of the witnesses."[158] He inveighed against the Constitution because it lacked a speedy trial guarantee; thus an accused could be subject to a "long, tedious, and painful" pretrial incarceration.[159] Once the accused got to trial, Holmes wondered whether the defendant would have an opportunity "to confront the witnesses" against him.[160] The federal Constitution, Holmes perceived, provided nothing but uncertainty.

In the North Carolina ratifying convention, Samuel Spencer raised similar concerns. He described juries as "the bulwarks of our rights and liberty" and demanded that local juries—juries of the vicinage—try all federal criminal offenses.[161] The Virginia ratifying convention shared such concerns and suggested the following amendment touching upon criminal jury trials:

> That in all capital and criminal prosecutions, a man hath a right to demand the cause and nature of his accusation, to be confronted with the accusers and witnesses, to call for evidence and be allowed counsel in his favor, and to a fair and speedy trial by an impartial Jury of his vicinage, without whose unanimous consent he cannot be found

guilty, (except in the government of the land and naval forces) nor can he be compelled to give evidence against himself.[162]

Anti-Federalist protests caused Madison to recommend the following to Congress: "In all criminal prosecutions, the accused shall enjoy the right to a speedy and public trial, to be informed of the cause and nature of the accusation, to be confronted with his accusers, and the witnesses against him; to have a compulsory process for obtaining witnesses in his favor; and to have the assistance of counsel for his defence."[163] Madison also suggested that in criminal cases, an accused be tried "by an impartial jury of freeholders of the vicinage, with the requisite of unanimity for conviction, of the right of challenge, and other accustomed requisites."[164]

The major division between the House and Senate was the vicinage provision, which would have guaranteed local juries. The Senate strongly opposed defining the locality of juries. Senators complained that "vicinage" was too vague, and state practice was far from uniform in choosing juries from specific geographic areas. After failed attempts to sway the senators, the House proposed the language "an impartial jury of the State and district wherein the crime shall have been committed." Hence, the conception of a vicinage requirement is tied to a "district," the boundaries of which are set by Congress.

Speedy Trial

The first clause of the amendment secures an accused's right to a speedy trial. This right dates back to the Magna Carta, which stated: "We will sell to no man, we will not deny or defer to any man either justice or right."[165] The Supreme Court has described the speedy trial guarantee as "an important safeguard to prevent undue and oppressive incarceration prior to trial, to minimize anxiety and concern accompanying public accusation and to limit the possibilities that long delay will impair the ability of an accused to defend himself."[166] In *Barker v. Wingo* (1972), the Court identified four factors that should be considered when adjudicating a speedy trial claim: (1) the length of the delay; (2) the reason for the delay; (3) the defendant's assertion of the right to a speedy trial; and (4) prejudice to the defendant as a result of the delay.[167]

Under current federal statutory law, a defendant who pleads not guilty to charges brought in an indictment or information is entitled to a trial "within seventy days from the filing date (and making public) of" the charging document "or from the date the defendant has appeared before a judicial officer of the court in which such charge is pending, whichever date last occurs."[168] Defendants can waive their speedy trial rights and often agree to case continuances so they can examine the government's evidence, plan a defense, or engage in plea negotiations. Upward of 90 percent of federal criminal defendants choose to negotiate with the government and plead guilty.

Public Trial

A public trial is also a component to the first clause of the amendment (and has First Amendment implications). According to the Supreme Court, the right to a public trial "has always been recognized as a safeguard against any attempt to employ our courts as instruments of persecution. The knowledge that every criminal trial is subject to contemporaneous review in the forum of public opinion is an effective restraint on possible abuse of judicial power."[169] Public trials encourage all participants—judges, lawyers, witnesses, and jurors—to responsibly perform their functions. The right to a public trial is typically traced to an English common-law privilege that predated the Norman Conquest. Indeed, prior to Norman rule all subjects in the local community were required to attend trials.

The Court has recognized that proceedings can be closed in certain circumstances. A courtroom closure must meet a four-part test crafted in *Waller v. Georgia* (1984): (1) the party seeking closure must advance an overriding interest that is likely to be prejudiced, (2) the closure must be no broader than necessary to protect that interest, (3) the trial court must consider reasonable alternatives to closing the proceeding, and (4) the trial court must make findings adequate to support the closure.[170] Closures are rare and typically concern national security matters, child victims, or undercover law enforcement agents.

Impartial Jury

In addition to a speedy and public trial, the Sixth Amendment guarantees an impartial jury. Scholars observe that "[a]t common law, jurors were 'impartial,' not because they knew nothing about the case, but simply because they had no family ties to any of the parties and no financial interest in the outcome."[171] The importance of impartiality is demonstrated by an early opinion of Chief Justice John Marshall in which he instructed that "[t]he jury should enter upon the trial with minds open to those impressions which the testimony and the law of the case ought to make, not with those preconceived opinions which will resist those

impressions."[172] Marshall did not demand that jurors be ignorant of the facts and issues involved—only that they make an ultimate decision based on the evidence presented at trial. In modern America, the Supreme Court has held that a jury free of bias is not enough for impartiality. In addition to lack of bias, "an impartial jury [must be] drawn from a cross-section of the community."[173] Intentional exclusion of any "social, religious, racial, political and geographical groups," according to the Court, undermines the "democratic ideals of trial by jury."[174]

Arraignment

An accused has a right to be informed of the charges against him or her. The Framers wanted a criminal process that operated in the light, not the shadows. No one brought to court for a criminal case should be puzzled at the accusations leveled. Though the accused might have a view of the facts different from the government's view, the Arraignment Clause ensures that the accused will be informed of exactly what is alleged to be the person's criminal activity. In modern practice, the federal judge conducting the arraignment offers to review the indictment or information with the defendant to make sure the accused understands the nature of the charges.

Confrontation

The amendment guarantees the right of defendants to confront their accusers. The right to confront one's accuser dates to the Roman Empire and is evidenced in legal proceedings brought against the Apostle Paul. The book of Acts contains excerpts from a letter written by the Roman procurator Porcius Festus concerning Paul and the demands of the Jewish religious leaders that Paul be delivered over to them. Festus informed King Agrippa, "I told them that it is not the Roman custom to hand over anyone before they have faced their accusers and have had an opportunity to defend themselves against the charges."[175]

Undoubtedly, the Framers also had in mind the injustice of 1618 when Sir Walter Raleigh was beheaded for high treason. Raleigh was convicted on the basis of ex parte affidavits and was denied the right to confront his accusers in court. His trial was more of a continental civil-law proceeding than a common-law trial featuring live testimony and adversarial testing. At the time, many lamented that the trial and execution were black marks on English justice.

The Supreme Court, in *Mattox v. United States* (1895), described "[t]he primary object" of the Confrontation Clause as avoidance of "depositions or ex parte affidavits, such as were sometimes admitted in civil cases, being used against the prisoner in lieu of a personal examination and cross-examination of the witness."[176] The Supreme Court has rejected interpreting the Confrontation Clause to apply only to "in-court testimony" and thus leave admission of out-of-court statements offered at trial to the applicable rules of evidence.[177]

To hold otherwise, the Court noted in *Crawford v. Washington* (2004), "would render the Confrontation Clause powerless to prevent even the most flagrant inquisitorial practices."[178]

Compulsory Process

A criminal defendant has the right to compulsory process for obtaining favorable witnesses. The Framers were aware that the early common law denied defendants use of compulsory process. By the time of the Revolution, English defendants did have access to compulsory process in treason and felony prosecutions. The Compulsory Process Clause sought to ensure this liberalized trend applied in federal court. The Supreme Court has noted that "[t]he right to offer the testimony of witnesses, and to compel their attendance, if necessary, is in plain terms the right to present a defense, the right to present the defendant's version of the facts as well as the prosecution's to the jury so it may decide where the truth lies."[179]

Assistance of Counsel

The final words of the Sixth Amendment guarantee the assistance of counsel. Until the mid-eighteenth century, the English common law forbade lawyers from appearing in court on behalf of defendants accused of felony offenses. The colonies, as distinguished from the mother country, employed more liberal standards, allowing the participation of counsel in trials of serious offenses. The Sixth Amendment constitutionalized this more liberal practice. Scholars agree, however, that the drafters and ratifiers of the Sixth Amendment intended only for a defendant to have the right to retain counsel and for that counsel to appear in court. There was no contemplation of appointed counsel at government expense.

In *Johnson v. Zerbst* (1938), the Supreme Court held that in federal criminal cases, an accused is entitled to counsel regardless of financial means.[180] The Court described the Sixth Amendment as containing "a realistic recognition of the obvious truth that the average defendant does not have the professional legal skill to protect himself when brought before a tribunal with power to take his life or liberty."[181] In *Gideon v. Wainwright* (1963), the

Court held that the Constitution mandates state courts to appoint attorneys for indigent defendants.[182] The Court described lawyers in criminal cases as "necessities" and pointed out that the "government hires lawyers to prosecute and defendants who have the money hire lawyers to defend themselves."[183]

Distortions

The Supreme Court has taken liberties in constitutionalizing safeguards such as the right to appointed counsel. Government-funded counsel was alien to the founding period.[184] Of course, with the complexities of modern criminal cases and discovery in some cases consisting of terabytes of data, a lawyer is very much a necessity; but the decision to fund counsel for indigents should be made by the accountable branches of government. The legislature is the body that makes policy and should decide whether appointed counsel is appropriate for all criminal cases, some criminal cases (for example, those involving a statutory penalty of more than five years'

imprisonment), or no criminal cases. The Court's decision that a defendant is entitled to counsel regardless of financial means might be good policy, but it is policy nonetheless. Making policy—whether we favor or abhor it—is not the function of the judiciary.

Discussion and Solutions

Scholars, lawyers, and citizens should challenge the courts to leave policy matters to the politically accountable branches. Living constitutionalism is but a legal theory that transfers decision-making from elected representatives to unelected judges. We must reject all its forms and facets, even when we agree with the ultimate outcome that it reaches. While the modern practice of appointing counsel for indigent defendants is wise, just as important is who makes that policy—unelected and unaccountable judges or elected representatives. If the judges are the appropriate authority, then we lose the advantages of republican government and move toward oligarchy.

AMENDMENT VII (RATIFIED 1791)

IN SUITS AT common law, where the value in controversy shall exceed twenty dollars, the right of trial by jury shall be preserved, and no fact tried by a jury, shall be otherwise re-examined in any Court of the United States, than according to the rules of the common law.

Purpose

The Seventh Amendment guarantees the right to jury trials in civil cases and prevents reexamination of facts found by a jury.

Background and Development

Article III guarantees the right to a jury trial in criminal cases. It is silent on jury trials in civil cases. As previously discussed, the Framers considered a jury guarantee for civil trials but did not include it in the Constitution because the several states took different approaches to distinguishing between cases at law (which involved jury trials) and cases at equity (in which the judge decided all issues). Hence, the Philadelphia Convention fretted that any division it made would be unsatisfactory and thus become an obstacle to ratification.

That omission was a mistake, and the Anti-Federalists launched effective attacks based on that mistake. The Federal Farmer, writing against ratification, argued that if the delegates in Philadelphia believed "no words could be found for the uniform establishment of" jury trials in civil cases, then the people should not expect Congress to be able to draft federal legislation protecting the right.[185] The Federal Farmer described jury trials in civil cases as "one of our fundamental rights" that would be put in jeopardy because of the decision to omit it from the Constitution.[186] Ratification of the Constitution without a protection for civil jury trials, the Federal Farmer continued, would be an indication that the people relinquished the right or simply did not care about it.

Patrick Henry was blunter in the Virginia ratifying convention. "How does your trial by jury stand? In civil cases gone."[187] Given the Constitution's omission of protection of civil jury trials, the Virginia ratification convention recommended the following amendment: "That in controversies respecting property, and in suits between man and man, the ancient trial by Jury is one of the greatest Securities to the rights of the people, and ought to remain sacred and inviolable."[188] Similar recommendations came from the ratifying conventions of Massachusetts, New York, New Hampshire, and Rhode Island.

In the face of objections and multiple demands to protect civil jury trials constitutionally, Madison's June 8 resolution recommended that "[i]n suits at common law, between man and man, the trial by jury, as one of the best securities to the rights of the people, ought to remain inviolate."[189] Madison also recommended prohibiting appellate courts from reexamining facts found by a civil jury. That recommendation answered Anti-Federalists' arguments that even if Congress established civil jury trials, the federal courts could cast aside jury findings based on their Article III jurisdiction to review law and fact.

Representative Samuel Livermore, who had served on New Hampshire's appellate bench, opposed the proposed Seventh Amendment because he did not believe that juries were suited to decide all civil cases. He preferred to leave Congress with the discretion to decide which category of civil cases required a jury. Livermore's objections, however, could not overcome the weight of Anti-Federalist demands. No other member spoke in like manner regarding civil juries.

The Senate inserted the Twenty Dollar Clause into what would become the Seventh Amendment. No state or Anti-Federalist writer ever suggested such wording. According to legal scholar Lawrence B. Solum, the "dollar" referred to is not a U.S. dollar, but "the Spanish silver dollar weighing 416 grains and possibly other dollars with closely approximate silver content."[190] Likely, the Senate desired to limit civil jury trials to significant cases, and in 1791, twenty dollars was no small amount.

What does the term "common law" mean in the Seventh Amendment? According to Justice Story in *United States v. Wonson* (1812), "the common law here alluded to is not the common law of any individual state, . . . but is the common law of England, the grand reservoir of all our jurisprudence."[191] Consequently, the Supreme Court has interpreted the Seventh Amendment as securing jury trial rights as they existed when the amendment was ratified in 1791. "In other words, a right of trial by jury exists for the legal claims historically pursued in the common law courts, but not for the equitable claims historically pursued in the chancery courts."[192]

Distortions

The administrative state poses a challenge to the Seventh Amendment right to a jury trial. Litigation is commonplace between citizens and federal agencies. The proceedings look very much like typical trial proceedings, except that the presiding officer is an administrative law judge (ALJ) and there is no jury to determine factual disputes. ALJs decide myriad cases dealing with enforcement of regulations, claims for benefits, licensing requirements, and the government's breach of its contracts. The ALJ decides all issues of law and fact. Although there is an appellate process, no jury will ever be involved in the case. As noted by Southwestern Law School's Richard Lorren Jolly, "Congress (with the judiciary's blessing) has developed an extensive system of tribunals that bypass the jury as a constitutional actor."[193]

In the past, the Supreme Court asserted that when Congress creates a non–Article III tribunal to decide a matter, "the Seventh Amendment poses no independent bar to the adjudication of that action by a nonjury factfinder."[194] The Court has adhered to this position and stated that "[t]his is the case even if the Seventh Amendment would have required a jury where the adjudication of those rights is assigned to a federal court of law, instead of an administrative agency."[195]

The Court, however, appears to be rethinking its Seventh Amendment jurisprudence. In *SEC v. Jarkesy* (2024), George Jarkesy argued that he was entitled to a jury trial in a Securities and Exchange Commission (SEC) proceeding in which the agency sought civil penalties for securities fraud.[196] The Court's majority agreed with him and held that "[t]he SEC's antifraud provisions replicate common law fraud, and it is well established that common law claims must be heard by a jury."[197] Key to the case was the Court's construction of the "public rights" exception to the Seventh Amendment, which allows Congress to assign some matters to agencies for adjudication, where no jury will be empaneled.

A public right is a matter that historically would have been determined by the executive or legislative branches. In construing the exception, the Court held that Jarkesy was entitled to a jury trial. The SEC sought a monetary remedy from Jarkesy to punish and deter him. In Anglo-American legal history, only law courts have had the power to order such penalties.

There are mechanisms Congress and the agencies can use to limit the *Jarkesy* decision. Claims sounding in equity do not require a jury. Rather than civil penalties, an agency could seek disgorgement, which is an equitable remedy. Hence, the SEC could demand that Jarkesy give up all illegal profits that unjustly enriched him. While not a perfect fit, workarounds are available to defeat the majority's opinion.

It is worth restating that the *Jarkesy* decision does not impact cases where the government is not seeking civil penalties. This is an area of law where significant developments are possible and will be followed with great interest.

Discussion and Solutions

The problems of the administrative state are not limited to nondelegation and separation of powers. (The constitutional problems of the administrative state are discussed under Article I, Section 1.) The administrative state raises significant questions about the right to a jury trial. For example, a breach of contract case is the quintessential common-law action heard by a jury. But if the federal government is in the mix, such matters are typically swept into the vortex of the administrative state, where juries are nonexistent. If the administrative state is indeed a fixture of American government, then we must demand that juries be incorporated into administrative proceedings. The Seventh Amendment requires jury trials, and our judges and congressmen should take heed and require the use of juries in all cases involving claims that historically were pursued in the common-law courts.

The Independent Guide recommends that Congress pass the following simple statute: "In administrative proceedings occurring in the agencies of the United States, the right to jury trial in all cases involving claims historically pursued in the common-law courts shall remain inviolate."

AMENDMENT VIII (RATIFIED 1791)

EXCESSIVE BAIL SHALL not be required, nor excessive fines imposed, nor cruel and unusual punishments inflicted.

Purpose

Citizens may not be kept in prison pending trial because an unnecessarily large bail amount has been set. When punishment is warranted after conviction, it should not lean toward the barbaric. A fine should be commensurate with the offense of conviction.

Background and Development

The language of the Eighth Amendment is derived from the English Bill of Rights. The English had suffered under the Stuarts and especially during the reign of Charles I, who made widespread use of the Star Chamber—"the English court sitting without a jury at the royal Palace of Westminster that frequently imposed arbitrary fines, sentences of imprisonment, and, most infamously, had a reputation for grotesque abuses of power and resorting to methods of torture."[198]

Anti-Federalists demanded protection against an American Star Chamber. In the Massachusetts ratifying convention, Abraham Holmes inveighed that Congress was "nowhere restrained from inventing the cruel and unheard-of punishments, and annexing them to crimes."[199] He feared that "racks and gibbets may be amongst the most mild instruments of their discipline."[200] Patrick Henry, in the Virginia ratifying convention, warned that "when we come to punishments, no latitude ought to be left, nor dependence put on the virtue of representatives."[201] The distinguished ancestors of Virginians would not stand for such leeway nor "admit of tortures, or cruel and barbarous punishment."[202]

New York, North Carolina, Pennsylvania, Rhode Island, and Virginia all requested amendments in the spirit of our current Eighth Amendment. Madison, in his June 8 resolution, proposed language closely tracking the English Bill of Rights. His proposal was accepted without alterations, although Representative Samuel Livermore of New Hampshire expressed concern that the proposal would deter authorities from whippings and cutting ears off, both of which he thought were necessary punishments in many circumstances.

In addition to cruel and unusual punishments, the Eighth Amendment prohibits excessive bail and fines. The prohibition on excessive fines dates back to the Magna Carta, which provided that "[a] freeman shall only be amerced for a small offence according to the measure of that offence. And for a great offence he shall be amerced according to the magnitude of the offence."[203] Hence, the Magna Carta required a proportionality between the economic penalties and the wrong done. In *Timbs v. Indiana* (2019), the Supreme Court considered the seizure of a Land Rover SUV that had been purchased for $42,000—more than four times the amount of the maximum fine assessable under state law for the defendant's drug conviction.[204] The Court held that the Excessive Fines Clause applies to the states and questioned the forfeiture but remanded the case to the state court for ultimate

disposition. Timbs eventually got his car back because the state court found that the forfeiture was grossly disproportionate to the gravity of the underlying offense.

Distortions

In modern times, a major focus of Eighth Amendment litigation has been abolishment of the death penalty. As a textual matter, that possibility would seem to be foreclosed by the language of the Fifth Amendment, which contemplates the taking of life, liberty, and property if procedural protections are provided. Moreover, capital punishment has been a fixture of the American criminal justice system since colonial times. The death penalty was also sanctioned by Jehovah in the book of Genesis long before the Mosaic law came into existence: "Whoever sheds the blood of man, by man shall his blood be shed, for God made man in his own image."[205]

Certain members of the Supreme Court, however, have argued that "[t]he Cruel and Unusual Punishment Clause must draw its meaning from the evolving standards of decency that mark the progress of a maturing society."[206] Justice William Brennan, for example, reasoned that "[t]his Court inescapably has the duty, as the ultimate arbiter of the meaning of our Constitution, to say whether, when individuals condemned to death stand before our Bar, moral concepts require us to hold that the law has progressed to the point where we should declare that the punishment of death . . . is no longer morally tolerable in a civilized society."[207] These death penalty opponents reject the idea that even if evolving standards and morality should be considered, the laws passed by the people's elected representatives are the proper measure rather than the preferences of unelected judges. So far, a majority of the Supreme Court has refused to declare the death penalty unconstitutional, but the Court does closely scrutinize how capital punishment is carried out.

There is also a trend in which courts are giving the Eighth Amendment a substantive reading, holding that the prohibition does not apply to the punishments inflicted but the reasonableness of a law. These decisions have occurred in the context of desperate municipalities attempting to address the homelessness crisis. For example, in *Martin v. City of Boise* (9th Cir. 2019), the Ninth Circuit held that the Cruel and Unusual Punishments Clause prohibits cities from enforcing a criminal law restricting public camping unless the violator has "access to adequate temporary shelter."[208] In *Johnson v. City of Grants Pass* (9th Cir. 2022), the court extended its decision in *Martin* to civil sanctions and also forbade the City of Grants Pass from enforcing its ordinance prohibiting camping on public property.[209]

In 2024, the Supreme Court examined the Ninth Circuit's substantive reading of the Cruel and Unusual Punishments Clause and held that recent decisions are contrary to original understanding. "The Cruel and Unusual Punishments Clause," the Court observed, "focuses on the question what method or kind of punishment a government may impose after a criminal conviction, not on the question whether a government may criminalize particular behavior in the first place or how it may go about securing a conviction for that offense."[210]

For example, had Grants Pass decreed that violators of the camping ordinance would suffer waterboarding, then a court would be correct to evaluate the propriety of the punishment inflicted. But the Ninth Circuit waded into the realm of policymaking, not the methods of punishment. The court disapproved of the cities, as a matter of public policy, prohibiting homeless persons from erecting shantytowns on public property and thus interfering with the public's use and enjoyment of that public property. While a policymaker could perhaps argue that there are more effective ways to reduce the stress on public property caused by the homeless crisis, the Supreme Court reminded that Ninth Circuit that policymaking is not part of the judicial duty.

Discussion and Solutions

The Constitution's Fifth Amendment expressly permits the death penalty. Clever manipulation of the Eighth Amendment cannot undo the Fifth Amendment's acknowledgment that a wrongdoer can be deprived of life, liberty, or property so long as government gives the process that is due. Legislatures, however, are free to reject capital punishment when drafting or updating a criminal code. Just because a punishment is constitutionally permissible does not mean that it must be utilized. If the evolving standards of society counsel against the death penalty, then representative bodies are the proper ones to banish capital punishment. Americans, whether pro- or anti-death penalty, should oppose any usurpations by the Supreme Court in prohibiting capital punishment. Such judicial overreaching amounts to a death sentence for republican government. With states serving as laboratories of democracy, the people can judge the deterrent effect of the death penalty, the cathartic effect on society, and myriad other matters that should inform the states' use or disuse of the death penalty.

> ## AMENDMENT IX (RATIFIED 1791)
> THE ENUMERATION IN the Constitution, of certain rights, shall not be construed to deny or disparage others retained by the people.

Purpose

The Ninth Amendment serves as a rule of construction to thwart an expansive interpretation of federal power that interferes with matters left to the ultimate sovereigns—namely, the people of the several states.

Background and Development

There are two primary competing interpretations of the Ninth Amendment. The first claims that it serves as a reservoir of fundamental or natural rights that are not specifically mentioned in the Constitution yet nonetheless are entitled to judicial protection.[211] The second claims that it is paired with the Tenth Amendment as a rule of construction to prevent, in the words of constitutional scholar Kurt T. Lash of the Richmond School of Law, "any interpretation of enumerated federal power that would allow federal authority to extend into subjects left, as a matter of right, to the sovereign control of the people of the several states."[212] The latter argument is best supported by the history of the ratification debates and early interpretations by commentators and courts.

Throughout the ratification debates, friends of the Constitution insisted, to quote James Madison in *Federalist* No. 45, that "[t]he powers delegated by the proposed Constitution to the Federal Government are few and defined. Those which remain in the State Governments are numerous and indefinite."[213]

In the Virginia ratifying convention, Edmund Pendleton assured his colleagues that "[t]he two governments act in different manners, and for different purposes."[214] The new general government would "operate in great national concerns," and the states "in mere local concerns."[215] Because the governments existed "for two different purposes" and were both "limited to the different objects, they can no more clash than two parallel lines can meet."[216] George Nicholas was more direct. In response to arguments that the federal government would possess a general power of legislation, he insisted that federal officials "cannot legislate in any case but those particularly enumerated."[217] "No gentleman," Nicholas continued, "who is a friend to the government, ought to withhold his assent from it for this reason."[218] Governor Edmund Randolph echoed Nicholas's reasoning. "But in the general Constitution, its powers are enumerated," Randolph averred. "Is it not, then, fairly deducible, that it has no power but what is expressly given it?—for if its powers were to be general, an enumeration would be needless."[219]

These grand statements did not satisfy Anti-Federalists. They wanted specific guarantees that the new government's powers were few and defined. They also wanted amendments to prevent a constitutional interpretation that would extend the powers of Congress to far-flung subjects. To address the first issue, the Federal Farmer suggested that the Constitution "declare all powers, rights and privileges, are reserved, which are not explicitly and expressly given up."[220] In addition, a constitutional rule of construction was needed to address the second issue. Brutus feared that the courts would interpret the Constitution "not only according to its letter, but according to its spirit and intention; and having this power, they would strongly incline to give it such a construction as to extend the powers of the general government."[221] In addition to Brutus's worry about construction, friends of the Constitution, in opposing a bill of rights, suggested that to specifically state, for example, that Congress had no power over free speech would imply that Congress through principles of construction did have power over other rights and privileges not specifically listed.

Based on these concerns, Virginia's ratifying convention proposed two amendments:

> First, That each State in the Union shall respectively retain every power, jurisdiction, and right which is not by this Constitution delegated to the Congress of the United States or to the departments of the Federal Government. . . .
>
> Seventeenth, That those clauses which declare that Congress shall not exercise certain powers be not interpreted in any manner whatsoever to extend the powers of Congress. But that they may be construed either as making exceptions to the specified powers where this shall be the case, or otherwise as inserted merely for greater caution.[222]

Other states, including New York, Rhode Island, and North Carolina, expressed similar sentiments. These states sought to ensure a system of few and defined federal powers

to guard against the dangers of a constitutional construction that would augment federal power.

In his June 8 resolution, Madison recommended an amendment expressing that powers not delegated to the general government were reserved (our Tenth Amendment), as well as an amendment aimed at preventing expansive construction that was the forerunner of our Ninth Amendment: "The exceptions here or elsewhere in the constitution, made in favor of particular rights, shall not be so construed as to diminish the just importance of other rights retained by the people; or as to enlarge the powers delegated by the constitution; but either as actual limitations of such powers, or inserted merely for greater caution."[223]

Madison's draft version of the Ninth Amendment underwent many changes. Virginia, led by Edmund Randolph, was so unhappy with the result that it contemplated rejecting both the Ninth and Tenth Amendments. Madison assured his friends back home that the final version of the Ninth Amendment accomplished the same thing sought by Virginia's seventeenth proposed amendment. Randolph admitted that Madison's interpretation of the Ninth Amendment was "plausible," but he still preferred the original Virginia proposal. Nonetheless, Virginia ultimately ratified both the Ninth and Tenth Amendments.

Madison's assurance to his friends on the meaning of the Ninth Amendment was genuine. Indeed, when arguing in the House against Hamilton's plan to create the Bank of the United States, Madison resorted to both the Ninth and Tenth Amendments. The Ninth, Madison contended, "guard[ed] against a latitude of interpretation," and the Tenth "exclud[ed] every source of power not within in the constitution itself."[224]

Justice Joseph Story interpreted the Ninth Amendment in a similar manner in his dissenting opinion in *Houston v. Moore* (1820).[225] At issue in *Moore* was when federal power is exclusive and when it is shared concurrently with the states. Story opined that unless the Constitution indicates that a grant to the federal government is exclusive, it should be understood that the states have concurrent authority. Story came to this conclusion "not only upon the letter and spirt of the [ninth] amendment of the constitution, but upon the soundest principles of general reasoning."[226] For Story, the Ninth Amendment was not a repository of natural or fundamental rights; rather, it provided a rule of constitutional interpretation. As Lash has observed, "Justice Story interpreted and applied the Ninth Amendment precisely the way James Madison and the state ratifying conventions intended—as a rule of construction preserving the retained right of local self-government."[227]

St. George Tucker, in his *View of the Constitution of the United States*, was in accord with Madison and Story. The Ninth Amendment, according to Tucker, was intended "to guard the people against constructive usurpations and encroachment on their rights."[228] The Ninth and the Tenth together, Tucker taught, require "that the powers delegated to the federal government, are, in all cases, to receive the most strict construction that the instrument will bear, where the rights of a state or of the people, either collectively, or individually, may be drawn into question."[229] In reviewing Tucker's words, it is helpful to remember, as constitutional scholar Raoul Berger pointed out, that rights and reserved powers were "two sides of the same coin" for the Founders.[230] We make a mistake if we try to segregate the Ninth

Amendment to the realm of individual rights and the Tenth Amendment to the realm of state powers. The Framers, with their emphasis on popular sovereignty and self-government, rejected such a dichotomy.

Distortions

In modern times, the Ninth Amendment is associated with *Griswold v. Connecticut* (1965), in which the Supreme Court held that an ancient Connecticut statute banning contraceptives violated a federal constitutional right to privacy found in the penumbras and emanations of the First, Third, Fourth, Fifth, and Ninth Amendments.[231] Justice Arthur Goldberg concurred in the opinion, but wrote separately to argue that the right to privacy was embodied in "the language and history of the Ninth Amendment."[232] Justice Goldberg then set forth the familiar argument that the Ninth Amendment was intended to be a repository of fundamental rights that government may not infringe. In dissent, Justice Hugo Black challenged Justice Goldberg's account of the Ninth Amendment and observed that the "Amendment was passed, not to broaden the powers of this Court or any other department of the General Government, but as every student of history knows, to assure the people that the Constitution in all its provisions was intended to limit the Federal Government to the powers granted expressly or by necessary implication."[233]

Interest in the Ninth Amendment has been renewed with the Supreme Court's decision in *Dobbs v. Jackson Women's Health Organization* (2022), in which the Court held that the Constitution contains no fundamental right to abortion.[234] Many abortion proponents have turned to the Ninth Amendment in criticizing the Court's decision. They contend that the freedom to end a pregnancy is a right retained by the people under the Ninth Amendment. Such arguments ignore the Ninth Amendment's role as a rule of construction. Aside from the original understanding of the Ninth Amendment, these critics ignore that the Ninth Amendment has never been applied to the states. There is simply no basis in history or modern constitutional law to use the Ninth Amendment to strike a state statute.

Discussion and Solutions

We must oppose any attempts by the courts to use the Ninth Amendment to increase federal power—whether it be legislative, executive, or judicial. The Ninth Amendment exists as a rule of construction to cabin federal power. It must not be used as a catchall justification when judges desire to strike a state policy decision with which they disagree. The right of self-government in the several states trumps jurists' desires to place preferred policy outcomes in the category of fundamental rights. By limiting the Ninth Amendment to a rule of construction, we avoid unresolvable scholastic disputations about which unenumerated rights are fundamental and why they should enjoy such a status. We ground the Constitution in its text rather than speculations that will empower unelected officials occupying the federal judiciary.

AMENDMENT X (RATIFIED 1791)

THE POWERS NOT delegated to the United States by the Constitution, nor prohibited by it to the States, are reserved to the States respectively, or to the people.

Purpose

The Tenth Amendment exists as a written guarantee that the general government, as promised by the Federalists, can exercise only delegated powers. Powers not delegated, no matter how convenient to the operation of the government, are off-limits.

Background and Development

The Tenth Amendment is modeled on a provision from the Articles of Confederation: "Each state retains its sovereignty, freedom, and independence, and every power, jurisdiction, and right, which is not by this Confederation expressly delegated to the United States, in Congress assembled."[235] Every state that requested amendments to the Constitution asked for something akin to the current Tenth Amendment. Massachusetts, for example, requested "[t]hat there it be explicitly declared that all Powers not expressly delegated by the aforesaid Constitution are reserved to the several States to be by them exercised."[236]

As mentioned in the discussion of the Ninth Amendment, friends of the Constitution uniformly preached that Congress's powers were limited and that the states had no reason to worry about a consolidation of power in the center. For example, Noah Webster, writing as "A Citizen of America," averred that "[t]he constitution defines the powers of Congress; and every power not expressly delegated to that body, remains in the several state-legislatures."[237] He further claimed that "the bounds of jurisdiction between the federal and respective state governments, are marked with precision."[238]

Anti-Federalists scoffed at such contentions. Pointing to provisions such as the Necessary and Proper Clause, An Old Whig questioned whether "any thing [can] be said to be reserved and kept back from Congress? Can it be said that Congress have no power but what is *expressed*?"[239] He further predicted that the "constitution, if adopted, will in great measure destroy, if it do not totally annihilate, the separate governments of the several states."[240] Similarly, Brutus complained that Congress's powers "are very general and comprehensive," so that the national legislature could "justify . . . almost any law."[241] He also feared that Congress could "entirely abolish the state legislatures."[242]

The Tenth Amendment, therefore, was meant to dispel the fears expressed in Anti-Federalist writings. In his June 8 resolution, Madison offered the following: "The powers not delegated by this constitution, nor prohibited by it to the states, are reserved to the states respectively."[243] Thomas Tudor Tucker of South Carolina moved that the word "expressly" be added so the clause would read "the powers not expressly delegated by this Constitution."[244] Madison opposed Tucker's motion "because it was impossible to confine a government to the exercise of express powers" inasmuch as "there must necessarily be admitted powers by implication."[245] Roger Sherman

of Connecticut supported Madison and observed "that corporate bodies are supposed to possess all powers incident to a corporate capacity without being absolutely expressed."[246] Tucker countered that "he thought every power to be expressly given that could be clearly comprehended within any accurate definition of the general power."[247] In other words, Tucker did not oppose necessary incidents to the grant of a power; he simply did not want the general government to claim additional powers not clearly delineated among the delegated powers. The House, however, rejected Tucker's motion despite the fact that Tucker's clarification was in accord with Madison's reasoning. For example, in his Report of 1800, Madison stated that "[i]f the powers granted be valid, it is solely because they are granted; and if granted powers are valid because granted, all other powers not granted must not be valid."[248]

The words "or to the people" were suggested by Daniel Carroll of Maryland. The addition reflects that the people of the several states are the ultimate sovereigns and that a state government might not be entitled to exercise a power if the people of that state have not granted it via the state constitution. Thus, in certain cases both the general government and state governments might not possess a power retained by the people.

Distortions

In his draft of the Kentucky Resolutions of 1798, Thomas Jefferson turned to the Tenth Amendment when arguing that the Sedition Act, which made criticism of the general government a crime, was void and of no force. Jefferson quoted the Tenth Amendment and searched the Constitution for any delegated power allowing Congress to restrict the press or the people's speech. Finding no such power, Jefferson argued that "all lawful powers respecting the same did of right remain, and were reserved to the States or to the people."[249] The states and the people "manifested their determination to retain to themselves the right of judging how far the licentiousness of speech and the press may be abridged without lessening their useful freedom."[250] Hence, Jefferson believed the Sedition Act "is not law, but is altogether void, and of no force."[251]

Since the late 1930s, the Supreme Court has shown little interest in confining Congress to its enumerated powers. In 1976, the Court attempted to revive the Tenth Amendment in *National League of Cities v. Usery*, which concerned whether the Fair Labor Standards Act's setting of minimum wages and maximum hours could apply to employees of states and their political subdivisions.[252] The Court held that the provision could not and cited the Tenth Amendment as declaring "the constitutional policy that Congress may not exercise power in a fashion that impairs the States' integrity or their ability to function effectively in a federal system."[253] The Court held that determination of pay and working hours for governmental employees was "an attribute of state sovereignty" and a traditional governmental function that could not be dictated by Congress using its commerce power.[254]

The *Usery* decision was short-lived. In *Garcia v. San Antonio Metropolitan Transit Authority* (1985), the Court gave up on determining what was or was not a traditional government function and ruled that the political process was the proper sphere for the states to protect their sovereignty from congressional encroachment.[255] *Usery* was thus overruled.

Discussion and Solutions

The Court's attempt to breathe life into the Tenth Amendment in *Usery* was too little, too late. The Court's expansive interpretations of the Commerce Clause, General Welfare Clause, and Necessary and Proper Clause had long ago mocked the clear command of the Tenth Amendment. The general government ceased to be bound by delegated powers many years ago. Although the Tenth Amendment has been ignored by proponents of energetic government, the people can still find hope in its plain meaning. If limited, constitutional government is ever to return to our shores, the Tenth Amendment will be a starting point. Thomas Jefferson, in opposing Hamilton's national bank, described the Tenth Amendment as the "foundation of the Constitution" and correctly predicted that "[t]o take a single step beyond the boundaries thus specially drawn around the powers of Congress, is to take possession of a boundless field of power, no longer susceptible of any definition."[256] Only by shoring up this foundation can we claim the limited government promised by the Constitution's proponents.

AMENDMENT XI (RATIFIED 1795)

THE JUDICIAL POWER of the United States shall not be construed to extend to any suit in law or equity, commenced or prosecuted against one of the United States by Citizens of another State, or by Citizens or Subjects of any Foreign State.

Purpose

The Eleventh Amendment recognizes that the states are sovereign jurisdictions and thus cannot be forced into court to answer complaints of private individuals absent a waiver of sovereign immunity.

Background and Development

Under Article III, Section 2, Clause 1, federal judicial power extends to suits brought against a state by citizens of other states as well as citizens or subjects of foreign states. But does Article III abrogate state sovereign immunity, which prohibits bringing a legal action against a government without its consent? As discussed previously (under Article III, Section 2, Clause 1), statements from Alexander Hamilton, James Madison, and John Marshall indicate that there was no surrender of sovereign immunity. The Supreme Court held otherwise in *Chisholm v. Georgia* (1793), in which a citizen of South Carolina and an executor of an estate brought suit in federal court against Georgia to recover a Revolutionary War debt.[257] Georgia refused to answer or appear in court on the ground of sovereign immunity. The Court rejected Georgia's immunity defense and held that the Citizen-State Diversity Clauses operated as a waiver of immunity.

Many were shocked by the decision—and especially Justice James Wilson's assertion that

the states were not sovereign in the union: "As to the purposes of the Union, therefore, Georgia is NOT a sovereign State."[258] Wilson further argued that in the United States, the amalgamated people are sovereign. He thus ignored that there was no national act of ratification and that the Constitution was instead adopted in the separate states.

The *Chisholm* decision stunned state and federal officials. The reaction was immediate and hostile. William A. Fletcher has pointed out that "[t]he Georgia House of Representatives passed a bill declaring that any persons attempting to levy a judgment in the case 'are hereby declared to be guilty of felony, and shall suffer death, without the benefit of clergy, by being hanged.'"[259] Massachusetts, at the urging of Governor John Hancock, passed a resolution "urging Congress to adopt 'such Amendments to the Constitution as will remove any clause or Article of the said Constitution which can be construed to imply or justify a decision that a State is compellable to answer in any suit by an individual or individuals in any Court of the United States.'"[260] Congress acted quickly, and by February 1795, the necessary twelve states had ratified the Eleventh Amendment to the Constitution.

The Eleventh Amendment is no mere historical artifact. It has been relevant in modern constitutional litigation. For example, in 1988 Congress enacted the Indian Gaming Regulatory Act ("Gaming Act"), which sought to establish a regulatory scheme for gambling on Indian reservations. Various types of gaming could be allowed under the Gaming Act pursuant to an agreement between a tribe and state authorities. To come to such an agreement, the Gaming Act required states to negotiate in good faith with Indian tribes. The Gaming Act allowed tribes to bring suit in federal district court if a state did not use good faith in dialogues with the tribe. Because Florida would not allow gambling as broadly as the Seminole Tribe would have liked, the tribe brought suit in district court and alleged that the state was acting in bad faith. Florida invoked sovereign immunity from the suit, and the tribe countered that Congress had abrogated immunity by passing the Gaming Act via its commerce power.

In *Seminole Tribe of Florida v. Florida* (1996), the Supreme Court upheld Florida's sovereign immunity pursuant to the Eleventh Amendment. "Even when the Constitution vests in Congress complete law-making authority over a particular area [such as commerce with the Indian tribes]," the Court reasoned, "the Eleventh Amendment prevents congressional authorization of suits by private parties against unconsenting States."[261] The Court did note that Congress can abrogate sovereign immunity when legislating pursuant to the Fourteenth Amendment, because that amendment contains a specific clause allowing for congressional legislative enforcement.

In *Alden v. Maine* (1999), the Court considered whether Congress could abrogate state sovereign immunity for suits brought in state courts.[262] At issue were overtime provisions of the Fair Labor Standards Act (FLSA), which state probation officers alleged Maine had violated. The probation officers' initial suit was

dismissed from federal district court because of *Seminole Tribe.* In *Alden*, the Supreme Court ruled "that the powers delegated to Congress under Article I of the United States Constitution [under which the FLSA was enacted] do not include the power to subject nonconsenting States to private suits for damages in state courts."[263] The Court came to this conclusion based on the framework of the federal system, which reserves to the states "a substantial portion of the Nation's primary sovereignty, together with the dignity and essential attributes inhering in that status."[264] The Court further discerned that the several states "form distinct and independent portions of the supremacy, no more subject, within their respective spheres, to the general authority than the general authority is subject to them, within its own sphere."[265]

The Court has even applied sovereign immunity in the context of the administrative state. In *Federal Maritime Commission v. South Carolina State Ports Authority* (2002), the Court considered whether state sovereign immunity precluded the Federal Maritime Commission (FMC) from adjudicating a private party's complaint that a state-run port violated the Shipping Act of 1984.[266] The complaint centered on South Carolina's policy of denying berths in the Port of Charleston to cruise ships whose primary purpose was gambling.

The Court began by observing that the several states, "upon ratification of the Constitution, did not consent to become mere appendages of the Federal Government. Rather, they entered the Union with their sovereignty intact."[267] It rejected the FMC's argument that sovereign immunity only shields states from exercises of judicial power and that administrative proceedings are not judicial in nature. The Court examined the administrative proceedings at issue and found them to mirror civil litigation in the federal courts. Based on the similarities between administrative proceedings and civil litigation, the Court held "that state sovereign immunity bars the FMC from adjudicating complaints filed by a private party against a nonconsenting State. Simply put, if the Framers thought it an impermissible affront to a State's dignity to be required to answer the complaints of private parties in federal courts, we cannot imagine that they would have found it acceptable to compel a State to do exactly the same thing before the administrative tribunal of an agency."[268]

Distortions

Unlike its Tenth Amendment jurisprudence, the Court's Eleventh Amendment decisions are trending in the right direction. Skeptics of state power, such as retired Justice Stephen Breyer, criticize the Court's sovereign immunity decisions as "set[ting] loose an interpretive principle that restricts far too severely the authority of the Federal Government to regulate innumerable relationships between State and citizen."[269] As an advocate of national power, Breyer cannot imagine a relationship between a citizen and state that the general government should not superintend. Our constitutional structure, however, expects the states to govern relationships with their citizens. Federal interference is the exception to the rule—warranted if, for example, a state denied black and white citizens access to the courts on equal terms.

Discussion and Solutions

Considering the trend in sovereign immunity decisions, no significant changes are offered. Citizens should support the Court's efforts to defend the states' sovereignty; the states are not mere administrative subdivisions of the national government but coequals in their reserved spheres. Sovereign immunity is part and parcel of the first principles of our federal union. A doctrine congruent with real federalism is worth defending and advancing when opportunities arise.

AMENDMENT XII (RATIFIED 1804)

THE ELECTORS SHALL meet in their respective states, and vote by ballot for President and Vice-President, one of whom, at least, shall not be an inhabitant of the same state with themselves; they shall name in their ballots the person voted for as President, and in distinct ballots the person voted for as Vice-President, and they shall make distinct lists of all persons voted for as President, and of all persons voted for as Vice-President, and of the number of votes for each, which lists they shall sign and certify, and transmit sealed to the seat of the government of the United States, directed to the President of the Senate;

—THE PRESIDENT OF the Senate shall, in the presence of the Senate and House of Representatives, open all the certificates and the votes shall then be counted;

—THE PERSON HAVING the greatest number of votes for President, shall be the President, if such number be a majority of the whole number of Electors appointed; and if no person have such majority, then from the persons having the highest numbers not exceeding three on the list of those voted for as President, the House of Representatives shall choose immediately, by ballot, the President. But in choosing the President, the votes shall be taken by states, the representation from each state having one vote; a quorum for this purpose shall consist of a member or members from two-thirds of the states, and a majority of all the states shall be necessary to a choice. And if the House of Representatives shall not choose a President whenever the right of choice shall devolve upon them, before the fourth day of March next following, then the Vice-President shall act as President, as in the case of the death or other constitutional disability of the President.

—THE PERSON HAVING the greatest number of votes as Vice-President, shall be the Vice-President, if such number be a majority of the whole number of Electors appointed, and if no person have a majority, then from the two highest numbers on the list, the Senate shall choose the Vice-President; a quorum for the purpose shall consist of two-thirds of the whole number of Senators, and a majority of the whole number shall be necessary to a choice. But no person constitutionally ineligible to the office of President shall be eligible to that of Vice-President of the United States.

Purpose

The Twelfth Amendment corrected the Framers' failure to foresee the rise of political parties. Under the amendment, presidential electors designate candidates for president and vice president. In the event no candidate receives a majority and thus the election is thrown to the House voting by states (as under prior law), only the top three candidates rather than five are presented to the House for consideration.

Background and Development

As discussed in connection with Article II, Section 1, Clause 3, the presidential elections of 1796 and 1800 exposed flaws in manner of choosing a president and vice president. In

1796, Federalist John Adams won the presidency and Republican Thomas Jefferson the vice presidency. It was not a marriage made in heaven, as the two men had very different visions for the direction of the country. The wheels came off in 1800, when the election, again featuring Adams and Jefferson, was thrown to the House of Representatives. Jefferson and his running mate, Aaron Burr, received an equal number of electoral votes because Republican electors were hesitant about throwing away electoral votes to ensure that Jefferson received a greater number than Burr. But for diplomacy and promises to keep on Federalist members of the civil service, a crisis would have arisen.

The difficulties of 1796 and 1800 demonstrate that the Framers did not foresee the rise of political parties and presidential candidates serving as party leaders. The Framers envisioned the president as a nonpolitical actor who was, in the words of Senator Joshua D. Hawley, "ever the servant of the . . . broader experiment in Congress-centered deliberative government."[270] The president was not supposed to enter office with a legislative agenda or as an advocate for certain public policies. But with the passing of George Washington from public life, presidential candidates became the chief spokesmen and advocates for political movements.

In light of this new role, Article II needed revamping. The Twelfth Amendment requires electors to identify which ballot cast is for president and which for vice president—thus preventing a tie between a party's presidential and vice presidential candidates, as happened with Jefferson and Burr. No longer does the runner-up in a presidential race become the vice president. If no presidential candidate receives a majority and thus the election is thrown to the House of Representatives, then the House, voting by states, chooses from no more than the top three candidates. Under former law, in which there was no designation of president and vice president, the names of the top five candidates were sent to the House. If the House does not choose a president by Inauguration Day, the Twelfth Amendment provides that the vice president will act as president in the same manner as if the president has a disability under Article II, Section 1, Clause 6. In case no vice presidential candidate receives a majority of electoral votes, the Senate chooses a vice president from the top two candidates for the office.

Alexander Hamilton praised the amendment because "the people should know whom they are choosing & because the present mode gives all possible scope to intrigue, and is dangerous as we have seen to the public tranquility."[271] Of course, there were dissenting voices. Senator Samuel White of Delaware objected that the constitutional change would degrade the office of vice president. A vice presidential candidate, White argued, would have value only insofar as his wealth, connections, and local political power "promote the election of a President."[272] Some also inveighed against the amendment for making it more likely that a candidate favored by the majority of the people would be chosen as president. Senator Uriah Tracy of Connecticut complained that the Twelfth Amendment deprived the small states of power in choosing a president because of designation and thus undermined federative features of the Constitution.

Only once has the Senate been called on to choose a vice president because no candidate received a majority of electoral votes. In the

1836 election, Martin Van Buren easily won the Electoral College vote and thus became president. His controversial running mate, Richard M. Johnson, however, did not receive the requisite number of electoral votes because of twenty-three "faithless electors" from Virginia who voted for another Democratic vice presidential candidate, Alabama's William Smith. The Senate, acting pursuant to the Twelfth Amendment and voting along party lines, chose Johnson to be vice president. Johnson found vice presidential duties to be boring and often left Washington to run his tavern and hotel back in Kentucky.

In the 2020 presidential election, a controversy arose about the vice president's authority to count electoral votes. President Trump and his legal team alleged that election irregularities raised concerns over the electoral count in several battleground states. They argued that Vice President Mike Pence, as the Senate's presiding officer, was charged with counting votes and resolving any disputed electoral votes. Vice President Pence, however, refused to reject electoral votes or delay the counting so state officials could investigate allegations of fraud. Pence opined that his duties were merely ministerial.

The Twelfth Amendment is ambiguous in directing how to resolve questions about the legitimacy of electoral votes. While the vice president, in the presence of both houses of Congress, must open the electoral certificates, the amendment then switches to passive voice and states that "the votes shall then be counted." The question is by whom? And does the counter(s) resolve disputes? In the 1876 presidential election, several states submitted competing slates of electoral votes. To decide the matter, a special electoral commission was

created. It included members of the House, the Senate, and the Supreme Court. The commission awarded Rutherford B. Hayes, the Republican candidate, the requisite electoral votes to catapult him to the presidency. In accepting this outcome, Democrats secured a promise that federal troops would be withdrawn from the Southern states and thus Reconstruction would end.

While there are some similarities between 1876 and 2020, there is one glaring difference. In 1876, a clear conflict existed, because Congress had received multiple slates of electors from the disputed states and each slate was signed by state officials. In 2020, state officials did not certify multiple slates. Hence, no person (Pence) or entity (Congress) had to decide between competing slates certified by state officials.

Because of the confusion in 1876, Congress enacted the Electoral Count Act of 1887 (ECA). The ECA provides that the electoral certificates are read by tellers previously appointed from among the membership of the House and Senate. Tellers are appointed by the presiding officer of each chamber based on recommendations from the leaders of the two major parties. The ECA provides that in the case of irregularities with an elector's vote or unlawful certification of the vote, a majority of both the House and Senate may reject the vote. Thus, by statute, Congress has claimed the authority to resolve questions about the legitimacy of electoral votes. The Trump legal team, of course, questioned the ECA's constitutionality and asserted it usurped the vice president's authority under the Twelfth Amendment.

Because the Twelfth Amendment is unclear about who counts and resolves disputes, the ECA reasonably lodges the decision-making with Congress. Congress is not constitutionally prohibited from that role. Members of Congress are drawn from all fifty states and must regularly present themselves to the people at the ballot box. Whereas often the vice president will have a personal stake in continuing in office, Congress is made up of politically accountable individuals with no personal stake in the outcome of the election, making it the logical choice. In the aftermath of the 2020 election, the ECA was amended to emphasize that "the role of the President of the Senate while presiding over the joint session shall be limited to performing solely ministerial duties."[273]

The Twelfth Amendment solved the problems evident in the presidential elections of 1796 and 1800. No presidential election has been thrown to the House since 1824. The Twelfth Amendment solution has worked well.

AMENDMENT XIII (RATIFIED 1865)

SECTION 1. NEITHER slavery nor involuntary servitude, except as a punishment for crime whereof the party shall have been duly convicted, shall exist within the United States, or any place subject to their jurisdiction.

SECTION 2. CONGRESS shall have power to enforce this article by appropriate legislation.

Purpose

The Thirteenth Amendment abolished slavery in the United States. It specifically makes an exception for individuals imprisoned after a conviction under the law of the land.

Background and Development

Many Americans assume that slavery ended in the United States with issuance of Lincoln's Emancipation Proclamation. This assumption is faulty. The Emancipation Proclamation, by its terms, declared the slaves free in the territory of the Southern states actively participating in the rebellion. The Proclamation did not affect slavery in Maryland, Kentucky, West Virginia, certain parishes in Louisiana, and certain counties of Virginia.

The language of the Thirteenth Amendment's first section is taken from the Northwest Ordinance of 1787: "There shall be neither slavery nor involuntary servitude in the said territory, otherwise than in the punishment of crimes whereof the party shall have been duly convicted."[274] The Thirteenth Amendment abolished the master-slave relationship. The categories of freeman and slave were wiped from American law. In the *Civil Rights Cases* (1883), the Supreme Court observed that "the amendment is not a mere prohibition of State laws establishing or upholding slavery, but an absolute declaration that slavery or involuntary servitude shall not exist in any part of the United States."[275]

In *Bailey v. Alabama* (1911), the Supreme Court used the Thirteenth Amendment to strike down a state peonage law.²⁷⁶ Bailey had agreed to work on a farm for one year and for the sum of $12 per month. Bailey received an advance of $15 and quit his job after approximately one month. An Alabama false pretenses law considered acceptance of an advance and the failure to repay it as evidence of fraud, and thus the law attempted to coerce workers to fulfill contractual obligations. Bailey was convicted and ordered to pay court costs and a fine. In the alternative to paying the fine and costs, a defendant would be sentenced to hard labor. The Supreme Court overturned the Alabama law as a form of peonage—compulsory service until a debt is paid. "The plain intention [of the Thirteenth Amendment] was to abolish slavery of whatever name and form and all its badges and incidents," the Court said, "to render impossible any state of bondage; to make labor free, by prohibiting that control by which the personal service of one man is disposed of or coerced for another's benefit, which is the essence of involuntary servitude."²⁷⁷

Congress is empowered to enforce the Thirteenth Amendment by appropriate legislation. In *Jones v. Alfred H. Mayer Co.* (1968), the Court interpreted this power broadly in upholding a federal statute that prohibited discrimination in the sale of real estate.²⁷⁸ "Surely Congress has the power under the Thirteenth Amendment rationally to determine what are the badges and the incidents of slavery," the Court averred, "and the authority to translate that determination into effective legislation."²⁷⁹ Such legislation, the Court noted, applies to private and governmental action.

Although the Court recognized a broad congressional power in Section 2 of the amendment outside the context of compulsory labor, Congress has yet to embrace what

could turn into a general police power. The criterion of rationality is a very low hurdle. Theoretically, under *Jones*, Congress could declare that all public or private monuments honoring individuals with politically incorrect views of race are "badges and incidents of slavery" that must be removed. Hence, Congress could order removal of the Washington Monument, the Lincoln Memorial, or a bust of Jefferson Davis in a private library.

Americans can take some hope from *City of Boerne v. Flores* (1997), in which the Court interpreted the enforcement power of the Fourteenth Amendment and held that Congress "has been given the power 'to enforce,' not the power to determine what constitutes a constitutional violation. Were it not so, what Congress would be enforcing would no longer be, in any meaningful sense, the provisions of [the Fourteenth Amendment]."²⁸⁰ Logic dictates that the enforcement power of both amendments, which are almost identically worded, should be interpreted in the same manner. This would impose a limit on what Congress decrees is a badge or incident of slavery. There is a strong argument that a *Boerne* interpretation applied to the Thirteenth Amendment would limit Congress to enforcement violations of "compulsory labor" arrangements, which probably exist in the United States only in the form of human trafficking. Under a *Boerne* analysis, Congress would be altering the heartland of the right protected under the Thirteenth Amendment if it delved into other social issues.

Distortions

Modern discussions of the Thirteenth Amendment are typically connected with the efforts of advocacy groups to apply the amendment to novel situations. For example, some law professors have argued that National Collegiate Athletic Association (NCAA) student-athletes suffer from involuntary servitude because colleges earn substantial amounts from football. Others contend that a state law prohibiting abortion requires women to carry and bear children and thus subjects them to involuntary servitude. So far, such far-flung interpretations have been rejected, and Section 1 has been limited to compulsory labor.

Discussion and Solutions

The Thirteenth Amendment is limited to compulsory labor arrangements, which form the heartland of the institution of slavery. The amendment should not be used as a vehicle to promote policies unconnected with slavery (such as payments to student-athletes or abortion on demand). To stretch the Thirteenth Amendment to such unique circumstances makes light of the wicked institution that it abolished. Accordingly, elected policymakers in the states should deal with matters such as payments to college football players or the scope of abortion regulations. Let us admire the monument that is the Thirteenth Amendment rather than contrive new uses for this constitutional provision that targeted a particular evil.

AMENDMENT XIV (RATIFIED 1868)

SECTION 1. ALL persons born or naturalized in the United States, and subject to the jurisdiction thereof, are citizens of the United States and of the State wherein they reside. No State shall make or enforce any law which shall abridge the privileges or immunities of citizens of the United States; nor shall any State deprive any person of life, liberty, or property, without due process of law; nor deny to any person within its jurisdiction the equal protection of the laws.

SECTION 2. REPRESENTATIVES shall be apportioned among the several States according to their respective numbers, counting the whole number of persons in each State, excluding Indians not taxed. But when the right to vote at any election for the choice of electors for President and Vice President of the United States, Representatives in Congress, the Executive and Judicial officers of a State, or the members of the Legislature thereof, is denied to any of the male inhabitants of such State, being twenty-one years of age, and citizens of the United States, or in any way abridged, except for participation in rebellion, or other crime, the basis of representation therein shall be reduced in the proportion which the number of such male citizens shall bear to the whole number of male citizens twenty-one years of age in such State.

SECTION 3. NO person shall be a Senator or Representative in Congress, or elector of President and Vice President, or hold any office, civil or military, under the United States, or under any State, who, having previously taken an oath, as a member of Congress, or as an officer of the United States, or as a member of any State legislature, or as an executive or judicial officer of any State, to support the Constitution of the United States, shall have engaged in insurrection or rebellion against the same, or given aid or comfort to the enemies thereof. But Congress may by a vote of two-thirds of each House, remove such disability.

SECTION 4. THE validity of the public debt of the United States, authorized by law, including debts incurred for payment of pensions and bounties for services in suppressing insurrection or rebellion, shall not be questioned. But neither the United States nor any State shall assume or pay any debt or obligation incurred in aid of insurrection or rebellion against the United States, or any claim for the loss or emancipation of any slave; but all such debts, obligations and claims shall be held illegal and void.

SECTION 5. THE Congress shall have power to enforce, by appropriate legislation, the provisions of this article.

Purpose

The Fourteenth Amendment overruled the *Dred Scott* decision, which held that blacks were not citizens of the United States. In connection with the establishment of national citizenship, the Fourteenth Amendment commands that all individuals—regardless of color—be treated the same under the law. Race must not be used when a legislature confers benefits or imposes penalties. All citizens are entitled to impartial and established judicial procedure before a state can interfere with their lives, liberties, or property.

Background and Development

The Fourteenth Amendment originated in the early years of Reconstruction as President Andrew Johnson and the Radical Republicans in Congress fought over who would lead efforts to reassemble the union. Johnson, like his predecessor Abraham Lincoln, favored a program of Reconstruction that moved expeditiously to restore the Southern states and end military rule. The Radical Republicans, on the other hand, were in no hurry to see the South restored to full membership and federal troops withdrawn. They realized that with the Three-Fifths Clause abrogated by the Thirteenth Amendment, the Southern states would enjoy augmented representation in the House and thus could challenge Republican rule. Radical leader Thaddeus Stevens averred that the Southern states should not be readmitted until measures had been taken "so as to secure perpetual ascendency to the party of the Union" (namely, the Republican Party).[281] The Radical Republicans claimed that Congress as then constituted spoke the general will of true Americans and that the executive branch existed to serve Congress rather than to challenge its vision for the nation.

The origins of the Fourteenth Amendment cannot be understood apart from the Civil Rights Act of 1866, which Congress enacted over President Johnson's veto. The Act, inter alia, defined U.S. citizenship and required that blacks and whites be treated equally under the law. The Act sought to ameliorate the situation of freedmen in the South who faced state Black Codes.[282] Some of the stricter codes prevented blacks from owning property, required blacks to carry a pass or a license when traveling, and declared any unemployed black man a vagabond. President Johnson raised significant constitutional questions concerning Congress's power to interfere with matters traditionally left to the state governments. Thus, the Joint Committee on Reconstruction created the Fourteenth Amendment. As observed by constitutional law scholar Henry J. Abraham, "The Fourteenth Amendment was passed by Congress on June 16, 1866, ratified by the required three-fourths of the states—ten of these then being Southern Reconstruction governments under duress—and was proclaimed in effect on July 28, 1868."[283] The amendment addressed the Northern demand that postwar governments in the South "be restrained in the future from discriminating against blacks and Northerners, and that this restraint be imposed without altering radically the structure of the federal system or increasing markedly the powers of the federal government."[284]

Section 1 and Citizenship

The first sentence of Section 1 of the amendment, like the first section of the Civil Rights

Act of 1866, addressed U.S. citizenship. This was in response to the *Dred Scott* decision, which held that blacks were persons under the Constitution but not citizens of the United States. Section 1 overturned that aspect of the *Dred Scott* ruling.

Many assume that Section 1 established birthright citizenship. A significant dispute exists, however, about whether the child of an illegal alien born on American soil is born "subject to the jurisdiction" of the United States. In *Elk v. Wilkins* (1884), the Supreme Court held that the language means "not merely subject in some respect or degree to the jurisdiction of the United States, but completely subject to their political jurisdiction and owing them direct and immediate allegiance."[285] If a child's parents owe allegiance to a foreign power, it is questionable whether the child owes no allegiance to the parent's country. More than a decade after the *Elk* decision, the Court held in *United States v. Wong Kim Ark* (1898), that a child born in the United States to permanent legal residents was a citizen, even though his parents were subjects of the emperor of China.[286] Importantly, no Supreme Court case has ever held that Section 1 provides automatic citizenship to anyone physically born within the borders of the United States.

Privileges or Immunities Clause

The next provision of Section 1 prohibits states from making or enforcing laws abridging "the privileges or immunities of citizens of the United States." But how can we determine what such privileges or immunities are? To quote Fourteenth Amendment scholar Raoul Berger, we must remember that "the purpose of the framers was to protect blacks

from discrimination with respect to specified 'fundamental rights,' enumerated in the Civil Rights Act and epitomized in the §1 'privileges or immunities' clause."[287] Even the Supreme Court in *McDonald v. City of Chicago* (2010), recognized that "it is generally accepted that the Fourteenth Amendment was understood to provide a constitutional basis for protecting the rights set out in the Civil Rights Act of 1866."[288] By fundamental rights, the Act's framers had in mind life, liberty, and property.[289] To secure these fundamental rights the Civil Rights Act, in pertinent part, provided:

> [All citizens without regard to race or color] shall have the same right, in every State and Territory in the United States, to make and enforce contracts, to sue, be parties, and give evidence, to inherit, purchase, lease, sell, hold, and convey real and personal property, and to full and equal benefit of all laws and proceedings for the security of person and property, as is enjoyed by white citizens.

This narrow interpretation of privileges or immunities corresponds with the historical understanding of the term as legal benefits granted to citizens by a governmental body.[290] Giles W. Hotchkiss, a Republican representative from New York, accurately described the purpose of the amendment in these narrow bounds as "to provide that no State shall discriminate between its citizens, and give one class of citizens greater rights than it confers upon another."[291] Similarly, Thomas D. Eliot, a Republican representative from Massachusetts, believed the Fourteenth Amendment would remedy the problem that "Congress has not the power to prohibit State legislation discriminating against classes of citizens or depriving any persons of life, liberty, or property without due process of law."[292]

Some commentators argue that the drafters and ratifiers of the Fourteenth Amendment believed that privileges or immunities included the first eight amendments to the Constitution. Indeed, some speakers during congressional debates on the Fourteenth Amendment said as much. Representative John Bingham of Ohio, for example, stated that the amendment would give Congress "the power to enforce the bill of rights as it stands in the Constitution today."[293] To the extent Bingham's statement represents the intent of the framers and ratifiers of the amendment, one would think that even the most inexperienced drafter of legislation could have done a better job expressing this intent in the amendment's text. Raoul Berger rightly describes Bingham as "a muddled thinker, given to the florid, windy rhetoric of a stump orator" and unacquainted with "the careful articulation of a lawyer who addresses himself to great issues."[294] Indeed, Bingham initially argued that the Bill of Rights already applied to the states, a proposition that lacked any support in American constitutional law at the time.[295]

Moreover, if the Privileges or Immunities Clause had made the Bill of Rights enforceable against the states, it would have caused a major change in state practice—especially in the criminal law context. States would have been required to augment the use of grand juries, to grant jury trials in all civil cases where the amount in controversy exceeded twenty dollars, and so forth. But opponents of the Fourteenth Amendment never made these obvious arguments against its adoption.[296] Why not? Because no one understood a few stray remarks about the Bill of Rights as embodying

the purpose of the Privileges or Immunities Clause. Moreover, the Privileges or Immunities Clause caused no great state constitutional revival—even in solidly Republican states—to conform state constitutional practice to the federal Bill of Rights. Surely, if the state legislatures that ratified the Fourteenth Amendment had understood it to incorporate the first eight amendments, some of the states would have then engaged in revision of their constitutional and statutory law. None did.

Also, if the Privileges or Immunities Clause were intended to incorporate the Bill of Rights, which includes the Fifth Amendment's due process provision, why does Section 1 of the Fourteenth Amendment have its own Due Process Clause? Is this a drafting error, double security for due process, or clear evidence that Congress did not believe the Bill of Rights was incorporated? The last explanation makes the most sense.

Further compelling evidence on this front is found in *Twitchell v Pennsylvania* (1868), in which the defendant contended that Pennsylvania denied him his rights under the Fifth and Sixth Amendments by failing to state with proper specificity in a charging document the manner in which the defendant was alleged to have caused the death of the victim.[297] The Supreme Court denied relief on the ground that the Bill of Rights did not apply to the states. Surely the justices of the Court, sitting in Washington and aware of the great debates that had taken place in Congress, would have understood that the Privileges or Immunities Clause had worked a constitutional revolution in applying the Bill of Rights to the states. The holding of *Twitchell* and the fact that the Fourteenth Amendment was not even mentioned in the decision speaks volumes about assertions regarding the first eight amendments.

Other scholars believe the privileges or immunities in the Fourteenth Amendment encompass natural, fundamental rights as spoken of by Justice Bushrod Washington in dicta in *Corfield v. Coryell* (1823) when he wrote of the Privileges and Immunities Clause in Article IV.[298] In addition to sonorous words about nature, Washington also included such matters as the right to travel, to sue, to be exempt from tax rates exceeding what other citizens pay, and to vote.[299] Some members of Congress did refer to the *Corfield* decision when discussing privileges or immunities in the Fourteenth Amendment. *Corfield*, however, is problematic, because the Civil Rights Act and the Fourteenth Amendment were sold as protections of civil rights as opposed to political or social rights. Voting rights, which Washington described as fundamental, are clearly among the matters that the amendment's framers considered political and thus beyond the scope of their work. Constitutional scholar Robert Bork has correctly described *Corfield* as a "singularly confused opinion" and observed that most commentators "have always thought that [the Constitution's Privileges and Immunities Clause appearing in Article IV] simply prevented a state from discriminating against out-of-staters in favor of their own citizens."[300] *Corfield* is not sturdy ground on which to build an interpretation and thus should not be used to import natural law principles into the Constitution.[301] As the University of Dallas's M. E. Bradford has recognized, "[n]o written constitution or limited government of laws such as the Framers intended can co-exist with such a doctrine."[302]

The Supreme Court first interpreted the Fourteenth Amendment's Privileges or Immunities Clause in the *Slaughterhouse Cases* (1873), holding that "privileges or immunities" were a limited set of rights that "owe their existence to the Federal government, its National character, its Constitution, or its laws."[303] The list included such matters as doing business with the federal government, petitioning the government for redress of grievances, and having access to the writ of habeas corpus. The *Slaughterhouse* Court, in the words of Justice Clarence Thomas, "all but read the Privileges or Immunities Clause out of the Constitution."[304] Thomas is a proponent of the *Corfield* approach but concedes the obvious: "Legal scholars agree on little beyond the conclusion that the Clause does not mean what the Court said it meant in 1873."[305]

Due Process

Section 1 prohibits the states from denying anyone due process of law. As discussed in connection with the Fifth Amendment's Due Process Clause, due process is best understood as requiring government to use the judicial process and to follow established and nondiscriminatory procedures under preexisting laws before punishing a citizen for some alleged violation. There is nothing in the debates on the Fourteenth Amendment to suggest otherwise. Indeed, when asked in the House debates what "due process" meant, Bingham replied that "courts have settled that long ago, and the gentleman can go and read their decisions."[306]

In the years after Reconstruction, the Supreme Court interpreted the Fourteenth Amendment's Due Process Clause as having a substantive component. The Court began to examine state laws to determine whether they were "reasonable." Too often, substantive due process was simply a mechanism for the Court to use to strike public policies with which it disagreed.

The classic judicial statement accepting substantive due process is *Lochner v. New York* (1905).[307] *Lochner* dealt with a New York statute prohibiting bakers from working more than sixty hours per week or ten hours per day. The state argued that the statute was a simple exercise of the police power—the reserved power to pass general legislation for the health, safety, and welfare of the people. The Supreme Court, however, held that the statute deprived bakers of liberty without due process of law because the right to freely contract was a fundamental right protected by the Fourteenth Amendment. The Court rejected the idea that reasonable legislators could conclude that working long hours near hot ovens was unhealthy and thus should be regulated. In short, the *Lochner* Court substituted its judgment for that of New York's elected representatives.

The Court continued to carefully scrutinize economic legislation into the 1930s. The Court got out of the business of protecting liberty of contract when the Brethren's aggressive review of New Deal legislation prompted President Franklin Delano Roosevelt to concoct a court-packing plan. Although the Court retreated from substantive due process in economic legislation, it held on to the power for individual liberties litigation.

The Court exercised substantive review in *Griswold v. Connecticut* (1965), when it struck down an ancient state statute that prohibited access to contraceptives.[308] Although different justices located a right to privacy in various

parts of the Constitution—shadow zones from the Bill of Rights, the Ninth Amendment, and the Due Process Clause—they ultimately agreed that certain unenumerated rights are so fundamental that no government can transgress them.

In dissent, Justice Hugo Black rebuked the majority with plain words of wisdom:

> I do not believe that we are granted power by the Due Process Clause or any other constitutional provision or provisions to measure constitutionality by our belief that legislation is arbitrary, capricious or unreasonable, or accomplishes no justifiable purpose, or is offensive to our own notions of civilized standards of conduct. Such an appraisal of the wisdom of legislation is an attribute of the power to make laws, not of the power to interpret them.[309]

Thirty-five years earlier, Justice Oliver Wendell Holmes expressed a similar sentiment.

> I have not yet adequately expressed the more than anxiety that I feel at the ever increasing scope given to the Fourteenth Amendment in cutting down what I believe to be the constitutional rights of the States. As the decisions now stand I see hardly any limit but the sky to the invalidating of those rights if they happen to strike a majority of this Court as for any reason undesirable. I cannot believe that the Amendment was intended to give us carte blanche to embody our economic or moral beliefs in its prohibitions.[310]

Lawmaking power is heady stuff that can be checked only by frequent elections. Because federal judges are not accountable at the ballot box, they should not be making public policy on controversial issues that by the original constitutional design belong to the people of the several states. Thus, with the Due Process Clause in tow, we were given the fundamental right to abortion (*Roe v. Wade*),[311] homosexual activity (*Lawrence v. Texas*),[312] and gay marriage (*Obergefell v. Hodges*).[313] These decisions have no roots in the text or history of the Constitution, and they certainly are not connected with the ancient concept of due process. They are mere public policy enactments of the Supreme Court. *Roe*, of course, was recently overturned in *Dobbs v. Jackson Women's Health Organization* (2022), but the Court made clear that it was not jettisoning the doctrine of substantive due process.[314] Relying on prior precedent, the Court simply held that for an unenumerated right to be discovered in the Due Process Clause, it must be deeply rooted in American history and tradition and implicit in the concept of ordered liberty. Because the alleged right to abortion did not fall within this framework, the Court overturned *Roe*.

The Court has also used the Fourteenth Amendment's Due Process Clause to apply much of the Bill of Rights to the states. The Due Process Clause became the vehicle because of the *Slaughterhouse* Court's narrow reading of the Privileges or Immunities Clause. Justice Hugo Black was a proponent of total incorporation and preferred such an approach to the picking and choosing ("selective incorporation") of various provisions of the Bill of Rights and the inevitable judicial creation of unenumerated rights. He feared the discretion that other approaches gave to unelected judges. As stated above in the discussion of the Privileges or Immunities Clause,

evidence for any type of incorporation is weak at best.

Equal Protection

The final portion of Section 1 prohibits the states from denying equal protection of the laws. The equal protection guarantee did not apply to all statutes. As mentioned above, there was general agreement in Congress that voting rights and other political rights were not covered in the Fourteenth Amendment. Moreover, we must remember, as legal historian Raoul Berger instructs, that "the concept of 'equal protection' had its roots in the Civil Rights Bill and was conceived to be limited to the enumerated rights."[315] Thus, concerning the enumerated rights listed in the Civil Rights Act (for example, to make and enforce contracts, bring lawsuits, and buy and sell property), blacks were not to be treated any differently than whites.

Until the second half of the twentieth century, the Equal Protection Clause was rarely invoked outside of racial discrimination cases. The Court tended to view equal protection claims in other cases, in the word of Justice Oliver Wendell Holmes, as "the usual last resort of constitutional arguments."[316] Today, the Equal Protection Clause is applied broadly to all government actions.

The beginning of modern equal protection theory is typically traced to a footnote penned by Chief Justice Harlan F. Stone in 1938. In *United States v. Carolene Products Co.* (1938), the Court upheld the power of Congress under the Commerce Clause to prohibit the shipment of filled milk, that is, skimmed milk compounded with any fat or oil.[317] The opponents of the regulation also brought equal protection and due process challenges.

The Court swiftly dealt with these by noting that removing filled milk from commerce furthered the goal of public health and thus Congress had a rational basis for passing the law.

In footnote 4, Chief Justice Stone hinted that judicial review might be more exacting in cases involving "discrete and insular minorities" or certain fundamental rights. Stone's thoughts on this matter were highly inchoate and were likely meant to spur a scholarly debate on the scope of equal protection. A debate did develop, ultimately leading to a revolution in equal protection and due process jurisprudence.

Major changes in the Court's equal protection jurisprudence occurred during the last decade of the Warren Court. In the 1960s, the Court developed a two-tier approach to equal protection cases. In addition to the deferential rational-basis standard for economic regulations, the justices created a new equal protection doctrine whereby they strictly construed certain classifications. This heightened scrutiny is also used when a fundamental right is in play. The use of strict scrutiny proved lethal to most laws under examination, as the Court required a close fit between the classification and legislative end. In addition, states could not simply put forward broad legislative goals, but had to show the Court that the classification furthered a compelling state interest. The Warren Court applied strict scrutiny to racial classifications but suggested that such matters as wealth and illegitimacy might also be subjected to heightened scrutiny.

A prime example of the new equal protection jurisprudence is *Shapiro v. Thompson* (1969), in which the Court examined laws (from Pennsylvania, Connecticut, and the District of Columbia) imposing a one-year residency requirement on indigents who sought public assistance.[318] The governments justified their laws on the ground that the legislation protected the fiscal integrity of the public purse by deterring indigents from migrating solely to take advantage of welfare benefits. That deterrence, in turn, would ensure that long-term residents falling on hard times would have access to adequate benefits.

The Court observed that the laws created a classification that distinguished residents who had resided in the jurisdictions for one year or more from residents who had resided there for less than one year. The Court then applied strict scrutiny because the legislation, in the Court's estimation, implicated the fundamental right to travel—a right nowhere enumerated in the Constitution. Although the laws denied no one entry to the jurisdictions in question, the Court reasoned that the limitation of welfare benefits served as a deterrent to interstate travel and thus infringed on the constitutional right of free movement among the states.

Justice John Marshall Harlan II dissented. Harlan protested that "[t]he 'compelling interest' doctrine [of strict scrutiny] constitutes an increasingly significant exception to the long-established rule that a statute does not deny equal protection if it is rationally related to a legitimate government objective."[319] He noted that strict scrutiny "had its genesis in cases involving racial classifications" but "apparently has been further enlarged to include classifications based upon recent interstate movement, and perhaps those based upon the exercise of any constitutional right."[320] Harlan complained that he could find no authority permitting the Court "to pick out particular human activities, characterize them as 'fundamental,' and give them added protection under an unusually stringent equal protection test."[321] Justice Harlan accused the Court, in so doing, of assuming the mantle of a "super-legislature" possessing a peculiar wisdom capable of leading the nation into a better world.[322]

Despite Justice Harlan's protests, the Court persisted in the new equal protection jurisprudence. It also added another tier to the framework. Today, equal protection jurisprudence can be summarized as follows: The top tier, as in *Shapiro*, remains strict scrutiny. To survive judicial review, a classification must serve a compelling state interest and be narrowly tailored to accomplish the stated goal. The classifications subject to strict scrutiny are race, national origin, religion, and alienage. In addition, if a classification burdens a right that the Court deems fundamental, strict scrutiny will apply. The second tier is often referred to as intermediate scrutiny. In defending a classification under this standard, the government must show that the classification serves an important government interest and that the classification is substantially related to serving that interest. Gender—not on the minds of the drafters of the Fourteenth Amendment— is the most frequent classification subjected to intermediate scrutiny. The final tier is rational-basis review. The classification is upheld so long as the government can show that the classification is rationally related to furthering a legitimate government interest.

The fate of state legislation challenged in the federal courts often depends on the level of scrutiny applied. Commentators quip that the highest level of scrutiny is strict in theory but fatal in fact. As for rational-basis review, they note that so long as the state can proffer

a plausible justification for the classification, it will typically pass muster. Of course, the liberality of the rational-basis standard is not always honored by the judiciary. Justice Clarence Thomas has observed that the "label the Court affixes to its level of scrutiny in assessing whether government can restrict a given right—be it 'rational basis,' . . . or something else—is increasingly a meaningless formalism. As the Court applies whatever standard it likes to any given case, nothing but empty words separate our constitutional decisions from judicial fiat."[323]

The Court's decision in *Obergefell* exemplifies how the Court uses due process and equal protection together to achieve desired egalitarian results.[324] Although a union between a man and a woman has been the common-law definition of marriage from colonial times, the petitioners argued that the traditional legal definition is "irrational" and thus counter to the Fourteenth Amendment. The state of Ohio and the other respondents contended that the traditional definition of marriage is rational and should be upheld. They linked the right to marry with potential procreative activity, explaining that society has chosen to channel such activity into a stable social and legal relationship: marriage.

The Supreme Court held that state restrictions of marriage to opposite-sex couples cannot stand under the Fourteenth Amendment. "The Due Process Clause and the Equal Protection Clause are connected in a profound way," the Court explained, as it declared a union between willing persons to be a marriage and thus fundamental.[325] The Court further concluded that this fundamental right must be available to all, regardless of the genders of the participants. Proffered reasons for the traditional definition of marriage were not rational, but rather the result of a desire to impose a "stigma and injury."[326]

As with *Lochner*, many libertarians have cheered *Obergefell* as an advancement of liberty. To applaud the decision requires the overcoming of several hurdles. First, same-sex marriage is not "deeply rooted in this nation's history and tradition" (the test used by the Court in recognizing fundamental rights): No state permitted same-sex marriage until a Massachusetts court held in 2003 that limiting marriage to opposite-sex couples violated the state constitution. Second, a state's decision to maintain the meaning of marriage that has been accepted in every culture throughout history can hardly be called irrational. Distinguishing between opposite-sex and same-sex couples is rationally related to a legitimate interest in preserving the traditional institution of marriage. If gender is not a reasonable criterion for marriage, one must wonder what is. Finally, until *Obergefell*, the Constitution did not enact any one theory of marriage. The people were free to change or keep the definition of marriage. Indeed, prior to the decision, voters and legislators in eleven states and the District of Columbia had changed their definitions of marriage to encompass same-sex couples. This liberty of action has been quashed. True freedom is diminished when decisions are taken away from the people and allocated to unelected and unaccountable actors.

Section 2 and Voting

Section 2 of the Fourteenth Amendment was meant to encourage Southern states to give blacks the right to vote and to secure a Republican ascendancy in Congress. Many of the Radical Republicans wanted to include a black suffrage requirement in the amendment, but they did not for fear that it would frustrate ratification. As constitutional law scholar William W. Van Alstyne has noted, in 1866, only "five states in the nation permitted Negroes to vote on equal terms with whites."[327] In 1865, "Connecticut, Minnesota, and Wisconsin voted down impartial suffrage by popular referendum."[328] With such Northern opposition, the best Congress could do was incentivize the South to grant freedmen the vote.

Section 2 decrees that if any state should deny the vote on account of race, then its representation in the House would be proportionately reduced. The decree also applied to Northern states, but given their small black populations, it was no threat to their congressional representation. In New England, for example, blacks were less than 1 percent of the population in 1860.[329] In the lower South, however, blacks were more than 43 percent of the population in 1860.[330]

The Republicans calculated that if the South chose to enfranchise blacks, all or most of these voters would be staunchly Republican. But if Southern states chose to prevent blacks from voting, they would lose representation and thus be unable win a majority in the House of Representatives. Either way, the Republicans reasoned, they would win.

The modern Supreme Court held that the Equal Protection Clause requires the states to structure their legislatures so that all the members of each house represent roughly the same number of people. Such a holding lacks any foundation in the Fourteenth Amendment. Section 2 is the only portion of the Fourteenth Amendment that deals with suffrage. Congress can reduce the representation of a state that denies the vote on account of race, but that is the limit of the authority granted by the Fourteenth Amendment.

Section 3 and Disqualification

Section 3 disqualified former Confederates who had previously taken an oath to support the federal Constitution from holding federal or state office. Although scholars are much more interested in issues surrounding Section 1's Privileges or Immunities and Due Process Clauses, Sections 2 and 3 were far more important to members of the Thirty-Ninth Congress. The Radicals did not want to see the likes of Alexander Stephens, John C. Breckinridge, and other Confederate leaders admitted to Congress. Section 3 serves as a bar absent a two-thirds vote in Congress to remove the disability. The Amnesty Act of 1872 removed office-holding disqualifications against most former Confederates except for a few hundred high-ranking leaders.

After 1872, Section 3 was mostly forgotten. As the 2024 presidential primary season approached, however, some commentators suggested a broad interpretation of the provision. The aim was to prevent Donald Trump from seeking a second term as president of the United States. Commentators argued that Trump engaged in an insurrection on January 6, 2021, and thus state secretaries of state and their subordinates could delete Trump from any presidential ballot.[331] The argument was further based on the idea that Section 3 is "self-enforcing," so no formal adjudication or congressional action is necessary.

The Colorado Supreme Court agreed that Trump was an insurrectionist and ordered the Colorado secretary of state to remove him from the Republican primary ballot and to disregard any write-in votes listing his name. In *Trump v. Anderson* (2024), all nine Supreme Court justices agreed that the state court decision should be reversed because the states lack the authority to enforce Section 3.[332] In accordance with the terms of Section 3, states have the power to disqualify persons from occupying a state office or running for state office; but there the states' power ends. A majority of justices, however, went further and held that only Congress using its enforcement power under Section 5 of the Fourteenth Amendment can enforce Section 3. Of course, Congress has enacted 18 U.S.C § 2383, which criminalizes inciting or participating in "any rebellion or insurrection against the authority of the United States or the laws thereof."[333] An offender "shall be fined under this title or imprisoned not more than ten years, or both; and shall be incapable of holding any office under the United States."[334] The statute requires a court adjudication in which the accused enjoys procedural protections, a jury trial, and the right to appeal the verdict. Three justices in the minority argued that Section 3 is self-executing and that congressional implementing legislation is not the sole mechanism by which federal authorities could enforce Section 3. They sought to preserve the federal courts' role in applying Section 3.

Section 4 and Debts

Section 4 declared that debts incurred by the general government in defeating the Confederacy were inviolable. This section prohibited either the general government or state governments from paying debts accumulated in supporting the Confederacy. Section 4 also foreclosed any claims by former slave owners—in loyal and rebel states—related to emancipation.

In the summer of 2023, the Biden administration contemplated invoking Section 4 to circumvent the federal debt ceiling. Rather than negotiate with Congress to increase borrowing or cut spending, President Biden asserted that Section 4 authorizes unilateral presidential action. Under Article I, Congress has the power of the purse and makes decisions about borrowing money. The contention that Section 4 displaces Congress's power of the purse is erroneous. Moreover, as Robert E. Wright of Augustana University has pointed out, all Section 4 requires is "that the Treasury has to service all the government's bonds and pay Social Security and certain other debt-like obligations before it can make other payments, including to federal government employees."[335] This can be accomplished with a government shutdown, spending cuts, or the sale of public lands to raise revenue. A limitation on more borrowing does not necessarily mean a debt repudiation or default.

The Enforcement Power

Section 5 grants Congress the power to enforce provisions of the Fourteenth Amendment "by appropriate legislation." Modern Americans mostly associate the Fourteenth Amendment with judicial decisions interpreting matters such as privileges or immunities, due process, and equal protection. It is doubtful that the framers of the amendment sought to aggrandize the judiciary, however. Section 1, for instance, was meant to overturn the judicial decision in *Dred Scott* holding that blacks could not be citizens of the United States. Trust in the Supreme Court was at its nadir when the amendment was drafted and sent to the states. Senator Jacob Howard made clear that Section 5 "casts upon Congress the responsibility of seeing to it, for the future, that all the sections of the amendment are carried out in good faith, and that no State infringes upon the rights of persons and property."[336]

The Supreme Court, in interpreting Section 5, has held that Congress does not possess "the power to decree the substance of the Fourteenth Amendment's restrictions on the States."[337] Enforcement of a constitutional right does not include the power to alter the right. "[Congress] has been given the power 'to enforce,' not the power to determine what constitutes a constitutional violation."[338] "The power to interpret the Constitution in a case or controversy," the Court has emphasized, "remains in the Judiciary."[339]

Distortions

The Fourteenth Amendment's color-blind Constitution has been traded for a system that confers benefits and burdens based on race. In modern America, to be an "anti-racist," one must view all interactions and situations through the prism of race.[340] In a push against this fixation with race, the Supreme Court, in *Students for Fair Admissions, Inc. v. President & Fellows of Harvard College* (2023), struck down the race-based admissions policies of Harvard and the University of North Carolina.[341] Both schools sought to achieve racial balance through admissions decisions that focused on an applicant's race. The Court recognized that the Fourteenth Amendment was meant to do away with state-sponsored discrimination and held that "both programs lack sufficiently focused and measurable objectives warranting the use of race, unavoidably employ race in a negative manner, involve racial stereotyping, and lack meaningful end points."[342] The reaction to the Court's decision was virulent, as American intellectuals demanded a system of racial balancing in higher education and other institutions. For example, the Biden administration's secretary of education, Miguel A. Cardona, compared the Court's decision to COVID-19 and promised "bold leadership and collaboration" to continue admissions policies focused on achieving racial diversity.[343]

Justice Sonja Sotomayor accused the majority of "cement[ing] a superficial rule of colorblindness as a constitutional principle in an endemically segregated society where race has always mattered and continues to matter."[344] In these words, there is no hope for a unity in shared citizenship. An immutable characteristic, Justice Sotomayor contends, defines us and always will. Citizens of different races are expected to perpetually fight to obtain government benefits for their particular racial groups. Unable to point to modern state-sanctioned discrimination against minorities, Sotomayor appealed to "systemic inequities" that require the government to consider race in its decision-making.[345] Hence, she would endorse continued discrimination in college admissions.

In addition to misuse of the Fourteenth Amendment to promote discrimination against legacy Americans, substantive due process remains a constitutional tapeworm feeding off what remains of our written charter. Substantive due process permits the federal courts to weigh the "reasonableness" of state laws, but that reasonableness has more to do with a judge's personal preferences than the law. Equal protection has become a vehicle for indulging extremist liberation theory and for destroying traditional structures and hierarchies. That course is far afield from the modest goals of the Civil Rights Act, including permitting citizens of all races to make and enforce contracts, sue in court, and purchase and sell property.

Discussion and Solutions

One can argue that the Fourteenth Amendment *is* the modern Constitution. As Paul Gottfried of Elizabethtown College has observed, "[u]nder contemporary jurisprudence, the Fourteenth Amendment can be stretched to 'defend' any imaginable 'right' beyond anything consistent with the original intent of the Amendment's authors."[346]

If America is to recover constitutional sanity, part of the process will be to put the Fourteenth Amendment in context. A sane and originalist jurisprudence will reject fantastical claims that the Fourteenth Amendment confers birthright citizenship on any person born within our borders, that the federal Bill of Rights applies to the states, and that "rights" deemed by the Court to be fundamental can be written into the constitutional text. Only by challenging the modern constitutional fallacies can we overturn our judge-made Constitution and return to the written document.

Our written charter is much preferable to a judicial ascendancy. The Constitution allows the people to govern themselves in their states and to experiment with policy decisions. While the Fourteenth Amendment wisely prohibits state and local government from discriminating against persons on the basis of race, it leaves the federal system's structural bones in place. That is how the amendment was offered to the people of the North: as affording freedmen protection in enjoying basic rights, yet otherwise leaving the states that fought to save the union to govern themselves as they always had. Senator Lyman Trumbull of Illinois, for example, announced that the amendment would have "no operation in Massachusetts, New York, Illinois, or most of the States in the Union" because such states levied no lawfare against freedmen.[347] The flexibility of the federal system is a strength of American government and must not be lost forever based on unsupportable interpretations of the Fourteenth Amendment.[348] We should interpret it in the same manner as it was explained to the people of the North.

AMENDMENT XV (RATIFIED 1870)

SECTION 1. THE right of citizens of the United States to vote shall not be denied or abridged by the United States or by any State on account of race, color, or previous condition of servitude.

SECTION 2. THE Congress shall have power to enforce this article by appropriate legislation.

Purpose

The Fifteenth Amendment prohibits denying the vote to citizens on account of race, color, or former status as a slave.

Background and Development

The Fourteenth Amendment left the matter of suffrage in the hands of the states. Many Radical Republicans wanted to address suffrage in the Fourteenth Amendment but realized that such a far-reaching measure would imperil ratification. The election of 1868 caused them to rethink matters. In 1868, Ulysses S. Grant won the presidency on a Republican platform declaring that voting rights were a matter of state legislative policy. Grant handily won the Electoral College vote, but triumphed over his rival by only a few hundred thousand votes nationally. Republican power was slipping. "What had so recently seemed impossible suddenly became a partisan necessity: black Americans had to be provided a constitutional right to vote."[349]

The lame-duck session of the Fortieth Congress went to work while the party clung to power in the state legislatures. Radical Republicans proposed sweeping reforms that would have struck at literacy tests, property requirements, and other mechanisms that restricted suffrage. Such proposals ran into trouble because these mechanisms were widely used in Northern states. Massachusetts, for example, used literacy tests, and Rhode Island imposed a property qualification on naturalized citizens. Radicals realized that if they were going to get an amendment passed and sent to the states, they would have to scale back their objectives. Consequently, they settled upon "race, color, or previous condition of servitude."

As with the Thirteenth and Fourteenth Amendments, Congress has the power to enforce the Fifteenth Amendment through appropriate legislation.

Distortions

One of the most notable pieces of legislation passed pursuant to the Fifteenth Amendment is the Voting Rights Act of 1965. This legislation, among other things, prohibited literacy tests, provided for federal oversight of voter registration in areas where less than half of the nonwhite population had not registered to vote, and prohibited certain enumerated jurisdictions from implementing any change affecting voting until the attorney general of the United States or the District Court for the District of Columbia determined that the change did not have a discriminatory purpose or effect.

The Supreme Court, in *South Carolina v. Katzenbach* (1966), rejected a challenge to the Voting Rights Act and found that the statute was a proper use of Congress's enforcement power under the Fifteenth Amendment.[350] The decision is questionable because the Reconstruction Congress specifically declined to prohibit literacy tests and other mechanisms targeted by the Voting Rights Act of 1965. As legal historian Alfred Avins has noted, "the framers of the amendment contemplated continued use of literacy tests despite their possible discriminatory effect and . . . legislation which purports to suspend such tests on that ground is not a legitimate exercise of congressional power."[351]

In *Shelby County v. Holder* (2013), an Alabama political subdivision challenged provisions in the congressionally reauthorized Voting Rights Act, under which covered jurisdictions—mostly in the South—were required to demonstrate that proposed voting law changes were not discriminatory.[352] Section 4(b) of the Act defined covered

jurisdictions as ones that had a voting test in place on November 1, 1964, and had a turnout of less than 50 percent for the 1964 presidential election. Noting that the Voting Rights Act was extraordinary legislation intended to be in effect for a temporary time period, the Court struck down Section 4 of the Act as lacking a logical relationship to current conditions. In making this point, the Court observed that in 1965 in Alabama, 69.2 percent of the white population was registered to vote versus 19.3 percent of the black population. In 2004, 73.8 percent of the white population was registered versus 72.9 percent of the black population—a gap of just 0.9 percent. Such statistics could not support the continued applicability of Section 4 of the Act.

There was hope that the common sense of *Shelby County* would extend to other issues involving voting rights, including the propriety of Section 2 of the Voting Rights Act, which prohibits voting practices or procedures that discriminate on the basis of race. In *Allen v. Milligan* (2023), the Supreme Court dealt with a Section 2 claim in which plaintiffs alleged that the statute required Alabama to redraw congressional districts so black voters could control House seats proportional to the state's black population.[353] Rather than interpreting Section 2 to govern access to the ballot or ballot-counting procedures, the Court held fast to the proposition that districting plans are covered and that race-based redistricting plans are often required by Section 2. While the Court acknowledged that racial gerrymandering as required by its Section 2 jurisprudence might carry the country away from the principle of color blindness, it declined to reconsider expansive Section 2 precedents. The

Court found that Alabama's congressional map likely violated Section 2 because it was possible to redraw the map and obtain two majority black districts rather than one. The Court rejected Alabama's use of computer-drawn maps that are not programmed to take race into account.

Discussion and Solutions

The Fifteenth Amendment prohibits denying the vote to citizens on account of race, color, or former status as a slave. The amendment was not designed to guarantee a certain legislative mix of black, white, or Hispanic representatives. When Congress and the courts use the Fifteenth Amendment to achieve racial balancing, they reject the principle of color blindness. People of a certain race are lumped together in a monolithic group perceived as sharing the same interests, ideas, and policy preferences. The value of the individual is reduced, and group identity is elevated. Americans should oppose such abuse of the Fifteenth Amendment and demand a return to an interpretation that guarantees a vote, not an outcome.

AMENDMENT XVI (RATIFIED 1913)

THE CONGRESS SHALL have power to lay and collect taxes on incomes, from whatever source derived, without apportionment among the several States, and without regard to any census or enumeration.

Purpose

The Sixteenth Amendment allows Congress to tax incomes without utilizing the Constitution's apportionment requirement.

Background and Development

The Sixteenth Amendment overturned *Pollock v. Farmers' Loan & Trust Co.* (1895), in which the Court held that income taxes were direct taxes and required apportionment among the states (previously discussed under Article I, Section 9, Clause 4). *Pollock* stood in the way of progressives' design to move American tax policy away from indirect taxes such as tariffs and toward direct income taxation. As Yale's Akhil Amar has pointed out, *Pollock* also stood in the way of the progressive hope of redistributionism—the reduction of "the great inequalities of wealth between rich and poor" through government transfers.[354]

The Sixteenth Amendment took life during the administration of President William Howard Taft, a Republican from Ohio. In 1909, Taft ascended to the presidency during a revenue shortfall and a fight over protective tariffs. Democrats plus a number of Republican insurgents wanted an income tax law passed so that the Supreme Court would have an opportunity to reverse *Pollock*. As a former jurist, Taft believed that such a course would lessen the standing of the Court and sought a compromise. According to Old Right polemicist Frank Chodorov, "[a] political deal was put over; the tariff bill was passed with a rider taxing corporation incomes [couched as an excise tax], and the opposition was promised a bill for a constitutional amendment."[355] Taft was no fan of an income tax amendment and did not believe it had much chance of ratification. Persuaded the amendment would be a dead letter, Taft signed off on the political horse trading. To his chagrin, the required thirty-six states ratified by 1913, and the Sixteenth Amendment became part of the Constitution.

The passage of the Sixteenth Amendment resulted in a revolution. J. Bracken Lee, a former governor of Utah, argued that "income taxation has made of the United States as completely centralized a nation as any that went before it."[356] As portions of the people's paychecks went to Washington, DC, their interest in national affairs as opposed to local affairs rose correspondingly. State officials, in Lee's experience, were "reduced to being procurement officers" and thus had to "play ball" with the federal government to receive "grants-in-aid."[357] Lee believed that only a repeal of the Sixteenth Amendment could restore meaningful home rule in state and local governments.

Distortions

The Sixteenth Amendment is the instrument that allows the general government to finance the welfare state. A desire to redistribute wealth birthed the Sixteenth Amendment, and government has worked for more than one hundred years to transfer wealth to its favorites. This is no modern distortion but is instead in accord with the intent of activists who demanded significant increases in government revenues.

Nonetheless, progressives are not content with the transfers made possible by the Sixteenth Amendment. They complain, in the words of the Institute for Taxation and Economic Policy, that the "problem with relying on income taxes is that much of the income received by the richest Americans is 'unrealized capital gains' which are not taxed."[358] This deferral "allows the net worth of the wealthiest to build up much more rapidly and substantially" to increase inequality.[359] To aid redistributionism, left-wing intellectuals are proposing a wealth tax (that is, a tax on net worth).

A wealth tax, however, like the income tax in *Pollock*, would likely run into the apportionment requirement. As the demand for the wealth tax gains steam, we should expect proposals for a constitutional amendment—à la the Sixteenth Amendment—removing the constitutional roadblock.

Discussion and Solutions

J. Bracken Lee was correct: A sure way to strike the welfare state and to revive federalism is to repeal the Sixteenth Amendment. Revenue from the income tax allows the general government an almost unrestrained capacity to fund programs that properly belong to the states. Education, poor relief, and policing are all local matters on which the general government spends billions. They are also areas where it has little or no constitutional authority.

Repealing the Sixteenth Amendment would restore the citizen's privacy. In collecting the income tax, the Internal Revenue Service (IRS) demands disclosure of gifts, how a citizen makes money, who the citizen gives that money to, and sundry other private matters. Pundits clamor about data collection efforts by the National Security Agency but ignore the far more invasive work of the IRS. The repeal of the Sixteenth Amendment would do more to further privacy than a vigorous enforcement of the Fourth Amendment.

AMENDMENT XVII (RATIFIED 1913)

SECTION 1. THE Senate of the United States shall be composed of two Senators from each State, elected by the people thereof, for six years; and each Senator shall have one vote. The electors in each State shall have the qualifications requisite for electors of the most numerous branch of the State legislatures.

SECTION 2. WHEN vacancies happen in the representation of any State in the Senate, the executive authority of such State shall issue writs of election to fill such vacancies: Provided, That the legislature of any State may empower the executive thereof to make temporary appointments until the people fill the vacancies by election as the legislature may direct.

SECTION 3. THIS amendment shall not be so construed as to affect the election or term of any Senator chosen before it becomes valid as part of the Constitution.

Purpose

The Seventeenth Amendment took from state legislatures the power to choose senators and transferred the power to voters in each state.

Background and Development

At the time of the Constitution's ratification, the Framers expected the Senate to serve as a guardian of the states' reserved powers. In the Philadelphia Convention, George Mason observed that the appointment of senators by state legislators would provide the states with a "power of self-defence."[360] Madison was unequivocal about the matter in *Federalist* No. 62: "[T]he equal vote allotted each state [in the Senate] is at once a recognition of the portion of sovereignty remaining in the individual states, and an instrument for preserving that residuary sovereignty."[361] No law could be passed, Madison continued, "without the concurrence of first a majority of the people, and then a majority of the States."[362] Importantly, the state ratifying conventions expressed a similar understanding. James Iredell of North Carolina, for example, described the Senate as the body charged with ensuring that the state governments "be preserved."[363] In commenting on the composition of the Senate, Pierce of Massachusetts echoed Madison and identified senators as "representatives of the sovereignty."[364] The state conventions also expected the state legislatures would exercise much control over the senators. Rufus King of Massachusetts believed that the legislatures would admonish and "instruct them" on the correct course of action.[365] Appointment and control of senators was seen by all as key to protecting the states' residuary sovereignty.

By the late 1800s, the Constitution's design for choosing senators appeared to many to be an anachronism. Progressives denounced the Senate as an oligarchic rich man's club and argued that democracy was the cure for ills wrought by industrialization and powerful business combinations. In response to pressure from progressives, thirty-three states eventually adopted a system of direct primaries for electing senators. The primaries operated much like the Constitution's Electoral College, with the state legislators promising to abide by the results of the primary when appointing senators. Going further than primaries, twelve states adopted the Oregon system for choosing senators. Under this system, candidates for the state legislature promised in their platforms either to abide by the people's choice of senators in the general election or to use their own judgment in appointing senators. Choosing the second option was political suicide, and therefore, as a practical matter, senators were elected by the people in the states using the Oregon system.

In 1912, the demand for popular election of senators was so strong that Congress submitted the Seventeenth Amendment to the states for ratification. Within eleven months, the requisite three-fourths of state legislatures approved the amendment and officially disenfranchised themselves. The debates in the early 1900s surrounding the Seventeenth Amendment evince little concern for the Senate's role as a protector of the states' reserved powers. In light of the outcome of the Civil War and the growing role of political parties, the people were forgetting the importance of federalism in the American system of government.

George Mason's Todd J. Zywicki has also pointed out that special interests and urban political machines were significant supporters of the Seventeenth Amendment "because popular election would increase their power by putting a premium on their unique power to organize and deliver voting blocks."[366] Political machines "were the only organizations who could organize the masses of voters necessary to win popular elections" and thus saw the amendment as a boon to their power.[367] Rather than transferring power to the people, Zywicki makes a compelling argument that special interests used the Seventeenth Amendment to extinguish "the systems of federalism and bicameralism which had previously checked expansionist federal activity."[368]

Though the role of the Senate was declining before ratification of the Seventeenth Amendment, it is no coincidence that the size of the national government expanded rapidly after 1913. Without the Seventeenth Amendment, one must wonder whether the Wilson administration would have succeeded in establishing the Federal Reserve, the Federal Trade Commission, or the "war socialism" used to control production and other facets of the economy during World War I.

As for the mechanics of the Seventeenth Amendment, Section 1 sets forth the qualification for electors and closely follows the original Constitution's wording regarding electors for the House of Representatives. Similarly, the first part of Section 2 of the amendment, dealing with vacancies, follows a similar provision in the original Constitution that dealt with vacancies for members of the House. In the case of a vacancy and prior to a special or general election, the governor of a state may make temporary appointments if permitted such authority by the legislature.

Distortions

The Seventeenth Amendment was not a transfer of power to the people. Instead, it served political machines and liberal interests intent on removing impediments to government expansion. The power to tax incomes, coupled with the extinguishment of the states as constituencies in the general government, paved the way for expansion of federal power. The modern state could not have thrived without additional taxing powers and the demise of federalism.

Discussion and Solutions

The year 1913 was a disastrous year for limited government. The income tax boosted Congress's ability to spend, and the Seventeenth Amendment removed institutional safeguards that might have impeded the growth of the welfare state. State representation in the Senate was a critical structural component of the Constitution. In light of Appomattox and the expansion of federal power, little thought was given to the consequences of rescinding state representation in Congress. Returning the Senate to its role as a guardian of the states' reserved powers will be key to any successful effort at reviving true federalism in the United States. This is especially true when shifting majorities of the Supreme Court shy away from protecting the states' reserved powers and instead argue that "the principal means chosen by the Framers to ensure the role of the States in the federal system lies in the structure of the Federal Government itself."[369] Following ratification of the Seventeenth Amendment, however, the states require assistance from all available sources in retaining what sovereign dignity they still possess.

AMENDMENT XVIII (RATIFIED 1919)

SECTION 1. AFTER one year from the ratification of this article the manufacture, sale, or transportation of intoxicating liquors within, the importation thereof into, or the exportation thereof from the United States and all territory subject to the jurisdiction thereof for beverage purposes is hereby prohibited.

SECTION 2. THE Congress and the several States shall have concurrent power to enforce this article by appropriate legislation.

SECTION 3. THIS article shall be inoperative unless it shall have been ratified as an amendment to the Constitution by the legislatures of the several States, as provided in the Constitution, within seven years from the date of the submission hereof to the States by the Congress.

Purpose

In a national effort to combat the vices associated with alcohol consumption and saloon culture, the Eighteenth Amendment prohibited the manufacture, sale, or transport of alcoholic beverages.

Background and Development

The American experiment with alcohol prohibition, according to W. J. Rorabaugh of the University of Washington, "was part of a global effort to ban or control alcohol and other drugs."[370] Abuse of alcohol has a long history in the United States: "By the 1820s, the average adult white male drank a half pint of whiskey a day."[371] In those days, the United States had a plentiful supply of surplus corn that was turned into alcohol. Whiskey was often safer to drink than water and cost less than nonalcoholic products such as coffee or milk. During the Second Great Awakening of the early nineteenth century, evangelical preachers sought to win souls and to promote sanctified living, which often meant opposing use of alcohol or encouraging people to switch to beer. During the 1850s, eleven states passed prohibition statutes. The temperance movement lost steam because of the tumult of the Civil War but regained momentum in the later decades of the 1800s. The Women's Christian Temperance Union and the Anti-Saloon League became forces in American politics. The progressive movement supported temperance, with William Jennings Bryan urging the Democratic Party to take a stand against alcohol.

World War I was a boon for the prohibition movement. In 1917, Congress passed the Food Control Act, which prohibited the distillation of foodstuffs. The statute also authorized President Wilson to use an executive order to further the temperance effort. Wilson cut the amount of grain available to brewers and decreed beer's alcohol content could be no greater than 2.75 percent. Most of the major breweries in the United States were owned by German Americans; during wartime, it was easy to smear the German community and their beloved beer as unpatriotic. The Kaiser's minions, American were told, swilled beer, while good democrats were teetotalers. So great was the wrath against the brewers that American politicians in both major parties refused to accept their campaign contributions. With the brewers' money verboten to both Republicans and Democrats, the temperance movement grew in power.

According to Rorabaugh, "[b]y late 1917, there were twenty-three dry states, seventeen of which had gone dry by popular vote."[372] Once the war ended, President Wilson and Congress continued the assault on alcohol—still using war powers—to ban the production of beer or wine after May 1, 1919, and the sale of alcohol after July 1, 1919.

The father of the Eighteenth Amendment was Morris Sheppard, a Democratic senator from Texas. On the Senate floor, Sheppard outlined his reasoning for supporting Prohibition:

[A]lcoholic poison works especial havoc. It impairs the highest functions of the brain, the sense of right, of moral conduct, of proper obligation to society and to God. It thus imperils virtue, integrity, respect for law and order—all that is sacred and pure in civilization. It is a chief source of immorality and crime. . . . [And] a hundred million bushels of grain and vast quantities of other foodstuffs intended by nature to be used in supporting life are converted into a beverage that corrupts and destroys it.[373]

The Eighteenth Amendment passed Congress and was sent to the states in late

December 1917. It was ratified on January 16, 1919. The text of the amendment prohibited the manufacture, sale, or transport of alcoholic beverages. Notably, it did not prohibit the consumption or possession of such beverages. Its targets were the saloons, breweries, and distilleries—not the average citizen who still wanted to imbibe.

In an interesting twist, the amendment granted the federal and state governments concurrent power to enforce Prohibition. Congress assumed that with such a groundswell of support for Prohibition, all levels of government would work together to enforce it. They did not. In many states, local officials ignored Prohibition and left the matter of enforcement to the general government.

The amendment gave the states seven years to ratify.

AMENDMENT XIX (RATIFIED 1920)

THE RIGHT OF citizens of the United States to vote shall not be denied or abridged by the United States or by any State on account of sex.

CONGRESS SHALL HAVE power to enforce this article by appropriate legislation.

Purpose

The amendment prohibits government from treating men and women differently when legislating on the franchise.

Background and Development

Many Americans erroneously believe that the U.S. Constitution deprived women of the right to vote until ratification of the Nineteenth Amendment in 1920. The Framers, however, left voter qualifications in the hands of the several states. The New Jersey Constitution of 1776 was the first state constitution that enfranchised both men and women who met certain property-holding requirements. Women voted in state and federal elections until 1807, when state law changed.

In the early 1900s, the women's suffrage movement gained energy when Theodore Roosevelt's Progressive Party became the first national political party to adopt a platform urging women's suffrage: "The Progressive party, believing that no people can justly claim to be a true democracy which denies political rights on account of sex, pledges itself to the task of securing equal suffrage to men and women alike."[374]

George Sutherland, a Republican senator from Utah and later a Supreme Court justice, argued for the Nineteenth Amendment in the Senate. Sutherland challenged his colleagues to support women's suffrage:

> Have women in the aggregate less native intelligence than men? Have they less desire for social and governmental righteousness? Are they less patriotic? Are they less interested in the common welfare? Have they less at stake? If not, wherein lies the superiority of the male portion of the population? . . .

We are told that if women are given the ballot the household will suffer. . . . The obvious retort is that if the workshop, and the farm, and the mine, and the office, and the countingroom continue in operation, notwithstanding the responsibility which now rests upon the male voter, the household may survive even if the women of the country study politics and take a few minutes off on election day to vote.[375]

Sutherland's appeals were successful. Congress passed the amendment in June 1919 and sent it to the states. It was ratified on August 18, 1920. As legal scholars Richard L. Hasen and Leah M. Litman have observed, "it is 'wildly inaccurate' to think of women's enfranchisement in the United States as happening in a single episode with the Amendment's approval. By the time of the Amendment's ratification in 1920, 'woman suffrage in some form was already a reality in nearly every state. Thirty states had [prior to ratification] changed their laws to do away with sex qualifications to vote in elections of national consequence.'"[376]

The only case in which the Supreme Court has applied the Nineteenth Amendment is *Breedlove v. Suttles* (1937), which dealt with a Georgia statute exempting nonregistered female voters, the aged, and blind persons from paying the poll tax.[377] The law was challenged by a white male who alleged that it unlawfully discriminated against him on account of sex. The Court rejected the man's challenge and averred that "[i]t is fanciful to suggest that the Georgia law is a mere disguise under which to deny or abridge the right of men to vote on account of their sex."[378] The Nineteenth Amendment, said the Court, was not intended "to regulate the levy or collection of taxes."[379]

Distortions

Activists seek to apply the Nineteenth Amendment to "transgender and gender-nonconforming voters."[380] They contend that vast discrimination exists when a volunteer poll worker asks for identification and the driver's license presented depicts, say, a man, when the voter appears to be female. According to the American Bar Association, "378,000 voting-eligible transgender adults do not have accurate ID documents, and nearly 105,000 of them face substantial barriers to voting and possible disenfranchisement in the twelve states with the strictest voter ID laws."[381] Legal activists seek to use the Nineteenth Amendment to strike down state laws requiring a voter to produce an accurate identification document at polling places.

In arguing their point, left-leaning activists point to *Bostock v. Clayton County* (2020), in which the Supreme Court held that Title VII of the Civil Rights Act of 1964's prohibition of workplace discrimination based on "sex" encompasses sexual orientation.[382] Hence, a person fired because of homosexual orientation or transgender status may, post-*Bostock*, bring a discrimination claim under federal law. Although many Americans agree with the policy result reached by the Court, all thinking persons should lament that six unelected lawyers usurped the role of Congress.

When engaging in statutory interpretation, the Court is supposed to implement congressional intent by examining the plain language of the statute. A statute's plain meaning is determined by reference to the ordinary definition of its words at the time of the statute's enactment.[383] In reaching its decision in *Bostock*, the

Court asserted that it was simply enforcing the plain terms of Title VII as those terms would have been understood in 1964. The Court's opinion cited the late Justice Antonin Scalia and assured readers that the Court was engaging in a textualism that would have made Scalia proud.

The Court conceded that "sex" as used in Title VII would have been understood by an average person in 1964 as meaning biologically male or female. The Court followed up with a remarkable statement, however: "[I]t is impossible to discriminate against a person for being homosexual or transgender without discriminating against that individual based on sex."[384]

If, for example, an employer fired all lesbians working for his company, he would not be discriminating because the targets of his wrath are biologically female but on account of their sexual orientation. Sex discrimination and sexual-orientation discrimination are two distinct categories of discrimination. The former falls within the plain meaning of Title VII; the latter does not.

For most of its history, this has been the common understanding of Title VII's prohibition of sex discrimination. As Justice Brett Kavanaugh pointed out in dissent, "in the first 10 Courts of Appeals to consider the issue, all 30 federal judges agreed that Title VII does not prohibit sexual orientation discrimination."[385] Indeed, for the first forty-eight years of its existence, the Equal Employment Opportunity Commission, charged with enforcing civil rights laws against workplace discrimination,

viewed sex discrimination and sexual-orientation discrimination as separate matters.

Congress certainly viewed sex and sexual-orientation discrimination as different. Over the years, various bills have been introduced to add sexual-orientation discrimination to Title VII. At different times, majorities in both the House and Senate have approved such a change, but they have yet to come together to send a bill to the president. In many other federal antidiscrimination statutes, Congress has specifically included sexual orientation. Thus, when Congress wants to prohibit discrimination based on sexual orientation, it knows how to do so. It did not do so in Title VII, however, and it certainly did not do so in the Nineteenth Amendment, passed and ratified at a time when most Americans never had contemplated the existence of transgenderism.

Discussion and Solutions

The interpretive jiggery-pokery, to borrow a phrase from Justice Scalia, used by the Court to reach a desired policy result in *Bostock* is now wielded by activists to distort the Nineteenth Amendment. *Bostock* was wrong; sex and sexual orientation are two different things. The former is at the heart of the Nineteenth Amendment, while the latter is a modern construct divorced from constitutional common sense. Originalists should oppose any efforts to foist the *Bostock* majority's interpretation on the Nineteenth Amendment, while at the same time demanding that *Bostock* be overturned.

AMENDMENT XX (RATIFIED 1933)

SECTION 1. THE terms of the President and Vice President shall end at noon on the 20th day of January, and the terms of Senators and Representatives at noon on the 3d day of January, of the years in which such terms would have ended if this article had not been ratified; and the terms of their successors shall then begin.

SECTION 2. THE Congress shall assemble at least once in every year, and such meeting shall begin at noon on the 3d day of January, unless they shall by law appoint a different day.

SECTION 3. IF, at the time fixed for the beginning of the term of the President, the President elect shall have died, the Vice President elect shall become President. If a President shall not have been chosen before the time fixed for the beginning of his term, or if the President elect shall have failed to qualify, then the Vice President elect shall act as President until a President shall have qualified; and the Congress may by law provide for the case wherein neither a President elect nor a Vice President elect shall have qualified, declaring who shall then act as President, or the manner in which one who is to act shall be selected, and such person shall act accordingly until a President or Vice President shall have qualified.

SECTION 4. THE Congress may by law provide for the case of the death of any of the persons from whom the House of Representatives may choose a President whenever the right of choice shall have devolved upon them, and for the case of the death of any of the persons from whom the Senate may choose a Vice President whenever the right of choice shall have devolved upon them.

SECTION 5. SECTIONS 1 and 2 shall take effect on the 15th day of October following the ratification of this article.

SECTION 6. THIS article shall be inoperative unless it shall have been ratified as an amendment to the Constitution by the legislatures of three-fourths of the several States within seven years from the date of its submission.

Purpose

The framers of the Twentieth Amendment designed it to curtail the significant period of time a defeated president or member of Congress would continue in office after failing to secure reelection.

Background and Development

The first sections of the Twentieth Amendment address constitutional issues exposed in 1800 when Thomas Jefferson was almost denied the presidency after his Republican Party soundly defeated the Federalists in national elections. As previously discussed (under Article II, Section 1, Clause 3), Jefferson and Aaron Burr (who was viewed by Republicans as their vice presidential candidate) tied with seventy-three electoral votes each. John Adams received sixty-five electoral votes, and Charles Pinckney (viewed by the Federalists as Adams's vice presidential candidate) received sixty-four. At that time, the Constitution did not allow electors to designate a presidential and vice presidential candidate, and thus Republican electors were afraid to waste a vote to ensure Burr had fewer electoral votes than Jefferson. Because they tied, the House of Representatives was called upon to decide between Jefferson and Burr. The Federalists worked doggedly to deny Jefferson the position of chief executive and relented only when Jefferson promised not to fire Federalist members of the civil service. The Constitution was soon amended to permit designation of presidential and vice presidential candidates, but nothing was done to address the issue of a lame-duck House choosing a president. The Twentieth Amendment fixed this problem so that a newly elected House, if constitutionally called upon, would elect a president. Prior to adoption of the Twentieth Amendment, the new Congress did not convene for its first session until December of the following year (more than a year after the elections). Under the amendment, the new Congress meets on the third day of January—just a few weeks after the election and before the end of the former president's term.

In addition to putting a lame-duck Congress out of the presidential election business, the amendment also abolished (or at least curtailed) the "short session" of the old Congress that under prior law did not terminate until the coming March. A rejected Congress thus had time to legislate and had no worries about facing the people at the ballot box. Framers of the amendment also believed that short sessions allowed special-interest groups to manipulate scheduling and other matters to frustrate popular measures. An example of attempted lame-duck lawmaking was the effort by President Warren Harding to persuade the lame-duck Congress to pass a ship subsidy bill, which would have given financial incentives to private companies that built cargo ships. The ship subsidy had been an important issue in the 1922 midterm elections, with many legislators losing their positions because they supported Harding's proposal. Ignoring the voice of the people, the House, convening in its short session, passed the subsidy. The Senate, however, defeated the bill through a filibuster.

While the lame-duck Congress, if it chooses, can still meet in late November and December after an election, the framers of the amendment expected Congress to stand at ease. Other than preparations for the incoming representatives, the framers did not expect that the work of legislation would go forward. Some have argued that under the spirit of the Twentieth Amendment, no valid legislation can be passed in November and December while the country awaits the assembly of the new Congress. The text of the amendment, however, does not support such a result.

Section 3 of the amendment provides that if the newly elected president dies before Inauguration Day, the vice president–elect becomes president. In the event the presidential election is thrown to the House of Representatives and the House has been unable to choose a president, the vice president–elect (who would have been chosen by the Senate under the Twelfth Amendment) would act as president until the House fulfilled its task. In the event neither the House nor the Senate act, Congress may via statute declare who shall act as president or how an interim president will be selected. In other words, the presidential succession statute kicks in. Under the current statute, the Speaker of the House would become president, and next in line is the president pro tempore of the Senate.

Section 4 of the amendment addresses the possibility that selection of the president devolves to the House (and selection of the vice president to the Senate), but a candidate dies before a selection can be made. Congress is authorized by law to address such a contingency via statute.

Congress provided that the states had seven years to ratify the Twentieth Amendment. Timing was not an issue. It was sent to the states in 1932 and ratified in 1933.

AMENDMENT XXI (RATIFIED 1933)

SECTION 1. THE eighteenth article of amendment to the Constitution of the United States is hereby repealed.

SECTION 2. THE transportation or importation into any State, Territory, or possession of the United States for delivery or use therein of intoxicating liquors, in violation of the laws thereof, is hereby prohibited.

SECTION 3. THIS article shall be inoperative unless it shall have been ratified as an amendment to the Constitution by conventions in the several States, as provided in the Constitution, within seven years from the date of the submission hereof to the States by the Congress.

Purpose

The Twenty-First Amendment ended the "noble experiment" known as Prohibition. The question whether to be a wet or dry jurisdiction was returned to the states and local governments.

Background and Development

Prohibition caused per capita consumption of alcohol to drop, and it ridded America of the male-only saloons where vice reigned.

The speakeasies that popped up across the country welcomed both men and women. The generation raised during Prohibition never became big drinkers.

Prohibition brought its own set of problems, however. Organized crime made millions of dollars supplying Americans with imported alcoholic beverages or beverages produced in illegal distilleries and breweries. The quality of the booze produced varied, and many Americans died or suffered paralysis from poisons in the product.[386] Thousands of elected officials and law enforcement officers took bribes from gangsters and ignored illegal activity occurring in their jurisdictions. Corruption was rampant.

Prohibition caused a substantial loss of tax revenues for the federal and state governments. When the economy crashed in 1929, the loss of revenue from alcohol taxation was felt more acutely as governments sought to provide aid to indigent Americans. At the 1932 Democratic convention, Franklin Roosevelt promised to seek the repeal of rohibition and was met with thunderous applause. Had he not cast his lot with the repeal movement, Roosevelt might not have secured the nomination.

Congress witnessed the people's approval of Roosevelt's repeal rhetoric and sent the Twenty-First Amendment to the states before the new president assumed office. Interestingly, the amendment specified that state ratification conventions should consider it rather than state legislatures. Congress believed the amendment stood a greater chance of ratification in conventions than in state legislatures because rural majorities, which typically favored Prohibition, held sway in many legislatures and could possibly block ratification. Prohibition, however, had fallen from favor across the nation. The amendment was ratified more quickly than any other in history (until the Twenty-Sixth Amendment).

Section 1 repealed the Eighteenth Amendment. Section 2 declared that the transportation or importation of alcohol into a state, in violation of the state's laws, was prohibited. Section 2 of the amendment has raised a bevy of questions. For example, does it give the states such complete control over alcohol that it trumps the federal government's power to regulate interstate commerce? Early Supreme Court precedent held that it does. Later cases retreated from this position.

Distortions

In *Granholm v. Heald* (2005), for example, the Court considered state laws that forbade out-of-state wineries from selling their product directly to consumers—a privilege allowed to in-state wineries.[387] The Court held that such economic discrimination violated the Commerce Clause and was not permitted by the Twenty-First Amendment. "The aim of the Twenty-First Amendment was to allow the states to maintain an effective and uniform system for controlling liquor by regulating its transportation, importation, and use," the Court averred.[388] It "did not give States the authority to pass non-uniform laws in order to discriminate against out of state goods."[389] Four dissenting justices would have held that the plain language of the "Twenty-First Amendment sanctions the right of a State to legislate concerning intoxicating liquors brought from without, unfettered by the Commerce Clause."[390]

Discussion and Solutions

The plain language of the Twenty-First Amendment permits the states to regulate all transportation or importation of alcohol into or from their jurisdictions. The amendment places no restriction on laws that discriminate against out-of-state goods. Pursuant to the amendment, the Court should leave the states alone and allow them to regulate the transportation or importation of alcohol as they see fit. The *Granholm* decision should be reconsidered at the appropriate time.

AMENDMENT XXII (RATIFIED 1951)

SECTION 1. No person shall be elected to the office of the President more than twice, and no person who has held the office of President, or acted as President, for more than two years of a term to which some other person was elected President shall be elected to the office of the President more than once. But this article shall not apply to any person holding the office of President when this article was proposed by the Congress, and shall not prevent any person who may be holding the office of President, or acting as President, during the term within which this article becomes operative from holding the office of President or acting as President during the remainder of such term.

SECTION 2. THIS article shall be inoperative unless it shall have been ratified as an amendment to the Constitution by the legislatures of three-fourths of the several states within seven years from the date of its submission to the states by the Congress.

Purpose

President George Washington established the precedent that American presidents should serve no more than two terms. The Twenty-Second Amendment constitutionalized that tradition in light of Franklin D. Roosevelt's choice to discard the example set by Washington.

Background and Development

Until Franklin D. Roosevelt, no president in American history served more than two terms in office. At the time Roosevelt won his third and fourth terms, there was no constitutional prohibition against serving more than two terms, but American tradition counseled against it. As noted by commentators Paul G. Wills and George L. Wills, "George Washington's refusal of a third term, erected into a political principle by the example of Thomas Jefferson, established a two-term tradition."[391] Jefferson believed that "service for 8 years with a power to remove at the end of the first four" was optimal.[392] He feared "the indulgence & attachments of the people will keep a man in the chair after he becomes a dotard, that re-election through life shall become habitual, & election for life follow that."[393] Jefferson believed that Washington's example, coupled with his own voluntary retirement, "and a few more precedents will oppose the obstacle of habit to anyone after a while who shall endeavor to extend his term."[394] Such a pattern, Jefferson speculated, "may beget a disposition to establish it by an amendment of the constitution."[395]

In 1875, when President Ulysses S. Grant contemplated a third term, the House of Representatives by a vote of 234 to 18 passed a resolution declaring that "the precedent established by Washington and other Presidents of the United States in retiring from the Presidential office after their second term has become, by universal concurrence, a part of our republican system of government, and that any departure from this time-honored custom would be unwise, unpatriotic and fraught with peril to our free institutions."[396] Because of such opposition, Grant declined to run in the 1876 election.

Republicans gained control of the House and Senate in the 1946 midterm election for the first time since the Hoover administration. Republican candidates had promised to support term limits for the president, and a constitutional amendment was introduced in the House on January 3, 1947. In the debates, Republicans appealed to the precedent established by Washington and Jefferson, while Democrats argued that it was improper to limit the people's choice for chief executive. Initial language for the amendment focused on an individual elevated to office through elections. But because the Constitution contemplated, in certain cases, elevation to

the presidency outside the electoral process, Senator Robert Taft of Ohio proposed the language targeting a person holding office or acting as president "for more than two years of a term to which some other person was elected President."

Of course, one can envision unlikely exceptions to the two-term goal of the language. For example, if Barack Obama ran for the House, was elected by the people of his district, and was then chosen as Speaker of the House, under the presidential succession statute there is a possibility he could become president again if, for example, both the president and vice president were killed in a terrorist attack. While such scenarios make for many law review articles, they are unlikely in practice.

AMENDMENT XXIII (RATIFIED 1961)

SECTION 1: THE District constituting the seat of government of the United States shall appoint in such manner as the Congress may direct: A number of electors of President and Vice President equal to the whole number of Senators and Representatives in Congress to which the District would be entitled if it were a state, but in no event more than the least populous state; they shall be in addition to those appointed by the states, but they shall be considered, for the purposes of the election of President and Vice President, to be electors appointed by a state; and they shall meet in the District and perform such duties as provided by the twelfth article of amendment.

SECTION 2. THE Congress shall have power to enforce this article by appropriate legislation.

Purpose

The Framers of the Constitution could not have envisioned Washington, DC, becoming the American Babylon with a population of more than seven hundred thousand residents.

Because the nation's capital is not within a state, its significant population cannot participate in national elections. The Twenty-Third Amendment addressed this disenfranchisement and gave residents of Washington, DC, the ability to participate in presidential elections.

Background and Development

The original Constitution provided no method for residents of the District of Columbia to participate in national elections. The Framers did not want the seat of government within a state (which can constitutionally participate in national elections) because of the danger of undue influence on national councils and the prospect that Congress might overawe state officials. As the powers of the federal government have grown, so has the population of the federal city.

The House Report on the Twenty-Third Amendment recognized the large population of the District of Columbia and that citizens residing there "have all the obligations of citizenship, including payment of Federal taxes, of local taxes, and service in our Armed Forces."[397] With such obligations, the report's authors reasoned, the people ought to be given the vote in presidential elections. The report was careful to note, however, that the "amendment would change the Constitution only to the minimum extent necessary to give the District participation in national elections. It would not make the District of Columbia a State."[398]

The amendment provides that the District shall have presidential electors equal to the numbers of senators and representatives it would be entitled to if it possessed statehood status, but in no event more than the least populous state. Currently, the District has three electors—the same number as Wyoming.

Distortions

The District of Columbia does not have voting representatives in Congress. Extremist political activists allege that the lack of voting power in Congress "is one way our political system disenfranchises and underrepresents voters of color."[399] Such statements are reckless because the Founders had no idea how large the District would become and did not envision it as a largely black enclave. Thus the "political system" has not targeted the District in an effort to harm minorities.

Advocates of the District having congressional representation have urged that Congress use its enforcement powers under Section 2 of the amendment to provide the District with senators and representatives. This would be a gross abuse of the enforcement power since the substance of the amendment simply provides for presidential electors and does not contemplate formal statehood. Statehood would require another constitutional amendment.

Discussion and Solutions

The District should never become a state. Its residents have a vested interest in the growth and power of the general government. The more federal employees in Washington, DC, the more income and job opportunities (in government or the service sector) for the District's residents. Such dependence on government is counter to the independence necessary for a republic's citizens.

It would be healthier for our government to disperse federal agencies and their employees. A metropolis where expanding government power and government budgets is the main business has corrupting effects and fosters groupthink. With technology and the success of teleworking during the pandemic, there is no reason the federal bureaucracy should remain consolidated in Washington, DC. For federal employees to work among average Americans in flyover country would have a salutary effect. Reduction of the centralized federal workforce would reduce the number of "unrepresented" Americans.

The employees would have full voting rights in the states of their residence and perhaps imbibe some of the values of the heartland.

AMENDMENT XXIV (RATIFIED 1964)

SECTION 1. THE right of citizens of the United States to vote in any primary or other election for President or Vice President, for electors for President or Vice President, or for Senator or Representative in Congress, shall not be denied or abridged by the United States or any state by reason of failure to pay any poll tax or other tax.

SECTION 2. THE Congress shall have power to enforce this article by appropriate legislation.

Purpose

States may not deny citizens the right to participate in national elections because of a failure to pay a tax.

Background and Development

A poll tax is "a tax of a specific sum levied upon each person within the jurisdiction of the taxing power."[400] Under the amendment, the right to vote for national offices may not be abridged for failure to pay the tax. It might appear at first blush that the Twenty-Fourth Amendment was part of the civil rights movement of the 1960s. It was not. In fact, the National Association for the Advancement of Colored People (NAACP) opposed the amendment because its leaders advocated a broad understanding of the Fourteenth Amendment and believed that poll taxes and other voting restrictions could be eliminated through congressional legislation.

As noted by scholars Bruce Ackerman and Jennifer Nou, the Twenty-Fourth Amendment had its roots in the New Deal and was

"an issue of class, not race."[401] New Dealers wanted to enfranchise poor white voters in hopes of extending electoral successes for years to come. President Roosevelt railed against "Polltaxia" and urged his party faithful to remove impediments that prevented the poor from voting. The Democratic Party believed a constitutional amendment was necessary because of the Supreme Court's decision in *Breedlove v. Suttles* (1937), which upheld a Georgia poll tax against a Nineteenth Amendment challenge.[402] What ultimately became the Twenty-Fourth Amendment was introduced by Senator Spessard Holland of Florida. Holland was a supporter of racial segregation but hated the poll tax because it allowed unscrupulous political machines to purchase the votes of citizens who could not pay the tax from their own resources. By the time the amendment was ratified, only five states in the union still used poll taxes as an impediment to voting.

The Supreme Court first considered the Twenty-Fourth Amendment in *Harman v. Forssenius* (1965), when it reviewed a Virginia statute that required prospective voters for federal elections to either pay a poll tax or to file a certificate of residence.[403] The Court found that the statute "erects a real obstacle to voting in federal elections for those who assert their constitutional exemption from the poll tax."[404] This obstacle, in the Court's words, "constitutes an abridgement of his right to vote by reason of failure to pay the poll tax."[405] Consequently, "[f]or federal elections, the poll tax is abolished absolutely as a prerequisite to voting, and no equivalent or milder substitute may be imposed."[406]

Distortions

Progressives argue that laws requiring a voter to present identification run afoul of the Twenty-Fourth Amendment.[407] Some even claim that requiring a voter to purchase a stamp to mail a ballot violates the amendment.[408] Such claims are absurd. Courts should resist the temptation to strike down generally applicable and nondiscriminatory voting regulations. Persons entering a federal building or boarding a flight must present identification. Such rules are modest efforts to ensure safety. Similarly, voter identification requirements are modest efforts to defeat fraud. One might as well argue that the cost of a city bus ticket, a gallon of gas, or the taxi fare necessary to get to a polling place is a de facto poll tax coming within the purview of the Twenty-Fourth Amendment. If postage stamps and trips to a department of motor vehicles are the new monsters in the realm of voting rights, then there must be no real monsters remaining; social justice warriors should celebrate rather than tilting at windmills.

Discussion and Solutions

Courts must reject attempts by progressives to use the Twenty-Fourth Amendment beyond the context of a true poll tax. The amendment is not a catchall justification to challenge nondiscriminatory, generally applicable rules. The amendment should be limited to its historical purpose: Citizens cannot be denied the right to vote for failing to pay a tax.

AMENDMENT XXV (RATIFIED 1967)

SECTION 1. IN case of the removal of the President from office or of his death or resignation, the Vice President shall become President.

SECTION 2. WHENEVER there is a vacancy in the office of the Vice President, the President shall nominate a Vice President who shall take office upon confirmation by a majority vote of both Houses of Congress.

SECTION 3. WHENEVER the President transmits to the President pro tempore of the Senate and the Speaker of the House of Representatives his written declaration that he is unable to discharge the powers and duties of his office, and until he transmits to them a written declaration to the contrary, such powers and duties shall be discharged by the Vice President as Acting President.

SECTION 4. WHENEVER the Vice President and a majority of either the principal officers of the executive departments or of such other body as Congress may by law provide, transmit to the President pro tempore of the Senate and the Speaker of the House of Representatives their written declaration that the President is unable to discharge the powers and duties of his office, the Vice President shall immediately assume the powers and duties of the office as Acting President.

THEREAFTER, WHEN THE President transmits to the President pro tempore of the Senate and the Speaker of the House of Representatives his written declaration that no inability exists, he shall resume the powers and duties of his office unless the Vice President and a majority of either the principal officers of the executive department or of such other body as Congress may by law provide, transmit within four days to the President pro tempore of the Senate and the Speaker of the House of Representatives their written declaration that the President is unable to discharge the powers and duties of his office. Thereupon Congress shall decide the issue, assembling within forty-eight hours for that purpose if not in session. If the Congress, within twenty-one days after receipt of the latter written declaration, or, if Congress is not in session, within twenty-one days after Congress is required to assemble, determines by two-thirds vote of both Houses that the President is unable to discharge the powers and duties of his office, the Vice President shall continue to discharge the same as Acting President; otherwise, the President shall resume the powers and duties of his office.

Purpose

The Twenty-Fifth Amendment deals with issues surrounding succession to the presidency and clarifies that, for example, on the death of the president, the vice president assumes the office and not just the duties of the president. The amendment also provides that when the vice presidency is vacant, the president can nominate a vice president, who must be approved by a majority of both houses of Congress. Finally, the amendment sets forth a procedure under which the vice president can become acting president if a presidential disability exists.

Background and Development

Concerns about succession to the presidency at the height of the Cold War prompted the Twenty-Fifth Amendment. A key event was a heart attack suffered by President Dwight D. Eisenhower in 1955. To recover, Eisenhower required a full month of rest. While Eisenhower convalesced, "the executive branch was dysfunctional, and it was often unclear . . . [who] was in charge of the federal government."[409] After the assassination of President John F. Kennedy, Lyndon Johnson assumed the presidency, and he was known to have serious medical conditions. No constitutional mechanism existed for President Johnson to name a vice president. Congress realized that constitutional clarification was needed in case of presidential disability and to ensure the vice president was in office.

Section 1 of the Twenty-Fifth Amendment makes clear that if the president dies, resigns, or is removed from office, the vice president becomes president, not simply the acting president. As discussed earlier (under Article II, Section 1, Clause 6), after President William Henry Harrison died in office, many objected when John Tyler, Harrison's vice president, declared himself the new president rather than the acting president. Congress ultimately accepted Tyler's claim to the office

and thus established the precedent that the office, rather than just its functions, transfers to the vice president when the presidency is vacant. Section 1 of the amendment constitutionalizes the precedent.

Section 2 provides that if the vice president dies in office, resigns, or ascends to the presidency, the chief executive must nominate a new vice president who must be confirmed by a majority of both the House and Senate. Section 2 proved a useful tool when Spiro Agnew, President Richard M. Nixon's vice president, resigned after pleading no contest to tax evasion charges. Congress easily confirmed Nixon's choice of Gerald Ford as the new vice president. When Nixon resigned because of the Watergate scandal and Ford became president, he nominated Nelson Rockefeller to the vice presidency, and Congress confirmed Rockefeller.

Section 3 provides a method for the president to transfer authority to the vice president when the president is unable to discharge his duties. For example, the president might make such a declaration prior to undergoing a serious surgical procedure or if incapacitated for a time by sudden illness. The president transmits a declaration to the speaker and president pro tempore informing them of the disability. Similarly, when the disability is ended, the president transmits a declaration informing them of his ability and resumption of duties.

Section 4 deals with the situation when the president is unable or unwilling to transmit a declaration of inability. The vice president and a majority of the cabinet may transmit a declaration of inability to congressional leadership, which allows the vice president to act as president. The president, upon recovery, may resume power by transmitting a declaration to the congressional leadership. If the vice president and the cabinet disagree that the president has recovered, they must transmit within four days a declaration that the inability persists. At this point, Congress decides whether the president should remain in authority or the vice president should become the acting president.

Distortions

Just prior to the 2020 presidential election, congressional Democrats urged Vice President Mike Pence to invoke the Twenty-Fifth Amendment because of concerns about President Donald Trump's health in relation to his COVID diagnosis and his unpredictable behavior. In the aftermath of the 2020 presidential election and the January 6, 2021 riot, congressional Democrats again urged Pence to invoke the amendment. Democratic calls for Pence and the cabinet to declare a presidential disability were nothing more than political showmanship. Pence responded to Democratic demands by declaring, "I will not now yield to efforts in the House of Representatives to play political games at a time so serious in the life of our Nation."[410] Pence also urged the Democrats "to avoid actions that would further divide and inflame the passions of the moment. Work with us to lower the temperature and unite our country as we prepare to inaugurate President-elect Joe Biden as the next President of the United States."[411]

In early 2024, Republicans played a similar political game regarding the competency of President Joe Biden. A special prosecutor found that Biden had mishandled classified material but declined to bring charges because a jury likely would find him a "sympathetic, well-meaning, elderly man with a poor memory." Remembering Democratic games with the Twenty-Fifth Amendment, Republicans called upon Kamala Harris to declare a presidential disability. The vice president, of course, declined to follow their advice.

Discussion and Solutions

The Twenty-Fifth Amendment addressed serious issues related to presidential succession. It also set forth a process to declare a presidential disability. The amendment deals with solemn matters and should not be a tool of partisan politics, as it was in 2020, 2021, and 2024. The American people must reject politicians who would use the amendment for political advantage or to harm a rival. If our political leaders continue to cry wolf on issues of presidential disability, they will not be taken seriously when a real issue surrounding presidential competency arises.

> ## AMENDMENT XXVI (RATIFIED 1971)
>
> SECTION 1. THE right of citizens of the United States, who are 18 years of age or older, to vote, shall not be denied or abridged by the United States or any state on account of age.
>
> SECTION 2. THE Congress shall have the power to enforce this article by appropriate legislation.

Purpose

The Twenty-Sixth Amendment guarantees the right to vote for citizens who are eighteen years of age or older.

Background and Development

In 1970, Congress passed amendments to the Voting Rights Act enfranchising eighteen-year-olds in state and federal elections, abolishing literacy tests, and abolishing state durational residency requirements for presidential elections. In *Oregon v. Mitchell* (1970), a divided Supreme Court, in a plurality opinion, struck portions of the statute allowing eighteen-year-olds to vote in state elections.[412] Justice Hugo Black, in the plurality opinion, believed Congress had sweeping powers over federal elections via Article I, Section 4, Clause 1, but reasoned that "[n]o function is more essential to the separate and independent existence of the States and their governments than the power to determine within the limits of the Constitution the qualifications of their own voters for state, county, and municipal offices."[413] The Equal Protection Clause of the Fourteenth Amendment, which was the basis for the 1970 amendments, "was never intended to destroy the States' power to govern themselves, making the Nineteenth and

Twenty-fourth Amendments superfluous."[414]

Oregon v. Mitchell posed a problem for states desiring, say, a voting age of twenty-one years old for state elections. These states would have been required to maintain different voting systems and structures for state and federal elections. This would have been expensive and complicated to pursue. In less than three months after the Supreme Court decision, Congress resolved this matter by sending the Twenty-Sixth Amendment to the states. The requisite number of states ratified within 107 days—the shortest ratification time for any amendment to the Constitution.

Distortions

Certain public interest lawyers allege that a nationwide conspiracy exists to threaten youth voting rights. Civil rights attorney Yael Bromberg argues that "[t]oday's young people face invidious threats to their voting rights through targeted voter identification restrictions," cuts in funding to voter registration programs, and polling sites located away from college campuses.[415] Bromberg argues that courts should embrace the Twenty-Sixth Amendment by strictly scrutinizing generally applicable voting requirements that might have a disparate impact on younger voters.

Bromberg would put a significant burden on a state to prove that, say, interests in preventing voter fraud "are real and not imagined."[416]

Discussion and Solutions

Courts should rebuff attempts by civil rights attorneys to label young voters as victims. The Twenty-Sixth Amendment simply prohibits state laws denying the franchise to citizens who are eighteen years of age or older. Having to show identification at the polling place or to travel from a dormitory to town to vote are not matters within the purview of the amendment. Our youth do not face invidious threats to their voting rights. The real problem centers on lawyers attempting to manufacture constitutional violations to boost their practices or their egos.

AMENDMENT XXVII (RATIFIED 1992)

NO LAW VARYING the compensation for the services of the Senators and Representatives shall take effect until an election of Representatives shall have intervened.

Purpose

The Twenty-Seventh Amendment requires an election to intervene before a congressional pay increase goes into effect. Thus, one-third of the Senate and the full House must face the people before enjoying the benefits of a pay raise.

Background and Development

As previously discussed (under Article I, Section 6, Clause 1), the Framers rejected the British model, in which members of Parliament were not entitled to compensation. Unpaid legislators, most of the Framers believed, would be more susceptible to the temptations of corruption. The Philadelphia Convention witnessed a vigorous debate on whether the states or the federal government should pay the salaries of members of Congress. Ultimately, the Framers decided that members of Congress should be paid by the federal government and left the matter of the amount to future legislation. Thus, the Constitution allows Congress to set its own pay.

Anti-Federalists recognized that a conflict of interest existed with such an arrangement and criticized the Constitution for allowing Congress such a power. For example, in the Virginia ratifying convention, Patrick Henry complained that "[t]he pay of the members is, by the Constitution, fixed by themselves, without limitation or restraint. They may therefore indulge themselves to the fullest extent."[417] Henry hoped that congressmen would be "good men" and thus resist the temptation to abuse the fixing of pay, but he pointed out that the Constitution was no barrier if they were corrupt men.

The ratification conventions of Virginia, New York, and North Carolina requested an amendment providing that no alteration in compensation should go into effect until a subsequent election. The obvious purpose was that one-third of the senators and all the representatives who voted themselves a pay raise would have to face election before receiving the benefit of the increase.

In his resolution of June 8, 1789, Madison proposed amending the Constitution as follows: "But no law varying the compensation last ascertained shall operate before the next ensuing election of representatives."[418] While it might seem odd that the amendment would start with "but," we must remember that Madison envisioned all of his amendments being incorporated into the text of the Constitution rather than appended at the end. In advocating for the compensation amendment, Madison doubted that Congress's power to set its pay would be abused "in the ordinary course of government."[419] He did admit to "a seeming impropriety in leaving any set of men without control to put their hand into the public coffers, to take out money to put in their pockets."[420] With the proposed amendment, Madison argued that any pay raise would not "operate until there is a change in the legislature; in which case it cannot be for the particular benefit of those who are concerned in determining the value of the service."[421] With but a little editing, Madison's proposed compensation amendment was adopted by the House and Senate.

This amendment garnered the ratifications of Maryland, North Carolina, South Carolina, Delaware, Vermont, and Virginia. It thus fell short and was not ratified. The compensation amendment lay dormant until 1873, when Ohio ratified the amendment in response to a congressional pay increase made retroactive to the beginning of the congressional session. According to constitutional historian Richard B. Bernstein, "[t]he increase thus provided all members with a $5,000 windfall—$2,500 per year for each of the previous two years."[422] The public protest caused Congress to repeal the so-called Salary Grab Act of 1873, but no other state followed Ohio's lead to ratify the compensation amendment. (Wyoming was the next state to ratify, but that was in 1978.)

In 1982, Gregory D. Watson "discovered" the compensation amendment while trying to find a topic for a paper in government class at the University of Texas at Austin. He received a C on the paper but was inspired to start a letter-writing campaign in which he urged state legislatures to ratify the compensation amendment. Maine (1983) and Colorado (1984) were the first states to heed Watson's call. Momentum gathered, and by 1992, the archivist of the United States ruled that the Twenty-Seventh Amendment had been ratified. Although some members of Congress expressed skepticism on the propriety of the archivist's declaration of ratification, no one pushed the matter further.

SUMMATION

The Constitution has been amended twenty-seven times. The first twelve amendments and the Twenty-Seventh are the work of the founding generation. Those amendments restricted the power of the general government or corrected deficiencies discovered (or suspected) in the original document. Judicial interpretation of the Fourteenth Amendment has caused much of the Bill of Rights (the first ten amendments) to be applied to the states. Through incorporation, the Supreme Court micromanages state policy decisions that neither the drafters of the Constitution nor Fourteenth Amendment envisioned. The Court passes judgment on state Christmas decorations, public health measures, and criminal penalties. The Fourteenth Amendment serves as the Court's Declaratory Act, because it claims the power to bind the states in all cases whatsoever. The Supreme Court is thus a second coming of the omnipotent British Parliament. It tramples on the right of self-government, which was the North Star of the American Revolution.

Congress's hands are by no means clean. As the Anti-Federalists feared, Congress has controlled the amendment process. Consequently, rather than a balanced budget amendment or term limits, we have the income tax amendment and disenfranchisement of the state legislatures. The general government engages in wealth redistribution and regulation of myriad aspects of life. Ill-conceived progressive-era amendments—coupled with abuses of the original delegated powers—have propelled the general government toward the despotic.

Strict construction would permit the country to gain its bearings and help direct us back to a true federal system. By simply examining how the drafters of the Fourteenth Amendment explained it to Northern public and then interpreting it accordingly, much of the mischief wrought by the courts could be undone. Strict construction originalism is not just for the Fourteenth Amendment or the first ten amendments, however; it is for the entire Constitution. Thus, rather than offering inventive interpretations for the likes of the Sixteenth and Seventeenth Amendments, *The Independent Guide* has recognized their progressive purposes and urged repeal. Though strict construction originalism does not always receive the same courtesy from its opponents, the honest and consistent approach offered here is our best hope going forward.

Afterword

WHERE DO WE go from here? This study shows that the substance of modern American government has little to do with the Founders' Constitution. It is almost impossible to discern a constitution of few and defined national powers focusing on external objects such as foreign trade and international relations.[1] The several states resemble administrative subdivisions of the center rather than the sovereign entities Publius promised, with powers "extending to all the objects, which, in the ordinary course of affairs, concern the lives, liberties and properties of the people."[2]

As for the foundational principle of popular sovereignty, it too is but a specter. In 1822, John Taylor of Caroline warned how this pillar of the American experiment could be turned on its head. "By our political theory," Taylor wrote, "the people are supposed to be the patrons of the government, and not the government the patron of the people."[3] A reversal of this tenet, Taylor warned, marked an "advance toward tyranny," with the government dictating constitutional regulations to the people and distributing their money and property to favored "individuals or combinations."[4]

One is hard-pressed to argue that the three departments of the national government do not dictate constitutional principles to the people. Without seeking amendments to the Constitution, the national government has claimed myriad new powers. For example, Congress regulates the amount of wheat a farmer can grow for personal consumption, the president sends the armed forces into "hot zones" without even a nod to the national legislature, and the Supreme Court strikes mundane state laws governing various internal matters. As for patron status, research shows that more than half of Americans receive federal subsidies, federal entitlement program payments, or both.[5] No wonder we have a $37 trillion national debt as the federal government has happily assumed the care and maintenance of much of the population. Based on Taylor's reasoning, we are not just advancing toward tyranny but have arrived at the station.

This state of affairs, whether we call it tyranny, the living Constitution, or something else, has not wrought political peace. Commentators see deep divisions and question whether the United States can survive as a nation. *Time* magazine's Ian Bremmer has correctly stated that "[t]here is no advanced industrial democracy in the world more politically divided, or politically dysfunctional, than the United States today."[6] A recent Zogby poll affirms this perception and reveals that 46 percent of Americans expect another civil war.[7]

A way out of this predicament is found in the Constitution of 1787 and specifically in its federalist principles. Maintaining a proper federalist balance between the states and national government is at the heart of strict construction originalism. Federalism is a system of dividing power between the general and state governments in which each is independent in its own sphere, but powers are limited by fundamental law (federal and state constitutions) as established by the people. The Founders' Constitution aimed to allow diverse and differing interests to coexist in a union. But key to coexistence was a demand of unity *only* in certain limited cases. For example, congressional regulation of foreign commerce (such as imposing high duties on the goods from countries having no commercial treaty with the United States) would be undermined unless all members of the union adhered to the national policy. Such external matters, requiring the states to speak with one voice, are obvious and few. In matters not implicating uniformity in dealing with the outside world, however, the states must be left to serve as laboratories of democracy. If they are not allowed to do so, we will remain at one another's throats.

Abortion is a prime example. In *Dobbs v. Jackson Women's Health Organization* (2022), the Supreme Court declared the obvious: the Constitution contains no fundamental right to abortion, and thus this controversial matter should be dealt with in the several states. Much of America went into apoplexy over the *Dobbs* decision. Citizens' and politicians' furor was fueled not because they lived in states where legislatures would likely restrict abortions, but because they could not stomach that other states might enact fetal heartbeat laws.

To our detriment, we think in terms of one-size-fits-all answers to difficult policy questions. An unwillingness to allow our neighbors in other states to craft answers different from our own engenders violent passions.

All-or-nothing politics erases the strength of a federal system. In a federation, the California wokester need not worry about how the people of South Carolina decide the abortion issue. In turn, the South Carolina evangelical need not lose sleep because of liberal California abortion regulations. As a constitutional and federalism matter, California's handling of abortion is as alien to the South Carolinian as is Finland's abortion policy. This same reasoning applies to myriad culture war matters that stoke the furnace of American politics, such as transgenderism, teaching of critical race theory in schools, and drug legalization.

Federalism requires a strict constructionist interpretation of the Constitution in which clauses are not twisted beyond recognition to augment federal power. Federalization of criminal law is a prime example of loose construction run amok. Under the Constitution, Congress can criminalize just a handful of matters, such as counterfeiting, piracy, crimes on the high seas, offenses against the law of nations, and treason. Today, most federal crimes have little to do with these enumerated subjects.

For example, under 18 U.S.C. § 922(g), it is a federal crime for a person previously convicted of a state or federal felony to possess a firearm. Congress claims the power to enact this statute because the firearm, its components, or the ammunition at some point in their existence moved in interstate commerce. Remington, to pick just one firearms company, manufactures its product in LaGrange,

Georgia. If a New York man with a felony conviction is found in possession of a Remington 9mm pistol, the federal government claims the right to prosecute him because the pistol, at some point in its existence, had to travel across states lines to reach New York. That travel could have been in 1970 prior to the New York man's birth, or it could have been last week with the man himself bringing the pistol from Georgia to New York.

By permitting Congress to regulate interstate commerce, the Framers did not contemplate restrictions on firearms. Instead, they sought to create a great free trade zone within the United States by removing internal trade barriers. A nationwide free trade zone, almost all agreed, would permit the states to take advantage of division of labor and lessen tensions as goods freely crossed borders. If the Commerce Clause is as elastic as modern judges and members of Congress claim, it would have been silly for the Framers to have specified piracy and counterfeiting as objects of federal criminal law, because counterfeiting undoubtedly affects commerce by reducing the purchasing power of legitimate mediums of exchange, and piracy directly interferes with foreign commerce by stopping the transport of merchandise. Modern Commerce Clause use and jurisprudence is simply untenable as it brings almost any activity within federal orbit.

The discussion of 18 U.S.C. § 922(g) provides just one example of congressional excess. A strict constructionist approach must be applied outside of the criminal law context and extend to the administrative state, federal spending, and the civil rights establishment. To live together, we must jettison the idea that the United States is a consolidated nation no different from Great Britian or France.

Americans must embrace life in a federation and the corresponding limits on the general government.

Of course, even if Congress and the people could be persuaded to interpret the enumerated powers in a strict constructionist originalist sense, we are still left with a Supreme Court micromanaging state policy decisions. The vehicles for micromanagement are the doctrines of incorporation via the Due Process Clause and strict scrutiny via the Equal Protection Clause. The Court claims the provisions of the federal Bill of Rights must be applied to the states and also discovers certain fundamental rights hidden in the words "due process." As discussed in the section on the Fourteenth Amendment, incorporation is folly. Inasmuch as overturning the *Dred Scott* decision was a key goal of the Fourteenth Amendment, it is unlikely that the amendment's framers intended to empower the Court. Had they meant to apply the Bill of Rights to the states or transform the judiciary into a permanent constitutional convention, this could have been easily accomplished with clear language. Today, many of the Court's blockbuster decisions involve state police-power regulations—matters the Founders assured us were reserved to the states and beyond federal interference. The Court regulates things such as state marriage laws, criminal procedure, and imposition of the death penalty.

Until the second half of the previous century, the Supreme Court rarely invoked the Equal Protection Clause outside of racial discrimination cases. That was logical because the purpose of the clause was to ensure equal treatment of blacks and whites and thus eliminate unequal justice. Today, the Equal Protection Clause is applied broadly to all government actions, and the Court strictly scrutinizes any classification that impacts a right the Court declares fundamental or a class of people to whom the Court grants special status. Although a state might rationally draw distinctions, say, between short- and long-term residents in providing poor relief, the Court rejects a mere rational basis test and applies a level of review that is strict in theory but fatal in fact. The result is micromanagement of state policy decisions.

Whether Congress strips jurisdiction from the Court, the justices voluntarily embrace judicial restraint, or judicial policymakers are removed by impeachment, the Court must be tamed if we choose a federal government over a consolidated government. Judicial supremacy is incongruent with popular sovereignty. It is a step back from the American Revolution inasmuch as an artificial body—the Supreme Court—creates and annuls fundamental law.[8]

The president's executive power would be curtailed if Congress restricted itself to the enumerated powers. But even with a Congress confined by the Constitution, the president can do much mischief on his own under theories of executive power that analogize his "implied powers" to those of an eighteenth-century British monarch. The president must accept that, just like Congress, his powers are enumerated in the Constitution. He cannot act without pointing to a specific provision of the Constitution that empowers him to act. The president does not have the power to suspend congressional statutes or to legislate through executive orders. His job is limited to executing congressional directives. This restricted function extends to use of the military. Absent a congressional declaration

of war, the president should not place troops in harm's way or intervene in the affairs of other countries.

Peaceful coexistence is the primary benefit of a revived federalism, but there are others worthy of mention. First, policy experimentation would flourish. All states could learn as they examined the outcomes and unintended consequences of the ideas implemented in sister states. Successful policies would spread throughout the country, while failures could be avoided. Of course, there is no one right way to accomplish objectives. Because of differences in culture, industry, temperament, and so on, there will always be a diversity of preference. In other words, while federalism has utilitarian aspects, it also accounts for intrinsic differences that cannot be explicated by data collection. Second, in a federal system, it is much easier for the people to vote with their feet if state policies are too liberal or conservative for their tastes. Under a consolidated government, the only other option people have is to move to a foreign country far away from friends and family. Often the distance and the legal complications of such a move keep people captive in their home country. Third, subsidiarity is furthered. The principle of subsidiarity holds that nothing should be undertaken by a larger and more complicated government which can be done as well by a smaller and modest government. Such a principle promotes limited government, freedom, and accountability. It is far easier for the people to make their voices heard and remove corrupt or inept representatives on the local level than at the national level. Moreover, a simple structure often is much more efficient than a complex one. Assigning something such as local poor relief to the national government is akin to using a howitzer rather than a claw hammer to pound in a nail.

If we want to have a peaceful union and to enjoy the other benefits of federalism, we have a blueprint in the Constitution of 1787 and the canon of construction given by St. George Tucker. Of course, the Constitution is not perfect. The Anti-Federalists were correct when they predicted that many provisions invited broad interpretation and centralization of power. The nation's almost 250 years of experience demonstrate where the major flaws are and how to correct them. The work will not be easy; however, we have little choice unless we are content with perpetual strife and claims that every policy issue has only one right answer.

THE UNITED STATES CONSTITUTION

We the People of the United States, in Order to form a more perfect Union, establish Justice, insure domestic Tranquility, provide for the common defence, promote the general Welfare, and secure the Blessings of Liberty to ourselves and our Posterity, do ordain and establish this Constitution for the United States of America.

ARTICLE I

Section 1

All legislative Powers herein granted shall be vested in a Congress of the United States, which shall consist of a Senate and House of Representatives.

Section 2

The House of Representatives shall be composed of Members chosen every second Year by the People of the several States, and the Electors in each State shall have the Qualifications requisite for Electors of the most numerous Branch of the State Legislature.

No Person shall be a Representative who shall not have attained to the Age of twenty five Years, and been seven Years a Citizen of the United States, and who shall not, when elected, be an Inhabitant of that State in which he shall be chosen.

Representatives and direct Taxes shall be apportioned among the several States which may be included within this Union, according to their respective Numbers, which shall be determined by adding to the whole Number of free Persons, including those bound to Service for a Term of Years, and excluding Indians not taxed, three fifths of all other Persons. The actual Enumeration shall be made within three Years after the first Meeting of the Congress of the United States, and within every subsequent Term of ten Years, in such Manner as they shall by Law direct. The Number of Representatives shall not exceed one for every thirty Thousand, but each State shall have at Least one Representative; and until such enumeration shall be made, the State of New Hampshire shall be entitled to chuse three, Massachusetts eight, Rhode-Island and Providence Plantations one, Connecticut five, New-York six, New Jersey four, Pennsylvania eight, Delaware one, Maryland six, Virginia ten, North Carolina five, South Carolina five, and Georgia three.

When vacancies happen in the Representation from any State, the Executive Authority thereof shall issue Writs of Election to fill such Vacancies.

The House of Representatives shall chuse their Speaker and other Officers; and shall have the sole Power of Impeachment.

Section 3

The Senate of the United States shall be composed of two Senators from each State, chosen by the Legislature thereof, for six Years; and each Senator shall have one Vote.

Immediately after they shall be assembled in Consequence of the first Election, they shall be divided as equally as may be into three Classes. The Seats of the Senators of the first Class shall be vacated at the Expiration of the second Year, of the second Class at the Expiration of the fourth Year, and of the third Class at the Expiration of the sixth Year, so that one third may be chosen every second Year; and if Vacancies happen by Resignation, or otherwise, during the Recess of the Legislature of any State, the Executive thereof may make temporary Appointments until the next Meeting of the Legislature, which shall then fill such Vacancies.

No Person shall be a Senator who shall not have attained to the Age of thirty Years, and been nine Years a Citizen of the United States, and who shall not, when elected, be an Inhabitant of that State for which he shall be chosen.

The Vice President of the United States shall be President of the Senate, but shall have no Vote, unless they be equally divided.

The Senate shall chuse their other Officers, and also a President pro tempore, in the Absence of the Vice President, or when he shall exercise the Office of President of the United States.

The Senate shall have the sole Power to try all Impeachments. When sitting for that Purpose, they shall be on Oath or Affirmation. When the President of the United States is tried, the Chief Justice shall preside: And no Person shall be convicted without the Concurrence of two thirds of the Members present.

Judgment in Cases of Impeachment shall not extend further than to removal from Office, and disqualification to hold and enjoy any Office of honor, Trust or Profit under the United States: but the Party convicted shall nevertheless be liable and subject to Indictment, Trial, Judgment and Punishment, according to Law.

Section 4

The Times, Places and Manner of holding Elections for Senators and Representatives, shall be prescribed in each State by the Legislature thereof; but the Congress may at any time by Law make or alter such Regulations, except as to the Places of chusing Senators.

The Congress shall assemble at least once in every Year, and such Meeting shall be on the first Monday in December, unless they shall by Law appoint a different Day.

Section 5

Each House shall be the Judge of the Elections, Returns and Qualifications of its own Members, and a Majority of each shall constitute a Quorum to do Business; but a smaller Number may adjourn from day to day, and may be authorized to compel the Attendance of absent Members, in such Manner, and under such Penalties as each House may provide.

Each House may determine the Rules of its Proceedings, punish its Members for disorderly Behaviour, and, with the Concurrence of two thirds, expel a Member.

Each House shall keep a Journal of its Proceedings, and from time to time publish the same, excepting such Parts as may in their Judgment require Secrecy; and the Yeas and Nays of the Members of either House on any question shall, at the Desire of one fifth of those Present, be entered on the Journal.

Neither House, during the Session of Congress, shall, without the Consent of the other, adjourn for more than three days, nor to any other Place than that in which the two Houses shall be sitting.

Section 6

The Senators and Representatives shall receive a Compensation for their Services, to be ascertained by Law, and paid out of the Treasury of the United States. They shall in all Cases, except Treason, Felony and Breach of the Peace, be privileged from Arrest during their Attendance at the Session of their respective Houses, and in going to and returning from the same; and for any Speech or Debate in either House, they shall not be questioned in any other Place.

No Senator or Representative shall, during the Time for which he was elected, be appointed to any civil Office under the Authority of the United States, which shall have been created, or the Emoluments whereof shall have been encreased during such time; and no Person holding any Office under the United States, shall be a Member of either House during his Continuance in Office.

Section 7

All Bills for raising Revenue shall originate in the House of Representatives; but the Senate may propose or concur with Amendments as on other Bills.

Every Bill which shall have passed the House of Representatives and the Senate, shall, before it become a Law, be presented to the President of the United States; If he approve he shall sign it, but if not he shall return it, with his Objections to that House in which it shall have originated, who shall enter the Objections at large on their Journal, and proceed to reconsider it. If after such Reconsideration two thirds of that House shall agree to pass the Bill, it shall be sent, together with the Objections, to the other House, by which it shall likewise be reconsidered, and if approved by two thirds of that House, it shall become a Law. But in all such Cases the Votes of both Houses shall be determined by yeas and Nays, and the Names of the Persons voting for and against the Bill shall be entered on the Journal of each House respectively. If any Bill shall not be returned by the President within ten Days (Sundays excepted) after it shall have been presented to him, the Same shall be a Law, in like Manner as if he had signed it, unless the Congress by their Adjournment prevent its Return, in which Case it shall not be a Law.

Every Order, Resolution, or Vote to which the Concurrence of the Senate and House of Representatives may be necessary (except on a question of Adjournment) shall be presented to the President of the United States; and before the Same shall take Effect, shall be approved by him, or being disapproved by him, shall be repassed by two thirds of the Senate and House of Representatives, according to the Rules and Limitations prescribed in the Case of a Bill.

Section 8

The Congress shall have Power To lay and collect Taxes, Duties, Imposts and Excises, to pay the Debts and provide for the common Defence and general Welfare of the United States; but all Duties, Imposts and Excises shall be uniform throughout the United States;

To borrow Money on the credit of the United States;

To regulate Commerce with foreign Nations, and among the several States, and with the Indian Tribes;

To establish a uniform Rule of Naturalization, and uniform Laws on the subject of Bankruptcies throughout the United States;

To coin Money, regulate the Value thereof, and of foreign Coin, and fix the Standard of Weights and Measures;

To provide for the Punishment of counterfeiting the Securities and current Coin of the United States;

To establish Post Offices and post Roads;

To promote the Progress of Science and useful Arts, by securing for limited Times to Authors and Inventors the exclusive Right to their respective Writings and Discoveries;

To constitute Tribunals inferior to the supreme Court;

To define and punish Piracies and Felonies committed on the high Seas, and Offences against the Law of Nations;

To declare War, grant Letters of Marque and Reprisal, and make Rules concerning Captures on Land and Water;

To raise and support Armies, but no Appropriation of Money to that Use shall be for a longer Term than two Years;

To provide and maintain a Navy;

To make Rules for the Government and Regulation of the land and naval Forces;

To provide for calling forth the Militia to execute the Laws of the Union, suppress Insurrections and repel Invasions;

To provide for organizing, arming, and disciplining, the Militia, and for governing such Part of them as may be employed in the Service of the United States, reserving to the States respectively, the Appointment of the Officers, and the Authority of training the Militia according to the discipline prescribed by Congress;

To exercise exclusive Legislation in all Cases whatsoever, over such District (not exceeding ten Miles square) as may, by Cession of particular States, and the Acceptance of Congress, become the Seat of the Government of the United States, and to exercise like Authority over all Places purchased by the Consent of the Legislature of the State in which the Same shall be, for the Erection of Forts, Magazines, Arsenals, dock-Yards, and other needful Buildings;-And

To make all Laws which shall be necessary and proper for carrying into Execution the foregoing Powers, and all other Powers vested by this Constitution in the Government of the United States, or in any Department or Officer thereof.

Section 9

The Migration or Importation of such Persons as any of the States now existing shall think proper to admit, shall not be prohibited by the Congress prior to the Year one thousand eight hundred and eight, but a Tax or duty may be imposed on such Importation, not exceeding ten dollars for each Person.

The Privilege of the Writ of Habeas Corpus shall not be suspended, unless when in Cases of Rebellion or Invasion the public Safety may require it.

No Bill of Attainder or ex post facto Law shall be passed.

No Capitation, or other direct, Tax shall be laid, unless in Proportion to the Census or enumeration herein before directed to be taken.

No Tax or Duty shall be laid on Articles exported from any State.

No Preference shall be given by any Regulation of Commerce or Revenue to the Ports of one State over those of another: nor shall Vessels bound to, or from, one State, be obliged to enter, clear, or pay Duties in another.

No Money shall be drawn from the Treasury, but in Consequence of Appropriations made by Law; and a regular Statement and Account of the Receipts and Expenditures of all public Money shall be published from time to time.

No Title of Nobility shall be granted by the United States: And no Person holding any Office of Profit or Trust under them, shall, without the Consent of the Congress, accept of any present, Emolument, Office, or Title, of any kind whatever, from any King, Prince, or foreign State.

Section 10

No State shall enter into any Treaty, Alliance, or Confederation; grant Letters of Marque and Reprisal; coin Money; emit Bills of Credit; make any Thing but gold and silver Coin a Tender in Payment of Debts; pass any Bill of Attainder, ex post facto Law, or Law impairing the Obligation of Contracts, or grant any Title of Nobility.

No State shall, without the Consent of the Congress, lay any Imposts or Duties on Imports or Exports, except what may be absolutely necessary for executing it's inspection Laws: and the net Produce of all Duties and Imposts, laid by any State on Imports or Exports, shall be for the Use of the Treasury of the United States; and all such Laws shall be subject to the Revision and Controul of the Congress.

No State shall, without the Consent of Congress, lay any Duty of Tonnage, keep Troops, or Ships of War in time of Peace, enter into any Agreement or Compact with another State, or with a foreign Power, or engage in War, unless actually invaded, or in such imminent Danger as will not admit of delay.

ARTICLE II

Section 1

The executive Power shall be vested in a President of the United States of America.

He shall hold his Office during the Term of four Years, and, together with the Vice President, chosen for the same Term, be elected, as follows:

Each State shall appoint, in such Manner as the Legislature thereof may direct, a Number of Electors, equal to the whole Number of Senators and Representatives to which the State may be entitled in the Congress: but no Senator or Representative, or Person holding an Office of Trust or Profit under the United States, shall be appointed an Elector.

The Electors shall meet in their respective States, and vote by Ballot for two Persons, of whom one at least shall not be an Inhabitant of the same State with themselves. And they shall make a List of all the Persons voted for, and of the Number of Votes for each; which List they shall sign and certify, and transmit sealed to the Seat of the Government of the United States, directed to the President of the Senate. The President of the Senate shall, in the Presence of the Senate and House of Representatives, open all the Certificates, and the Votes shall then be counted. The Person having the greatest Number of Votes shall be the President, if such Number be a Majority of the whole Number of Electors appointed; and if there be more than one who have such Majority, and have an equal Number of Votes, then the House of Representatives shall immediately chuse by Ballot one of them for President; and if no Person have a Majority, then from the five highest on the List the said House shall in like Manner chuse the

President. But in chusing the President, the Votes shall be taken by States, the Representation from each State having one Vote; A quorum for this Purpose shall consist of a Member or Members from two thirds of the States, and a Majority of all the States shall be necessary to a Choice. In every Case, after the Choice of the President, the Person having the greatest Number of Votes of the Electors shall be the Vice President. But if there should remain two or more who have equal Votes, the Senate shall chuse from them by Ballot the Vice President.

The Congress may determine the Time of chusing the Electors, and the Day on which they shall give their Votes; which Day shall be the same throughout the United States.

No Person except a natural born Citizen, or a Citizen of the United States, at the time of the Adoption of this Constitution, shall be eligible to the Office of President; neither shall any Person be eligible to that Office who shall not have attained to the Age of thirty five Years, and been fourteen Years a Resident within the United States.

In Case of the Removal of the President from Office, or of his Death, Resignation, or Inability to discharge the Powers and Duties of the said Office, the Same shall devolve on the Vice President, and the Congress may by Law provide for the Case of Removal, Death, Resignation or Inability, both of the President and Vice President, declaring what Officer shall then act as President, and such Officer shall act accordingly, until the Disability be removed, or a President shall be elected.

The President shall, at stated Times, receive for his Services, a Compensation, which shall neither be encreased nor diminished during the Period for which he shall have been elected, and he shall not receive within that Period any other Emolument from the United States, or any of them.

Before he enter on the Execution of his Office, he shall take the following Oath or Affirmation:--"I do solemnly swear (or affirm) that I will faithfully execute the Office of President of the United States, and will to the best of my Ability, preserve, protect and defend the Constitution of the United States."

Section 2

The President shall be Commander in Chief of the Army and Navy of the United States, and of the Militia of the several States, when called into the actual Service of the United States; he may require the Opinion, in writing, of the principal Officer in each of the executive Departments, upon any Subject relating to the Duties of their respective Offices, and he shall have Power to grant Reprieves and Pardons for Offences against the United States, except in Cases of Impeachment.

He shall have Power, by and with the Advice and Consent of the Senate, to make Treaties, provided two thirds of the Senators present concur; and he shall nominate, and by and with the Advice and Consent of the Senate, shall appoint Ambassadors, other public Ministers and Consuls, Judges of the supreme Court, and all other Officers of the United States, whose Appointments are not herein otherwise provided for, and which shall be established by Law: but the Congress may by Law vest the Appointment of such inferior Officers, as they think proper, in the President alone, in the Courts of Law, or in the Heads of Departments.

The President shall have Power to fill up all Vacancies that may happen during the

Recess of the Senate, by granting Commissions which shall expire at the End of their next Session.

Section 3

He shall from time to time give to the Congress Information of the State of the Union, and recommend to their Consideration such Measures as he shall judge necessary and expedient; he may, on extraordinary Occasions, convene both Houses, or either of them, and in Case of Disagreement between them, with Respect to the Time of Adjournment, he may adjourn them to such Time as he shall think proper; he shall receive Ambassadors and other public Ministers; he shall take Care that the Laws be faithfully executed, and shall Commission all the Officers of the United States.

Section 4

The President, Vice President and all civil Officers of the United States, shall be removed from Office on Impeachment for, and Conviction of, Treason, Bribery, or other high Crimes and Misdemeanors.

ARTICLE III

Section 1

The judicial Power of the United States, shall be vested in one supreme Court, and in such inferior Courts as the Congress may from time to time ordain and establish. The Judges, both of the supreme and inferior Courts, shall hold their Offices during good Behaviour, and shall, at stated Times, receive for their Services, a Compensation, which shall not be diminished during their Continuance in Office.

Section 2

The judicial Power shall extend to all Cases, in Law and Equity, arising under this Constitution, the Laws of the United States, and Treaties made, or which shall be made, under their Authority;--to all Cases affecting Ambassadors, other public Ministers and Consuls;--to all Cases of admiralty and maritime Jurisdiction;--to Controversies to which the United States shall be a Party;--to Controversies between two or more States;--between a State and Citizens of another State, --between Citizens of different States,--between Citizens of the same State claiming Lands under Grants of different States, and between a State, or the Citizens thereof, and foreign States, Citizens or Subjects.

In all Cases affecting Ambassadors, other public Ministers and Consuls, and those in which a State shall be Party, the supreme Court shall have original Jurisdiction. In all the other Cases before mentioned, the supreme Court shall have appellate Jurisdiction, both as to Law and Fact, with such Exceptions, and under such Regulations as the Congress shall make.

The Trial of all Crimes, except in Cases of Impeachment; shall be by Jury; and such Trial shall be held in the State where the said Crimes shall have been committed; but when not committed within any State, the Trial shall be at such Place or Places as the Congress may by Law have directed.

Section 3

Treason against the United States, shall consist only in levying War against them, or in adhering to their Enemies, giving them Aid and Comfort. No Person shall be convicted of Treason unless on the Testimony of two Witnesses to the same overt Act, or on Confession in open Court.

The Congress shall have Power to declare the Punishment of Treason, but no Attainder of Treason shall work Corruption of Blood, or Forfeiture except during the Life of the Person attainted.

ARTICLE IV

Section 1

Full Faith and Credit shall be given in each State to the public Acts, Records, and judicial Proceedings of every other State. And the Congress may by general Laws prescribe the Manner in which such Acts, Records and Proceedings shall be proved, and the Effect thereof.

Section 2

The Citizens of each State shall be entitled to all Privileges and Immunities of Citizens in the several States.

A Person charged in any State with Treason, Felony, or other Crime, who shall flee from Justice, and be found in another State, shall on Demand of the executive Authority of the State from which he fled, be delivered up, to be removed to the State having Jurisdiction of the Crime.

No Person held to Service or Labour in one State, under the Laws thereof, escaping into another, shall, in Consequence of any Law or Regulation therein, be discharged from such Service or Labour, but shall be delivered up on Claim of the Party to whom such Service or Labour may be due.

Section 3

New States may be admitted by the Congress into this Union; but no new State shall be formed or erected within the Jurisdiction of any other State; nor any State be formed by the Junction of two or more States, or Parts of States, without the Consent of the Legislatures of the States concerned as well as of the Congress.

The Congress shall have Power to dispose of and make all needful Rules and Regulations respecting the Territory or other Property belonging to the United States; and nothing in this Constitution shall be so construed as to Prejudice any Claims of the United States, or of any particular State.

Section 4

The United States shall guarantee to every State in this Union a Republican Form of Government, and shall protect each of them against Invasion; and on Application of the Legislature, or of the Executive (when the Legislature cannot be convened) against domestic Violence.

ARTICLE V

The Congress, whenever two thirds of both Houses shall deem it necessary, shall propose Amendments to this Constitution, or, on the Application of the Legislatures of two thirds of the several States, shall call a Convention for proposing Amendments, which, in either Case, shall be valid to all Intents and Purposes, as Part of this Constitution, when ratified by the Legislatures of three fourths of the several States, or by Conventions in three fourths thereof, as the one or the other Mode of Ratification may be proposed by the Congress; Provided that no

Amendment which may be made prior to the Year One thousand eight hundred and eight shall in any Manner affect the first and fourth Clauses in the Ninth Section of the first Article; and that no State, without its Consent, shall be deprived of its equal Suffrage in the Senate.

ARTICLE VI

All Debts contracted and Engagements entered into, before the Adoption of this Constitution, shall be as valid against the United States under this Constitution, as under the Confederation.

This Constitution, and the Laws of the United States which shall be made in Pursuance thereof; and all Treaties made, or which shall be made, under the Authority of the United States, shall be the supreme Law of the Land; and the Judges in every State shall be bound thereby, any Thing in the Constitution or Laws of any State to the Contrary notwithstanding.

The Senators and Representatives before mentioned, and the Members of the several State Legislatures, and all executive and judicial Officers, both of the United States and of the several States, shall be bound by Oath or Affirmation, to support this Constitution; but no religious Test shall ever be required as a Qualification to any Office or public Trust under the United States.

ARTICLE VII

The Ratification of the Conventions of nine States, shall be sufficient for the Establishment of this Constitution between the States so ratifying the Same.

AMENDMENTS TO THE
CONSTITUTION OF THE UNITED STATES OF AMERICA

AMENDMENT I
RATIFIED DECEMBER 15, 1791

Congress shall make no law respecting an establishment of religion, or prohibiting the free exercise thereof; or abridging the freedom of speech, or of the press; or the right of the people peaceably to assemble, and to petition the Government for a redress of grievances.

AMENDMENT II
RATIFIED DECEMBER 15, 1791

A well regulated Militia, being necessary to the security of a free State, the right of the people to keep and bear Arms, shall not be infringed.

AMENDMENT III
RATIFIED DECEMBER 15, 1791

No Soldier shall, in time of peace be quartered in any house, without the consent of the Owner, nor in time of war, but in a manner to be prescribed by law.

AMENDMENT IV
RATIFIED DECEMBER 15, 1791

The right of the people to be secure in their persons, houses, papers, and effects, against unreasonable searches and seizures, shall not be violated, and no Warrants shall issue, but upon probable cause, supported by Oath or affirmation, and particularly describing the place to be searched, and the persons or things to be seized.

AMENDMENT V
RATIFIED DECEMBER 15, 1791

No person shall be held to answer for a capital, or otherwise infamous crime, unless on a presentment or indictment of a Grand Jury, except in cases arising in the land or naval forces, or in the Militia, when in actual service in time of War or public danger; nor shall any person be subject for the same offence to be twice put in jeopardy of life or limb, nor shall be compelled in any criminal case to be a witness against himself, nor be deprived of life, liberty, or property, without due process of law; nor shall private property be taken for public use, without just compensation.

AMENDMENT VI
RATIFIED DECEMBER 15, 1791

In all criminal prosecutions, the accused shall enjoy the right to a speedy and public trial, by an impartial jury of the State and district wherein the crime shall have been committed, which district shall have been previously ascertained by law, and to be informed of the nature and cause of the accusation; to be confronted with the witnesses against him; to have compulsory process for obtaining witnesses in his favor, and to have the assistance of counsel for his defence.

AMENDMENT VII
RATIFIED DECEMBER 15, 1791

In Suits at common law, where the value in controversy shall exceed twenty dollars, the right of trial by jury shall be preserved, and no

fact tried by a jury, shall be otherwise reexamined in any Court of the United States, than according to the rules of the common law.

AMENDMENT VIII
RATIFIED DECEMBER 15, 1791

Excessive bail shall not be required, nor excessive fines imposed, nor cruel and unusual punishments inflicted.

AMENDMENT IX
RATIFIED DECEMBER 15, 1791

The enumeration in the Constitution, of certain rights, shall not be construed to deny or disparage others retained by the people.

AMENDMENT X
RATIFIED DECEMBER 15, 1791

The powers not delegated to the United States by the Constitution, nor prohibited by it to the States, are reserved to the States respectively, or to the people.

AMENDMENT XI
RATIFIED FEBRUARY 7, 1795

The Judicial power of the United States shall not be construed to extend to any suit in law or equity, commenced or prosecuted against one of the United States by Citizens of another State, or by Citizens or Subjects of any Foreign State.

AMENDMENT XII
RATIFIED JUNE 15, 1804

The Electors shall meet in their respective states, and vote by ballot for President and Vice President, one of whom, at least, shall not be an inhabitant of the same state with themselves; they shall name in their ballots the person voted for as President, and in distinct ballots the person voted for as Vice-President, and they shall make distinct lists of all persons voted for as President, and of all persons voted for as Vice-President, and of the number of votes for each, which lists they shall sign and certify, and transmit sealed to the seat of the government of the United States, directed to the President of the Senate; --The President of the Senate shall, in the presence of the Senate and House of Representatives, open all the certificates and the votes shall then be counted;--The person having the greatest number of votes for President, shall be the President, if such number be a majority of the whole number of Electors appointed; and if no person have such majority, then from the persons having the highest numbers not exceeding three on the list of those voted for as President, the House of Representatives shall choose immediately, by ballot, the President. But in choosing the President, the votes shall be taken by states, the representation from each state having one vote; a quorum for this purpose shall consist of a member or members from two-thirds of the states, and a majority of all the states shall be necessary to a choice. And if the House of Representatives shall not choose a President whenever the right of choice shall devolve upon them, before the fourth day of March next following, then the Vice-President shall act as President, as in the case of the death or other constitutional disability of the President. The person having the greatest number of votes as Vice-President, shall be the Vice-President, if such number be a majority of the whole number of Electors appointed, and if no person have a majority, then from the two highest numbers on the list, the Senate shall choose the Vice-President; a quorum for the purpose shall consist of two-thirds of the whole number of Senators, and a majority of the whole number shall be necessary to a choice. But no person constitutionally ineligible to the office of President shall be eligible to that of Vice-President of the United States.

AMENDMENT XIII
RATIFIED DECEMBER 6, 1865

Section 1. Neither slavery nor involuntary servitude, except as a punishment for crime whereof the party shall have been duly convicted, shall exist within the United States, or any place subject to their jurisdiction.

Section 2. Congress shall have the power to enforce this article by appropriate legislation.

AMENDMENT XIV
RATIFIED JULY 9, 1868

Section 1. All persons born or naturalized in the United States, and subject to the jurisdiction thereof, are citizens of the United States and of the State wherein they reside. No State shall make or enforce any law which shall abridge the privileges or immunities of citizens of the United States; nor shall any State deprive any person of life, liberty, or property, without due process of law; nor deny to any person within its jurisdiction the equal protection of the laws.

Section 2. Representatives shall be apportioned among the several States according to their respective numbers, counting the whole number of persons in each State, excluding Indians not taxed. But when the right to vote at any election for the choice of electors for President and Vice President of the United States, Representatives in Congress, the Executive and

Judicial officers of a State, or the members of the Legislature thereof, is denied to any of the male inhabitants of such State, being twenty-one years of age, and citizens of the United States, or in any way abridged, except for participation in rebellion, or other crime, the basis of representation therein shall be reduced in the proportion which the number of such male citizens shall bear to the whole number of male citizens twenty-one years of age in such State.

Section 3. No person shall be a Senator or Representative in Congress, or elector of President and Vice President, or hold any office, civil or military, under the United States, or under any State, who, having previously taken an oath, as a member of Congress, or as an officer of the United States, or as a member of any State legislature, or as an executive or judicial officer of any State, to support the Constitution of the United States, shall have engaged in insurrection or rebellion against the same, or given aid or comfort to the enemies thereof. But Congress may by a vote of two-thirds of each House, remove such disability.

Section 4. The validity of the public debt of the United States, authorized by law, including debts incurred for payment of pensions and bounties for services in suppressing insurrection or rebellion, shall not be questioned. But neither the United States nor any State shall assume or pay any debt or obligation incurred in aid of insurrection or rebellion against the United States, or any claim for the loss or emancipation of any slave; but all such debts, obligations and claims shall be held illegal and void.

Section 5. The Congress shall have power to enforce, by appropriate legislation, the provisions of this article.

AMENDMENT XV
RATIFIED FEBRUARY 3, 1870

Section 1. The right of citizens of the United States to vote shall not be denied or abridged by the United States or by any State on account of race, color, or previous condition of servitude.

Section 2. The Congress shall have power to enforce this article by appropriate legislation.

AMENDMENT XVI
RATIFIED FEBRUARY 3, 1913

The Congress shall have power to lay and collect taxes on incomes, from whatever source derived, without apportionment among the several States, and without regard to any census or enumeration.

AMENDMENT XVII
RATIFIED APRIL 8, 1913

The Senate of the United States shall be composed of two Senators from each State, elected by the people thereof, for six years; and each Senator shall have one vote. The electors in each State shall have the qualifications requisite for electors of the most numerous branch of the State legislatures.

When vacancies happen in the representation of any State in the Senate, the executive authority of such State shall issue writs of election to fill such vacancies: Provided, That the legislature of any State may empower the executive thereof to make temporary appointments until the people fill the vacancies by election as the legislature may direct.

This amendment shall not be so construed as to affect the election or term of any Senator chosen before it becomes valid as part of the Constitution.

AMENDMENT XVIII
RATIFIED JANUARY 16, 1919

Section 1. After one year from the ratification of this article the manufacture, sale, or transportation of intoxicating liquors within, the importation thereof into, or the exportation thereof from the United States and all territory subject to the jurisdiction thereof for beverage purposes is hereby prohibited.

Section 2. The Congress and the several States shall have concurrent power to enforce this article by appropriate legislation.

Section 3. This article shall be inoperative unless it shall have been ratified as an amendment to the Constitution by the legislatures of the several States, as provided in the Constitution, within seven years from the date of the submission hereof to the States by the Congress.

AMENDMENT XIX
RATIFIED AUGUST 18, 1920

The right of citizens of the United States to vote shall not be denied or abridged by the United States or by any State on account of sex.

Congress shall have power to enforce this article by appropriate legislation.

AMENDMENT XX
RATIFIED JANUARY 23, 1933

Section 1. The terms of the President and Vice President shall end at noon on the 20th day of January, and the terms of Senators and Representatives at noon on the 3d day of January, of the years in which such terms would have ended if this article had not been ratified; and the terms of their successors shall then begin.

Section 2. The Congress shall assemble at least once in every year, and such meeting shall begin at noon on the 3d day of January, unless they shall by law appoint a different day.

Section 3. If, at the time fixed for the beginning of the term of the President, the President elect shall have died, the Vice President elect shall become President. If a President shall not have been chosen before the time fixed for the beginning of his term, or if the President elect shall have failed to qualify, then the Vice President elect shall act as President until a President shall have qualified; and the Congress may by law provide for the case wherein neither a President elect nor a Vice President elect shall have qualified, declaring who shall then act as President, or the manner in which one who is to act shall be selected, and such person shall act accordingly until a President or Vice President shall have qualified.

Section 4. The Congress may by law provide for the case of the death of any of the persons from whom the House of Representatives may choose a President whenever the right of choice shall have devolved upon them, and for the case of the death of any of the persons from whom the Senate may choose a Vice President whenever the right of choice shall have devolved upon them.

Section 5. Sections 1 and 2 shall take effect on the 15th day of October following the ratification of this article.

Section 6. This article shall be inoperative unless it shall have been ratified as an amendment to the Constitution by the legislatures of three-fourths of the several States within seven years from the date of its submission.

Amendment XXI
Ratified December 5, 1933

Section 1. The eighteenth article of amendment to the Constitution of the United States is hereby repealed.

Section 2. The transportation or importation into any State, Territory, or possession of the United States for delivery or use therein of intoxicating liquors, in violation of the laws thereof, is hereby prohibited.

Section 3. This article shall be inoperative unless it shall have been ratified as an amendment to the Constitution by conventions in the several States, as provided in the Constitution, within seven years from the date of the submission hereof to the States by the Congress.

Amendment XXII
Ratified February 27, 1951

Section 1. No person shall be elected to the office of the President more than twice, and no person who has held the office of President, or acted as President, for more than two years of a term to which some other person was elected President shall be elected to the office of the President more than once. But this Article shall not apply to any person holding the office of President when this Article was proposed by the Congress, and shall not prevent any person who may be holding the office of President, or acting as President, during the term within which this Article becomes operative from holding the office of President or acting as President during the remainder of such term.

Section 2. This article shall be inoperative unless it shall have been ratified as an amendment to the Constitution by the legislatures of three-fourths of the several States within seven years from the date of its submission to the States by the Congress.

Amendment XXIII
Ratified March 29, 1961

Section 1. The District constituting the seat of Government of the United States shall appoint in such manner as the Congress may direct:

A number of electors of President and Vice President equal to the whole number of Senators and Representatives in Congress to which the District would be entitled if it were a State, but in no event more than the least populous State; they shall be in addition to those appointed by the States, but they shall be considered, for the purposes of the election of President and Vice President, to be electors appointed by a State; and they shall meet in the District and perform such duties as provided by the twelfth article of amendment.

Section 2. The Congress shall have power to enforce this article by appropriate legislation.

Amendment XXIV
Ratified January 23, 1964

Section 1. The right of citizens of the United States to vote in any primary or other election for President or Vice President, for electors for President or Vice President, or for Senator or Representative in Congress, shall not be denied or abridged by the United States or any State by reason of failure to pay any poll tax or other tax.

Section 2. The Congress shall have the power to enforce this article by appropriate legislation.

AMENDMENT XXV
RATIFIED FEBRUARY 10, 1967

Section 1. In case of the removal of the President from office or of his death or resignation, the Vice President shall become President.

Section 2. Whenever there is a vacancy in the office of the Vice President, the President shall nominate a Vice President who shall take office upon confirmation by a majority vote of both Houses of Congress.

Section 3. Whenever the President transmits to the President pro tempore of the Senate and the Speaker of the House of Representatives his written declaration that he is unable to discharge the powers and duties of his office, and until he transmits to them a written declaration to the contrary, such powers and duties shall be discharged by the Vice President as Acting President.

Section 4. Whenever the Vice President and a majority of either the principal officers of the executive departments or of such other body as Congress may by law provide, transmit to the President pro tempore of the Senate and the Speaker of the House of Representatives their written declaration that the President is unable to discharge the powers and duties of his office, the Vice President shall immediately assume the powers and duties of the office as Acting President.

Thereafter, when the President transmits to the President pro tempore of the Senate and the Speaker of the House of Representatives his written declaration that no inability exists, he shall resume the powers and duties of his office unless the Vice President and a majority of either the principal officers of the executive department or of such other body as Congress may by law provide, transmit within four days to the President pro tempore of the Senate and the Speaker of the House of Representatives their written declaration that the President is unable to discharge the powers and duties of his office. Thereupon Congress shall decide the issue, assembling within forty-eight hours for that purpose if not in session. If the Congress, within twenty-one days after receipt of the latter written declaration, or, if Congress is not in session, within twenty-one days after Congress is required to assemble, determines by two-thirds vote of both Houses that the President is unable to discharge the powers and duties of his office, the Vice President shall continue to discharge the same as Acting President; otherwise, the President shall resume the powers and duties of his office.

AMENDMENT XXVI
RATIFIED JULY 1, 1971

Section 1. The right of citizens of the United States, who are eighteen years of age or older, to vote shall not be denied or abridged by the United States or by any State on account of age.

Section 2. The Congress shall have power to enforce this article by appropriate legislation.

AMENDMENT XXVII
RATIFIED MAY 7, 1992

No law varying the compensation for the services of the Senators and Representatives shall take effect, until an election of Representatives shall have intervened.

Resolutions on State and Federal Power

From the American Revolution to the crisis of the Alien and Sedition Acts, state legislatures have used resolutions to set forth first principles and outline a course of action against oppressive or unconstitutional governmental measures. In this spirit, we offer the following as model resolutions to be adopted in the several state legislatures. These resolutions declare the spirit in which the Constitution was adopted, its limited purposes, and the role of the states in the federal system.

1. Resolved, that the Constitution of 1787 was recommended to the people as creating a federal government of few and defined powers. Consequently, the Founders expected the authority of the states to extend to numerous and indefinite matters as governed by their own constitutions.

2. Resolved, that the general government's few and defined powers were to extend primarily to external objects such as war, peace, diplomacy, and foreign commerce, whereas the states' numerous and indefinite powers were to encompass subjects pertaining to the health, welfare, and morals of the people.

3. Resolved, that the division of governmental powers in the federal system was one of the grandest experiments ever attempted in political science and distinguished the art of government in the United States from the unitary states of Europe.

4. Resolved, that because of fears of encroaching federal authority, various state ratification conventions demanded additional security in the form of the Ninth and Tenth Amendments, the latter of which asserts that "[t]he powers not delegated to the United States by the Constitution, nor prohibited by it to the states, are reserved to the states respectively, or to the people."

5. Resolved, that power is of an encroaching nature and that the general government, over a course of years, has substantially passed the limits assigned to it by the Constitution so that it resembles a European unitary state rather than the grand experiment designed by the Founders.

6. Resolved, that the United States today is a diverse country with a population exceeding 330 million; therefore, the people of the several states hold many different views on public policy questions such as abortion, the definition of marriage, and the role of religion in a free society.

7. Resolved, that by nationalizing these public policy questions rather than permitting the states to serve as laboratories of democracy, the general government has sown seeds of division and distrust among the people.

8. Resolved, that our only hope for peaceful coexistence is in a union of states wherein the general government's activities are limited to external matters that, by their very nature, cannot be governed by the several states.

9. Resolved, that the legislature of the state of _____, hereby advises and instructs members of the state's congressional delegation to oppose all matters of legislation—whether they be wise policy in the members' eyes or foolish—that exceed Congress's enumerated powers under the Constitution of the United States.

10. Resolved, if the members of this state's congressional delegation believe that legislation on matters outside of Congress's enumerated powers is required for the good of the union, the members should propose amendments to fundamental law using the process outlined in Article V of the Constitution.

11. Resolved, that the legislature of this state recognizes that adherence to these instructions likely will cause inconveniences in conducting business in the Congress of the United States; however, sundry departments and initiatives of the federal government are so far removed from the powers delegated by the people through the Constitution that inconvenience is small price to pay for a serious examination and adherence to the fundamental law of the union.

NOTES

Preface

1. *SGT View* 105.
2. *Id.* at 103.
3. John Taylor observed that "[t]here are two kinds of construction; one calculated to maintain, the other to corrupt or destroy the principles upon which governments are established; one visible to common sense, the other consisting of filaments so slender, as not to be seen except through some magnifying glass; one which addresses the understanding, the other which addresses prejudice or self-interest." John Taylor, *Construction Construed* 21 (2009) [1820]. Taylor believed that strict construction belonged to the first category and loose construction to the second category.
4. James Madison's Speech on the Bank Bill (1791), reprinted in *Liberty and Order* 73 (Lance Banning ed., 2004).
5. TJ to William Johnson (1823), *VCCG* 269.
6. The Old Republicans were a faction of the Jeffersonian party and believed, inter alia, that "centralized power represents an ever-present threat to individual liberty and that human liberty in America is best protected by the diffusion of power among the several states in exercising their reserved rights." Norman K. Risjord, *The Old Republicans* 281 (1965).
7. John Randolph, Speech on Surveys for Roads and Canals (1824), reprinted in Russell Kirk, *John Randolph of Roanoke* 424 (1951).
8. *Id.* at 425.
9. Annals of Congress, 6th Congress (January 1800), p. 403.
10. John C. Calhoun, Exposition and Protest (1828), reprinted in *Union and Liberty* 314 (Ross M. Lence ed., 1992).
11. *Id.* at 314–15.
12. Abel Parker Upshur, *Our Federal Government* 149 & 152 (2015) (1868).
13. Modern originalism is divided into three basic schools, respectively focused on the original intent of the Framers, the original understanding of the ratifiers, and the original public meaning. *See* Cass Sunstein, *How to Interpret the Constitution* 24–34 (2023). In this book, originalism is understood as the interpretation most consistent with how the advocates of the Constitution (and subsequent amendments) explained the document and its particular provisions to the people of the several states during the push for ratification.
14. For a selection of modern originalist writings, see *Originalism: A Quarter-Century of Debate* (Steven G. Calabresi ed., 2007).
15. Akhil Reed Amar, *America's Constitution* 107 (2005).
16. Jesse Merriam, *A Better Legal Conservativism*, The American Mind, May 24, 2021, https://americanmind.org/features/a-new-conservatism-must-emerge/a-better-legal-conservatism/.
17. Jonathan Gienapp, *Against Constitutional Originalism* 190 (2024).
18. Quoted in Michael Wildman, *Originalism Run Amok at the Supreme Court* (2022), https://www.brennancenter.org/our-work/analysis-opinion/originalism-run-amok-supreme-court.
19. To be clear, the Hamiltonians were not living constitutionalists. They advocated for loose construction—a type of construction they denied would be possible when they spoke in ratification debates and in newspaper essays.
20. Louis Michael Seidman, *On Constitutional Disobedience*, Georgetown Public Law and Legal Theory Research Paper No. 12-002, at 7.
21. Adrian Vermeule, *Common Good Constitutionalism* 1 (2022).
22. *Id.* at 34.
23. Cass R. Sunstein, *How to Interpret the Constitution* 164 (2023).
24. *Id.* at 73.

25. William J. Brennan, Speech to the Text and Teaching Symposium (1985), reprinted in *Originalism: A Quarter-Century of Debate* 61 (Steven G. Calabresi ed., 2007).

26. Cass R. Sunstein, *How to Interpret the Constitution* 71 (2023).

27. Thomas Jefferson, Draft of the Kentucky Resolutions (1798), reprinted in *Liberty and Order* 236 (Lance Banning ed., 2004).

28. John Taylor, *Tyranny Unmasked* 195 (1992) (1822) ("The theoretical maxims best established by our political principles, is, that the people by special conventions have a right to make or alter their constitutions or forms of government, and that the government itself can do neither.").

29. *JM Notes* 70.

30. Alexis de Toqueville described the American union as "only an assemblage of confederate republics." Alexis de Toqueville, 1 *Democracy in America* 117 (1990) (1835).

31. Thomas Ritchie, To the Publick (1820), reprinted in John Taylor, *Construction Construed and Constitutions Vindicated* ii (2019).

32. The Virginia Declaration of Rights (1776), *VCCG* 3.

33. Gordon S. Wood, *The Creation of the American Republic* 598 (1969).

34. See John C. Calhoun, From a Public Letter to Governor James Hamilton (1832), reprinted in *The Essential Calhoun* (Clyde N. Wison ed., 1992) (observing that "the Constitution is the work of the people of the States, considered, as separate and independent political communities—that they are its authors—their power created it—their voice clothed it with an authority—that the Government it formed is in reality their agent—and that the Union, of which it is the bond, is a Union of States, and not of individuals").

35. Spencer Roane, Algernon Sidney Essay No. 3 (1821), reprinted in David Johnson, *Irreconcilable Founders* 168 (2021) ("The constitution was adopted by them, not as *one* people, but by the several states, by the people thereof, respectively.").

36. *JM Notes* 348.

37. Thomas Jefferson, Draft of the Kentucky Resolution (1798), reprinted in William J. Watkins Jr., *Reclaiming the American Revolution* 172 (2004).

38. "[T]he Federal government was authorized to interfere in the internal affairs of the states in a few predetermined cases in which an indiscreet use of their independence might compromise the safety of the whole Union." Alexis de Toqueville, 1 *Democracy in America* 116 (1990) (1835).

39. *Federalist* No. 45, at 236 (James Madison) (Bantam Books, 1982).

40. Forrest McDonald, *Novus Ordo Seclorum* 1 (1985).

41. William J. Watkins Jr. *Crossroads for Liberty: Recovering the Anti-Federalist Values of America's First Constitution* (2016).

42. *Creating* 3.

43. *JM Notes* 195.

44. *Id.* at 210.

45. George Washington, First Inaugural Address (1789), https://www.archives.gov/exhibits/american_originals/inaugtxt.html.

46. Randy Barnett & Evan Bernick, *The Original Meaning of the Fourteenth Amendment* 1 (2021).

47. *The Reconstruction Amendments' Debates* 200 (Alfred Avins ed., 1967). *See also id.* at 155 (remarks of Bingham denying the amendment would apply to New York).

48. *Slaughterhouse Cases*, 83 U.S. 36, 82 (1872).

Preamble and Article I

1. Articles of Confederation of 1781, art. III.

2. *Farrand's Records* 4:183.

3. Brutus, Essay XII (1787), *TAF* 457.

4. *Elliot's Debates* 3:44.

5. *See id.* at 301.

6. *Id.* at 259.

7. *Federalist* No. 17, at 80 (Alexander Hamilton) (Bantam Books, 1982).

8. *Id.* at 81.

9. *Black's Law Dictionary* 813 (6th ed. 1991).

10. Mr. Madison's Report of 1800, *VCCG* 198.

11. 197 U.S. 11, 22 (1905).

12. Annals of Congress, 5th Congress, 2d sess. (June 16, 1798), p. 1957.

13. John W. Welch & John A. Heilpern, *Recovering Our Forgotten Preamble*, 91 S. Cal. L. Rev. 1021, 1029 & 1133 (2018).

14. See e.g., Constitutional Authority Statement for H.R. 988 (112th Cong.), introduced March 9, 2011 by Rep. Schiff.

15. 2 U.S. 419, 471 (1793).

16. *Federalist* No. 39, at 192 (James Madison) (Bantam Books, 1982).

17. 19 U.S. 264, 389 (1821).

18. Akhil Reed Amar, *America's Constitution* 21 (2005).

19. John Taylor, *Construction Construed and Constitutions Vindicated* 47 (2009) (1820).

20. *JM Notes* 385.

21. For the distinction between ultimate sovereignty and governmental sovereignty, *see* William J. Watkins Jr., *Reclaiming the American Revolution* 61 & 192–93 n.27 (2004). Michael Kammen describes popular sovereignty as "a belief that public authority and the legitimacy of governmental actions originate in the people-at-large." Michael Kammen, *Sovereignty and Liberty* 13 (1988). "[W]e have adopted the policy of transferring this illimitable power called sovereignty, from the government to the people." John Taylor, *Construction Construed and Constitutions Vindicated* 68 (2009) (1820).

22. Abel Parker Upshur, *Our Federal Government: Its True Nature and Character* 88 (2015) (1868).

23. *JM Notes* 353.

24. 1 William Blackstone, *Commentaries* *156.

25. John W. Welch & John A. Heilpern, *Recovering Our Forgotten Preamble*, 91 S. Cal. L. Rev. 1021, 1111 (2018).

26. *McCulloch v. Maryland*, 17 U.S. 316, 403 (1819).

27. Some critics might bristle at the candid and often critical assessment of Lincoln's extraconstitutional government. They should remember that even the celebrated historian and political scientist Clinton Rossiter acknowledged that Lincoln undertook "a number of unconstitutional and dictatorial actions" during his presidency. Clinton Rossiter, *Constitutional Dictatorship* 11 (2002). The question is not whether Lincoln acted unconstitutionally, but whether the "necessity" of preserving the union—Lincoln's stated reason for going to war—excuses his actions despite the dangerous precedents he set.

28. Lincoln's Gettysburg Address (1863), reprinted in *American Historical Documents* 415 (Charles W. Elliot ed., 1980).

29. Articles of Confederation of 1781, art. IX.

30. *Black's Law Dictionary* 624 (6th ed. 1991).

31. Even absent the "herein granted" language, there would be no reasonable argument that Congress could exercise powers outside of the actual enumeration. The structure of the Constitution and arguments made by its friends are counter to such a contention.

32. M. J. C. Vile, *Constitutionalism and the Separation of Powers* 15 (1998).

33. *Federalist* No. 47, at 244 (James Madison) (Bantam Books, 1982).

34. Massachusetts Constitution (1780), *TFC* 1: 13–14.

35. Vince Eisinger, *Auxiliary Protections: Why the Founders' Bicameral Congress Depended on Senators Elected by State Legislatures*, 31 Touro L. Rev. 231, 241 (2015).

36. *TFC* 2:30.

37. *Federalist* No. 51, at 264 (James Madison) (Bantam Books, 1982).

38. *JM Notes* 193.

39. *JW Works* 1:698.

40. *JCC* 6:1102.

41. *JM Notes* 218.

42. *Id.*

43. *Id.*

44. *Elliot's Debates* 2:236.

45. *Id.*

46. James Burnham, The Managers Shift the Locus of Sovereignty (1941), reprinted in *The Paleoconservatives* 50 & 53 (Joseph Scotchie ed., 1999).

47. *Id.* at 50.

48. *Id.* at 53.

49. *Id.*

50. *Id.*

51. *Id.* at 54.

52. *Id.* at 55.

53. Ronald J. Pestritto, *Woodrow Wilson and the Roots of Modern Liberalism* 222 (2005).

54. *Id.* at 228.

55. *Id.* at 234.

56. *Id.* at 221.

57. John Locke, *Second Treatise of Government* 74 (C. B. Macpherson ed., 1980) (1690) (emphasis omitted).

58. Thomas Jefferson, Notes on the State of Virginia (1781), reprinted in *The Complete Jefferson* 653 (S. Padover ed., 1943).

59. *J.W. Hampton, Jr., & Co. v. United States*, 276 U.S. 394, 406 (1928).

60. *Id.* at 409.

61. 293 U.S. 388 (1935).

62. 295 U.S. 495 (1935).

63. 139 S. Ct. 2116, 2121 (2019).

64. 145 S. Ct. 2482 (2025).

65. *Loper Bright Enterprises v. Raimondo*, 603 U.S. 369 (2024).

66. *Chevron U.S.A., Inc. v. NRDC*, 467 U.S. 837 (1984).

67. William J. Watkins Jr., *The Constituent Power as a Remedy for the Administrative State*, 26 Independent Rev. 65 (2021).

68. *See* Peter B. McCutchen, *Mistakes, Precedent, and the Rise of the Administrative State: Toward a Constitutional Theory of the Second Best*, 80 Cornell L. Rev. 1 (1994).

69. 462 U.S. 919 (1983).

70. *Id.* at 977 (White, J., dissenting).

71. *Id.* at 959.

72. *Id.* at 967–68 (White, J., dissenting).

73. Gary Lawson, *The Rise and Rise of the Administrative State*, 107 Harv. L. Rev. 1231, 1231 (1994).

74. *JM Notes* 39.

75. *Id.* at 167.

76. *Id.*

77. *Id.* at 168.

78. *Federalist* No. 52, at 267 (James Madison) (Bantam Books, 1982).

79. Cato, Letter V (1787), *TAF* 21.

80. *Elliot's Debates* 2:5.

81. *Id.* at 10.

82. *Id.*

83. *Id.* at 16.

84. *JM Notes* 401.

85. *Elliot's Debates* 2:100.

86. *Id.* at 439.

87. U.S. Const. amend. XV, XIX, XXIV, XXVI.

88. 376 U.S. 1, 7–8 (1964).

89. 462 U.S. 725, 727 (1983).

90. *Baker v. Carr*, 369 U.S. 186, 332 (1962) (Harlan, J., dissenting).

91. *Id.*

92. *Evenwel v. Abbott*, 578 U.S. 54, 88 (2016) (Thomas, J., dissenting).

93. *Id.*

94. *JM Notes* 174.

95. *Id.*

96. *Id.* at 406.

97. *Id.* at 407.

98. *Id.* at 406.

99. 514 U.S. 779, 827 (1995).

100. *U.S. Term Limits*, 514 U.S. at 845 (Thomas, J., dissenting).

101. Thomas Jefferson (TJ) to Joseph C. Cabell (1814), *TFC* 2:81.

102. *Id.*

103. Aristotle, *Politics* 49 (Benjamin Jowett ed., 2000).

104. Articles of Confederation of 1781, art. V.

105. An Officer of the Late Continental Army, Reply to Wilson's Speech (1787), reprinted in *The Debate on the Constitution* (Bernard Bailyn, ed., 1993)) 1:99–100.

106. A Columbian Patriot, *Observations on the New Constitution* (1788), https://digfir-published.macmillanusa.com/roarksources/roarksources_ch8_6.html.

107. Dickinson Draft (1776), *JCC* 5:548.

108. *JCC* 6:1100.

109. Merrill Jensen, *The Articles of Confederation* 146 (1940).

110. *JM Notes* 260.

111. *Id.* at 277.

112. *Id.* at 266.

113. *Id.* at 268.

114. *JM Notes* 266.

115. 536 U.S. 452, 475 (2002).

116. *Evans*, 536 U.S. at 510 (Thomas, J., dissenting) (internal citation omitted).

117. *Elliot's Debates* 3:32.

118. *Federalist* No. 56, at 285 (James Madison) (Bantam Books, 1982).

119. *Federalist* No. 55, at 282 (James Madison) (Bantam Books, 1982).

120. Charles Loius de Secondat, Baron de la Brède et de Montesquieu, *The Sprit of the Laws* 176 (David Wallace Carruthers ed., 1977) (1748).

121. 385 F.3d 641 (6th Cir. 2004).

122. *Id.* at 644.

123. *Id.* at 649.

124. *Id.*

125. Massachusetts Constitution (1780), *TFC* 1:16.

126. *See* Russell Spivak, *Anybody's Gavel: Why Congress Can Choose a Speaker from Outside Its Ranks*, 2019 U. Ill. L. Rev. Online 9 (2019).

127. Jonathan Turley, *Congress as Grand Jury: The Role of the House of Representatives in the Impeachment of an American President*, 67 Geo. Wash. L. Rev. 735, 773 (1999).

128. *JM Notes* 30.

129. *Id.* at 42.

130. *Id.*

131. *Id.* at 82.

132. *Id.*

133. *Id.* at 84.

134. *Id.* at 82.

135. *Id.* at 190.

136. *Federalist* No. 62, at 314 (James Madison) (Bantam Books, 1982).

137. *JM Notes* 354.

138. *TFC* 2:225.

139. *Id.*
140. Centinel, Letter II (1787), *TAF* 54.
141. Cato, Letter V (1787), *TAF* 21.
142. John DeWitt, Essay IV (1787), *TAF* 508.
143. *Elliot's Debates* 1:361.
144. *Id.*
145. *JM Notes* 193.
146. *Elliot's Debates* 2:214.
147. *Id.*
148. U.S. Senate, About the Senate and the U.S. Constitution: Senate Classes, https://www.senate.gov/about/origins-foundations/senate-and-constitution/senate-classes.htm (last visited Feb. 15, 2025).
149. *JM Notes* 415.
150. *Federalist* No. 62, at 313 (James Madison) (Bantam Books, 1982).
151. *Id.*
152. *JM Notes* 418.
153. *Id.* at 419.
154. *Id.*
155. Paul E. Salamanca & James E. Keller, *The Legislative Privilege to Judge the Qualifications, Elections, and Returns of Members*, 95 Ky. L.J. 241, 282 (2007).
156. *JM Notes* 596.
157. *Id.*
158. *Id.*
159. *Elliot's Debates* 4:26.
160. Richard Albert, *The Evolving Vice Presidency*, 78 Temp. L. Rev. 811, 824–25 (2005).
161. Roy E. Brownell II, *A Constitutional Chameleon: The Vice President's Place Within the American System of Separation of Powers, Part I: Text, Structure, Views of the Framers and the Courts*, 24 Kan. J.L. & Pub. Pol'y 1, 77 n.123 (2014).
162. Jefferson quoted in Andrew N. Shindi, *Concocting the Most Insignificant Office Ever Contrived: The Vice Presidency During the Early Republic*, 104 Geo. L.J. 1029, 1048 (2016).
163. Joel K. Goldstein, *Constitutional Change, Originalism, and the Vice Presidency*, 16 U. Pa. J. Const. L. 369, 397 (2013).
164. Aaron-Andrew P. Bruhl, *Burying the "Continuing Body" Theory of the Senate*, 95 Iowa L. Rev. 1401, 1454 (2010).
165. *JM Notes* 56.
166. *Id.*
167. *Id.* at 333.
168. *See* Raoul Berger, *Impeachment: Constitutional Problems* 263–309 (1974) (discussing the Johnson impeachment).
169. *Federalist* No. 65, at 332 (Alexander Hamilton) (Bantam Books, 1982).
170. *Id.*
171. *Elliot's Debates* 4:44.
172. *Elliot's Debates* 3:366.
173. *Id.* at 49.
174. 144 S. Ct. 2312 (2024).
175. Brian C. Kalt, *The Constitutional Case for the Impeachability of Former Federal Officials: An Analysis of the Law, History, and Practice of Late Impeachment*, 6 Tex. Rev. L. & Pol. 13, 17 (2001).
176. *TFC* 2:150–51.
177. *JM Notes* 424.
178. *Id.*
179. *Id.* at 423.
180. *Id.*
181. Cato, Letter VII (1788), *TAF* 30.
182. Brutus, Essay IV (1787), *TAF* 404.
183. Centinel, Letter I (1787), *TAF* 41.
184. *Elliot's Debates* 4:71.
185. *See Elliot's Debates* 2:50–51; 3:202–3.
186. *Elliot's Debates* 3:661.
187. *Federalist* No. 59, at 300 (Alexander Hamilton) (Bantam Books, 1982).
188. *Republican Party of Pennsylvania v. Boockvar*, 141 S. Ct. 1 (2020).
189. *Id.*
190. *Id.*
191. *Id.* at 3.
192. 570 U.S. 1 (2013).
193. *JM Notes* 398.
194. *Id.*
195. *Id.*
196. *Id.*
197. *Id.*
198. *Id.* at 399.
199. *Id.*
200. *Id.*
201. *Id.*
202. *Id.*
203. *Id.* at 400.
204. *JS Exposition* 117.
205. The Whigs were supporters of parliamentary power versus the power of the monarchy.
206. 395 U.S. 486 (1969).
207. *JM Notes* 428–29.
208. *Id.* at 429.
209. *Id.* at 430.
210. *Elliot's Debates* 2:249.
211. 144 U.S. 1, 6 (1892).
212. *JS Exposition* 118.

213. *Id.*

214. *JM Notes* 431.

215. *See* Congressional Research Service, Expulsion of Members of Congress: Legal Authority and Historical Practice (2023).

216. *See id.*

217. *In re Chapman*, 166 U.S. 661, 669 (1897).

218. Articles of Confederation of 1781, art. IX.

219. *JM Notes* 434.

220. *Id.*

221. *Id.*

222. *Marshall Field & Co. v. Clark*, 143 U.S. 649, 671 (1892).

223. *Elliot's Debates* 3:60.

224. *Id.*

225. *Id.* at 404.

226. *Id.* at 348.

227. *Id.* at 659.

228. Alexander Tytler, quoted in Richard E. Wagner, *Richard Epstein's* The Classical Liberal Constitution: *A Public Choice Refraction*, 8 N.Y.U. J.L. & Liberty 961, 963 (2014).

229. *Elliot's Debates* 3:367.

230. *Id.* at 406.

231. *Id.* at 367–68.

232. *Id.* at 368.

233. *Id.* at 409.

234. *JM Notes* 108.

235. *Id.* at 172.

236. *Id.* at 171.

237. *Id.*

238. *Id.*

239. *Id.* at 199.

240. *Id.*

241. *Elliot's Debates* 3:368.

242. *Id.* at 369.

243. 2 U.S.C. § 4501.

244. Ida A. Brudnick, *Salaries of Members of Congress: Recent Actions and Historical Table* 2 (Congressional Research Service, 2021).

245. *Boehner v. Anderson*, 30 F.3d 156, 162 (D.C. Cir. 1994).

246. 207 U.S. 425, 446 (1908).

247. *Id.* at 445.

248. *See Long v. Ansell*, 293 U.S. 76, 82 (1934).

249. Articles of Confederation of 1781, art. V.

250. The Bill of Rights (1689), reprinted in *From Magna Carta to the Constitution* 40 (David L. Brooks ed., 1993).

251. *JW Works* 2:855.

252. Thomas Jefferson, A Manual of Parliamentary Practice (1854), reprinted in *The Complete Jefferson* 704 (S. Padover ed., 1943).

253. *Gravel v. United States*, 408 U.S. 606, 625 (1972).

254. *Id.*

255. 443 U.S. 111, 114 (1979).

256. *Id.* at 130 (internal quotation marks omitted).

257. Akhil Reed Amar & Neal Kumar Katyal, *Executive Privileges and Immunities: The Nixon and Clinton Cases*, 108 Harv. L. Rev. 701, 702 (1995).

258. *TFC* 2:346.

259. *Id.*

260. *Id.*

261. *Id.* at 347.

262. *Id.*

263. *Id.*

264. *JM Notes* 450.

265. *Id.* at 451.

266. *TFC* 2:346.

267. *A Dictionary of the English Language* (Samuel Johnson ed., 1755).

268. 302 U.S. 633, 636 (1937).

269. *See, e.g.*, David J. Shaw, *An Officer and A Congressman: The Unconstitutionality of Congressmen in the Armed Forces Reserve*, 97 Geo. L.J. 1739, 1740 (2009).

270. 418 U.S. 208 (1974).

271. *See* Michael Stokes Paulsen, *Is Lloyd Bentsen Unconstitutional?*, 46 Stan. L. Rev. 907, 908 (1994).

272. *JM Notes* 416.

273. Tessa L. Dysart, *The Origination Clause, the Affordable Care Act, and Indirect Constitutional Violations*, 24 Cornell J.L. & Pub. Pol'y 451, 482 (2015).

274. *JM Notes* 444.

275. *Id.* at 445.

276. Priscilla H. M. Zotti & Nicholas M. Schmitz, *The Origination Clause: Meaning, Precedent, and Theory from the 12th to 21st Century*, 3 Brit. J. Am. Legal Stud. 71, 95 (2014).

277. *Elliot's Debates* 3:375.

278. *Id.*

279. *Id.* at 376.

280. *Id.*

281. 495 U.S. 385, 387 (1990).

282. *Id.* at 397.

283. *Id.* at 398.

284. 760 F.3d 1 (2014).

285. *JM Notes* 32.

286. *Id.*

287. *JM Notes* 338.

288. *Id.*

289. *Id.* at 340.

290. *Id.* at 63.

291. *Id.*

292. *Id.* at 62.

293. *Id.*

294. *Federalist* No. 73, at 372–73 (Alexander Hamilton) (Bantam Books, 1982).

295. *Id.* at 373.

296. *Id.*

297. *Elliot's Debates* 4:74.

298. *Id.* at 75.

299. Pennsylvania Convention Minority Address (1787), *TAF* 539.

300. Impartial Examiner, Essay IV (1788), *TAF* 670.

301. Federal Farmer, Letter XIV (1788), *TAF* 267.

302. 462 U.S. 919 (1983).

303. *Id.* at 977 (White, J., dissenting).

304. *Id.* at 959.

305. 524 U.S. 417, 431 (1998).

306. *Id.* at 438.

307. *Id.* at 448.

308. *Id.* at 469 (Scalia, J., dissenting).

309. 279 U.S. 655, 680 (1929).

310. Butler C. Derrick Jr., *Stitching the Hole in the President's Pocket: A Legislative Solution to the Pocket-Veto Controversy*, 31 Harv. J. on Legis. 371, 372 (1994).

311. A good study of the structure of the Confederate Constitution is Randall G. Holcombe, *The Distributive Model of Government: Evidence from the Confederate Constitution*, 58 S. Econ. J. 58, no. 3, 1992, at 762–69. Another valuable work is Marshall L. DeRosa, *The Confederate Constitution of 1861* (1991).

312. *JM Notes* 465.

313. 3 U.S. 378 (1798).

314. U.S. Const. art. V.

315. *Hollingsworth*, 3 U.S. at 382.

316. Sopan Joshi, *The Presidential Role in the Constitutional Amendment Process*, 107 Nw. U. L. Rev. 963, 965 (2013).

317. Keith L. Dougherty, *Collective Action Under the Articles of Confederation* 53 (2001).

318. James Madison (JM) to TJ (March 27 & 28, 1780), *TRL* 1:136.

319. *JM Notes* 7.

320. *See* Grant of a Power to Collect Import Duties (1781), reprinted in 1 *The Documentary History of the Ratification of the Constitution* 140 (Merrill Jensen ed., 1976).

321. Grant of Temporary Power to Collect Import Duties . . . (1783), reprinted in 1 *The Documentary History of the Ratification of the Constitution* 146 (Merrill Jensen ed., 1976).

322. *Elliot's Debates* 2:73.

323. *Id.*

324. *Elliot's Debates* 3:57.

325. *Id.* at 34.

326. Federal Farmer, Letter III (1787), *TAF* 163.

327. *Id.*

328. *Id.* at 163–64.

329. *Id.* at 165.

330. Richard Henry Lee to Governor Edmund Randolph (1787), *TAF* 365.

331. *Elliot's Debates* 3:442.

332. *Id.* at 449.

333. *Elliot's Debates* 2:338.

334. *Elliot's Debates* 3:466.

335. *Federalist* No. 41, at 209 (James Madison) (Bantam Books, 1982).

336. *Id.* at 210.

337. Alexander Hamilton, Report on the Subject of Manufactures (1791), reprinted in *Liberty and Order* 101 (Lance Banning ed., 2004).

338. Mr. Madison's Report of 1800, *VCCG* 168.

339. *Id.* at 169.

340. 112 U.S. 580, 594 (1884).

341. *Id.*

342. 112 U.S. 580, 594 (1884).

343. 297 U.S. 1 (1936).

344. *Id.* at 65.

345. *Id.* at 66.

346. 483 U.S. 203 (1987).

347. *Id.* at 207 (internal quotation marks omitted).

348. 567 U.S. 519 (2012).

349. *Id.* at 541–42.

350. *Id.* at 542.

351. *Id.* at 581.

352. 462 U.S. 74, 77 (1983).

353. *Id.* at 85.

354. *Id.* at 78.

355. For an excellent discussion of a proposed balanced budget amendment, see J. Huston McColloch, *An Improved Balanced Budget Amendment*, 17 Ind. Rev. 219 (2012).

356. John Menton, *Ridding Congress of Riders: The Case for a Single Subject Amendment* (2018), https://www.jamesmadison.org/wp-content/uploads/2018/05/Menton.pdf.

357. Articles of Confederation of 1781, art. IX.

358. *Id.*

359. Clarence B. Carson, The Constitution and Paper Money 166 (1983), reprinted in *The Foundations*

of American Constitutional Government (Robert D. Gorgolione, comp., 1996).

360. *Elliot's Debates* 5:434.

361. *Id.* at 435.

362. *Id.*

363. *Id.*

364. *Id.*

365. *Id.*

366. Brutus, Essay VIII (1788), *TAF* 430.

367. *Id.* at 431.

368. *SGT View* 189.

369. *Id.* at 190.

370. 12 Stat. 345 (1862).

371. 79 U.S. 457, 529 (1870).

372. *The Legal Tender Cases*, 110 U.S. 421, 450 (1884).

373. Frederic Bastiat, *The Law* 7 (2007) (1850). Bastiat described government transfer programs as legalized plunder.

374. *SGT View* 191.

375. *JM Notes* 551.

376. *Elliot's Debates* 1:373.

377. *Elliot's Debates* 3:78.

378. Agrippa IX (1787), *Debate on the Constitution* 1:629.

379. *Federalist* No. 42, at 214 (James Madison) (Bantam Books, 1982).

380. *Id.*

381. *Federalist* No. 11, at 53 (Alexander Hamilton) (Bantam Books, 1982).

382. *Id.*

383. State Soldier, Essay II (1788), reprinted in *Friends of the Constitution* 124 (Colleen A. Sheehan & Gary L. McDowell, eds., 1998).

384. *United States v. Lopez*, 514 U.S. 549, 586 (1995) (Thomas, J., dissenting).

385. *SGT View* 346.

386. A Freeman, Essay I (1788), reprinted in *Friends of the Constitution* 92 (Colleen A. Sheehan & Gary L. McDowell eds., 1998).

387. 22 U.S. 1, 203 (1824).

388. 156 U.S. 1, 12 (1895).

389. Articles of Confederation of 1781, art. IX.

390. 301 U.S. 1 (1937).

391. *Id.* at 37.

392. 317 U.S. 111, 125 (1942).

393. *Id.* at 127–28.

394. 514 U.S. 549 (1995).

395. 567 U.S. 519 (2012).

396. *Id.* at 552.

397. *Id.*

398. *Id.*

399. 597 U.S. 215 (2022).

400. Articles of Confederation of 1781, art. IV.

401. James E. Pfander & Theresa R. Wardon, *Reclaiming the Immigration Constitution of the Early Republic: Prospectivity, Uniformity, and Transparency*, 96 Va. L. Rev. 359, 384 (2010).

402. *Federalist* No. 42, at 215 (James Madison) (Bantam Books, 1982).

403. 15 U.S. 259, 269 (1817).

404. *Federalist* No. 42, at 217 (James Madison) (Bantam Books, 1982).

405. Frederick P. Corbit, *The Founding Fathers' Influence on Bankruptcy Law*, Am. Bankr. Inst. J., July/August 2007, at 50, 51.

406. *Sturges v. Crowninshield*, 17 U.S. 122 (1819); *Hanover Nat'l Bank v. New York*, 186 U.S. 181 (1902).

407. Russell H. Markwell, *Bankruptcy—Validity of Proceedings Under the Texas Assignment for Creditors Act*, 10 Tex. L. Rev. 197 (1932).

408. See Matthew J. Lindsay, *Immigration, Sovereignty, and the Constitution of Foreignness*, 45 Conn. L. Rev. 743, 746 (2013).

409. For a discussion of the statute, see William J. Watkins Jr., *Reclaiming the American Revolution: The Kentucky and Virginia Resolutions and Their Legacy* 35–37 (2004).

410. Kentucky Resolution of 1798, reprinted in *id.* at 166.

411. Lydia Saad, *Americans Showing Increased Concern About Immigration* (February 13, 2023), https://news.gallup.com/poll/470426/americans-showing-increased-concern-immigration.aspx.

412. Articles of Confederation of 1781, art. IX.

413. Current coin is any coin the issue and circulation of which as money, in any state or territory, have been authorized by law.

414. Joseph Story, *Commentaries on the Constitution* (1833), reprinted in *TFC* 3:11.

415. Richard H. Timberlake, *Constitutional Money* 35 (2013).

416. 110 U.S. 421, 462 (1884) (Field, J., dissenting).

417. Richard H. Timberlake, *Constitutional Money* 35 (2013).

418. *Juillard*, 110 U.S. at 464 (Field, J., dissenting).

419. *Id.*

420. 110 U.S. at 448.

421. Bettina Bien Graves, *How to Return to the Gold Standard* (1995), https://fee.org/articles/how-to-return-to-the-gold-standard.

422. H.R. 2435, 118th Cong. (2023–24).

423. *Id.*

424. *Id.*

425. *JM Notes* 473.

426. *Id.*

427. *Id.*

428. *See Fox v. Ohio*, 46 U.S. 410 (1847).

429. *See United States v. Marigold*, 50 U.S. 560, 569–70 (1850).

430. Lewis D. Solomon, *Local Currency: A Legal and Policy Analysis*, Kan. J.L. & Pub. Pol'y, Winter 1996, at 59, 86.

431. Articles of Confederation of 1781, art. IX.

432. *JM Notes* 638.

433. *Id.*

434. *SGT View* 207.

435. Robert G. Natelson, *Founding-Era Socialism: The Original Meaning of the Constitution's Postal Clause*, 7 Brit. J. Am. Legal Stud. 1, 55 (2018).

436. *Id.* at 55–56.

437. TJ to JM (March 6, 1796), *TRL* 2:924.

438. *Id.*

439. Christina M. Bates, *From 34 Cents to 37 Cents: The Unconstitutionality of the Postal Monopoly*, 68 Mo. L. Rev. 123, 135 (2003).

440. *See Searight v. Stokes*, 44 U.S. 151 (1845) (Daniel, J., dissenting).

441. 96 U.S. 727, 731 (1877).

442. *JCC* 23:672–73.

443. 1 Stat. 232, 236.

444. George L. Priest, *The History of the Postal Monopoly in the United States*, 18 J. of Law & Econ. 33, 54 (1975).

445. *See Brennan v. U. S. Postal Serv.*, 439 U.S. 1345, 1346 (1978).

446. Lysander Spooner, *The Unconstitutionality of the Laws of Congress Prohibiting Private Mails* 5 (1844).

447. Chris Edwards, *Privatizing the U.S. Postal Service* (2016), https://www.cato.org/tax-budget-bulletin/privatizing-us-postal-service.

448. *See* Paul E. Schaafsma, *An Economic Overview of Patents*, 79 J. Pat. & Trademark Office Soc'y 241–44 (1997).

449. An Act concerning Monopolies and Dispensations with Penal Laws . . . , 21 Jac. I, ch. 3 (1623).

450. *JS Exposition* 152.

451. *Id.*

452. *Id.*

453. TJ to Isaac McPherson (1813), *TFC* 3:42.

454. *Id.*

455. *Id.*

456. 1 Stat 109 (1790).

457. *Id.*

458. 35 U.S.C. § 101.

459. Articles of Confederation of 1781, art. IX.

460. *Id.*

461. *JM Notes* 32.

462. *Id* at 71.

463. *Id.*

464. *Id.* at 72.

465. *Id.* at 319.

466. *Id.* at 70.

467. *Elliot's Debates* 1:370.

468. *Elliot's Debates* 3:521.

469. *Elliot's Debates* 4:155.

470. *Id.*

471. Donald H. Zeigler, *Twins Separated at Birth: A Comparative History of the Civil and Criminal Arising Under Jurisdiction of the Federal Courts and Some Proposals for Change*, 19 Vt. L. Rev. 673, 691 (1995).

472. Articles of Confederation of 1781, art. IX.

473. Sarah H. Cleveland, William S. Dodge, *Defining and Punishing Offenses Under Treaties*, 124 Yale L.J. 2202, 2212 (2015) (explaining the understanding of the law of nations at the time of the founding).

474. Edmund Randolph, James Duane, and John Witherspoon, Report to Congress (1781), *TFC* 3:66.

475. *JM Notes* 474.

476. Chad DeVeaux, *Rationalizing the Constitution: The Military Commissions Act and the Dubious Legacy of* Ex Parte Quirin, 42 Akron L. Rev. 13, 91–92 (2009) (internal quotation marks omitted).

477. *Federalist* No. 42, at 212 (James Madison) (Bantam Books, 1982).

478. *SGT View* 210.

479. 120 U.S. 479, 488 (1887).

480. 317 U.S. 1, 28, modified sub nom. *U.S. ex rel. Quirin v. Cox*, 63 S. Ct. 22 (1942).

481. 548 U.S. 557, 601–2 (2006) ("There is no suggestion that Congress has, in exercise of its constitutional authority to 'define and punish . . . Offences against the Law of Nations,' U.S. Const., Art. I, § 8, cl. 10, positively identified 'conspiracy' as a war crime.").

482. Some commentators argue that Congress has complete power to define and enact statutes pursuant to the law of nations without court interference. *See* Eugene Kontorovich, *The "Define and Punish" Clause and the Limits of Universal Jurisdiction*, 103 Nw. U. L. Rev. 149, 150 (2009).

483. *See* Beth Stephens, *Federalism and Foreign Affairs: Congress' Power to Define and Punish Offenses Against the Law of Nations*, 42 Wm. & Mary L. Rev. 447 (2000).

484. *Id.* at 449.

485. Louis Fisher, *Presidential War Power* 1 (2014).

486. Articles of Confederation of 1781, art. IX.

487. *JM Notes* 475.

488. *Id.* at 476.

489. *Id.*

490. *Id.*

491. *Id.*

492. *Elliot's Debates* 2:528.

493. *Id.*

494. JM to TJ (April 2, 1798), *TRL* 2:1032.

495. *Id.*

496. James Madison, Helvidius Number IV (1793), *PHD* 87.

497. *Id.*

498. *Id.*

499. *Id.*

500. Granting letters of marque and reprisal, 3 *Modern Constitutional Law* § 34:6 (3rd ed.).

501. 115 Stat. 224 (emphasis added).

502. 87 Stat. 555, § 3.

503. *Id.* at § 5(c).

504. Bruce Ackerman & Oona Hathaway, *Limited War and the Constitution: Iraq and the Crisis of Presidential Legality*, 10 Mich. L. Rev. 447, 458 (2011).

505. Letter to President Biden (Jan. 26, 2024), https://www.documentcloud.org/documents/24377843-congress-letter-to-president-biden.

506. *JM Notes* 481.

507. *Id.* at 482.

508. *Id.*

509. Virginia Declaration of Rights, § 13 (1776), *TFC* 3:173.

510. *Elliot's Debates* 2:136.

511. *Elliot's Debates* 3:380.

512. Federalist No. 8, at 34 (Alexander Hamilton) (Bantam Books, 1982).

513. *Elliot's Debates* 2:81.

514. *Id.* at 98.

515. 245 U.S. 366, 378 (1918).

516. Daniel Webster, *On the Draft: Text of a Speech Delivered in Congress* (Dec. 9, 1814), https://oll.libertyfund.org/title/webster-daniel-webster-on-the-draft-text-of-a-speech-delivered-in-congress-december-9-1814.

517. Doug Bandow, *America Has No Need for a New Draft*, L.A. Times, June 14, 1987, http://latimes.com/archives/la-xpm-1987-06-14-op-story.html.

518. *Wyden, Paul, DeFazio, Davis Introduce Bipartisan Bill to Abolish the Selective Service* (Apr. 14, 2021), https://www.wyden.senate.gov/news/press-releases/wyden-paul-defazio-davis-introduce-bipartisan-bill-to-abolish-the-selective-service.

519. Articles of Confederation of 1781, art. IX.

520. *JM Notes* 482.

521. *Federalist* No. 4, at 16 (John Jay) (Bantam Books, 1982).

522. *Id.*

523. *Elliot's Debates* 3:428.

524. *Id.* at 429.

525. *JM Notes* 482.

526. David F. Forte and Mackubin Owens, Military Regulation, in *The Heritage Guide to the Constitution* 136 (Edwin Meese III ed., 2005).

527. James B. Roan & Cynthia Buxton, *The American Military Justice System in the New Millennium*, 52 A.F. L. Rev. 185, 187 (2002).

528. *Solorio v. United States*, 483 U.S. 435, 436 (1987).

529. 395 U.S. 258 (1969).

530. *JM Notes* 31.

531. *Id.* at 45.

532. *Id.*

533. *Id.* at 121.

534. *Elliot's Debates* 1:371.

535. *Federalist* No. 29, at 138 (Alexander Hamilton) (Bantam Books, 1982).

536. *Elliot's Debates* 3:378.

537. *Id.* at 381.

538. *Id.*

539. *Elliot's Debates* 3:378.

540. Quoted in *Martin v. Mott*, 25 U.S. 19, 29 (1827).

541. *Id.* at 30.

542. S.T. Ansell, *Legal and Historical Aspects of the Militia*, 26 Yale L. J. 471, 471 (1917).

543. 1 William Blackstone, *Commentaries* *397.

544. William S. Fields & David T. Hardy, *The Militia and the Constitution: A Legal History*, 136 Mil. L. Rev. 1, 7 (1992).

545. Saul Cornell, *A Well-Regulated Militia* 13 (2006).

546. *JM Notes* 513.

547. *Id.*

548. *Elliot's Debates* 1:371.

549. *JM Notes* 515.

550. 1 Stat. 271 (1792).

551. Washington's Farewell Address (1796), reprinted in *American Historical Documents* 246 (Charles W. Eliot ed., 1980).

552. *Id.*

553. Fla. Stat. § 251.001(2) ("The Florida State Guard is created to protect and defend the people of Florida from all threats to public safety and to augment all existing state and local agencies.").

554. Florida State Guard, *Purpose*, https://www.floridastateguard.org/purpose (last visited Feb. 15, 2025).

555. Mark S. Scarberry, *Historical Considerations and Congressional Representation for the District of Columbia: Constitutionality of the D.C. House Voting Rights Bill in Light of Section Two of the Fourteenth Amendment and the History of the Constitution*, 60 Ala. L. Rev. 783, 873 (2009).

556. *JM Notes* 378.

557. *Id.* at 379.

558. *Id.* 435.

559. *Id.*

560. *Elliot's Debates* 2:99.

561. *Elliot's Debates* 3:439.

562. *Federalist* No. 43, at 219 (James Madison) (Bantam Books, 1982).

563. *Elliot's Debates* 2:545.

564. *Elliot's Debates* 3:431.

565. *Id.*

566. 1 Stat. 130 (1790).

567. Randy E. Barnett, *The Original Meaning of the Necessary and Proper Clause*, 6 U. Pa. J. Const. L. 183, 186–87 (2003).

568. An Old Whig, Essay II (1787), *TAF* 324.

569. *Id.* at 325.

570. Federal Farmer, Letter IV (1787), *TAF* 174.

571. Centinel, Letter V (1787), *TAF* 80.

572. Brutus, Essay I (1787), *TAF* 377.

573. James Wilson, Speech (1787), reprinted in *Friends of the Constitution* 246 (Colleen A. Sheehan & Gray L. McDowell eds., 1998).

574. *Federalist* No. 33, at 156 (Alexander Hamilton) (Bantam Books, 1982).

575. *Id.*

576. Alexander Hamilton, Plan for a Nation Bank (1791), reprinted in *Legislative and Documentary History of the Bank of the United States* 15 (M. St. Clair Clarke & D. A. Hall eds., 1832).

577. *Id.*

578. *Id.*

579. *Id.* at 18.

580. *Id.* at 47 (Fisher Ames).

581. *Id.* at 51 (Theodore Sedgwick).

582. *Id.* at 53 (John Lawrence).

583. *Id.* at 53.

584. *Id.* at 42 (James Madison).

585. Gary Lawson & Patricia B. Granger, *The "Proper" Scope of Federal Power: A Jurisdictional Interpretation of the Sweeping Clause*, 43 Duke L. J. 267, 272 (1993).

586. *Id.*

587. Edmund Randolph, Opinion on the Bank (1791), reprinted in *Legislative and Documentary History of the Bank of the United States* 89 (M. St. Clair Clarke & D. A. Hall eds., 1832).

588. U.S. Const. amend. X.

589. Thomas Jefferson, Opinion on the Bank (1791), reprinted in *Legislative and Documentary History of the Bank of the United States* 91 (M. St. Clair Clarke & D. A. Hall eds., 1832).

590. *Id.* at 93.

591. Alexander Hamilton, Opinion on the Bank (1791), reprinted in *Legislative and Documentary History of the Bank of the United States* 95 (M. St. Clair Clarke & D. A. Hall eds., 1832).

592. *Id.* at 99.

593. 17 U.S. 316 (1819).

594. *Id.* at 401.

595. *Id.* at 409–10 & 413.

596. *Id.* at 421.

597. 130 S. Ct. 1949 (2010).

598. *Id.* at 1956.

599. Hampden Letter No. 1 (1819), reprinted in *Irreconcilable Founders* 127 (David Johnson ed., 2021).

600. *Elliot's Debates* 2:452.

601. *Id.*

602. *JM Notes* 502.

603. *Id.* at 503.

604. *Id.*

605. *Id.* at 504.

606. *Id.*

607. *Id.* at 505.

608. *Id.*

609. *Id.* at 530.

610. *Id.* at 532.

611. Thomas Jefferson, Sixth Annual Message (1806), reprinted in *The Complete Jefferson* 424 (Saul K. Padover ed., 1943).

612. Dumas Malone, *Jefferson the President: Second Term 1805–1809* 541 (1974).

613. M. Andrew Holowchak, Turning Back the Clock from the Race-First 1619 Project to the Virginia-First 1607, in *Virginia First: The 1607 Project* 257–58 (Brion McClanahan ed., 2024).

614. Nigel Biggar, *Colonialism: A Moral Reckoning* 53-54 (2023).

615. *Id.* at 54-55.

616. 3 William Blackstone, *Commentaries* *129.

617. Anthony Gregory, *The Power of Habeas Corpus in America: From the King's Prerogative to the War on Terror* 283 (2013).

618. *JM Notes* 486.

619. Massachusetts Constitution (1780), *TFC* 1:22.

620. *Elliot's Debates* 2:137.

621. Clinton Rossiter, *Constitutional Dictatorship* 227 (2002).

622. 17 F. Cas. 144, 149 (1861).

623. James A. Bayard Jr., *Two Speeches Delivered in the United States Senate* 24 (1863).

624. *Id.*

625. 62 U.S. 506 (1859).

626. *Id.* at 526.

627. *Boumediene v. Bush*, 553 U.S. 723 (2008).

628. *Johnson v. Eisentrager*, 339 U.S. 763, 769 (1950).

629. Todd E. Pettys, *State Habeas Relief for Federal Extrajudicial Detainees*, 92 Minn. L. Rev. 265, 270 (2007).

630. *SGT View* 232.

631. Duane L. Ostler, *The Forgotten Constitutional Spotlight: How Viewing the Ban on Bills of Attainder as a Takings Protection Clarifies Constitutional Principles*, 42 U. Tol. L. Rev. 395, 396-97 (2011).

632. *SGT View* 233.

633. *Federalist* No. 84, at 435 (Alexander Hamilton) (Bantam Books, 1982).

634. *JM Notes* 510.

635. *Id.*

636. 381 U.S. 437, 447 (1965).

637. 3 U.S. 386, 394, 1 L. Ed. 648 (1798) (Chase, J.).

638. For an argument that the clause should apply to civil cases, see Evan C. Zoldan, *The Civil Ex Post Facto Clause*, 2015 Wis. L. Rev. 727, 783 (2015) ("The dispute turns on the professional meaning of the term *ex post facto*, a phrase that was well known to the professional class of American judges and lawyers in the decades leading up to the framing of the Constitution. The phrase, as recorded in colonial and early state court cases, was used by these professionals to describe not only criminal laws, but civil laws as well.").

639. *Weaver v. Graham*, 450 U.S. 24, 31 (1981).

640. 386 F. Supp. 2d 980, 1006 (2005).

641. *Id.*

642. 576 U.S. 644 (2015).

643. *Id.* at 28–29.

644. *Id.* at 29.

645. *Elliott's Debates* 3:229.

646. *Elliot's Debates* 2:91.

647. The Federal Farmer, Letter IX (1788), *TAF* 220.

648. Robert G. Natelson, *What the Constitution Means by "Duties imposts, and Excises"—and "Taxes" (Direct or Otherwise)*, 66 Case W. Res. L. Rev. 297, 318 (2015).

649. *Black's Law Dictionary* 145 (6th ed. 1991).

650. *SGT View* 233.

651. Robert G. Natelson, *What the Constitution Means by "Duties imposts, and Excises"—and "Taxes" (Direct or Otherwise)*, 66 Case W. Res. L. Rev. 297, 334 (2015).

652. *TFC* 3:357.

653. *Elliot's Debates* 2:42.

654. *Id.*

655. 3 U.S. 171 (1796).

656. *Id.* at 174.

657. *Id.*

658. 102 U.S. 586 (1880).

659. Robert Higgs, *Crisis and Leviathan* 97 (1987).

660. 158 U.S. 601, 618 (1895).

661. 157 U.S. 429, 558, *opinion vacated on reargument*, 158 U.S. 601 (1895).

662. *See* Dawn Johnsen, Walter Dellinger, *The Constitutionality of a National Wealth Tax*, 93 Ind. L.J. 111, 118 (2018).

663. *JM Notes* 499.

664. *Id.* at 501.

665. *Id.* at 468.

666. *Id.* at 500.

667. *Id.* at 467.

668. 517 U.S. 843 (1996).

669. *Id.* at 846.

670. *Id.* at 854 (internal quotation marks omitted).

671. *See id.* at 850.

672. *JM Notes* 532–33.

673. *JS Exposition* 135.

674. *Pennsylvania v. Wheeling & Belmont Bridge Co.*, 59 U.S. 421 (1855).

675. *Id.* at 435.

676. Edward S. Corwin, *The Constitution and What It Means Today* 81 (1958).

677. *Federalist* No. 58, at 297 (James Madison) (Bantam Books, 1982).

678. *Elliot's Debates* 3:233.

679. *Elliot's Debates* 3:459.

680. *Id.* at 170.

681. *Elliot's Debates* 2:347.

682. *Elliot's Debates* 3:460.

683. 12 U.S.C. § 5497(a)(1).

684. 144 S. Ct. 1474, 1482 (2024).

685. *Id.* at 448 (Alito, J., dissenting).

686. *United States v. MacCollom*, 426 U.S. 317, 321 (1976).

687. 1 William Blackstone, *Commentaries* *153.

688. *Id.*

689. *Id.*

690. Articles of Confederation of 1781, art. VI.

691. Thomas Jefferson to George Wythe (August 13, 1786), https://founders.archives.gov/documents/Jefferson/01-10-02-0162.

692. Burke quoted in John C. Meleney, *The Public Life of Aedanus Burke* 85 (1989).

693. *Id.*

694. *SGT View* 234.

695. Articles of Confederation of 1781, art. VI.

696. *SGT View* 234.

697. Douglas R. Hume, *Between "The Rock" and a Hard Case: Application of the Emoluments Clauses for a New Political Era*, 2018 Pepp. L. Rev. 68, 73–74 (2018).

698. *Federalist* No. 22, at 108 (Alexander Hamilton) (Bantam Books, 1982).

699. *Federalist* No. 44, at 226 (James Madison) (Bantam Books, 1982).

700. *JM Notes* 29.

701. *Id.* at 15.

702. *JM Notes* 542.

703. *Federalist* No. 44, at 226 (James Madison) (Bantam Books, 1982).

704. *Home Bldg. & Loan Ass'n v. Blaisdell*, 290 U.S. 398, 454 (1934) (Sutherland, J., dissenting).

705. Northwest Ord. art. II.

706. *JM Notes* 542.

707. *Id.*

708. *Elliot's Debates* 1:376.

709. 10 U.S. 87 (1810).

710. 17 U.S. 518 (1819).

711. Douglas W. Kmiec & John O. McGinnis, *The Contract Clause: A Return to the Original Understanding*, 14 Hastings Const. L.Q. 525, 534 (1987) ("Thus, the history of the Clause suggests that it was aimed at all retrospective, redistributive schemes in violation of vested contractual rights, of which debtor relief was merely a prime example.").

712. 25 U.S. 213 (1827).

713. *Id.* at 259.

714. *Federalist* No. 44, p. 227 (James Madison) (Bantam Books, 1982).

715. 290 U.S. 398 (1934).

716. *Id.* at 437.

717. *Id.* at 438.

718. *Id.* at 450 (Sutherland, J., dissenting).

719. *Camps Newfound/Owatonna, Inc. v. Town of Harrison, Me.*, 520 U.S. 564, 628 (1997) (Thomas, J., dissenting).

720. *JM Notes* 7.

721. *Id.*

722. *Id.*

723. *Elliot's Debates* 3:67-68.

724. Brutus, Essay 1 (1787), *TAF* 376.

725. *Id.*

726. *Id.* at 377.

727. *Elliot's Debates* 3:481.

728. *Id.*

729. *See Brown v. Maryland*, 25 U.S. 419 (1827).

730. 75 U.S. 123 (1868).

731. *Comptroller of Treasury of Maryland v. Wynne*, 575 U.S. 542, 572 (2015) (Thomas, J., dissenting).

732. *Camps*, 520 U.S. at 637 (Thomas, J., dissenting).

733. *SGT View* 248.

734. *Id.*

735. Erik M. Jensen, *Quirky Constitutional Provisions Matter: The Tonnage Clause, Polar Tankers, and State Taxation of Commerce*, 18 Geo. Mason L. Rev. 669 (2011) (internal quotation marks omitted).

736. *Id.*

737. *JM Notes* 645.

738. 434 U.S. 452, 473 (1978).

739. James Madison, Speech on the Bank Bill (1791), reprinted in *Liberty and Order* 73 (Lance Banning ed., 2004).

ARTICLE II

1. Thomas Jefferson, A Draft Constitution for Virginia (1783), reprinted in *The Complete Jefferson* 114 (S. Padover ed., 1943).

2. Gordon Wood, *The Creation of the American Republic* 136 (1969).

3. M. J. C. Vile, *Constitutionalism and the Separation of Powers* 148 (1998).

4. *JM Notes* 46.

5. *Id.*

6. *Id.* at 31.

7. *Id.* at 46.

8. *Id.*

9. *Id.* at 58.

10. *Id.* at 59.

11. *Id.* at 60.

12. *Id.* at 46.

13. *Id.*

14. *Id.* at 310.

15. *Federalist* No. 72, at 367 (Alexander Hamilton) (Bantam Books, 1982).

16. *JM Notes* 312.

17. *Id.*

18. *JS Exposition* 205.

19. *Id.*

20. *Elliot's Debates* 3:56.

21. *Elliot's Debates* 4:311.

22. An Old Whig, Essay V (1787), *TAF* 343.

23. Philadelphiensis IX, *Freeman's Journal*, Feb. 6, 1788, https://csac.history.wisc.edu/wp-content/uploads/sites/281/2017/07/Philadelphiensis_IX.pdf.

24. Americanus II (1787), reprinted in *The Debate on the Constitution* 417 (1993).

25. *Id.*

26. Washington's Neutrality Proclamation (1793), *PHD* 1.

27. U.S. Const. art I, § 1 (emphasis added).

28. Pacificus No. 1 (1793), *PHD* 13.

29. *Id.* at 16.

30. Robert G. Natelson, *The Original Meaning of the Constitution's "Executive Vesting Clause"—Evidence from Eighteenth-Century Drafting Practice*, 31 Whittier L. Rev. 1, 29 (2009).

31. Helvidius No. 1 (1793), *PHD* 58.

32. *Id.* at 59.

33. See William Michael Treanor, *Gouverneur Morris and the Drafting of the Federalist Constitution*, 21 Geo. J.L. & Pub. Pol'y 1, 19 (2023).

34. *Myers v. United States*, 272 U.S. 52, 230–31 (1926).

35. John Yoo, *Military Interrogation of Alien Unlawful Combatants Held Outside the United States* 5 (2003), https://www.aclu.org/sites/default/files/pdfs/safefree/yoo_army_torture_memo.pdf.

36. Bureau of Justice, *Executive Orders on Privacy and Civil Liberties and the Information Sharing Environment*, https://bja.ojp.gov/program/it/privacy-civil-liberties/authorities/executive-orders (last visited Feb. 15, 2025).

37. *Id.*

38. *Id.*

39. Tara L. Branum, *President or King? The Use and Abuse of Executive Orders in Modern-Day America*, 28 J. Legis. 1, 21–22 (2002).

40. American Presidency Project, *Executive Orders by President*, https://www.presidency.ucsb.edu/statistics/data/executive-orders (last visited Feb. 15, 2025).

41. *Id.*

42. *Remarks by the President on Immigration* (June 15, 2012), https://obamawhitehouse.archives.gov/the-press-office/2012/06/15/remarks-president-immigration.

43. Michael Muskal, *"I Am Not King": Obama Tells Latino Voters He Can't Conjure Immigration Reform Alone*, L.A. Times, Oct. 25, 2010, https://www.latimes.com/archives/la-xpm-2010-oct-25-la-pn-obama-immigration-reform-20101026-story.html.

44. "Improving Education Outcomes by Empowering Parents, States, and Communities," White House, March 20, 2025, https://www.whitehouse.gov/presidential-actions/2025/03/improving-education-outcomes-by-empowering-parents-states-and-communities/.

45. TJ to Benjamin Rush (June 13, 1805), https://www.loc.gov/item/mtjbib014807/.

46. *JM Notes* 48.

47. *Id.* at 525.

48. *Id.*

49. *Id.* at 48.

50. *Id.* at 308.

51. *Id.* at 309.

52. *Id.* at 50.

53. *Id.* at 51.

54. *Id.*

55. *Id.* at 574.

56. *Id.* at 576.

57. *Id.* at 576–77.

58. *Id.* at 577.

59. *Federalist* No. 68, at 345 (Alexander Hamilton) (Bantam Books, 1982).

60. *Id.*

61. *Id.*

62. *JS Exposition* 207.

63. Early Argument Against the Electoral College, https://www.usgopo.com/anti-federalist-paper-72/ (last visited Feb. 25, 2025).

64. *Id.*

65. Mercy Otis Warren, *Observations on the new Constitution, and on the foederal and state conventions* (1788), https://quod.lib.umich.edu/e/evans/N16431.0001.001/1:2?rgn=div1;view=fulltext.

66. *Id.*

67. Alex Woodward, *Hillary Clinton Calls for Electoral College to Be Abolished After Casting First Vote in New York for Biden*, Independent, Dec. 15, 2020, https://www.independent.co.uk/news/world/americas/us-election-2020/hillary-clinton-biden-electoral-college-vote-b1773891.html.

68. @AOC, Twitter (Oct. 5, 2018).

69. *JM Notes* 577.

70. *Id.*

71. *Id.*

72. *Federalist* No. 10, at 43 (James Madison) (Bantam Books, 1982).

73. *Id.*

74. *Elliot's Debates* 4:105.

75. *Id.*

76. Seth Lipsky, *The Citizen's Constitution* 124 (2009).

77. *JS Exposition* 211.

78. *Id.* at 212.

79. *JM Notes* 575.

80. James C. Ho, Presidential Eligibility, in *The Heritage Guide to the Constitution* 190 (Edwin Meese III ed., 2005).

81. *Farrand Records* 3:61.

82. *Id.*

83. Lawrence B. Solum, *Originalism and the Natural Born Citizen Clause*, 107 Mich. L. Rev. First Impressions 22 (2008).

84. *Id.*

85. *Ex parte Grossman*, 267 U.S. 87, 108–9 (1925).

86. 1 William Blackstone, *Commentaries* *354.

87. *Id.* at *357.

88. *Id.*

89. Michael D. Ramsey, *The Original Meaning of "Natural Born,"* 20 U. Pa. J. Const. L. 199, 221 (2017).

90. 1 Annals of Congress of the United States 404 (Joseph Gales ed., 1834).

91. Valere Gaspard, *The Millions of Americans Who Are Ineligible to Be President Are Excluded from an Important Part of the American Dream* (March 10, 2022), https://blogs.lse.ac.uk/usappblog/2022/03/10/the-millions-of-americans-who-are-ineligible-be-president-are-excluded-from-an-important-part-of-the-american-dream/.

92. *Id.*

93. Edward J. Larson, *A Constitutional Afterthought: The Origins of the Vice Presidency, 1787 to 1804*, 44 Pepp. L. Rev. 515, 519 (2017).

94. *Id.*

95. *See* Oliver Perry Chitwood, *John Tyler: Champion of the Old South* 205 (1996).

96. Congressional Research Service, *Presidential Succession: Perspectives and Contemporary Issues for Congress* 4 (2020).

97. *Id.* at 5.

98. William F. Brown & Americo R. Cinquegrana, *The Realities of Presidential Succession: "The Emperor Has No Clones,"* 75 Geo. L.J. 1389, 1396 (1987).

99. *JM Notes* 52.

100. *Id.* at 55.

101. *Federalist* No. 73, at 371 (Alexander Hamilton) (Bantam Books, 1982).

102. *Id.*

103. *Farrand's Records* 2:172.

104. *JM Notes* 536.

105. *Id.*

106. *Westminster Confession of Faith* 22.1.

107. *WCF* 22.2.

108. *WCF* 22.3.

109. James E. Pfander, *So Help Me God: Religion and Presidential Oath Taking*, 16 Const. Comment. 549, 550 (1999).

110. *Id.*

111. Edward S. Corwin, *The Constitution and What It Means Today* 99 (1958).

112. Robert J. Reinstein, *The Limits of Executive Power*, 59 Am. U. L. Rev. 259, 310 (2009).

113. *JM Notes* 47 (internal quotation marks omitted).

114. *Farrand's Records* 2:171–72.

115. *Federalist* No. 69, at 350 (Alexander Hamilton) (Bantam Books, 1982).

116. *Elliot's Debates* 4:107.

117. *JM Notes* 488.

118. *Elliot's Debates* 5:131.

119. *JM Notes* 646.

120. John Yoo & James C. Ho, Commander in Chief, in *The Heritage Guide to the Constitution* 195 (Edwin Meese III ed., 2005).

121. Louis Fisher, *Domestic Commander in Chief: Early Checks by Other Branches*, 29 Cardozo L. Rev. 961, 962 (2008).

122. Washington, quoted in *id.* at 975.

123. Thomas Jefferson, Special Message to Congress on Foreign Policy (1805), reprinted in 2 *American State Papers* 613 (William Lowrie & Matthew St. Clair Clarke, eds., 1832).

124. *Id.*

125. *Id.*

126. Martin S. Sheffer, *Does Absolute Power Corrupt Absolutely? Part I. A Theoretical Review of Presidential War Powers*, 24 Okla. City U. L. Rev. 233, 234–36 (1999).

127. Robert J. Pushaw Jr., *Justifying Wartime Limits on Civil Rights and Liberties*, 12 Chap. L. Rev. 675, 684 (2009).

128. 343 U.S. 579, 582 (1952).

129. *Id.* at 587.

130. Alan L. Feld, *The Shrunken Power of the Purse*, 89 Boston U. L. Rev. 487, 489 (2009).

131. *JM Notes* 517.

132. JM to TJ (June 30, 1789), *TRL* 1:621.

133. *Id.*

134. *Id.* at 621–22.

135. *Free Enter. Fund v. Pub. Co. Acct. Oversight Bd.*, 561 U.S. 477, 513–14 (2010).

136. *See Seila L. LLC v. Consumer Fin. Prot. Bureau*, 140 S. Ct. 2183, 2192 (2020).

137. 140 S. Ct. 2183 (2020).

138. *Id.* at 2197.

139. *Id.* at 2203.

140. *Edmond v. United States*, 520 U.S. 651, 663 (1997).

141. *JM Notes* 461.

142. *Id.*

143. Louis Fisher, *Congressional Participation in the Treaty Process*, 137 U. Pa. L. Rev. 1511, 1512 (1989).

144. *Federalist* No. 64, at 327 (John Jay) (Bantam Books, 1982).

145. Hampden, *A Note Protesting the Treaty-Making Provisions of the Constitution* (1788), https://famguardian.org/Publications/AntiFederalist-Papers/afp75.htm.

146. *Id.*

147. Louis Fisher, *Congressional Participation in the Treaty Process*, 137 U. Pa. L. Rev. 1511, 1515 (1989).

148. *Federalist* No. 75, at 380–81 (Alexander Hamilton) (Bantam Books, 1982).

149. *JM Notes* 599.

150. *Elliot's Debates* 4:135.

151. *Id.*

152. *Federalist* No. 67, at 342 (Alexander Hamilton) (Bantam Books, 1982).

153. Hamilton quoted in Jonathan Turley, *Constitutional Adverse Possession: Recess Appointments and the Role of Historical Practice in Constitutional Interpretation*, 2013 Wis. L. Rev. 965, 978 (2013).

154. 573 U.S. 513, 538 (2014).

155. *Id.* at 575 (Scalia, J., concurring).

156. *SGT View* 280.

157. Keith E. Whittington, *The State of the Union Is a Presidential Pep Rally*, 28 Yale L. & Pol'y Rev. 37, 47 (2010).

158. *Federalist* No. 69, at 352 (Alexander Hamilton) (Bantam Books, 1982).

159. *Id.*

160. Alexander Hamilton, Pacificus I (1793), *PHD* 15.

161. James Madison, Helvidius III (1793), *PHD* 75.

162. William Rawle, *A View of the Constitution* 119 (1993) (1825).

163. *JW Works* 2:878.

164. The Bill of Rights (1689), reprinted in *From Magna Carta to the Constitution* 39 (David L. Brooks ed., 1993); *see also Kendall v. U.S. ex rel. Stokes*, 37 U.S. 524, 525, 9 L. Ed. 1181 (1838) ("This doctrine cannot receive the sanction of this Court. It would be vesting in the President a dispensing power, which has no countenance for its support in any part of the constitution; and is asserting a principle, which if carried out in its results to all cases falling within it, would be clothing the President with a power to control the legislation of congress, and paralyze the administration of justice.").

165. Kiel Brennan-Marquez, *The Philosophy and Jurisprudence of Chief Justice Roberts*, 2014 Utah L. Rev. 137, 149 (2014).

166. Richard A. Epstein, *Why the Modern Administrative State Is Inconsistent with the Rule of Law*, 3 N.Y.U. J.L. & Liberty 491, 496 (2008).

167. *Black's Law Dictionary* 186 (6th ed. 1991).

168. *JS Exposition* 223.

169. Paul J. Larkin, *Wholesale-Level Clemency: Reconciling the Pardon and Take Care Clauses*, 19 U. St. Thomas L.J. 534, 553 (2023).

170. Nixon, quoted in Encyclopedia.com, *Impoundment*, https://www.encyclopedia.com/law/encyclopedias-almanacs-transcripts-and-maps/impoundment (last visited Feb. 15, 2025).

171. *But see Kendall v. U.S. ex rel. Stokes*, 37 U.S. 524, 525 (1838) ("To contend that the obligations imposed on the President to see the laws faithfully executed, implies a power to forbid their execution; is a novel construction of the constitution, and is entirely inadmissible."). Many scholars contend that "*Kendall* may only be cited for the proposition that a writ of mandamus is available to compel performance of a nondiscretionary, 'ministerial' obligation to pay prior contractual claims." Irwin R. Kramer, *The Impoundment Control Act of 1974: An Unconstitutional Solution to a Constitutional Problem*, 58 UMKC L. Rev. 157, 159 (1990).

172. Louis Fisher, *Constitutional Freedoms in Times of National Crisis*, 33 Vt. L. Rev. 627, 637 (2009).

173. U.S. Const. art. III, § 3, cl. 1.

174. *Black's Law Dictionary* 132 (6th ed. 1991).

175. Ford, quoted in Evan Gerstmann, *Impeachable Offences Are "Whatever a Majority of the House of Representatives Considers Them to Be,"* Forbes

(Jan. 11, 2021), https://www.forbes.com/sites/evangerstmann/2021/01/11/impeachable-offences-are-whatever-a-majority-of-the-house-of-representatives-considers-them-to-be/.

176. *JM Notes* 605.

177. *Id.*

178. *Id.* at 606.

179. Stephen B. Presser, *Would George Washington Have Wanted Bill Clinton Impeached?*, 67 Geo. Wash. L. Rev. 666, 674 (1999).

180. *Federalist* No. 65, at 331 (Alexander Hamilton) (Bantam Books, 1982).

181. *See* Buckner F. Melton Jr., *Let Me Be Blunt: In Blount, the Senate Never Said That Senators Aren't Impeachable*, 33 Quinnipiac L. Rev. 33, 38 (2014).

182. Edmund Randolph, Governor Edmund Randolph's Reasons for Not Signing the Constitution (1787), reprinted in *The Debate on the Constitution* 610 (1993).

183. *Elliot's Debates* 3:397.

184. Benjamin Cassady, *"You've Got Your Crook, I've Got Mine": Why the Disqualification Clause Doesn't (Always) Disqualify*, 32 Quinnipiac L. Rev. 209, 267 (2014).

Article III

1. James I, Speech to the Judges in Star Chamber (1616), reprinted in *The Stuart Constitution* 84 (J. P. Kenyon ed., 1986).

2. *Id.* at 85.

3. Declaration of Independence (1776), *TFC* 1:10.

4. Articles of Confederation of 1781, art. IX.

5. *Id.*

6. *JM Notes* 32.

7. *Id.*

8. *JM Notes* 67.

9. *Id.* at 575.

10. *Id.* at 67.

11. *Federalist* No. 78, at 393 (Alexander Hamilton) (Bantam Books, 1982).

12. *Id.*

13. *SGT View* 291.

14. *Id.*

15. *Id.*

16. *Farrand's Records* 2:638.

17. Brutus, Essay XV (1788), *TAF* 478.

18. *Federalist* No. 78, at 393 (Alexander Hamilton) (Bantam Books, 1982).

19. *Id.* at 394.

20. 14 U.S. 304, 331 (1816).

21. Martin H. Redish & Curtis E. Woods, *Congressional Power to Control the Jurisdiction of Lower Federal Courts: A Critical Review and a New Synthesis*, 124 U. Pa. L. Rev. 45, 58–59 (1975).

22. *See* Robert N. Clinton, *A Mandatory View of Federal Court Jurisdiction: Early Implementation of and Departures from the Constitutional Plan*, 86 Colum. L. Rev. 1515, 1585 (1986).

23. *See, e.g.*, Steven G. Calabresi & Kevin H. Rhodes, *The Structural Constitution: Unitary Executive, Plural Judiciary*, 105 Harv. L. Rev. 1155 (1992).

24. Victoria J. Haneman, *Changing the Estate Planning Malpractice Landscape: Applying the Constructive Trust to Cure Testamentary Mistake*, 80 UMKC L. Rev. 91, 99 (2011).

25. Thomas O. Main, *Traditional Equity and Contemporary Procedure*, 78 Wash. L. Rev. 429, 430 (2003).

26. *JM Notes* 536.

27. John R. Kroger, *Supreme Court Equity, 1789–1835, and the History of American Judging*, 34 Hous. L. Rev. 1425, 1486 (1998).

28. *Farrand's Records* 2:39.

29. *JM Notes* 538.

30. *Id.* at 539.

31. *Id.*

32. *Id.*

33. 9 U.S. 344, 348 (1809).

34. *See* 28 U.S.C.A. § 1331 (defining federal question jurisdiction for the lower courts).

35. *Osborn v. Bank of U.S.*, 22 U.S. 738 (1824).

36. 246 U.S. 297 (1918).

37. *Id.* at 302.

38. 506 U.S. 224, 235 (1993).

39. *JM Notes* 120.

40. *Federalist* No. 78, at 393 (Alexander Hamilton) (Bantam Books, 1982).

41. Articles of Confederation of 1781, art. IX.

42. *Chisholm v. Georgia*, 2 U.S. 419, 475 (1793).

43. *Id.*

44. Articles of Confederation of 1781, art. IX.

45. *Chisholm*, 2 U.S. at 475.

46. *Black's Law Dictionary* 476 (6th ed. 1991).

47. *Federalist* No. 81, at 414 (Alexander Hamilton) (Bantam Books, 1982).

48. *Elliot's Debates* 3:533.

49. *Id.* at 555.

50. 134 U.S. 1, 11 (1890).

51. 18 U.S.C. § 1332.

52. 13 U.S. 292, 322 (1815).

53. *JM Notes* 32. The proposed council could also review congressional decisions to nullify state law. Under the Virginia Plan, Congress would have had the power to review state legislation.
54. *Id.* at 61.
55. *Id.* at 340.
56. *Id.* at 61.
57. *Id.* at 341.
58. *Id.* at 336.
59. *Id.* at 337.
60. *Id.*
61. Sylvia Snowiss, *Judicial Review and the Law of the Constitution* 60 (1990).
62. *Federalist* No. 78, at 395 (Alexander Hamilton) (Bantam Books, 1982).
63. *Id.*
64. *Id.*
65. *Id.* at 395.
66. *Id.*
67. *Id.* at 396.
68. *Kamper v. Hawkins*, 3 Va. (1 Va. Cas.) 20 (1793). For the ease of the reader, pinpoint citations will be to the Westlaw citation: 1793 WL 248, *1 (Va. Nov. 16, 1793). For a good discussion on the background to *Kamper*, see Charles T. Cullen, *St. George Tucker and Law in Virginia* 120–26 (1971) (Ph.D. dissertation University of Virginia).
69. *Black's Law Dictionary* 540 (6th ed. 1991).
70. *Kamper*, 1793 WL at *60.
71. *Id.* at *35.
72. *Id.* at *36.
73. *Id.* at *42.
74. Advertisement in Report of a case . . . 84 (A. M'Kenzie & Co. 1794).
75. *Id.*
76. TJ to Abigail Adams (September 11, 1804), reprinted in *The Adams-Jefferson Letters* 279 (Lester J. Cappon ed., 2012).
77. *Id.*
78. *Id.*
79. *Id.*
80. *Id.* Jefferson was not the only president to adhere to departmentalism. *See* Keith E. Whittington, *Presidential Challenges to Judicial Supremacy and the Politics of Constitutional Meaning*, 33 Polity 367, 369 (2001).
81. Thomas Jefferson, *Notes on the State of Virginia* 221 (William Peden ed., 1954) (1785).
82. TJ to William Johnson (June 12, 1823), in *VCCG* 270.
83. Abel Parker Upshur, *Our Federal Government* 82 (2015) (1868); *see also* John C. Calhoun, *Exposition and Protest* 345 (1828), reprinted in *Union and Liberty* (Ross M. Lence ed., 1992).
84. *Id.* at 104.
85. *Black's Law Dictionary* 593 (6th ed. 1991).
86. Alexander Bickel, *The Supreme Court and the Idea of Progress* 112 (1970).
87. *Black's Law Dictionary* 760 (6th ed. 1991).
88. 5 U.S. 137 (1803).
89. *Marbury*, 5 U.S. at 147.
90. *Elliot's Debates* 3:559–60.
91. *Federalist* No. 81, at 417 (Alexander Hamilton) (Bantam Books, 1982).
92. 74 U.S. 506 (1868).
93. *Id.* at 514.
94. *Id.* at 515.
95. *Federalist* No. 81, at 416 (Alexander Hamilton) (Bantam Books, 1982).
96. U.S. Const. amend. VII.
97. For a good discussion of scholarship aimed at limiting congressional authority over the federal courts, see John Eidsmoe, *The Article III Exceptions Clause: Any Exceptions to the Power of Congress to Make Exceptions?*, 19 Regent U. L. Rev. 95, 129–43 (2006).
98. William J. Quirk, *Courts & Congress: America's Unwritten Constitution* 35 (2008).
99. *Id.* at 213.
100. 29 U.S.C. § 101.
101. William J. Quirk, *Courts & Congress: America's Unwritten Constitution* 36 (2008).
102. Declaration of Independence (1776), *TFC* 1:10.
103. *See* William E. Nelson, *Americanization of Common Law* 28–29 (1975).
104. *See id.*
105. *See* Federal Farmer, Letter XV (1788), *TAF* 275.
106. *JM Notes* 630.
107. Lochlan F. Shelfer, *How the Constitution Shall Not Be Construed*, 2017 B.Y.U. L. Rev. 331, 351 (2017).
108. The Federal Farmer, Letter III (1787), *TAF* 169.
109. 195 U.S. 65, 68 (1904).
110. *Lewis v. United States*, 518 U.S. 322, 326 (1996).
111. *Elliot's Debates* 2:109–10.
112. *Elliot's Debates* 4:154.
113. *Id.*
114. Amendments Passed by the House of Representatives (1789), reprinted in Richard Labunski, *James Madison and the Struggles for the Bill of Rights* 274 (2006).
115. U.S. Const. amend. VI.

116. John Gramlich, *Only 2% of Federal Criminal Defendants Go to Trial, and Most Who Do Are Found Guilty* (June 11, 2019), https://www.pewresearch.org/short-reads/2019/06/11/only-2-of-federal-criminal-defendants-go-to-trial-and-most-who-do-are-found-guilty/.

117. Monika Jain, *Mitigating the Dangers of Capital Convictions Based on Eyewitness Testimony Through Treason's Two-Witness Rule*, 91 J. Crim. L. & Criminology 761, 775 (2001) (internal quotation marks omitted).

118. *Elliot's Debates* 3:469.

119. 2 William Blackstone, *Commentaries* *75.

120. James G. Wilson, *Chaining the Leviathan: The Unconstitutionality of Executing Those Convicted of Treason*, 45 U. Pitt. L. Rev. 99, 105 (1983).

121. Monika Jain, *Mitigating the Dangers of Capital Convictions Based on Eyewitness Testimony Through Treason's Two-Witness Rule*, 91 J. Crim. L. & Criminology 761, 775 (2001).

122. An Act Declaring What Shall be Treason (1776), *TFC* 4:430.

123. *Federalist* No. 43, at 219 (James Madison) (Bantam Books, 1982).

124. An Act Declaring What Shall be Treason (1776), *TFC* 4:430.

125. Akhil Reed Amar, *America's Constitution* 244 (2005).

126. 8 U.S. (4 Cranch) 75 (1807).

127. *Id.* at 126.

128. An Act Declaring What Shall be Treason (1776), *TFC* 4:430.

129. *Federalist* No. 43, at 219 (James Madison) (Bantam Books, 1982).

130. *Wallach v. Van Riswick*, 92 U.S. 202, 210 (1875).

Articles IV–VII

1. Articles of Confederation of 1781, art. IV.

2. *JM Notes* 546.

3. *Id.*

4. Timothy Joseph Keefer, *DOMA as a Defensible Exercise of Congressional Power Under the Full-Faith-and-Credit Clause*, 54 Wash. & Lee L. Rev. 1635, 1643 (1997).

5. 28 U.S.C. § 1738.

6. 570 U.S. 744, 770 (2013).

7. Mark D. Rosen, *Why the Defense of Marriage Act Is Not (Yet?) Unconstitutional: Lawrence, Full Faith and Credit, and the Many Societal Actors That Determine What the Constitution Requires*, 90 Minn. L. Rev. 915, 940 (2006).

8. Articles of Confederation of 1781, art. IV.

9. Robert G. Natelson, *The Original Meaning of the Privileges and Immunities Clause*, 43 Ga. L. Rev. 1117, 1166 (2009).

10. *See id.* at 1192.

11. *Livingston v. Van Ingen*, 1812 WL *1156 (N.Y. 1812), overruled by *N. River Steamboat Co. v. Livingston*, 1825 WL *1859 (N.Y. 1825).

12. *Campbell v. Morris*, 3 H. & McH. 535, 554 (Md. Gen. 1797), *rev'd* (June 1800).

13. Kurt T. Lash, *The Origins of the Privileges or Immunities Clause, Part i: "Privileges and Immunities" as an Antebellum Term of Art*, 98 Geo. L.J. 1241, 1263 (2010); *see also* Randy E. Barnett, *Restoring the Lost Constitution* 193 (2004) ("This somewhat enigmatic provision was originally meant to protect the rights of out-of-state citizens from discrimination when they traveled to another state.").

14. 6 Fed. Cas. 546 (C.C. E.D. Pa. 1823).

15. Robert H. Bork, *The Tempting of America* 181 (1990).

16. 436 U.S. 371 (1978).

17. *Id.* at 388.

18. *Id.*

19. 470 U.S. 274 (1985).

20. *Id.* at 281.

21. Articles of Confederation of 1781, art. IV.

22. *Michigan v. Doran*, 439 U.S. 282, 287 (1978).

23. *Id.* at 289.

24. 65 U.S. 66 (1861).

25. *Id.* at 109–10.

26. *Id.* at 110.

27. *Puerto Rico v. Branstad*, 483 U.S. 219, 230 (1987).

28. Northwest Ord. art. VI.

29. *JM Notes* 546.

30. *Elliot's Debates* 4:286.

31. 1 Stat. 302 (1793).

32. 41 U.S. 539 (1842).

33. 3 Wis. 1 (1854).

34. *Ableman v. Booth*, 62 U.S. 506 (1858).

35. *JM Notes* 552.

36. *Id.*

37. *Oregon ex rel. State Land Bd. v. Corvallis Sand & Gravel Co.*, 429 U.S. 363, 370 (1977).

38. William Michael Treanor, *The Case of the Dishonest Scrivener: Gouverneur Morris and the Creation of the Federalist Constitution*, 120 Mich. L. Rev. 1, 99 (2021).

39. David F. Forte, New States Clause, in *The Heritage Guide to the Constitution* 278 (Edwin Meese III ed., 2005).

40. David Benner, *Secession Hypocrisy: The Case of West Virginia* (2016), https://www.abbevilleinstitute.org/secession-hypocrisy-the-case-of-west-virginia/.

41. *Federalist* No. 38, at 188 (James Madison) (Bantam Books, 1982).

42. *United States v. Gratiot*, 39 U.S. 526, 537 (1840).

43. Kevin R. C. Gutzman, *The Politically Incorrect Guide to the Constitution* 96 (2007).

44. Jefferson Davis, 1 *Rise and Fall of the Confederate Government* 70 (1990).

45. 60 U.S. 393 (1857).

46. *Id.* at 450.

47. Carl Brent Swisher, *Roger B. Taney* 508 (1933).

48. *Examining Bd. of Engineers, Architects & Surveyors v. Flores de Otero*, 426 U.S. 572, 596 n.28 (1976); *United States v. Lebron-Caceres*, 157 F. Supp. 3d 80, 89 (D.P.R. 2016), *amended* (D.P.R. Jan. 15, 2016).

49. *Kleppe v. New Mexico*, 426 U.S. 529, 539 (1976) (cleaned up).

50. *Id.* at 536.

51. *Id.* at 536–37.

52. *See* Jeffrey M. Schmitt, *Limiting the Property Clause*, 20 Nev. L.J. 145, 146 (2019) ("In spite of the principle that Congress is limited to its enumerated powers, the federal government effectively has a police power over one-third of the country.").

53. Draft of Articles of Confederation (1776), reprinted in 1 *Constitutional Documents and Records, 1776–1797* 81 (Merrill Jensen ed., 1976).

54. *JM Notes* 32.

55. *Id.* at 104.

56. *Farrand's Records* 1:206.

57. *JM Notes* 322.

58. *JM Notes* 475.

59. *Federalist* No. 43, at 220 (James Madison) (Bantam Books, 1982).

60. *Id.* at 221.

61. William Rawle, *A View of the Constitution* 234 (1993) (1825).

62. *Id.* at 235.

63. *See* William J. Watkins Jr., *Crossroads for Liberty: Recovering the Anti-Federalist Values of America's First Constitution* 49–50 (2016).

64. *See Luther v. Borden*, 48 U.S. 1, 47 (1849).

65. Articles of Confederation of 1781, art. XIII.

66. *JM Notes* 104.

67. *Id.*

68. *Id.* at 69.

69. *Id.* at 609.

70. *Id.*

71. *Id.*

72. *Id.* at 649.

73. *Id.*

74. An Old Whig, Essay I (1787), *TAF* 318.

75. Federal Farmer, Letter IV (1787), *TAF* 179.

76. *Id.*

77. *Elliot's Debates* 3:49.

78. *Id.* at 101.

79. *Elliot's Debates* 4:178.

80. *See Hollingsworth v. Virginia*, 3 U.S. 378 (1798).

81. *See* James Kenneth Rogers, *The Other Way to Amend the Constitution: The Article V Constitutional Convention Amendment Process*, 30 Harv. J. L. & Pub. Pol'y 1005, 1021 (2007).

82. William J. Quirk & Robert Wilcox, *A 28th Amendment: Democracy and Constitutional Change*, Chronicles, July 1996, at 20.

83. *Federalist* No. 43, at 223 (James Madison) (Bantam Books, 1982).

84. *Legislative and Documentary History of the Bank of the United States* 15 (M. St. Clair Clarke & D. A. Hall eds., 1832).

85. Articles of Confederation of 1781, art. XII.

86. U.S. Treasury, What Is the National Debt?, https://fiscaldata.treasury.gov/americas-finance-guide/national-debt/#:~:text=The%20national%20debt%20is%20the,)%2C%20a%20budget%20deficit%20results (last visited March 29, 2025).

87. *JM Notes* 320.

88. *Id.* at 512.

89. *Id.*

90. *Federalist* No. 43, at 223 (James Madison) (Bantam Books, 1982).

91. Articles of Confederation of 1781, art. XIII.

92. *JM Notes* 31.

93. *Id.* at 44.

94. *Id.* at 88.

95. *Id.*

96. *Id.*

97. *Id.*

98. *Id.* at 89.

99. *Id.* at 203.

100. *Id.* at 305–6.

101. *Id.* at 390.

102. *Id.* at 626.

103. An Old Whig, Essay II (1787), *TAF* 326.

104. Brutus, Essay I (1787), *TAF* 375.

105. *Id.*

106. A Federal Republican, *A Review of the Constitution* (Nov. 28, 1787), https://teachingamericanhistory.org/document/a-federal-republican-a-review-of-the-constitution.

107. *Federalist* No. 33, at 155 (Alexander Hamilton) (Bantam Books, 1982).

108. *Id.* at 155–56.

109. *SGT View* 304.

110. *Id.*

111. *Id.*

112. *Virginia Uranium, Inc. v. Warren*, 139 S. Ct. 1894, 1901 (2019). Some commentators, such as Mark Pulliam, believe that the Supremacy Clause forbids considering nullification as a constitutional option. *See* Mark Pulliam, *Nullification of the Constitution* (2024), https://lawliberty.org/forum/nullification-or-the-constitution/. All the Supremacy Clause declares is that statutes made pursuant to the Constitution are supreme law throughout the union. The real question is who has the final word on whether a statute is consistent with the Constitution. The Supremacy Clause does not settle this issue.

113. *Black's Law Dictionary* 815 (6th ed. 1991).

114. *Hoagland v. Town of Clear Lake*, 415 F.3d 693, 696 (7th Cir. 2005).

115. *Id.* (internal quotation marks omitted).

116. *Id.* (internal quotation marks omitted).

117. Paul Wolfson, *Preemption and Federalism: The Missing Link*, 16 Hastings Const. L.Q. 69, 88 (1988).

118. *Wyeth v. Levine*, 555 U.S. 555, 587 (2009) (Thomas, J., concurring).

119. *Id.* at 587–88.

120. *Id.* at 588.

121. *See Lipschultz v. Charter Advanced Servs. (MN), LLC*, 140 S. Ct. 6, 7 (2019) (Thomas, J., concurring).

122. *JM Notes* 33.

123. *Federalist* No. 44, at 231 (James Madison) (Bantam Books, ed., 1982).

124. Matthew Spalding, Oaths Clause, in *The Heritage Guide to the Constitution* 295 (Edwin Meese III ed., 2005).

125. *Elliot's Debates* 2:118.

126. *Id.* at 119.

127. *JM Notes* 33.

128. *Id.* at 70.

129. *Id.* at 126.

130. *Id.* at 348.

131. *Id.* at 350–51.

132. *TFC* 1:6.

133. Gordon S. Wood, *The Creation of the American Republic 1776–1787* 309 (1969).

134. Alexis de Tocqueville, 1 *Democracy in America* 55 (1990) (1835).

135. Willi Paul Adams, *The First American Constitutions* 20 (2001) ("In Massachusetts the signal step was taken of formally separating the legislative activity and the task of creating a constitution."); Pauline Maier, *Ratification* 139 (2010) (describing how Massachusetts "transformed popular sovereignty from a theory to a process"). *But see* Marc W. Kruman, *State Constitution Making in Revolutionary America* 15–33 (1997) (Massachusetts receives too much credit inasmuch as other states understood the constituent power and had elected special conventions to draft constitutions; the difference between Massachusetts and several other states is that the former submitted the constitution for popular ratification, while the latter did not).

136. Elisha P. Douglas, *Rebels and Democrats* 188 (1955); R. R. Palmer, *The Age of Democratic Revolution* 222 (1959).

137. Thomas Jefferson, Notes on the State of Virginia (1781–85), reprinted in *The Complete Jefferson* (Saul K. Padover ed., 1943).

138. *SGT View* 20.

139. *Id.* at 19.

140. *JW Works* 718–19.

141. *Id.* at 728.

142. *Elliot's Debates* 2:497 & 499.

143. Akhil Reed Amar, *Of Sovereignty and Federalism*, 96 Yale L.J. 1425, 1520 (1987).

144. *Elliot's Debates* 3:37.

145. *Id.*

146. *JM Notes* 278.

147. Declaration and Resolves of the First Continental Congress, reprinted in *From Magna Carta to the Constitution* 53 (David L. Brooks ed., 1993).

148. Dumas Malone, *Jefferson and the Ordeal of Liberty* 402 (1962).

149. James Madison, Report of 1800, *VCCG* 160.

150. *Id.* at 161.

151. TJ to William H. Crawford (June 20, 1816), https://founders.archives.gov/documents/Jefferson/03-10-02-0101#:~:text=if%20any%20state%20in%20the,in%20saying%20'let%20us%20separate.

152. Alexis de Tocqueville, 1 *Democracy in America* 387 (1990) (1835).

153. Rebert Remini, 3 *Andrew Jackson and the Course of American Democracy* 31 (1984).

154. 74 U.S. 700 (1868).

Amendments

1. *JM Notes* 630.
2. *Id.*
3. Federal Farmer, Letter IV (1787), *TAF* 173.
4. *Id.* at 174.
5. A Maryland Farmer, Essay I (1788), *TAF* 560.
6. Brutus, Essay II (1787), *TAF* 385.
7. *Id.* at 387.
8. *Id.*
9. *Id.*
10. *Id.*
11. *JW Works* 1:171.
12. *Id.* at 172.
13. *Id.*
14. *Id.*
15. *Id.*
16. JM to TJ (April 22, 1788), *TRL* 1:534.
17. Proceedings of the Meetings at Harrisburg (1788), *Elliot's Debates* 2:543.
18. *Id.*
19. *Id.*
20. *Gazette of the United States*, June 10, 1789, *Creating* 65.
21. *Daily Advertiser*, June 9, 1789, *Creating* 64.
22. *Gazette of the United States*, June 10, 1789, *Creating* 65.
23. *Gazette of the United States*, June 10, 1789, *Creating* 64.
24. *Gazette of the United States*, June 10, 1789, *Creating* 68.
25. Amendments to the Constitution, September 28, 1789, *Creating* 3.
26. 32 U.S. (7 Pet.) 243, 250 (1833).
27. *Id.*
28. *Elliot's Debates* 3:658–59.
29. Kevin R. C. Gutzman, *James Madison and the Making of America* 44 (2012).
30. James Madison, Memorial and Remonstrance Against Religious Assessments (1785), *TFC* 5:82.
31. Madison Resolution (1789), reprinted in *Creating* 12.
32. *Id.* at 157.
33. *Id.*
34. TJ to The Danbury Baptist Association (1802), reprinted in *The Complete Jefferson* 519 (S. Padover ed., 1943).
35. *Reynolds v. United States*, 98 U.S. 145, 164 (1878).
36. Northwest Ord. art. III.
37. George Washington, *Thanksgiving Proclamation* (1789), https://founders.archives.gov/documents/Washington/05-04-02-0091.
38. *JS Exposition* 316.
39. *Creating* 58.
40. Office of Legal Policy, *Religious Liberty Under the Free Exercise Clause* 7 (August 13, 1986).
41. *Id.* at 9.
42. *Federalist* No. 84, at 437 (Alexander Hamilton) (Bantam Books, 1982).
43. Mr. Madison's Report of 1800, *VCCG* 203.
44. *SGT View* 382.
45. Emmanuel Hiram Arnaud, *The Dismantling of Dissent: Militarization and the Right to Peaceably Assemble*, 101 Cornell L. Rev. 777, 787 (2016).
46. The Bill of Rights (1689) in *From Magna Carta to the Constitution* 39 (David L. Brooks ed., 1993).
47. *Creating* 151.
48. *Id.* at 152.
49. 403 U.S. 602 (1971).
50. *Lamb's Chapel v. Ctr. Moriches Union Free Sch. Dist.*, 508 U.S. 384, 398, (1993) (Scalia, J., concurring).
51. 492 U.S. 573, 598 (1989).
52. 545 U.S. 844, 881 (2005).
53. 545 U.S. 677, 691 (2005).
54. *Id.* at 691–92.
55. 2022 WL 2295034 (June 27, 2022).
56. *Id.*
57. *Id.*
58. 142 S. Ct. 1987 (2022).
59. *Id.* at 1997.
60. *Id.* at 1998.
61. 494 U.S. 872 (1990).
62. *Id.* at 874.
63. *Id.* at 888.
64. 573 U.S. 682 (2014).
65. 6 F.4th 1160, 1181 (10th Cir. 2021).
66. *See Masterpiece Cakeshop, Ltd. v. Colorado C.R. Comm'n*, 138 S. Ct. 1719, 1724 (2018).
67. *303 Creative LLC v. Elenis*, 600 U.S. ___, slip op. at 14 (2023) (cleaned up).
68. *Id.* at 12.
69. *Id.* at 15.
70. 142 S. Ct. 1583 (2022).
71. *Id.* at 1587.
72. 413 U.S. 15 (1973).
73. *Id.* at 27.
74. 299 U.S. 353, 364 (1937).
75. *Ward v. Rock Against Racism*, 491 U.S. 781, 791 (1989).

76. The Bill of Rights (1689) in *From Magna Carta to the Constitution* 40 (David L. Brooks ed., 1993).

77. James Warner, *Disarming the Disabled*, 18 Geo. Mason U. Civ. Rts. L.J. 267, 274 (2008).

78. Stephen P. Halbrook, *The Founders' Second Amendment* 5 (2008).

79. *Elliot's Debates* 3:659.

80. *Creating* 17.

81. Address of the Minority of the Pennsylvania Convention (1787), *TAF* 530.

82. Federal Farmer, Letter XVIII (1788), *TAF* 305.

83. Madison Resolution (1789), in *Creating* 12.

84. Coxe, quoted in Stephen P. Halbrook, *The Founders' Second Amendment* 257 (2008).

85. *Id.*

86. Eugene Volokh, *The Commonplace Second Amendment*, 73 N.Y.U. L. Rev. 793, 801 (1998).

87. *Id.*

88. *Id.* at 806–7.

89. 554 U.S. 570 (2008).

90. 561 U.S. 742 (2010).

91. 142 S. Ct. 2111, 2122 (2022).

92. *Id.*

93. *Id.* at 2164 (Breyer, J., dissenting).

94. *TFC* 5:212.

95. *TFC* 5:214.

96. *JS Exposition* 319.

97. *See, e.g.,* John Paul Stevens, *The Supreme Court's Worst Decision of My Tenure*, The Atlantic, May 14, 2019, https://www.theatlantic.com/ideas/archive/2019/05/john-paul-stevens-court-failed-gun-control/587272/.

98. 307 U.S. 174 (1939).

99. *Id.* at 178.

100. MoveOn, *Repeal the Second Amendment Now*, https://sign.moveon.org/petitions/repeal-the-second-amendment-6 (last visited Feb. 15, 2025).

101. *Heller*, 554 U.S. at 634 (emphasis in original).

102. The Bill of Rights (1689) in *From Magna Carta to the Constitution* 38 (David L. Brooks, ed., 1993).

103. *Elliot's Debates* 3:659.

104. Madison Resolution (1789), in *Creating* 12.

105. 381 U.S. 479 (1965).

106. Mark Puls, *Samuel Adams: Father of the American Revolution* 35 (2006).

107. James Otis, *Against Writs of Assistance* (1761), https://constitutioncenter.org/the-constitution/historic-document-library/detail/james-otis-against-writs-of-assistance-february-24-1761.

108. *Elliot's Debates* 3:588.

109. Brutus, Essay II (1787), *TAF* 388.

110. *Id.*

111. Madison Resolution (1789), in *Creating* 12–13.

112. 338 U.S. 25, 27–28 (1949).

113. 232 U.S. 383, 386 (1914).

114. Bradford P. Wilson, The Fourth Amendment as More Than a Form of Words: The View from the Founding, in *The Bill of Rights: Original Meaning and Current Understanding* 157 (Eugene W. Hickok ed., 1991).

115. 389 U.S. 347, 351 (1967).

116. *Id.*

117. *Id.* at 360 (Harlan, J., concurring).

118. 495 U.S. 91 (1990).

119. 525 U.S. 83 (1998).

120. 138 S. Ct. 1518, 1524 (2018).

121. 439 U.S. 128 (1978).

122. As Alexander Bickel has noted, American "[d]iversity implies less rather than more law, and certainly less centralized, national law." Alexander Bickel, *The Supreme Court and the Idea of Progress* 116 (1970).

123. *Elliot's Debates* 2:111.

124. *Id.*

125. *Elliot's Debates* 2:177.

126. *Creating* 13.

127. *TFC* 5:251.

128. *Id.*

129. *Id.* at 252.

130. *Id.*

131. *United States v. Mandujano*, 425 U.S. 564, 571 (1976).

132. 4 William Blackstone, *Commentaries* *335.

133. *Creating* 22.

134. *Elliot's Debates* 2:550.

135. G. Robert Blakely, Double Jeopardy, in *The Heritage Guide to the Constitution* 333 (Edwin Meese III ed., 2005).

136. *Creating* 12.

137. *TFC* 5:262.

138. *Puerto Rico v. Sanchez Valle*, 136 S. Ct. 1863, 1867 (2016).

139. 139 S. Ct. 1960 (2019).

140. *Id.* at 1964.

141. *Id.* at 1980 (Thomas, J., concurring).

142. § 2.10(c) History of the Privilege, 1 Crim. Proc. § 2.10(c) (4th ed.).

143. 384 U.S. 436, 444 (1966).

144. *Id.* at 519 (Harlan, J., dissenting).

145. 530 U.S. 428 (2000).

146. Magna Carta (1215) in *From Magna Carta to the Constitution* 9 (David L. Brooks ed., 1993) (emphasis added).

147. Hugo LaFayette Black, *A Constitutional Faith* 33 (1968).

148. Sir Edward Coke, 2 *Institutes* § 46, reprinted in *The Selected Writings of Sir Edward Coke* 849 (Steve Sheppard ed., 2003).

149. *SGT View* 148.

150. William Rawle, *A View of the Constitution* 114 (Walter D. Kennedy & James R. Kennedy eds., 1993).

151. *Fuentes v. Shevin*, 407 U.S. 67, 80 (1972).

152. *Bd. of Regents of State Colleges v. Roth*, 408 U.S. 564, 576 (1972).

153. *Id.* at 577.

154. *Pennsylvania Coal Co. v. Mahon*, 260 U.S. 393 (1922).

155. 505 U.S. 1003, 1019 (1992).

156. 545 U.S. 469 (2005).

157. *Elliot's Debates* 2:109.

158. *Id.* at 110.

159. *Id.*

160. *Id.* at 111.

161. *Elliot's Debates* 4:154.

162. *Elliot's Debates* 3:658.

163. *Creating* 13.

164. *Id.*

165. Magna Carta (1215) in *From Magna Carta to the Constitution* 9 (David L. Brooks ed., 1993).

166. *United States v. Ewell*, 383 U.S. 116, 120 (1966).

167. 407 U.S. 514, 530 (1972).

168. 18 U.S.C. § 3161(c)(1).

169. *Gannett Co. v. DePasquale*, 443 U.S. 368, 380 (1979).

170. 467 U.S. 39 (1984).

171. Caren Myers Morrison, *Jury 2.0*, 62 Hastings L.J. 1579, 1618–19 (2011).

172. *United States v. Burr*, 25 F. Cas. 49, 50 (C.C.D. Va. 1807).

173. *Thiel v. S. Pac. Co.*, 328 U.S. 217, 220 (1946).

174. *Id.*

175. *Acts* 25:16 (NIV).

176. 156 U.S. 237, 242 (1895).

177. *Crawford v. Washington*, 541 U.S. 36, 50–51 (2004).

178. *Id.*

179. *Washington v. Texas*, 388 U.S. 14, 19 (1967).

180. 304 U.S. 458 (1938).

181. *Id.* at 462–63.

182. 372 U.S. 335 (1963).

183. *Id.* at 344.

184. Michael R. Dreeben, *The Right to Present a Twinkie Defense*, 9 Green Bag 2d 347, 350 (2006) ("It is certainly true that the Sixth Amendment, as implemented by the Framers, did not encompass the right to appointed counsel.").

185. Federal Farmer, Letter IV (1787), *TAF* 176.

186. Federal Farmer, Letter XVI (1788), *TAF* 284.

187. *Elliot's Debates* 3:47.

188. *Id.* at 658.

189. *Creating* 13.

190. Lawrence B. Solum, *Originalist Methodology*, 84 U. Chi. L. Rev. 269, 282 (2017).

191. 28 F. Cas. 745, 750 (C.C.D. Mass, 1812).

192. Ann M. Scarlett, *Shareholders in the Jury Box: A Populist Check Against Corporate Mismanagement*, 78 U. Cin. L. Rev. 127, 141 (2009).

193. Richard Lorren Jolly, *The Administrative State's Jury Problem*, 98 Wash. L. Rev. 104 (2023).

194. *Granfinanciera, S.A. v. Nordberg*, 492 U.S. 33, 53–54 (1989).

195. *Atlas Roofing Co. v. Occupational Safety & Health Rev. Comm'n*, 430 U.S. 442, 455 (1977).

196. *SEC v. Jarkesy*, 144 S. Ct. 2117 (2024).

197. *Id.* at 2127.

198. John D. Bessler, *A Century in the Making: The Glorious Revolution, the American Revolution, and the Origins of the U.S. Constitution's Eighth Amendment*, 27 Wm. & Mary Bill Rts. J. 989, 1011 (2019).

199. *Elliot's Debates* 2:111.

200. *Id.*

201. *Elliot's Debates* 3:447.

202. *Id.*

203. Magna Carta (1215) in *From Magna Carta to the Constitution* 6 (David L. Brooks ed., 1993).

204. 139 S. Ct. 682 (2019).

205. *Genesis* 9:6 (ESV).

206. *Gregg v. Georgia*, 428 U.S. 227, 227 (1976) (Brennan, J., dissenting) (internal quotation marks omitted).

207. *Id.* (internal quotation marks omitted).

208. 920 F.3d 584, 617 & n.8 (9th Cir. 2019).

209. *Johnson v. City of Grants Pass*, Nos. 20-35752, 20-35881 (July 5, 2023).

210. *City of Grants Pass v. Johnson*, 144 S. Ct. 2202, 2216 (2024).

211. *See, e.g.*, Randy E. Barnett, *The Ninth Amendment: It Means What It Says*, 85 Tex. L. Rev. 1 (2006).

212. Kurt T. Lash, *The Lost Jurisprudence of the Ninth Amendment*, 83 Tex. L. Rev. 597, 604 (2005).

213. *Federalist* No. 45, at 236 (James Madison) (Bantam Books, 1982).

214. *Elliot's Debates* 3:301.

215. *Id.*

216. *Id.*

217. *Id.* at 451.

218. *Id.*

219. *Id.* at 464.

220. Federal Farmer Letter XVI (1788), *TAF* 281.

221. Brutus, Essay XII (1788), *TAF* 455.

222. *Creating* 19 & 21.

223. *Id.* at 12 & 14.

224. James Madison's Speech on the Bank Bill (1791), reprinted in *Liberty & Order* at 77.

225. 18 U.S. 1 (1820).

226. *Id.* at 49 (Story, J., dissenting).

227. Kurt T. Lash, *The Lost Jurisprudence of the Ninth Amendment*, 83 Tex. L. Rev. 597, 597 (2005).

228. *SGT View* 105.

229. *Id.*

230. Raoul Berger, *The Ninth Amendment*, 66 Cornell L. Rev. 1, 3 (1980).

231. 381 U.S. 479, 484 (1965).

232. *Id.* at 487 (Goldberg, J., concurring).

233. *Id.* at 520 (Black, J., dissenting).

234. 2022 WL 2276808 (June 24, 2022).

235. Articles of Confederation of 1781, art. II.

236. *Creating* 14.

237. A Citizen of America, An Examination into the Leading Principles of the Federal Constitution (1787), reprinted in *Friends of the Constitution* 405 (Colleen A. Sheehand & Gary L. McDowell eds., 1998).

238. *Id.*

239. An Old Whig, Essay II (1787), *TAF* 324.

240. An Old Whig, Essay IV (1787), *TAF* 335.

241. Brutus, Essay I (1787), *TAF* 377.

242. *Id.*

243. *Creating* 14.

244. *Id.* at 197.

245. *Id.*

246. *Id.*

247. *Id.*

248. Mr. Madison's Report of 1800, *VCCG* 161.

249. Thomas Jefferson, Draft of the Kentucky Resolutions (1798), in *Liberty and Order* 234 (Lance Banning ed., 2004).

250. *Id.*

251. *Id.*

252. 426 U.S. 833 (1985).

253. *Id.* at 843.

254. *Id.* at 845.

255. 469 U.S. 528, 531 (1985).

256. Thomas Jefferson, Opinion on the Bank (1791), reprinted in *Legislative and Documentary History of the Bank of the United States* 89 (M. St. Clair Clarke & D. A. Hall eds., 1832).

257. 2 U.S. 419 (1793).

258. *Id.* at 457.

259. William A. Fletcher, *A Historical Interpretation of the Eleventh Amendment: A Narrow Construction of an Affirmative Grant of Jurisdiction Rather Than a Prohibition Against Jurisdiction*, 35 Stan. L. Rev. 1033, 1058 (1983).

260. *Id.*

261. 517 U.S. 44, 72 (1996).

262. 527 U.S. 706 (1999).

263. *Id.* at 712.

264. *Id.* at 714.

265. *Id.* (internal quotation marks omitted).

266. 535 U.S. 743 (2002).

267. *Id.* at 751 (cleaned up).

268. *Id.* at 760.

269. *Id.* at 788 (Breyer, J., dissenting).

270. Joshua D. Hawley, *The Transformative Twelfth Amendment*, 55 Wm. & Mary L. Rev. 1501, 1514 (2014).

271. *TFC* 5:452.

272. *TFC* 5:459.

273. 3 U.S.C. § 15(b)(1).

274. Northwest Ord. art. VI.

275. 109 U.S. 3, 20 (1883); "While the thirteenth article of amendment was intended primarily to abolish African slavery, it equally forbids Mexican peonage or the Chinese coolie trade, when they amount to slavery or involuntary servitude; and the use of the word 'servitude' is intended to prohibit all forms of involuntary slavery of whatever class or name." *Slaughter-House Cases*, 83 U.S. 36, 37 (1872).

276. 219 U.S. 219 (1911).

277. *Id.* at 241.

278. 392 U.S. 409 (1968).

279. *Id.* at 440.

280. *City of Boerne v. Flores*, 521 U.S. 507, 519 (1997) (cleaned up).

281. Stevens, quoted in Clarence B. Carson, *The Sections and the Civil War* 187 (1985).

282. William E. Nelson, *The Fourteenth Amendment* 43 (1988).

283. Henry J. Abraham, *Freedom and the Court* 44 (1988).

284. William E. Nelson, *The Fourteenth Amendment* 197 (1988).

285. 112 U.S. 94, 102 (1884).

286. 169 U.S. 649 (1898).

287. Raoul Berger, *Government by Judiciary* 64 (1997); *see also* Alfred Avins, Reader's Guide, in *The Reconstruction Amendments' Debates* xi (1967); Alexander M. Bickel, *The Original Understanding and the Segregation Decision*, 69 Harv. L. Rev. 1, 58 (1955) (noting that "section 1 of the fourteenth amendment, like section 1 of the Civil Rights Act of 1866, carried out the relatively narrow objectives of the Moderates, and hence, as originally understood, was meant to apply neither to jury service, nor suffrage, nor antimiscegenation statutes, nor segregation.").

288. 130 S. Ct. 3020, 3023 (2010).

289. See Virginia Commission on Constitutional Government, *The Reconstruction Amendments' Debates* 164 (1967).

290. *See* Robert G. Natelson, *The Original Meaning of the Privileges and Immunities Clause*, 43 Ga. L. Rev. 1117, 1166 (2009).

291. Virginia Commission on Constitutional Government, *The Reconstruction Amendments' Debates* 160 (1967).

292. *Id.* at 215.

293. *Id.* at 157.

294. Raoul Berger, *Government by Judiciary* 164 (1997).

295. See Virginia Commission on Constitutional Government, *The Reconstruction Amendments' Debates* 158 (1967); *see also* Kurt T. Lash, *The Origins of the Privileges or Immunities Clause, Part II: John Bingham and the Second Draft of the Fourteenth Amendment*, 99 Geo. L.J. 329, 335 (2011).

296. See Charles Fairman, *Does the Fourteenth Amendment Incorporate the Bill of Rights?*, 2 Stan. L. Rev. 5, 137 (1949).

297. 74 U.S. 321, 325 (1868).

298. 6 F. Cas. 546, 551 (C.C.E.D. Pa. 1823).

299. *Id.* at 552.

300. Robert H. Bork, *The Tempting of America* 181 (1990).

301. For the argument that privileges or immunities includes natural rights and "is a broader term that includes additional rights," see Randy E. Barnett, *Restoring the Lost Constitution* 60–61 (2004).

302. M. E. Bradford, *Original Intentions* 120 (1993). "Under the pressure of all the excited feeling growing out of the war, our statemen have still believed that the existence of the State with powers for domestic and local government, including the regulation of civil rights—the rights of person and of property—was essential to the perfect working of our complex form of government, though they have thought proper to impose additional limitations on the States, and to confer additional power on that of the Nation." *Slaughter-House Cases*, 83 U.S. 36, 82 (1872).

303. 83 U.S. 36, 79 (1872).

304. *Saenz v. Roe*, 526 U.S. 489, 521 (1999) (Thomas, J., dissenting).

305. *Id.* at 523 n.1 (Thomas, J., dissenting).

306. Virginia Commission on Constitutional Government, *The Reconstruction Amendments' Debates* 157 (1967).

307. 198 U.S. 45 (1905).

308. 381 U.S. 479 (1965).

309. *Id.* at 513 (Black, J., dissenting).

310. *Baldwin v. State of Missouri*, 281 U.S. 586, 595 (1930).

311. 410 U.S. 113 (1973).

312. 539 U.S. 558 (2003).

313. 576 U.S. 644 (2015).

314. 142 S. Ct. 2228 (2022).

315. Raoul Berger, *Government by Judiciary* 202 (1997).

316. *Buck v. Bell*, 274 U.S. 200, 208 (1927).

317. 304 U.S. 144 (1938).

318. 394 U.S. 618 (1969).

319. *Id.* at 568 (Harlan, J., dissenting).

320. *Id.*

321. *Id.* at 662 (Harlan, J., dissenting).

322. *Id.* at 661 (Harlan, J., dissenting).

323. *Whole Woman's Health v. Hellerstedt*, 136 S. Ct. 2292, 2327 (2016) (Thomas, J., dissenting).

324. *Obergefell v. Hodges*, 576 U.S. 644 (2015).

325. *Id.* at 19.

326. *Id* at 18.

327. William W. Van Alstyne, *The Fourteenth Amendment, the "Right" to Vote, and the Understanding of the Thirty-Ninth Congress*, 1965 Sup. Ct. Rev. 33, 70 (1965).

328. *Id.*

329. *Data Analysis: African Americans on the Eve of the Civil War*, https://tildesites.bowdoin.edu/~prael/lesson/tables.htm (last visited Feb. 15, 2025).

330. *Id.*

331. Steven Calabresi, *Trump Is Disqualified from Being on Any Election Ballots*, The Volokh Conspiracy (Aug. 10, 2023), https://reason.com/volokh/2023/08/10/

trump-is-disqualified-from-being-on-any-election-ballots.

332. 601 U.S. 100 (2024).

333. 18 U.S.C § 2383.

334. *Id.*

335. Robert E. Wright, *Eliminating the Debt Ceiling: Is There Anything the 14th Amendment Can't Do?*, The Beacon (May 24, 2023), https://blog.independent.org/2023/05/24/eliminating-debt-ceiling-14th-amendment/.

336. Virginia Commission on Constitutional Government, *The Reconstruction Amendments' Debates* 221–22 (1967).

337. *City of Boerne*, 521 U.S. at 519.

338. *Id.*

339. *Id.* at 524.

340. Ibram X. Kendi, *How to Be an Antiracist* (2019).

341. 143 S. Ct. 2141 (2023).

342. *Id.* at 2175.

343. Mark Walsh, *Secretary Cardona Says Affirmative Action Decision Will Challenge All Education Leaders*, Education Week, July 26, 2023, https://www.edweek.org/policy-politics/secretary-cardona-says-affirmative-action-decision-will-challenge-all-education-leaders/2023/07.

344. *Id.* at 2226 (Sotomayor, dissenting).

345. *Id.* at 2235 (Sotomayor, dissenting).

346. Paul Gottfried, *No Surrender After Dobbs*, The American Mind (August 11, 2022), https://americanmind.org/salvo/no-surrender-after-dobbs.

347. Virginia Commission on Constitutional Government, *The Reconstruction Amendments' Debates* 200 (1967). *See also id.* at 155 (remarks of Bingham denying the amendment would apply to New York).

348. Perhaps the boldest and most efficient route would be to declare that the Fourteenth Amendment is a nullity because it was not properly ratified. As Forrest McDonald has observed, there were myriad problems with the creation and adoption of the amendment:

> President Andrew Johnson questioned the legitimacy of an amendment proposed by a Congress that represented only twenty-five of the thirty-six states. Three northern states that ratified the proposal later rescinded their votes. All the southern states except Tennessee at first voted against the amendment, despite an implied threat that they would not be readmitted to the Union; they

changed their stands only after the threat was made explicit. And throughout the debates on the amendment, friends and foes alike disagreed as to whether approval of three-quarters of twenty-five states or of thirty-six would be necessary.

Forrest McDonald, *Was the Fourteenth Amendment Constitutionally Adopted?*, 1 Ga. J.S.L. Hist. 1, 1 (1991). Even Justice Felix Frankfurter, an FDR appointee, argued in *The New Republic* that "[t]he due process clause [of the Fourteenth Amendment] ought to go." Alexander Bickel, *The Supreme Court and the Idea of Progress* 25–26 (1970).

349. Richard M. Re & Christopher M. Re, *Voting and Vice: Criminal Disenfranchisement and the Reconstruction Amendments*, 121 Yale L.J. 1584, 1630 (2012).

350. 383 U.S. 301 (1966).

351. Alfred Avins, *The Fifteenth Amendment and Literacy Tests: The Original Intent*, 18 Stan. L. Rev. 808, 808 (1966).

352. 570 U.S. 529 (2013).

353. 143 S. Ct. 1487 (2023).

354. Akhil Reed Amar, *The Constitutional Virtues and Vices of the New Deal*, 22 Harv. J. L. & Pub. Pol'y 219, 221–22 (1998).

355. Frank Chodorov, *The Income Tax: Root of All Evil* 32 (1954).

356. J. Bracken Lee, Foreword, in *id.* at iv.

357. *Id.*

358. Steve Wamhoff, *The U.S. Needs a Federal Wealth Tax* (2019), https://itep.org/the-u-s-needs-a-federal-wealth-tax.

359. *Id.*

360. *JM Notes* 190–91.

361. *Federalist* No. 62, at 314 (James Madison) (Bantam Books, 1982).

362. *Id.*

363. *Elliot's Debates* 4:38.

364. *Elliot's Debates* 2:22.

365. *Elliot's Debates* 2:47.

366. Todd J. Zywicki, *Beyond the Shell and Husk of History: The History of the Seventeenth Amendment and Its Implications for Current Reform Proposals*, 45 Clev. St. L. Rev. 165, 188 (1997).

367. *Id.*

368. *Id.* at 233.

369. *Garcia v. San Antonio Metro. Transit Auth.*, 469 U.S. 528, 550 (1985).

370. W.J. Rorabaugh, *Prohibition: A Concise History* 1 (2018).

371. *Id.* at 2.

372. *Id.* at 44.

373. Sheppard, quoted in Scott Schaeffer, *The Legislative Rise and Populist Fall of the Eighteenth Amendment: Chicago and the Failure of Prohibition*, 26 J.L. & Pol. 385, 392–93 (2011).

374. *Progressive Party Platform* (1912), https://www.presidency.ucsb.edu/documents/progressive-party-platform-1912.

375. George Sutherland, *Speech in the United States Senate* 4–5 (1914), https://www.scmlaw.com/wp-content/uploads/2019/12/1914-woman-suffrage-speech-to-us-senate.pdf.

376. Richard L. Hasen & Leah M. Litman, *Thin and Thick Conceptions of the Nineteenth Amendment Right to Vote and Congress's Power to Enforce It*, 108 Geo. L.J. 27, 44 (2020).

377. 302 U.S. 277 (1937).

378. *Id.* at 284.

379. *Id.* at 284.

380. Michael Milov-Cordoba & Ali Stack, *Transgender and Gender Non-conforming Voting Rights after* Bostock, 24 U. Pa. J.L. & Soc. Change 323, 323 (2021).

381. Adam P. Romero, *The Nineteenth Amendment and Gender Identity Discrimination* (2020), https://law-journals-books.vlex.com/vid/the-nineteenth-amendment-and-908043444.

382. 140 S. Ct. 1731 (2020).

383. "It is certainly true that an undefined term must be construed in accordance with its ordinary and plain meaning." *Stenberg v. Carhart*, 530 U.S. 914, 993 (2000).

384. *Id.* at 1741.

385. *Id.* at 1833 (Kavanaugh, J., dissenting).

386. A common estimate is fifty thousand. *See Bootleggers and Bathtub Gin*, https://prohibition.themobmuseum.org/the-history/the-prohibition-underworld/bootleggers-and-bathtub-gin/#:~:text=This%20%E2%80%9Crotgut%E2%80%9D%20liquor%20used%20in,from%20tainted%20alcohol%20during%20Prohibition (last visited Feb. 15, 2025).

387. 544 U.S. 460 (2005).

388. *Id.* at 484.

389. *Id.* at 484–85.

390. *Id.* at 517 (Thomas, J., dissenting) (internal quotation marks omitted).

391. Paul G. Wills & George L. Wills, *The Politics of the Twenty-Second Amendment*, 5 Western Pol. Q. 469, 469 (1952).

392. TJ to John Taylor (Jan. 6, 1805), https://www.loc.gov/resource/mtj1.032_0169_0169/?st=text.

393. *Id.*

394. *Id.*

395. *Id.*

396. The Springer Resolution, quoted in Bruce G. Peabody & Scott E. Gant, *The Twice and Future President: Constitutional Interstices and the Twenty-Second Amendment*, 83 Minn. L. Rev. 565, 591 (1999).

397. H.R. Rep. No. 1698, 86th Cong., 2d Sess. 1, 2 (1960).

398. *Id.*

399. Maya Efrati, *DC Statehood Explained* (Mar. 18, 2022), https://www.brennancenter.org/our-work/research-reports/dc-statehood-explained.

400. *Black's Law Dictionary* 804 (6th ed. 1991).

401. Bruce Ackerman & Jennifer Nou, *Canonizing the Civil Rights Revolution: The People and the Poll Tax*, 103 Nw. U. L. Rev. 63, 71 (2009).

402. 302 U.S. 277 (1937).

403. 380 U.S. 528 (1965).

404. *Id.* at 541.

405. *Id.* at 542.

406. *Id.*

407. *See* Brendan F. Friedman, *The Forgotten Amendment and Voter Identification: How the New Wave of Voter Identification Laws Violates the Twenty-Fourth Amendment*, 42 Hofstra L. Rev. 343 (2013).

408. Samuel Ackerman, *"Stamping" Out the Postage Poll Tax*, 55 Colum. J.L. & Soc. Probs. 331 (2022).

409. *See* Ryan T. Harding, *Preventing Presidential Disability Within the Existing Framework of the Twenty-fifth Amendment*, 40 U. Ark. Little Rock L. Rev. 1 (2017).

410. Mike Pence to Nancy Pelosi (January 12, 2021), https://int.nyt.com/data/documenttools/pence-letter-to-pelosi/38989457c7d0c1b8/full.pdf.

411. *Id.*

412. 400 U.S. 112 (1970).

413. *Id.* at 125.

414. Id. at 126.

415. Yael Bromberg, *Youth Voting Rights and the Unfulfilled Promise of the Twenty-Sixth Amendment*, 21 U. Pa. J. Const. L. 1105, 1107–8 (2019).

416. *Id.* at 1116.

417. *Elliot's Debates* 3:368.

418. *Creating* 12.

419. *Id.* at 84.

420. *Id.*

421. *Id.*

422. Richard B. Bernstein, *The Sleeper Wakes: The History and Legacy of the Twenty-Seventh Amendment*, 61 Fordham L. Rev. 497, 534 (1992).

Afterword

1. *Federalist* No. 45, p. 236 (James Madison) (Bantam Books, 1982).

2. *Id.*

3. John Taylor, *Tyranny Unmasked* 195 (1992) (1822).

4. *Id.*

5. Chris Edwards, *How Many Americans Get Subsidies?*, Cato at Liberty, July 29, 2020, https://www.cato.org/blog/how-many-americans-get-subsidies; Merrill Matthews, *We've Crossed The Tipping Point: Most Americans Now Receive Government Benefits*, Forbes, July 2, 2014, https://www.forbes.com/sites/merrillmatthews/2014/07/02/weve-crossed-the-tipping-point-most-americans-now-re-ceive-government-benefits/; Rich Morin, Paul Taylor & Eileen Patten, *A Bipartisan Nation of Beneficiaries* (December 18, 2012), https://www.pewresearch.org/social-trends/2012/12/18/a-bi-partisan-nation-of-beneficiaries/.

6. Ian Bremmer, *Why Is America So Divided Today?*, Time, January 16, 2021, https://time.com/5929978/the-u-s-capitol-riot-was-years-in-the-making-heres-why-america-is-so-divided/.

7. *The Zogby Poll: Will the U.S. Have Another Civil War?* (2021), https://zogbyanalytics.com/news/997-the-zogby-poll-will-the-us-have-an-other-civil-war.

8. In a previous book, I have looked at length at just how to curb judicial power. *See* William J. Watkins Jr., *Judicial Monarchs: Court Power and the Case for Restoring Popular Sovereignty in the United States* 135–47 (2012).